Inventing Mark Twain

Inventing Mark Twain

THE LIVES OF
SAMUEL
LANGHORNE
CLEMENS

Andrew Hoffman

QUILL
WILLIAM MORROW
NEW YORK

It is the policy of William Morrow and Company, Inc., and its imprints and
affiliates, recognizing the importance of preserving what has been written, to print
the books we publish on acid-free paper, and we exert our best efforts to that end.

Library of Congress Cataloging-in-Publication Data

Hoffman, Andrew Jay.
   Inventing Mark Twain : the lives of Samuel Langhorne Clemens /
Andrew Hoffman. — 1st ed.
     p. cm.
   ISBN 0-688-16110-3
   1. Twain, Mark, 1835-1910—Biography. 2. Authors, American—
19th century—Biography—History and criticism. 3. Biography as a
literary form. 4. Autobiography. I. Title
   PS1331.H53 1997
818'.409   96-34611
[B]—DC20   CIP

Printed in the United States of America

First Quill Edition 1998

   2 3 4 5 6 7 8 9 10

BOOK DESIGN BY MISHA BELETSKY

www.williammorrow.com

For my mother,
who gave me—
among many precious gifts—
a love of books

Contents

Prologue

Truth is stranger than fiction, but it is because Fiction is obliged to stick to possibilities; Truth isn't.
—"Pudd'nhead Wilson's New Calendar" (1897)

You can find in a text whatever you bring, if you will stand between it and the mirror of your imagination.
—"A Fable" (1909)

Mark Twain is the most recognizable figure in American letters. After Shakespeare, he is perhaps the most widely known writer the world has yet produced. Nearly everyone knows those two mythic figures of American childhood, Tom Sawyer and Huck Finn; most literate adults treasure a Twain quotation or story. Mark Twain wrote several books that have already lasted a century and will likely last centuries more: *The Adventures of Tom Sawyer*, *Adventures of Huckleberry Finn*, *A Connecticut Yankee in King Arthur's Court*, and *Roughing It*. A couple of dozen shorter works stand with these as testimony to his skill, imagination, and acuity. Nearly a century after the death of the man who invented the creature we know as Mark Twain, things Twain never said, funny and telling assessments of the human character, continue to be attributed to him. He appears in movies and on popular television shows. Newspapers and magazines report on him with startling frequency. Scholars, too, keep themselves busy excavating both the life and work of Mark Twain, with a phalanx of fine academicians publishing books and articles about him.

Because he appears to be alive, Twain grows and changes so frequently that writing a biography of him is like writing a biography of a liar. We will never know the complete truth about Mark Twain, because he changes shape as we study him. A fool, a tyrant, a philosopher, a humorist, an unschooled literary genius, a friend to revolution, a confidant of presidents and industrialists, an insatiable and sophisticated reader of history, a glad-hander, a sham, a self-destructive narcissist: Each of these epithets describes Mark Twain; their contradictions create a persona that is at once both larger and smaller than a real person.

The unreality of Mark Twain is the primary reason this book cannot be a biography of him. To write a biography of Mark Twain would be as absurd as writing a biography of Huckleberry Finn, or any invented character, with one significant difference: Huck Finn lived in a fictional world, and Mark Twain lived in the real one. Mark Twain had a biographable life, but it is the life of a public image, not a flesh-and-blood man. When railroads and telecommunications knit the diverse postbellum American empire into a more cohesive whole, Samuel Langhorne Clemens became the first expert, the first beneficiary, and the first victim of the new phenomenon. For nearly forty years, except for a hiatus during which his creator attempted to squelch him, Mark Twain was the most interviewed, most photographed, and most recognizable figure in North America and Europe.

Samuel Langhorne Clemens invented Mark Twain, grooming him and seeking out influential people who could help his invention's career as a public persona. He married a wealthy, intelligent, and insightful woman, Olivia Langdon of Elmira, New York, who helped him fashion Mark Twain and who provided some of the capital necessary to build him on an enormous scale. Sam Clemens maintained and refined Mark Twain's image by conscious effort, with well-placed interviews and lecture tours, magazine articles and lawsuits, books and political pronouncements, public gestures and good works. He reaped the rewards of fame: wealth, luxury, and friends of the highest caliber. He also found fame's shortcomings: endless requests for money and autographs, the absence of privacy, and the loss of self to the public. This last, most subtle demon of fame proved inescapable: When Samuel Langhorne Clemens tired of being Mark Twain, he could not destroy him. In the course of constructing Mark Twain, Clemens deeded his proprietary rights to a public that defined Mark Twain's limits for him.

This book is a biography of Samuel Langhorne Clemens. By necessity, it includes the story of Mark Twain as well, but the focus on Clemens makes this a departure from previous biographies. Since Sam Clemens' death in 1910, biographies of Mark Twain have appeared at an average of nearly one per year, though only two are truly significant. The first, the mammoth *Mark Twain: A Biography*, by Albert Bigelow Paine, was issued two years after Clemens' death. Paine was Mark Twain's official biographer, and his nearly two-thousand-page work is in many ways more an autobiography than a biography. Paine's willingness to portray Mark Twain as Clemens dictated him produced a curious mix of confessions and lies, a semblance of truth nearly indistinguishable from truth itself. The book is indispensable for understanding how Clemens lived with Mark Twain.

The second distinguished biography, though it begins only after Clemens' thirtieth birthday, is Justin Kaplan's 1966 *Mr. Clemens and Mark Twain*, winner of the Pulitzer Prize and the National Book Award and a standard of the biographer's art for three decades. Time does not treat biography well, however: Scholarship has revealed new information, alternative interpretations have grown more accepted, and the style of biography itself has changed. Biography, when it is good, explains a remarkable person to a generation; when a new generation comes along, with different conceptions of what it means to be a remarkable person, it needs a new biography to comprehend that person. To contemporary readers, it sometimes appears that Justin Kaplan missed the essence of Samuel Langhorne Clemens. I fully expect that, if this book survives even half as long as *Mr. Clemens and Mark Twain*, people will point out how much I missed, too.

I have tried to be thorough. In the course of my research, I have read nearly every letter Clemens wrote, reviewed all of his notebooks, explored his unpublished manuscripts and autobiographical dictations, and absorbed most of the several hundred books and several thousand articles that contribute to what we know of Samuel Langhorne Clemens. These primary and secondary materials have led me to conclude that received interpretations of Clemens' life are about as likely to be wrong as right. For example, on June 2, 1872, Clemens' firstborn child died; on August 21, 1872, he sailed for England alone, on a hastily arranged trip of indefinite duration. Why did he travel so soon after the death of his only son? Tradition and slim evidence indicate he left the country with the intention of writing a book, one he never even began. Common sense argues he wanted to get away from his wife and her unbearable sorrow.

The facts of a life are one thing, and mostly discoverable, but it is the reasons underlying those facts that matter in biography, and those reasons are mostly obliterated by time, deception, and forgetfulness. Confessions by the biographical subject are more likely to be rationalizations than honest depictions of the state of mind that produced the action. For Clemens, recollections always had the primary purpose of adding to Mark

Twain's image. As Clemens noted himself, "No man is straitly honest to any but himself and God," and he did not consistently believe in God. We can only divine, through circumstantial evidence and guesswork, why Clemens went to England.

Speculation is a necessity in biography. As a biographer, I could blur the facts to create a reason, or I can admit the uncertainty of knowledge—and guess. An interesting thing happened once I began to guess about the uncertainties in Clemens' life. These surmises—not random choices, but conclusions built of circumstantial evidence—began to form patterns. Earlier guesses determined later ones, forcing certain conclusions. If I had continually guessed wrong—that is, misunderstood the state of Clemens' mind at these crucial points—it would have become increasingly difficult to make the guesses suit the known facts. In fact, Clemens' habits of mind became clearer as I went along. I cannot say that I proved myself right; I can only say it began to seem less and less likely that I was wrong.

Despite traditional arguments and Clemens' own recollection that he went to England in 1872 to write a book, I concluded that he went to put an ocean between himself and his wife. That answer was consistent not only with the facts, but also with his own father's habit of separating himself from his family. It seemed more consistent with what I knew of Sam Clemens' state of mind, despite the fact that it countered accepted knowledge. It occurred to me that only by setting aside past assumptions could I divine a true, cohesive portrait of the man. By building my portrait from the ground up, with assistance from some extraordinary recent scholarship, I have ended up with a man who will be unfamiliar even to some experts in Mark Twain. Hundreds of small discoveries, some of which I believe to be of major significance, such as his youthful homosexual experiences and his later secret business ventures, create a fresh portrait of Clemens.

In writing this study of Samuel Langhorne Clemens, I encountered one fundamental, overreaching problem. Traditional interpretation of the man dictated that Clemens had such a large personality that he needed a separate persona in which to carry it. That premise seemed to me fundamentally false. Anyone who has ever performed, whether on the stage or at a dinner party, knows that maintaining a false persona places a huge strain on one's ego. The larger the ego, in fact, the more difficult it becomes to sustain the invention. To live as someone else, to fully inhabit an invented self, the root self must have nearly no ego, or at least one so handicapped by insecurities that it might as well not exist. It became clear to me that Sam Clemens could play Mark Twain to such success for so long only because his fundamental self was so unstable and uncertain. This hollowness at Clemens' core resulted from the odd configuration of his childhood: his very early acceptance of responsibility for the deaths of loved ones; his flighty mother; his distant but demanding father, whose death as young Clemens entered adolescence determined much of his adult identity. Later experiences in his life reinforced his perception that it was the image of the person that truly mattered in life, and not the essential identity, which was likely to be callow, cruel, frightened, and selfish. His faith in the sharp separation between image and identity resulted in the nearly seamless presentation of an invented self named Mark Twain.

In my view, the greatest of all Clemens' accomplishments is his invention of Mark Twain. Mark Twain was, and still is, a nearly complete human being, constructed on a scale at the very edge of imagination. Rather than make of Mark Twain someone entirely distinct from Sam Clemens, Clemens made him a near match. When Mark Twain "remembered" something from his childhood, he remembered Sam Clemens' childhood; he had no childhood of his own, since he arrived in the world full-grown at age twenty-seven. If a Clemens memory did not suit Mark Twain's persona, Clemens re-created it, "remembering" something that had happened differently. He became two people occupying the same body: the brilliant, though acerbic, public man of letters known as Mark Twain; and the cowed, uncertain, and underdeveloped boy-man Sam Clemens. His financial success, both as Mark Twain and through marriage, necessitated another invented persona, that of a Victorian literary gentleman known as S. L. Clemens, a more appropriate alter ego for Mark Twain than was Sam Clemens. Installed in a mansion in New England's most fashionable suburb, Nook Farm, now part of Hartford, Connecticut, S. L. Clemens hosted dinner parties and young people's soirees, raised funds for charities, and overall lived a life for which neither his own childhood nor his success as a writer and performer had prepared him. He invented S. L. Clemens to help him cope with the obligations of an unfamiliar world to which Mark Twain bought his admission.

During Clemens' life, Mark Twain was as much a cultural phenomenon as a writer. He came to notice as a funnyman, and at the beginning of his career his comic stage performances were as integral to his persona as anything he wrote. He changed from an untamed humorist into a distinguished writer and then from a writer into a social philosopher—and he did it without losing his audience, in part because these transformations mirrored the growing sophistication of the American public. The combination of his wild adventures along the frontier and his solid social values as a member of the eastern establishment made Mark Twain an emblem of the United States' rise to prominence. He symbolized, both for Americans and the world at large, the drive, imagination, and liberty that converted our sprawling domestic landscape into a vision of the future.

Among Clemens' most important contributions was the invention of the modern concept of fame itself, a phenomenon of a world just coming into being. Fame—and the manipulation of personal image that fame implies—has become the defining characteristic of American culture. It is an entity apart from what we typically think of as high culture, but it is in fact a high art form. We praise artists as much for the management of their careers as for their art. Fame has huge commercial and imperialist value; culture is the United States' second largest export, after munitions. In creating an international hegemony for stars of American music and movies, we still use the models of inventing personas and exporting fame Samuel Langhorne Clemens developed for Mark Twain a century and more ago. His use of his image and his ideas concerning its relationship to his identity continue to fuel not only American but international concepts of fame.

I have a picture postcard of Mark Twain, not in his wild youth or his successful middle age, but in his final years (see last page of photographic insert). He sits propped up in bed, his white dressing-gown contrasting with his even whiter shirt, which is buttoned tight up against his flaccid neck; its sleeves are rolled up to expose half of his forearm. Visible behind him is one of the removable carved-wood angels that make so distinctive the bedstead he and his wife Livy bought in Venice in the 1870s. Their daughters got to sleep with an angel when they were ill, and the girls often played dress-up with these guardians of the parental bed, in which Sam and Livy always slept facing the large headboard. In the photograph, Mark Twain's gray-blue eyes gaze down at a pad of paper, supported by a book he uses as a writing tablet, which he holds still with his left hand. The hand itself looks much younger than seventy years, Twain's age when the picture is taken. His right hand, a little blurred, holds a pen nearly the thickness of a cigar. His cigar itself sits neglected in an ashtray on the barely visible side-table, just within reach of his left hand. Scattered across the empty side of the bed are books and newspapers.

Mark Twain's large head, made gigantic by his wild mane and aquiline nose, seems preternaturally still. The expression on his face—not only the eyes, but the raised left brow, the tightened cheek, the furrows rising like a ladder to his hairline—communicates concentration. I always make myself quiet when I gaze at this photograph, afraid to disturb the writer at work. Twain seems so absorbed in his writing that he does not notice the incursion of a photographer into his private sanctum. The image is iconic. When I think about a great writer writing, I think about that picture: the wise man, his aged head bent to his labor, painfully squeezing his thoughts drop by drop from pen to paper.

This picture always takes me in; that's why I kept it by me while writing this book. Like almost every photograph of Mark Twain in existence, this one is posed, not candid. The bed, the books, and the cigar on the nightstand have a legitimate place in the frame. The pad and the pen, however, have a more doubtful provenance. While he could have been writing a letter when the photographer came, very few other possibilities for serious composition existed during 1906, when the picture was taken. He was not writing much that year, especially in his Fifth Avenue home in New York. The writing he did do he might have done in bed, but he had better places to work, and probably would have chosen them. And why is he wearing his shirt buttoned up to his neck? Had he been fully dressed when the photographer came and then undressed for the picture, or had he been relaxing and then buttoned himself up out of decency? Both answers point in the same direction: This seemingly candid photograph is anything but. It is a performance, like almost everything we know of Mark Twain. Mark Twain's entire existence, almost, was an act of public proclamation of self.

But that phrase is an oxymoron. If the self is the essential person—the man or woman within—then what is this public proclamation except a claim for a limited and false version of the self to be taken as the whole self? Can anyone present themselves unaltered? Could someone as acutely aware of performance as Samuel Langhorne Clemens at age seventy regard public proclamation as anything but an opportunity for shading the true self? The answer becomes obvious when one reflects on what Clemens was really doing during the hours he spent propped up in that very bed during that year.

In January, Albert Bigelow Paine, who had recently completed a biography of Clemens' friend, cartoonist Thomas Nast, asked Clemens to consider him for the position of Mark Twain's official biographer. Without hesitating, without checking Paine's references or reading his work, and without contemplating whether or not he wanted an official biographer at all, Clemens said yes. Within days, Paine and Clemens began the project. Most every morning, Paine would show up at 21 Fifth Avenue with Josephine Hobby, a stenographer, and the two of them, sometimes joined by others, would take chairs in Clemens' bedroom, beside the Venetian carved-mahogany bed with the detachable angels. With the huge headboard against the wall and Sam propped up at the foot, there weren't many places for company, but the size of the audience did not matter to Clemens. He made these performances—morning after morning through most of 1906, into 1907 and then more sporadically for another year or more—to be recorded, not to be admired or celebrated in themselves. They were like the photograph described above, created in a certain moment to be absorbed later.

Like the photograph, too, these sessions with Paine were posed. In the picture, Twain succeeded in looking like a writer writing. Clothed in white amid white bedclothes, Mark Twain's head and hands stand out; the body virtually disappears. The photo reduces the writing process to its essence: ideas and composition, with luck overseen by an angel. But Sam only needed to hold his writerly pose for ten seconds to achieve the desired exposure. His real performance during those days lingered for hours each day, almost every day. He propped himself up in the same position he occupied in the picture, cigar at hand and books around him, angels looking over his shoulders, and he talked. The biographer lobbed in questions and the stenographer recorded every word, but mostly Mark Twain talked—about the people he had known, the life he had led, the worlds he had seen. Clemens performed Mark Twain's life in retrospect, mimicking and altering the performed life he had made since he had assumed the persona of Mark Twain.

Most of his performances, during most of his life, had been ephemeral. He stood on a stage, offering an hour or more of Twainian insight and humor, and then went away. The books, stories, and essays were permanent records, but they were records of an imagined life. Even the first-person narratives of trips actually taken, like *The Innocents Abroad* or *A Tramp Abroad*, were records at second hand: Sam Clemens went on the trip, but Mark Twain reported on the experience as though it had been his alone. The ephemerality and inherent falseness of Mark Twain's existence called for a reformulation of his identity. Lying in his bed talking, Sam Clemens amended his life, looking for a way to make the ephemeral permanent and the false true. He wanted to leave behind a Mark Twain as nearly lifelike as he could make him. And so, for hours, days, and months he used his talk to pose Mark Twain as a real man not significantly different from his creator, Samuel Langhorne Clemens. He would erase the differences that Clemens had employed throughout his life to keep Mark Twain at a distance, and he could go to his grave satisfied with the believability of his lies.

For generations, since he died at the age of seventy-four in 1910, that false union of Samuel Langhorne Clemens and Mark Twain has appeared true. Mark Twain's recollections of Sam Clemens' life adhere to fact so neatly that they seem to support the idea that Mark Twain was really nothing more than a different name for Sam Clemens, that they possessed in fact a single identity. Those reminiscences, which scholars call the autobiographical dictations, disguise the historical truth, however. The dictations, like the photograph taken at the same time, intentionally misrepresent the lived life. The truth was that Sam Clemens lived in an uneasy alliance with Mark Twain, the alternate persona who occupied his very bones. The fundamental tension between the essential man and his assumed face was the core fact of Sam Clemens' life, a fact that remained hidden by his masterful performance in front of Albert Bigelow Paine and Josephine Hobby.

Those tensions—between one's true self and one's public one; between the experienced life and the recollected one; and between the pose and the person composing the pose—are the real subject for this book. Before Mark Twain, no one had achieved his kind of fame, except perhaps, briefly and accidentally, Voltaire. Mark Twain maintained his cultural prominence over several decades through concerted effort, and in the end Sam Clemens had to live the peculiar life such fame creates. With no models to follow, Clemens had to make it up as he went along, coping with the strange existence as best he could. The void between private self and public persona has grown since Sam Clemens died, and now all of us living in a complex, media-driven world have to cope with the distance between image and identity as a daily factor of our existence. This book recalls how the pioneer did it, and what strategies he used to bridge the void, and what brought him to that Venetian carved bed, talking, talking, talking to fill that vacuum with the semblance of a unified life.

At the dawn of the twenty-first century, the multiple personas of Sam Clemens, Mark Twain, and S. L. Clemens remain surprisingly modern. The indefinite identity that allowed for the creation of Clemens' personas prefigures contemporary neuroses; our technology—from television to telecommunication, computers to reproduction of all types—enhances the power of image and promotes the importance of image over that of identity. When this uncertainty of self is combined with vast ambition, as was the case with Samuel Langhorne Clemens, we have a portrait of American life reduced to its most typical characteristics. As a nation of immigrants, most Americans suffer from an uncertain identity. Americans cannot say, "This is us!" as we point to specific defining events of our past; we can only say, "This is us, and this, and this, and this too!" And like Clemens, too, our nation harbors huge ambitions, and the absence of a definable national identity will not restrain us. We assume an idealized identity instead and make that assumed identity stand in for us. It is represented by freedom, by justice, by democracy, and by prosperity. These values, which we even now assign to the persona of the United States, are in fact the very same ones that Sam Clemens assigned to Mark Twain as the nation's foremost public representative. His modernity, together with the enduring quality of the best of his literary efforts, keeps Mark Twain alive for us.

In his vision of who we have become, Samuel Langhorne Clemens was a pioneer of the American soul. In his writing as Mark Twain, in his social life as S. L. Clemens, and in his internal one as Sam Clemens of Hannibal, Missouri, he continues to give us succor and direction. As I explore the nature of his life, his times, his literature, and his wit in these pages, I have tried to capture in a visceral, feeling sense his experience of his own life. It is my hope that by understanding how Clemens lived his lives, we might better understand how we live our own.

Inventing Mark Twain

1 | *Inventing Sam Clemens*

*Training is everything. The peach was once a bitter
almond; cauliflower is nothing but cabbage with a college
education.*
—"Pudd'nhead Wilson's Calendar" (1894)

Two months premature and weighing five pounds, the baby born to John Marshall and Jane Lampton Clemens on November 30, 1835, in the frontier hamlet of Florida, Missouri, had the worst possible prospects. "A lady came in one day," Jane Clemens wrote later, and "said you don't expect to raise that babe do you. I said I would try. But he was a poor looking object to raise."

The most auspicious element in the child's birth was the presence of Halley's Comet in the sky. The Clemenses and Jane's extended family, the largest and most prominent among the local pioneers, were literate people, but that didn't stop them from subscribing to a host of superstitions. No one had yet heard of Charles Darwin; the mysterious complexity of life seemed more a result of contesting angels and demons than of predictable laws discernible by science. Such powerful forces as electricity had been investigated, but not tamed, and even the most learned among Missouri frontiersmen believed that a little luck, courted by the right ritual, would take a person further than the latest scientific knowledge. The presence of the comet seemed an omen to the Clemens clan, though whether for their new son or their new home they could not guess. Jane's family—her sister, father, uncle, brother-in-law, cousins, nephews, and nieces—brought their jovial warmth to bear on making the comet's lucky powers apply to both Sam and their town. Without them, the boy would almost certainly have followed the fate of the Clemenses' third child, Pleasant, born half a dozen years before and dead within three months.

John Marshall Clemens named his son Samuel Langhorne; his wife felt so hopeless about the child's survival that she relinquished her usual claim to name him. "Samuel" came from John's father, who had died when John was a boy. In a search for new land, cheaper and less settled than in Virginia, the Clemenses had crossed the Appalachian Mountains to Kentucky. Only two years later, the senior Samuel had died, crushed in an accident at a house-raising. John never forgot feeling slighted that his father had not kissed him before he left that day. His mother was soon remarried, to a man who took little interest in the children of her first marriage. John, in a hurry to leave that household, accepted an offer for an apprenticeship back in Virginia from a relative named Langhorne. After a few years, however, John dolefully returned from the land his father had left to the hills of Kentucky; he had been a conspicuous failure in the Old Virginia territory toward which settlers farther west looked with pride and nostalgia. Now back on the frontier, even farther west, John Marshall Clemens bestowed the ambiguous names Samuel Langhorne on a child he expected to die. The names would bury John's own failure in Virginia and his father's default as a pioneer and free him to look to the future in Missouri. He did not think what a haunting burden they might be to his son, if the child had the fortune to survive.

Writing as Mark Twain, Samuel Langhorne Clemens would claim that Florida, Missouri, "contained a hundred people and I increased the population by one per cent. It is more than the best man in history ever did for any other town." In 1835, the hamlet consisted of just two dusty roads and as many shacks as were needed to house a few hundred people a day's horse-ride away from the nearest Mississippi River community. Laid out in 1831, Florida sat on high, fertile ground where the north and south forks of Salt River joined thirty land miles from the Mississippi and seemed a likely spot to mill and ship the products of the outlying farms. By 1835, the first horse-powered mill gave way to a few water-powered ones; small, flat-bottomed boats carried produce the eighty river miles down to the town of Louisiana, Missouri, where Salt River joined the Big Muddy.

John Clemens brought big dreams to this tiny place. A lawyer who entered the bar in Kentucky in the fall of 1822, he tried to help two brothers named Lampton forestall their bankruptcy. Though he was unsuccessful in court, he wooed Benjamin Lampton's elder daughter Jane—a vivacious redhead, a notable dancer with a laconic way of talking and a peculiar sense of humor. Like the Clemenses, the Lamptons were refugees from Virginia, but they carried an even higher distinction, a shadowy claim to British nobility; family legend held that Benjamin's father William had left England after a fight with his father, the earl of Durham. The Lamptons often acted the role of gentry, whether or not they had the property to back up the claim. When Jane's distinguished maternal grandfather died in 1816—memorably, he was buried sitting upright in the chair to which he'd been confined for years—he left Ben Lampton with a disappointing inheritance. In October 1818, when Jane was fifteen, her mother died, and the Lamptons' debts slowly but stubbornly brought them to financial ruin. Desperate, Jane jumped into a marriage with the somber young lawyer John Clemens. A bit eccentric, given to flightiness and flamboyance, Jane later claimed that a failed romance with someone more promising had driven her to accept the cadaverous John Clemens "in a pet." The marriage between Jane and John Clemens was "courteous, considerate and always respectful, and even deferential," their son Sam remembered; "they were always kind toward each other, but . . . there was nothing warmer."

The couple lingered in Jane's hometown of Columbia, Kentucky, for a few years, but then moved on, first to Gainesboro, Tennessee, where on July 17, 1825, Jane gave birth to Orion—named by his mother, with the stress on the first syllable. The family crossed the Cumberland Mountains to a sandy patch of ground called Jamestown, the seat of a new county. By 1827, John Clemens' studiousness and Virginian ways impressed his Tennessee neighbors sufficiently for them to appoint him county commissioner and court clerk of Fentress County. He opened a store and dispensed legal advice. He began buying land, thousands of acres of it, encouraging his and Jane's relatives to buy in, too. The land Clemens bought, however, could grow nothing more than potatoes. Also, after settling some early land disputes, Clemens got very little legal work. Men gathered at his Jamestown store to drink and talk, but not to transact much business. As the town's growth stalled, he developed the habit of pouring a drink for himself whenever he poured one for a customer. Soon, though, frightened by his drinking, John Clemens swore off alcohol.

The family grew: a daughter, Pamela—emphasis on the second syllable, again named by Jane—in 1827; the short-lived Pleasant Hannibal a little over a year later; and Margaret in 1830. A year later, the Clemenses moved nine miles north to Pall Mall, Tennessee, for better farmland. There, Benjamin, the Clemenses' fifth child, arrived on June 8, 1832. The failure of Jamestown, the expanding clan, and the tightening resources combined to bring debilitating migraines upon John Clemens, which he termed "sun-pain." The Clemenses' promising future quickly became a desperate present. By 1834, with his vast acreage around Jamestown representing value only when Tennessee grew, the Clemenses looked west, to Missouri. They believed in the westward dreams of America, and the land beyond the Mississippi seemed capable of accommodating John Clemens' vision. Jane's sister, Martha Ann, whom she called Patsy, had married a robust pioneer named John Quarles, who kept a store in Florida, Missouri. Their father had followed with his second wife after settling his debts. They all harmonized on the same theme: "Come!"

Florida gave John Clemens a new beginning. Soon after he arrived, he adopted the project of raising money to straighten and dredge Salt River. Though the town's economic future depended on opening the river to navigation, its political future depended on its becoming the county seat. John Clemens, experienced in constituting new counties, fought hard for Florida through 1835. The town lost to a more central one, but the defeat did not dampen Clemens' civic energy. He lobbied the state legislature to establish the Salt River Navigation Company, which could raise money necessary for his main project. Operating a store with his brother-in-law John Quarles, Clemens began to practice law again.

Pregnant when they arrived in Florida, Jane busied herself setting up frontier housekeeping in this new town, a task she had accomplished without much help twice before. Now she had family around. While John Clemens was cramped and unforgiving, Jane was expansive and boundlessly optimistic. To Jane, Florida felt like a return to the warm family circle of her Kentucky days in Columbia, before the loss of fortunes and beloved relatives. Though the house in which Sam Clemens came prematurely into the world had little to recommend it, being nothing but a two-room cabin with a lean-to kitchen, the village's promise and his mother's relatives made that cabin a hopeful starting point for the family's new life. Though Jane remembered that Sam spent his first several years under the threat of death—and she avidly read all the health publications she could find, and employed their often painful cure-alls—the Lampton clan provided continual amusement and attention for the children.

The Lamptons and Quarleses possessed good fellowship in abundance. Old Ben Lampton had a reputation as a singer. Jane loved to dance and always was ready to turn the simplest gathering into a full-blown party. Patsy set a prodigious table, and John Quarles was a garrulous storyteller. As in John Clemens' earlier store, the new concern could always provide another shot of the locally produced whiskey. The store was the town's social center, and the Lamptons attracted other members of the community to their circle. The town's thriving ambition—as well as Sam's unexpected survival into childhood—built up great hope for the future. Only the March 1837 death of Jane's father, Ben, dampened the settlers' enthusiasm. On November 6, 1837, John Clemens became a judge in the Monroe County Court. Good news kept coming for the Lampton sisters, too: They were both pregnant, both due in June of 1838. The sisters' simultaneous pregnancies promised to bind their families even closer together in the coming success of their town.

Young Sam, steeped in the family's endless storytelling, confessions, musings about their aspirations, and bickering about politics, seemed destined to become happy and convivial, so different from his siblings Orion and Pamela, their early years dominated by the hardscrabble, joyless life in Tennessee isolated from any family beyond their parents, whose kind but loveless union did not provide much. In John Quarles and Ben Lampton, Sam saw adult men who met life with joy, as opposed to his own father's rigor and seriousness. John Clemens had drive, dignity, and the respect of his community, all personal assets that Sam would eventually crave, but his uncles and cousins preferred the brighter qualities of wit, playfulness, and delight. Nurtured by the attentions of his older siblings and cousins and the ministrations of his worried mother, Sam developed a taste for center stage. He early picked up skills in occupying more of the limelight, like his languorous style of speech, adopted from his mother. His slow talk, seeming both labored in its deliberateness and effortless in its calm, always made people laugh.

Jane's family began to trickle into Missouri shortly after 1820, when the sparsely settled territory became a state as part of the Missouri Compromise. The young union had nearly broken up over the issue of slavery, until Congress agreed to admit Missouri as a slave state and to separate Maine from New Hampshire and admit it as a free state. That preserved the balance of representation and kept the fragile Republic together, but at a high cost. The Missouri Compromise also required that Congress not entertain any legislation relative to slavery. As the years passed, the conflict the Compromise had intended to quell burned ever hotter, and what could not get a public airing in Washington became an issue for feverish debate in the states. The Bible justified slavery, or so Sam heard in the sermons preached on Sundays at Florida's churches. Most Missouri settlers came from slaveholding states, and they believed that organic differences between the races made equality unthinkable. In rural Missouri in the 1830s, abolition was not only a theoretical and impractical notion, but also a harsh threat to economic survival.

Born into this slave culture, Sam Clemens assimilated the belief that difference in skin color meant a difference not only in caste but in fundamental rights. His household included a slave, Jennie, who had been with them since Jane and John's marriage and who served as nursemaid to young Sam and his siblings. The Quarleses also owned several slaves, mostly blood relatives, and the slave community in the Florida area formed a separate society that Sam enjoyed. He had a special affection for a slave in the Quarles household, Uncle Dan, about thirty in 1835 and a father figure for the boy. The slaves watched over the children, overseeing the supervision of the younger ones by the older. During busy planting and harvesting seasons, the children watched the slaves work. They all had free run of the small town, but the places where the slaves gathered were the parts Sam liked best—within limits. Blacks and whites never ate together; this type of segregation was total. Whites could interrupt blacks with impunity, but blacks could never interrupt whites. All his life, Sam remembered one harrowing incident that represented the brutal power relations underlying the caste differences. Once, when Jane and Jennie bickered, Jennie raised her hand to strike Jane. John Clemens intervened; he dragged Jennie outside, bound her hands with a bridle, and whipped her as six-year-old Sam watched. It would take him decades to escape his tangled feelings about race and slavery.

In Missouri in the 1830s, however, owning slaves did not ensure success. Economic vagaries could derail even the soundest investments. John Clemens' hopes for Florida, Missouri, suffered immense reversals just as he achieved his greatest personal success. The battle that the determinedly democratic President Andrew Jackson waged against the business-backed Bank of the United States rose to a crisis when the bank fought back by strangling its own financial resources. The bank refused aid to the government and called in other loans, leading to a nationwide monetary collapse in 1837. The same year, to protect the state from the national crisis, the Missouri Legislature established a State Bank to print money, but only in denominations above ten dollars; sums less than that had to be in gold or silver. Suddenly, the legal tender people used for their everyday debts had no value.

Because of these economic contractions, there was no money for John Clemens' Salt River Navigation Company, despite the rapid growth of Missouri's population. In only a few years, Missouri had ceased to be the newest frontier; now it was only the gateway to the West, first to Santa Fe, then to California, and at last to Oregon and the Pacific Northwest. By 1835, St. Louis boasted more than ten thousand inhabitants and the state as a whole more than fifty thousand. New towns sprang up every-

where, many of them founded upon one utopian social principle or another. For a short while, Missouri was a land where hope grew even more
rapidly than hemp or grain or pigs. The seeming permanence of the state,
however, with its elected officials, public buildings, and dozens of newspapers, was only an economic mirage brought about by the promise of
wealth from the West, a promise erased by the nation's first massive
economic shutdown. The financial disaster erased many Missouri towns—
like Florida.

The Clemenses and the Quarleses looked to escape the dying town.
John Quarles bought farmland toward the North Fork of Salt River. John
Clemens went back to Tennessee in the fall of 1838 to attend to his property there, and when he returned to Florida, he opened a general store
across the street from the Quarleses', a separation of assets preparatory
to Quarles' move into farming. Though Jane and Patsy stayed together
during their bittersweet pregnancies and the nursing afterward of Henry,
Jane's last child, the breakdown in relations between the brothers-in-law
contaminated Jane Clemens' relationship with her extended family. When
the Quarleses moved to their family farm, the family amity Jane found so
delightful ended.

The prolonged absence of his father and the birth of Henry Clemens
had a disturbing effect on Sam, now three. He was accustomed to his
position as the center of family attention, and the breakdown in family
cohesiveness and the sudden appearance of a competitor started explosions
of unprovoked rage. By day, Sam became wild and unmanageable, except
during his periods of illness, which diverted Jane's attention from the rival
child, Henry. At night, he began sleepwalking, almost always toward
Jane's bed. The world that Sam knew had shattered. Every day, friends and
family abandoned Florida; his father's departure seemed permanent to him.
His favorite spots fell still: The mills stopped; the flat-bottomed boats remained tied up at the wharf. The slaves, anxious about their fate in the new
order, shunned Sam. These events deeply unsettled the little boy.

Then came an incident that cemented the development of the boy's
young psyche. His mother Jane, who perceived Sam as a sickly, sensitive
boy, saw his sleepwalking as evidence of second sight. She believed he
was clairvoyant; his survival after his birth during the presence of Halley's
Comet indicated supernatural abilities. A handsome child, noted for ex-
citability and his red curls, Sam played to this perception. Even before
his fourth birthday, he provided his family a disturbing confirmation of
his special abilities. One August night, in 1839, Sam rose and walked, still
asleep, into the room where his sister Margaret, nine, lay ill. With his
small hand, he plucked at the coverlet of his sister's bed, a gesture asso-

ciated in the Missouri folk-mind with imminent death. A few days later, Margaret died. The family concluded that Sam had foreseen the event.

Sam did not understand the odd way everyone looked at him after his sister's death; he confused his supposed foreknowledge of Margaret's death with a responsibility for it. In his own mind, he became the instrument of his sister's demise. By confirming his mother's belief that he had a clairvoyant's gift, Sam also created a profound and reflexive guilt in himself. Though his later religious training emphasized guilt, his direct experience with it made those feelings endure vividly into adulthood, long after Sam Clemens had discarded almost every other trapping of his original religion. Throughout his life, that powerful, almost primal, guilt would resurface when anyone close to him died.

The removal of the family from Florida a few months after Margaret's burial deepened Sam's feelings of responsibility. Coming so soon after Margaret's death, the move seemed to Sam the direct result of it. With this one change, Sam lost not only his cousin-playmates, but his good-hearted and expansive Uncle John and the wise and tender slave Uncle Dan. In return for these losses, he gained only the regular presence of the taciturn and unbending John Clemens. Jane, mourning both Margaret and the loss of her family's support, relinquished most of her joy. John Clemens traded his local holdings for a few small housing lots and a new hotel in the Mississippi river town Hannibal, a magnet for Missouri's disaffected, from washed-out utopians, like those of Marion City, to recession-frozen hopefuls, like the Clemenses of Florida. Since most of the human personality is formed before the age of five, Florida was as fundamental to Samuel Langhorne Clemens as Mark Twain would later make Hannibal appear. In the eyes of a four-year-old, the move from the safe and convivial Florida felt like a payment for his ambiguous responsibility for the death of his sister, a banishment from Eden. It was an imitation of death. Later, in his fiction, Mark Twain named his imaginary blend of Hannibal and Florida St. Petersburg, for the heaven that stands closed off behind the gates Saint Peter guards.

Becoming Tom Sawyer

We get our morals from books. I didn't get mine from
books, but I know that morals do come from books—
theoretically at least.
—Remarks at the opening of the Mark Twain
Library (1908)

AMERICA'S ECONOMIC SPASMS had the curious
effect of energizing Hannibal, Missouri, founded in 1819,
with many of its one-thousand-plus residents involved in
one of the few reliable enterprises of the era: Mississippi River traffic.
John Clemens, part of the first boom in Hannibal's growth, was well placed
to capitalize on this good fortune—possessed of goods to sell, houses to
rent, and the title of judge to impress his fellow citizens. The deal that
brought the Clemenses to Hannibal, however, was not an even exchange;
John Clemens faced a series of payments that constantly threatened him
with financial ruin. In the short term, the move improved the Clemenses'
style of living. Occupying relatively luxurious rooms at their recently
acquired hotel, the Virginia House, they gained further income both from
rental property and from the contents of the store the judge had brought
with him. His indebtedness and lack of ability prevented John Clemens
from thriving as the town did. This contrast between Hannibal's growth
and the family's declining fortunes framed Sam Clemens' experience of the
town that Mark Twain would later mythologize.

Hannibal presented Sam with frightening and entrancing adventures.
Though he had been transplanted from a familiar town to one made up

primarily of strangers, the great Mississippi River flowed just a hundred yards from the door of the Virginia House. Living on the Mississippi meant living on America's new Main Street. Traffic up and down the river in all but the coldest months brought to the growing town a variety of strangers, goods, and amusements, nearly all of which Sam embraced. The town sat in a small valley between Holliday's Hill to the north and Lover's Leap to the south; about the latter Sam heard an oft retold but apocryphal tale of the suicide of forlorn Indian lovers. Bear Creek zigzagged through the valley, a dangerous but open invitation to all children. The sixty-foot-wide streets of Hannibal—impassably muddy in winter and chokingly dusty in summer—gave it a perpetually unsettled look, as though the buildings could not possibly rise high enough to match the grand space allotted them. Truck farmers sold their daily produce on the hundred-foot-wide Market Street, which ran straight up from the river. Campaigning politicians and traveling performers set up there, too. The rich farmland to the west provided pork-packing and rope-making work for the men of the town. The meat-processing industry kept coopers busy making barrels, and transporting goods to the river gave the draymen regular work. In the earliest days of the Clemenses' tenure in Hannibal, steamboats stopped at the cobblestone harbor three times a week; soon they came more frequently. A free-black drayman named John Hannick announced their arrival before anyone else by booming out across the town, "S-t-e-a-m-boat a-comin'!" The whole town turned out when they heard John Hannick's call.

Despite John Clemens' deepening financial problems, the family still paid for the children's schooling; free education had barely begun anywhere in America. Just four and frail when the family arrived in this wonderful new place, Sam began school that fall, but he still didn't rove far from his one-year-old brother, Henry, or his mother, who satisfied her longing for her extended family by adopting an extravagant variety of animal life, notably cats. Otherwise, life in the struggling household patterned itself on John Clemens' chilly grimness. Sam rarely tried to make his distant father laugh; John was so impervious to humor that he once scolded his son Henry for planting his marbles in hopes they would sprout more. Jane, on the other hand, was so susceptible to Sam's humor that she began her admonitory lectures knowing that Sam would break them up with a quip. The store and the hotel at first provided Sam with all the excitement and relief from home he could want, but soon he ventured out onto the streets and down to the river, where the constant influx of settlers and travelers created an everlasting performance that compared favorably with the funereally tedious tension of home.

Judge Clemens sought to make his way in the new place by becoming a central figure in civic affairs. He befriended members of Hannibal's Old Guard, including Judge Zachariah Draper of South Carolina and Dr. William Humphrey Peake of Virginia. The town's elite welcomed their new member, and John Clemens' association with them confirmed his Whiggish political leanings. The Whigs, gaining power in the post-Jacksonian 1840s, supported states' rights and decried government interference; they were the party of the rising American gentry, of which John Clemens considered himself a member. John eschewed any labor other than legal work, deputizing his oldest son, Orion, to be clerk at the store. A dreamy fourteen-year-old when the family moved to Hannibal, Orion proved himself unsuited to keeping accurate records or monitoring the store for shoplifting. The store failed to provide the Clemenses with a living. Nothing else did either: They had little experience running a hotel; the tenants on the other property didn't always pay their rent; legal work came only sporadically. The debt John Clemens had incurred in the move hamstrung all his efforts to turn the town's growth into personal profit. If John had had fewer scruples about paying his bills, he might have thrived on credit, but operating under the eyes of Judge Draper and Dr. Peake, he feigned a gentlemanly unconcern about money. Sam later wrote that Hannibal was "soft, sappy, melancholy; but money had no place in it. To get rich was no one's ambition," but that nostalgic view encompassed only his own family. The townspeople, Orion noted, "greatly prefer the study of pork and flour barrels, tape, cordwood and the steamboat's whistle" to more esoteric concerns.

Because of these divided sensibilities, money became a Clemens family obsession, marked by a continual scratching for cash, which even six-year-old Sam observed when the family sold their slave Jennie, whom Sam missed severely; her disappearance hardened life in the Clemens house. John Clemens transferred title of their Hannibal landholdings into the name of their largest creditor and the family moved into more modest quarters. Then, in the winter of 1842, John left home to extract payment from a Mississippi man who owed him money. When he returned from this trip stoically empty-handed, Jane rebuked him for spending money instead of raising it; it was one of the few hostile exchanges between them their children would remember.

Sam absorbed this ambiguous obsession with money. He never wanted to appear to care about it, but getting rich and staying that way became the dominant motivation in his life. Much as he manifested his father's attitude toward wealth, he dreaded repeating his father's financial mistakes. John Clemens was so coldly impersonal that his economic well-being—or lack of it—became the feature about him that his son best remembered, and he could never help but compare his own prosperity with his father's economic failures. What John Clemens' example taught his son—to crave a social position which required money, but which regarded ambition for it as distasteful—created a moral quandary for the ambitious youngster.

The people of Hannibal respected John Clemens, despite his inability to earn a living. In September 1841, he sat on a jury in Palmyra, the Marion County seat, at a trial of three abolitionists who had ushered a handful of slaves north to freedom. The slaves had returned on their own and turned in their liberators. Some people lobbied to lynch the men whom the *Daily Missouri Republican* called "that species of character . . . who will pray for you at evening and steal your negro at midnight." The jury quickly returned a guilty verdict, with a stiff sentence of twelve years in the state penitentiary. The rhetoric surrounding this trial, along with the ongoing debate about the place of slavery in the territories of the West, made the trial a community referendum on slavery, and Judge Clemens returned to Hannibal amid cheers. This dramatic foretaste of the coming Civil War ripened Sam's attitude toward race: His father had received his greatest accolade for his unyielding support of slavery.

The only break in John Clemens' solid appearance of rectitude came in the wake of another family tragedy, the death in spring 1842 of Ben, not quite ten years old. John and Jane both grieved more at the passing of Ben than they had at the earlier death of Margaret at much the same age. His demise allowed the Clemenses to express not only their grief but also their anxiety over the diminishment and dislocations resulting from their move to Hannibal. Orion remembered that in their grief, his parents kissed each other, a sight new in his experience. It took a cataclysm to create a fissure in the reserve that ruled the house.

Ben's death affected Sam as profoundly as had his sister Margaret's three years earlier. Although there was no gesture of clairvoyance about this tragedy, six-year-old Sam still found a dark place in himself where his feelings about this event resided. As an adult, he remarked on Ben's death in his journals with several odd phrases: "The case of memorable treachery" and "Dead Brother Ben. My treachery to him." His unshakable feelings of responsibility for Margaret's passing made him believe he carried the seed of death in him. After Ben died, Sam's guilt drove him to punish himself. Risking his own destruction, he let himself come close to drowning several times. At eight, he sneaked into the quarantined sickroom of his friend Will Bowen, daring himself to catch the measles, which had already killed many of the town's children. The precariousness of his health had long since strained Jane's homeopathic skills and gave her cause to call often on Dr. Peake, Dr. Meredith, and Dr. Grant, who ran the pharmacy across Hill Street from the Virginia House. Medical emergencies replicated Sam's drama of self-destructiveness, but after the death of his older brother, his health improved. He replaced medical melodramas with behavioral ones—smoking, swearing, skipping school, staying out late, and slipping off to places off limits with people equally off limits. The sudden disappearance of Sam's bad health convinced his mother that her cures had worked, but it is more accurate to say that Sam found symptoms he enjoyed more.

During the hot Missouri summers, Jane took the children to the Quarles farm. She grasped every opportunity to spend time with her sister and provide her children with their cousins' companionship, stretching these visits to the country into weeks and months. John Clemens came infrequently, since he had the store, his legal practice, and his debts to occupy him in Hannibal. Orion, too, now a teenager, stayed in Hannibal, first to clerk in the store and later to serve an apprenticeship in a Hannibal newspaper printshop. These trips back to Florida improved Sam's disposition. In a sweet gesture his cousins always remembered, he would bring his favorite Hannibal cat to the farm. Reacquainting himself with his cousins, his uncle, and the slaves, whose energies and affections so vitalized him, Sam inhabited the farm as though it were his own private Eden. He loved the freedom from the humorlessness of John Clemens' house during these summers, despite the fact that he attended school a few days a week with the Quarles children. Mark Twain later re-created these blissful days in his fictions about a mythic and fatherless Missouri boyhood.

The summer after Ben's death, Sam's relationship with his father took a terrifying turn. The family left for the Quarles farm in two stages; almost everyone rode in the wagon on one day, with John Clemens to follow by horse with Sam the next. Preoccupied, Sam's father rode off without him and didn't notice the absence until he got to the farm, half a day's ride away. An uncle of Jane's rode the thirty miles back to Hannibal to find young Sam, weeping, hungry, and angrily draining meal out of a small hole he'd made in a burlap sack. The resentment Sam bore his father for this abandonment never abated. This incident, conflated with his guilt over his siblings' deaths, exaggerated beyond hope of repair the dread and anger inspired by his remote father. Replicating his abandonment by his own father, John Clemens made a habit of deserting his sons, occurring primarily in his frequent absences; he had also left Orion behind when the family moved from Florida. The memory of his own abandonment so enraged Sam that years later he blunted it by misrecalling Orion's abandonment in Florida for his own at a much younger age in Hannibal.

Soon after Ben's death, Jane Clemens, a dilettante when it came to religion, joined the Presbyterian church in Hannibal. Presbyterians came in two stripes: the more reflective and conventional sort typical elsewhere, and the Campbellite or Cumberland Presbyterians, who believed that only by unquestioning faith in Jesus, who by His crucifixion had atoned for the sins of mankind, could people find salvation from their sinful nature. They favored the experience of an emotional conversion. The church in which young Sam attended his second Sunday school echoed his mother's haphazard but moderate approach to religion; but the revivalist camp meetings in Hannibal brought as much show as religiosity, and Sam adored a show. These traveling preachers worked as much to stir the excitement of the crowd as to save their souls or teach them the Bible. Preachers summoned a panoply of oratorical effects in their efforts to raise the emotions to a godly hysteria. With fervent songs and prayers, sobbing penitents moved forward to join the circles of the reborn. Passionate sinners cried in awful guilt and fell prostrate on the ground. Camp meetings of this sort were such regular events that the people of Hannibal set aside spots outside of town for them; however, these religious carnivals actually differed little from the more secular ones that stopped in any river town large enough to repay the cost of setting up the tent. Critics complained that the traveling preachers sold excitement but no moral value. One contemporary observer noted that young women at these meetings were often "regrettably careless," echoing Mark Twain's later observation in *Huckleberry Finn* that "some of the young folks was courting on the sly" at a camp meeting. This conjunction of godliness and deviltry affected the religious training of Missouri youth as much as more conventional Sunday school did.

Aiming to occupy the center of attention, young Sam Clemens found the preachers' spellbinding techniques inspiring and worth appropriating. Public speaking—not only for religious purposes, but in court, on the campaign trail, and at all community celebrations—was the consummate art in frontier Missouri. Given the transience of the population and the absence of more established vehicles for acculturation, such as colleges, theaters, and the like, the orations bound the frontier citizenry together. Every significant social event promised speechmaking. At political rallies, July Fourth celebrations, and school graduations, the keynote orator typically held forth for two hours. Colorful figures of speech found their way into newspaper summaries of the presentations and onto the lips of the people fortunate enough to have heard them. The more muscular and immediate the image, the greater the effect, and orators commanded significant fees if they could be counted on to excite the audience with their words. From them, Sam learned to use language colorfully, and later, Mark Twain would commandeer their techniques, even as he satirized their styles and substance, in *Adventures of Huckleberry Finn* and *A Connecticut Yankee in King Arthur's Court.*

The boy also had a more conventional education. His first teacher, at Mrs. Horr's dame school, was Mary Ann Newcomb, a family friend from Florida, who also dined with the Clemens family regularly as a paying guest. After attending Mrs. Horr's until the third grade, Sam fell under the tutelage of William Cross, an Irishman who taught Latin and French. For the final two years of his formal education, he attended a school run by J. D. Dawson. Sam never excelled, except in spelling. His family's scholarly predilections and his own voracious appetite for reading compensated for the fact that he attended classes mostly when the weather made the shelter of school more attractive than roaming Bear Creek, Holliday's Hill, or Glasscock's Island, a mile straight across the Mississippi from town. The schools commonly indulged in corporal punishment, and Sam, whose histrionics and mischievous restlessness frequently pushed him beyond the code of accepted behavior, came in more regularly for such punishment than for praise. Already rebellious, he often played hooky and rebelliously underachieved exactly because scholastic excellence was the norm in his family. His poor performance in school agitated them, which pleased him.

He also got a better education on the streets of Hannibal than he could in the classroom, and had more fun in the process. The Mississippi itself was a vital source of information, the trunk line of the vast national system of communication. Sam spent time stolen from school observing the characters the Big Muddy delivered to Hannibal's shore. The town had more than its share of oddities and challenges to convention. During Sam Clemens' boyhood, the town witnessed a number of murders vastly out of proportion to the population. On September 4, 1843, when Sam was not quite eight, two men came to town; after drinking, they fell into an argument and one stabbed the other through the heart. Townspeople carried the body to the office of John Clemens, the justice of the peace, and took the murderer into custody. Sam, having skipped school that day, returned after sunset and decided to sleep in his father's office to forestall his inevitable punishment at home. As his eyes adjusted to the dark, he later recalled, a pale moonbeam illuminated first the dead man's hand and at last his bloody wound. "I went out at the window," he would later write, "and I carried the sash along with me; I did not need the sash, but it was handier to take than it was to leave it, and so I took it."

Sixteen months later, Hannibal had a showier murder, which Sam may have seen firsthand and would remember years later. One Friday noon, Sam Smarr, a gentle and honest man who grew abusive when drunk, sassed a well-to-do shopkeeper, William Owsley. Owsley shot him twice before calmly walking away. After the crowd carried Smarr into the apothecary shop of Dr. Grant, a mob reportedly threatened to hang Owsley, but he faced them down. Evidence that a mob followed Owsley is only hearsay—Mark Twain offers the only report, in Chapters 21 and 22 of *Huckleberry Finn*—but word of Owsley's facing down the hostile mob had stuck with him. At his trial, Owsley won acquittal, most probably because of his standing in Hannibal. John Clemens took depositions in the case.

Sam found adventure and eccentricity not just on the streets and the river, but in the Clemenses' own circle. Dr. William Humphrey Peake was so proud of his past as a member of the First Families of Virginia that he never discarded the habits of his glory days, and he wore the knee breeches, buckle shoes, and pigtail of his colonial ancestors. Despite his standing as a physician, pharmacist, and upright citizen, Dr. Grant suffered a number of puncture wounds in a streetfight conducted with sword-canes—walking sticks with a long narrow blade concealed inside. A man named Pavey, a Hannibal hotelkeeper, chased his daughter through the streets threatening to whip her; the girl took shelter at the Clemens house, and Sam's mother held her ground against the enraged innkeeper.

Judge Clemens had his own peculiarities. He once restored order in his court by striking a contestant on the head with a mallet. As an impoverished gentleman, he cut an increasingly ridiculous figure in town. The family avoided the shame of homelessness only by the grace of a wealthy St. Louis cousin, James Clemens, who bought some of John Clemens' property and leased it back to the family for a pittance. At seventeen, Orion found a position as a compositor in St. Louis, sending home a portion of his pay. He studied Benjamin Franklin's *Autobiography*, his bible of self-improvement, but he was so much of a prig that his coworkers, tiring of his efforts to convert them to his religion of the month, nicknamed him Parson Snivel. Pamela, always ill at ease, remained unmarried, but made money for the family by giving music lessons in small towns around Hannibal. Only Henry, three years Sam's junior, appeared absolutely normal, except for his preternatural goodness. Since the deaths of Margaret and Ben, more than eight years separated the older siblings from the younger brothers. Sam and Henry battled as devil and angel in every department of their lives, from school to decorum; Henry was Sam's distressingly good example, and Sam invented new forms of bad behavior more as a way to distinguish himself publicly than for the sake of the behavior itself. This inclination to shock would burden Sam as an adult when he sought more conventional acceptance.

Sometime in 1843 or 1844, in a last blush of prosperity, Judge Clemens built a house on Hill Street, uphill from the river, behind the hotel. The house held many attractive qualities for Sam. The front door opened directly onto the street and left one just a half block off the main commercial strip and just two blocks from the river. Across Hill Street lived the Hawkins family, whose blond daughter Laura was an early and lasting object of Sam's affections. Tom Blankenship, on whom Mark Twain later based Huck Finn, lived with his drunken father and enormous clan in a barnlike structure just a shade up Hill Street from the new house. Townspeople looked down on the Blankenships, about whom rumors of drunkenness and prostitution flowed. Though near neighbors, the Clemenses thought the Blankenships belonged in a completely different social sphere, one with which they would never have any contact. Naturally, John and Jane Clemens preferred that Sam choose other company, but the one-story wing off the back of the house gave their wild son a ready escape from his bedroom. Neither parental disapproval nor school could keep Sam in his bed after dark, especially when Tom Blankenship had an adventure in mind. Older than Sam by four years, Tom Blankenship was bred to the sort of trouble Sam enjoyed. On Tom's signal, Sam would climb out his window and into the night.

Sam and his friends—Tom Blankenship, John Briggs, Will Bowen, John Garth, John Robards, and dozens of others mostly a year or two younger than he—took frequent trips to Glasscock's Island, where they would spend the day swimming, fishing, hunting for turtle eggs, and smoking. Around town, they raided fields and orchards for melons and apples. They played marbles and games of imagination hiding in the high jimsonweed that covered many of the town's unimproved lots. They became Indians and pirates and highwaymen as easily as the suggestion came from someone's mouth, most often from Sam, whose brazen leadership the friends all acknowledged. He could never let a dare pass or forgo an opportunity to show off for his friends. Even alone, Sam had a daredevil quality, an almost self-destructive passion for effect, an urge to contradict convention and his father as outrageously as possible. At age nine, for example, he boarded a steamboat headed south as a stowaway. Discovered by a member of the crew, he disembarked thirty miles downriver, in the town of Louisiana, Missouri, where he spent the night with Lampton kin, who brought him to Hannibal in the morning, delighted by the uproar he had caused.

Good-hearted, harmless, and untamed, Tom Blankenship provided the model for Sam's rejection of authority. Also, because Tom lay outside the bounds of acceptable society, he defined the outer limit for Sam's own misbehavior: As long as Sam behaved better than Tom Blankenship— staying somewhat clean and well dressed, attending school at times, practicing pranks with no direct harm—he could maintain enough respectability to stay clear of any extreme punishment from his family. Sam and Tom also learned some valuable social lessons from Tom Blankenship's older brother, Benson, a fisherman. When Ben encountered a runaway slave on Sny Island, across the Mississippi from Hannibal, he ignored the reward, preferring instead to feed and shelter the hounded man. Weeks later, bounty hunters chased the poor slave into a swamp, where he vanished. A few days later, while Sam and some friends were fishing near the island, the slave's body rose to the surface, "much mutilated" as the local paper reported. Both terrifying and inspiring, this incident opened Sam's imagination to the power hidden in the juxtaposition of compassion and the grotesque, a theme he would develop in his later writing. The scene in *Tom Sawyer* in which the evil Injun Joe stalks Tom and Becky—based on Laura Hawkins—through a cave and then dies there replicated this association of the horrible and the just.

The actual cave, tucked under the promontory south of Lover's Leap, was one of Hannibal's foremost attractions, and Tom Blankenship led the younger boys through its fascinating and dangerous paths. Sam, through Tom, had an intimate knowledge of the adventures possible in this secluded, womblike but treacherous environment. Anyone initiated into its intricacies could hide in the cave without discovery for as long as he liked, an option taken by several outlaws who worked this territory. Some of the cave's features became so well known among Sam's Hannibal friends that they used them as points of assignation. The presence of the cave placed a physical limit on parental authority; a child wanting freedom from chafing restrictions could simply escape to McDowell's Cave.

The cave itself contained one of Hannibal's most bizarre elements. The property containing the entrance had been acquired by a Dr. Joseph Nash McDowell, a notable physician who founded a St. Louis medical school. In the 1840s, Dr. McDowell used the cave to store a cache of weapons for the war against Mexico, but he also had the notion to turn the cave into a mausoleum. He suspended a glass-lined copper cylinder— containing a corpse, said to be the doctor's own fourteen-year-old daughter, in an alcohol solution—in one of the cave's deep recesses. He hoped the corpse would petrify; if the experiment proved a success, he thought he could sell space in the cave to people who would rather petrify their dead than bury them. All the townspeople knew about the corpse in the cave, and they visited it often in the mid to late 1840s, before word got out to tourists. When Dr. McDowell learned that steamboats were stopping below the town to give the interested a chance to sneak a peek at the dead girl, he removed the corpse.

Peculiar though it might be, Hannibal had become an economic hub, as the first major town on the Mississippi north of St. Louis, the chief port on the way to Keokuk, Iowa, where the Des Moines River joined the Mississippi. Brick commercial buildings lined Market Street and large warehouses rose by the river. Sumptuous houses of stone and brick and fancy clapboard went up where rustic pioneer cabins had once stood as people made fortunes in the burgeoning trade passing through Hannibal. Houses were trimmed with wooden finery and stores were filled with valuable trinkets. Steamboats now stopped as many times each day as they had formerly stopped each week. Pork packing remained the dominant industry, along with hemp and timber. Hannibal also began making steamboat hulls, to be floated downriver and outfitted in St. Louis. At one of the first boat launchings, when Sam was nine, people gathered by the shore to cheer as the hull splashed into Bear Creek. No sooner had the hoopla begun than Sam appeared on deck, waving his hat to the excited crowd. No amount of punishment could erase the glory he garnered from this stunt.

Neither Hannibal's rising prosperity nor help from generous cousin James could lift the Clemens family finances, and by 1847, after occupying the house on Hill Street for three years, John Clemens faced bankruptcy. This crisis worsened his already fragile health. To quell his painful migraines, Clemens often went on extended trips, unprofitably following the circuit court; distance from the family relieved his symptoms. Despite these pressures, he not only continued to abstain from alcohol, but also determined to help reform Hannibal's most prominent drunkards; according to Mark Twain, however, he "was not a professional reformer. In him the spirit of reform was spasmodic. It only broke out now and then, with considerable intervals between." Though he resisted alcohol, Judge Clemens found another vehicle for his addiction, consuming Cook's pills several times a day. His need to feed his addiction to this standard concoction of aloe, calomel, rhubarb, and a narcotic could easily account for his financial failure in Hannibal. When money got tight, John Clemens' friend Dr. Grant invited the Clemenses to live with his family in its quarters above the pharmacy just across Hill Street; Jane cooked for the household, a task she detested. The presence of an apothecary on the first floor of their new quarters enhanced John Clemens' willingness to take charity from Dr. Grant.

John Clemens, mortified by the need to accept a friend's charity for his family, determined to run for the office of clerk of the county court, which would at least offer him a wage. Though he was a firm Whig in a Democratic town, his election seemed a certainty; in an era when newspapers were party organs, the campaign occurred with a surprising absence of partisanship, in part as an act of charity toward a good man fallen on hard times. Though constrained by his poverty and his personality, John Clemens had enough drive to work on projects to improve Hannibal. He advocated the construction of a railroad and a surfaced road connecting the town on the river with St. Joseph's, the point of departure for the Oregon Territory. He also served as president of the Hannibal Library Institute, which he had helped found. This explosion of civic interest benefited the judge's campaign for public office; no one could blame the man for cloaking the shame of his poverty in the mantel of public service. Anticipating election, he closed his law office, took a position as a clerk in a trading house, and made some unsuccessful efforts to sell his Tennessee land.

In March of 1847, before the election, John Clemens went to Palmyra, the county seat some dozen miles west of Hannibal, where he hoped to raise some cash through a court battle with William Beebe, a Hannibal merchant and slave trader. On his way home, John found himself caught in a sleet storm and arrived at Dr. Grant's cold, tired, and sick. He took to bed, suffering first from pleurisy and then pneumonia. He weakened. The family gathered—Pamela from Florida and Orion from St. Louis, and Jane, Sam, and Henry, all living together with the Grants. In his last days, he cautioned the family to keep a tight hold on the still unprofitable land in Tennessee, which he believed would bring the family its fortune. As death drew nearer, he beckoned nineteen-year-old Pamela from the group, to bestow on her, and not Jane, his final kiss. On March 24, 1847, Judge John Marshall Clemens died. He was forty-eight years old.

Sam was eleven and a half. The ambiguous sense of responsibility Sam bore for the death of his siblings took on a gigantic power with the death of his father, whom he feared, respected, and loathed to the point of wanting him out of the way. The complex of grief and satisfaction at his father's passing grew to an impossible weight, a burden that enraged Sam even more after he obtained a horrifying glimpse, through a keyhole, of Dr. Hugh Meredith opening his father's body for an autopsy. The dissection reduced his physical father to an assemblage of inert organs, but the transformation somehow made the man himself more powerful in his son's imagination.

Little of a practical nature changed immediately in Sam's life. He continued to attend school, though he worked at some odd jobs, delivering newspapers and assisting a variety of storekeepers for extra cash. His true apprenticeship, however, with Joseph Ament, editor and publisher of the *Missouri Courier*, did not start until almost two years after his father's death. Years later, Sam declared, "It was pretty hard sledding. I was not one of the burdens, because I was taken from school at once, upon my father's death, and placed in the office of the Hannibal *Courier*, as printer's apprentice." None of this was true, however. It was a myth, convenient to Mark Twain's purposes and easy on Sam's own psyche. Convinced he bore some guilt for his father's demise, Sam misremembered what were in fact two years of boyish freedom from John Clemens' oppressive presence. Despite that freedom, his father was not entirely absent from Sam's life. He lingered as he always had, both present and remote, not in the house but in Sam's mind. His mother Jane loved to tell the story of how, the night after John Clemens died, she was awakened by the spooky apparition of a shroud approaching her bed. It turned out to be Sam, wrapped in a sheet, still asleep.

3 | Seeing with Huck Finn's Eyes

What's the use you learning to do right, when it's troublesome to do right and ain't no trouble to do wrong, and wages is just the same?
—*The Adventures of Huckleberry Finn* (1884)

IN THE YEARS directly following his father's death, young Sam Clemens moved from careless mischief to extreme unruliness. With his friend John Briggs, Sam worked for several days to loosen a huge boulder high up on Holliday's Hill. When they finally unearthed the monster, they shoved it down the hill toward a cooper's shop. The huge stone hopped over the road, over the head of a startled black drayman, and landed smack in the middle of the shop, destroying it. Only luck prevented injury; no one was in the shop. In another reckless act, he and Tom Nash determined to skate on the Mississippi as the river began to thaw. As they heard the rumbling of the ice, they headed for shore, floe to floe. Sam made it back, but Nash landed in the frigid river, contracted scarlet fever afterward, and lost his hearing as a result. Quarrelsome, Sam waged an ongoing war with his teacher's son Theodore Dawson, whom he despised for his priggishness. The showiness that had characterized Sam's play before his father's death gave way now to a brazen disregard for consequences. Judge Clemens had rarely employed violence against his children, but his fierce rectitude compelled at least a measure of obedience. Now, with Jane preoccupied with making ends meet, Orion in St. Louis, and Pamela often teaching music elsewhere,

Sam suffered little restriction. Driven by his conflicting emotions, he pushed his misbehavior beyond truancy, smoking, and swearing. His younger brother Henry's relentless obedience, studiousness, and politeness made it all but impossible for Sam to stake a claim on familial and worldly attention by good behavior.

The onset of puberty aggravated Sam's wild reaction to his father's death. A popular, attractive boy with a quick wit, he valued the high regard of his peers, both male and female. Though the licentiousness occurring around the camp meetings was in conflict with its high-minded, conservative morality, Hannibal society in the 1840s accepted both. Most magazines of the day only acknowledged the existence of respectable women, who were divided into pure girls and elderly mothers, without reference to how they moved from one category to the other. Idealized conceptions dominated public discussion about women and their social roles. On the Hannibal streets in which Sam came of age, sex was a common but secret subject. Like any town catering to travelers, Hannibal had its brothels. Sam knew of the unproven allegations against the Blankenship girls, one of whom was his pal Tom's twin sister. In 1850, at age fourteen, Sam witnessed a shooting connected to the sex trade when, on one of his late-night escapades, he saw a woman use a gun to discourage an undisciplined customer who had come across the river for a frolic. Sam and his cronies could easily satisfy any anatomical curiosity they had in McDowell's Cave. The preserved corpse of the fourteen-year-old girl gave any boy who could brave the chill of death a long look at a female body; Sam would prize adolescent beauty his entire life. The cave itself provided the town's youth a secret hideaway from public scrutiny.

The nature of sexuality in the pre-Civil War Mississippi Valley emerged in startling detail in the murder trial of John Wise in Palmyra, Missouri, just a dozen miles from Hannibal. In the summer of 1849, Wise shot his friend Thomas Hart, pistol-whipped him, and then stabbed him, in full view of more than a dozen witnesses, because Hart and Wise's wife were having an affair. A simple case, the trial generated massive interest only because the lovers' passionate and explicit letters were read into the court record. This act turned into evidence what would otherwise be considered pornography, thus suspending the rules banning the discussion of sex from public discourse. Preachers castigated the lead prosecutor Richard Blennerhassett for his bold action, but even by talking about the trial itself the clergy appeared to aggravate its sensationalism. Newspapers four states away published the correspondence, and many newspapers printed broadsides of the titillating letters. The *Missouri Courier*, where Sam apprenticed, gave reports of the trial, though the editor reprinted the salacious correspondence "omitting, however, such portions of it as are too indecent for publication." Sam had access to the full text of the letters and probably supplied copies to his friends from the stash at the office.

Though Sam Clemens never referred to them later, these events—both the Wise-Hart affair and the publication of the letters during the murder trial—symbolized animalistic depravity throughout his life. Capitalizing on its obscure reference and its inherently funny sound, he always used the name Blennerhassett as a buried emotional sign representing wildness, sexuality, and violence. "Blennerhassett" became a verbal key to this doorway, usually locked, between the sunlit parlor of good girls and elderly mothers and the dark underside of human sexuality, widely practiced and never discussed.

Hannibal did attempt to morally educate its young. Jane sent Sam to Sunday school all through this period, but Sam seldom actually made it all the way to the church. Typically, Jane tested her son by asking him to repeat the Bible text the teacher had used, and just as typically Sam would memorize a quote for the purpose. One Sunday when he preferred play to church, he rushed home wearing his cloak inside out, with the bright plaid lining showing. Jane asked him how he'd been able to stay warm in church on such a cold day. He claimed he'd never taken off his cloak. Indicating the glaring swath of exposed plaid, Jane asked, "Didn't that attract any attention?" Despite her difficulty in managing her son during his adolescence, Jane never turned to John Quarles or one of John Clemens' men friends for help. Infuriating as he could be, Jane relished Sam's wildness and prized his casual disregard of authority. She might not have been so sanguine if, despite Sam's later claims to constant absence from school and church, he had not gained a steady education in grammar, geography, and the Bible.

The practical life of the Clemens family improved between 1847 and 1850; perhaps John Clemens had cost the family more than he'd brought in. Only a few months after John's death, they returned to their own house across Hill Street from the Grants; James Clemens of St. Louis, the wealthy cousin, still owned the place, and Orion arranged the family's return to it. Except for Sam's outrageous and dangerous behavior, life for the Clemens clan grew steadier with its feckless patriarch gone. With everyone in the family now bringing in some money, and John not spending it on his addictions and his expensive associations with the town's elite, the Clemenses' fortunes became more certain, if no more promising. At last, after three years of wildness, Sam, nearing fifteen, began to settle down, due as much to external events as to a truce with the demons unleashed by his father's death.

The discovery of gold in California signaled a marked change in the life of Hannibal and in the makeup of Sam's associations. Sam watched with envy as a large number of Hannibal residents left for California—more than 5 percent of the population, including many of Sam's closest friends. As Hannibal became a way station for easterners taking the overland route to the goldfields, the intimacy of the town decreased. Strangers began occupying stores, homes, and street corners that before had harbored only familiar faces. The moral tone of Hannibal suffered; prospectors rarely showed signs of refinement as they passed through town. The wholesale change of Hannibal's population eliminated the community in which Sam Clemens had grown up, and did so in a matter of months.

Another external change quieted Sam, too: He left school and began his apprenticeship at the *Missouri Courier*. As the only male member of the family to have reached his majority, Orion made the arrangements for Sam, legally his ward. Though Sam's skill in spelling made a career as a compositor an appropriate one, Orion chose a printshop apprenticeship for him as much because it was his own career as to answer any particular aptitude he perceived in his brother. As an apprentice, Sam had the filthy jobs of cleaning the floor, the press, and the type. After a newspaper page or advertising broadside had run through the press, Sam painstakingly separated the letters from the frame of type and returned them to their correct bins in the compositor's box. An observer of the day gives the following description of a small-town newspaper office:

> Here is a great iron concern with big bars, levers, rollers and screws, standing exactly in the middle of the floor, occupying just twice as much room as it would have anywhere else, and looking far better suited for a machine shop, than a young literary emporium. Then there are papers of all sizes from a seven-by-nine, up to a mammoth, scattered all around the room and tables, just as if a young whirlwind had been frolicking among them. Then such a paraphernalia—a deformed inkstand, an empty wafer box, an old rusty steel pen, a big bottle with something green in it, (we never have learned what it is) a big pair of shears which we are told bears the very respectful title of "assistant editor."

An apprentice such as Samuel Langhorne Clemens occupied the lowest rung in the editorial hierarchy; he was as likely to carry wood for the stove as haul paper to the press. Sam felt lonely at Ament's, sleeping on the floor of the printshop on a pallet and eating with his printshop cronies at the Ament family home. Sometimes he came unannounced late at night to his mother's home and slept in the parlor, just to have familiar surroundings.

Sam's apprenticeship inducted him into the world of men, and he responded with a theretofore unknown maturity. He rarely skipped out of his work obligations. The difference between his unreliable attendance at school and his reliable performance as an apprentice reflects the seriousness with which he took this rise in status. As an apprentice, Sam did not make money—Ament's obligations extended to room, board, clothing, and training—but he earned respect. A quick study and a fine speller, Sam proved early on his ability to read proof and set clean type. He formed a close alliance with one journeyman in Ament's shop, Wales McCormick, with whom he pilfered potatoes and onions from the Aments' cellar to cook on the stove at work. McCormick's bold disregard for authority— when he was chastised for setting "J.C." in place of Jesus Christ, he revised it to read "Jesus H. Christ"—showed Sam how an adult male could be his own man while working for someone else. He could also succeed in a way his father had not. McCormick's freewheeling attitude reassured Sam—who had no prospects, little education, and a high-spirited, almost frantic independence—that he could be true to himself and still have the security of a good trade.

Yet he did not entirely abandon his fickle youth when he began his apprenticeship. In 1850, he joined the Cadets of Temperance, a junior arm of a national temperance group, for the sole purpose of gaining the right to wear the Cadets' colorful regalia in a parade. His name appeared at the very top of the membership list and Sam occupied a notable position in the Cadets. But abstention from profanity, tobacco, and liquor eventually proved too steep a price to pay for the limited benefit of wearing the regalia on May Day and July Fourth. After the holidays, Sam withdrew from the Cadets of Temperance and resumed his already well-developed habits of swearing, smoking, and drinking, and settled into more adult versions of the showy, but less dangerous, forms of play he had favored as a child, before his father's death. When a traveling hypnotist stopped in Hannibal for a two-week stint, Sam volunteered to be a subject, but failed to succumb. Embarrassed by the failure, he decided to fake the trance and mimic the actions of a person under the influence, even refusing to flinch when stuck with needles. He capped his first night as mesmeree by chasing a school bully with a revolver, using the opportunity to get back at someone he detested. His father's old friend, Dr. Peake, doubted hypnotism until Sam, as though traveling across space and time, described the burning of a Virginia theater, an event he had happened to overhear Peake himself describe many years before. Sam performed so well that his mother forever after refused to believe he had faked his submission, despite his willingness to prove it to her by again not flinching while she stuck him with needles.

Though Sam seemed destined to follow his brother into the printing business, he would later claim that a particular event led him to his true calling. One day, a page of a book blew across his path. He snatched it out of the air and read it; it contained a snippet of the life of Joan of Arc. Sam was skeptical: Joan's story seemed no more possible than his childhood dreams of piloting a steamboat. He asked his brother Henry, the family scholar, what he knew about Joan, and Henry told him how she had led her people to freedom after receiving instructions from God, and how she had died a martyr at the stake. Whether or not Sam learned of Joan in this chance way, the actuality of her existence made a deep impression on him. It stunned him that a book could reveal an astounding truth. He began to regard literature seriously for the first time. Trying to make sense of a rapidly changing life, he had already begun to write, but this leaf from Joan of Arc's story hinted at how powerful writing could be. He read more hungrily, not the romances that had consumed him as a boy, but history and literature. As a printer's apprentice, he filled the perfect position from which to launch himself into a writing life. Orion had chosen a fortuitous apprenticeship for Sam; Orion's idol, American legend Benjamin Franklin, had begun his remarkable life working in a printshop, as had many writers.

His older brother's position as Sam's guardian had more legal than practical standing. Though he tried to direct his younger brother, he was woefully inept as a father figure. Orion was just as dedicated to his principles as was John Clemens, but, like his mother, he changed them often. Where the Judge avoided any circumstance that might threaten his dignity, Orion seemed to cultivate foolishness. Unaware that his family had left the Grants' household, Orion arrived on a late boat from St. Louis, entered the house stealthily, and climbed into what he thought was his brother Henry's bed. It turned out that Dr. Meredith and his sisters had taken up residence with the Grants, and to Dr. Meredith's horror Orion had climbed into bed with one of the sisters. Orion scampered out into the night half clothed.

Orion was like his father in some matters: He struggled to make a living; he endorsed visionary projects designed to materially and morally uplift humanity; and he was too proud to ask anyone for help. Though he had made a powerful friend in Edward Bates, an architect of Missouri's 1820 state constitution and the state's most powerful member of the new Republican party, Orion did not exploit this connection for personal advancement. Despite his shortcomings, Orion undertook a paternal role with his two much-younger siblings. He supervised family finances and kept an eye out for opportunities to bring wealth to the family. The gold-rush exodus provided a chance when a Hannibal newspaperowner succumbed to the temptation of California and shut down his paper. In the fall of 1850, Orion purchased fifty dollars' worth of printing supplies and stepped into the gap left by his departure. Orion expected Sam, too, to work on his newspaper.

Though Orion began publishing his *Hannibal Western Union* in September of 1850, it was January 1851 before Sam could break free of his commitment to Joseph Ament. Orion promised Sam a salary of $3.50 a week as enticement, but Sam couldn't have refused even if he had known then what he would soon discover: that Orion would never be able to give him a penny for his work. The *Western Union* was a family venture; Orion's enterprise included cousin Dr. Jim Lampton and uncle John Quarles as sales agents. Sam began his new position with a flourish, printing in the January 16, 1851, issue a comic squib about the Clemenses' new apprentice Jim Wolfe's reaction to a minor fire. Wolfe fretted pointlessly until the matter was taken care of and then declared, "If that thar fire hadn't bin put out, thar'd a'bin the greatest *confirmation* of the age!" Sam tried to spice up the newspaper with local color, local stories, and local language, but his brother filled the pages with moralistic lectures, generic-sounding schoolgirl compositions, and distillations of national news.

Orion found it difficult, as did most border-state newspapermen, to articulate a course between the unfolding activism on both sides of the slavery issue. The Compromise of 1850, which gave new states the right to determine by vote whether to permit slavery, attempted to replicate the truce that had brought Missouri into existence thirty years before, but in fact had already begun to draw blood in Kansas, where armed hooligans intimidated abolitionist voters. Waffling between defending slavery and advocating abolition, Orion's editorial policy could never have satisfied Sam, who would have found reason to object, if only to contradict his brother. Sam's lighthearted humor, his focus on Hannibal life, and his playfulness with printing conventions would have improved the *Western Union*, but as Judge Clemens' heir, Orion slapped down his brother's nonsense as a matter of course.

In the fall of 1851, as Sam neared his sixteenth birthday, the Clemens family received two bits of good news from the hills of Kentucky and

Tennessee. On September 20, Pamela married Will Moffett, a successful merchant in Hannibal who had known the Clemens family since he and John ran competing stores in Florida. Though family legend tells that the marriage in Kentucky was prearranged, it surprised the Hannibal contingent. Pamela proved a good judge of prospects: Will Moffett sold out his Hannibal business and set up as a commission merchant, a wholesaler, in St. Louis, the city through which passed almost all the trade with the growing western territories. Also in the fall, the family received notice of the sale of some Tennessee land, that Holy Grail of financial salvation the dying Judge Clemens had held out for. This good news soon paled when the farmer who made the purchase discovered the soil's unsuitability. Orion went to Tennessee to resolve the matter, staying away two months, leaving the paper in the inexperienced but steady hands of Dr. Hugh Meredith. Orion's foray to Tennessee proved fruitless, and the Tennessee land lay as unprofitable as on the day John Clemens bought it.

Despite the newspaper's failure to provide much money, Orion saw himself as successful. Now renamed the *Journal*, his paper had the largest circulation of any in the area. Orion filled it with distinguished material, both original and lifted from other sources, the latter an acceptable practice in the days before copyright. In truth, newspapers in Missouri typically brought no one money. Successful printers survived on government contracts for printing laws and court transcripts, contracts that rewarded editorial support for the dominant party, which in Missouri was the Democrats. As neither a savvy businessman nor a Democrat, Orion seemed incapable of making this sort of backroom deal. He had to survive on advertisements and subscriptions, and like most Missouri editors accepted produce in lieu of cash. With the printshop resembling a store more than a newspaper office, Sam felt that Orion could manage the *Journal* with greater wisdom. Also, Orion's luck seemed as uncertain as his judgment. No sooner had he returned from his useless trip to Tennessee than the office caught fire and burned. Orion set up shop again quickly in the Hill Street house where Jane, Orion, Sam, Henry, and the apprentice Jim Wolfe all lived. A few months later, another fire broke out, but the family soon got the paper back into circulation, if not exactly on its feet.

The older brother had only one effective control over Sam: He could decline to print Sam's writing. Sam, however, refused to accede to his brother's power over him and submitted his writing elsewhere. The May 1, 1852, issue of *The Carpet-Bag*, a journal whose rustic humor provided filler material for all the Hannibal papers, carried a brief sketch titled "The Dandy Frightening the Squatter" bearing the signature initials "S.L.C." It tells of a steamboat dandy attempting to gain the attentions of the female passengers by his bravery, only to be bested by a Hannibal native. The *Philadelphia American Courier* carried a description of Hannibal a week later, signed again by "S.L.C." Sam, then sixteen, did not let his accomplishments go unnoticed by Orion, who found his younger brother's impudence infuriating. Nor did Sam allow his publications to escape unadored by the girls who interested him. He took advantage of his access to a press to print poems on fabric as love tokens. Despite his charm, achievements, and humor, he suffered typical adolescent failures in romance. Comparing himself with his hapless brother, Sam had more reason to question Orion's authority over him. Sam wrote better copy, set good type faster, and excited more admiration than his brother. Why should Orion run his life?

Sam had the opportunity in September 1852 to demonstrate his growing mastery of the newspaper trade. Orion left town for a week and turned over the reins of the *Journal* to Sam, who promptly set off some journalistic bombs that rocked Hannibal's fourth estate. Hoping to liven up the dreary hamlet, Sam satirized the newly arrived editor of the *Hannibal Tri-Weekly Messenger*, who had made himself the target of gossip by leaving a suicide note and heading off to drown himself in Bear Creek over a dashed love affair. A friend found him wandering in the shallows unable to take the plunge. Sam trumpeted what had only been whispered about before, captioning a caricature he drew himself under the heading " 'Local' Resolves to Commit Suicide":

> "[L]ocal" . . . contemplates Suicide. His "pocket-pistol" (i.e. the *bottle*) failing in the patriotic work of ridding the country of a nuisance, he resolves to "extinguish his chunk" by feeding his carcass to the fishes of Bear Creek. . . . Fearing, however, that he may get out of his depth, he *sounds the stream with his walking-stick.*

Responding to retaliation in the *Messenger*, the following issue of the *Journal* continued the attack in two more sketches. Enraged, the abused "local" stormed the rival paper's office expecting to throttle Orion. Instead, he found Sam, not quite seventeen, sitting placidly in the editor's chair.

Another significant event occurred during Orion's brief absence: Sam Clemens' first use of a pen name. W. Epaminondas Adrastus Blab, a pseudonymous observer of local life, wrote satirically about the rowdy doings of a drunk living with his large and poor family on Holliday's Hill—at a time when alcohol and poverty were topics usually left unmentioned in the paper. Lambasting the drunk for his violence, Sam has "Blab" wryly report on the brute's savage beating of his wife as "an extreme case of matrimony." He lightened this drama of domestic abuse with a long story about a young, shy rube (probably a nod to apprentice Jim Wolfe) who pays to see an exhibit called "Bonaparte Crosses the Rhine"—in this case, a bony part of a pig laid across a pork rind. Confident with his material, Sam could translate his bold ease into writing.

While not wildly out of keeping with the norms of frontier journalism, Sam Clemens' work during his brief tenure as editor included material equal to the best of small-town newspaper writing, the standards of which Mark Twain ridiculed throughout his life as abysmally low. While the prose does not distinguish itself in its own right, it does reveal some characteristics the boy will eventually transform into Mark Twain. As in his later writing, Sam's comedy covered the brimstone of his raging conscience with the scent of flowers. Orion's return snuffed out both Sam's blooming humor and his fiery satire.

Sam's conscience had cause to torture him a few months later, in late January 1853. Mark Twain told in his 1882 *Life on the Mississippi* how a drunk, wandering the streets harassed by a troop of little boys, wants matches for his pipe. Sam, feeling sympathy for the man, helps him out. Later that night the man is arrested and placed in jail, a solid small brick structure down by the water. At two in the morning, fire bells break the still night, the tramp has set fire to his bed and his cell's wooden interior catches fire. Unable to break down the door, the people can only watch as the poor man bakes to death. In *The Adventures of Tom Sawyer*, published in 1876, Mark Twain transforms the same tale. The drunk, now dubbed Muff Potter, is wrongly accused of murder and languishes in jail, even though Tom knows that Injun Joe is the real killer. Feeling guilty, Tom goes to the jail and gives Potter some matches and tobacco, which prompts Muff to say, "You've been mighty good to me, . . . better'n anyone else in this town. . . . Shake hands—yourn'll come through the bars, but mine's too big. Little hands, and weak—but they've helped Muff Potter a power, and they'd help him more if they could." Muff Potter faces hanging for a crime he did not commit, but Tom Sawyer eventually summons the courage to testify against Injun Joe and thus free Muff.

What really happened to cause the drunk to burn up in the cell remains unclear, but in 1870 Sam recalled to his boyhood friend Will Bowen how "we accidentally burned up that poor fellow in the calaboose." If Sam had started the fire in the cell, he bore a direct responsibility for the drunk's death. His complicity in the death and his inability to take direct blame for it even years later connects backward to the deaths of his sister, brother, and father. It looks forward to his willingness—perhaps need—to live his life in disguise. Sometimes a blameless man feels overwhelming guilt; what then of the man whose true guilt remains undiscovered?

When Orion decided to publish the *Journal* daily, it gave Sam an opportunity to write more material, but also severely overworked him. Henry, now employed alongside his brothers, set type poorly, which forced Sam to stay up well into the night, crying with rage and frustration, fixing Henry's proofs. Tensions reached incendiary proportions when, as a result of Orion's editorial policy of raising the tone of the paper by removing anything of local interest from it, the rival *Messenger* began outselling the *Journal*. In May, Orion again left Sam in charge of the paper and, in an attempt to mimic the controversy of his last interim posting, Sam concocted a controversy. He subtitled a love poem from another contributor "To Katie of H———l," regarding the purposeful confusion of Hannibal and Hell "as a perfect thunderbolt of humor." Writing under various pseudonyms, he then objected to the dedication, objected to the objection, and so on. This series of replies and counters failed to equal the sparks of his earlier efforts. Upon his return, Orion again squelched his younger brother, at least for a week and a half, after which he at last gave Sam his own space, pointedly called "Our Assistant's Column." The column ran in only three issues.

In a 1904 paean to his idol, Mark Twain wrote, "In Joan of Arc at the age of sixteen there was no promise of a romance. She lived in a dull little village on the frontiers of civilization; she had been nowhere and seen nothing. . . . And now, aged seventeen, she was made Commander-in-Chief . . . and marched to Orleans." Sam at seventeen felt his own urge to march. Though he lacked a divine call, he still needed to leave Hannibal, to divest himself of the cloak of failure first his father and then his brother had sought to drape over his shoulders. He told his mother he would go to St. Louis as a journeyman compositor and stay with Pamela and her husband, the increasingly successful Will Moffett. Jane knew she never could restrain Sam, so—as he recalled it later—she exacted a promise from him not to "throw a card or drink a drop of liquor while I am gone."

By the end of May 1853, he had left Hannibal behind—and left his brother in the lurch. Without Sam's help, Orion failed to publish his daily *Journal* for a whole month. He thought Sam would come back soon, hanging his head, and he explained the lapse of the daily paper in his weekly version for June 30, 1853, by saying that his "hands . . . have gone off on a sort of 'bust.'" In fact, Sam Clemens—with his wry wit, his fresh good looks crowned by auburn curls, his fierce refusal to bow to authority, his deeply hidden well of guilt, and his astounding ear for humor and language—had gone for more than a bust. And he'd gone farther than St. Louis. He'd broken free of his boyhood cage of Hannibal, and he vowed he would never let a place trap him again.

4 | On the Road, On His Own

The dreamer's valuation of a thing lost—not another
man's—is the only standard to measure it by, and his
grief for it makes it large and great and fine, and is
worthy of our reverence in all cases.
—"My Boyhood Dreams" (1900)

Hannibal could not hold Sam Clemens, and neither could St. Louis. Sam soon gave up the idea of staying with Pamela, Will, and their ten-month-old daughter, Annie. At seventeen, he had very little patience for children, often referring to them as "trundle-trash." Besides, living with family, no matter how easygoing or congenial, did not suit his adventuresome frame of mind. Since Pamela and Will had yet to set up house but were boarding instead in a well-to-do neighborhood, Sam had to pay more to stay with them than he would for modest quarters elsewhere.

St. Louis had grown into a bustling city of 100,000 by the time Sam arrived in the summer of 1853 and boasted a peculiar mix of sophistication and barbarity. Rich with trade from both east and west, the city offered both imitation western liberty and the luxuries and affectations of eastern culture. Theaters, art exhibits, and lecture societies competed with less cultural attractions like beer halls and nightclubs. As the biggest city in the West, St. Louis also pulled ruffians, drifters, and gamblers from up and down the Mississippi all the way from the Atlantic to the east. Sam could have found himself any number of dangerous, expensive amusements there if he had not vowed to his mother to avoid cards and liquor. A fellow typesetter recalled that "it was the proud prerogative of printers to be able to drink more red whiskey than men of any other trade. But Clemens, so far as I can remember, never took a drink." Sam did not want to just spread his wings; he wanted to fly.

Despite what he had told his mother about moving to the big city to become a printer, Sam went to St. Louis intending to stay just long enough to acquire the fare to New York City. The stories about the World's Fair there, which had come over the wire to Hannibal, enchanted him enough to include them in his short-lived column. New York was also the nation's undisputed metropolis, the premier accomplishment of New World civilization. St. Louis had its attractions, but they were mostly the attractions of Hannibal writ large. The river traffic that stirred sleepy Hannibal to life a few times a day never rested in St. Louis, with dozens of landings and departures daily. The growth that gave Hannibal its wild edge made St. Louis explosive. There, tensions over slavery, unions, and politics frequently burst into violent exchanges, with not only principles but the lives of the battlers at stake. Journalistic competition among newspapers put Sam's satirical sketches in the *Hannibal Journal* to shame, as he saw up close setting type for the *St. Louis Evening News*. These excitements were just bigger than what Sam had known, not different.

Without telling his mother, he boarded a boat on Friday, August 19, 1853, to begin a five-day journey to New York by boat and train. Remembering the envy he felt watching so many friends striking out for the goldfields of California, Sam believed he was doing them all one better, going east against the prevailing tide, the way his father had done at the same age, attempting unsuccessfully to meet his Virginia relative's expectations. Sam wrote Jane the day he arrived in New York, calling the journey "an awful trip" and charming his mother with this opening: "You will doubtless be a little surprised, and somewhat angry when you receive this, and find me so far from home; but you must bear a little with me, for you know I was always the best boy you had, and perhaps you remember the people used to say to their children—'Now don't do like Orion and Henry Clemens but take Sam for your guide!' "

Orion published Sam's letter in the *Journal*. Most of it describes a pair of freaks he saw on public display in New York, but he also showed off his ingrained southern prejudice by observing, apropos of an incident of "infernal abolitionist" resistance to fugitive slave laws, "I reckon I had better black my face, for in these Eastern States niggers are considerably better than white people." A few months later, he wrote that he "would like amazingly to see a good, old-fashioned negro." The fugitive slave laws, which made it a crime *not* to report anyone suspected of being an escaped slave, would make anyone of African descent suspicious, close-mouthed, and hostile to a white man traveling alone, especially one with as pronounced a southern accent as Sam's. The publication and wide success of Harriet Beecher Stowe's *Uncle Tom's Cabin* in 1852 had begun to galvanize public opinion against slavery, particularly in the Northeast. Private militias drilled on the streets of New York. The most adamant activists on both sides already believed that the issue of slavery would bring on civil war, but Sam observed the signs of the turmoil without recognizing the political upheaval they represented. People from the border states, anticipating that the burden of conflict would fall disproportionately on them, believed that the two sides would come to terms somehow, but abolitionists saw no room for compromise. Sam himself had no solution to these historic upheavals, of course, and could barely think of how they might affect him; he only had dreams of his own future. He journeyed to the beach to put his feet in the Atlantic Ocean and imagined not making war, but making his mark.

The ambitious seventeen-year-old found a position at John A. Gray's job-printing concern, the second largest in the city after Harper and Brothers. In addition to books, Gray's set type for magazines and journals. Printers in New York had broken into two separate unions; chaos governed their compensation. Compositors received pay on a piecework basis, so much per 1,000 ems of type set. Sam entered at the bottom of the scale, at 23 cents per 1,000 ems, a wage he called "villainous" and which barely covered his room, board, and incidentals. True, he was getting paid, as he had not been when working for his brother; but life on his own in a new city proved discouraging. He did not want to admit his anxiety, but the bravado in his letters to Pamela did not fool her. "If you have a brother nearly eighteen years of age," he wrote, "who is not able to take care of himself a few miles from home, such a brother is not worth one's thoughts."

Most disconcerting for Sam was the lack of communication from friends and family left behind. Toward the end of September—while Sam sweated out his hours at Gray's and returned to his Duane Street boarding house to food he had trouble stomaching—Orion sold the *Journal* and moved the family north to Muscatine, Iowa. Sam's departure had made it nearly impossible to continue the newspaper, but Orion had also experienced one of his frequent changes of heart, this one political. His move to Muscatine put him on free soil and out of the untenable confusion about slavery that ran rampant in northern Missouri. Because he had not received any letters, Sam guessed but did not know that his family had moved away from Hannibal. He felt horribly adrift. For a while he gave up his only lifeline home, writing letters, because he had no idea where to send them. The letters he did write bear repeated messages of despair: "Tell Jim and all the rest of them to write"; "Tell Ella I intend to write to her soon, whether she wants me to or not." He complained that the few letters he received from friends "are not written as they should be," because they included no information about home; after he read them, Sam knew "no more about what is going on there, than the man in the moon."

New York offered Sam none of the warmth and hospitality he had grown up with in Hannibal; while his letters constantly remark on the variety and immensity of the city's population, they mention no individual by name. The printer's union maintained a free library, and Sam kept company primarily with books, reading Swift's *Gulliver's Travels*, among others. He went to see the World's Fair, awed that the exhibition attracted six thousand visitors a day, twice the population of Hannibal. The machinery on display impressed him most; he said it would take a week to examine all the wares. Even the mundane details of supplying water to a city the size of New York, over half a million people in the 1850s, filled him with admiration.

New York satisfied Sam's startling capacity for wonder, but the strain of living in poverty proved too much for him, and in the middle of October, after little more than eight weeks in New York, he moved on to Philadelphia. In Philadelphia, Sam found it difficult to acquire work, though when he finally did, it paid better wages than he had earned in New York. The best position involved night work as a substitute typesetter at the *Philadelphia Inquirer*. His first letter from Philadelphia to his brother, whose whereabouts remained a mystery to him, offered Orion the same bravado he had shown Pamela. "I fancy they'll have to wait some time till they see me downhearted or afraid of starving while I have strength to work and am in a city of 400,000 inhabitants."

After several weeks, the family at last reported their move to Sam: Orion had taken charge of a new paper, the *Muscatine Journal*, with Henry assisting him. Sam wrote about his new city for his brother's paper, reporting on a visit to Benjamin Franklin's grave, which he knew would have a special interest for Orion. Living in a boarding house and working from seven in the evening till three in the morning, Sam boasted, he could go to the theater matinees and to work, and still have the afternoon to himself. The language in his letters showed an increasing maturity. He copied his reports of the Philadelphia sights from a guidebook, but altered the descriptions into a style much more muscular and direct, using simplified sentence structure, tactile descriptions, and apt similes. Inspired by the great orators who had visited Hannibal, he embraced writing that was as immediate as speech.

In February, he took a "flying trip" to Washington, D.C., as much to allay the cold as to satisfy his brother's desire for a greater variety of subjects. In surefooted prose that captured the contradictions of the young nation's capital, he wrote:

> The public buildings of Washington are all fine specimens of architecture, and would add greatly to the embellishment of such a city as New York—but here they are sadly out of place looking like so many palaces in a Hottentot village. . . . The [other] buildings, almost invariably, are very poor—two and three story brick houses, and strewed about in clusters; you seldom see a compact square off Pennsylvania Avenue. They look as though they might have been emptied out of a sack by some Brobdignagian gentleman, and when falling, been scattered abroad by the winds.

He played tourist to the hilt, traipsing through snow and wind to the Smithsonian, the National Theater, the Patent Office Museum, and finally the Capitol, where he spotted Thomas Hart Benton amid the jabbering congressmen. A senator for the first thirty years of Missouri's statehood, Benton had lost his seat in 1850, and then returned in 1853 to the lowly House of Representatives, where his efforts at forging a compromise solution to the slavery issue not only failed but also earned him deep enmity at home. Sam described him as "a lion imprisoned in a cage of monkeys." He would die in 1858, before he could witness the bloody end to his frustrated efforts.

Sam returned to Philadelphia for a while and then went again to New York. Unable to find a job—a fire at the Harper and Brothers printshop had put many experienced printers out of work—Sam gave up his sojourn in the East.

The foray had proved at once broadening and disillusioning. In his eight months far from home, he had just barely earned his own living, and without the occasional convivial and gustatory largesse of his family he found the short wages and long hours grinding. Though he wrote letters to distant friends and correspondence to his brother's newspaper, he could not muster the courage to repeat his early success in publishing elsewhere. He did encounter high culture, or what passed for it in the America of the 1850s: He explored the great Philadelphia Water Works; saw Edwin Forrest act; witnessed America's unique democracy in action;

and visited museums, like the one at the Patent Office in Washington where he saw Benjamin Franklin's printing press. The very cogs of Franklin's press embodied history, but Sam's admiration for it was mere sentiment. Franklin's press was almost laughable when compared with the 1854 presses capable of printing twenty thousand sheets an hour. Sam's preoccupation with the conflict between the sentiment of history and the efficiency of technology took root in him, and his enthusiasms for both would create conflicts for him in future years. Much as he adored inventions, he recognized their limits: Technology could improve everything human, he concluded, except human nature.

Despite all he gained from his time away from home, the fact that he felt impelled to return galled him. He felt like a failure when he compared himself with his brother, who had left Hannibal for St. Louis at eighteen. Orion had sent his family a portion of his pay weekly, but Sam could send his mother one gold dollar to show for his entire eight months away. Orion stayed in St. Louis for many years, flitting from one passionate interest to another, but studying the law part-time and making influential friends; Sam could not hold on for a year, and he met no one except the people with whom he worked or boarded. He took the train west in the spring of 1854, anxiously sitting up several days in the smoking car. He stopped for a short visit with his sister in St. Louis before boarding a steamer north to Iowa, sleeping the entire thirty-six hours it took to get there. Going to Muscatine was not going home. He had no home; he had no life in Iowa; he had no life anywhere. What Sam had so forcefully run away from the summer before no longer existed.

Once in Iowa, Sam flirted with the idea of staying in Muscatine to work with his brother. The town was like Hannibal, a little larger perhaps, but not nearly so interesting. Orion had only grown more preoccupied and his move to Muscatine took place with little forethought; Jane and Henry followed because Orion needed their help. The *Muscatine Journal* read no better than the Hannibal incarnation Sam had ventured to improve. Though Sam befriended a couple of the town's intelligentsia, a bookseller and a teacher, and so found Muscatine convivial enough, his family circle remained difficult for him. Orion's confusion had significant consequences for him in the summer of 1854: He had proposed marriage— to two women. Unable to resolve the matter for himself, he allowed one of them, Mary Eleanor Stotts—called Mollie, and the daughter of a childhood friend of Jane's—to make up his mind for him. They married before the end of the year. Although Sam lingered with his mother and brothers until the summer of 1854, Orion still could not pay him from the earnings of the newspaper. Unwilling to be his brother's indentured servant and unable to manage life with this madcap family in Muscatine, Sam returned to St. Louis by the middle of July 1854. Jane found Mollie a trifle intimidating and followed Sam south to St. Louis a few months later, taking up residence with her daughter's family.

Working as a compositor for the *St. Louis Evening News*, Sam found a room in a section of town that catered to students. He roomed with Jacob Burrough, a ravenous reader and journeyman chair-maker. Testing the waters as a journeyman himself, Sam became fast friends with Burrough. In a letter to Burrough after he had become famous, Sam acknowledged that he had been "a callow fool, a self-sufficient ass, a mere human tumble-bug, stern in air, heaving at his bit of dung, imagining he is remodeling the world." In short, he was an adolescent know-it-all, but one who after the loneliness and deprivation of eastern travels now found St. Louis life to his taste. For excitement, there were election riots involving the Know-Nothing party, whose platform of xenophobia and bigotry prompted hot-tempered violence. Sam joined other young men of the city as a volunteer citizen-policeman, but he fearfully backed out as his division marched toward the rioting mob. For culture, he attended lectures and the theater, often amateur productions featuring his friends. Having renewed his childhood ambition to enter the St. Louis–New Orleans steamboat trade, Sam took French lessons; an ability to speak the language would give him an advantage there. He even asked the old family benefactor, wealthy James Clemens, for help in gaining a post on a boat, but his relative told Sam to stick with the printing trade.

Soon after Sam's arrival in St. Louis, he resumed writing correspondence for Orion's *Muscatine Journal*. Pregnant and craving friends and family, Orion's wife Mollie wanted to leave Muscatine for her home in Keokuk; she belonged to one of the town's premier families. So in June 1855, Orion sold his share of the newspaper, moved Henry and Mollie to Keokuk, halfway between Hannibal and Muscatine, and bought the Ben Franklin Job Printing Office. Sam came up to escape the fierce heat of the St. Louis summer and Orion offered him a job, at five dollars a week and board at Keokuk's best hotel. By fall 1855, the three brothers were together again, working under the name of Orion's hero.

Before settling in at Keokuk, Sam took a trip back to Hannibal and Florida, Missouri. Closing in on twenty, he had sufficient maturity to conduct business on the family's behalf, at least under the watchful eye of Uncle John Quarles. He went to Florida to claim his mother's share of an inheritance due from the estate of her father. The notebook that Sam had intended to contain only his French lessons became an omnibus of an 1850s young male American's varied interests, including legal documents,

chess moves, anecdotes, street directions, personal comments, and phren-
ological observations. Sam copied these last, with slight emendations, from
a book on phrenology by a St. Louis Universalist pastor, the Reverend
George Summer Weaver. Phrenology, a popular psychological theory in
nineteenth-century America, claimed that discrete parts of the brain represented different aspects of one's character, and that the exercise of
certain characteristics enlarged that portion of the brain, as if the brain
were a muscle. This enlargement produced a detectable bulge in the cra-
nium, which a gifted phrenologist could detect. An examination of the
head thus revealed the patient's character. The practice had a sincere,
dedicated following among amateurs looking for a physiological key to the
human mind, and phrenology attracted both gifted practitioners and char-
latans. Popularizers of this system turned phrenology into a parlor game,
with the language of phrenology entering common discourse. Referring to
a sanguine, bilious, or nervous temperament invoked not only the older,
supplanted system of humors, which determined character and health by
assessing bodily fluids, but also the newer belief in the meaning of the
contours of the human skull.

Sam bought phrenology wholesale. He copied Weaver's summaries of
each temperament, with special attention to "the sanguine," because he
identified that as his own, amending Weaver's assertion that the sanguine
temperament went with blue eyes to "blue or gray," as his were variously
described. According to Weaver, the sanguine temperament

> gives activity, quickness, suppleness to all the motions of
> body and mind; great elasticity and buoyancy of spirit; read-
> iness, and even fondness for change; suddenness and intensity
> of the feelings; impulsiveness, and hastiness in character;
> great warmth of both anger and love; it works fast and tires
> soon; runs its short race and gives over. . . . It loves excite-
> ment, noise, bluster, fun, frolic, high times, great days, mass
> meetings, camp meetings, big crowds. It is also predominant
> in those active, stirring, noisy characters that are found in
> every community.

Adding his own views to this surprisingly accurate description of
young Sam Clemens, Sam incorporated the following sentences of his own
into Weaver's text: "It is very sensitive and is first deeply hurt by a
slight, the next emotion is violent rage, and in a few moments the cause
and the result are both forgotten for the time being. It often forgives, but
never entirely forgets an injury." Sam also concerned himself with Orion,

to whom he had committed himself, looking for a bright side to his coming association. Copying Weaver's portrait of a nervous temperament, Sam parenthetically inscribed his brother's name and noted that the nervous temperament "makes geniuses, precocious children, people of purely intellectual habits and tastes." The comments document Sam's emotional preparations for his reconciliation with Orion.

Although the pressure of working with his brother threatened to drive Sam off into another bout of journeyman work, Orion's domestic concerns gave his younger brother some breathing room. After his daughter Jennie was born on September 14, 1855, Orion undertook to assemble and print Keokuk's first city directory, leaving the remainder of the business to Sam's guidance. Sam found companionship in Henry, now seventeen, and in Mollie's circle of women friends. Keokuk proved so companionable that it held Sam for over a year. His high spirits, his slow and poetic manner of speaking, his quick wit, and his wide intelligence made him a favorite with Keokuk's smart set. He befriended the Taylor girls, Annie and her younger sisters, the daughters of Hawkins Taylor, a former steamboat captain soon to become mayor of Keokuk. The father of another friend, Ella Creel, would also become mayor. Mollie's sister, Belle Stotts, was Ella Creel's inseparable companion.

Both Sam and Henry slept in the printing office, which was located on the third floor of a building in the center of town. At night after the work was done, the office became a gathering place. Edward Brownell, who worked in the bookstore downstairs, often came up to join Sam, Henry, and Dick Higham, who also worked for Orion. A music teacher named Oliver Isbell conducted classes in the evening on the second floor and disliked the racket made by the young men above. One night, he impolitely let Sam's rowdies know. The next night Sam retaliated with a bowling match using cobblestones and wine bottles. Isbell banged on the door to no avail and accosted Sam the next day. Sam then organized his friends into a minimilitia and drilled them—bootstep after bootstep— while Isbell tried to teach below. Catching on at last, Isbell apologized with humor, which won Sam over. The teacher joined the social circle and even induced Sam to bring his fine tenor to the chorale.

Sam developed close ties with several women in his clique, writing poems and letters to them. All through the winter and spring of 1856, he felt happy and relaxed, a popular beau free from his mother's supervision and Orion's meddling. His popularity opened a new opportunity for him. At a banquet on January 17, 1856, which Orion organized for the town's printers to honor Ben Franklin on the 150th anniversary of his birth, "Sam Clemens was loudly and repeatedly called for, and he responded in a speech 'replete with wit and humor, being interrupted by long and continuous bursts of applause.' " It was a tremendous accolade for a man just twenty. That dinner inaugurated Sam's career as a public speaker. He returned to writing, then, and began to think again about a career.

As spring slipped into summer, however, Keokuk began to lose its charm. Orion's disorganized approach to business frustrated him. Not surprisingly, Orion could not pay him the promised five dollars a week, so he instead made Sam a partner in the Ben Franklin Job Printing Office, which paid only honor. He and Orion divided the labor, with Orion attending to the city directory and Sam to the smaller jobs that naturally came his way as the charming man-about-town. Once Sam had the jobs in hand, however, Orion claimed the compositors or the presses for the directory, and Sam could not deliver the material when he promised it. Orion also knocked down whatever price Sam had fetched, hoping for repeat business, but ending up only operating at a loss.

Keokuk also dimmed because Sam was in love with bright, funny Annie Taylor, who was away at Iowa Wesleyan College. Sam wrote fancifully to her of a colloquium of bugs gathered around him as he worked the press. They saw each other whenever Annie came home, but their relationship did not develop more seriously. Growing up in a prudish household, devoid of affectionate touching, Sam felt uncomfortable initiating any intimacy. He did not know how to approach women. Neither his parents' marriage nor that between Orion and Mollie gave him any clues as to how even to talk to a girl who interested him.

In fact, the honorable expression of physical affection was the norm in their circle: Belle Stotts had been romantically linked in rumor to the music professor, Oliver Isbell, so much so that the announcement of his marriage to someone else caused an uproar within the Stotts household. Even quiet Henry, head over heels in love with Mary Jane Taylor, could express more of his feelings toward his object of desire than could Sam. Though Sam couldn't tell Annie how he felt, he did confide in Henry somewhat. In a letter he wrote to his younger brother during the summer of 1856, Sam couldn't contain his enthusiasm about seeing his beloved, interjecting several variations of the simple sentence "*Annie* is well," "Annie *is* well," "Annie is *well*."

Despite his feeling for Annie, or perhaps because of his failure to make the relationship progress, Sam felt the urge to take to the road again. In the very same letter to Henry that bubbled with joy over seeing Annie, Sam discussed his intention to leave not only Keokuk and the Mississippi River Valley but the United States. Reports about the bounty of the Amazon had drifted back with the first explorers, and Sam, in consultation with a Keokuk physician who envisioned a pharmaceutical fortune, had determined to go to South America to set up in the coca business.

There was no business there yet—no plantations, no roads, not even regular boat transport between North and South America—but Sam wanted to get rich by getting there first, and coca leaves, the raw ingredient of cocaine, seemed the perfect opportunity. He had already told his mother of his plans, but warned Henry not to tell Orion, who had the mistaken impression that Sam would serve as the United States agent for colleagues already in the Amazon. However, "that don't suit me. My confidence in human nature does not extend quite that far," Sam wrote of such an arrangement. "Ma knows my determination, but *even she* counsels me to keep it from Orion. She says I can treat him as I did her when I started to St. Louis and went to New York."

Only one thing stood in the way of Sam's next high adventure: He needed money. Though in his last years, he would claim to have discovered a fifty-dollar bill blowing down the streets of Keokuk, he found the resources to leave Keokuk more conventionally; he probably lied to discourage people from digging up his juvenilia. He arranged with George Rees, the editor of the *Keokuk Post*, to publish sketches of the big city written from the point of view of a country bumpkin, at five dollars apiece. By the middle of October, he had gone to St. Louis.

Though he did not stay long, St. Louis gave Sam both a dose of family life and inspiration for his correspondence to the Keokuk newspaper. Jane's much younger half-brother, Dr. James Lampton, Orion's contemporary, and his pretty wife Ella were now living in St. Louis, too. Jim and Ella took in Dr. John McDowell to live with them. McDowell, the brother of the fourteen-year-old corpse that had hung in the cave south of Hannibal, began an affair with Ella that was obvious to everyone but Jim Lampton. Sam, confused by his own earlier desire for Ella, rebelled at witnessing her affair with Dr. McDowell. The fusion in his imagination of Ella and of McDowell's dead sister added to his confusion and helped drive him away.

St. Louis did prove literarily ripe for Sam. His letters to the Keokuk paper, signed "Thomas Jefferson Snodgrass," employed a fictional narrator—and not merely a pseudonym—for the first time. Writing in a marginally literate voice was a common stratagem in this era; newspapers all over the Mississippi Valley published correspondence of a similar sort. The bumpkin narrator made the western readers feel superior and laugh at the rube's idiocy; eastern papers published the same sort of thing, only with a westerner in place of the rube. Describing the din at the theater one night, Snodgrass wrote, "Gals! Bless your soul, there was gals of every age and sex, from three months up to a hundred years, and every cherubim of 'em had a fan and an opery glass and a—tongue—probably two or three of the latter weepon, from the racket they made. No use trying to estimate the oceans of men and moustaches—the place looked like a shoe brush shop."

He returned briefly to Keokuk to bargain for a higher price for subsequent Snodgrass letters, and then went on through Chicago to Cincinnati, the center of the western publishing trade, where he expected to find work as a compositor. Sam boarded with a man named Macfarlane, an autodidact who never made personal disclosures, never even confiding his line of work, but who contentedly discussed philosophical matters with Sam for hours. He outlined his pre-Darwinian theory of evolution, maintaining that man's consciousness was a developmental dead end, a fact that bumped humans from the top of the evolutionary ladder to the bottom. Sympathetic to the blamelessness of nonconscious animals, Sam began to regard the human race with deep ambivalence. He questioned whether the capacity for thought, which distinguished humans from lower animals, actually did raise the moral value of human beings. At the same time he entertained Macfarlane's radical philosophy, Sam harbored an ambition that only consciousness made possible. Working as a typesetter at T. Wrightson and Company, the city's largest printer, he helped set *James's River Guide*, the authoritative handbook to the Ohio and Mississippi river valleys and the touchstone of that brave American creature who would eventually become so central to Samuel Clemens' myth of Mark Twain: the river pilot.

Not yet twenty-one, the young journalist got off to a roaring literary start in Cincinnati, sending two extended pieces back to the *Keokuk Post*. He issued another Snodgrass letter, concerning Sam's roundabout journey from St. Louis to Cincinnati, which showed his comic side as Snodgrass masters the subtle rules of train travel after only a few missteps. Arriving in Chicago, he writes that "bimeby my vallis made its appearance, with shirts and cravats hangin out at one end, and socks and collars at t'other—lookin considerable like a Irishman that jest got out of a New Orleans l'ection riot—and dern my cats if I'd a knowd it was a vallis at all." Snodgrass indicated he wanted to publish a "diarrea," following the example of other authors of comic correspondence from fictional semiliterates, but he never did. Sam Clemens' work as Snodgrass helped him develop his stylistic reach by writing in imitation of his elders, but it did not represent a distinctive voice of his own.

Sam's productivity those first few weeks soon slackened. The long hours at Wrightson's and his boardinghouse companions kept him from taking up his pen, but he also began to suspect that making a fortune in South America, even in as promising a commodity as coca leaves, was not the most realistic prospect. The bitter Cincinnati winter, together with an early freezing of the Ohio River that prevented the city from receiving enough coal, made life there unbearably difficult. On February 15, 1857, just three and a half months after arriving in Cincinnati, Sam boarded the steamboat *Paul Jones*, bound for New Orleans. Since the middle of November, he had done little but work, freeze, and think.

Though Sam still felt excitement about the Amazon just a few weeks before left Cincinnati, he took the *Paul Jones* to explore a different opportunity. Horace Bixby, the boat's pilot, was heading for a posting on a boat in the St. Louis–New Orleans trade, and Sam found himself wanting to realize his wistful boyhood ambition of piloting a riverboat. If Sam could convince Bixby to take him on as a trainee—cub pilot or steersman, they were called—he might live the dream of every boy growing up along the great Mississippi. He could also become wealthy, admired, and independent. That was what appealed to him about writing, after all, but in the winter of 1857 the odds against his success as a writer were much greater than the odds against becoming a pilot.

5   *Life on the Mississippi*

*On the river front some of the houses was sticking out
over the bank. . . . Such a town as that has to be always
moving back, and back, and back, because the river's
always gnawing at it.*
—The Adventures of Huckleberry Finn (1884)

MARK TWAIN LATER wrote that a pilot on the
Mississippi, in the years when the river was America's
Main Street,

was the only unfettered and entirely independent human being that lived in the earth. Kings are but the hampered servants of parliament and people; parliaments sit in chains
forged by their constituency; . . . but in the day I write of,
the Mississippi pilot had *none*. The captain could stand upon
the hurricane-deck, in the pomp of a very brief authority,
and give him five or six orders while the vessel backed into
the stream, and then that skipper's reign was over. The moment that boat was under way in the river, she was under
the sole and unquestioned control of the pilot.

Steamboat traffic dominated the economically and politically vital Mississippi River trade, carting everything of value produced in the Ohio, Missouri, and Mississippi river valleys to New Orleans and St. Louis, from
which they were sold to the increasingly industrialized Northeast. The

tentacles of the river and its trade seemed to reach around the world. No wonder that Sam—first as a boy and then as a young man on his own but not independent—felt hypnotized by the power of the steamboat pilot. If Sam could take control of such a boat, it would remove from his life both the ghostly hand of his father's authority and his brother Orion's surrogate version of it. And, showman that he was, piloting a riverboat would put Sam center stage in the gaudiest ongoing performance in western life. The job would also resolve his persistent anxiety over money, which so often gnawed at Sam—Mississippi riverboat pilots earned more than the Vice President of the United States. Shivering through the Cincinnati winter, Sam realized he had left Hannibal nearly four years before, aiming for greatness, and yet only labored long, undistinguished, and unpromising hours as a compositor, as he had before he left Hannibal. Only the size of the shop and the size of the city differed.

While some of his boyhood friends had gone on to California's goldfields, others had gone to the river as pilots. His best friend, Will Bowen, had joined his brothers Bart and Sam as a pilot by 1857, bringing pride and prosperity to his clan. The Bowens were so well known to the river trade that Sam used Will's name as a reference when importuning pilot Horace Bixby to take him on as a cub. Bixby resisted Sam's pleading as the boat bobbed west along the Ohio and then south along the Mississippi. Taking advantage of a mishap that stranded the *Paul Jones* for a day on some rocks, Sam lingered around the texas, the area from which the pilot steered, offering unwanted help whenever he perceived a need. Sam's charm and humor eventually persuaded Bixby to accept him as a trainee, for a consideration: $500. Sam had never possessed a tenth of that sum. When the *Paul Jones* docked in New Orleans, Horace Bixby went off in search of a berth on a Mississippi boat and Sam investigated the possibility of reviving his South American dream of entering the coca trade. No boats went to South America from New Orleans, ever. An adventurer with cash could find a vessel, but not a poor twenty-one-year-old typesetter.

Promising payment on arrival in St. Louis, Sam began his training on the upstream journey, attending to Bixby, who had found a position as pilot on a boat bound for the seasonal Missouri River trade. Bixby kept up a stream of chatter, pointing out landmarks, aspects of the river, crossings, and best approaches to the river's obstacles. Piloting on the Mississippi demanded utmost attention—just days before their journey began, the *Cora Anderson* had rammed the *Ben Franklin* a day's travel above the city. Safe, prosperous voyages depended on a pilot's vast storehouse of knowledge about sandbars, submerged snags and boat carcasses, landings, and ever-changing depths of the river. Finally, Bixby turned to Sam and asked him to name the first point above New Orleans. "I was gratified to be able to answer promptly, and I did," Mark Twain later wrote. "I said I didn't know." Bixby immediately exploded at him:

> "What did you suppose I told you the names of those points for?"
> I tremblingly considered a moment, and then the devil of temptation provoked me to say:
> "Well to—to—be entertaining, I thought."
> This was a red rag to the bull. He raged and stormed [and] . . . threw open a window, thrust his head out, and such an irruption followed as I never had heard before.

Bixby told Sam to "get a little memorandum book" and take down everything. Sam talked a clerk out of a partly filled account ledger and began taking detailed notes about the river.

In St. Louis, his family rejoiced at the news that Sam would someday be a pilot; his niece Annie, not quite five, recalled as one of her first memories the hubbub caused by the announcement. After the celebration, reality set in: Sam would need $100 right away to secure his tuition. He went to his wealthy cousin James Clemens to borrow the cash, but returned to his sister's house disappointed. Will Moffett, Pamela's husband, excelling in business, took Sam aside and gave him the money. Delighted and grateful, Sam went to find Bixby, who had equally good news: The pilot responsible for ramming the *Ben Franklin* would be dismissed from the *Cora Anderson*, and Bixby would take his place. The captain of the *Cora Anderson* refused to allow Bixby to take Sam Clemens along as a pilot in training, however, and more than a month passed before Bixby got himself and his new steersman a place.

Sam filled his time in part by writing another Snodgrass letter for the *Keokuk Post*. Incommunicado with his editor for four months, Sam felt a pressing need for the $7.50 each letter brought him. Snodgrass berates the bureaucratic tangle involved in getting poor people coal during the frigid winter in Cincinnati, and then drifts into a bizarre story about an infant given to him by a woman on the street. Snodgrass attempts to quiet the baby by forcing it through a hole in the ice. Mixing violence and humor was another hallmark of the marginally literate narrator, but Sam failed to find an effective balance between Snodgrass' public-spirited critique and his wild disregard for custom and law. After he finished the letter, Sam took a brief trip to Keokuk to deliver the manuscript, see his family, and boast to his old friends. When Sam failed to convince his editor to increase his pay for the Snodgrass letters to ten dollars, he declined to write more of them.

On the Mississippi by the end of April 1857, Sam found the shipboard pattern of four hours on duty and four hours off difficult and disruptive. He despaired of ever learning the river. Even if his memory could capture every nuance of the one trip he'd made from New Orleans to St. Louis, he would still know less than one half of the upriver course, and that only in one season. The downstream features and the upstream portions passed off-watch or at night remained a mystery to him. In his memorandum book he cryptically recorded such notations as "Bird's II.—Hd towh br, & 250 under hd of II—9 ft. D. S.—faint circle fm pt to hd towh, S open on pt." Soon his book could hold no more, but neither could he write down what he needed to know. Not only were the shapes and colors of the river impossible to describe, but every detail of the river revised itself in different weather and different seasons.

Bixby also challenged Sam at every turn: "What is the shape of Walnut Bend?" "How much water did we have in the middle crossing at Hole in the Wall, trip before last?" He taught Sam to hold an exact picture of the river in his head and refuse to believe his eyes and ears if they contradicted what he absolutely knew about the Mississippi. Once Bixby left Sam in charge at a simple crossing, and then schemed with the leads-man to make Sam think the river had turned shallow. Even though Sam entered the crossing knowing he had plenty of water there, the leadsman's false calls made him swear he saw a reef in front of him. He "flew to the speaking tube, and shouted to the engineer: 'Oh, Ben, if you love me, *back* her! Quick, Ben! Oh, back the immortal *soul* out of her!'" He suffered weeks of teasing for his cowardly gaffe, but he learned to trust his own sense of the Mississippi.

He also feasted on steamboat life, absorbing the legends and language as he mastered the landings and levees. Carrying 130 passengers plus freight, Sam's boat glittered stem to stern with fancy woodwork and paint. Liveried texas-tenders brought the pilots ices. The texas often hosted crowds of unemployed pilots, who could hook a ride on any boat on the pretense of "taking a look at the river," reeducating themselves about the Mississippi. Once, under the watchful eyes of a dozen pilots, Bixby ne-gotiated a difficult river crossing as calmly as he would traverse his own parlor, and his astonished audience declared him "a lightning pilot," mak-ing Sam proud to be his pupil. Pilots boasted without seeming to, just by telling stories about treacherous crossings and "sawyers"—submerged logs carried along by the current, invisible under the muddy water. Sam heard fanciful ghost stories he later brought home to his niece, and he witnessed ghastly cruelty in the feuds that plagued the small towns along the Mississippi. He learned the songs of the leadsmen, who dropped a line off the bow of the boat and sang back special melodies that indicated how much water in fathoms lay beneath the boat: "Quarter-less three!" and "Mark twain!"—this last meant two fathoms, or twelve feet, safe water for any steamboat.

Just before Sam signed on, the pilots organized themselves into a union, the Western Boatman's Benevolent Association. The union had two purposes: to keep salaries high by limiting the number of licensed pilots; and to take care of sick or unemployed pilots and their families. From the start, Sam, a member of the printers' unions wherever he had worked, took an active interest in the organization. The WBBA could protect pilots from owners and salve the painful outcomes of the tragedies endemic to this dangerous mode of travel.

No union, however, could protect anyone aboard a steamboat from the gamblers, roughnecks, and desperadoes who plied the Mississippi during the steamboat era. Violent men boarded boats in gangs, taking over the cabins for all-night card games, drunken revels, and cursing marathons. Captains and pilots risked their lives standing up against the pistols, rifles, and bowie knives that the hustlers brought to their card tables. Sam learned prodigious cursing on the steamboats, but he also learned how to subdue a hostile crowd with his humor and his presence. He became an adept mimic of rivermen's boasts. "I put my hand on the sun's face and make it night in the earth; I bite a piece out of the moon and hurry the seasons; I shake myself and crumble the mountains! Contemplate me through leather—*don't* use the naked eye!" Everything he learned on the river—the language, the feel of command, the ways of the rapscallions and rajas of the trade—became ballast for his imagination, to be kept in the hold until his writing called on it.

By the middle of the summer of 1857, Sam had made five runs up and down the river on several different boats. Bixby, wanting to pilot the more lucrative Missouri and feeling that Sam would benefit from another pilot's tutelage, traded his cub to the pilots of the *John J. Roe*, a slow-moving agricultural barge with a congenial crew that seemed to Sam like his uncle John Quarles' Florida farm set upon the water. Becoming friends of Beck Jolly and Zeb Leavenworth, the pilots of this groaning and un-romantic river freighter, Sam joined in the festivities with the "friends of the captain" who rode along; the boat was not licensed to carry legal, paying passengers. He sang, danced, and entertained with his comical stories. He grew singularly unattractive muttonchop sideburns, the fashion among pilots.

Now a confident steersman, Sam joined other boats Bixby arranged for him, settling in under the ornery but skilled pilot William Brown on the lavish steamboat *Pennsylvania*. In late November, his boat encountered the *Vicksburg* heading upstream thirty miles outside of New Orleans. The boats signaled one another—and a race was on. Steamboat racing, dangerous and illegal, formed a fundamental part of river culture. The pilot called to the engineers to build up steam. Since the hotter the fire the greater the steam pressure driving the paddle wheels, engineers tossed not only knotty wood but also whole barrels of tar and turpentine into the boilers. The *Pennsylvania* had the early advantage in the race, but then the other boat came alongside her. To avoid losing his lead, pilot William Brown crowded the *Vicksburg* between the sandbar and Sam's boat. The *Vicksburg* had to crash or stop, perhaps destroying itself in the process. It crashed, and the *Pennsylvania*, severely damaged in the collision, had to be towed back to New Orleans for repairs.

The captain of the *Pennsylvania*, John Klinefelter, had a special interest in keeping Sam Clemens happy, because Sam would be a powerful witness in the trial for damages that would result from the race and collision. Still under contract, Sam found his way up to St. Louis for the holidays. Since he made no money during his apprenticeship, he worked as a watchman on the docks for a few dollars, staying out all night to protect the cargo. He resisted the temptation to write for money, as he told Orion and Mollie in March of 1858, "because when one is learning the river, he is not allowed to do or think about anything else." Orion had given up the Ben Franklin Job Printing Office in June 1857; by the end of summer he had moved with Mollie and little Jennie back to the inauspicious town of his family's roots—Jamestown, Tennessee. Revising his ambitions once again, he planned to sell the family land and finish the study of law he began in St. Louis under Edward Bates years before. Idle and directionless, nineteen-year-old Henry had come down to St. Louis, where he contented himself just reading books. Sam got Henry a berth on the *Pennsylvania* as a mud clerk, keeping track of the cargo and fuel as they came on and off the boat. Providing young Henry with a job, Captain Klinefelter enticed Sam to testify to the relative blamelessness of the *Pennsylvania* crew during his deposition toward the end of March. Sam qualified his statements competently: "I think she was steady"; "I am not exactly certain whether I was in a position to see"; "I do not know whether she had any signal lights up." The owners of the *Pennsylvania* escaped with only a light penalty.

Sam soon began to regret that he had made this bargain. William Brown, the pilot he had defended in his statement and under whom he served as steersman, proved to be a mean-spirited, small-minded, foul-mouthed tyrant. He talked to hear himself and would not listen to anyone else; more than likely he found Sam's engaging manner irritating in the extreme. Brown's philistinism seemed all the more egregious when compared with the refinement of the other pilot on board the *Pennsylvania*, George Ealer, who played the flute and read Shakespeare aloud. The winter of 1858 proved bitter and icy, and more than once Sam found himself out on a yawl in the middle of the frigid river searching out a clear passage for the boat bearing down on him. Whether because of Brown's tyranny, the morally dangerous game of giving testimony in exchange for work, the quietus in his love life, or the extra responsibility he bore for his brother, the winter he spent aboard the *Pennsylvania* dragged along ominously.

Spring promised a change in Sam's dreary mood. Women were increasingly on his mind. His last romantic episode ended when Annie Taylor, the belle of Keokuk, dropped him. Writing her the summer before from New Orleans, he complained of her faltering correspondence. "I imagined that as you had got started once more, you would continue to write with your ancient punctuality." She didn't, and Sam didn't even tell her about his new career. Spring 1858 brought Sam a new love. While docked in New Orleans, Sam went aboard the *John J. Roe*, tied up alongside the *Pennsylvania*, to visit with Beck Jolly and Zeb Leavenworth. There he met Laura Wright, a small, slim fourteen-year-old girl with long hair, a fine mind, and a grave demeanor. A cousin of the Leavenworths, Laura was on a vacation from her central Missouri home where her wealthy father was a judge. For the several days the boats were at the levee together, so were Sam and Laura. The eight years separating them—he was twenty-two now—were not unusual for a courtship at that time and in that place, but the opportunity for such extensive unchaperoned time was quite atypical, and Sam and Laura formed a deep bond. When the *Pennsylvania* began backing out, Sam had to vault the rails of the two boats to cling to his post.

Sam bored his brother Henry with tales of Laura; but then a disturbing dream alarmed him enough that he told his family about it. Sam saw Henry, dressed in Sam's clothes, laid out in a metal coffin, a bouquet of white roses with a single red one in the middle on his breast. The nightmare woke Sam, whose suspicion of his own clairvoyance made such a vision unnerving. His mother and sister pooh-poohed his worry, and Sam's mind returned to Laura. They wrote letters, but his training and her return home kept them apart.

Then a disaster utterly altered Sam's romance with the river. On the run down from St. Louis at the beginning of June 1858, Henry came into the pilothouse to give William Brown a message from Captain Klinefelter to stop at a certain landing. Brown passed the landing without stopping and the captain came up to the pilothouse to admonish him. Brown claimed he never got the message, and when Henry showed up Brown jumped all over him verbally and physically. "I was wild from that moment," Sam wrote Mollie. "I left the boat to steer herself, and avenged the insult—and the Captain said I was right—that he would discharge Brown in N. Orleans if he could get another pilot, and would do it in St. Louis anyhow. Of course both of us could not return to St. Louis on the same boat—no pilot could be found, and the Captain sent me to the *A. T. Lacey*, with orders to her Captain to bring me to St. Louis."

Fuming his way back upriver on June 13, 1858, two days behind his old boat, Sam received terrible news. The boilers of the *Pennsylvania* had exploded. Dozens of people were killed and hundreds wounded. Henry, asleep above the boilers, was blown into the air and then landed back among the debris. Swimming into the wreckage to help others, Henry inhaled steam and burned himself inside and out. Captain Klinefelter also behaved bravely, and survived with small injury, but William Brown was killed instantly. The *Pennsylvania* caught fire, drifted a few miles downriver, and sank. Henry, exposed to the elements for hours before his rescue, was brought to Memphis, where the Exchange became an emergency hospital. Sam arrived on June 15, and a newspaper reporter noted, "He hurried to the Exchange to see his brother, and on approaching the bedside of the wounded man, his feelings so much overcame him, at the scalded and emaciated form before him, that he sunk to the floor overpowered."

Sam nursed his brother for a week. As Henry floated in and out of consciousness, his gentle manner and Sam's tender dedication to his injured brother earned the admiration of everyone in attendance and repeated mention in the extensive newspaper coverage of the accident. Sam wrote his sister-in-law that Henry received "five—aye, ten, fifteen, *twenty* times the care and attention that any one else has had." Henry seemed to recover a little. The doctor in charge told Sam to get a medical student to give Henry some morphine if he should wake. During the night of June 20, Henry woke in pain, and Sam pleaded with a student to give him some relief. The man nervously administered the dose. Henry settled into sleep, and he did not wake up again. He died on the morning of June 21, 1858.

Sam was so distraught that friends accompanied him and Henry's body back to St. Louis, as a protection against Sam's suicidal despair. The people of Memphis had been so affected by Henry's bravery and Sam's loyalty that they bought Henry a metal coffin and a bouquet of roses: white, with a red one in the center. Henry was dressed in Sam's clothes.

Sam's prescience of Henry's death, as with the death of Margaret nearly two decades before, reinforced his powerful guilt. His mind raced with recriminations: If he had not lobbied for a job for Henry; if he had not fought Brown over family honor; if he had done something more to help Klinefelter find a pilot, or not testified for him in March; if he had done something to stop the race in November, before the boat's boiler had suffered damage; if he hadn't pressed the physician for morphine; if he hadn't conducted a twenty-year-long rivalry with his brother, then, maybe, Henry would still be alive. Orion hurried west from Tennessee; Mollie from Keokuk; and Jane, Sam, Pamela, and Will Moffett from St. Louis. The family buried him at Hannibal on June 26, 1858.

The second week in July, in order to get Sam back on the river, Bart Bowen brought him onto his boat as a steersman. Then, in early August, Bart's brother Sam got him a spot on the Memphis–St. Louis packet *John H. Dickey*, captained by Dan Able, whom Sam knew from Hannibal. Sam wanted both to be on the river and to remain in close touch with family after the loss of Henry, and the short runs to Memphis allowed him weekly visits. Captain Able owned the *Dickey*, the linchpin of the Memphis–St. Louis trade, previously served only by tramp steamers. The Bowens' plan of getting Sam back on the river sped his recovery after Henry's death. The success of Captain Able, who had commanded his first boat when he was Sam's age, stirred Sam's ambition. During the summer and fall of 1858, Sam witnessed the growth of the cotton trade along this line. A fortune was being made under his feet as he steered, and he resolved to make a future fortune himself.

Soon confident of his river knowledge, Sam started to write again, for St. Louis and Memphis papers. He penned some puffery extolling the *Dickey*, Captain Able, and the city of Memphis, cross-fertilizing his interests in piloting and writing. He also wrote fanciful contributions to the *Memphis Appeal*, one satirizing the journalistic habit of inventing "calls" to traveling performers—requests for performances by public figures—to pump up interest in the performance. In Sam's piece, brimming with silly canine puns, the performer is a dog, and the invitation reads, in part, "We, dear sir, have recognized your artistic genius as displayed by leaping over the many obstructions thrown in your way by the manager, prompter and public." The artist refuses the offer, maintaining, "I have, during my stay here, been treated like a dog."

The pace of Sam's life picked up dramatically after the tragedy of Henry's death. Sam's interest in Laura Wright, with whom he kept up correspondence, intensified. The death of his brother moved Sam toward wanting a family of his own; he was the only surviving Clemens sibling without a family. Henry's death also concentrated Sam's ambition. He wanted not only to make a fortune, but also to make a name for himself. Having once been content to follow whatever paths appeared before him, with an eye for adventure and quick money, he now seemed reborn with sudden determination and energy. By November, Horace Bixby returned to piloting the Mississippi and took Sam along with him on two of the finest boats on those waters. On April 9, 1859, Sam received his license to pilot boats on the Mississippi between St. Louis and New Orleans. He had achieved his great goal in under two years. Sam quickly proved himself a trusted and capable pilot and, after his first posting beside Bart Bowen on the *A. T. Lacey*, he went on to pilot a boat almost continually over the next two years. Most of his postings were on the larger boats plying the Mississippi, and, after his first berth, he never served his captain for only a single sailing, a sign of the confidence he inspired. Cautious and reliable at the wheel, he caused no accidents, except two harbor crashes for which his captains took the blame. He ran aground only once, an excellent record. A year after receiving his license, Sam wrote Orion:

> I am also lucky in having a berth, while all the other young pilots are idle. This *is* the luckiest circumstance that ever befell me. Not on account of the wages—for that is a secondary consideration—but from the fact that the *City of Memphis* is the largest boat in the trade and the hardest to pilot, *and* consequently I can get a *reputation* on her, which is a thing I never could accomplish on a transient boat. I can "bank" in the neighborhood of $100 a month on her, and that will satisfy me for the present (principally because the other youngsters *are sucking their fingers*). Bless me! what a pleasure there is in revenge!—and what vast respect Prosperity commands!

Despite his claim in this epistolary victory dance that the money did not matter to him, it clearly did. Sam derived deep pleasure from his affluence. He cherished membership in the elite club of pilots in part because of the prestige, but also because of the gloating rights membership granted him. Besting the once-superior younger pilots gratified Sam's competitive rage. In a single coup, he had surpassed his brother and exceeded his father's greatest accomplishment. Still, his father's and brother's uneasy relationship with the commercial world kept Sam apprehensive about his fortunes; his own feelings of unworthiness, drawn more sharply by Henry's death, made him doubt the justice of receiving the very money he craved. Money appeared to be an objective measure of a man's worth, but Sam's current affluence did little to assuage his doubt about himself.

Orion felt Sam's letter stingingly. After Henry's death, he had returned to Keokuk but found nothing there to occupy him except politics. Abolitionism had become a political litmus test: A person either subscribed to it or was considered an enemy. To forward their powerful agenda, abolitionists had organized a new political party from the ashes of the Whigs and had settled on an Illinois lawyer, Abraham Lincoln, as the 1860 Republican party's presidential candidate. Committed to the antislavery cause, Orion worked actively for Lincoln, whose candidacy was at once magnetic and divisive. Orion's efforts on behalf of the eventual President interfered with his ability to earn a living in his wife's hometown, and by the spring of 1860 he moved to Memphis, Missouri, to open a law practice and represent the Republicans. The St. Louis portion of the clan succeeded in putting behind them their grief over the loss of Henry, in part because of the birth of a son, Samuel Moffett, to Pamela in November 1860. Despite the scandal it caused among her neighbors, Jane began attending services at the Jewish temple. Always eccentric, she claimed she went to the temple merely because she liked the music; Jane Clemens was always a woman to whom the content of religion mattered less than the feeling of peace it brought her.

Now a man of influence and fortune, Samuel Langhorne Clemens at age twenty-five absorbed himself completely in his new role. Pilots had one foot in bourgeois prosperity and another in bohemian sensationalism, and Sam Clemens prided himself on his mastery of both of the river pilot's worlds. He dressed expensively and flamboyantly with a keen eye on the newest fashions. He prided himself on knowing the chic slang and using it right, dancing the most modern steps elegantly, and holding his own with the finest of the fine men who commanded the great boats along the Mississippi River. In Memphis or New Orleans, he always ate at the most expensive restaurants and hobnobbed with community notables. Sliding easily from the gaming tables of shipboard ruffians to the dining tables of the elite, from the domestic solidity of the Moffett household to the wild walks of nighttime New Orleans, Sam Clemens was a natty high-roller. Expressing his uncertainty about his affluence the only way he knew how, he speculated on the commodities the riverboats carried, buying produce low and shipping it where he could sell it high.

Not content to make his reputation as a pilot, he also desired fame, and he believed it would come to him through his pen. Sam experimented with full-fledged stories, Gothic tales of murder and revenge and the sort of ghost stories told by steamboatmen; those were the first pieces he had written that would be out of place in a newspaper. By the time he became a pilot, newspapering had been a part of his life for more than a decade. Though he had no easy venue for the fiction he wrote, turning his droll wit and travel adventures into print became second nature for him. While on his first boat, he authored a piece of waggery mercilessly satirizing Captain Isaiah Sellers, who had been a fixture on the river since Missouri joined the Union. Sellers contributed his unmistakable "River Intelligence" to various newspapers, recounting events forty years past to support his prognostications about the condition of today's Mississippi. Sam, who served as cub under Bixby when Sellers piloted the other watch, found his old icon of steamboating egotistical, long-winded, and incapable of trimming a tale to his audience—this last an unforgivable sin in Sam's eyes. Sam deflated Sellers through his narrator Sergeant Fathom, who claimed to have been a cub pilot since before the American Revolution. As Sergeant Fathom concluded, "The gradual *widening* and *deepening* of the river is the whole secret of the matter." Sam had no intention of publishing the cruel satire, but Bart Bowen, his copilot, gave it to a friendly editor, making sure that the introductory paragraph gave enough information to identify Sam as the author. Sellers found the insult so galling he refused to write another newspaper snippet. Sam regretted how hard the old man took it, but the piece earned Sam a reputation among pilots as a daring, funny man.

In the summer of 1860, as the country marched toward civil war, the world Sam piloted so deftly was about to disappear. The Mississippi River knit the nation together, but the political division between the North and the South had become a gulf so vast that even the Big Muddy could not bridge it. It was clear to everyone, even someone as steadfastly apolitical as Sam Clemens, that the compromises that had kept the nation at peace since the Revolution had reached an end. Sam maintained his faith in the remedy of compromise for as long as possible, since a war would destroy the river trade that gave him his place in the world. Even southerners who disliked slavery—and such dislike was nearly universal among the more cosmopolitan southerners—rebelled at granting the federal government power over what had always been a state's decision. Sam could not determine which principles ought to take precedence. Also, with the outcome of the conflict so unpredictable, he did not know which way to jump. He determined to stand pat.

As though reflecting the nation, Sam's life careened out of control. He went to visit Laura Wright in Warsaw, Missouri, but something in this trip led to the disruption of the relationship. Laura's mother may not have approved of a man who made his living consorting with ruffians. Perhaps Laura impetuously threw herself at Sam more forcefully and romantically than he could accept. Sam's growing interest in another woman he had met, Myra Robbins of St. Louis, might also have confused his intentions. He left Warsaw with the relationship irretrievably broken, but Laura had engraved herself in his imagination as his romantic ideal. Soothing his hurt with other feminine contacts, Sam went to Keokuk and saw his friends there. He wrote to Belle Stotts, "*Con*found me if I wouldn't *eat up* half a dozen of you small girls if I just had the merest shadow of a chance this morning. Here I am, now, about 3 weeks out from Keokuk, and 2 from St. Louis, and yet I have not heard a word from you." Sam returned to his river life, and asked Myra Robbins' father for permission to court his daughter. Robbins *père* refused; he didn't approve of rivermen.

Meanwhile, in both the North and South, young men organized independent military units, to defend their state or to preserve the Union. Newspapers overflowed with fiery rhetoric attacking slavery or maintaining the inviolability of states' rights. On the river, everyone speculated on how the conflict would affect the Mississippi trade. As weeks slid by, it became more difficult to remain uncommitted. Sam's captain, David DeHaven, was "flamboyantly secessionist" and his friend Will Bowen's sympathies lay with the South. Once he spoke about Abraham Lincoln's campaign and the United States so disrespectfully that he and Sam got into a shipboard fistfight. Caught between his southern training and his brother's abolitionism, in November Sam voted for John Bell of Tennessee, a minor-party candidate advocating both Union and slavery. Lincoln's election, however, made civil war inevitable. In December 1860, a New Orleans citizens' party forced Sam's commander from the *Pennsylvania*, Captain Klinefelter, a Union sympathizer, out of town. In January, Louisiana seceded. Silence seemed the safest course: Sam's letters home say nothing political and his notebooks contain only river notes and a dialogue from Voltaire.

Like many people caught up in a vast conflict, Sam did not feel strongly enough about either side of the issue to take up arms. He did not know what to do, especially since it seemed that everyone he knew had declared himself willing to die for one side or the other. His conflicting emotions filled a February 1861 letter to his brother recounting a visit to a famous fortune-teller, Madam Caprell. He used the psychic's reading to try to make sense of his history and perhaps point him in a direction, while at the same time laughing off her predictions. The fortune-teller astounded Sam by describing Laura Wright perfectly—"not remarkably pretty, but very intelligent—is educated, and accomplished—and has property—5 feet 3 inches—is slender—dark-brown hair and eyes." She divined what disrupted the affair: "that about the girl's [mother] being 'cranky,' and playing the devil with me, *was* about the neatest thing she performed—for although I have never spoken of the matter, I happen to know that she spoke the truth. The young lady has been beaten by the old one, though through the romantic agency of intercepted letters, and the girl still thinks *I* was in fault." Madam Caprell touched a nerve when she said that no matter whomever else Sam courted, he would always think of Laura Wright first. The fortune-teller also struck gold in detecting Sam's father's death, which, Sam was told, "threw you upon the world and made you what you are." Yet he had achieved success in a career despite obstacles "which would have deterred nineteen out of any twenty men." And, she told Sam, "you have written a great deal; you write well—but you are rather out of practice; no matter—you will be *in* practice some day." She also described Orion as "too visionary—is always flying off on a new hobby." She saw that Orion craved a political appointment to repay his efforts for the new administration and said he should "devote himself to his business and politics, with all his might, for he must hold offices under government, and 6 or 8 years from this time, he will run for Congress."

Six weeks later, President Lincoln named Orion Clemens secretary to the newly formed Nevada Territory, thanks not to Madam Caprell but to Lincoln's new attorney general, Edward Bates. Bates, Orion's mentor in St. Louis, supported this appointment with a tepid letter to Lincoln's new secretary of state, William Seward, "I consider him an honest man of fair mediocrity of talents & learning. . . . Without being very urgent with you, I commend Mr Clemens to you." Now thirty-five, Sam's brother at last had something significant in hand: a sinecure, and a stepping-stone to a livelihood. A territorial position out west was the equivalent of having the government cover the expense of speculation. Going west had always been the best option for people who had failed in the East, and to go with the guarantee of a livelihood was nearly as good as piloting a Mississippi steamboat. Of course, Orion didn't have the money for the trip to Nevada, but he felt sure he would find it. Orion quit Missouri and went to Keokuk, where Mollie and Jennie planned to stay until he could get settled in Carson City and send for them. At least Nevada would provide Orion with an escape from the war.

While America's Civil War began in earnest with the firing on Fort Sumter in April 1861, it had begun along the Mississippi earlier, when armed units took positions on both banks. On a quick trip to Hannibal,

Sam found the town patrolled by a Home Guard loyal to the Union, while his friends whispered about their obligation to defend Missouri's right to self-determination. They begged Sam to heed the governor's call for loyal Missourians to resist Union oppression, but Sam returned to the river uncommitted. All he wanted to do was pilot his boat, but Union forces would inevitably close the river at the southernmost point of Union sympathies, Cairo, Illinois, which would strangle trade to St. Louis.

After the first May run south to New Orleans, Sam's secessionist captain, David DeHaven, decided to limit his boat to a Memphis–New Orleans route. Sam could either stay with the boat and therefore choose the Confederacy, or head home and keep his neutrality a little longer. Sam took passage north on the steamer *Nebraska*, piloted by Zeb Leavenworth, Laura Wright's cousin. At Cairo, Union soldiers searched the boat. Just below St. Louis, they fired a warning shot and then heavy ordnance at the *Nebraska*, shattering the glass in the pilothouse, with Sam in it. The boat wheeled into the St. Louis levee on the morning of May 21, 1861. It was the last boat allowed north. If he had missed the point before, he could not miss it now: There would be no more steamboat traffic up and down the Mississippi. His career had ended just two years after it began.

The next six weeks forced Sam into choices. All of history seemed to converge on him. Now that his job no longer vied with his judgment, which side would he choose? To Sam, both arguments seemed equally virtuous, but he still kept personal concerns, and not moral ones, at the forefront of his deliberations. A rumor ran around the Association Rooms that the Union Army would impress pilots into service, at gunpoint if necessary. Annie Moffett remembered Sam hiding from Union soldiers during his first days in St. Louis, but he did not keep his presence in St. Louis a complete secret, since he took his second degree at the Polar Star Masonic Lodge on June 12. Sam's absence of allegiance drove him to contradictory actions: Once, his niece later remembered, he "helped some boys make Confederate cockades and only shortly afterward became furiously angry when they burned the Union flag." Even when he made a choice as a mere whim, he could not hold to it. He did not believe in either cause enough to fight for it.

By mid-June, however, Sam could no longer maintain his disinterest. His Hannibal friends organized the secessionist Marion (County) Rangers, and Sam joined them. Although it might have seemed a lark to some of the members of the group, many of whom had played at soldiering side by side with Sam as a child, no one could mistake the deadliness of the enterprise. Union passions ran high in Hannibal. The Marion Rangers convened inland, away from the town, hoping to unite with the governor's troops in the southern portion of the state. As second lieutenant of the Rangers, Sam was second-in-command, but since these friends would not obey one another's orders, chain of command mattered little. They managed to live off the generosity of farmers sympathetic with the Southern cause, and found transportation along the way. Soon, however, the weather turned rainy. The men were cold, hungry, wet, and apprehensive. They heard constant reports that Union troops, under the command of Ulysses S. Grant, were approaching. Fear began to eat away at even the most enthusiastic supporters.

Sam left the Rangers after a fire broke out in the loft where they were sleeping and Sam rolled out of the barn to save himself, spraining his ankle. During his recovery, his troop moved on and, relieved, he went back home. Mark Twain later wrote that the Rangers gunned down a man traveling alone, and when they gathered around to watch him die he realized "that all war must be just that—the killing of strangers against whom you feel no personal animosity; strangers whom, in other circumstances you would help if you found them in trouble, and who would help you if you needed it." He invented this, though: There was no stranger and no battlefield realization, only the raw elements and the fear. Sam got as far as his birthplace, Florida, where perhaps the Quarleses told him not to be a fool. He headed back to St. Louis and struck a deal with his brother. If Orion named him secretary to the secretary of the Nevada Territory, Sam would finance their trip to Nevada. Sam thought the fighting would end in three months and that he could then resume his position on the river. On July 10, 1861, Orion and Sam headed west to St. Joseph's, the jumping-off place for the Nevada mining country. Sam was out of the conflagration of the Civil War, forced away from his river idyll like Adam and Eve from Eden. That Eden was gone forever, though Sam would try again and again to recapture it through his writing.

6 | Out West

*Consider well the proportions of things. It is better to be
a young June-bug than an old bird of paradise.*
—"Pudd'nhead Wilson's Calendar" (1894)

Sam and Orion Clemens left St. Joseph, at the
western edge of Missouri, by coach on July 26, 1861, taking
the northern route through Salt Lake City. Sam relinquished his identity as a riverboat dandy even before he left Missouri. A
weight limit of twenty-five pounds of luggage per person forced the brothers to pare down their carefully stored finery to only their most durable,
coarse-woven clothes. Averaging one hundred miles a day, the coach traveled steadily west with stops only for brief, inedible meals and changes
of horses and staff. At first, Sam, Orion, and their traveling companion
tried sleeping on the seats, with the dozens of mail sacks crammed all
around them, but they soon simply spread the sacks along the floor and
stretched out among them. Without women along, the men felt no obligation to observe any rules of decency, and so stripped down to their
skivvies in the hot weather. They smoked, talked, and observed the glorious scenery, which had been only fable before. Though stagecoach travel
risked both Indian attack and highway desperadoes, it also offered solid
pleasure. Sam would:

sit up and contemplate the majestic panorama of mountains and valleys spread out below us and eat ham and hard boiled eggs while our spiritual natures reveled alternately in rainbows, thunderstorms, and peerless sunsets. Nothing helps scenery like ham and eggs. Ham and eggs, and after these a pipe—an old, rank, delicious pipe—ham and eggs and scenery, a "down grade," a flying coach, a fragrant pipe and a contented heart—these make happiness. It is what all the ages have struggled for.

The trip cost approximately $500. Orion's annual salary was $1,800. There was no salary for the secretary to the secretary of the Nevada Territory. Sam would take out in education what he could not get as income. His experiences in the Wild West as a political operator, prospector, and frontier journalist would become central not only to how he thought of himself, but also to his future life as a public man, and to the second persona he would acquire while beyond the Rocky Mountains.

Sam had always considered himself a good raconteur of Mississippi River stories, but the stagecoach stories he heard on this trip had a different edge to them. While the dangers of river travel grew out of unpredictable nature, the dangers out west were decidedly human; stories of violence and pillage by desperadoes dominated. Most memorable for Sam were the tales about J. A. Slade, a fearless and unrepentant killer. Slade, it was said, once captured a sworn enemy, bound him to a post, and used him for target practice before killing him; he then cut off his ears and kept them in his pocket. Sam met Slade during the trip, before he heard the stories about him. The former outlaw now kept the road between Julesberg, Colorado, and Salt Lake City in good running order for the stagecoach company, a task he managed with kindliness when possible and with the barrel of his gun when not. During the stop at Slade's station, Sam finished off the station's coffee. Back on the road, the tales of the desperado's ruthlessness made Sam worry that Slade would repay him, someday, for taking that last cup.

The Mormons also intrigued Sam. Hounded out of Missouri and Illinois in the 1840s, the new religious sect settled in Utah, where they at last built a home far from intolerance and interfering governments. Under the dictatorial direction of Brigham Young, the Mormons governed the entire Utah Territory, which had stretched from the western foothills of the Rocky Mountains all the way to California. In response to Mormon hegemony over the region, and the Mormons' mocking disregard of secular authority, the federal government had recently sliced their holdings in half, establishing a separate Nevada Territory, also called Washoe, secure from the religious hierarchy in Salt Lake City. Mormon disregard for federal authority had earlier provoked an armed response from Washington. In the late 1850s, Brigham Young had called the Washoe settlers back to Salt Lake City to defend their enclave against attack by federal troops. Jefferson Davis, now Confederate president, had, as secretary of war under President Franklin Pierce in the mid-1850s, encouraged anti-Mormon fervor so that he could send a division of the United States Army away from the conflict that he suspected would follow secession. Now, the Union tried to settle into a more peaceful arrangement with the Mormons. Orion Clemens, as the first secretary to the Nevada Territory, paid visits to Union representatives and ranking Mormons. Sam attended some of these meetings, but showed more interest in the Mormon institution of polygamy. He enjoyed the titillating tales that the Salt Lake City gentiles told about the harems of the church elders. Though for many other Americans the Mormons were considered a dangerous sect, to Sam they were an unconventional curiosity, an experiment in living; his mother's religious eccentricities had made him tolerant of alternative creeds.

Sam and Orion reached Carson City on August 14, 1861. Because the embattled United States government had created the Nevada Territory both to add a state to the Union side before the 1864 presidential election and to confine Mormon influence, Orion's job there was to make Nevada conform to constitutional and congressional requirements for statehood. Only after his arrival did Orion discover the politics that had led to his appointment. William Seward, former New York governor and senator, had lost the Republican battle for the presidential nomination, and Abraham Lincoln had named Seward secretary of state as a consolation. Seward gave the territorial governorship to his shrewd campaign coordinator, former New York City Commissioner of Police James Nye. Nye accepted, knowing that he could become a U.S. senator when Nevada achieved statehood. Seward turned over all further territorial appointments to Nye, except territorial secretary, which Lincoln had reserved for Edward Bates, Orion's old friend and patron, for resigning *his* presidential candidacy earlier in the convention. Orion, the only Bates appointee in a sea of Seward politicos, entered the territorial government with political naïveté and high ideals. Even at this point of greatest career promise, odds did not favor Orion's success.

In Carson City, Sam distanced himself from Orion by moving into an upstairs dormitory occupied primarily by Governor Nye's camp followers. Carson itself, though "*surrounded* by sand, . . . is built upon what was once a very pretty grassy spot," Sam wrote his mother. "The houses are mostly frame, unplastered, but 'papered' inside with flour-sacks sewed together—and the handsomer the 'brand' upon the sacks is, the neater the house looks." Nevada weather astounded Sam with its ridiculous extremes, the most outrageous of which was the Washoe Zephyr, a sudden wind so strong it would upend houses and blow trash clear across the desert.

Sam spent his first month in town learning the territorial ropes and assessing the economic forces that drove Nevada. Mining and its related businesses remained the only reasons people had settled the area, he judged. Under the relentless Washoe desert lay veins of quartz rich in silver and gold. The epicenter was the Comstock Lode, one of the richest mineral deposits in the continental United States. Discovered in 1856, the lode had started a mining fever in Nevada in 1859. On the dusty streets of Carson City and in every saloon east of San Francisco, people traded "feet" of unworked mines. Not quite the same thing as stock in a company, mining "feet" represented inexact interests in a particular dig. People traded paper interest in promising holes in the ground in order to raise the cash to work the mines. Shysters did the same thing simply to squeeze money out of newcomers' hopes for sudden fortune.

Though Sam acquired some "feet" during his first weeks in Nevada, he realized that Nevada's profits went not to miners but to those who supplied them. Since most of Nevada was desert, and wood came at a premium, Sam decided to stake a timber claim. He and a new friend headed off to Lake Tahoe, a dozen miles from Carson, to find a stand of virgin timber. To mark a claim, they had to build a structure on the land and fence it. They hacked down a couple of trees to imply a fence and tossed a couple of branches together to suggest a house. Camping out, Sam neglected their fire, which spread to the dry floor of the forest. In a matter of minutes, the claim had turned to flame. Sam and his friend faced the inferno, their backs to the lake. He wrote his mother afterward:

> The level ranks of flame were relieved at intervals by the standard-bearers, as we called the tall dead trees, wrapped in fire, and waving their blazing banners a hundred feet in the air. . . . Occasionally, one of us would remove his pipe from his mouth and say,—"*Superb! magnificent! Beautiful!*—but—by the Lord God Almighty, if we attempt to sleep in this little patch to-night, we'll never live till morning!"

They returned to Carson, their claim destroyed and one shot at fortune gone.

Working with his brother, Sam helped organize the first territorial legislature, which Governor Nye wanted convened on October 1, 1861. The governor himself offered no help in this hapless enterprise; he had gone to California for most of September, leaving Orion as acting governor. Still, the legislature did its work of making the government profitable for its appointees. It granted Orion, as territorial secretary, the right to pocket fees for use of the territorial seal. It incorporated so many toll roads across the territory that "the ends of them were hanging over the boundary line everywhere like a fringe," as Mark Twain later wrote. The legislature divided the territory into counties and assigned clerks and judges to each, providing positions for the minions who had come west with Governor Nye.

Sam had no interest in a permanent government position, though he did become party to legislative shenanigans, especially a burlesque institution imported from California called the third house, which legislators convened after the official legislature adjourned and during which they mocked their own efforts at government. Sam also found an old friend from Keokuk, Billy Claggett, who had come to Carson as a legislator and left it as a notary public for Humboldt County, home to the Buena Vista Mining District. People coveted notarial appointments because they were so lucrative where mining claims needed to be registered. After the close of the legislature, Sam accompanied Billy Claggett to Unionville, Humboldt's county seat and now a tiny boomtown. Sam declined to invest there—he had his eye on the Esmeralda district near the California border—but as he told his mother he had faith that "before I can go to Esmeralda and get back to Humboldt, they will have laid, with the certainty of fate, the foundations of their fortunes."

On his return to Carson City, Sam found Orion in a predictable conflict with Governor Nye. James Nye was a politician and Orion Clemens an idealist: Orion pledged to execute territorial laws as handed him by the federal government and the territorial legislature, and Governor Nye refused to be bound by impractical bureaucrats in Washington, preoccupied by the more pressing matter of the Civil War. The conflict between the two men threatened to explode, and the loser would certainly have been Orion, whose patron, Attorney General Bates, possessed less pull than Secretary of State Seward. Sam intervened on his brother's behalf, miraculously smoothing the ruffled feathers of these two territorial peacocks and managing to become a favorite of the governor in the process. Whatever deal Sam offered, Nye kept him in Carson City until April of 1862, when he had intended to go to Esmeralda in February.

Just as Sam had assumed the patois of the Mississippi, mining slang now infected his speech and correspondence. He became part of the Nevada scene as quickly as it became a part of him. He showed Orion how to make a living out of selling his seal and signature to speculators while hobnobbing with influential Nevadans such as Bob Howland and Tom Nye, respectively the governor's nephew and brother. Both men also planned to go to Aurora, Esmeralda's county seat, Nye to prospect and Howland to be marshal of Aurora.

Sam also wrote for newspapers in Keokuk and Nevada, while trying to entice his brother-in-law Will Moffett to invest in Nevada mines; in Washoe, everyone was rich in paper mining claims, but few people had the cash to work those claims. Sam's three-month Nevada sojourn had grown to six, and he still hadn't gotten his hands dirty in a mine. Besides, with the war raging on back east, he felt no desire to return. He could not muster any enthusiasm for the Union cause, and the Southern effort had grown increasingly repellent. Nevada allowed the young Samuel Clemens to go wild, in a way that his driving ambitions had never allowed him before. As a Mississippi pilot he had adventure, but he also had to maintain the dignity of his position. In Nevada, Sam was merely the loafing brother of the secretary of the territory. He drank voluminously, played poker all night, speculated in mining stock, and sought out easy female company. He wrote to his sister-in-law Mollie:

> I never *will* marry until I can afford to have servants enough to leave my wife in the position for which I designed her, viz.—as a *companion*. I don't want to sleep with a threefold Being who is cook, chambermaid and washerwoman all in one. I don't mind sleeping with female servants as long as I am a bachelor—by *no* means—but *after* I marry, that sort of thing will be "played out," you know.

Orion added in his own missive to his wife, "I am told that female society here is not much better than the male society. There is a fashion of loose language among them that disgusts men of refinement. Loose manners are frequent. In California great numbers of the women are loose characters." In fact, very few women lived in Nevada. In the two largest towns, Carson and Virginia—Nevadans regarded as superfluous the "City" attached to both place names—women represented under 5 percent of the population. Almost all of them were Indians, the wives and daughters of wealthy mill operators, or prostitutes. For the first few months of 1862, Sam gave himself over to nearly unbroken dissipation.

In April, he finally made his way down to Aurora. Week after week, he attempted to wrench a fortune from the earth. He secured an agreement from Orion to attend exclusively to his duties as secretary and recorder which, if worked properly, could generate enough capital to finance Sam's mining. "Don't buy *anything* while I am here—but save up some money for me," Sam wrote Orion. "Don't send any money home. I shall have your next quarter's salary spent before you get it, I think. I mean to make or break here within the next 2 or 3 months." Of course, Orion did not listen to his brother and continued to buy mining feet from his position in Carson. Sam irately responded, "The pick and shovel are the only claims I have any confidence in now. My back is sore and my hands blistered with handling them today." The dirtiest he ever got came early one morning when some rowdies jumped his claim—that is, got to the mine before Sam and his cohorts did—and then would not budge from it. A similar incident just days before had left another miner dead. The next morning, Sam and his friends got to the mine first and took over again, but a court ordered Sam to pay off his combatants with a one-eighth interest in the claim. Brute power commanded justice in mineral-rich Nevada.

In fact, Sam had only a passing acquaintance with the pick and shovel. He spent most of his time in Esmeralda coordinating the work of other people, registering claims, and investigating the process of milling rock. Sam liked milling because it paid whether the rock had silver in it or not. He hoped to learn an Esmeralda mill operator's excellent new method of extracting value from ore and then take the secret to Humboldt. After only a few weeks in Esmeralda, he wrote Billy Claggett that "if I hadn't started in here, I would clear out for Humboldt immediately. But since I *have* got interests here, I will hold on a little, and see if I can make anything out of them." He had to give up his plan for moving to Humboldt after a week of learning the new refining process, however, because the mercury and other chemicals used there made him ill.

Sam soon surrendered any passionate interest in mining: "I have been here as long, now, as it is in my nature to stay in one place—and from this out I shall feel as much like a prisoner as if I were in the county jail." Tight money sent prices for scarce supplies sky-high. In his hopeless dissatisfaction with mining, he began writing correspondence, signed "Josh," for Nevada's oldest and most prominent newspaper, the Virginia City *Territorial Enterprise*, where his legislative friend William Barstow worked in the business office. By the summer of 1862, Sam would gladly have walked away from Aurora for a writing job; in August, the *Territorial Enterprise* offered him a full-time reporter's position. Sam wrote a tentative acceptance, but then ran off with prospector Calvin Higbie to search for the legendary lost Whiteman mine, a find so rich and abundant the mere rumor of its whereabouts sent prospectors scurrying into the desert. Sam, reluctant to give up on his vanishing dream of instant wealth, wanted to extend his freedom before taking his first job in five years.

Though he never relished his position as an impoverished silver magnate, it was the only identity he now had. Giving it up meant finding a new one. He wrote Billy Claggett on September 9, 1862, "I can't stand another winter in this climate, unless I am obliged to. I have a sneaking notion of going down to the Colorado mines 2 months from now." Sam said nothing to his close friend about mining or about going to work for a newspaper, though he fills several pages with political opinions, indicating that in his mind he had already switched over to his new line of work. Passing through Carson City, where Orion was building a small house in excited anticipation of the arrival of his wife and daughter, Sam shook the rock dust out of his clothes, shaved his raggedy beard, and went on to Virginia City to assume his position as a member of the fourth estate.

7 | Inventing the First Mark Twain

*That awful power, the public opinion of a nation, is
created in America by a horde of ignorant, self-complacent
simpletons who failed at ditching and shoemaking and
fetched up in journalism on the way to the poorhouse.*
—"License of the Press" (1873)

UNDER THE DIRECTION of Joseph Goodman, a visionary and sensitive editor two years younger than Sam, the Virginia City *Territorial Enterprise* had become the finest paper between Missouri and California. Goodman had acquired the *Enterprise* with Denis McCarthy after the pair had left San Francisco's *Golden Era*, the West's premier literary journal. Writers for the *Enterprise*—including Rollin Daggett, a founder of the *Golden Era*, and William Wright, who under the name Dan De Quille had become Nevada's mining authority—held to the highest journalistic standards in matters of fact, but they enjoyed tremendous latitude elsewhere in the paper. The legitimacy of the *Enterprise*'s news reporting supported the distribution of its more fanciful articles in newspapers all over Nevada, California, and the Pacific Northwest. It helped, too, that Virginia City was the true center of the Nevada Territory. Carson may have been home to the governor and the legislature, but Virginia City had the silver, and silver ran Nevada. Joe Goodman hired Sam on the basis of his letters from the Esmeralda mining camps, but he had another, better reason for wanting Sam on staff. As territorial secretary, Orion Clemens commissioned all government printing, a lucrative contract for the publisher lucky enough to win the bid.

While Goodman could not hire an incompetent to cover the legislative session, by hiring Sam he acquired for the *Enterprise* both a skilled reporter and an edge on the territorial contract.

Virginia City was the West's most prominent boomtown. It was a strange and violent place. Not quite five years old in 1862, Virginia boasted more than forty thousand residents. Set into the side of Mount Davidson, the streets of the city terraced the hillside and gave a physical manifestation to its social hierarchy. C Street, the main commercial road, led south to neighboring Gold Hill and north to the Henness Pass route to San Francisco. Farther up the hill on A and B streets lived the wealthy and respectable. D Street offered bars, whorehouses, and other amusements for the hardworking miners. Below that were slums, then Chinatown, and at the bottom of the hill the Indians who, it was said, lived off the white man's trash. No one planned cross streets for this burgeoning metropolis; people literally and figuratively clawed their way up chance alleys from the depths toward A Street. Virginia City was San Francisco's far-flung counterpart. San Francisco money built Virginia City, and Virginia City sent back as much as $20 million a year in tribute. The goal of every miner was to have a house on Nob Hill; the A Street mansions merely provided luxurious way stations until their residents could live well in San Francisco.

Local lore held that the first twenty-six graves in the Virginia City cemetery were occupied by murdered men. The search for sudden wealth had turned these entrepreneurs from the settled states to the east into desperate and marginal creatures. The major mines—the Ophir, the Gould and Curry, the Spanish or Mexican, and a few others—operated around the clock, as did the enormous and noisy ore mills just outside of town. After twelve hours of scraping rock out of a hole in the ground, the miners needed raucous fun, so the saloons and brothels never closed. A panorama of prostitutes plied the streets, from the raging siren "Buffalo Jo" Dodge, who physically attacked rivals in public, to the refined madam Julie Bulette, who brought Paris fashions to the Nevada desert. Among the men, disagreements often ended in blood, unless they involved mining money, in which case they went into the courts. (There were over three hundred lawsuits during Sam's first year in Virginia.) The murders received little notice from newspapers or from the law. Sam interrupted a letter to his mother with "I have just heard five pistol shots down the street—as such things are in my line, I will go and see about it." He concluded the tale in a second postscript: "5 A.M.—The pistol did its work well—one man . . . shot two of my friends, (police officers), through the heart—both died within three minutes." The murderer, Missourian John Campbell, escaped.

Virginia City's untamed quality came straight from San Francisco, which had established a vigilance committee in 1856 to force its brigands out of town. By 1860, San Francisco had shipped its dark and violent recklessness inland and rebuilt itself as a cosmopolitan city of 100,000 people; when San Francisco could no longer afford desperadoes, it provided the money to build Virginia City for them.

The town's unique birth resulted in an odd mix of democracy and aristocracy. Everyone smoked and drank, but what you smoked or drank defined your social position—cigarettes for the Mexicans, fine pipes for the gentry. Entertainment included several theaters and several more hurdy-gurdy houses, with rowdy music and dancing girls. The rich settled their differences with pistols as commonly as did ruffians, but the elite observed the rules of dueling—involving challenges, seconds, and rhetorical indignity—while the lower classes simply shot one another. Duels exacted more legal retribution in Virginia City than did outright murders. People from all strata mixed freely, and the myth that a sudden find could elevate a filthy prospector to social eminence kept snobbery to a minimum.

The *Territorial Enterprise* gave Sam a partial immunity from the violence of Virginia City; he was a witness to the scene, a commentator on it, not an actor in it. He found the culture at the *Enterprise* uplifting and gratifying. His fear that returning to newspaper work would mean another period of servitude proved false. Writers at the *Enterprise* saw themselves as a desert outpost of cosmopolitan Bohemians, whose challenge to traditional values created a stir in New York and San Francisco. Joe Goodman, Rollin Daggett, Dan De Quille, and Steve Gillis showed him how to wash the miner's dirt from his hands and replace it with printer's ink. Writing all together at one long and broad wooden table, the reporters at the *Enterprise* did not even have to leave to eat, since the paper's Chinese cook tossed bowls of oriental cuisine in front of them. Dan showed Sam, who had never reported regularly, what constituted news for the paper, while Joe set the journalistic standards. After they put the paper to bed for the night, the staff headed to their favorite establishment, a D Street brewery that sold beer at a dollar a gallon and served it with platters of Limburger cheese, radishes, and mustard.

The facts and figures of the mining beat bored Sam—he'd had enough of holes in the ground during his four months in Esmeralda—but Dan De Quille's fanciful sketches, which he called "quaints," intrigued him. Dan, at thirty-three the old man on the paper, had a kindly, gentle manner both personally and in print, and people appreciated and admired even his most outrageous hoaxes. One article, titled "The Travelling Stones of

Pahrangat Valley," minutely detailed the mysterious and random movements of some boulders in the Nevada desert. When newspapers around the country and around the world reprinted the article without qualification, it created a scientific stir. Sam loved hoaxes, and hardly three weeks into his tenure he wrote "The Petrified Man," reporting that a corpse had been found "in the mountains south of Gravelly Ford," as petrified as the rock around it. Judge Sewall, who had annoyed Sam during his brief stay in Humboldt, rushed to the spot to hold an inquest. Sam's description of the deceased hid the clues to the hoax: "The body was in a sitting posture . . . the attitude was pensive, the right thumb resting against the side of the nose; . . . the right eye was closed and the fingers of the right hand were spread apart." The petrified man was thumbing his nose at his readers, but few editors noticed and the squib found gullible audiences in newspapers hundreds of miles away. Sam confessed to his brother that the story was "an unmitigated lie, made from whole cloth. I got it up to worry Sewall. Every day, I send him some California paper containing it." Sam discovered from the episode his awesome journalist's power. For the first time in his life, he had colleagues who could help him develop his imagination and literary skills.

Whatever gaps might have remained in Sam's mining education after his first year in Nevada disappeared quickly at the *Enterprise*. In Virginia City, people sold false claims as blithely as they'd buy a drink. "Salted" mining samples were the rule; the perpetrators of one notorious con hadn't even bothered to fully melt the coins they used to salt their sample. Even the more established companies assessed their stockholders for payments without warning or cause, and then resold the stocks of delinquent investors. Rumor caused stock prices to fluctuate wildly; as a reporter, Sam could make prices turn somersaults. Owners and agents made gifts of mining feet to reporters, who would then raise the stock's value with a timely squib. Company assessments on these feet soon made them a dead loss, so the trick came in selling them quickly. Sam acquired a trunkful of stock certificates, but because he didn't unload them until he was strapped for cash, his dreams of making a fortune from mining remained locked in his valise.

In November of 1862, Sam went to Carson City for the legislative session. It took him a few weeks to learn how to report on the legislative proceedings and he took a ribbing for his shortcomings from his *Virginia City Union* rival, Clement Rice. Sam retaliated in print by stating that although Rice's reports were perhaps technically correct, they were wholly unreliable. He referred to Rice as "the Unreliable," attributing to him a legendary drunken boorishness, while implying for himself the opposite

quality by signing his own correspondence "Reliable." The conflict between the two was an elaborate hoax; the friends divided their reportorial
duties to gain a more comprehensive view of the Carson City action. Their
combined coverage of the legislature earned an official thanks at the end
of the session—a rare compliment to reporters in any era. With the arrival
of Mollie Clemens in early October, the territorial secretary's house became the locus of Carson City society. Mollie presided over many balls
and receptions during the legislative session. Sam attended these gatherings, earning renown as a storyteller and parlor entertainer. He broke up
serious musical entertainment with his sonorous rendition of "Old Horse
Named Jerusalem." He mimicked legislators and played off Unreliable
Rice, also always in attendance. The two men participated in the burlesque "third house," and Sam's antic performance there spread his reputation across the Nevada Territory.

Back in Virginia City, Sam gave Dan De Quille a hyperbolic send-
off, blaming his departure on

> a scarcity of pack-trains and haywagons. These had been the
> bulwark of the local column; his confidence in them was like
> unto that which men have in four aces; murders, robberies,
> fires, distinguished arrivals, were creatures of chance, which
> might or might not occur at any moment, but the pack-trains
> and the hay-wagons were certain, predestined, immutable!
> When these failed last week, he said *"Et tu, Brute,"* and gave
> us his pen.

After Dan's departure, the packtrains and hay wagons fell to Sam, along
with the mining reports and numerous, if irregular, explosions of violence.
The dull repetition of the daily mill of local tidbits proved discouraging
to Sam. "They let me go, about the first of the month, to stay twenty-
four hours in Carson, and I staid a week," he wrote his mother and sister.
"Perhaps they haven't much confidence in me now."

Sam spent the week visiting Orion and Mollie and cruising the parties
with Clement Rice, who came along. Rice, like most of the newspapermen
in Nevada, felt an affinity with the Bohemians, whose rejection of convention gave Rice and others license to drink endlessly, keep wildly irregular hours, and act without further ideological constraint. Sam
appreciated Rice's approach to life in Nevada; he regarded the entire
western half of the continent as a playground. Though he had come west
with Governor Nye's New York party, Rice didn't allow his political
ambitions interfere with having a good time.

The letters Sam sent back to Virginia that week were his first signed "Mark Twain." He needed a catchy replacement for the temporary pseudonym Reliable, which only had life as a counterpoint to Rice, the Unreliable. People who knew Sam in Nevada said that he arrived at the pseudonym by entering a saloon and calling out in the leadsman's singsong intonation "Mark twain!"—meaning the bartender should pour two drinks and mark them down on the debit ledger. Sam wrote in his first letter from Carson at the end of January 1863, "The Unreliable intruded himself upon me in his cordial way, and said, 'How are you, Mark, old boy? when d'you come down?'"—implying that his pseudonym already existed for him as a nickname. Later, and throughout his life, Mark Twain maintained that he had adopted his pseudonym from Captain Isaiah Sellers, whom he had parodied as Sergeant Fathom. According to Twain, Sellers had used the name Mark Twain and when Sellers died, Sam had appropriated his pen name. Unfortunately, the name Mark Twain does not appear in any newspaper prior to Sam Clemens' use of it, and Sellers did not die until months after Sam first used the name. Sam began telling his version of the origin of his pen name a decade after he first used it and, despite witnesses' testimony in favor of its barroom roots, Mark Twain steadfastly adhered to this fabrication throughout his career.

Mark Twain's three letters from Carson recount parties he attended, and the Unreliable occupies a prominent place at all of these gatherings. Mark Twain accuses the Unreliable of stealing his fine kid boots and his gold watch, forcing his way into a party of dignitaries and consuming all the food, challenging him to a duel and then feigning illness to escape it, impersonating the best man at a wedding reception, wilting all his dance partners "with the horrible fragrance of his breath," and stealing seventeen silver spoons. Despite his companion's transgressions, Mark Twain never strays from the Unreliable's company. The Unreliable served as a literary shield. Just as Sam, as a boy, had escaped punishment by behaving better than Tom Blankenship, Mark Twain could establish himself as a moral commentator because he had a sidekick who behaved more reprehensibly than he did. Whatever Mark Twain might do, the Unreliable was always worse.

The shield had another function, as well. The daily newspaper gibes between Mark Twain and the Unreliable created barroom conversation, but they also sparked the rumor mill. He and Rice lived together in Virginia City, and the fact that they escaped together for a week of revelry in Carson suggested a deeper bond than that of just two friends on a lark. Mark Twain's reports of his activities with the Unreliable hid the intimacy between Sam Clemens and Clement Rice under exaggeration, personal differences, and grotesque humor. Still, the conclusion to his second letter, about a wedding reception he and Rice supposedly crashed, offered a glimpse of his secret:

"It was all pleasant, and jolly, and sociable, and I wish to thunder I was married myself. I took a large slab of the bridal cake home with me to dream on, and *dreampt that I was still a single man*, and likely to remain so, if I live and nothing happens—which has given me a greater confidence in dreams than I ever felt before." The exact nature of sexuality in the American West will remain a mystery, but behavior in Nevada took its cue from San Francisco, which even in its early days showed a surprising acceptance of sexual bonds between men. Though most western men appear to have visited female prostitutes, they also typically lived in male pairs, sharing resources and beds; this was especially true among prospectors. Many ties between men were strong and loving, and mining partnerships were often understood as metaphorical marriages.

How often western men physically expressed their affection escapes determination. There is no simple way to define the sexual connection between two men who visit a bordello together and then go home to sleep in the same bed. Are there any changes detectable between a relationship that moves from simultaneous masturbation to mutual masturbation? We recognize that this change in sexual behavior redefines the relationship, but those definitions themselves grow from our contemporary ideology of relationships. In the mid-nineteenth century, the rules were different; only the Bohemians, that rebellious group of artists and philosophical fellow-travelers who traced their roots through Paris' Left Bank, publicly acknowledged sexual flexibility. But even the Bohemians—with whom Sam Clemens implicitly identified when he took his place among the writers at the *Territorial Enterprise*—were defined more by their social attitudes than their aesthetics, and disguised their unconventional sexual behavior in print.

The frequency, even predominance, of homoerotic relationships among nineteenth-century men of note, from Henry David Thoreau to the Reverend Henry Ward Beecher, originates in the rigid social standards of the era's formal society, in which men and women occupied separate spheres, and relationships between men were seen as a kind of practice for the later and more socially fundamental relationship of marriage. There is little evidence for the existence of a discrete homosexual subculture prior to the emergence of the Bohemians, though the practice appears to have been common among the educated and wealthy, where social norms kept the sexes apart. Even modest bohemian forthrightness about same-sex relationships, as exemplified by the poetry and persona of Walt Whitman, brought forward both radical ideas of personal freedom and an elitism that celebrated the homoerotic structure of upper-class society.

With the rise of abolitionism, and women's increasingly dominant role in public debate, this structure began to disappear. As men encountered women in the normal progress of society, people abandoned the long-held tolerant view of same-sex romantic friendships. Men and women who pursued such bonds risked appearing to indulge in eccentric behavior. The American West during the Civil War was a sanctuary not only from the actual battleground back east, but also from these social changes. Socially advantaged men in their twenties comprised the largest demographic segment in the West by far, and the acceptance of homoerotic behavior there was something of an upper-class holdover. Still, homoeroticism was such a fundamental part of life in San Francisco that it was not unusual for a merchant's male clerks to dress in women's clothing. Sam Clemens' bohemian aspirations only put him in the vanguard of homoerotic expression; the behavior itself was far from unusual. Only the later prominence of Mark Twain makes his relationship with other men appear out of the ordinary. Although proof of these ties is unlikely ever to surface, the silhouette of Sam Clemens' relationship with Clement Rice shows behind the twin masks of Mark Twain and the Unreliable.

The name Mark Twain gave Sam's work in the *Enterprise* a unique and clever moniker by which readers could remember him. Sam began to develop a reputation as a brilliant, irascible man with a withering wit. Stories about him circulated throughout the West. For example, newspapers hundred of miles from Virginia City reported that a man he had excoriated in Mark Twain's column threatened to kick Sam across Nevada. "Well, if you think you've got money enough to put me over all these toll-roads," Sam drawled to his victim, "just start in!" Goaded as much by his newspaper colleague Rollin Daggett's deep social sarcasm as by the gentle whimsy of Dan De Quille, still on leave to visit his family in Iowa, Mark Twain commented on police murderer John Campbell, still at large but supposedly seen entering a mine in Gold Hill. The timid residents refused to go in after him, closing the mine with rocks instead. When they roused enough hands, the townspeople reopened the tunnel to reveal five dead Indians, "smothered by the foul atmosphere. . . . The intention of the citizens was good, but the result was most unfortunate. To shut up a murderer in a tunnel was well enough, but to leave him there all night was calculated to impair his chances for a fair trial."

Sam reserved his great personal charm for his closest friends and for public events such as balls, receptions, and the legislative meetings. Those who came into only incidental contact with him found him prickly and inconsistent, as liable to enrage them over some personal insult as to make them laugh. His office mates at the *Enterprise* called him "the Incorrigible" and dubbed his fantastically foul-smelling pipe "the Remains." Sam's touchiness almost begged his coworkers to nettle him, in part just to generate his colorful curses. He preferred his work materials just so—a candle instead of a lamp, a certain pen, an eyeshade—and someone, often the game and scrappy printshop foreman Steve Gillis, would hide them just to get Sam started. He would begin with a slow amble around the long writing table, building up to his peculiar skipping, bouncing gait. Then his slow rumble of curses would pick up volume and ferocity. Once when he was in full blather, Franklin Rising, one of the young ministers whose friendship Sam liked to cultivate, dropped by to see him. Sam tried to moderate his language but finally gave up, saying, "I know, Mr. Rising, I know it is wicked to talk like this; I know it is wrong. I know I shall certainly go to hell for it. But if you had a candle, Mr. Rising, and those thieves should carry it off every night, I know that you would say, just as I say, Mr. Rising, G—d d——n their impenitent souls, may they roast in hell for a million years." In a town like Virginia City, known for its outrageous behavior, Sam augmented his reputation by cultivating his peculiarities. Some people considered him nothing but a buffoon; some, fooled by his slow talk and odd walk, believed him little more than a drunken idiot. A slight man with a large head, he exaggerated his shambling appearance with unkempt hair and ratty clothes. His beauty— auburn hair, commanding brow, straight nose, flashing blue-gray eyes— served as a counterpoint to his sometimes cranky demeanor. Most everyone respected him, if only for the damage his pen might inflict. Sam never felt comfortable sharing his private life, and few could claim him as a close friend.

Pressed by the demands of his reporting during the first few months of 1863, Sam allowed most of his personal correspondence to languish. He no longer attempted to entice his family and friends to Nevada, but instead actively discouraged them. He liked his freedom; moreover, his family would not approve of his late hours, extensive drinking, and close friendships with other men. Also, the persona of Mark Twain gave Sam a liberty he had only begun to explore. Writing as Mark Twain, he developed a style and language more concise, authoritative, and energetic, but he had not yet constructed for his new voice a public persona different from Sam Clemens. To a man whose fluid and uncertain personality had allowed him to take on the protective coloration of his environment, his pseudonym made a new, distinct self seem possible, but he needed freedom from old friends and family in order to discover the nature of this invention.

As spring came to Washoe, Sam felt he needed a vacation, and so around the first of May 1863 he took off for San Francisco. Joe Goodman, filling in for him, acknowledged the importance of Mark Twain's contributions to the paper, dedicating almost twelve inches of type to the notice that Twain "has abdicated the local column . . . where by the grace of Cheek he so long reigned." Goodman ridiculed Sam for having "gone to display his ugly person and disgusting manners and wildcat on Montgomery street. In all of which he will be assisted by his protegee, the Unreliable."

In the company of Clement Rice, the young journalist spent two months in San Francisco, finding the city entirely to his liking. Nevada stocks enjoyed a sudden vogue around the time Sam hit the city, and so he could readily raise cash whenever needed by peddling the contents of his valise. Staying at the luxurious Lick House, Sam and Rice "fag ourselves completely out every day," he wrote his mother with surprising bad-boy frankness, "and go to sleep without rocking, every night. We dine out, & we lunch out, and we eat, drink and are happy—as it were. After breakfast, I don't often see the hotel again until midnight—or after. I am going to the Dickens mighty fast." Putting his feet in the Pacific, he remembered stepping into the Atlantic Ocean a decade before and felt the vastness of America. Yet even in this huge land, he ran into people he knew from the river and Virginia City so frequently that "it is just like being in Main Street in Hannibal." Sam and Rice perpetually haunted the Bella Union and the Willows, two entertainment centers that featured dancing, casinos, and shows.

Though he did only minimal work for the *Enterprise* while in San Francisco, he did quite a bit of work for himself, not only in making deals for mining stock but also, and more important, in arranging to write for the *Golden Era* and for the *San Francisco Morning Call*. The *Call* was the cheapest and least respectable of San Francisco's numerous newspapers, but it was also one of the most popular. The *Golden Era*, though in format like an eight-page newspaper, was a weekly magazine that published the best essays, poetry, and fiction written in the West, along with some sensationalist serialized novels, both pirated and original. The *Era*, intended to appeal to both the farmer and the city sophisticate, dominated the market thanks to the eclectic mix developed by editor Joe Lawrence, whose office was not only the literary heart of the city, but also, according to bohemian poet Joaquin Miller, "the most gaudily carpeted and most gorgeously furnished that I had then seen." Lawrence introduced Sam to Miller and the other wild men and women of the San Francisco scene. The welcome literary San Francisco gave Sam and his work elevated his faith that Mark Twain might amount to something. Writing his first letter to his family after his return to Virginia City in early July, he signed it "mark," but the name didn't sit well with his mother, and he thereafter refrained from its use in his letters home. It was his first experience of the limits of his invented persona, and of the resistance his family would always have to that public self.

Virginia City's first boom peaked in the summer of 1863. Population had expanded so rapidly that houses rented before they were built and new buildings and hotels rose on every available lot. On July 8, 1863, Mark Twain spoke at the dedication of the new Collins House hotel, and within a few weeks Tom Maguire, a San Francisco theater impresario, opened a sixteen-hundred-seat theater. Gould and Curry, the most profitable mine on the Comstock Lode, built an enormous and showy silver mill near town. After a fire forced Sam and Clement Rice out of their rooms in late July, Sam roomed alone in an A Street mansion, seemingly ending his close ties with Rice. He ate at a bargain price at the Collins House, repayment for his writing up the place—"so much for being a reporter," he told his mother. A few weeks later, a bigger fire wiped out a huge portion of the city. The citizens rebuilt, not in flimsy wood, but in brick. Even the *Territorial Enterprise* moved to new offices in a three-story brick building, introducing steam-powered printing to Nevada. The rowdy celebration at the *Enterprise* went on for days, culminating in a serious duel between Joe Goodman and Tom Fitch, Clement Rice's boss at the *Union*. Interrupted once by the law and required to put up a $5,000 bond each for disturbing the peace, the duelists met the next day in secret. Joe Goodman crippled Fitch with a shot to the leg.

These raucous excitements and long hours left Sam hamstrung with an unshakable cold. Unable to complete his local column, he asked Unreliable Rice to fill in for him, even though they worked for rival newspapers and their two editors had just conducted a public duel. Rice took advantage of Sam by publishing as Mark Twain a deadpan apology to the notables and "a host of others whom we have ridiculed from behind the shelter of our reportorial position. . . . We ask their forgiveness, promising that in the future we will give them no cause for anything but the best of feeling toward us." Angered by the Unreliable's impudent twist on their journalistic compact, the next day Sam pulled himself out of his sickbed "to annul all apologies he coined as coming from us, and to hold him up to public commiseration as a reptile endowed with no more intellect, no more cultivation, no more Christian principle than animates and adorns the sportive jackass rabbit of the Sierras. We have done." Sam's ferocious response shows three things about him: He was a man one imposed upon only at great peril; he could never take a joke; and he meant what he said. He terminated his friendship with Rice immediately, notwithstanding their romantic history, and he never referred to the Unreliable thereafter.

Sam's cold lingered. Orion, worried that his brother led a life of dissipation, penned him a sermon about it. Sam disingenuously responded to Pamela and Jane, "As I don't dissipate, & never expect to, & am man enough to have a good character & keep it, I didn't take the trouble to answer it. He will learn after a while, perhaps, that I am not an infant, that I know the value of a good name as well as he does." Now that Sam's importance had once again begun to eclipse his brother's, he bridled even more under the territorial secretary's tutelage. He went to Lake Tahoe to cure his cold, but fell in with a fast crowd there, staying up late drinking too much champagne. He looked for a cure at Steamboat Springs, where he covered his bill by writing up the resort for both the *Enterprise* and the *Morning Call*. He returned to Virginia for less than two weeks, holding his own against his cold only until Dan De Quille could complete his sojourn east. Then, on September 5, 1863, Dan relieved Sam of his duties as a local editor, and Sam headed to San Francisco. He stayed just a month this time, recovering his health and writing articles for the *Era* and correspondence to the *Enterprise*. By the middle of October, he was back in Nevada. Then, he and Dan took up rooms together in a new building owned by Rollin Daggett and the recovered Tom Fitch.

Dan's return and the restoration of Sam's health emboldened him to try another hoax, but one with a purpose. Mark Twain intended "A Bloody Massacre Near Carson" to be a satire of the San Francisco papers that criticized the scheming financial practices of Nevada mining companies while ignoring the same "dividend cooking" being done in California. The satire, unfortunately, was so subtle because of the gory details in which it was couched that readers, including editors, missed it. In the story, Twain told of a man, P. Hopkins, living between Empire City and Dutch Nick's, who had scalped his wife, stabbed his nine children—two of whom survived—and then slit his own throat. He rode into Carson in that condition before collapsing, dead, outside the Magnolia Saloon, clutching the bloody scalp of his wife. The cause of the tragedy? Hopkins had taken all of his money out of Nevada mining stocks and put it into the Spring Valley Water Company of San Francisco, a dividend cooker whose stock went suddenly flat, leaving Hopkins broke and desperate.

Papers far and wide picked up the ghastly story, but not the satire. Fascinated readers couldn't stop talking about the gory image of Hopkins, throat cut, falling from his horse, his wife's bloody thatch of hair in his hand. The horror of that picture obscured the fact that Dutch Nick's and Empire City were one and the same place, that the pine forest described as nearby couldn't exist in such a desert, or that P. Hopkins was the name of the man who ran the Magnolia Saloon in front of which the imaginary murderer collapsed. When Twain published a retraction the next day, editors castigated both the author and his paper for perpetrating the fraud. Many swore never again to trust a story reported in the *Territorial Enterprise*. Taken aback by the controversy his hoax had provoked, Sam offered his resignation to Joe Goodman, but Joe and Dan De Quille advised him to wait, believing people would laugh once their anger at being fooled subsided.

Wisely, he left Virginia for a month to cover the proceedings of the constitutional convention in Carson. The constitutional convention—and the Union party convention a few weeks later—started an imbroglio lasting beyond Sam's tenure in Nevada. The legislature had called the constitutional convention into being under a faulty measure, which had gone to Governor Nye with blanks in it. The new constitution itself, while generally an able document, had one key flaw. It included a provision for taxing not just working mines but undeveloped claims as well, which would have destroyed the silver industry by dousing the fervor with which miners pursued claims. Further, a procedural question threatened to make a circus out of the whole effort of organizing Nevada into a state, a dangerous situation, since the government in Washington counted on the presence of another state to add moral force to their efforts in the Civil War. Since the ratification of the constitution and the election of state officers would go before the voters simultaneously, if the constitution didn't pass, the election wouldn't matter. With Orion running for secretary of state, Sam had a special interest in the balloting. To relieve these pressures, the constitutional convention held a "third house," electing Mark Twain burlesque governor. Sam directed this farcical government with great aplomb. Not only did his election prove the regard Nevada's leaders had for Sam's wit and intellect, but his on-stage performance as Governor Mark Twain amply demonstrated his ability to deliver in person the same incisive humor he showed in print. The riotous "third house" was so successful that a committee of citizens asked Sam to deliver another speech as Governor Mark Twain, to benefit a church.

Between the constitutional convention and the Union party nominations, one event changed the course of Mark Twain's career and gave him the inspiration to establish his persona more richly and publicly. The West had sufficient population and hunger for culture now that it attracted the East's most popular acts. Performers would start a tour in San Francisco and then travel inland to Sacramento, Virginia, and smaller towns. Some performers had already made the trip to Virginia City, but in December 1863, Artemus Ward arrived, and he was a phenomenon, a sensation, a high-caliber star of both print and stage. Nearly a year before, President Abraham Lincoln had opened a Cabinet meeting by reading a Ward column aloud, and then, as his aides laughed helplessly, he presented the Emancipation Proclamation for approval.

Artemus Ward, supposedly a showman with a traveling waxworks display who commented in his illiterately misspelled columns on manners and current events, was invented in 1858 by Maine native Charles Farrar Browne, a flamboyant member of the New York bohemian scene and one of the most frankly homosexual men in the entire literary circle. Recently resigned from his post as editor of the bohemian magazine *Vanity Fair*, Browne transformed his literary persona into a popular stage performance, which he took on tour. His performance, advertised as "Artemus Ward," made him rich; his first San Francisco show netted him more than $1,500. A gaunt man with a large nose, Browne played his refined sense of humor against his illiterate bumpkin print character Ward. His act, a stand-up comedy performance, was utterly new; people attended plays, concerts, and lectures, but they had never listened to one man speak with no higher purpose than to entertain. Ward deadpanned his way through two hours of "goaks" and one-liners, leaving the audience no time to recover from one convulsive fit before sending them into another. "I give you Upper Canada!" went one grave Artemus Ward toast. And then, after a lingering pause, "Because I don't want it myself." His advance man, E. P. Hingston, cultivated relationships with the press, assuring Ward of both publicity and shining reviews, which Hingston would use to trumpet Ward at his next stop.

When Artemus Ward came to Virginia City, he gravitated to the offices of the *Territorial Enterprise*, home of Washoe's most distinguished writers. Ward even helped write the newspaper so that he, Mark Twain, Dan De Quille, and Joe Goodman could go drinking. Sam and Ward found that, as teenagers, they had both contributed to the same Boston humor magazine, *The Carpet-Bag*. Together, they drank gallons of wine, one night feeling so high that Ward took Sam on a walk across the rooftops, where they nearly were shot as thieves. Drunk, Ward, Twain, and De Quille— that is, Charles Farrar Browne, Sam Clemens, and William Wright—

"climbed into the big bed together. When they were comfortable, nimble-witted Ward remarked: 'Three Saints! Mark, Luke and John.' "

Ward, prepared to like Mark Twain by the regard with which he was held in San Francisco, and enamored of Sam's wit upon meeting him, promised an introduction to an editor at New York's *Sunday Mercury*, where Ward thought Mark Twain might find an outlet. Ward also invited Sam to join him on the European leg of his tour the next summer, to which Sam, cultivating their relationship, eagerly agreed. Throwing himself into a flash romantic attachment with Ward, Sam also watched this traveling star carefully for clues to his success. If this was not love on Sam's part, it was arrant sycophancy. As Arthur McEwen, a San Francisco reporter who knew Sam, noted, "Mark, being a man of sense, never neglected his interests. The fact that to know a particular man might at some time be advantageous did not deter Mr. Clemens from making his acquaintance."

A few days later, Ward wrote Sam romantically from his next stop, Austin, Nevada:

> My dearest Love,—I arrived here yesterday a.m. at 2 o'clock. It is a wild, untamable place, but full of lion-hearted boys. I speak to-night. See small bills.
>
> Why did you not go with me and save me that night?—I mean the night I left you drunk at that dinner party. I went and got drunker, beating, I may say, Alexander the Great, in his most drinkinist days, & I blackened my face at the Melodeon, and made a gibbering, idiotic speech. God-damit! . . . I shall always remember Virginia as a bright spot in my existence, as all others must or rather cannot be, as it were. . . .
>
> Good-bye, old boy—and God bless you! The matter of which I spoke to you so earnestly shall be just as earnestly attended to— . . . I am Faithfully, gratefully yours,
>
> Artemus Ward

Still reeling from his ten-day drinking binge with Ward, Sam wrote his mother, "When Artemus Ward gets to St. Louis, invite him up to the house & and treat him well, for behold, he is a good fellow. But don't ask him too many questions about me & Christmas eve, because he might tell tales out of school." He added, "Beside, I have promised to go with him to Europe in May or June." Despite the Virginia City fling, nothing came of the promised trip to Europe. Perhaps the pledges Ward made in the flush of first acquaintance evaporated after the hangover wore off, or perhaps Ward made the same promises to other men in other towns, promises now forgotten because they were not made to Mark Twain.

Sam returned to Carson to report the Union convention and the third territorial legislature, from January 9 to February 20, but he also wrote some articles for the *Mercury*, as Artemus Ward had suggested. Ward also influenced Sam's speech as Governor Mark Twain, which a disgusted critic from the *Virginia City Union* panned: "The style of the burlesque Governor is . . . disconnected from genial originality and variation. His originality is like that of the literary bubble known as 'Artemus Ward.' " Two hopeful politicians presented Sam with a gold watch inscribed to Governor Mark Twain both as a token honor for his presentation and a simple bribe "to obtain publicity in the most powerful organ in the Territory." Neither a triumph nor a disaster, the speech solidified Sam's reputation and gave him the chance to imagine how he might follow Artemus Ward's path to success.

The January 19, 1864, election brought the Clemenses mixed results. Orion won the post of secretary of state, but the electorate rejected the constitution, negating his accomplishment and throwing Nevada's statehood into doubt. Piling tragedy on disappointment, the day following Governor Mark Twain's appearance in Carson at the sold-out benefit, Jennie Clemens, the eight-year-old daughter of Orion and Mollie, took sick. She died of meningitis a few days later. The legislature adjourned to attend Jennie's funeral, and a couple of days later Sam vented his rage at fate in a vituperative article in the *Enterprise* about the larcenous practices of the only undertaker in Carson City. Sam sympathized with Orion, who expected familial closeness after this sad loss, but Sam could not set aside the antagonism he felt toward his brother. Orion's constant attempts to lecture him, to drive him to a more moral life, to father him, only drove Sam further away. He wrote to his sister Pamela, "Mollie & Orion are all right, I guess. They would write me if I would answer there letters—but I won't."

Soon after Sam's return to Virginia City in late February, the town received another notable guest from the same New York bohemian community to which Artemus Ward belonged. Adah Isaacs Menken—Jewish, Southern, and unapologetic about her secessionist politics—reminded her audiences of her wild personal life with her most alarming performance, *Mazeppa*, in which she played a Polish nobleman caught in an affair with a powerful man's wife. Mazeppa is punished by being lashed naked to a horse and sent riding into the barren mountains. Menken's sexually ambiguous striptease and circus performance as a naked-seeming woman portraying a violated man never ceased to please her mostly male audience.

The notorious Menken, celebrated in Nevada as much for her affair with a horse trainer as for her performances, asked for Sam's opinion of her Whitmanesque free verse—"She is a literary cuss herself," he wrote his sister. She also invited Sam and Dan to an intimate luncheon with Ada Clare, called the Queen of Bohemia for her efforts to import Left Bank Parisian ways to New York. Despite the fact that Sam did not much like Menken, her presence in Virginia City taught him some important lessons about fame: Don't overstay your welcome; find a public persona you can maintain without disturbing too many people; and don't *live* outrageously if you want to *perform* outrageously. Eventually, Sam adopted each of these principles for Mark Twain.

Before Menken left Nevada, Joe Goodman took off for Hawaii, leaving Sam and Dan in charge of the paper. The roommates worked and lived well together. Dan wrote of their digs to the *Golden Era*, "We (Mark and I) have the 'sweetest' little parlor and the snuggest little bedroom . . . all to ourselves. Here we come every night and live—breathe, move and have our being, also our toddies." This was as public a declaration of their relationship as any of the Bohemians had ever managed. Their rooms became a satellite *Enterprise* office, a center of revelry and work. Dan said, "We went merrily along, laughing and joking and never feeling the weight of the work we were doing in the whirl and excitement of the times." The *News* from nearby Gold Hill reported on the doings of this duo frequently, putting the rumors concerning Mark and Dan into black and white: "*To be married.*—Dan de Quille and Mark Twain are to be married shortly. About time." The men worked and lived and played together almost every hour of every day. Despite the pressure of work, "Mark and I agreed well as room-mates. Both wanted to read and smoke about the same length of time after getting into bed, and when one got hungry and got up to go down town for oysters the other also became hungry and turned out." To relax, they went to the gym, where once Sam menacingly shadowboxed a man known as the town's best boxer. The man thought Sam meant to fight and floored him with one punch, bloodying Sam's nose. Dan satirized Mark's wounds in his column, which began some playful badinage in print. The *Golden Era* reprinted the entire sequence of teasing comments between Nevada's celebrity duo.

Joe Goodman returned in mid-April, and within six weeks Sam left Virginia City for good. Though Sam had a good life there, he sabotaged it so thoroughly that, in May of 1864, departure became inevitable. Mark Twain later wrote, "I wanted to see San Francisco. I wanted to go somewhere. I wanted—I did not know *what* I wanted. I had the 'spring fever' and wanted a change, principally, no doubt." The sequence that led to his banishment from Nevada began with a simple wager in which Sam had a trivial part. In Austin, Nevada, a Southern sympathizer named Reuel Gridley—a Hannibal native who had once tossed Sam into Bear Creek— bet that "if a Republican Mayor were elected there, he would give [his opponent] a 50-pound sack of flour, and carry it to him on his shoulder, a mile and a quarter, with a brass band at his heels playing 'John Brown.' " Gridley lost the bet, but instead of paying it off as he originally promised, he auctioned off his flour sack, with the proceeds to benefit the United States Sanitary Fund, the precursor of the American Red Cross. The flour sack netted $5,300 for the Sanitary Fund, and Gridley then began a raucous procession around Nevada, whipping up the competitive juices between communities to see who could pledge the most money for the sack. Sam, encouraged by his sister Pamela, who supported the fund in St. Louis, led the coverage of this fund-raising parade. " 'Tone' was given to the procession by the presence of Gov. Twain and his staff of bibulous reporters," the *Gold Hill News* reported on May 17, "who came down in a free carriage, ostensibly for the purpose of taking notes, but in reality in pursuit of free whiskey." Each stop brought thousands of dollars to the fund.

The flour sack did not get to Carson, the state capital, prompting a joke among the reporters, which Sam wrote down as part of his column.

> The reason the Flour Sack was not taken from Dayton to Carson, was because it was stated that the money raised at the Sanitary Fund Fancy Dress Ball, recently held in Carson for the St. Louis Fair, had been diverted from its original course, and was being sent to aid a Miscegenation Society somewhere in the East; and it was feared the proceeds of the sack might be similarly disposed of.

Mark Twain's snippet included an admission that this comment was a hoax, "But not all a hoax, for an effort is being made to divert their funds from their proper course." This was dynamite. Mollie Clemens had, of course, been instrumental in organizing the Carson affair, and her friends were aghast: The accusation that anyone would assist in the sexual mixing of the races inevitably bred an explosive response. After the notice appeared, Sam wrote a lame and equivocal apology to Mollie:

> We kept that Sanitary spree up for several days, & I wrote & laid that item before Dan when I was not sober (I shall not get drunk again, Mollie,)—and said he, "Is this a

joke?" I told him "Yes." He said he would not like such a joke as that to be perpetrated on him, & that it would wound the feelings of the ladies of Carson. He asked me if I wanted to do that, & and I said "No, of course not." While we were talking, the manuscript lay on the table, & we forgot it & left it there when we went to the theater. . . . I suppose the foreman [Steve Gillis], prospecting for copy, found it, & seeing that it was in my handwriting, thought it was to be published, & carried it off.

When the *Enterprise* refused to publish a protest from the women of Carson, Sam could not avoid challenges from the women's husbands.

Sam dug more trouble out of the Sanitary Fund by writing an editorial ridiculing the *Virginia City Union* for not paying its pledge. His accusation was ill-timed; they paid before the editorial hit the streets. James Laird, publisher of the *Union*, responded, and—goaded by hot-tempered Steve Gillis—Sam challenged Laird to a duel. At last, on May 24, the *Enterprise* published the challenges, counterchallenges, and refusals, and Laird had no choice but to accept the duel. Sam and his coterie went off to practice one morning, but Sam literally could not hit even the barn door to which his friends attached the target. His courage wavered as he missed shot after shot and collapsed when he heard Laird shooting nearby. Then, as Laird and his party approached, Gillis took the gun and shot the head off a small bird. A Laird second asked, "Who did that?" and Gillis answered that Sam did, and that he could do it every time. The second told Laird, "You don't want to fight that man. It's just like suicide. You'd better *settle* this thing, now." They did, but printing the challenges had advertised that Sam had broken the law against dueling. Furthermore, the husbands of the Carson City women demanded Sam's skin. Short of announcing himself a coward, a drunk, and a criminal, Sam had no way out of his dilemmas. Even in the Wild West, there were costs to playing by one's own rules, and Sam had put himself heavily in debt. His habit of risking what he most cherished had lost him his berth at the *Territorial Enterprise* and his uniquely high standing in Nevada society.

So on May 29, 1864, Sam Clemens—known as Mark Twain, the Washoe Giant, and the Wild Humorist of the Pacific Slope—boarded the stage to San Francisco with Steve Gillis. Joe Goodman, intending only to accompany the pair out of town, enjoyed his ride so much that he stuck with them all the way. Sam's experience on the *Territorial Enterprise* had refined his raw writing gifts and given him a well-placed platform from which to demonstrate his abilities. He had named his literary persona and sketched the first outlines of Mark Twain's paper identity. Mark Twain stood just far enough outside the mainstream to satirize convention. Though Sam only hazily understood its implications in the spring of 1864, this identity offered him a clear direction in which to take his alter ego. San Francisco would, he hoped, give him a higher apex from which to survey the world he wanted to conquer.

8 | Hostage to Bohemia

Prosperity is the best protector of principle.
—"Pudd'nhead Wilson's New Calendar" (1897)

MUCH ABOUT SAM Clemens' twenty-one months in San Francisco, from June of 1864 until March 1866, remains unaccounted for. He left little documentary evidence, and in *Roughing It*, his book-length autobiographical portrait of his western years, Mark Twain dedicates barely eleven pages to his two years in San Francisco—2 percent of the book for one third of his tenure beyond the Rockies. This suppression leaves a tantalizing vacuum, which the city itself fills with suggestive answers to the mystery of what happened to Sam Clemens there.

In its own mind, San Francisco was the future of the nation; for a country obsessed with progress, the city was the New World to which it aspired. The city wanted the first taste of the latest excitement, be it new technology or bohemianism. The transcontinental telegraph had eclipsed the Pony Express, and San Francisco grew anxious to join the Union not just politically, but via the railroad, already under construction. Railroads, bohemianism, telegraphs, and large-scale agriculture all promised the future for 1860s San Francisco. Since the war only hampered that future, any western forbearance for the Southern cause had disappeared. By the summer of 1864, the Confederacy had been reduced to resistance, one that threatened to drain national resources while California and its glittering pinnacle San Francisco thrived in peace. Comprising more than half the city's population, men in their twenties who had declined to die for the Union cause, like Sam Clemens, curried their patriotism a safe distance from the battlefields. The town was rich—the growth of San Joaquin Valley farming more than made up for the decline of Washoe silver—but it took a great deal of money to support the bohemian arts subculture to which Sam wished to belong. Money made possible the city's taste for the new.

Sam arrived in San Francisco with a shining reputation based on his contributions to the *Golden Era* and the *Morning Call*, and his columns in the *Enterprise*. The city had great literary expectations ever since the early 1850s, when an Army engineer named George Derby, publishing under the name John Phoenix, had pioneered a style of Wild Western humor to which hordes of followers now aspired. Mark Twain seemed poised to improve even on John Phoenix. Fitz Hugh Ludlow, a visiting New York Bohemian who had created a sensation in 1857 with his drug confession *The Hasheesh Eater*, had "published a high encomium upon Mark Twain" as a part of his November 1863 "Good-Bye Article" in the *Era:* "In funny literature, that Irresistible Washoe Giant, Mark Twain, takes quite a unique position. He makes me laugh more than any Californian since poor Derby died. He imitates nobody. He is a school by himself."

Instead of capitalizing on Mark Twain's uniqueness, however, Sam chose a job and a literary style that marked him as just one of a crowd. Settling in at the posh Occidental Hotel with Steve Gillis, he accepted a position as the local reporter for the *Call*, at forty dollars a week in gold; combined with his occasional pay from the *Era*, his earnings now nearly equaled his salary as a pilot. He felt boundless joy at living in San Francisco. Perhaps he would not accompany Artemus Ward on a glamorous trip to Europe, but he would live recklessly high in San Francisco and be paid well for it. "I lived at the best hotel, exhibited my clothes in the most conspicuous places, infested the opera," Mark Twain wrote later. "I attended private parties in sumptuous evening dress, simpered and aired my graces like a born beau, and polked and schottisched with a step peculiar to myself—and the kangaroo. In a word, I kept the due state of a man worth a hundred thousand dollars."

Twain would also claim that his high spending lasted only until the bottom dropped out of the stock market. After the crash, he "had not now as much as fifty dollars when I gathered together my various debts and paid them. I removed from the hotel to a very private boarding house. I took a reporter's berth and went to work." But these assertions are at best revisions of the facts of Sam Clemens' life. His stock had little value and he began working at the *Call* within a week of arriving in San Francisco. He could not pay his debts and sank deeper into them. He frequented fine restaurants, drank champagne, and attended expensive parties because the name Mark Twain brought him a line of credit. Now a literary prospector more expectant than ever of striking gold, Sam lived on anticipated fame. When it came to him—imminently he believed—he would be rich enough to repay whatever he had charged.

The high confidence with which Sam came to San Francisco lasted through the summer of 1864. He wrote Dan De Quille about his and Steve's hijinks, including how they threw "their empty bottles out of the window at the Chinamen below," brandished weapons at the help, and ran women to their room, "sometimes in broad daylight—bless you, [we] didn't care." Their first few months in the city, Sam and Steve changed their lodgings a half-dozen times. But despite his wild times with Steve Gillis, part of Sam remained wistful for the life he had shared with Dan. He wrote increasingly desperate letters to his betrayed Virginia City roommate, but, as Mark Twain retold it, he "could not hear from Dan. My letters miscarried or were not answered." Hurt and angry, De Quille refused to respond to Sam's reports about his new life in San Francisco with Steve Gillis.

Bret Harte, a regular contributor to the *Golden Era* and San Francisco's leading literateur, signed on as Sam's literary adviser. Harte had an administrative position with the San Francisco Mint and occupied an office in the same building as the *Call*. Harte's government job—which he had obtained through art patron Jessie Benton Frémont, the daughter of Missouri Senator Thomas Hart Benton and the wife of early California adventurer and former presidential candidate John Frémont—freed him from journalistic drudgery. Sam also befriended wealthy Martha Hitchcock, doyenne of San Francisco's literary clique, whom he met at the Occidental Hotel, where he received his mail and ate during his frequent relocations. Hitchcock, recently returned from Paris, was a contributor to the staid *Alta California*, the *Call*'s morning competition, and a reputed Southern spy. Hitchcock had a daughter, Lillie, then eighteen, who was already making herself known for her unrestrained approach to life—occasionally cross-dressing, smoking cigars at poker games, racing horses out to the Cliff House, and riding the cowcatcher on the Napa Valley railroad. Hitchcock, Harte, and *Golden Era* editor Joe Lawrence introduced Sam to every California literary figure of note.

Sam's exuberance over his San Francisco life, however, began to dissipate as the summer of 1864 drew to a close. He alluded to his disaffection in a *Morning Call* sketch about a mid-August drunken foray to San Jose with Steve and six other newspapermen. Instead of recounting the adventure as he had experienced it, Sam posed Mark Twain as the recipient of an inebriated report about the bibulous excursion, implying that he did not himself participate. By placing this literary distance between himself and his own pleasures, Mark Twain signaled Sam's alienation from his summer of raucousness. By fall, Sam took only intermittent pleasure from his position on the *Call*. Though he rebelled at the tedium of his news beat, he did discover the satisfaction of flexing his muscles as a journalist. Once, having been refused information by the coroner's office, he wrote an article exposing the close relationship between the coroner and the city's leading undertaker—undertakers had been a useful literary target since his brother Henry's death. When the coroner died soon after, Sam mobilized on behalf of a certain candidate for the appointment. He proudly wrote to his mother about his political machinations:

> I had a candidate pledged to take the lucrative job . . .
> & I went into the Board of Supervisors & button-holed every
> member & worked like a slave for my man. When I began
> he hadn't a friend in the Board. He was elected, just like a
> knife. . . . I learned to pull wires in the Washoe Legislature,
> & my experience is, that when a bill is to be put through a
> body like that, the only thing necessary to insure success is
> to get the reporters to log-roll for it.

Sam always prided himself on both his political savvy and his personal power. During his western years, politics seemed dirty to him only when it involved outright thievery.

Never engaged by his work as a reporter—covering the police, the courts, the fires, and the political meetings—by mid-September Sam worked only half days at the *Morning Call*, at a reduced salary. He hoped to equal the loss in wages by writing regularly for a new literary magazine, the *Californian*, started by Bret Harte and Charles Henry Webb, an exile from New York's Bohemia. Unlike the middle-brow *Golden Era*, the new magazine imitated the best eastern journals in layout and design and aimed its material at a more cosmopolitan audience. But despite his popular contributions to the magazine, such as his farcical series "Answers to Correspondents," one of the first satires on advice columnists, Sam's debts continued to mount. He gambled both aboveboard in the stock market, about which he wrote a *Californian* article called "Daniel in the Lion's Den—and Out Again All Right," and in the many quasi-legal casinos around the city, one of which was run by the older brother of Sam's close Hannibal buddy John Briggs.

Personally, Sam felt adrift. Closing out his twenties, he found the joys of life as a single man wearing thin. He wrote his family in St. Louis and Nevada that his friend Steve Gillis was to marry heiress Emmelina Russ on October 24, with Sam to stand up for him "as chief mourner." Though Sam had reason to question the sincerity of Steve Gillis' engagement to Russ, it was a serious enough possibility to make him rue his lost matrimonial opportunity. "What has become of that girl of mine that got married?" he plaintively asked his mother and sister. "I mean Laura Wright." As fall sped along, he looked for an escape through his brother's political ambitions. The grapevine whispered that Orion would snag the nomination to the United States Senate from the new state of Nevada, whose constitution, without the onerous tax provision that had killed the earlier one, earned President Lincoln's ratification on October 31, 1864, just in time for November's election. Viewing his Virginia City associates with a newly jaundiced eye, Sam wrote Orion that his newspaper colleague Rollin Daggett and rival editor Thomas Fitch "will be likely to euchre you out of the nomination. . . . I know Daggett & Fitch both, & I swear a solemn oath that I believe that they would blast the characters of their own mothers & sisters to gain any great advantage in life. I know both dogs well." The rumor proved incorrect, in that Orion was not up for senator but rather secretary of state, as before. In any case, Orion did not need the help of Sam's erstwhile friends to destroy his political opportunity; he "was hit with one of his spasms of virtue on the day that the Republican party was to make its nominations," as his brother later described it. "He could not be persuaded to cross the threshold of a saloon. The paper next morning contained the list of chosen nominees. His name was not in it."

Within a few weeks of reducing his hours at the *Call*, Sam had proven to himself and to the paper that he could not suit himself to conventional newspaper duty. He would not be satisfied writing columns covering the mundane occurrences of city life without a byline. Besides, the *Call* restricted him in ways the *Territorial Enterprise* never had. In one of his periodic efforts to make Mark Twain something of a public conscience, Sam wrote a strong condemnation of the official abuses heaped on the immigrant Chinese; the *Call* refused to run it because the newspaper's core readership was Irish, and the Irish didn't like the Chinese. Sam was let go, "with a charity I still remember with considerable respect," he later recalled, since he was given "an opportunity to resign my berth and so save myself the disgrace of a dismissal." Sam's off-hour habits—drinking, gambling, high living with a fast crowd—contributed to his untimely release from newspaper moil.

California had disappointed Sam as it had disappointed many young men who came west. It galled him to have come to San Francisco so full of promise and yet failed to top the fame he had achieved in Nevada. His writing never elevated him above the pack of bohemian scribblers around him. The fame, and the fortune he expected from it, never grew. "For two months my sole occupation was avoiding acquaintances. . . . I became very adept at 'slinking.' I slunk from back street to back street, I slunk away from approaching faces that looked familiar, I slunk to my meals." Sam still had credit, but the size of his debt made him reluctant to use it. Falling into a dark financial hole, he couldn't write his way out of it or act outrageously enough for people to forgive his debt. What had passed for outrageous behavior in Virginia City was tame in San Francisco. New York bohemianism had emerged from the dingy cellar bar called Pfaff's— Walt Whitman had been a prewar habitué of the place. Now a crowd of artists, writers, and performers from that cultural hot spot had brought their wild ways west. Still a small-town boy, much as he hated to admit it, Sam was out of his depth in the drinking and libertinism, not to mention the sexual variety, that characterized the Bohemians: Charles Warren Stoddard, a twenty-one-year-old poet, had gone to Hawaii in late 1864 to recover from a nervous collapse brought on by his difficulty accepting his homosexuality; Stoddard's roommate Ina Coolbrith, also a poet, had a secret past and a love for women. However bold Sam had felt in Virginia City, he couldn't compete with the dark histories, nervous breakdowns, and other behavioral extremes of San Francisco's artistic crowd.

Even in his writing, Sam found himself unable to compete, insufficiently skilled to compose the polite essays fashionable among Bohemians. As chief contributor and interim editor at the *Californian*, Bret Harte was the unofficial arbiter of West Coast taste. Harte's effete sensibilities and impeccable rhetorical skills embodied the fine-arts ideal of San Francisco's literary world. Though a year younger than Sam, Harte seemed to have the perfect life, enjoying both urban bohemianism and suburban bourgeois comfort, financed by his sinecure at the mint. In his columns for the *Californian* toward the end of 1864, Sam tried to make himself into another Bret Harte. He imitated one of Harte's signature forms, the condensed novel. He also wrote picaresque essays which leapt pointlessly from subject to subject, never connected to the title he chose. He retold Caesar's assassination in contemporary journalese, but he introduced the satire in the strained language of genteel literature. The narrative drive, the wild humor, and the muscularity of language that had made Sam's writing notable in Nevada thinned in the foggy air of literary San Francisco.

Harte, described by poet Joaquin Miller as "the cleanest man he had ever met," made this verbal sketch of Sam Clemens in San Francisco: "He had the curly hair, the aquiline nose, and even the aquiline eye—an eye so eagle-like that a second lid would not have surprised me—of an unusual and dominant nature. His eyebrows were very thick and bushy. His dress was careless, and his general manner one of supreme indifference to surroundings and circumstances." What Harte read as indifference, at least late in 1864, was in fact depression. Sam, to whom identity was a mutable, liquid thing, had lost track of his own identity in the months since leaving Nevada. Dan De Quille wouldn't answer his letters. Steve Gillis' odd engagement had failed, leaving his friendship with Sam in doubt. Steve only wanted to drink and brawl, and Sam had to bail him out; once, when he accompanied Steve, Sam got arrested himself. His breakup with the turbulent Gillis was wreaking emotional havoc. He had no job, no steady income, and a mountain of debt. To make matters worse, Sam's muckraking columns against the police had prompted them to begin harassing him. Most difficult of all, Sam's best cues to his own identity—his fame, his skill in writing, his easy money, his outrageous behavior—had lost ground in the stiffer competition of the big city. Turning twenty-nine, Sam faced a dwindling opportunity for the fame and fortune he desired. He needed to get away and take stock.

He left San Francisco on December 4 for the Jackass Hill cabin of Jim Gillis, Steve's older brother; Jim had invited him to see what was left of California gold country. He later remembered taking $300 with him; the fact that $300 wouldn't soothe his creditors indicates just how steep his debt was. Jim Gillis modeled his life after Thoreau's, living in the played-out Tuolumne Hills, not in the hope of making a big gold strike but to enjoy the hills' beauty. Jim's cabin stocked a fine library, and conversation around the fire was refreshing and erudite. Even Bret Harte had taken refuge at the cabin in his penurious schoolteacher days. Sam chummed around with Jim and his cabin mate Dick Stoker and young Billy Gillis for twelve weeks.

Sam felt comfort and companionship in the hills. He stayed seven weeks in the cabin on Jackass Hill, and then went with Jim to another spot near Angel's Camp for the next month. Once during this emotional convalescence, Sam accepted Billy Gillis' offer of a partnership in a pocket mine—in which a miner pans across a small area and triangulates his way uphill to the narrow point from which rain had washed gold into the dirt below—but he never lifted a pick or panned any of the dirt. The hole that Billy Gillis worked yielded about $700 in ten days. Billy made good on his partnership offer, but Sam refused it. "The knowledge of mining I acquired," he said, "and the pleasure it gave me, is better equivalent for my time and labor than that little dab of money." Though Sam did no mining during those twelve weeks, he did a tremendous amount of listening—to the talk around the fire, to the Tuolumne Hills, and to himself. He began to keep a notebook again, trying to renew Mark Twain's singular voice.

Returning to San Francisco on February 26, 1865, Sam found waiting for him a letter from Artemus Ward, which, as he noted in his journal, asked him "to write a sketch for his new book of Nevada Territory travels which is soon to come out. Too late—ought to have gotten these letters 3 months ago. They are dated early in November." Still, the request from Ward served another, more important, purpose: It reminded Sam that he wanted to achieve more than success among the San Francisco Bohemians, against whose standards he mistakenly had judged himself. He imagined a future not just at the bars frequented by his friends, but one like Artemus Ward's, on the broader national stage.

The end of the Civil War and the assassination of President Lincoln, though they caused no discernible ripple in Sam's daily life, reopened the larger world to him. With the war over and the Union preserved, the nation was now poised to fully occupy the continent—and beyond. It was a bold new country, and it seemed to require a bold new voice. Writing again for the *Californian*, Sam recaptured his old style with material harvested from Jackass Hill and Angel's Camp. His language and subject matter demonstrated the same authority that had marked his Virginia City writing, while incorporating some of the associative logic that passed for structure in the bohemian aesthetic. He wrote with an energy and determination that had escaped him most of the preceding year. Looking to earn money, he made unsigned contributions to the *Dramatic Chronicle*, a free sheet alerting tourists to the city's entertainments, and began a daily letter to the *Territorial Enterprise*, giving not only the standard stock reports, lists of visitors from Washoe, and cultural reviews, but also more pungent commentary like his continuing critique of San Francisco's corrupt police force, indictments always copied by the big city's press. His *Enterprise* platform gave him a better foothold in San Francisco than any of the writing he did for the local publications. Eschewing the polite literature Bret Harte favored for the leaner, earthier work which came more naturally to him, Sam's *Californian* contributions earned the attention of the East Coast journals. For example, he concluded a satire of the instructive tales of bad little boys typical of Sunday school books, "He grew up, and married, and raised a large family, and brained them all with an axe one night, and got wealthy by all manner of cheating and rascality, and now he is the infernalest wickedest scoundrel in his native village, and is universally respected, and belongs to the Legislature." Sam raised Mark Twain's literary outrageousness to an extreme none of his bohemian competitors could match, elevating tired forms into something elegantly and alarmingly funny.

Though his work gives evidence of his literary growth, Sam's physical whereabouts during most of 1865 remains sketchy. In *Roughing It*, Mark Twain skips over the entire year—one sixth of the period the book supposedly covers—with a one-paragraph bridge between Jackass Hill and the Sandwich Islands, which would be his destination in March of 1866. "When my credit was about exhausted," Twain wrote in his abbreviated history, "I was created San Francisco correspondent of the *Enterprise*, and at the end of five months I was out of debt, but my interest in my work was gone; for my correspondence being a daily one, without rest or respite, I got unspeakably tired of it." His memory, however, disguised the truth. His $100 a month from the *Enterprise* could not eliminate a debt that the $300 he took with him to Jackass Hill could not significantly diminish.

Further, this period of what he recalled as mindless drudgery also gave him his first real taste of fame. The last few months of 1865 proved a watershed for both Sam Clemens and his literary mouthpiece Mark Twain. In mid-October, the *Dramatic Chronicle* reprinted wild praise for Mark Twain from the editor of New York's *Round Table*. Citing some exciting new humor writing coming from California, the New York editor compared Mark Twain with the legendary John Phoenix:

> The foremost among the merry gentlemen of the California press, as far as we have been able to judge, is one who signs himself "Mark Twain." Of his real name we are ignorant, but his style resembles that of "John Phoenix" more nearly than any other, and some things we have seen from his pen would do honor to the memory of even that chieftain among humorists. He is, we believe, quite a young man, and has not written a great deal. Perhaps, if he will husband his resources and not kill with overwork the mental goose that has given us these golden eggs, he may one day rank among the brightest of our wits.

This tribute spurred Sam to write his first letter in a year to Orion, who had recently sent him a letter, once again preaching to Sam about his dissolute style of living. "It is one of the few sermons I have read with pleasure," he replied. "I do not say profit, because I am beyond the reach of argument now." Then, in the most specific declaration of his intentions he had made to his family since leaving the river, Sam acknowledged a calling "to literature, of a low order—*i.e.* humorous. It is nothing to be proud of, but it is my strongest suit." Sam offered his brother a deal: "I will drop all trifling, & sighing after vain impossibilities, & strive for a fame—unworthy & evanescent though it must of necessity be—if you will record your promise to go hence to the States and preach the gospel." He also jovially but revealingly told Orion, "You had better shove this in the stove— . . . I don't want any absurd 'literary remains' & 'unpublished letters of Mark Twain' published after I am planted." Although Sam Clemens' personal correspondence had never been wholly trustworthy evidence of his inner life, it is clear that from this point on his concept of an audience moderated everything he wrote, no matter how privately.

Despite this measure of resolution and success, Sam despaired openly to his brother, "There is a God for the rich man but none for the poor." He concluded, "If I do not get out of debt in 3 months,—pistols or poison for one—exit *me*. (There's a text for a sermon on Self-Murder—Proceed.)" Sam gave himself three months to achieve his ambitious goals—that is, until his thirtieth birthday. He failed to kill himself; a marginal note that Sam scribbled in 1909 states that he tried, "but wasn't man enough to pull the trigger."

Thoughts of suicide left his mind when he achieved a startling success in late November. Sam's sketch for Artemus Ward's book did arrive in New York too late, but the publisher passed it along to the editor of the struggling *Saturday Press*, which ran it as "Jim Smiley and His Jumping Frog."

In the story, the first truly lasting work the young writer had created, Mark Twain reports, as though in a letter to Ward himself, the result of a favor Ward himself had supposedly asked. Ward has sent Twain to the laconic Simon Wheeler to inquire after his lost friend the Reverend Leonidas Smiley, but Wheeler knows nothing about him. Instead, he unleashes a rambling account of another man named Smiley, one so addicted to gambling that "If there was two birds setting on a fence, he would bet you which one would fly first." This Smiley gets his comeuppance when a stranger fills his pet jumping frog with buckshot. The stranger's funny refrain—"I don't see no points about that frog that's any better'n any other frog"—had kept Sam and Jim Gillis doubled over laughing when they'd heard the original version of the story told at Angel's Camp. By the end of the "letter," Mark Twain finally realizes that Ward set him up as a victim of the long-winded Wheeler. This work, which would later become "The Celebrated Jumping Frog of Calaveras County," was a bold effort. It publicized Sam's connection to Ward and implied Ward's ill-treatment of him, albeit obliquely. It demonstrated Mark Twain's capacity for dialect and caricature, but did not impose on Twain the class identity of a marginally literate narrator, like Thomas Jefferson Snodgrass. He confidently handled a story which moved in three directions at once—the tale of Jim Smiley, the answer to Ward's invented request, and the implied joke by Ward on Mark Twain. The comic desperation powering each of these narratives reflected, at a distance, Sam Clemens' own desperate drive to succeed.

Impeccably written, more deft than anything Twain had written before—indeed, more resonant than anything by Ward and equal to the very best work of any American humorist—the story made Mark Twain the signature voice of the western school. The piece soon became as celebrated as the frog itself, running in newspapers and journals all over the East Coast. The New York correspondent to the *Alta California* wrote back that "The Jumping Frog" had "set all New York in a roar, and he may be said to have made his mark. I have been asked fifty times about it and its author. . . . It is voted the best thing of the day."

The success of the story failed to relieve Sam's onerous debt, but it did lift his spirits. He wrote home a month after his splash into fame, "To think that after writing many an article a man might be excused for thinking tolerably good, those New York people should single out a villainous backwoods sketch to compliment me on!" Sam's excitement encouraged him to resurrect the notion of writing books rather than articles. He had two books in mind, one about piloting on the Mississippi, and another about the Nevada silver-mining boom, both to be seen through the eyes of Mark Twain. He still didn't know exactly who Mark Twain was or what he would bring to the worlds Sam had experienced, but Mark Twain was a valuable commodity now, and Sam Clemens had a monopoly on him.

His leap into fame brought another exciting effect: He was one of fifty-two San Franciscans invited to take passage on the steamer *Ajax* on its maiden voyage to the Sandwich Islands, later known as Hawaii. Sam declined the invitation, "because there would be no one to write my correspondence while I was gone. But I am so sorry now. If the *Ajax* were back I would go—quick!—and throw up the correspondence." Though Sam missed the *Ajax*'s first sailing on January 13, 1866, it planted the idea that he could go to Hawaii as a correspondent and develop a book on the islands. He had heard great things about the Sandwich Islands from his old editor Joe Goodman. Bohemian poet Charley Stoddard had often referred to his mystical journey there to recover his mental balance, and the languageless intimacy he found with young natives. Stoddard praised this experience in a letter to Walt Whitman, "For the first time I act as my nature prompts me. It would not answer in America, as a general principle,—not even in California, where men are tolerably bold." A trip to the islands sounded ideal.

Just getting away from the daily grind of his *Enterprise* correspondence and the constant burden of his indebtedness to San Francisco creditors would have made a trip to Hades attractive to Sam. The unexpected death of Will Moffett in August 1865 had left Pamela and Jane in financial uncertainty even greater than Sam's own. This deeply worried Sam, who felt guilty at being unable to provide for his mother, sister, and niblings. He arranged with a friend, a mining speculator named Herman Camp, to act as agent for the family's Tennessee land, offering Camp favorable terms in the hope of at last cashing in on the property the family had held for decades. Sam wrote Orion that Camp "says the land is valuable now that there is peace & no slavery, even if it have no oil in it." Camp produced an offer even better than Sam hoped: He would buy the land himself for $200,000 and turn the hills into vineyards. This deal would free the family from all money worries, repay Sam's debts, and allow him time to write. Unfortunately, Orion's continued belief in temperance precluded selling the land to grow grapes for wine. He quashed the deal and left Sam livid. Having taken responsibility for bringing security to his family, Sam could not bear his brother's autocratic paternalism. He determined not to write his brother again for a year and washed his hands of the land forever. "I am in poverty & exile now because of Orion's religious scruples," he raged to Mollie a few months later. "I want no such religion. He has got a duty to perform by us—will he perform it?"

On February 24, wanting to put some distance between himself and his troubles, he went up to Sacramento with Charles Webb, erstwhile editor and founder of the *Californian*, to hammer out an arrangement with the *Sacramento Union*, a wealthy and generous paper, for a series of letters from the Sandwich Islands. The development of steamer traffic to the islands and the rapid expansion of the sugar industry there made them seem like the next American frontier, and interest in the Pacific kingdom ran high. Sam wrote his mother and sister that "I am to remain there a month & ransack the islands, the great cataracts & the volcanoes completely, & write twenty or thirty letters to the Sacramento *Union*—for which they pay me as much money as I would get if I staid at home."

On March 7, 1866, as Sam Clemens sailed west out of the Golden Gate, he regarded the city of San Francisco with a strange mixture of joy and terror. He had nearly ruined himself, nearly lost himself, and nearly killed himself there. Was there anything left to Sam Clemens worth keeping? Well, there was Mark Twain, whose increasing fame and talent seemed to take up more of Sam Clemens' life. Though Sam could not fully identify this Mark Twain who shared his very skin, he thought that perhaps this alter ego could rescue him from the trouble he had made for himself in San Francisco, the city he once believed was his paradise.

9 | Hawaiian Correspondence

*Soap and education are not as sudden as a massacre, but
they are more deadly in the long run.*
—"The Facts Concerning the Recent Resignation"
(1867)

ON BOARD THE *Ajax*, the voyaging writer immediately jumped into his work, writing three letters to the
Union about his steamer trip alone. A few pages into his
notebook he wrote across the middle of the page: "Moral Phenomenon."
It was a sobriquet applied half jokingly to Mark Twain since his early
days on the *Enterprise;* he now wanted to wear the mantle with more
seriousness. Moral outrage had fueled his writing since well before Mark
Twain came into being; the "extreme case of matrimony" and other abuses
he had witnessed in Hannibal provoked some of Sam's best, and funniest,
adolescent work. He recognized that ethical indignation separated a clown,
like Artemus Ward, from a literary humorist. He would be satisfied if
Mark Twain became a successful clown, but Sam dreamed of making him
a voice for something finer than simple laughter.

Even in his notebooks, Sam practiced Mark Twain's morality. He
noted on March 15, not far below his sobriquet, that he had a case of the
mumps, "a d——d disease that children have—I suppose I am to take a
new disease to the Islands & depopulate them, as all white men have done
heretofore." Some doubt exists whether Sam had the mumps; it is possible
that his actual malady was venereal in nature, as a rival newspaperman

in San Francisco implied in a column, and that Sam disguised his diagnosis in his notebook for the sake of future readers of these private papers. In any case, his public-spirited concern was well placed: The native population of Hawaii had been literally decimated by syphilis, cholera, influenza, and other diseases in the previous hundred years.

Sam resurrected for Mark Twain a crass companion called Brown, who played the role the Unreliable had pioneered. Expressing bigoted opinions about the islands and their inhabitants, Brown served as Mark Twain's foil: Anything too base for Mark Twain to say could come from Brown. Brown's callously rude quips about missionaries, natives, and the Hawaiian monarchy allowed Sam the space and sophistication to define Twain not only as a moralist, but more importantly as a sympathetic iconoclast. Brown prided himself on being boorish and reactionary, but Mark Twain always looked for the more noble aspects of what Brown ridiculed. For example, in Honolulu, Brown looks over Mark Twain's shoulder as he writes a panegyric to the Hawaiian paradise and interrupts:

> "Yes, and hot. Oh, I reckon not (only 82 in the shade)! Go on, now, put it all down, now that you've begun; just say, 'And more "santipedes," and cockroaches, and fleas, and lizards, and red ants, and scorpions, and spiders, and mosquitoes and missionaries'—oh, blame my cats if I'd live here two months, not if I was High-You-Muck-a-Muck and King of Wawhoo, and had a harem full of hyenas!"

Brown, mistakenly pronouncing *wahine* (Hawaiian for "woman"), also mocks the unctuous praise of the travel writer, which frees Mark Twain to evaluate his experience more honestly.

As an experienced reporter, Sam knew that his fellow newspapermen would provide him with Hawaii's home truths. He befriended the founder and editor of the *Pacific Commercial Advertiser*, the oldest and most distinguished of the three English-language newspapers in Honolulu, with an eye toward augmenting his pay while in the islands. The editor had no need for his work, though he later recalled that Sam's "occasional joke played on an unsuspecting victim . . . and racy items of news, made the stranger's visits very welcome. . . . He was not only an inveterate joker but also a smoker, at least one box of cigars disappearing every week on an average." The *Advertiser* staff paid for whatever pleasure Sam's visits brought not only in cigars, but also in information and introductions. Using these connections for both knowledge and access, Sam wrote eleven

Mark Twain letters for the *Union* in the first month, covering such diverse topics as the Hawaiian whaling industry, the islands' prison, and a mysterious sandy patch of land outside of town scattered with human bones. As he had always done, Mark Twain made frequent comic use of animals, particularly horses, but truthfully Sam was so poor a rider that even the best horse seemed to him the very devil. He wrote about one horse he rented, alluding to his jumping frog story, "I could see that he had as many fine points as any man's horse, and I just hung my hat on one of them, behind the saddle."

In his letters to the *Union*, Mark Twain proved as insightful as he was amusing, especially when he wrote of the history and economy of the islands. Arguing forcibly for the inclusion of the islands as a territory of the United States, he astutely observed not only their social structure, but also the European and American personalities who had come to dominate Hawaii and its political future. Twain unmercifully castigated the Anglican bishop—who served as the head of the official state religion in a country whose natives, the Kanaka, had been forced to relinquish their tribal ways—as "a weak, trivial-minded man," spiteful, gossipy, and stupid. Marred only by his lack of sympathy for King Kamehameha V—who disliked Americans because his skin color had barred him from a steamboat's dining room when visiting the States—Mark Twain's letters won an immediate audience for their sparkling humor, their forceful discernment of Hawaiian politics, and their vividness of detail.

Samuel Clemens himself impressed the Americans living in the Sandwich Islands even more than Mark Twain did his readers back in California. His auburn curls, full and carefully trimmed mustache, and sharp wit collided with his apparently drunken manner, slouchy dress, and languorous speech. Though he drank sometimes, the poor quality of the liquor, its cost, and the short hours of the saloons kept his inebriation in Hawaii to a minimum. Sam claimed to his childhood friend Bill Bowen, with whom he could reestablish ties now that the war was over, "I know better than to get tight oftener than once in 3 months. It sets a man back in the esteem of people whose good opinions are worth having." Sam also spent much of his social time with divines, such as his temporary landlord, the Reverend Samuel Damon, who generously lent books from his extensive library, and his old Nevada pal the Reverend Franklin Rising, who had come to Hawaii for his health just before Sam had arrived. The missionaries had insights into Kanaka ways that interested Sam, but he also believed that his role as Moral Phenomenon required close association with traditional ethical authorities. He neglected the demimonde, membership in which he had habitually pursued in Nevada and California.

Despite his more conservative associations, or perhaps because of them, Sam often behaved outrageously while in Hawaii. To combat the heat while riding, he took to wearing a long brown linen duster—and not much else. The duster was too large for him and would periodically drop off one of his sloped shoulders. Sam would adjust it, but it would soon just drop off the other. Savoring any amenity he could, he also had no scruples about asking straight out for the best tobacco and liquor a host could offer. If the smoke and drink agreed with him, he would stay into the small hours, repaying his host's generosity with stories. Word got around what a good talker he could be when properly moved, and so he was often well treated, despite the odd impression he made.

The slow pace of island life pleased him. In his notebook he remarked, "Californians ought to come here twice a year to soothe down their harassing business cares." Sam lingered on Oahu into April to attend a sumptuous dinner with the king's grand chamberlain, David Kalakaua, who the very next day brought Sam to meet King Kamehameha V. The king impressed Sam more with his high degree of Masonry than with his royalty. Sam had suspended his association with the Masons after achieving his third degree, but Kamehameha V had achieved a stratospheric rank in the group. Revealing the ambition lingering just below his democratic ideology, Sam admired the king's rank among the Masons because it was a distinction to which Sam might himself aspire. He could never become a king.

Planning to range over most of the Sandwich Islands in six weeks and then return to California, Sam discovered that the islands were not so easily traversed as he imagined. He spent five weeks in Maui before returning to Honolulu to report on the Hawaiian Legislature. Then he boarded another small boat for the island of Hawaii, where he went to see Kilauea from the volcano's very rim. A new hotel had opened for that very purpose, and the owner, eager for a positive write-up, waived Sam's bill. The planters on the outward islands made life hospitable for him, but he exhausted himself riding from plantation to plantation to take advantage of the hospitality. Despite all this good fellowship, he felt a deeper loneliness. Regarding one planter's daughter, he remarked to his mother and sister that "If I were worth even $5,000 I would try to marry that plantation—but as it is, I resign myself to a long & useful bachelor-dom as cheerfully as I may." He wrote to Jane and Pamela from Honolulu a week later that "I rushed too fast. I ought to have taken five or six weeks" for that plantation trip. He complained of getting lost, of sleeping in huts with natives and living like a dog. At the end of his trip on the island of Hawaii, Sam was laid up with saddle boils for weeks. The pleasures Charley Stoddard had found could not compensate for the degraded conditions Sam experienced in the villages.

Three important events kept Sam in Hawaii longer than he anticipated. First, the king's sister, Princess Victoria, died, necessitating a month-long period of mourning complete with new and interesting cultural events for Mark Twain to report. Second, two American diplomats stopped for a month in Hawaii—Anson Burlingame, headed to China, and Robert Van Valkenburgh, off to Japan. And third, a miraculous story, a reporter's dream, simply dropped into Sam's lap. Fifteen men had arrived in Hilo after surviving forty-three days in an open boat. The *Hornet*, their original ship, had caught fire, and the crew boarded three separate boats to escape. After a few days, the three small boats cast off from one another, increasing their odds of finding either land or, better yet, a ship. Only one boat, carrying more than a dozen crewmen, succeeded, though most of the men were very close to death when they arrived. Sam interviewed the survivors, with the help of Anson Burlingame, whose son adored Mark Twain. Burlingame asked questions while Sam wrote and reclined gingerly on his painful posterior. Sam stayed up all night to complete the story in time to get it aboard the next ship heading to San Francisco. The *Hornet* disaster story went on to occupy the entire front page of the *Union* and was subsequently carried by wire across the country, scooping the month's most exciting news event.

Anson Burlingame, an immensely able diplomat, flattered Sam with his attention. Sam wrote home that the diplomat was "going to do me the honor to call on me this morning, & that accounts for my being out of bed now. You know what condition my room is always in when you are not around." Burlingame not only helped Sam get the *Hornet* story, but also invited him to share his house in Peking while covering China as Mark Twain. The plan was that Sam would first go back to the States, then on to China, and after that to the Paris World's Fair. Though Sam did not yet know the effect of his Sandwich Island letters, Burlingame's "throwing away invitations to dinner with the princes & foreign dignitaries, & neglecting all sorts of things to accommodate me" gave him sudden confidence. Burlingame told him, "You have great ability; I believe you have genius. What you need now is the refinement of association. Seek companionship among men of superior intellect and character. . . . Never affiliate with inferiors; always climb." No record exists indicating that Burlingame actually gave that advice, but the legendary diplomat unquestionably had a tremendous effect on Sam Clemens. Sam felt this interest in him by Anson Burlingame, a man of the same character of democratic greatness later embodied by Ulysses S. Grant, as a sort of anointment. Burlingame's enthusiasm encouraged Sam to believe that Mark Twain could rejuvenate the petrified genre of travel writing, a growing field since the explosion of American wealth and technological improvements in transportation sent more Americans abroad than ever before. Those Americans could use Mark Twain's moral pungency to replace the characterless claptrap most contemporary travel writers supplied.

Burlingame also provided Sam with access to the complex and often lascivious rites of mourning for Princess Victoria. The waning native Kanakan culture, under assault by the Christian morality of the missionaries, suffered severe restrictions on its traditional songs, dances, and other rituals. Even the treasured erotic hula dance now required a license and a ten-dollar fee, and could only be performed in its true state of near nakedness in strict privacy. The king, divided between Western and traditional religion, encouraged the dance but enforced the restrictions. Sam accepted a deal whereby he could watch the wild ceremonies with Burlingame, but could never write that he had. In fact, the king had closed the grounds to whites because the last royal funeral had caused too much comment overseas. The jarring differences between the cultures affected Sam, too. His letters to the *Union* praised Princess Victoria's musical talents, her leadership, and her support for missionaries; but in his notebooks he admitted that Victoria had kept a harem of thirty-six men busy satisfying her sexually and that she "died in forcing abortion." Hiding his arrangement and his privilege, Mark Twain exposed Sam's discomfort with the proceedings. He discussed some of the differences between current rites of mourning and those practiced in the past, and praised the American missionaries for moderating the former excesses to the more modern "singing and wailing every night—queerly enough, but innocently and harmlessly."

On July 19, 1866, Sam boarded the *Smyrniote* and set sail for the mainland. He had filled his head with exotic sights, but his Hawaiian excursion had given him only a holiday from his debt, which awaited him in San Francisco. The ship spent weeks becalmed, giving Sam the opportunity to consider what the journey had meant for him. Several of the *Hornet* survivors were on board, and he copied the journals they had written while adrift. He saw himself as also adrift at sea, barely holding on, not through forty-three days of privation, but through two years of a swelling tide of debt. The support of Anson Burlingame reinforced the success of the jumping frog story, and it made him realize what he might attain as Mark Twain. His exposure to the lasciviousness surrounding the burial rites of Princess Victoria allowed him to see that his own sexual and social choices had seemed wild only in comparison with the restrictive morality of the American Protestantism in which he had been raised; it was merely rebellion for rebellion's sake. If he was not willing to toss all hopes of a family life aside and disregard convention the way the Bohemians Charley Stoddard, Ina Coolbrith, and Prentice Mulford had done, then he had better focus his attention on achieving some stability and human connection in his own life. The day before he had left Honolulu, Sam noted that the gossipy village had "let me off comparatively easy." He perceived this as a failure of his public persona. "I don't thank them for it because it argues that I wasn't worth the trouble of blackguarding." If his outrageousness couldn't get Mark Twain lead billing in as small a town as Honolulu, Sam clearly needed to improve his act if he hoped to perform it on the world's stage.

10 | *At Home, On Stage*

I cannot see how a man of any large degree of humorous perception can ever be religious—except he purposely shut the eyes of his mind & keep them shut by force.
—Notebook (1888)

ON AUGUST 13, 1866, the day Sam landed in San Francisco, he noted to himself, "Home again. No—*not* home again—in prison again—and all the wild sense of freedom gone. The city seems so cramped, & so dreary with toil & care & business anxiety." Encountering Orion in Sam's own desperate San Francisco contributed to his anxiety; he still loathed his brother for quashing the Tennessee land deal that would have saved the entire family. Since leaving government office, Orion had tried to make enough money for the trip home to Iowa by writing, speculating, practicing law, and trying to sell the house in Carson City, all while living in the forsaken town of Meadow Lake, Nevada. Now, at the end of August, in San Francisco with Mollie before shipping off for points east, Orion tried to make peace with his brother. Tense, worried, and depressed, the two Clemens boys who had come west with such high hopes five years earlier faced each other as two men made brittle by political and financial reverses. In spite of Orion's peripatetic nature, his western experiences had changed him very little, but Sam had grown acutely from the twenty-five-year-old riverboat pilot who had tagged along with his older brother. Hard-eyed, determined, and weary, he now had a clear idea of the Mark Twain he wanted to become, but as he saw off his brother and sister-in-law, he possessed neither money nor fame beyond the ephemeral celebrity of his Hawaii letters.

Settling quickly down to work, Sam finished the last of his twenty-five letters due to the *Sacramento Union*, whose editors had been so pleased with his performance that they gave him not only his regular pay, but a $300 bonus as well. He turned the *Hornet* disaster into an article he hoped would find favor in a distinguished eastern journal such as *Harper's*, and he penned some humorous pieces for less distinguished venues like the *New York Weekly Review*.

The popularity of his Sandwich Island letters led him to conclude that he could follow Artemus Ward's path to fame by giving a humorous lecture based on his travel experiences. By actually putting Mark Twain on the stage, as a performed self, Sam could go Ward one better, making Mark Twain himself a theatrical attraction rather than just using the nom de plume to attract an audience to hear the actual author, as Charles Farrar Browne used the name Artemus Ward. His success as Governor Mark Twain of the "third house" in Nevada boosted his belief that he might earn enough talking as Mark Twain to pull Sam Clemens out of debt.

Sam reserved Maguire's Academy of Music and wrote up handbills to whet the public appetite for the live performance:

A SPLENDID ORCHESTRA
IS IN TOWN, BUT HAS NOT BEEN ENGAGED.

Also
A DEN OF FEROCIOUS WILD BEASTS
WILL BE ON EXHIBITION IN THE NEXT BLOCK.

MAGNIFICENT FIRE WORKS
WERE IN CONTEMPLATION FOR THIS OCCASION,
BUT THE IDEA HAS BEEN ABANDONED.

A GRAND TORCHLIGHT PROCESSION
MAY BE EXPECTED; IN FACT, THE PUBLIC ARE PRIVILEGED
TO EXPECT WHATEVER THEY PLEASE.

This last joke was not entirely funny to Sam, who worried that no one would show up at Mark Twain's premiere. Successful writers starved, while successful performers got rich; if he could get a good audience and strong reviews, he could take the lecture on an inland tour, as Ward had, and earn enough money to pay off all his creditors. His friend Denis McCarthy, formerly co-owner of the *Territorial Enterprise*, had already agreed to serve as Sam's stage manager and advance man. Sam suggested his anxiety in the handbill's tag line: DOORS OPEN AT 7 O'CLOCK. THE TROUBLE BEGINS AT 8 O'CLOCK.

The lecture was a smashing success. The hall had no vacant seats, and many who came late hoping for a standing-room ticket went away unsatisfied. Since many of the people in the audience were friends of Sam Clemens—or creditors—they greeted his appearance in the wings with a thunderous applause, which only increased as Mark Twain shambled toward the lectern. Twain opened with a joke about a trombone player he'd engaged to play during the lecture, but who refused to honor his contract without a band to support him. He went on to intersperse observations about the Sandwich Islands with humorous anecdotes and gorgeous word-pictures of the glorious sights there. The audience roared over Mark Twain's account of how the Kanaka treat their dogs, "a species of little mean, contemptible cur, that a white man would condemn to death on general principles. . . . They feed this dog, pet him, take ever so much care of him, and then cook and eat him." He encouraged his listeners to think of the animal as "only our cherished American sausage with the mystery removed." The audience responded with over an hour of constant laughter, giving Sam a standing ovation and calling for an encore.

Nearly all the newspapers praised his performance, claiming that Mark Twain bettered Artemus Ward and harked back to the greater humor of San Francisco's literary pioneer John Phoenix. One reviewer chastised his colleagues for exaggerating their adulation of Twain, accusing them of fearing what Sam would write about them if they didn't, but conceded that even he had to "regard this subject with mingled awe and admiration, and approach him with hesitation. Nature must have been in one of her funniest moods when she fashioned this mixture of the sublime and the ridiculous." Mark Twain had brought out a better lecture than his model Ward, everyone agreed, not only in providing comparable delivery of better jokes, but also by containing his humorous jabs in an organized and substantive lecture. Sam could not have hoped for more.

Except when it came to the receipts. Only then did he realize what a poor arrangement he had made in taking the hall at half price, in exchange for the promise of sharing half the $1,200 gate with theater owner Tom Maguire. After expenses, Sam netted only $400 for his efforts. Still, for one night's work and a few weeks of anxious preparation, that was excellent pay, and the reviews in the San Francisco press were all Sam needed to take Mark Twain on tour. He stayed in San Francisco another week, and then took to the road with Denis McCarthy, stopping for shows in Sacramento, Marysville, Grass Valley, Nevada City, Red Dog, and You Bet before heading into Nevada for the first performance there, in Virginia City, on October 31, 1866. Blurbs from the San Francisco reviews brought out full and enthusiastic houses. All along the trail he used the same sort of misdirection in his advertisements, such as "THE CELEBRATED BEARDED WOMAN! Is not with this circus."

McCarthy escorted a jubilant Mark Twain into his old stomping grounds. Sam had worried about his reception by old friends, especially Steve Gillis and Dan De Quille, but the whole *Enterprise* crew welcomed him. Puffing his performance as well as itself, the newspaper noted, "It was while in residence here and associated with the *Enterprise* that he assumed the name 'Mark Twain' and developed the rich and inexhaustible vein of humor which has made the title famous." The paper claimed that his comedy rested "upon the solid foundation which was originally laid in our native alkali and sagebrush." With the help of his friends, Sam received handsome treatment not only in Virginia City, but also, to his surprise, in Carson City. Even there, the newspapers printed welcomes from the town's notables; everyone but Sam seemed to have forgotten his insult to the ladies of Carson. But still he was not entirely at ease with the success of Mark Twain. Sam grumbled to Tom Fitch—the man he had called a two-faced dog to Orion but who was his host while lecturing in Washoe City—that he felt like a fraud on the lecture platform. Fitch tried to cheer him up, telling him he had "taken in over $200." Twain responded, "Yes, and I have taken in over 200 people." Always aware of his finances, he cheered himself up with the thought that he could play every town in the country and take them too, at least once.

A disturbing event on the evening of November 10 ended his plans for Mark Twain to lecture in more Nevada towns. Crossing the divide between Gold Hill and Virginia City as they walked home in the dark after a performance, Sam and Denis were waylaid by robbers. The desperadoes relieved them of their evening's take and Sam's fine gold watch inscribed to GOV MARK TWAIN. Though Sam kept his composure throughout the ordeal, the experience frightened him badly. He waited by the roadside as long as the robbers had commanded him to—and then he waited longer, just to be sure. Back in Virginia City, he commiserated with his *Enterprise* buddies in a C Street saloon and composed a brief report of the theft and a plea for the return of his watch, to which he had a sentimental attachment. His friends kept straight faces—but they knew that McCarthy and Gillis had planned the robbery stunt together. They all thought the fake robbery a hoot, and they thought Sam would think so, too. Though Gillis and company intended the hoax to demonstrate that they still considered him one of their merry band, they had forgotten that Sam never liked to be the butt of practical jokes. Remembering Anson Burlingame's advice to always climb, Sam began to regard the Nevada gang as his slumming buddies; he wanted to transcend both Nevada and the Sam Clemens who had debauched himself there. When he discovered the ruse, Sam canceled several performances and stalked off for San Francisco, where he found that the news of the robbery, but not its resolution, had beaten him to town.

He arranged for a second Sandwich Island lecture in the city on Friday, November 16, hoping to bring in a new audience by adding some material about the robbery. He called the show his Farewell Benefit—that is, a benefit for himself—and planned to leave for the East, and greater fortune, by boat on the following Monday. The lecture, however, did not match his first; the audience came, but the mediocre performance garnered only tepid reviews. He was not yet sanguine enough about his friends' practical joke to turn the robbery into comedy. He decided to delay his departure. Sam wanted a grand California send-off for "The Wild Humorist of the Pacific Slope," and a so-so performance there might mean that Mark Twain would fizzle in New York. More important, the several thousand dollars he netted on his inland sweep had not satisfied his creditors. They attached the money from his second San Francisco show, said one newspaper account; the *Gold Hill News* also attributed his remaining in California to a "severe attack of impecuniosity." Sam took Mark Twain's lecture to San Jose, Petaluma, and Oakland, with mixed success. In San Jose, he introduced a gambit that guaranteed a laugh, offering to demonstrate the cannibalism practiced in Hawaii, if only a young mother would offer him her child for a subject. In Oakland, however, he had only a minuscule audience. Even *Harper's* December publication of his *Hornet* article, "Forty-three Days in an Open Boat," was bittersweet. It had been published under the misnomer "Mark Swain." Though Mark Twain later claimed in "My Debut as a Literary Person" that this was both a mistake and a disappointment, it is possible that he doubted the wisdom of debuting in *Harper's* with this story just enough that he misspelled his name when signing the manuscript. The sensational, real-life drama of the *Hornet* survivors was news, however well told, and Sam, trying to define his alter ego's persona, did not envision Mark Twain as a reporter.

Back in San Francisco, Sam picked up a crucial element of success he felt he needed before quitting California. The prestigious *Alta California* newspaper signed him on as a roving correspondent; though his exact destination remained uncertain, the editors agreed to pay his travel expenses as well as a fee for a weekly letter from wherever he landed. He thought of going to Paris and China, with stops in exotic climes along the way. The Reverend Franklin Rising, Sam's Nevada friend, convinced him that the only Americans he would meet in many parts of the world would be missionaries, and that references from religious people at home would improve his reception abroad. He wrote his family at the beginning of December, "I am thick & thieves with the Rev. Stebbings, & I am laying for the Rev. Scudder & the Rev. Dr. Stone. I am running on preachers, now, altogether." Sam wanted introductions to famous preachers, such as Henry Ward Beecher, in the hope that his association with notable religious leaders would make Mark Twain a more believable and successful Moral Phenomenon to an East Coast audience.

The *Alta California* helped Sam with his final send-off by publishing a call from eminent westerners, including governors, generals and judges, for another San Francisco lecture. On December 10, 1866, Mark Twain gave his Sandwich Island performance once again, enjoying a reprise of his first rousing success. He ended by ballyhooing his adopted home: "California is the Crown Princess of the new dispensation! She stands in the center of the grand highway of nations; she stands midway between the Old World and the New, and both shall pay her tribute." Jokingly predicting a population of 450 million for San Francisco alone, he said, "Half the world stands ready to lay its contributions at her feet. Has any other State so brilliant a future? Has any other city a future like San Francisco?" The crowd gobbled up every bit of Mark Twain's panegyric to the city he was so eager to leave. Writing home on December 15, Sam almost gloated, "I sail tomorrow . . . leaving more friends behind me than any newspaper man that ever sailed out of the Golden Gate, Phoenix not excepted." He had managed in the four short months since his return from the Sandwich Islands to undo most of the damage to his reputation he had recklessly accumulated in the four years before. Sam Clemens— and Mark Twain—boarded the steamer *America* bound for New York, sailing south along the Pacific Coast for Nicaragua, where he would cross to the Gulf of Mexico a new man.

11 | *On the Make in the East*

When I reflect upon the number of disagreeable people
who I know have gone to a better world, I am moved to
lead a different life.
—"Pudd'nhead Wilson's Calendar" (1894)

WHAT EXACTLY DID Sam Clemens hope to accomplish once he got to New York? He never put his aspirations down on paper. The first letter he sent after boarding the *America* out of San Francisco went to E. P. Hingston, Artemus Ward's manager, whom Sam boldly asked to abandon Ward in England and come manage him in the States. Though he wanted to replicate Ward's success, he had no intention of parading himself as a genius, one of those self-parodying bohemian writers he ridiculed as "people who dash off weird, wild, incomprehensible poems with astonishing facility, & then go & get booming drunk & sleep in the gutter." In his notebook covering the journey from San Francisco to New York, Sam worried more about his first-cabin privileges than his genius. His health concerned him, too; he was frequently laid low by a mysterious complaint on the first leg of the journey. He kept his spirits up through such mischief as getting the ship's monkey drunk, and by getting to know Ned Wakeman, the captain of the *America*, a burly, tattooed raconteur. On board ship, Sam little resembled as a writer or personality the Mark Twain he hoped to become. He wrote satirical doggerel about fellow passengers and attempted a burlesque of Victor Hugo's *Toilers of the Sea*. He also exhibited remarkable bigotry toward a Jewish man on board. Sam recorded in his notebook that Ned Wakeman allowed Sam to lie on the captain's sofa, and that the Jewish man assumed the same privilege. That outraged Sam; the Jew was, after all, "In good health, though not to our thinking a white man." Sam enjoyed a cruel revenge when Wakeman fed the man a laxative.

The train-and-boat trip across Nicaragua interested Sam little, but boarding the *San Francisco* for the final leg of the journey began a nightmare, which Sam noted the day after setting sail: "Two cases of cholera reported in steerage today." In all, seven people died before the vessel docked in New York ten days later. As the sickness and death mounted, Sam took a reporter's professional interest in the details of the plague. He corralled the ship's surgeon, a fellow Mason, who explained that the disease was swift, virulent, and deadly, and that the *San Francisco* had no medicine. Sam went untouched by cholera, but his entry into New York was harrowing and portentous.

Upon arrival, Sam labored like a madman for Mark Twain's success, making contacts with newspapers and hunting up western friends who had since moved east, such as Charles Henry Webb, a bohemian comrade, and Frank Fuller, former governor of Utah and now a businessman. Within a few weeks, Sam had closed deals to contribute material to the *Sunday Mercury*, the *Evening Express*, and the *New York Weekly*, all at good rates. Mark Twain began appearing regularly as an original contributor to the established eastern press but he did not have much luck in placing his collection with a book publisher. Webb set up an interview with George Carleton, publisher of Sam's friendly competitor Bret Harte, but Carleton dismissed Sam without even looking at his work. "The fountains of his great deep were broken up," Mark Twain later recalled, "and for two or three minutes I couldn't see him for the rain. It was words, only words, but they fell so densely they darkened the atmosphere." Carleton told him, "Books—look at those shelves! Every one of them is loaded with books that are waiting for publication. Do I want any more?" After only a few weeks, Webb decided he would publish the book himself. Sam agreed with trepidation, since he had seen Webb drive himself to the edge of bankruptcy in San Francisco by backing the *Californian*, to which both Bret Harte and Mark Twain had contributed. Still, he was in a hurry to succeed and saw no compelling reason to hesitate.

Meanwhile, Frank Fuller agreed to manage Mark Twain's stage appearances. Within the first few weeks of his arrival, Fuller and Clemens had planned Mark Twain's eastern stage debut. In preparation, Sam attended lectures, including a notable one by the fiery Anna Dickinson, who had begun her platform career while still a teenager, railing against slavery, and had continued after the war as a sharp-tongued supporter of women's rights. After starting to make arrangements for his speaking performances, though, Sam decided to hold off awhile. His lectures in San Francisco had created ripples of excitement among the community of former westerners in New York, but Sam felt uncertain that Mark Twain could pull in a large audience based on that reputation alone.

A project hatched by yet another successful platform speaker helped decide the timing for Mark Twain's coming-out party. Henry Ward Beecher organized a tour of Europe and the Holy Land through his Plymouth Church, in Brooklyn, and Sam wanted to join it. Beecher was the nation's preeminent preacher, the leader of a loose wing of theologically liberal ministers whom Mark Twain ironically characterized as "the fast nags of the cloth." Beecher and his comrades espoused a morality of wealth, based on the principle that earthly success was God's reward for righteousness, a theology which played well to a post-Civil War audience poised to take the spoils of victory. In early February, Sam attended services at the moneyed Plymouth Church with Moses Beach, a New York editor and a neighbor of Henry Ward Beecher. Complete with General William Tecumseh Sherman as a passenger, the six-month tour cost $1,250, plus another $500 for land expenses. Sam talked his editors at the *Alta California* into paying his way, in exchange for two letters a week, not just one. With a bohemian literary friend, Edward House—just returned from having escorted Artemus Ward to Europe—Sam went to book passage when the two men were drunk. House presented Sam to the cruise's captain, Charles C. Duncan, as the Reverend Mark Twain, recently arrived from San Francisco. Twain was a Baptist, House explained, but he hoped that his orthodoxy wouldn't conflict with the more liberal teachings of the tour's host minister, Beecher. Duncan was flabbergasted by the display, and inclined against accepting Twain. When Sam confessed his actual identity and paid his $125 nonrefundable deposit, Duncan gladly accepted; the press had more enthusiasm for the pricey trip than did paying passengers.

Though New York had not treated him well almost a decade and half before, this time Sam swiftly established himself as a promising presence. In two months, he had not only sold his short work to the New York press, arranged with Charles Webb to publish his back work as a book, and begun preparations to lecture as Mark Twain in New York, but he had also cemented plans that would determine his life for nearly a year to come. Though his plans called only for more travel, Sam Clemens' life hadn't been so determined since he had abandoned riverboat piloting six years before.

Just as many years had passed since he had seen his family. Having set his career on full steam, Sam Clemens boarded a night train from New York on March 3, 1867, and reached St. Louis two days later for a month-long visit with his mother Jane, sister Pamela, and her children, fourteen-year-old Annie and six-year-old Sammy. Though he had not returned rich or famous, as he had vowed years before to do, he did come clad in more brilliant success than his brother had managed. In the several months since Orion and Mollie had returned home, Orion had neither found productive work nor sold the Tennessee land. Mollie had settled in with her family in Keokuk, to wait for her husband to make enough money to support a household. Jane, Pamela, and the children made their modest ends meet with William Moffett's insurance settlement. As the successful son returning to his roots, Sam sought to redefine his relationship with his family. His mother, now sixty-four, had as much esprit and religious eclecticism as ever. Pamela had a generous heart, and her children delighted Sam. He even made up with his brother and promised he would look into a political position for Orion when he went to Washington before sailing for Europe.

During his first three weeks in the Midwest, Sam renewed contact with his Masonic and riverboat cronies, and he forged alliances with editors who could spread his pseudonym around the Mississippi River Valley. These connections helped during the second half of his stay. Invited to speak on March 25 and 26, 1867, he placed a letter in the *Missouri Republican* on the twenty-fourth. "I wish you would mention it in your paper, that I am going to lecture for the benefit of a Sunday School, so they will see it in California, because . . . if I were merely to say it myself, without any endorsement," he wrote using frontier slang, "they would copper it." He claimed there would be a contest associated with his performance, and offered as one prize a public park. In another newspaper attempt at self-promotion, Sam replicated his youthful trick of creating a false controversy between invented correspondents. Mark Twain, "as a husband and father," satirizes women in public life, joking that if they could vote "Every woman in the commonwealth of Missouri would let go everything and run for State Milliner." Mark Twain's "wife" and other nonexistent female relatives write in to protest his opinions. This satire exploited the rapidly growing concern with women's issues without giving any real clue as to Sam's true opinions, except that such issues were ripe topics for newspaper humor. Mark Twain gave lectures while visiting Sam's old haunts, including one at Hannibal and another at Keokuk, performances that brought him both travel money and hometown acclaim. He left St. Louis in mid-April, unsure of when he might return.

Back in New York, Sam reentered the whirlwind he had set in motion a month and a half before. The Plymouth Church Europe and Holy Land tour promoters were now using the name Mark Twain to entice prospective pilgrims onto the *Quaker City*, the cruise's steamship. Charles Webb had Mark Twain's book, *The Jumping Frog of Calaveras County and Other Sketches*, in press, though Sam's absence precluded his reading its proofs. Frank Fuller had set up Mark Twain's New York debut for May 6, 1867, at the large Cooper Institute hall. At Sam's behest, Frank Fuller went to Washington to ask his fellow former territorial governor James Nye, now a Nevada senator, to introduce Mark Twain to his first eastern audience. The senator agreed. Fuller fronted the money for advertising and hall rental, expecting repayment in ticket sales.

The show took on a sadly auspicious quality with the news that Artemus Ward had died of an infection in England, at age thirty-three. The death of the man who had given Sam a vision of his future was a personal loss but a professional gain: Comparisons between Ward and Mark Twain, who had commandeered Ward's stage manner so effectively, made Twain Ward's unofficial successor.

Frenzied preparations attended Mark Twain's eastern premiere right up to the moment the curtain rose. Though Sam's press connections produced positive advance notice of Mark Twain's performance, the box office disappointed Fuller and frightened Sam. "Everything looks shady, at least, if not dark," he wrote his family five days before his appearance. "I have taken the largest house in New York & cannot back water. Let her slide! If nobody else cares, I don't." Fearing an empty auditorium, Sam asked Fuller to send complimentary tickets to area schoolteachers. When Sam rehearsed his lecture in his backer's office, Fuller raved about the performance, but fretted about Sam's dress. Sam had adopted an outrageous costume—"heavy arctics on his feet . . . a slouch hat, pulled carelessly out of shape . . . a high-collared overcoat"—to define himself as a humorist. Fuller wanted Sam in formal evening dress and had a suit tailored for him, but Sam raged at the stupidity of the tailor who had sewn the buttonholes of the suit jacket closed. Though Fuller explained that suit jackets weren't buttoned, Sam cut an opening and buttoned it anyway. Sam and Fuller went to Nye's hotel to escort him to the Cooper Institute, but the senator had either forgotten his promise or purposely snubbed Mark Twain. Sam hurried to the theater only to find a mob outside; the free tickets and advertising had produced an overflow crowd. Mark Twain shambled on stage to applause and feigned searching for some lost object. After a long, curious search, he explained that he was looking for the missing Senator Nye. With that moment, Mark Twain seized his audience. "The mantle of the lamented Artemus Ward seems to have fallen on the shoulders of Mark Twain," the *New York Tribune* announced, "and worthily does he wear it."

The demand for tickets led Clemens and Fuller to schedule more appearances for Mark Twain in New York. He spoke twice more, but, having let his lectures interfere with his writing, "I am obliged to give up the idea of lecturing any more," he told fellow humorist Corry O'Lanus. He had only three weeks before sailing and nearly a dozen newspaper and magazine pieces to write. "Confound me if I won't have a hard time catching up anyhow. I shall stick in the house day & night for 2 weeks & try, though, anyhow." Sam had to forgo lucrative lecturing opportunities, not only in New York, but in the communities nearby. Excited by the big-city press, small-town lecture committees sent Fuller requests for an appearance by Mark Twain. Still uncertain of his fame, Sam felt that before he went on tour he needed to develop greater name-recognition for Mark Twain through magazines, newspapers, and primarily his book. But *The Jumping Frog of Calaveras County and Other Sketches* sold only a few hundred copies, primarily to friends and transplanted westerners. Charles Webb had little experience as a businessman, and Mark Twain's collection of old sketches, many of them dated or too western in their sensibilities, did not sell well. Sam asked Bret Harte to review his book kindly, even though "it is full of damnable errors of grammar & deadly inconsistencies of spelling." By the time he left New York, he had soured on the book even more, telling his family, "I published it simply to advertise myself & not with the hope of making anything out of it." Sam realized that almost everything in the book was disposable periodical work given an artificially long life by publication between hard covers. The ephemeral nature of the work by which he made his living appalled him. Before he had fulfilled his obligations to the various newspapers and journals, he was sick of writing. He regretted not taking to the lecture field. He had no illusions about the durability or moral value of performance; it merely paid better and provided more pleasure than writing.

Sam had reason to gloat over what he had accomplished in the five months since he had left California. He had made Mark Twain a published author, a popular lecturer, and a paid celebrity correspondent on a luxury cruise. But the stultifying work of grinding out copy, and his savage and perpetual dissatisfaction with himself, kept him from deriving pleasure from his success. He fretted over the opportunities he might miss by traveling, but wanted nothing more than to get away. The depreciation of the widely touted Holy Land cruise eerily mirrored Sam's disappointment in himself. The two leading celebrities, whose presence would have attracted a more distinguished clientele, canceled in the weeks before sailing: Henry Ward Beecher decided to stay home and write a novel; General Sherman went west to fight the Indian wars. In the end, the *Quaker City*, outfitted for well over a hundred passengers, carried just over half its capacity.

Sam spent the day before departure, June 5, 1867, drinking wine with *New York Tribune* editors to cement his deal to report on the voyage for them as well as for the *Alta California*. "Now I feel good—I feel d——d good—& I could write a good correspondence—can, anyway, as soon as I get out of this most dismal town. *You'll see*," he wrote one of the owners of the *Alta*, which had invested nearly $2,000 in Sam. As he sought to elude through travel the very work that gave him success, he wrote his family that he felt "wild with impatience to move—move—*Move!* . . . Curse the endless delays! They always kill me—they make me neglect every duty & then I have a conscience that tears me like a wild beast. I wish I never had to stop *any*where a month. I do more mean things, the moment I get a chance to fold my hands & sit down than ever I can get forgiveness for."

12 | *An Innocent Vandal*

*It liberalizes the Vandal to travel. You never saw a
bigoted, opinionated, stubborn, narrow-minded, self-
conceited, almighty* mean man *in your life but he had
stuck in one place ever since he was born and thought God
made the world and dyspepsia and bile for* his *especial
comfort and satisfaction.*
—"The American Vandal Abroad" (1868)

T HE *QUAKER CITY* cruise's mixture of high ideals
and vulgar execution annoyed Sam from the start. Also,
much as the role flattered him, he could not adjust to
being the ship's only real celebrity—and one whose celebrated persona
existed separate from his basic identity. Until he boarded the *Quaker City*,
he had remained Sam Clemens except when writing, lecturing, or posing.
Now he felt uncertain when to be Mark Twain and when not to be,
especially with the puzzling audience he found himself among. The pious
quietude of this shipboard congregation ran counter to his natural bois-
terousness, and the quirks of individual passengers pushed him into sudden rages of impatience. Overall, the more than sixty pilgrims seemed to
Sam elderly, serious, well-to-do sheep. These *Quaker City* comrades were
impervious to his overtures. They either did not get his jokes or refused
to laugh if they did. Refusing Sam's humor deprived him of his ability to
charm.

Still, he found some congenial company. Mary Mason Fairbanks, traveling without her husband, *Cleveland Herald* publisher Abel Fairbanks, became the maternal magnet for the younger people on the ship. Though
she was only seven years his senior, Sam fell easily into calling her Mother

Fairbanks, as did the other younger travelers: Charlie Langdon, the desultory son of a rich coal merchant in Elmira, New York; Julius Moulton of St. Louis, taking a break from a position with his father's railroad; Jack Van Nostrand, a socially awkward twenty-year-old; and the seventeen-year-old Emeline Beach, traveling with her father Moses, who as a dignitary at Henry Ward Beecher's Plymouth Church became the de facto civilian authority aboard ship. These five became Mary Fairbanks' "cubs"; she was assisted in their supervision by Solon and Emily Severance, other prominent Clevelanders.

This group became Sam's editorial circle, to whom he read aloud his letters to the *Alta* and the *Tribune*. He elicited the group's reactions, but only Mrs. Fairbanks' opinion swayed him. Solon Severance once watched Sam throw a day's production into the Mediterranean Sea because it didn't suit Mother Fairbanks. Sam had not read work-in-progress aloud since his river days; he resurrected this method of composition in part because he wanted to reconstitute himself and thought he could best accomplish that by reconstituting his family in the group aboard the *Quaker City*, falling back on familial habits born in Missouri. His solitary creativity had encouraged him to develop the combustible sarcasm, which was his signature out west, but he thought that Mark Twain needed a gentler satire to reach his ideal audience. This small, controlled audience represented the larger anonymous one and thus allowed him to evolve a kinder humor. Unfortunately, this also forced him to act like Mark Twain for his friends, and the exhausting demands of this bunch made him hungry for company in which he could just be Sam Clemens. Emma Beach, whom Sam allowed to win at chess, later remembered that Sam not only belonged to her circle but also to "the smoking-room set": with his roommate Dan Slote, Dr. Abraham Jackson, and a few others, Sam could drink and swear and say outrageous things with impunity. When Sam would disembark from the *Quaker City* as a tourist, he went with his smoking-room set, occasionally including some male "cub" as a reward for good behavior.

He needed this support to counter the religious solemnity of the pilgrims. Instead of spending their first night at sea dancing, the passengers held services and sang hymns. Sam did feel somewhat heartened when Captain Duncan rejected one religious enthusiast's notion of stopping the ship each Sabbath. Once the voyage got under way, Sam found another irritant: Everyone wrote. Most only intended to keep a journal of their travels for themselves or their families, but more than a dozen of the almost seventy passengers wrote for newspapers. Mary Fairbanks wrote for her husband's *Herald*, Moses Beach for his own *New York Sun*, Dr. Jackson for the *Monroe County Democrat* in Pennsylvania, and Julius Moulton for the *Missouri Republican* of St. Louis. Even the ship's photographer, hired by Beach to create a stereoscopic record of the journey, wrote for publication. None had as lucrative a contract as Mark Twain, and none could expect the same attention, but at first Sam found this "reporter's congress" disconcerting. Once the journal keepers found something more pleasant to occupy their time, however, the writing mania settled down.

The arrival at the Azores on the morning of June 21, 1867, generated an exuberance mostly because of the break from the tedium of sea travel. The pilgrims tramped ashore at Horta, the village on Faial where they landed, moved by their first taste of the exotic. In Horta, Sam established the pattern for touring he would follow throughout his journey. He sought out intriguing details, such as the varied headdresses worn by Azorean women, which signaled their island of origin, and the blight that had ended the islands' wine production a decade before. Calling on the United States consul to the Azores for more information, he recorded his observations with businesslike efficiency.

Though Mark Twain's humor did not typically rely on stereotypes, Sam's prejudices fueled his first reactions to the exotic. He noted that Faial was "eminently Portuguese—that is to say, it is slow, poor, shiftless, sleepy and lazy. . . . The people lie, and cheat the stranger, and are desperately ignorant, and have hardly any reverence for the dead." Ethnic categorizations worked well in the newspapers back home, as long as Twain's humor refrained from lambasting any significant portion of his potential audience. Still, he shied away from the comedy of intolerance, netting more laughs from the imponderable differences between the dollar and other currencies. Twain also found humor in the ignorant ineptitude of his fellow travelers. He dubbed the ship's master of malapropisms "the Oracle," who in turn divinely named another passenger, Bloodgood Haviland Cutter, "the Poet Lariat." Cutter went into a spasm of doggerel at the least provocation and handed out broadsides of his poetry printed on the ship's press. Despite these real-life caricatures, Mark Twain called upon his old imaginary sidekick Brown to voice his cruder jokes. For example, when the art-weary Brown obligatorily views Leonardo da Vinci's "Last Supper" and at last learns that the artist is dead, the fact of Da Vinci's demise "seemed to give Brown great satisfaction, and the gloom passed away from his countenance." Sam believed that Mark Twain's higher humor needed Brown's earthiness to succeed.

People read Mark Twain's correspondence for more than its humor. Challenging the New World chroniclers' visions of Old World wonders, Twain gave Americans a new way to view their European roots. He lampooned the myths travelers heard upon arriving in a new place, and instead offered his own judgments about a particular foreign city's charms, based less on its intrinsic interest than on such plainspoken criteria as the cleanliness of the inhabitants, the cost of good cigars, and the competence and kindness of the guides he hired. He made it acceptable to worry more about whether the hotel had soap and less about whether the old masters moved you. In the Holy Land, his questioning would reach an apogee; everything he saw seemed dirtier, ruder, and smaller than Christian legend and guidebook prattle described them. Mark Twain brought the Gospels down to earth and gave his readers an alternative to the guidebooks' mindless homage to Western civilization.

From the Azores, the *Quaker City* sailed six days to Gibraltar, where the passengers temporarily dispersed. Many of the pilgrims decided to traverse Spain to Paris, but the thought of racing through the countryside for three days had no appeal for Sam. Instead, adventure called the smoking-room set aboard a steamer crossing the Strait of Gibraltar to Tangier. They sought a place "thoroughly and uncompromisingly foreign—foreign from top to bottom—foreign from centre to circumference—foreign inside and outside and all around—nothing anywhere about it to dilute its foreignness—nothing to remind us of any other people or any other land under the sun. And lo! in Tangier we have found it." Islamic Africa seemed wild to Sam, a chance to rediscover untamed life. Tangier so satisfied Sam that he bought a Moorish costume and wrote two articles about the one day he spent there. Allowing himself to get lost there, he relieved himself of the pressure of being Mark Twain every day by covering himself in alien dress, customs, and flavors.

On the evening of July 1, the *Quaker City* left Gibraltar for Marseilles. En route, the passengers held a Fourth of July celebration, to which Sam, Dan Slote, and Dr. Jackson wore their Moroccan garb. Many toasts were given and drunk, and dances danced, but the pious pilgrims disliked the raucous festivities and banned dancing aboard ship thereafter. Sam and his buddies could not wait to disembark. They boarded an overnight train for Paris, where Sam met up with his San Francisco friend, the notorious cross-dressing Hitchcock, whom he "did so yearn to kiss." He also beheld Versailles and glimpsed the emperor Napoleon III. When the *Quaker City* left Marseilles at noon on the thirteenth, the three renegades were back on board. The next morning, after the ship arrived in Genoa, Sam, Dan, and the doctor went off again for a month-long tour of Italy, including stops in Milan, Lake Como, Venice, Florence, Pisa, Naples, and Rome. Dr. Jackson demonstrated his wickedly perfect deadpan humor, asking the Genoese guide about Columbus, "Is he . . . dead?" This line became the refrain of these less-than-innocent Americans abroad.

While in Italy, Sam decided to accept an offer from Nevada Senator William Stewart to become his private secretary. In the nineteenth century, government posts often went to people expected to do little government work; the jobs supported their writing, as the San Francisco Mint sinecure supported Bret Harte. Eager for the opportunity to concentrate on serious writing, without the bifurcating drain of lecturing, Sam wrote Fuller, "Don't make any arrangements about lecturing for me. I have got a better thing, in Washington. . . . Winter after next will be early enough to dare that,—& I may be better known, then." Telling his family the news of his appointment a full month later, Sam wrote, "I believe it can be made one of the best paying berths in Washington. Say nothing of this."

In Naples, the *Quaker City* first encountered a problem that plagued the remainder of the voyage: As a precaution against cholera, local authorities quarantined passengers aboard ship. That enraged Sam because to his pragmatic American mind, the natives could protect themselves more effectively with a liberal application of soap and water than by restricting the movements of fastidious American travelers. The ship left Naples on August 11 and reached the port of Athens three days later, but again a quarantine threatened to keep the pilgrims from a destination that keenly interested them. To nineteenth-century Americans, the flowering of democracy, drama, philosophy, and military excellence in ancient Athens seemed their rightful inheritance, which was best claimed by visiting the Acropolis. The harbor police did not share the pilgrims' perception of the matter and threatened anyone caught running the quarantine with imprisonment. The challenge enticed Sam and three others, who slipped ashore under cover of darkness and walked for two hours through vineyards and over mountains to reach the great Greek city. They roused the guards at the Acropolis and toured the grounds in darkness before hurrying to reach the ship by first light. The men boasted of their adventure, only to discover that Moses Beach had gone ashore in full daylight, hired a carriage to Athens, seen the sights, dined, and returned to the ship safe and comfortable.

After a stop in Constantinople, which impressed Sam both in its appearance from the water and in the number and extent of its cripples, the *Quaker City* steamed along toward Odessa, a newly built and beautiful resort on the Black Sea. Rumors began to swirl on board that the passengers might get an audience with Czar Alexander II. As negotiations for this honor progressed, it became clear that the owners of the ship, the Leary brothers, had agreed to lease the *Quaker City* for the cruise primarily to attract a buyer for the vessel. Daniel Leary, representing his family's interests in the boat, heard that the czar was in the market for a ship, and negotiations for its sale led to a royal audience at the summer palace in Yalta on August 26, 1867. Gathering to host a luncheon for the traveling Americans—and to show off their palaces and yachts—were the czar, his wife, and their two children, along with an array of dukes, admirals, and other dignitaries. Sam composed a strikingly ceremonious address, which began, "We are a handful of private citizens of the United States, travelling simply for recreation—and unostentatiously, as becomes our unofficial state—and, therefore, we have no excuse to tender for presenting ourselves before your Majesty." Though Sam told his family "I didn't mind" writing the speech, "because I have no modesty & would as soon write an Emperor as to anybody else," he wrote with relief in his notebook: "That job is over.—Writing addresses to Emperors is not my strong suit." Royalty awed him. The czar declined to buy the ship.

After the excitement, Sam quickly grew embarrassed by the speech he had given, which the crew of the ship ridiculed mercilessly by repeating the opening line whenever they could squeeze it in within Sam's hearing. "I never was so tired of any one phrase as the sailors made me of the opening sentence of the Address," Mark Twain wrote, reluctant as ever to be the butt of any joke he did not make himself.

The ship returned to Constantinople for a few more days, and then went on to Smyrna, from which Sam visited Ephesus and Beirut, where it arrived on September 10. Ephesus, an ancient Greek city in what is now Turkey and site of "the temple of Artemis, considered one of the Seven Wonders of the ancient world," had only recently been the subject of excavation. Archaeology impressed Sam deeply. He marveled at the statuary that had lain buried from view for more than a millennium and the theater that took two years to reveal, proving himself vulnerable to the charms of history, provided few historians and fewer awed travel writers intervened between him and his contact with the past. "It is a world of precious relics, a wilderness of marred and mutilated gems," Twain wrote. "And yet what are these things to the wonders that lie buried here under the ground?"

At Beirut, Sam and seven others engaged an escort for their overland trip to Jerusalem through Syria, Lebanon, and Palestine. They hired a dragoman to make arrangements for five dollars a day, only to discover that the price included bedsteads, fluffy mattresses, carpets, silver candlesticks, and better cuisine than they got on board the *Quaker City*. "They call this camping out," he declared. "At this rate it is a glorious privilege to be a pilgrim in the Holy Land." Sam enjoyed the luxurious camping, but their ill-cared-for and unruly horses disgusted him. His own horse,

Jerico, had "only one fault. His tail has been chopped off or driven up, and he has to fight the flies with his heels. This is all very well, but when he tries to kick a fly off the top of his head with his hind foot, it is too much variety." The gang inspected the ruins at Baalbek and moved on to Damascus, where Sam succumbed to an intestinal bug. "I had nothing to do but listen to the pattering of the fountains and take medicine and throw it up again. It was dangerous recreation, but was pleasanter than traveling in Syria." Fortunately, one of the eight travelers, coincidentally also from Hannibal, was a physician who got Sam back in the saddle after twenty-four hours. The disease left Sam weak and he tired of travel in the hot sun. Though he prized his tent full of sinners, he "developed a profound distaste" for his more sanctimonious companions. They refused to ride on Sunday, unconcerned about the hardship this caused the rest of the party or—worse, in Sam's view—the animals, which would then have to ride more than twelve hours a day in the broiling sun to make up for the days off. His illness and irritation influenced his perception of all of the Holy Land as feeble, decrepit, and vermin-ridden. The biblical sights, which should have inspired any Christian, repulsed him. About Jerusalem, Twain wrote:

> Rags, wretchedness, poverty, and dirt, those signs and symbols that indicate the presence of Moslem rule more surely than the Crescent flag itself, abound. Lepers, cripples, the blind, and the idiotic, assail you on every hand, and they know but one word of but one language—the eternal "bucksheesh." To see the numbers of maimed, malformed and diseased humanity that throng the holy places and obstruct the gates, one might suppose that the ancient days had come again, and that the angel of the Lord was expected to arrive at any moment to stir the waters of Bethesda.

Sam's pilgrimage had reached the Christian's Mecca, and he felt only disappointment and disgust. Further explorations of biblical landmarks brought the same wretched feelings.

Mark Twain's newspaper correspondence concluded with his dyspeptic travelogue of Palestine. He had fallen behind in his obligations and, after rejoining the *Quaker City* at Jaffa on September 30, 1867, fretted about fulfilling his contracts. Exhausted and irritated by almost everyone around him, he found writing a nagging chore, made worse by Sam's distaste for the religious fanatics, who charitably allowed forty American refugees from a failed messianic cult on deck during the rocky voyage to Alexandria, but stingily barred them from the empty staterooms. Once in Egypt, Sam discovered he was even further behind in his correspondence than he had thought: More than a dozen of his letters had failed to reach the States. He would have to spend the voyage home reconstructing his journey.

Except for a few days visiting the pyramids and a week's foray into Spain, the touring was now behind the passengers. Cholera canceled stops at nearly all the other destinations, inciting a squabble about the itinerary. The cruise's rules dictated that a unanimous vote could change the ship's ports of call, but it took threats and abuse to bring one difficult passenger around to skipping Valencia for Cadiz, in Spain. Typically, Sam would have found the entire hubbub amusing, but the necessity to work now allowed him little time to laugh, and his dislike of his fellow travelers made their arguments more annoyingly petty. In spite of his deadlines, Sam, with Julius Moulton, Dr. Jackson, and Julia Newell—a game correspondent for a Wisconsin newspaper to whom the married Jackson had recently grown attached—left the boat in Gibraltar for five days of knocking about Andalusia. They reboarded on October 25, 1867, and the ship left the Mediterranean. As they headed homeward, the simmering disagreements began to heat up, completely spoiling the atmosphere of the *Quaker City*, as gossiping and backbiting became the foremost occupation of all the passengers. Captain Duncan issued niggling edicts about smoking and lights-out, most of which Sam prominently and blithely ignored. Sam wrote Joe Goodman from Spain, "This pleasure party of ours is composed of the d——dest, rustiest, ignorant, vulgar, slimy, psalm-singing cattle that could be scraped up in seventeen States." At the end of six months of travel, everyone aboard the cruise just wanted to abandon the boat, its forced companions, and travel itself. Only a miraculously pleasant four-day refueling stop at Bermuda interrupted the boiling dissatisfaction Sam and the rest of the pilgrims felt.

When the *Quaker City* docked in New York at 10:00 A.M. on November 19, Sam could not wait to escape both his fellow passengers and the persona of Mark Twain, a role his celebrity had forced him to assume more often than he liked. He found it nearly impossible to maintain Mark Twain's genial humor for more than short periods, and the animosity he had aroused in many of the *Quaker City* pilgrims proved that Sam's first experiment living as Mark Twain had not succeeded. He wanted nothing more than to reclaim his fundamental identity, and he spent his first day ashore visiting friends who knew him as "Sam," ending up at the offices of the *New York Herald* at six in the evening. Ignoring a dinner and theater engagement he had with Charlie Langdon and Mary Mason Fairbanks, he "wrote a long article that will make the Quakers get up & howl in the morning." The *Herald* burned with Mark Twain's indictment of the "extraordinary voyage" of the *Quaker City*. "Well, perhaps it was a pleasure excursion, but it certainly did not look like one; certainly it did not act like one. . . . The pleasure ship was a synagogue, and the pleasure trip was a funeral excursion without a corpse." Sam felt that his column let the enterprise off easy, but he hoped it would "bring out bitter replies from some of the *Quaker City*'s strange menagerie of ignorance, imbecility, bigotry, & dotage, & so give me an excuse to go into the secret history of the excursion." He signed his private letters to *Tribune* editor John Russell Young "Sam. L. Clemens," following the public convention regarding a writer's pseudonym: Mark Twain was merely a name he used in print and on stage; in his correspondence and elsewhere, Sam Clemens remained Twain's controlling intelligence.

But he was fed up with Mark Twain, just as he was fed up with his forced familiarity with religious pilgrims. Anxious to take up his new post as a Washington political hack, he undervalued his recent adventures and achievements. Not only had he seen the wider world at last, he had written about it in such a way that a hundred thousand Americans now had a vocabulary with which to discuss the experience. Through his correspondence, Mark Twain had transformed Europe and the Holy Land from a vast temple to our past into a simple foreign destination. An American traveler could approach the old masters with reverence only at risk of ridicule, and few readers could contemplate Jesus in Jerusalem without thinking first about filth and fleas. Mark Twain had struck a blow for the freedom of the American soul, but Sam Clemens could not wait to get back to his own life.

A Gypsy Again

> *It could probably be shown with facts and figures that
> there is no distinctly native American criminal class except
> Congress.*
> —"Pudd'nhead Wilson's New Calendar" (1897)

FRESH FROM HIS tour of Europe, and equipped with a new perspective on the mores of his own nation, Sam arrived in Washington, D.C., in late November 1867. He had planned to spend the winter there, but opportunities to establish Mark Twain as a force on the American scene ran him up and down the East Coast. Despite Sam's request that Mark Twain not lecture over the winter, Frank Fuller had forged ahead, figuring that one month on the road would earn Sam just as much as his senatorial clerkship. Though Sam calculated a $1,000 profit for the month of lecturing, the following months of idleness made the plan seem less wise than his position with Senator Stewart. He felt certain he would repay Governor Fuller's help with a more profitable tour once Mark Twain became better known. Besides, Fuller injured Sam's pride with the size of the towns into which he booked him. "I won't start in the provinces, Gov," Sam told him. "I won't do it."

Mark Twain's lambasting of the *Quaker City* tour in the *New York Herald* strained Sam's friendship with Mary Fairbanks and earned him a public rebuke from Moses Beach, whose daughter Emma captivated Sam as the trip came to an end. On the other hand, the controversy attracted the attention of Elisha Bliss of the American Publishing Company, who wrote from his office in Hartford, Connecticut, "If you have any thought of writing a book, or could be induced to do so, we should be pleased to see you." Bliss' company published by subscription, selling its wares through traveling agents, mostly ministers and schoolteachers interested in a second income. The agents canvassed their territories door to door, taking orders for elaborately bound and illustrated Bibles and giftbooks from people who did not frequent bookshops. Bliss' company had recently sold 100,000 copies of a first-person account of eighteen months in a Confederate prison. Since Charles Webb had sold only a few thousand copies of Mark Twain's first book, Sam answered Bliss excitedly.

Meanwhile, Sam began to make himself at home in Washington, serving as Senator Stewart's unofficial proxy on some committees and befriending both government officials and the press corps. He rapidly learned to imitate Stewart's signature well enough to use the senator's franking privilege for his personal mail. Though he claimed to have an eye out for his brother Orion's benefit, he noted in a letter home, "I could get a place pretty easily, because I have friends in high places who offer me such things—but it is hard to get them interested in one's relatives." As his acceptance in Washington grew, however, Sam's affiliation with Senator Stewart degenerated. Within weeks of his arrival, Mark Twain mocked his experience in government in a *New York Tribune* article, "The Facts Concerning the Recent Resignation." "I have resigned," he wrote. "I could no longer hold office and retain my self respect." He explained that, though he was appointed clerk of the Committee on Conchology, they "allowed me no amanuensis to play billiards with."

He also apologized to Frank Fuller, acknowledging "I believe I have made a mistake in not lecturing this winter. I did not suppose I was any better known when I got back than I was before I started—but every day I find additional reasons for thinking I was mistaken about that." By Christmas, his notoriety—originally from his *Quaker City* letters, but increased by his more recent articles—had produced a vast array of options for him: offers of a California sinecure; a position on a diplomatic mission to bring the Sandwich Islands under American control; an assignment as consul to China; and more writing assignments, including a book for Bliss about his *Quaker City* cruise. He remained torn by his desires to roam overseas as a diplomat, to live a writer's life, and to get rich on the lecture circuit. He preferred the anticipation of receiving a plum contract and the wistfulness about forgone opportunities to the practical work any contract might have entailed.

In New York City for the holidays, where he stayed with his *Quaker*

City roommate Dan Slote, Sam met Charlie Langdon's family for supper one night and on New Year's Eve joined them to hear Charles Dickens read at Steinway Hall. Charlie's twenty-two-year-old sister, Olivia, whose image on an ivory miniature Sam later claimed to have admired on the *Quaker City*, proved the most charming member of the party. Sam paid his first New Year's Day call at the house where Olivia Langdon, known as Livia to her family and Livy to her friends, received company with her friend Alice Hooker, a niece of Henry Ward Beecher. He neglected all his other calls. "We sent the old folks home early, with instructions not to send the carriage till midnight, & then I just staid there & deviled the life out of those girls." He added, to his mother and sister, "I'm going to spend a few days with the Langdon's, in Elmira, New York, as soon as I get time, & a few days at Mrs. Hooker's, in Hartford."

The appeal of Livy Langdon did not blind him to his "old *Quaker City* favorite," Emma Beach; his later claim to have fallen in love with Olivia Langdon via her miniature is false: He remembered being in love, but mistook the object of his affection. Despite her father's public dispute with Mark Twain, Sam and Emma dined together at Henry Ward Beecher's house the following Sunday. There Sam met *Uncle Tom's Cabin* author Harriet Beecher Stowe, whose reputation and success he revered. In a letter to his family, he gloried in his acquaintance with the most influential family in American public life.

> We had a very gay time, if it *was* Sunday. I expect I told more lies than I have told before in a month. We had a tip-top dinner, but nothing to drink but cider. I told Mr. Beecher that no dinner could be perfect without champaign, or at least some kind of Burgundy, & he said that privately he was a good deal of the same opinion, but it wouldn't do to say it out loud. I went back, by invitation, after the evening service, & finished the blow-out, & then staid all night at Mr. Beach's. Henry Ward is a brick.

Sam's ten days of flirtation reminded him of his response a few weeks earlier to Mother Fairbanks' suggestion that Sam marry. "You are only just proposing luxuries to Lazarus. That is all. I want a good wife—I want a couple of them if they are particularly good—but where is the wherewithal?" Sam earned enough from his writing to house and feed himself while he traveled, stay in good hotels, and dine with the elite, but he did not have the resources to occupy a position in society. He certainly could not afford to be the husband to women such as Emma

Beach or Livy Langdon. Fairbanks did not understand why Sam could not "turn an inkstand into Aladdin's lamp," as Sam put it to her.

Lecturing could provide the money, and Sam discovered upon his return to Washington in early January that a friend had put Mark Twain up to speak for two nights. He went into a fever writing a lecture purporting to tell "The Frozen Truth" about the *Quaker City* tour, all the while sweating about the publicity, his lack of preparation, and what size audience would attend. Although a good crowd turned out, Sam canceled Mark Twain's second performance, because the *Washington Evening Star* published a synopsis of the lecture. "[O]ne never feels comfortable, afterward, repeating a lecture that has been partially printed," he wrote to the *Alta;* "and worse than that, people don't care about going to hear what they can buy in a newspaper for less money." The same week, Mark Twain made news with another public performance, which he proudly declared "Speaker [of the House of Representatives, Schuyler] Colfax said was the best dinner-table speech he ever heard at a banquet." The Washington Newspaper Correspondents Club had asked Mark Twain to toast to Woman. "What, sir, would the peoples of the earth be, without woman?" he said in part. "They would be scarce, sir—almighty scarce!"

Sam soon was on his way to Hartford to meet Elisha Bliss. He stopped in New York to refresh his relationship with the *Herald*, which would give him more money and greater latitude than the *Tribune*, and to get pointers from Henry Ward Beecher, experienced in negotiating subscription-book contracts. Bliss offered Sam a $10,000 outright purchase. Following Beecher's advice, Sam held out for a royalty, a high one for the time, 5 percent of the cover price of books sold. Excited by the conclusion of the deal, Sam wrote a spate of bragging letters from the Hookers' fashionable house in the tony Hartford suburb of Nook Farm, where he was staying. He was not a terrific guest, apparently, and quickly exhausted the Hookers' welcome: His bohemian manners might have appealed to the upper class' younger set, but they grated on his actual hosts.

Upon his triumphant return to Washington, California Senator John Conness suggested that Sam become postmaster of San Francisco. The competition for this appointment raged for weeks, because any rascal could easily double the position's handsome salary of $4,000 a year. Sam rejected the job when he heard that a friend on the *Alta California* wanted it, but then a "complacent idiot" had "suddenly turned up on the inside track." Sam swung into action. "I got a dozen Senators pledged against him, & had Judge Field of the Supreme Bench get out of his sick bed & visit the president early in the morning," he crowed to his family. "It was jolly." Having defeated the rival, Sam again refused the appointment, "because it was plain enough that I could not be postmaster & write the book, too." Instead, he begged Bliss and the American Publishing Company to advance him $1,000. "If I can stand the *loss*, on the correspondence, of $300 a month for three months," he wrote Bliss, "don't you think you could stand the *loan* of it, you being capitalists & I being considerably otherwise?" Another alluring opportunity arose when diplomat Anson Burlingame, now serving the Chinese government as envoy to the West, accepted Sam as a part of his delegation to Europe, once he finished his book.

In early March 1868, however, the *Alta* presented Sam with an impediment to his plans. The newspaper's editors had heard about Sam's book deal, but they felt that their investment in Mark Twain's travels meant they owned his letters; they had even taken the rare precaution of copyrighting them to prevent such a dispute. To make their position clear, they decided to reissue the letters as a book. Sam learned of the editors' intentions on March 8 and promptly boarded a steamer out of New York. He wrote Mrs. Fairbanks that "if the *Alta*'s book were to come out with all those wretched, slangy letters unrevised, I should be utterly ruined." He needed to get to California immediately not only to stop the edition, but also to solve the problem of who owned Mark Twain's correspondence.

Once in San Francisco, Sam began his negotiations with the *Alta;* conferred with diplomat Anson Burlingame, on his way east from China, determining he couldn't yet accompany him to Europe, but could join the delegation later; and set about making money with a lecture tour. Now that Mark Twain had become a celebrity in the East, San Francisco embraced him as a hometown boy made good. On April 14, less than two weeks after reaching California, Mark Twain spoke to a full house and Sam netted some $1,600, enough to live on while in San Francisco. He took Mark Twain's lecture inland to Sacramento and Nevada, but Sam did not make much money there. The *Alta*'s copyright had dissuaded newspapers from reprinting his *Quaker City* letters; people outside the city did not know enough about the tour for Twain to make a successful stand lecturing in the provinces. When he returned to San Francisco, he asserted that the *Alta*'s copyright had already cost him $10,000 in lecture receipts. Would they now try to rob him further? The editors, made uncertain of the market for their book by the failure of Mark Twain's tour, relinquished their copyright in exchange for a simple acknowledgment in any eventual volume incorporating the letters.

Sam settled down to his labors. He found, to his amazement, that the correspondence he had sent to the *Alta* would not make even half the text needed for a subscription book. He worked from midnight, after dinner and revelry, until morning, writing new chapters, pasting previously printed letters on fresh pages, and surrounding the newsprint with corrections and additions. Six weeks later, he claimed he had nearly twenty-five hundred pages of manuscript. "I wish you could revise this mountain of MSS. for me," he wrote Mother Fairbanks, but Sam already had another, more experienced editor on hand. Sam's friendly competitor Bret Harte, now hard at work producing the first issue of his new magazine, the *Overland Monthly*, took time out to tell Sam, as he later put it, "what passages, paragraphs & *chapters* to leave out." Harte encouraged Sam to feature Mark Twain, to give him the full responsibility for the insights, both reverent and irreverent, which made the work's view of Europe so revealing and refreshing. Purging every vestige of the low-class clown Brown, Sam produced a manuscript that had Mark Twain's verve and Bret Harte's elegant restraint. Sam wrote to Elisha Bliss on June 23, 1868, that the book was finished.

He organized one more lecture, to be presented on July 2 for the "benefit of the future widows and orphans of Mark Twain," comically opening with an expression of sham gratitude to the capacity audience. There had been "such a wide-spread, such a furious, such a determined opposition to my lecturing . . . I never had such a unanimous call to— to—to leave, before." When he left San Francisco a few days later, his fame was so great that the steamer company wouldn't let him pay for his own ticket out of town. Not quite two years had passed since his last departure through the Golden Gate, but his entire world had changed, and would soon change a hundredfold more.

14 | Love and Money

*In whatsoever position you place a woman she is an
ornament to society and a treasure to the world. As a
sweetheart she has few equals and no superiors—as a
cousin she is convenient; . . . —as a wet nurse she has no
equal among men!*
—"Woman—an Opinion" (1868)

*I see that I was mistaken about Eve in the beginning; it
is better to live outside the Garden with her than inside it
without her.*
—"Extracts from Adam's Diary" (1893)

ELISHA BLISS, SAM'S publisher, had said he would
issue the book in December, and Sam, seeing the plain
connection between lecturing and book sales, wanted Mark
Twain on the road around that time, to excite public interest in the book.
In Hartford for ten days to deliver the still-untitled *Quaker City* manuscript, Sam listened as Bliss explained that he wanted the text to wrap
around the book's two hundred-plus illustrations. An experienced compositor, Sam understood that this required more tedious typesetting and
that none of the manuscript could go to type before all the illustrations
had been engraved—which would put off the release of the book until
March 1869. Without the book on the market, he would be lecturing for
money only and not to promote the book. In New York around the middle
of August, Sam turned to booking agencies to arrange his lectures, since
Frank Fuller could no longer act as his agent—he was preoccupied with
the rubber company he had recently bought. Though Sam wanted to join
the delayed Burlingame delegation when it moved on to Europe, he
wanted more to stay close to his publisher. He attributed the failure of
his first book not only to Charles Webb's inexperience, but also to his
own inattention during production.

After completing the manuscript, Sam needed company. Mary Fairbanks had visited the Langdons in Elmira over the summer, and Sam wished he could have joined her there. He wanted to see fellow *Quaker City* "cub" Charlie and reacquaint himself with Olivia for a few days, and then continue west with him to stay with "the old bear" Mother Fairbanks in Cleveland. Perpetually inept at reading timetables, Sam boarded a local train from New York to Elmira on August 21, cabling Charlie along the route, noting his slow progress. "Train stops every fifteen minutes and stays three quarters of an hour," one cable read. "Figure out when it will arrive and meet me." Charlie welcomed Sam, and Livy proved herself every bit as engaging as she had been on New Year's Day eight months before.

Occupying with its grounds an entire city block, the Langdon house offered sumptuous comforts, and the clan itself was "the pleasantest family I ever knew," Sam wrote to his mother. Olivia's father, Jervis, had made his money in coal, but other than their fortune, the family had few characteristics that typified capitalists. Ardent abolitionists, the Langdons had made their home a stop on the Underground Railroad, helping writer and orator Frederick Douglass to freedom. In 1854, Jervis Langdon had persuaded Thomas K. Beecher, the youngest of the prodigious Beecher clan, to serve as pastor of the alternative, abolitionist Park Church. The Langdons also generously supported Elmira Female College, the decade-old college for women offering degrees comparable to those of men's institutions. Thanks to the Langdons, Elmira was a forward-thinking place, an idyllic fusion of commerce and enlightenment. In a movement that promised lasting peace between capital and labor, even before the tensions between those forces were entirely clear, many small cities across the industrial North had become, like Elmira, beacons of social progress characterized by the ideals of universal education and shared prosperity and havens of compassion and equality.

Jervis and Olivia Lewis Langdon had three children. Susan, only a few months younger than Sam, had been adopted by the Langdons early in their marriage. Ten years later, Livy was born, followed by Charlie. Susan, who married Theodore Crane in 1858, lived in an apartment in the Langdon house; her husband was the financial manager of Jervis Langdon's coal business. Sue was unflappable, funny, and unerringly thoughtful, but Charlie and Livy caused their parents worry. The family had sent Charlie, a lackluster student and incipient drunkard, on the *Quaker City* cruise to get him the education he refused to obtained from books—and to put him among virtuous company that might curb his drinking. Sweet, intelligent Livy, on the other hand, had suffered a severe illness. Although well-to-do and underemployed women of the late nineteenth century sometimes found emotional compensation and a sense of identity in the purposeful practice of invalidism, Olivia Langdon's incapacitation was testimony not to her society, but to her body. Following a fall on the ice at age sixteen, Livy had been stricken with Pott's disease, or tuberculosis of the spine, which in many cases led to paralysis. She had spent two years in New York City away from her family, confined to her bed in a special clinic. By the time Sam met her, she was as healthy as she had been in years, but she was still not able to walk much farther than from one room to another. This experience had made a resolute woman out of the sweet girl. It also kept her from the dances and suitors typical for wealthy young women, and preserved the child in her, a feature which appealed deeply to Sam. To him, Livy was reminiscent of Laura Wright: small, slight, with opalescent skin, deep brown hair, and dark eyes. Her serenity contributed to her beauty—her peaceful spirit derived as much from the Langdon wealth as from the progressive Christian faith that saw her through her treatment and cure.

Livy's seriousness, studiousness, and quietude—emphasized by her weak eyes, for which she wore glasses, and uneven teeth, which made her reluctant to smile—made her a curious match for the funny, indolent, and garrulous Sam Clemens, but Sam determined to woo her. Livy's companion during this first visit, her witty cousin Hattie Lewis, bridged the gap between Sam's levity and Livy's gravity. "Mr. C. evidently greatly preferred her sense to my nonsense," Lewis would observe later. "I think I discovered the fact almost as soon as he did, himself, and I thought it would be a most suitable match for both." For a man bred in the formality and reticence of his Hannibal home and accustomed to making his own way in a rough world, the Langdon circle—with its money, social concern, and forthright love—seemed a heavenly beacon. Sam wanted to join the circle more than he had ever wanted anything. He brashly lingered at the Langdon estate not for two days, but for two weeks, falling ever more deeply in love with Livy. She was not merely Sam's best romantic opportunity, she was the epitome of all he desired: moral integrity and social position, wrapped in a physical package that matched his romantic ideal.

Following the custom of the time, Sam approached Livy's father to ask his consent to pay court to his daughter. Jervis Langdon, nearing sixty, suffered chronic pains in his belly; as his health began to fail, he regarded the younger man as a possible redeemer, who might bring peace to his final days. With Sue married and Charlie attached to Ida Clark, of another notable Elmira family, Livy was his only unsettled child. Her selectivity, dubious health, and quiet ways made her difficult to marry off. In Sam

Clemens, Jervis Langdon saw a man who despite his bohemianism was not only charming and brilliantly funny, but one whose incipient fame as Mark Twain implied sufficient resources to provide for a wife. He consented to Sam's attempt to win Livy's hand, saying he would allow a marriage if Sam got himself situated in life with a regular position, a regular address, a regular life, with exceptions made for his fame, such as extensive travel and currying of publicity.

Taking an informed risk, Sam instantly proposed. Livy naturally refused. Not only was their two-week acquaintance in Elmira too short a time for a serious young woman to entertain a proposal of marriage, but custom dictated that a woman always refuse a man's first proposal. Livy signaled her interest, however, with an insistence that Sam treat her as a sister. Insecure and untutored in upper-class courtship, Sam misunderstood this coded encouragement. Livy's refusal seemed another example of how women regarded him; he once wrote his friend Will Bowen, "Women appear to like me, but d———n them, they don't *love* me." Sam wrote Livy the night before he and Charlie left for Cleveland.

> My Honored "Sister"—
> The impulse is strong upon me to say to you how grateful I am to you and to all of you for the patience, the consideration & the unfailing kindness which has been shown me ever since I came within the shadow of this roof, and which has made the past fortnight the sole period of my life unmarred by a regret. Unmarred by a regret. I say it deliberately. For I do not regret that I have loved you, still love & shall always love you. I accept the situation, uncomplainingly, hard as it is. Of old I am acquainted with grief, disaster & disappointment, & have borne these troubles as became a man. So, also, I shall bear this last & bitterest, even though it break my heart.

For her own part, Livy saw the relationship as an almost certain match. She marked his letter "1st"; she went on to number all Sam's courtship letters.

Over the next two months, Sam wrote to Livy, composed his lecture, worked on his book, and prepared for his tour. Apprehension peppered his correspondence with Mother Fairbanks, but only a "gloomy preoccupation" indicated the state of his heart to anyone else. His visit to St. Louis for a week in late September was a muddle of worry relieved by the receipt of his first letter from his beloved, enclosing her picture. "I could not believe it possible, under the circumstances, that you could write a letter that would not give me pain, no matter how hard you might try to avoid it," he responded. "But you did.—It was almost a miracle." Jervis Langdon also wrote Sam "a very jolly letter," but these clues to his courtship's future success could not calm Sam's misunderstanding mind. Three days later, he wrote Mother Fairbanks that he only wanted "a cheerful day—an untroubled spirit. . . . There is something in my deep hatred of St. Louis that will hardly let me appear cheery even at my mother's own fireside." What could he do to change Livy's attitude toward him? How could he prove himself successful on Jervis Langdon's terms?

On Sam's next visit to Elmira in late September 1868, Jervis Langdon's stomach caused him severe and constant pain. Sam's naturally high spirits, augmented by his proximity to Livy, did not suit the somber hospital atmosphere of the Langdon house, and the visit ended awkwardly. Then, as Charlie accompanied Sam to the train station, the horses drawing the wagon they were in started, knocking them both backward and onto the pavement. Charlie received a nasty cut. Sam was stunned. He tarried awhile in Elmira, allowing Livy to nurse him. As a result, Sam confided in Mother Fairbanks, the courtship "bears just a *little* pleasanter aspect than it did when I saw you last & I am *just about* that much more cheerful over it, you know." The wounds, Livy wrote her friend Alice Hooker the day after Sam left, "did not prove to be serious in either case—We all enjoyed Mr. Clemens stay with us very much indeed—" Encouraged by the visit, Sam let his next letter to Livy strain against the artificial construct of sibling love that allowed Livy to correspond with propriety. A week later, in Hartford again, he regretted sending it. "I'll bet I have written a letter that will *finish* me," he bemoaned to Mother Fairbanks.

But Livy did not dismiss him for his impetuous letter; she only rebuked him. At last Sam recognized Livy's refusal as mere form and not actual rejection, and he responded to her contritely. "I sinned, but it was in hot-blooded heedlessness—not deliberate intent to do wrong." He probed the courtship game's boundaries, telling Livy about a new friend of his who praised the efficacy of a woman's prayers, but discounted the prayers of sisters, who are obligated to pray for their brothers. Mocking the artifice of their relationship, he added, "You seem so much my sister that I could say naught against his argument, & so said nothing." Understanding, as well, that the courtship game had a predetermined ending, Sam ridiculed such artifice by writing a burlesque of puppy love, including all the shams of romance, such as absurd gifts, showing off, and sickness induced by rejected love. Set in the era of his own boyhood, the manuscript shows that he was of two minds in his courtship of Olivia Langdon, frustrated in love but also demonstrating by his satire an emotional distance inconsistent with a man anxiously hopeful of success.

The new friend with the religious turn of mind was Joseph H. Twichell, the pastor of Hartford's Asylum Hill Congregational Church, a church established by the prominent families in Nook Farm and the nearby neighborhood of Asylum Hill. Twichell, a few years younger than Sam, was a man of immense grace who saw any act of simple kindness as divine virtue. Sam "met him at a church sociable," where a photo of the church under construction caught his eye. Sam drawled, "Why, yes, this is the Church of the Holy Speculators." Elisha Bliss' wife warned him that the pastor was standing right behind him, eager to meet him. Working on his manuscript in Hartford until the end of the month, Sam spent most of his time with Joe and Harmony Twichell, who had an infant son. He liked Hartford enough to want to settle there, but he couldn't locate any opportunity in the city that would satisfy Jervis Langdon's requirements. His plans were wrapped up in Livy now; if she agreed to marry him, he would need to find a permanent situation somewhere. If she didn't, he could go anywhere, but he would go with a broken heart.

With more at stake than ever before, the writer and suitor grew edgy over the prospect of his tour, set to begin in Cleveland on November 17, 1868, and continue through the winter. Civic groups, such as Young Men's Christian Associations and library and literary organizations, sponsored lecture series, both to raise money and as an educational service. From the abstruse Ralph Waldo Emerson to the showy temperance exhorter John Gough, speakers would travel from town to town throughout the fall and winter, performing mostly in drafty, ill-lit halls. Each speaker received a set fee, with the sponsor taking the loss on a small turnout and pocketing the profit when someone filled the hall. Sam asked Mother Fairbanks "to write the first critique on this lecture—& then it wouldn't be *slurred over* carelessly, anyhow." He had three dozen engagements already, with more coming in weekly. Mark Twain, one of few humorists working the lecture trade, could be counted on to bring out a crowd to the usually didactic series.

Sam, new to the game, worried about delivering a good show night after night, often traveling overnight to the next engagement. His lecture, extracted from his forthcoming book and calculated to advertise a product that, as it turned out, would not reach the market for months, attracted sponsors willing to pay Sam $100 a night for Mark Twain, out of which fee Sam had to cover his own transportation costs. For this money, a bit higher than average, series organizers expected Mark Twain to deliver something substantial along with his jokes. If Sam failed and his first lecture season became his last, he risked losing a lucrative chance to prove his worth to Livy and her parents. He arrived in Cleveland more than a week before his first lecture to work on it with Mother Fairbanks, who helped him balance the elements of humor and insight. He would speak there on November 17, in Pittsburgh on the nineteenth, and in Elmira on the twenty-third. He wanted the lecture to be perfect by then.

In Cleveland and Pittsburgh, Mark Twain made splendid successes, filling the halls even against bad weather and stiff competition. Mary Mason Fairbanks published a lavish review on the front page of her husband's paper, praising her friend especially for "having conclusively proved that a man may be a humorist without being a clown. He has elevated the profession by his graceful delivery and by recognizing in his audience something higher than merely a desire to laugh." While the Pittsburgh performance did not earn universal praise, the enthusiastic response elicited an offer from the sponsor for a return engagement. Mark Twain was a new sensation on the lecture circuit. Performers in the late nineteenth century depended on a lavish theatricality, filled with grand gestures, emphatic melodrama, and emotional articulation, but Twain's naturalness on stage merited widespread admiration. His unforced presence, calm demeanor, and patient delivery embodied something intriguing and entirely new; even Artemus Ward's performances seemed like an act when compared with Mark Twain's amazing nonchalance. He would cross the stage like a man crossing his front yard; he would speak to a thousand people as though carrying on a conversation with his neighbor. The audience saw Mark Twain speaking, not Sam Clemens acting; the real disappeared entirely, leaving the false—but wholly believable—Mark Twain in his place. Sam's performance was the perfect semblance of honesty.

Sam arrived in Elmira on Saturday morning feeling ecstatic. He proudly showed reviews that praised both Mark Twain's humor and insight. Livy, for her part, felt ready to leap beyond the sisterly construct through which the relationship had progressed, and looked forward to his performance with girlish anticipation. Sam wrote to his new friend, the Reverend Joseph Twichell, of the transformation:

> She felt the first symptoms last Sunday—my lecture, Monday night, brought the disease to the surface—Tuesday & Tuesday night she avoided me & would not do more than be simply polite to me because her parents said *NO* absolutely (almost,)—Wednesday they capitulated & marched out with their side-arms—Wednesday night—she said over

& over & over again that she loved me but was sorry she
did & hoped it would yet pass away—Thursday I was telling
her what *splendid, magnificent* fellows you & your wife were,
& when my enthusiasm got the best of me & the tears sprang
to my eyes, she jumped up & said she was *glad & proud* she
loved me!—& Friday night I left, (to save her sacred name
from the tongues of the gossips[)]—& the last thing she said
was: "Write *immediately* & just as often as you can!" Hurra!
(Hurricanes of applause.) There's the history of it.

If the Langdons harbored serious doubts about Sam Clemens' character,
they would not have allowed him to hang about their house or, for that
matter, Elmira; instead, they invited him to Thanksgiving dinner. Jervis
Langdon still played both sides against the middle, encouraging Sam in
his suit while supporting his wife in her caution concerning him. Afterward, Sam wrote to Mother Fairbanks that he had special reasons for
giving thanks, because "Mr. and Mrs. L. have yielded a *conditional* consent—Livy . . . isn't my sister any more—but some time in the future
she is going to be my wife, & I think we shall live in Cleveland." Declaring
his success to Mother Fairbanks, Sam also asked if Abel Fairbanks would
sell him an interest in the *Cleveland Herald*, which would provide him the
sort of position that would satisfy Livy's father's provisions and overwhelm her mother's objections.

But Sam was not convinced he needed a place on a newspaper; lecturing paid well enough. Even in this, his first year on the circuit, entered
into late and irregularly, Sam would clear over $2,500 in four months,
which compared well with the $4,000 a year he would have made as San
Francisco postmaster. Platform stars such as John Gough, or—in Mark
Twain's humorous line—Petroleum Vesuvius Nasby, received nightly fees
several times what Twain was earning; Gough earned $30,000 a year lec-
turing. Even at his current level, Sam's lecture income outpaced what he
earned as a journalist, and a lecture tour reached potential book-buyers
who might not read the latest sketch by Mark Twain in their local paper.
Sam felt sure he could convince the Langdons that the stage was both a
reputable and rewarding path to security and fortune.

Of course, he also had to amend his behavior to satisfy Livy. Sam
vowed not to drink spirits anymore, but to "be a *Christian*. I shall climb—
climb—climb toward this bright sun that is shining in the heaven of my
happiness," as he told Mother Fairbanks. "I shall be *worthy*—yet. Livy
beli[e]ves in me." The conditional betrothal required stratagems to protect Livy from rumor; between Mark Twain's fame and the Langdons'

money, the couple risked notice in the press, Sam's bread and butter but unacceptable for a woman of Livy's station. Sam could no longer address his correspondence directly to Livy; instead, he had to send letters to her enclosed in envelopes addressed to Charlie. Sam accepted the stricture without complaint. He made every effort to appear a completely righteous man.

After he left Elmira, letters went out to people who might evaluate the prospective son-in-law. Supplying names of West Coast acquaintances for the Langdons to pursue through their own means, Sam himself asked several others to write letters of recommendation to the Langdons. Livy's mother wrote Mary Fairbanks acknowledging that "a great change had taken place in Mr Clemens . . . The question, the answer to which, would settle a most weaning anxiety, is,—from what standard of conduct,— from what habitual life, did this change . . . commence?" Had Sam gone from an immoral man to a moral one, she wanted to know, or from a man of the world, as men typically saw other men, to a Christian? Though she was politically progressive, she was socially cautious, and she greatly preferred a devout and upright son-in-law to one merely moral and law-abiding.

Over the next three months, Sam lectured dozens of times in an awkwardly organized tour that ran him from New York to Iowa. Twice when he had the opportunity for a few days' rest, he hurried to Elmira, for an overnight in mid-December and several days at the beginning of February. In between, he wrote Livy long letters of love—more than fifty thousand words during the days and weeks his lecture tour kept them apart. Though he now began to sign almost all his other letters "Mark Twain," even those to Mother Fairbanks and Joe Twichell, he used his real name with Livy. He had begun to find more successful ways to be Mark Twain than he had mastered on board the *Quaker City*, but he wanted Livy to fear no falseness from him. She was in love with Sam Clemens and recognized Mark Twain as his adopted persona. Her acceptance delighted Sam, but he did not dare express himself with total honesty. He was fully sincere in his declarations of love, laden with praise of his intended, but he feigned a religious faith he did not have. He wrote of the condition of his soul from Lansing, Michigan, where he spent Christmas. They discussed sermons they heard and annotated published ones for one another. He pondered his unworthiness and his inability to pray. "God forbid that you should be an angel," he wrote Livy. "I am not fit to mate with an angel—I could not *make* myself fit. But I can reach your altitude, in time, & I *will*. I mean as near to it as God will permit." Amending his original "God has" to "God will"—and thus implying a conscious change from the Calvinist concept of God of his childhood toward the more for-giving Christianity to which he supposedly aspired—Sam queried Livy on the rigidity of her religious principles. He wanted to know how much of a Christian he must become in order to pass muster with her.

Eventually, Sam resolved this problem by making Livy his religion. He already loved her; loving God became a simple matter of transference. "You are a living, breathing sermon; a blessing delivered straight from the hand of God; a messenger, that, speaking or silent, carries refreshment to the weary, hope to the despondent, sunshine to the darkened way of all that come & go about you." By the time Sam arrived in Elmira in early February, his strategy had worked. Whether strictly Christian or not, his spirit achieved an elevation that at least satisfied Livy. All reli-giosity, except noncommittal asides such as "God bless you" and "I will pray," disappeared from his letters.

More assured of Livy's affections, Sam's letters—her side of the cor-respondence no longer exists—now replaced the religious ruminations with observations about the traits of a good wife. Livy blamed herself for not having enough fire to fight publicly for justice, as did women's rights activist and powerful platform speaker Anna Dickinson, a Langdon family friend. "You cannot do Anna Dickinson's work, & I can freely stake my life upon it, she cannot do yours," Sam soothed. "I am thankful that you are not the sort of woman that is her ideal, & grateful that you never *can* be, Livy, darling." Accepting the role of protective prospective husband, he directed Livy's secular reading. After praising Swift's *Gulliver's Travels*, he offered it to her, but only after he could "mark it & tear it until it is fit for your eyes—for portions of it are very coarse & indelicate. . . . You are as pure as snow, & I would have you always so—untainted, untouched even by the impure thoughts of others." His letters are filled with in-structions to her to watch her health, to sleep more, to undertake less.

Describing how to be his perfect wife, Sam also offered Livy hus-bandly concessions in the form of dreams. Sam told Livy a dream about riding on a train's cowcatcher, as wild Lillie Hitchcock once did on a dare; in the dream Livy "came & ordered me to get off it, & I obeyed. You did perfectly right." This confession was provoked by a recent scandal involving Hitchcock, who had interrupted a date with one man in order to marry another, and then returned to the first without telling him she was now Mrs. Howard Coit. Sam had defended Lillie Hitchcock to Livy, calling her "as generous & warm-hearted a girl as you ever saw," but writing Livy this dream reassured her that, though he was tempted by the outrageous bohemian edge occupied by his friend Lillie Hitchcock, Sam would shun scandal for Livy's sake.

His promised rectitude did not extend to his love letters themselves, in which Sam not only concealed the truth but actively misrepresented it to Livy, especially when a lie would improve his worth as a husband in the Langdons' eyes. Soon after gaining conditional consent for the marriage, he wrote, "I say to you, now, Livy, on my word of honor as a man, that I never yet made an individual a friend, *called* him my friend, & lost him." The five-year hiatus in his friendship with Will Bowen turned out to be a temporary disaffection, but he had scrapped his friendships with Clement Rice and Dan De Quille. In a more egregious act of dissembling, he even revised his personal history, answering one of Livy's parents' greatest concerns, his rootlessness. He wrote, "Your father & mother are overlooking one thing, Livy—that I have been a wanderer from necessity, three-fourths of my time—a wanderer from choice only one-fourth." In fact, almost continually from the time he first left home, Sam had found it impossible to stay in one place. Travel had become his fundamental means of escape from himself; in his own mind, perpetual motion protected him both from acts he regretted and time to repent them. He never longed for the comforts of home, regular habits, or domesticity. He craved only movement.

Now touring was tempering his pleasure in travel. Though some of the tour passed joyfully enough, with good accommodations and convenient travel over relatively short distances, many legs involved grueling all-night train rides, demanding hosts, and unheated halls. Several times, Sam found himself speaking after forgoing sleep for thirty-six hours. Though he liked having time alone before appearing on stage, his sponsors often insisted on taking him to dinner, where they expected brilliant conversation for the price of a meal. Despite the cost, Sam preferred to stay not at a sponsor's often luxurious home, but at a shabby hotel, where he could smoke at will and sleep as late as his schedule allowed. Even the few hours he lectured, normally islands of pleasure in the tedious ocean of trains, hotels, and unpleasant company, sometimes failed to sustain him. In Ottawa, Illinois, on January 13, 1869, he experienced "another botch of the lecture!" The association's "idiot president" introduced Mark Twain as the crowd entered, and more people streamed in until Sam shouted at the doorkeeper to close the doors to the remainder. "I just hobbled miserably through, apologized, bade the house good-night, & then gave the President a piece of my mind, without any butter or sugar on it. And now I have to pray for forgiveness for these things—& unprepared, Livy, for the bitterness is not all out of my bad, foolish heart yet." Another time, still abed at nine one morning in an Iowa City hotel, Sam cursed the landlord, who had knocked to see if he needed anything. An hour later, wanting coffee and finding no bellpull, he began slamming doors and screaming, which again brought the landlord, whose calm responses shamed Sam into silence. He wrote the hotel manager an apology, but not before the *Iowa City Republican* told of Mark Twain's public tantrum in a story that ended with a chilling remark, especially for a man whose betrothal remained probationary. The lecture's sponsors "were wretchedly imposed upon by Mark Twain, and so of course were the audience. He is the only one engaged for the course whose personal character was unknown."

The veiled danger implicit in this cutting comment became explicit and ugly as reports arrived from California, assessing the character of Sam Clemens while he and Mark Twain lived there. As Sam wrote to his friend Charles Warren Stoddard, the respondents "said with one accord that I got drunk oftener than was necessary & that I was wild & Godless, idle, lecherous & a discontented & unsettled rover & they could not recommend any girl of high character & social position to marry me—but as I had already said all that about myself beforehand there was nothing shocking or surprising about it to the family." In fact, he had revealed only portions of his true history, and only to Jervis Langdon, but the letters must have made even Mr. Langdon uncomfortable, especially when a note from a prominent California clergyman calling Sam Clemens a "humbug" fell into the hands of the entire family, including Livy and her mother. This deprecation "came within an ace of breaking off my marriage," Sam told Stoddard. Only Jervis Langdon's willingness to set aside the bad reports overcame Mrs. Langdon's doubt, and Sam's personal life resolved itself happily and quickly. A mere six months passed from the time he fell in love with Livy until the engagement became official and public.

Though the clergyman's letter did not destroy his engagement, the episode draws in high relief the amazing malleability of Sam's personality. In California, on the *Quaker City* cruise, in Washington afterward, and during the months in California he spent writing his book, he lived and acted as his referees described him, and perhaps worse than that. Only when the prospect of marriage to Olivia Langdon offered itself did he change. On New Year's Eve, he wrote Livy how grateful he was for the passing of 1868. The year

> found me a waif, floating at random upon the sea of life, & it leaves me freighted with a good purpose, & blessed with a fair wind, a chart to follow, a port to reach. It found me listless, useless, aimless—it leaves me knighted with noble ambition. . . . If I forget all else it has done for me I shall still

remember that it gave me your love, Livy, & turned my wandering feet toward the straight gate & the narrow way.

At age thirty-three, unsettled, lonely, and bored with rakishness, Sam needed a reason to improve his conduct. Livy's love and money provided it, though even a prestigious marriage to an angelic woman could not completely erase what drove him to that behavior to begin with, his insecure identity and guilt over the deaths of his siblings. Trying on new identities, drinking to excess, and traveling had seemed like attractive salves for these emotional wounds but marriage, success, and the persona Mark Twain offered better solutions. When Sam tired of being himself, he could be Mark Twain instead. Financial success, the true measure of value in nineteenth-century America, could assuage his feelings of unworthiness. Livy's love and their impending marriage justified his life more profoundly than any achievement he might manage on his own.

On February 4, 1869, the day after Sam arrived in Elmira for a stay of a week, Olivia Langdon and Sam Clemens received permission from her parents to marry. Sam announced the news to his family by noting the juncture of romance and finance. "It may be a good while before we are married, for I am not rich enough to give her a comfortable home right away, & I don't want *anybody's* help. I can get an eighth of the *Cleveland Herald* for $25,000 . . . & if I can do no better elsewhere, I shall take it."

15 | *Unsettling Down*

Truth is the most valuable thing we have. Let us economize it.
—"Pudd'nhead Wilson's New Calendar" (1897)

Loyalty to petrified opinions never yet broke a chain or freed a human soul.
—"Consistency" (1887)

Bᴀᴄᴋ ᴏɴ ᴛʜᴇ lecture circuit shortly after his betrothal, Sam grew ever more assured in his public performance of Mark Twain. By naturalistically exaggerating his characteristic drawl and slouch, he replicated in Mark Twain the small-town, whiskey-drinking, cracker-barrel tale-teller. Sam revised and amplified this staple of American humor into something more by his very subject—travel—which removed this character from his country store and brought him into contact with the greater world. Mark Twain alternated his stories and one-liners with pointed insights into his foreign experience and gorgeous verbal portrayals of famous sights of the Old World. His set piece on the Sphinx, for example, received newspaper notice at almost every stop. He praised American Vandals, as he called his tourists, as always self-possessed and unabashed in the presence of kings, "even in the presence of the Sphinx. The Sphinx, whose great face was so sad, so earnest, so longing, so patient. . . . If ever image of stone *thought*, it was thinking. . . . It was MEMORY—RETROSPECTION—wrought into visible tangible form, . . . that reveals to one something of what he shall feel when he stands at last in the awful presence of God!" This passage, coming near the beginning of his lecture, had a startling effect.

Advertised as a funnyman and often introducing himself with comical immodesty, Mark Twain courageously sprang a serious turn on an audience that expected only to laugh. Sam knew he could raft along on a current of laughter all evening, but he wanted to make Mark Twain known as a writer-performer of both humor and insight, someone worth listening to not only for the jokes, but for the wisdom as well.

Livy Langdon influenced this design of Sam's complex stage persona. As he wrote to Mother Fairbanks, "Anybody who could convince [Livy] that I was not a humorist would secure her eternal gratitude! She thinks a humorist is something perfectly awful. I never put a joke in a letter to her without feeling a pang." In trying to prove that Mark Twain had more to him than humor, Sam's performance also emphasized an ironic distance between himself and his invention, by sometimes stepping out of character to comment to the audience on Mark Twain's performance. These two strategies of impressing Livy with his personal seriousness worked against one another: If Mark Twain was both serious and funny, then he did not need Sam Clemens' ironic distance from him. Sam employed such contradictory strategies because he had conflicting goals: He wanted Mark Twain to appear worthy of the bourgeois life that marriage to Livy promised, but he also wanted his persona to epitomize a morally renegade Bohemian.

These twin drives surfaced, soon after he left Elmira, in a letter to his future mother-in-law attempting to answer the lingering doubts of Langdon friends who might look askance at Livy's marriage to an iconoclastic stage and newspaper humorist from a family of unknown character. In the letter, which Sam insisted he had written with "no restraint in it, no expediency, no policy, no diplomacy," Sam denied that his romance was motivated by his desire for money. "As far as I am concerned, Mr. Langdon can cut [Livy] off with a shilling—or the half of it. . . . I have paddled my own canoe since I was thirteen." He went on to argue illogically that the unfavorable reports on his character from California resulted from the conflation of Mark Twain and Sam Clemens. Though confusion between the public and private man could only hurt the reputation of Twain and improve that of Clemens, or vice versa, Sam contended that "my private character is hacked, & dissected, & mixed up with my public one, & both suffer the more in consequence." He advised Mrs. Langdon to trust Livy—"My own mother & sister do not know me half so well as she does."

Jervis Langdon's difficulties in accepting Sam fully were less moral than social and economic. Langdon wanted his son-in-law settled, and Sam had so far taken only small, ineffectual steps in that direction. In addition to asking Abel Fairbanks about obtaining a share of the *Cleveland Herald*, he approached General Joseph Hawley, former governor of Connecticut and editor of the *Hartford Courant*, with an eye toward buying into that paper, but Hawley's partner, the writer Charles Dudley Warner, had gone to Europe for several months and Sam could get no answer until he returned. Sam put more effort into showing interest than into actually resolving the matter. He did little more than broach the subject with a few people he knew would assure Jervis Langdon of his active interest, even though his network of journalists extended across the continent. Since Sam had no capital, he could only buy into a newspaper by mortgaging his future. Besides, he felt that his career as Mark Twain was zooming ahead, and that once his book came out he would have no need for any job but that of author and lecturer. Terrified of being tied down not only to a wife but to a job as well, he planned his temporary escape: yet another trip to California.

But in late February, Langdon pressed Sam more aggressively, inviting him to attend a business meeting, to introduce Sam to the family enterprise and perhaps attract him to join it. The strategy did not work. As Sam wrote Livy with frank irony, "The subject of coal is very thrilling. I listened to it for an hour—till my blood curdled in my veins." The meeting only moved Sam to write a sarcastic attack on Cornelius Vanderbilt, ridiculing the same sort of shrewd practices he witnessed at the Langdon meeting; he eased the sting by urging Vanderbilt to "Go and surprise the whole country by doing something right," as the Langdons typically did. Except for the money it generated, big business had no appeal for Sam. The meeting was not a total waste, though, since Sam made a friend of John D. F. Slee, Langdon's man in Buffalo.

Sam went to Hartford in early March to look into the progress of his book, which he had tentatively called *The New Pilgrim's Progress*, despite the irreverence toward the canonical work by John Bunyan. The fabulous illustrations struck a balance between elegance and humor, but Elisha Bliss had few finished ones to show Sam. With July now the likeliest date for publication, Sam had to put off his California trip until after he finished reading proof. He lingered in Hartford, rereading the book for places he might improve it and distracting himself by catching the performance of famed platform character Petroleum Vesuvius Nasby, the creation of David Ross Locke, editor of the *Toledo* (Ohio) *Blade*, on stage on March 9, 1869. Petroleum Nasby merged humor and politics by first voicing a variety of common but reactionary opinions about race, gender roles, money, and war; then, as Nasby explicated his opinions, he would reveal the irrational prejudices behind them. He came onto the platform full of bluster and left it a man enlightened by his own reasoning. Locke commanded high fees for this complex performance; he also complimented Sam and his creation Mark Twain by visiting him at his hotel afterward. The two lecturing newspapermen sat up late talking shop until Sam agreed to accompany Locke to Boston. There, Locke introduced him to "the literary lions of the 'Hub,'" including Oliver Wendell Holmes, whose *Autocrat of the Breakfast Table* Sam had annotated for Livy as a courtship book. Locke also tried, but failed, to introduce Sam to James Redpath, who had recently established a new lecture bureau. Locke suggested that Sam join him on the staff of the *Blade*.

Returning to Elmira, Sam stayed with the Langdons for much of the next seven weeks. During their separation, Sam and Livy wrote almost daily letters that, taken together, diagrammed how their relationship had matured. He used less restrained language and more comic stratagems, such as only lightly crossing out something he pretended he did not want her to read. (When he really wanted to obscure something, he marked it through with a spiral and then added the loops of false letters above and below the line.) Livy's open acceptance of Sam doubled his courage. They communicated frankly about his wild past, about which he admitted, "I fear me I have been in the wrong. Twichell says, 'Don't *sow* wild oats, but *burn* them.'" He submitted himself to Livy's perspective. "You must lead, till the films are cleansed from my eyes & I see the light." They wrote one another as an established couple, with Livy reminding Sam of his social obligations and Sam—recalling his early pursuit of Livy—confessing "my desperate temerity in venturing to locate myself for two weeks in a house where I was a stranger." Together as spring began, Sam and Livy achieved a peaceful and sustaining connection surprising in so young a relationship.

Elisha Bliss sent the book's proofs to Elmira for Sam to read; he and Livy worked side by side revising the manuscript. They settled on a title: *The Innocents Abroad, or The New Pilgrim's Progress;* devaluing the allusion to Bunyan to a subtitle, he lightened the irreverence. The couple took breaks from their work by playing cribbage and euchre and singing in the evenings. Sam paid scant attention to acquiring interest in a newspaper. "[A] man in love *don't* bother about business much, & that is a petrified fact—but bye-&-bye—bye-&-bye," he wrote Mother Fairbanks in explaining why he had not pursued the opportunity at the *Cleveland Herald*. Livy had doubts about moving to Cleveland, and the *Herald* itself didn't seem like just the right paper. The *Hartford Courant* seemed a more attractive option, and Hartford a more attractive city, but General Hawley was busy in politics and Charles Dudley Warner still in Europe. Sam flirted with David Ross Locke's offer to join Nasby in the pages of the *Toledo Blade*, but with only half a heart. Discussing all his career matters with Livy, Sam called her his "business manager" and assigned her the job of keeping his scrapbook of newspaper clippings. Mostly, Sam felt inclined to stay in Elmira, fill himself with Livy's company, and make himself a part of the Langdon clan.

This bounty of pleasure had begun to raise some eyebrows, however. Newspapers ran squibs about the impending nuptials; and Mother Fairbanks, Mrs. Langdon, and even Jane Clemens wondered in their letters if Sam's staying so long in the same household with Livy was altogether proper. Sam talked the matter over with Livy, who wanted him around. They continued to work on *The Innocents Abroad* until early May, when Sam accompanied Charlie to New York City. "You drove me away from Elmira at last," he wrote Mother Fairbanks. "Livy spoke right out, & said that to leave was unnecessary, uncalled-for, absurd, & utterly exasperating and foolish—but I smoothed her feathers down at last by insisting that your judgment in this matter, just as usual, was solid good sense." Much as he enjoyed the Langdons' hospitality, Sam felt the need to move on. He had not yet given up the idea of going to California once *Innocents* came out, and he still had thoughts of following Anson Burlingame to Europe on his China mission.

Back in Hartford, reading the final pages of proof, Sam came to an agreement with James Redpath, of the Boston Lyceum Bureau, to manage Mark Twain's next lecture tour. Sam had a book in mind concerning his experiences out west and intended to write a new lecture called "Curiosities of California" to support it. He wrote articles for newspapers and magazines. In "Personal Habits of the Siamese Twins," one of his most enduring sketches, Mark Twain completely fictionalized Chang and Eng, the original Siamese twins, exaggerating their differences: Chang is a Catholic and Eng a Baptist; Chang fought for the Confederacy and Eng for the Union ("They took each other at Seven Oaks"); one is a drunk and the other a teetotaler. He concluded by asserting that "the Siamese Twins are respectively fifty-one and fifty-three years." The zany humor of two personalities yoked in a permanent arrangement and taken as one reflected Sam's mind as he approached marriage. Moreover, the image of twins also symbolized Sam Clemens' relationship with Mark Twain. This short piece revealed one of Sam's most remarkable talents: the ability to displace his own psychological dissonance and then reproduce it as humor.

In early summer, two concurrent events solidified Sam's position with the Langdon clan. Intervening on his future father-in-law's behalf, Sam asked the new managing editor at the *New York Tribune*, Whitelaw Reid, to print a notice about the half-million dollars the city of Memphis, Tennessee, owed Jervis Langdon for paving their streets. Langdon appreciated this helpful turn and saw Mark Twain's clout with the press; even without a steady berth, Sam might be a useful son-in-law. Then the Langdons came to Hartford to attend the wedding of Livy's childhood friend, Alice Hooker. The unity of the Langdon family at the wedding gave Sam a feeling of inclusion, which Jervis Langdon felt, too. He made his future son-in-law an offer. Sam wrote to his sister that the *Cleveland Herald* had returned as a serious candidate for investment: "If they will take sixty thousand dollars for one-third of the paper, I know Mr. Langdon will buy it for me. This is strictly private."

This secret promise had a huge effect on Sam. It galvanized his efforts to acquire a part of a newspaper, since Langdon's money meant he could do so without encumbering his future. He conferred at long last with Charles Dudley Warner about buying into the *Courant*, though after some initial excitement the plan suddenly cooled. Sam pursued the opportunity in Cleveland, only to find that Abel Fairbanks was an unreliable negotiator. Fairbanks withdrew the old offer and changed the terms to $50,000 for a one-fourth interest, a price too high for a share too small. Langdon executive John Slee, in Buffalo, opened negotiations for a piece of the *Buffalo Express*. Sam stopped there in late July to accept the deal that Slee worked out for him with Jervis Langdon's money.

The closure of his hunt for a situation did not bring Sam unmitigated joy. Not only did Buffalo lie far from the center of culture, but Langdon's gift also made it impossible for Sam to resist the arrangement. Taking issue with the offer would unveil his resistance to settling down, a precondition of his acceptance into the Langdon fold. But the threat of being anchored in Buffalo, combined with the irresistible goodwill of his benefactors, agitated him. He took out his frustration on Elisha Bliss. Where was *The Innocents Abroad*? he demanded. "I think you will do me the justice to say that I have borne these annoying & damaging delays as patiently as any man with bread & butter & reputation at stake could have borne them. I cannot think I have been treated just right." Elisha Bliss copyrighted the book on July 28, 1869, just before responding calmly to Sam's assault. Once he settled himself in Buffalo, Sam caught his breath and apologized.

He set to work at the *Buffalo Express* with surprising energy. The first week on the job he redesigned the newspaper and frequently contributed to its pages. A reporter later recalled his shockingly informal personal style. "At the outset he bought a comfortable lounging chair with a writing board hinged on to the arm." Sam sat in the chair, "a pipe in his mouth and only a negligee shirt, trousers and socks in evidence as costume. His collar and shoes would most likely be in a waste basket." As he feared, the new position meant he had to put Mark Twain's lectures in abeyance, since, as he told James Redpath, "one requires two months to get ready to marry & three more to get used to it." He thought he might stop in St. Louis on the way to California, but he told his family not to expect him. He had sent some baggage ahead, with a note that he would arrive in a week or so, but his new job forced him to scuttle his plan to see Jane, Pamela, niece Annie, nephew Sam, Orion, and Mollie. "I have been waiting, waiting, for you," his mother wrote. "There is no excuse for a child not to go and see his old mother when it is in his power. . . . If a carrige or omnibus comes near the gate we are shure it is Sam. You can immagine the rest." These pathetic promptings from his family and inquiries from the Langdons about his relationship with them renewed his efforts to move his mother, sister, and the children east.

Now that he had a job and he could begin to create a life for Livy, the family set a date for the marriage, first in December, then January, and finally for February 4, 1870. Sam expected to bury himself in work during the week and on weekends join Livy in Elmira. Unfortunately, Redpath replied that he had already promised Mark Twain for a number of lecture dates. Sam conceded to be booked wherever Redpath could manage from the first of November until the end of January. "When I once start in lecturing," he wrote Livy, "I might as well consent to be banged about from town to town while the lecture season lasts, for it would take that shape anyhow." During September and October, Sam visited Elmira occasionally, but his consuming efforts at the *Express* did not allow him to travel as often as he had planned; the frantic wedding activity there also discouraged him from making the trip to see Livy.

Moved by the old thrill of newspapering, Sam excitedly threw himself into a new project. The Langdons had determined to send Charlie on a round-the-world tour with Darius Ford, a professor at Elmira College. Ford agreed to send Sam observations and information from their many destinations. Mark Twain would rewrite these as his own, creating a circumnavigational extravaganza by proxy. It seemed the perfect scheme, since Sam would not have to leave Livy to assemble another travel book. Reinvigorated by the prospect of writing about far-flung places while he was in the midst of settling down, he began immediately to record auto-biographical recollections of his journey west nearly ten years before, composing six articles while waiting for Ford to arrive someplace interesting and report back. This new project affected his lecture plans, since the process of composing new material on his western experience made that subject too uncertain and changeable for the repetitive use he would put it to in the lecture tour beginning November 1, 1869. Instead, he relearned his old standby presentation on the Sandwich Islands.

With *The Innocents Abroad* actually on the market now, public interest in Mark Twain rose to a new pinnacle. The lecture circuit was postwar America's broadcast medium, and Twain became the lyceum's leading comic voice. In the northern states—to which Sam limited his lecture tour and where Bliss concentrated his sales force—*The Innocents Abroad* seized its audience with bold irony. This region confidently enjoyed the spoils of the Civil War. The machinery of munitions, built to subjugate the southern rebellion, was quickly turned to the mass production of consumer goods. Wealth grew enormously. America, long a poor relation of the European centers of finance and culture, began to make claims to social and economic equality. Mark Twain's irreverent take on European primacy gave his audience, who for the first time might be able to afford a tour of the Old World, a new view of the icons of their erstwhile cultures and a firm confidence in a bold new American attitude.

In his book, Sam made a deliberate effort to indict almost every feature of Old World history, saving his admiration for the very few which met his standards of excellence, such as the Sphinx. He exercised his democratic outrage especially trenchantly in his consideration of the old masters.

> Raphael pictured such infernal villains as Catherine and Marie de Medici seated in heaven and conversing familiarly with the Virgin Mary and the angels (to say nothing of higher personages), and yet my friends abuse me because I am a little prejudiced against the old masters—because I fail sometimes to see the beauty that is in their productions. I cannot help but see it now and then, but I keep on protesting against the groveling spirit that could persuade those masters to prostitute their noble talents to the adulation of such monsters.

From lambasting the Renaissance, he moved on to ridiculing the Romans, whose brief flirtation with republicanism American political rhetoric had transformed into a democratic paradigm. Twain satirized the blindness of such reverence with a mock program from the

> ROMAN COLISEUM. UNPARALLELED ATTRACTION! NEW PROPERTIES! NEW LIONS! NEW GLADIATORS! . . . The whole to conclude with a chaste and elegant GENERAL SLAUGHTER! In which thirteen African Lions and twenty-two Barbarian Prisoners will war with each other until all are exterminated.

All history was fair game, Twain implied. If America was going to lead the way to the future, we had best start by devaluing the past.

He did not spare the Holy Land, either. Encountering some goats and sheep, he noted: "The shepherds that tended them were the very pictures of Joseph and his brethren. . . . These chaps would sell their younger brothers if they had a chance, I think." While Mark Twain held himself back from ridiculing the actual characters and creeds of the Christian faith, he made the world from which they emerged seem so dirty, so paltry, and so repulsive that his American audience could not help but find themselves stirred to religious doubt. Any commonplace American, he hinted, would be a Christ to these moral pygmies.

The Innocents Abroad captured, and the lecture tour reinforced, the grandest hopes of the new American era. As a siren of the future, Mark Twain showed his countrymen how to meet the future by breaking the shackles of the past, untroubled by the widespread religious decline foreshadowed in his book. Sam made sure that Mark Twain stepped on the lecture platform with the same relaxed equanimity and the same semblance of reality as he did before he'd had a book to sell. He was not trying to persuade people of a doctrine; he was only trying to make them laugh their way to a new perspective.

During the fall, friendly reviews of *The Innocents Abroad* began rolling in. Sam's genial relationships with editors around the country and Mark Twain's successful lecture tour and oft-reprinted articles assured the book wide notice. Most reviews struck the exact tone Sam wanted for Mark Twain, praising its humor and insight in equal measure. Though a number chastised Mark Twain for his irreverence, Sam, a shrewd old Bohemian, knew that irreverence invited controversy, which sold books. Bret Harte wrote a satisfying review in his *Overland Monthly*, calling the book "six hundred and fifty pages of open and declared fun." The most surprising notice came from William Dean Howells of the *Atlantic Monthly*, the citadel of elite publishing that seldom deigned to notice books published by subscription. Sam was extremely grateful for this review, which regarded

Mark Twain as deserving "something better than the uncertain standing of a popular favorite." The reviews sparked interest in the lecture, and reports of the lecture boosted sales. The book sold over fifteen thousand copies by November and showed every sign of selling several times that amount. By giving America confidence in its prospects, Mark Twain had assured Sam Clemens of his own fortune.

16 | On the Road Again

The holy passion of Friendship is of so sweet and steady and loyal and enduring a nature that it will last through a whole lifetime, if not asked to lend money.
—"Pudd'nhead Wilson's Calendar" (1894)

FACING LONG, UNINTERRUPTED years on the *Buffalo Express*, and with his wedding only a few months away, Sam threw himself into the current tour with the relish of a man going on his final bender. He craved the attention Mark Twain commanded from the stage. Although he worried about losing income from the *Express* and from his freelance writing while on the road, he believed that the publicity surrounding Mark Twain's appearances would compensate for his losses by boosting sales of *The Innocents Abroad*. He seldom worried about his performance, except when some thoughtless journalist printed a synopsis of his lecture, robbing him of the element of surprise. The only aspect of touring he dreaded was actually *visiting* the town in which he spoke. If he could guarantee himself a good hotel at each stop—and no obligatory show-and-tell of the town's highlights by his sponsors—Sam could enjoy full-time the attention and the independence of living life as Mark Twain.

James Redpath had no trouble organizing a congenial schedule for Sam. Requests for appearances by Mark Twain poured into his office, and, with Mark Twain available to the lecture circuit only half the length of the normal season, Redpath could now choose the most convenient locations, the most lucrative offers, and the best-equipped halls available. No longer would Sam have to abide overnight trains running him ragged from this small-town church to that run-down auditorium. In Pittsburgh, for his first lecture, thirty newspapermen organized a sumptuous oyster dinner for him. Then he traveled to New York and Hartford, and on to Boston by November 6, where he roomed at Young's Hotel, a quiet place on a back street known for its comfortable beds and excellent table. Lecturers staying at Young's created a salon there, featuring humorists like Nasby and Josh Billings and roving conscience Frederick Douglass, with whom Sam swapped stories about the Langdons. Redpath arranged Mark Twain's engagements so that Sam could stay at Young's almost the entire month of November, boarding afternoon trains to nearby towns and returning to the Hub after the show.

Boston was the literary center of America, home to such gray eminences as James Russell Lowell, Oliver Wendell Holmes, Henry Wadsworth Longfellow, and Ralph Waldo Emerson, as well as to newcomers Thomas Bailey Aldrich and William Dean Howells. Sam went to the office of *The Atlantic* to thank editor James T. Fields and Howells, who at age thirty-two was the probable successor to the editor's chair, for the encouraging review of *The Innocents Abroad*. Even on this call, Sam dressed the part of roving humorist. Howells later recalled him "wearing a sealskin coat, with the fur out. . . . With his crest of dense red hair, and the wide sweep of his flaming moustache, Clemens was not discordantly clothed in that sealskin coat, which afterward, in spite of his own warmth in it, sent the cold chills through me when I once accompanied it down Broadway, and shared in the immense publicity it won him."

Only his impending local appearance caused Sam the slightest apprehension; he defined "a Boston audience—4,000 critics." Common touring wisdom dictated that success in Boston meant success in all the subsequent New England shows. Failure in Boston meant fighting to reclaim audiences in small towns from Maine to Connecticut. But Mark Twain dazzled the Boston audience the night of November 10, 1869. The next day's *Boston Advertiser* described the event fully:

> Mark Twain is a very good looking man. He is of medium height and moderately slender build, has light brown hair, a reddish brown moustache, regular features and a fresh complexion; and he has a queer way of wrinkling up his nose and half closing his eyes when he speaks. The expression on his face is as calm and imperturbable as that of the sphinx. Looking at him you feel it to be an impossibility that he

should ever hurry or ever be out of temper, and you might suppose him to be incapable of a joke, if it were not for the peculiar twinkle in his merry eyes. . . . His style of speaking is unique to the last degree. . . . He delivers his sentences without haste, and in a tone of utter indifference.

After perhaps one hundred performances as Mark Twain, Sam had finally achieved a satisfactory definition of the stage persona.

That persona, so accurately described by the *Advertiser* review, contrasted with the frequently agitated mien of his creator. For Sam Clemens, lecturing was performance: On stage, he acted the part of a three-dimensional being. No other lecturer came to the stage as a wholly believable character; even Nasby was merely a caricature intended to lampoon the era's common prejudices. Though Sam experimented with breaking the illusion of Mark Twain's reality by stepping out of the performance to comment on it—trying to lighten the spellbinding effect of his description of the eruption of Kilauea, for example, by expressing relief at having "got that volcano off my mind"—he soon relinquished these antics for a more complete semblance of authenticity.

The Boston reviewer also captured the unique quality of the performance. "[T]he perception of the fun is unmeasurably heightened by the apparently serious intention of the general discourse, and at times by an air of half seriousness in the joke itself. The audience gets into a queer state after a while. It knows not what to trust; for while much is meant to be seriously taken, the fun is felt to be the real life of the thing; and yet they never know where the fun will come in." His audience's anticipation of humor from this widely heralded funnyman, reminiscent of the expectant prurience attending Adah Isaacs Menken's performance in *Mazeppa*, allowed Mark Twain tremendous flexibility. Once he got the audience in the state he wanted, he could vary the lecture to include whatever anecdote suited the crowd. Sam thought this reviewer got his performance as Mark Twain right. Only his inclusion of a synopsis jarred Sam; he excised those paragraphs when he sent the clipping to Livy for his scrapbook.

During his quiet days, Sam prepared for his nuptials, buying his wedding clothes and shipping them to Elmira. He wrote to his sister, emphasizing how much her attendance would mean to Livy. "Her heart is thoroughly set upon it, & I don't like to have the child disappointed. *Purchase no outfit.* Come as you are." Sam had not yet given up hope that his mother or brother would attend, though he worried that his mother would refuse out of anger at Sam's earlier inability to travel to St. Louis.

Bringing the entire family would cost close to $1,000, which Sam would have willingly spent, though his frustration with Orion had only grown. Orion had worked for months to straighten out the claims on the family's long-unsold Tennessee land, only to inexplicably turn down an offer of $30,000 which Sam had secured from Jervis Langdon. Orion later reversed his position and wanted Sam to get Langdon to revive the proposal. Sam would not.

At the end of November, Hartford gave Mark Twain and Sam such a positive reception that it rekindled hopes that he and Livy might eventually make a home there. Joe Twichell, warm as ever, agreed to officiate at the wedding with Thomas K. Beecher of the Langdons' Park Street Church. Sam met again with Charles Dudley Warner of the *Hartford Courant*, and the two writers struck up an instant rapport. Warner, however, confused Sam with his excitement at "the prospect of what we could do with the Courant now that I have achieved such a sudden & sweeping popularity in New England." Sam was willing to entertain a revival of the mysteriously terminated negotiations with the *Hartford Courant*, but he could only leave the *Buffalo Express* at a cost of nearly $10,000. That money would have to come from Jervis Langdon, a man Sam increasingly regarded as a father, and thus entailed the same difficulties involved in asking any parent for so large a sum. Meanwhile, Sam learned from Joe Twichell that the previous round of negotiations with the *Courant* had nearly succeeded, but Samuel Bowles, the editor of the *Springfield* (Mass.) *Republican*, who had known Sam in his wilder days, had convinced General Hawley and Warner that they couldn't trust him. Sam's revenge on Hawley and Warner—"wicked, & unchristian & in every way unbecoming . . . (But it is powerful sweet, anyway)"—came when they directly petitioned Mr. Langdon to free Sam from Buffalo. Langdon refused, but Hawley's and Warner's enthusiasm for Mark Twain and the success of *The Innocents Abroad* confirmed Jervis' wise judgment in backing Sam's engagement to Livy.

Sam was now a full member of the Langdon family. He met Livy and her father in New York City to shop for Livy's trousseau, while Mrs. Langdon wrote Mary Fairbanks, "We are all increasingly attached to Mr. Clemens, every time he leaves us loving him better than when he came." Sam even gave up his favorite room at the Westminster Hotel in New York in favor of joining the Langdons at the St. Nicholas from just after his and Livy's birthdays—they were born just three days shy of a decade apart—until December 7, when he left to lecture in Philadelphia and Washington, D.C. Livy reported that Jervis Langdon would not settle down for the night until all the packages of her trousseau had been opened, checked, and put away; his tender pleasure in preparing for his daughter's wedding greatly impressed Sam.

The week with Livy and her father had a mixed effect on him, however. His first surviving letter after they parted again retells a wretched dream in which Livy rejects Sam and, in their period of separation, falls in love with a mysterious old inamorato. Catching her alone, he sees tragedy in Livy's dream face: "There was no more *true* happiness for you on earth—nothing but a feverish fascination, & then a vapid, vacant existence, then Death." Although it is unclear what moved Sam to write this implicit threat to his beloved, tensions surrounding the wedding drove a temporary wedge between the lovers. Two days later, however, peace returned. Sam concluded his letter, "I love you so, Livy, that I . . . *have* to commune with you, even if it be in simply a few sentences, scratched with a vile, blunt pencil. I was afraid something was the matter, but I am content, now that I have heard from my darling."

On the envelope of this letter, Livy calculated the costs of their housekeeping, including the costs of three servants and a horse. With an income of $4,000 a year, she concluded, they could manage comfortably. Sam would have exploded if he had known that Livy intended for them to have several servants. Although exuberant about the success of *The Innocents Abroad*, which sold thirty thousand copies in its first six months of release, he did not feel confident that as newlyweds he and Livy could afford more on their own than to board, albeit in a well-appointed house. He had asked John Slee to rent a place for them in Buffalo, and Slee had written Sam of his successful efforts at finding "a place on one of our most pleasant streets . . . a delightful cozy nest." In Buffalo between lectures, Sam tried to locate Slee, so he could get a look at the house, but Slee never seemed to be in town when Sam was. Sam's worries about affording marriage had diminished since he had wondered to Mother Fairbanks eighteen months earlier how he might manage it. The lecture tour grossed about $5,000, of which he cleared three fourths, and his *Innocents* royalties from December alone reached $2,500. For the first time since leaving the river, Sam had money of his own, and though he owed his future father-in-law for his share of the *Buffalo Express*, he fully planned to enjoy the comfortable living he earned his own way. On the other hand, he knew that Livy would be an expensive wife, perhaps more expensive than even a successful writer and performer could afford, and Sam did not know what to expect from the Langdon coffers to help with the upkeep.

After lecturing out of Boston until Christmas, Sam arrived in Elmira for a week on New Year's Day. The date for the wedding had moved yet again, this time to February 2, 1870, and it seemed clear that only Pamela and her daughter Annie, now seventeen, would serve as Clemens family emissaries. Letters flooded Mrs. Fairbanks to make certain that Sam would have at least one mother as a witness to his marriage. The couple naturally indulged in a final premarital disagreement, about Sam's smoking. Livy noted the health risks, the dirtiness, and the odors of the habit, but Sam responded; "I shall treat smoking just exactly as I would treat the fore-finger of my left hand: If you asked me in all seriousness to cut that finger off, & I saw that you really meant it, & believed that the finger marred my well-being in some mysterious way, & it was plain to me that you could not be entirely satisfied & happy while it remained, I give you my word that I would cut it off." She tabled her objections, and by the final letter of their courtship correspondence, all ill feeling had been put away. Sam wrote with a self-conscious delight about the hundreds of pages that had passed between them. The correspondence now "becomes a *memory*. A memory to be laid reverently away in the holy of holies of our hearts & cherished as a sacred thing. A memory whose mementoes will be precious while we live, & sacred when either one shall die." Livy observed the end of the exchange on the envelope of Sam's final premarital missive: "184th—Last letter of a 17-months' correspondence."

With his attention now riveted on the enormous changes marriage would bring to his life, estate, and social position, Sam finished up his lecture series almost half asleep. His final hurrah as a single man complete, he wrote to Mother Fairbanks at the beginning of his upstate New York swing, "I lecture no more after this season, unless dire necessity shall compel me." Two lectures just outside Buffalo gave him the best and the worst of the road. In Fredonia, he had such a full and intelligent audience that he determined to situate his mother, sister and her children there. In Jamestown, not far away, an irritated local wrote blistering notices to the newspaper, claiming that Mark Twain had "offended the good taste and religious scruples of the sober portion of this community." Sam Clemens could not charm everyone, even as Mark Twain.

17 | *Wedded Bliss*

A man should not be without morals; it is better to have bad morals than none at all.
—Notebook (1894)

W ITH TREMENDOUS SATISFACTION, Sam concluded what he vowed was Mark Twain's final lecture
tour, which had brought money, fame, and a book-buying
audience. Newspapers reported his upcoming marriage to an heiress not
so much because of Olivia's family fortune as because of Mark Twain's
swelling popularity. *The Innocents Abroad* continued to sell, bringing Sam
more than $1,000 a month in royalties, in addition to his editor's salary
and income from his share of the *Buffalo Express*. In Elmira, where he would
stay with the Langdons for the days leading up to the wedding, Sam
expressed a boundless confidence both in his capacities as a writer and in
Mark Twain's future as a commodity. "I can get a book ready for you
any time you want it," he told Elisha Bliss. He was confident, too, that
the American Publishing Company could turn anything by Twain into a
gold mine. "I'll back you against any publisher in America, Bliss—or
elsewhere." Writing to his old companion Jim Gillis in California, Sam
traced all of his luck and prosperity to the day he had heard the jumping
frog story, "the one gleam of jollity that shot across our dismal sojourn
in the rain and mud of Angel's Camp."

In the days before the nuptials, Sam felt a curious blurring of the boundaries between his private and public selves, since newspapers reported the marriage of Mark Twain, an invented persona. Not all could resist a poke at the humorist. "It was not the act of a desperate man," Ambrose Bierce, opined of the wedding in his San Francisco column; "it was the cool, methodical, cumulative culmination of human nature, working in the breast of an orphan hankering for some one with a fortune to love." In the public's mind, Mark Twain would marry a millionaire's daughter; few cared that Samuel L. Clemens was the name on the marriage certificate. Just before the wedding, Bliss relieved Sam's unnerving loss of identity with news of *Innocents'* impressive quarterly earnings: Despite the name on the book's spine, Sam Clemens got the money. The wedding capped his rising fortunes.

The quiet, unostentatious event Sam and Livy desired proved impossible. Instead of two dozen close friends and relatives at a midday ceremony, more than a hundred crowded into the Langdons' parlor at seven in the evening. Sam mediated the first meetings between his sister and niece and the Langdons. Unlike Sam himself, who had grown accustomed to moneyed ways, Pamela and Annie Moffett felt uneasy in the company of millionaires. The wedding of Olivia Louise Langdon and Samuel Langhorne Clemens celebrated her family's style of wealth. The two charming ministers, the opulence of the Langdon house, Livy's shoulder-length gloves and breathtaking gown, the sumptuous food at the reception, and the Langdons' characteristic ease all made Sam's family feel like frontier strangers.

Pamela and Annie also sensed that their hosts were keeping a secret from them, which they were, for fear that they would tip off Sam. Through a railroad-magnate friend, Jervis Langdon had secured a private car for the train ride back to Buffalo; Livy's parents, Mother Fairbanks, the Moffetts, and the Beechers joined them. John Slee arranged for sleighs to carry the bridal couple through Buffalo's dark and icy streets to their new home, but the sleigh carrying Livy and Sam got separated from the others. Sam, worried about Livy's exposure to the cold and annoyed at having had little time alone with her, cursed Slee for choosing a boardinghouse so difficult to find. But the driver had gotten Sam lost on purpose in order to give the others time to light the way. When their driver finally turned into Delaware Avenue, Buffalo's "Street of Palaces," Sam remarked to Livy, "Oh, this won't do. People who can afford to live in this sort of style won't take boarders." Sam saw the wedding party at 472, a three-story brick house with a mansard roof, but could not see the surprise until Livy explained that the house itself was theirs, a gift from her father.

And not only the house awaited them, but the furnishings, a cook, a housemaid and a coachman in livery, and a generous check to keep the household running. Livy had not only been party to the scheme but had spent most of her separation from Sam decorating the place, which Jervis Langdon had purchased in November. He had spent close to $50,000 on this surprise, which—together with his purchase of Sam's share of the *Express* and his offer to help the Clemens family with the Tennessee land— pushed his investment in this union to over $100,000. He wanted to guarantee his precious daughter luxury, but he also was fearful, as he told young Annie Moffett, that "Sam will go far, and Livy has been brought up so quietly and so simply that I sometimes wonder if she will be able to hold him." Langdon, applying the skills that had made him his millions, calculated his investment as much to obligate Sam as to provide for Livy.

Sam thanked the Langdons for the obligation which turned him into "Little Sammy in Fairy Land," as he unironically called himself. He gloried in his new possession, now boasting that he never thought about work or even left the house. While that was not strictly true, Sam fittingly enjoyed the salutary leisure during his stay-at-home honeymoon. He responded to his old friend Will Bowen's congratulations, "Your letter has stirred me to the bottom. The fountains of my great deep are broken up & I have rained reminiscences for four & twenty hours." After regaling Bowen with pages of memories, he finds himself brought "violently back unto this day & the generation. For behold I have at the moment the only sweetheart I ever *loved*, & bless her old heart she is lying asleep upstairs in a bed that I sleep in every night, & for four whole days she has been *Mrs. Samuel L. Clemens.*"

Livy communicated the honeymoon bliss even more touchingly when she interlined her own comments in Sam's letters. When Sam teased Livy in a letter to her family—"Now this morning she had a mackerel fricaseed with pork & oysters & I tell you it was a dish to stir the very depths of one's benevolence. We saved every single bit of it for the poor"—Livy jotted one word: "False." After another silly joke she noted, using her exclusive nickname for him, "Isn't he a funny Youth?" The couple gave another sign that marriage agreed with them: Livy became pregnant almost immediately. As Livy scribbled on a letter Sam wrote Mother Fairbanks, "Samuel is a pretty boy—He is good too—I like um." This auspicious start to the marriage demonstrated the deep and powerful bond that would survive the uproars, tragedies, and plain hard work of the life ahead of them.

The new couple's domestic patterns conformed more to Sam's desires than to Livy's. They acquired a number of cats; it was the first time that Sam could indulge his affection for pets after so many years without a home of his own. They rose late for breakfast, having it served after nine o'clock. Sam seldom ate lunch and preferred an early dinner, to leave time for evening conversation, company, and reading. Together they studied the recently published autobiography of legendary promoter P. T. Barnum and read the poetry of both Robert and Elizabeth Barrett Browning. The *Express* did not interfere with Sam's domestic pleasures, partially because his enthusiasm for the newspaper faded in the realization that Langdon had paid too much for Sam's share, which had been overvalued in anticipation of having Mark Twain publish there; Mark Twain's magic, which had turned so much paper to gold, did not dramatically improve the *Express'* sales or circulation. He went to the office once a week, and then only for an hour, he claimed to Bliss. To another friend he wrote that the rule for his new life was "To Work No More than is Absolutely Necessary. I've got plenty of money & plenty of credit." Even so, Sam entertained offers from other publishers, if only to force Bliss' American Publishing Company into offering a 50 percent higher royalty, 7½ percent, for the next project. He turned down another publisher's offer of 10 percent, out of obligation to Bliss.

Though he denied working much, he did try to write. To Mary Fairbanks he admitted, "Every day I nerve myself, & sieze my pen & dispose my paper, & prepare to buckle on the harness & *work*! And then I pace the floor—back & forth, back & forth, with vacuous mind—& finally I lay down the pen & confess that my time is not come—that I am utterly empty. But I must work, & I *will* work." The death of Anson Burlingame, on February 23, 1870, moved Sam to write the great diplomat an eloquent tribute, rich with the feeling of opportunities forgone. Determining to rearrange his work life, he told James Redpath that he would not lecture again. He gave up on the "Round the World" letters both because Elmira professor Darius Ford proved an undependable correspondent, and because Sam found he could not apply Mark Twain's voice to someone else's experience. Sam published Ford's first letter without emendation and without taking credit. He returned to his idea of a book about his western experience, expanding upon his contributions to the "Round the World" series.

Sam also accepted a deal with *The Galaxy*, New York's answer to *The Atlantic*, for Mark Twain to edit a ten-page monthly "Memoranda" of original sketches, observations, tales, and reports culled from other sources. He wrote Mother Fairbanks, "I just came to the conclusion that I would quit turning my attention to making money especially & go to writing for enjoyment as well as profit. I needed a *Magazine* wherein to shovel any fine-spun stuff that might accumulate in my head, & which

isn't entirely suited to either a daily, weekly, or *any* kind of newspaper."
Sam's arrangement with *The Galaxy* broke new ground in the publishing
world, because, as he told his family, "I am to *rent* the matter to them,
not sell it—& so I can use it in book form afterwards without sharing
the proceeds with them." Now he would not have to fight for control of
his own writing, as he had had to do with the *Alta California*. This arrangement also prefigured the modern-day standard for publication in periodicals. Sam did not yet realize that any separate deal for a book made
from the material would conflict with his contractual obligations to the
American Publishing Company.

During their first few months of married life, the new couple spent
most of their time alone together in their big new house, except for one
quick trip that Sam took to Washington. While there, he met President
Ulysses S. Grant. Neither of them had anything to say until Sam offered,
"Mr. President, I am embarrassed. Are you?" He also renewed his acquaintance with some scalawags in the Senate and "gathered material
enough for a whole book!" American politics, rife with dirty backroom
deals, begged to be the subject of satire, and Sam hungrily wrote about
his experience with the Nevada territorial legislature.

As joyful as Sam and Livy found their life together, and as satisfying
as it was for Sam to get back to work, Buffalo proved a difficult city to
settle into socially. It took both Sam and Livy a while to learn the rules
of visiting in Buffalo. Going out on calls, Livy got lost in her new city
and left her card, with a note, at the house of a total stranger. She met
few women her own age. Sam liked John Slee, and the Slees and the
Clemenses dined together regularly, but without the spark of intimacy;
because John was Jervis Langdon's delegate in Buffalo, the Slees took too
parental an interest in Sam and Livy to make for good friendship. Only
poet and editor of the *Buffalo Courier* David Gray and his wife held real
potential for friendship, but even that alliance developed slowly. Sam and
Livy planned instead to vacation in the summer with the Twichells.

Family claimed an increasing share of Sam's and Livy's attention.
After the wedding, Pamela and Annie traveled to Fredonia, New York, to
find a house to rent for themselves, Jane, and eleven-year-old Sammy
Moffett. Jane put the best face she could on Sam's decision to move the
family near, but not too near, his new home. Sam and Livy also spent
unexpectedly large amounts of time in Elmira. Pregnant, Livy wanted the
care of her own doctor, Dr. Rachel Gleason, who, with her husband, was
the proprietor of the Elmira Water Cure and one of the nation's first
female physicians. She also craved contact with her family; a sharp decline
in Jervis Langdon's health called them home more frequently. "We were

snatched away suddenly by an urgent call to come to Elmira & help nurse Mr. Langdon for a couple of weeks at some Pennsylvania Springs he was going to visit," Sam wrote his sister in the middle of June. "But he decided not to go, & so we simply rested a moment & then hurried back here." By midsummer, calls for Sam and Livy to come to Elmira became more insistent. They canceled their vacation with the Twichells when it became inescapably clear that Jervis Langdon was dying of stomach cancer. Charlie was sent for. Everyone sat up shifts with Langdon, Sam included; Jervis Langdon had replaced John Clemens as Sam's model for his future life as father and social activist. For days at a time, Langdon's health improved, but the decline never reversed. After an exhausting and depressing siege, Jervis Langdon, the man who had become Sam's surrogate father, died on August 6, 1870.

18 | *The Horrible Year*

> *Nothing that grieves us can be called little: by the eternal laws of proportion a child's loss of a doll and a king's loss of a crown are events of the same size.*
> —"Which Was the Dream?" (1897)

"MY WIFE IS nearly broken down with grief and watching," Sam wrote Elisha Bliss a few days after the death of Jervis Langdon. The combination of her pregnancy and the death of her cherished father left Livy prostrate. Her invalidism, which had lightened in the year before her marriage, now returned; she could hardly walk. After a few weeks, when the Clemenses returned to Buffalo, Livy began to manage a little better, but just how little a letter Sam wrote Mother Fairbanks makes clear: "Livy is getting along tolerably well, now—takes a sleeping potion every night & sleeps refreshingly."

Sam also found Jervis Langdon's death difficult, especially as it reminded him of his own father's death. In Mark Twain's August 1870 *Galaxy* "Memoranda," he offered "A Memory" of John Clemens, who did not compare well with Jervis Langdon. When the son in the sketch combines his father's love of the poem "Hiawatha" and his higher love for the poetry of the law by rendering a legal document in the singsong rhythm of "Hiawatha," the father erupts in violent anger at the travesty. Mark Twain's comic rendition of the wrath of John Clemens revealed how poignantly Sam missed Jervis Langdon's kindness.

In Buffalo, Livy had the comfort of a beloved guest, her childhood friend Emma Nye, who arrived in late August. Nye planned to amuse her bedridden friend for a few days before heading on to a teaching appointment in Detroit, but unfortunately was soon bedridden herself. Nye's health deteriorated, and Livy, though bent with sadness, had to attend to her friend. Sam wrote to Mother Fairbanks, "Miss Emma Nye lingered a month with typhoid fever, & died here in our own bedroom on the 29th Sept. She was buried in Elmira." Following this siege, Livy relapsed and returned to her bed. She could not travel to Elmira for the October 12 wedding of her brother Charlie to his childhood sweetheart Ida Clark; Sam stayed in Buffalo with her. In early November, Livy's doctor advised that "she may drive a hundred yards every day, but I am a little afraid of it." Sam had good reason to fear. Two days later, November 7, 1870, Livy gave birth to a sickly, premature boy. The trauma of the birth left Livy gravely ill. The child, named Langdon Clemens, weighed less than five pounds. Sam and Livy could not expect him to survive.

Meanwhile, Elisha Bliss had decided to publish a journal to publicize his own authors and books. To be called *The American Publisher*, the paper would straddle the line between journalism and advertising. Bliss wanted Mark Twain to edit it, but Sam refused, even at $4,000 a year. Transparently trying to obligate his temperamental but profitable author, Bliss told Sam he'd reserve the job for Orion at $100 a month. "[W]e have no real place just now for him, but would like for *your sake to create a position* for him, if possible." Orion, in St. Louis setting type and tinkering, needed Sam's help. He had invented a drilling machine for use in factories and gotten a manufacturer interested, but he needed time to perfect the gadget. If only he had a job that gave him evenings free for refining his machine, he wrote his brother, he would be happy. The job also allowed Sam to pay a psychological debt by moving his hapless brother to Hartford, the city Sam wished to call home, while he lingered in frustrating Buffalo. Orion dithered awhile before accepting.

In the face of growing tragedy at home, and fearing that like any fad Mark Twain's run of popularity would fade before long, Sam became urgent about his work. His September and October contributions to *The Galaxy* were remarkably full and varied, from a funny sketch portraying Mark Twain's attempt to write a serious column on "Political Economy" while enduring interruptions by a lightning-rod salesman, to an epistolary essay from a hopeful Chinese immigrant shamefully abused in San Francisco ("Goldsmith's Friend Abroad Again"). He got his Twainian reconstruction of his western years under way, as he told Bliss, "driveling along tolerably fairly on the book—getting off from 12 to 20 pages, (M.S.) a day. I am writing it so carefully that I'll never have to alter a sentence." Mark Twain made a splash with a juvenile spoof of the big-city newspaper maps of the Franco-Prussian War; his crudely drawn "Map of Paris," placing the Erie Canal and Jersey City nearby, included "Official Commendations" from Bismarck, Napoleon, and others. Sam also implored Bliss to throw him a dinner celebrating the success of *The Innocents Abroad*. Sam wouldn't attend the dinner—no one would, so it wouldn't cost anything—but the newspapers could reprint the speech he would have delivered, and as a result they would sell more copies of *Innocents*! Sam believed so completely in the income potential of this scheme that he ignored the fact that it crossed the lines of honesty and journalistic propriety.

Sam hatched another cockamamie plan he felt certain would take the world by storm. Just as the reports of gold in California in 1849 had sent tens of thousands of prospectors to endure the hardships of the mining country, reports of the discovery of diamonds in South Africa were having the same effect on Europeans. Sam read about the exodus and determined to send a proxy to South Africa. Unlike the "Round the World" project, which relied on correspondence, Sam wanted to send James H. Riley—a close friend from California and Washington whom Twain had glorified wildly in his November *Galaxy* "Memoranda"—to South Africa for a short time, debrief him, and then write a "first-person" Mark Twain book based on Riley's report. Riley would receive passage, a salary of $100 a month, and free claim to the first $5,000 worth of gems harvested from the diamond fields. Sam asked Bliss to split the up-front costs, with the money to serve as an advance against Sam's earnings if the book reached completion. Bliss accepted the terms, offering a high royalty rate of 8½ percent. "Keep this whole thing a dead secret—" Sam wrote his publisher, "else we'll have somebody standing ready to launch a book on our big tidal wave and swim it into a *success*." Although Riley felt reluctant to drop his senatorial clerkship, Sam enticed him at last. On December 5, 1870, Riley telegraphed, "Plan approved. Will get ready to go."

Sam also secretly employed a new pseudonym, "Carl Byng," in the *Buffalo Express*, preparing for what he believed would be Mark Twain's inevitable demise. Humorists' pseudonyms typically had only a few years of life before audiences tired of their character and style of comedy. To capitalize on Mark Twain while he could, Sam agreed with Isaac Sheldon, *The Galaxy* publisher, to issue an illustrated pamphlet of Mark Twain's humor, which Sam spent a week arranging in New York in early December. Sam knew but did not care that this publication strained his contract with Bliss; when he paid Charles Webb $1,500 for the return of the *Jumping*

Frog plates and copyright, Sam used the provision to explain to Webb that he couldn't republish the substandard book "without vitiating my contracts with my present publishers and creating dissatisfaction." Bliss handled this forced crisis with intelligent restraint, accepting Sam's argument that a pamphlet did not abrogate the provision against publishing another Twain book. Instead, he negotiated for his own illustrated pamphlet for the next holiday season as well as a collection titled *Mark Twain's Sketches*, to be published before the release of the book about the West. When Bliss wondered if the book of sketches wouldn't interfere with the sale of *The Innocents Abroad*, which still boomed along, selling more than twenty-five hundred copies a month, Sam countered that he would hurry along the western book instead, if Bliss could publish it before summer.

In his urge to exploit the current success of Mark Twain, his creator trod very close to other limits of propriety, too. Just before Jervis Langdon's death, Sam had borrowed—he preferred the word "smouched"—some material for one Mark Twain sketch in *The Galaxy*. The source, a Philadelphia writer using the pen name John Quill, returned fire, and then made the mistake of borrowing from Twain. Twain then lambasted him as "A Literary 'Old Offender' in Court with Suspicious Property in his Possession." Then, in another incident at the beginning of 1871, Boston literary mogul Thomas Bailey Aldrich accused Mark Twain of hiding behind a new pseudonym to write a weak imitation of Bret Harte's newly famous poem, typically called "The Heathen Chinee." Sam responded first with a violent denial, then with a tardy request to Aldrich to suppress the denial, and finally with praise for Harte, who, Sam wrote, "trimmed & trained & schooled me patiently until he changed me from an awkward utterer of coarse grotesquenesses to a writer of paragraphs & chapters that have found a certain favor in the eyes of some of the very decentest people in the land."

In fact, Bret Harte's success had put Sam in a black funk. Sam wrote Riley that Harte had lately come east "in a perfect torchlight procession of eclat & homage," the newly anointed king of letters, crowned with his best-selling collection *The Luck of Roaring Camp* and brandishing a $10,000 contract for a year of monthly contributions to *The Atlantic*. It galled Sam to have accepted a quarter of that amount for a year in *The Galaxy*. Moreover, he felt uncertain that he could even get an article accepted by *The Atlantic*; Mark Twain's prose did not have the refinement necessary to satisfy that arbiter of American culture. Whatever pinnacle Mark Twain had reached, Bret Harte had leaped clear above him, and Aldrich's accusation that Twain had imitated Harte made Sam feel desperate about both his talent and his future. As Sam saw it, Harte's ascendancy threatened

Mark Twain's prospects. Given the melancholy state of family life in Buffalo, Sam needed Mark Twain's success to buck up his spirits.

Neither baby Langdon nor Livy recuperated much. The baby fell in and out of trouble. The Clemenses hired a wet nurse and a caretaker for the boy; Livy could do almost nothing. Langdon's helpless cries kept the household in a state of constant worry. Sam wrote Orion and Mollie early in 1871 that "the baby's weight has increased to 7½ pounds & his personal comeliness in proportion." Though they had only fragile hopes for the boy, the new parents took solace from the fact that Sam had himself survived an unlikely infancy.

Then, in early February, Livy collapsed, this time with typhoid fever, the disease that had killed Emma Nye. Sam felt certain that Livy too would die. To clown before the public while his wife lay dying horrified him. He begged the publishers of *The Galaxy* to withhold his March "Memoranda" and delay the publication of his pamphlet, *Mark Twain's (Burlesque) Autobiography*. Only Herculean effort withdrew the column from the magazine, further indebting Sam to *The Galaxy* just as he wanted to reduce his obligations there. He wrote Bliss, "Sometimes I have hope for my wife,—so I have at this moment—but most of the time it seems to me impossible that she can get well. I cannot go into particulars—the subject is too dreadful." Livy's sister Susan Crane, Livy's friend Clara Spaulding, and Elmira physician Dr. Rachel Gleason all came to Buffalo to help nurse Livy. At last, Livy retreated, slowly and uncertainly, from the edge of death.

The run of misery in the Clemens household became unbearable, and in March of 1871, Sam finally exploded. Issuing his valedictory, his last column for *The Galaxy* blurred the line between Mark Twain and his creator: "For the last eight months, with hardly an interval, I have had for my fellows and comrades, night and day, doctors and watchers of the sick! During these eight months death has taken two members of my home circle and malignantly threatened two others. All this I have experienced, yet all the time been under contract to furnish 'humorous' matter once a month for this magazine." When he could not be funny, he could not sustain the mask he required to assume his alternate persona. Humor not only defended Sam from the world; it was also the catalyst in the creative process that resulted in Mark Twain. Using rage to defend himself when he could not muster comedy, Sam wrote a long, blistering letter telling his brother—and through him Elisha Bliss—to stop asking him to contribute to *The American Publisher*. "Haven't I risked cheapening myself sufficiently by a year's periodical dancing before the public but I must continue it?" he fumed. "I lay awake all last night aggravating myself with this prospect of seeing my hated nom de plume (for I do loathe the very sight of it) in print *again* every month." Playing the jovial clown became more of a burden than a release. A week later, he raged directly to Bliss. "Do you know that for seven weeks I have not had my natural rest but have been a night-and-day sick-nurse to my wife?" he wrote. "I thought that the vials of hellfire bottled up for my benefit *must* be about emptied. By the living God I don't believe they ever *will* be emptied."

Sam exorcised his wrath in the company of movers packing boxes and lawyers drawing up contracts. Despair, sickness, and death had proved too much for them, and Sam and Livy had decided to leave Buffalo as soon as her health permitted. They put Jervis Langdon's gifts—the house and Sam's share of the *Buffalo Express*—on the market. After a summer in Elmira to recover their health and wits, he wrote to Riley in Africa, they would "build a house in Hartford just like this one." Livy and little Langdon were loaded onto mattresses and taken to the train. The simultaneous failure of *Mark Twain's (Burlesque) Autobiography*, the pamphlet published in defiance of Sam's contract with Bliss, meant nothing. Normally, the failure of a literary enterprise would have sent Sam into mourning, but he was too dispirited to grieve.

19 | A New Life

*Duties are not performed for duty's sake, but because
their neglect would make the man uncomfortable. A
man performs but one duty—the duty of contenting his
spirit, the duty of making himself agreeable to himself.*
—"What Is Man?" (1906)

In the bosom of Livy's family home, the beleaguered clan attempted to recover. With Livy and the infant Langdon in capable, familial hands, a calmer Sam shifted his focus back to his work. Daily, Sam hiked from the house in town up to Quarry Farm, Jervis Langdon's summer retreat, which Livy's sister "Saint Sue" Crane later used to provide milk to the poor. The hilltop house at the farm and the occasional company of Sue made it easy for Sam to concentrate. For all the loathing he'd expressed for his pen name only weeks before, the pen itself claimed his heart and promised him salvation from travail. Hiking the mile up East Hill to Quarry Farm each morning, Sam rose above the painful shambles of his first year of married life and devoted himself to mythologizing his memories of his days out west. He wrote his brother that his book was "booming along. And what I am writing now is so much better than the opening chapters, or the Innocent Abroad either, that I do *wish* I could spare time to . . . write some of them over again."

Although committed to Elisha Bliss and his American Publishing Company, Sam flirted with Isaac Sheldon, who had published Mark Twain's costly and unfunny *(Burlesque) Autobiography*. He outlined an idea for a novel; Sheldon sent an encouraging response. In early April 1871, Sam wrote of his new interest in this genre, "I begin to think I can get up quite a respectable novel, & mean to fool away some of my odd hours in the attempt, anyway." Perhaps sensing both Sam's potential defection and recovering concentration, and having held his tongue during the earlier crisis over the pamphlet, Elisha Bliss finally loosed an understated rebuke. Declaring that Mark Twain's popularity depended on his image and not on Sam Clemens' talent, Bliss made it plain that the fate of Mark Twain's image depended not only on Sam but also on Bliss. Without the American Publishing Company's glowing advertisements and impressive prospectuses, Mark Twain would sell no more books through subscription than he had copies of his misbegotten pamphlet.

Bliss' letter stopped Sam's progress on the book for a few days, and Sam instructed Livy to halt all his letters from Hartford. The spotty sales and insulting newspaper reviews of *(Burlesque) Autobiography* at last fired an anxiety about his literary and financial future. In his despondent torpor after receiving Bliss' letter, Sam wrote Mary Fairbanks that his new book "will have no success. The papers have found at last the courage to pull me down off my pedestal & cast slurs at me—& that is simply a popular author's death rattle. Though he wrote an inspired book after that, it would not save him."

Joe Goodman, Sam's friend and editor in Virginia City, came to Elmira to encourage him. Goodman was writing a novel, and the two friends worked on their manuscripts side by side on the Quarry Farm porch, overlooking the Chemung River Valley south of the town and the Pennsylvania border beyond. As spring drifted into summer, Sam's enthusiasm for his book returned. "This book will be pretty readable, after all; and if it is well and profusely illustrated," he told Bliss, "it will crowd the 'Innocents.'" His passion for his and Riley's story-by-proxy of the South African diamond rush diminished in his excitement over this firsthand narrative. Sam made startling progress on his book. By the middle of May, he had "1200 pages of MS already written and am now writing 200 a week—more than that, in fact; during the past week wrote 23 one day, then 30, 33, 35, 52 and 65.—How's that?" Writing the story as the autobiography of a fictional person, he subsumed his experience into the myth of Mark Twain, replacing his own identity with something new. Knitting together his own past and the image of Mark Twain's persona he derived from performing him on the lecture circuit, Sam invented a new man: a clever bungler, an innocent learning the ways of a dirty world. Sam revised his own profligate western adventures, creating from them a palatable history for Mark Twain.

This transformation allowed Sam to see the possibility of finding a future beyond his own misfortunes. Now that Livy was able to walk a few steps at a time, supporting herself on a chair back, and Langdon, though still small and sickly, seemed to gain strength, Sam recovered a feeling of control over his life. Moreover, just as Jervis Langdon's generous life had revived his memories of his father's constricted one, Jervis' death had freed Sam, not from John Clemens' terminal sobriety, but from a tyranny of kindness. Had Livy's father lived, Sam could not have sold the house and the investment in the newspaper; he would have been stuck in Buffalo indefinitely. Now Sam could not only shake off the complex financial and emotional chains of filial loyalty; he could also assume a paternal role himself. He and Livy together held the purse strings both of her inheritance and of his own success.

His feeling of freedom and authority induced him to write a new lecture and reopen his relationship with lyceum agent James Redpath. Instead of casting wildly about for strange literary schemes, he resumed his faith in his success as Mark Twain. Public performance affirmed this belief and extended Sam's reinvented Mark Twain from manuscript to life. He wrote of his experiences in Nevada and California by recasting Sam Clemens' life of debt, frustration, guilt, and drunkenness as Mark Twain's adventures in a wild land. This not only erased Sam's messy past, but also freed him to pursue a new future. By applying P. T. Barnum's philosophy of self-promotion to Elisha Bliss' reminder that Mark Twain's success depended on his image, Sam allowed his western book to literally make him the author of his own life.

By the summer of 1871, after six productive months in Elmira, he had good reasons for confidence. He had Mark Twain under lucrative contracts for two books and a lecture tour; taking advantage of Sam's renewal of faith, Bliss journeyed to Elmira in mid-July to sign him to a contract for yet another book. Livy had survived a birth and an illness, each of which came close to killing her. Now she was pregnant again and feeling good, with her first child appearing at last to have found his health. Consulting with Sue's husband, Theodore Crane, and Charlie Langdon, Livy determined they could spend $30,000 building a new house, with several thousand more for the land and furnishings. Once Livy was strong enough, the young family would rent a house in Hartford and create lives for themselves there. In August, Sam brought his newly completed manuscript to Hartford and, while there, rented the house of John Hooker, in which he had stayed when he'd first visited Connecticut three years before, and in which Livy's friend Alice Hooker Day had grown up.

In Hartford, Sam visited with his mother and his niece Annie, who had come to see Orion and Mollie in their new town. Orion was "as queer & heedless a bird as ever," Sam reported to Livy. Orion had alarmed his own housemaid by cooling off in the bath with his head under water and his rear end in the air. The maid screamed to Mollie that Orion had drowned in the tub; when Mollie saw her husband's position, she asked the maid, "How do you know it is Mr. Clemens?" Even Livy's despairing letters, prompted by the anniversary of her father's death, couldn't suppress Sam's joy in his arrival at the gates of his new home. Sam soothed her: "If you are taken away I will love the baby & have a jealous care over him.—But let us hope & trust that both you & I shall tend him & watch over him till we are helped from our easy-chairs to the parlor to see his children married."

Hartford had simple attractions for both Sam and Livy. Livy had lifelong friends there. Sam had made a friend in Joe Twichell and hoped that Orion could settle into a durable way of life nearby. The overtures Sam had received from the *Hartford Courant*'s Charles Dudley Warner and his wife, Susan, advanced his expectation of a professional and personal acceptance from the city's leadership. Elisha Bliss and his American Publishing Company flourished in Hartford, so Sam's move also brought him closer to the source of Mark Twain's fame and fortune. The lifestyle in Hartford and particularly at Nook Farm—neither as literary as Boston nor as mercenary as New York—allowed the pursuit of money and a life in letters to combine honorably. The Hartford insurance companies had survived the financial debacle of claims resulting from the Great Chicago Fire of 1871, which had destroyed the industry elsewhere. The Civil War had made the Colt Arms factory immensely wealthy, and the postwar industrial expansion did the same for Pratt and Whitney machines. The subscription book business, following the business model fashioned by the insurance companies, thrived in America's ebullient climate.

An intellectual bourgeois utopia such as Nook Farm could only have developed in the wealthiest city in the East. In Nook Farm, neighbors entered one another's houses without knocking, exchanged social and political ideas at biweekly meetings, and self-consciously advanced family, hospitality, generosity, intellectual growth, and healthful recreation as cardinal virtues. This ethic attracted entire clans. Charles Dudley Warner's brother George lived there; George Warner's wife Lilly was the daughter of Senator Francis Gillette, who had helped his brother-in-law John Hooker establish Nook Farm. His relatives Edward and William lived there too, as did Charles and Thomas Perkins, both prominent lawyers. The Beechers had four contributors to Hartford and Nook Farm society: Catherine Beecher, who founded and ran the Hartford Female Seminary;

Isabella Beecher Hooker; Mary Beecher Perkins, wife of Thomas Perkins; and Harriet Beecher Stowe, who occupied the celebrated literary position to which Sam aspired. Nook Farm virtues were expensive to maintain because they required large houses with artistic flair, modern conveniences, and open green spaces surrounding them. Nook Farmers dedicated relatively small amounts of time to work so as to allow time for family readings, theatricals, games, and conversation. Large houses meant servants and private carriages, a luxury calling for horses, a stable, and a staff to tend both. Travel for intellectual improvement and emotional regeneration became as much of a social norm as charity benefits, spontaneous whist parties, and long walks, the preferred form of exercise. Despite the experiment's success, the cost of Nook Farm life periodically sent most residents into temporary exile. Fortunately, renters from other communities wanted to take up temporary residence at Nook Farm, despite the ruinous tariff.

John and Isabella Beecher Hooker were the architects of this enclave for right-thinking, successful men and women of letters and business; living in their house put the Clemenses at the center of Nook Farm life. John Hooker's colonial lineage and reputation as a lawyer gave him a conspicuous position in Hartford society from which to spearhead his socially progressive ideas. His wife, a member of the prodigious Beecher clan, had made herself a leader in the women's movement, after hiring Anna Dickinson as her personal tutor in suffragist politics. Isabella Hooker's spiritualist feminism, less radical than that of Susan B. Anthony, Elizabeth Cady Stanton, or free-love advocate Victoria Woodhull, still resided on the political fringe, which hurt her husband's legal practice. The Hookers needed to rent their house to curtail their expenses. The Nook Farm aesthetic encouraged an activism that sometimes made it difficult to earn enough money to live there.

Sam could have moved to Hartford in a more economical way than by leasing the Hookers' house. His lecture tour and Livy's confinement in Elmira the following spring would keep him away from his new city most of the next eight months. He could have found a smaller place rented on a shorter term, but locating at the center of Nook Farm brought perquisites. Sam immediately received an invitation to join the Monday Evening Club, Hartford's male intellectual leadership, which met every other week from October to May to discuss an essay written by a member. Sam and Livy had chosen Hartford because of the life implicit in belonging to this club; why stint on rent if it cost them membership? Between Mark Twain's fame and Livy's inheritance, Sam believed, he could meet the expensive demands of the life he wanted for himself and his family. *The*

Innocents Abroad had sold about ninety thousand copies by fall of 1871, making it one of the best-selling books of the nineteenth century. With a royalty of 5 percent of the cover price, Sam had netted $20,000 from the book, a substantial sum.

The publisher earned several times that, of course, which is why Elisha Bliss pursued Sam's signature on book contracts so energetically, even at a 7½ percent royalty. The success of *Innocents* meant a ready-made audience for future works; Mark Twain was by now a trade name Bliss could bank on. Subscription publishers like Bliss waged a fierce war with trade publishers. Trade publishers sold books of higher quality, printed on better paper with more care. They published both popular novels and serious literature, as opposed to subscription publishers' travel narratives, Bibles, and personalized histories of great events. Trade books received reviews in the literary press, unlike subscription books, which were noticed only in newspapers. To entice buyers, subscription book agents carried a prospectus, a thin mock-up of the book, bound in leather and gilt, laden with illustrations and dramatic snippets of the narrative. Subscription publishers began printing only after orders came in, which with the large markup per volume made their enterprise colossally lucrative, especially for books by a sensational new author like Mark Twain. Elisha Bliss' American Publishing Company led the Hartford subscription houses on the combined strength of Bliss' acumen and a handful of notable successes. In the first flush of *Innocents'* sales, Sam had praised Bliss' mastery of the subscription trade. "It is easy to see, when one travels around, that one must be endowed with a deal of genuine generalship in order to maneuvre a publication whose line of battle stretches from end to end of a great continent, and whose foragers and skirmishers invest every hamlet and besiege every village hidden away in all the vast space between." The truth is that Sam, as a hero in this war between subscription and trade publishers, did not alter his style to suit eastern taste, but instead wanted the eastern literary establishment to accept him on his own terms. A century of praise for Mark Twain has obscured the radical nature of the aesthetic—of earthy subjects written of in immediate language—to which he aspired.

In Mark Twain, Bliss had the nation's most popular author committed to him for many years, with Orion's job an additional obligation of author to publisher. The course of Orion's employment had not run smoothly, however, as Sam discovered after his arrival in Hartford. His older brother had accepted the position as editor of *The American Publisher* with the understanding that he would edit the newspaper and still have time to work on the inventions that so preoccupied him. His drilling machine had not gone far, but together with Sam, Orion had developed an adjustable clothing strap, for which the brothers began pursuing a patent. Even the work on the paper itself had caused problems between Orion and his employer. To Orion, editing a journal meant writing for it too, but Bliss had no patience for Orion's painstaking method of composition; besides, he expected Orion to serve as his errand boy on other projects, too. Orion's dissatisfaction divided Sam between his obligations to Bliss and his obligations to blood. With Nook Farm's ideals glittering within reach, Sam needed Elisha Bliss and his American Publishing Company; he refused to intervene on Orion's behalf.

After escorting his mother and niece as far as Elmira, Sam rushed to Washington, D.C., to spend five days researching and patenting his clothing strap. He was deeply excited about obtaining this patent, which he regarded as both a certificate of originality and his ticket to a level of wealth far beyond what Mark Twain could earn. In the middle of September, Sam returned to upstate New York, first to Elmira to see to Livy and Langdon, and then to Buffalo to close the sale of the house and the newspaper share. His portion of the *Buffalo Express* sold for only $15,000, a dead loss of $10,000. The house on Delaware Avenue, however, brought $25,000 free and clear. These combined deals left them $15,000 and their furnishings to the good, but as a trustee of the Jervis Langdon estate, Sam considered himself liable for the debt incurred by leaving Buffalo so precipitously. He returned to Elmira in the final days of September 1871, to help Livy with the move to Hartford. Sam and Livy took over the Hooker home on Forest Street on October 1, 1871.

Exhausted from travel, her pregnancy, and worry over the still-sickly Langdon, Livy settled in uncomfortably as mistress of the house she had visited many times. Though she and Sam would have valued a few weeks of quiet to recover from their move and make a life together in this new place, Mark Twain was scheduled to return to the platform on October 16, 1871. Life in Nook Farm required money and the lecture platform provided it. Sam barely had time to give Livy a lover's welcome, make sure Bliss had Mark Twain's version of the Wild West, and prepare his lecture before boarding a train out of Hartford. Sam wrote to Riley, lately returned from his Mark Twain-financed exploration of the South African diamond bonanza, that their planned collaboration would have to wait. Sam no sooner had arranged himself in his own eastern utopia than he had to bid it farewell.

| # *Hell on Rails*

To be good is noble, but to show others how to be good is nobler, and no trouble.
—"Pudd'nhead Wilson's New Calendar" (1897)

SAM DID NOT plan his lecture tour with his typical clearheadedness. The summer before moving to Hartford, he claimed to James Redpath, "Without really intending to go into the lecture field, I wrote a lecture yesterday just for amusement to see how the subject would work up, but now that I have read it I like it so much that I want to deliver it." The fib sounded like angels' harps to Redpath, who had lost thousands of dollars in business the year before when Sam refused to lecture. Mark Twain's absence from the platform had only whetted the public's desire to hear him perform; Redpath could set Mark Twain lecturing daily until spring, and demand as much as $150 a night. Sam gave his manager conflicting mandates: refusing to lecture in Buffalo, then agreeing to lecture in Buffalo, but only for a certain group; or telling Redpath to limit him to New England and then permitting him to send him anywhere. "I am different from other women; my mind changes oftener," Sam eventually confessed. "You must try to keep the run of my mind, Redpath, it is your business being the agent, and it always was too many for me."

His attention to the minutiae of his schedule would have been better applied to refining his lecture. His first draft, satirically advocating voting rights for boys, was discarded almost immediately. After a couple other attempts, he finally prepared for the road with a hash of thumbnail sketches he called "Some Uncommonplace Characters I Have Chanced to Meet," a loose net intended to hold jokes and pathos about the human condition as seen by Mark Twain. It came across to his audiences as a hopeless mess. He wrote from Amish Pennsylvania, "Livy darling, this lecture will *never* do. I *hate* it & won't keep it. I can't even handle these chuckleheaded Dutch with it." He delivered the lecture three times before canceling the next two shows to give himself time to assemble a new one. Even as he got out of his obligations with a lie about family illness, Sam complained to Livy, "I seem doomed to be always in the papers about private matters."*

Because the Artemus Ward segment of "Uncommonplace Characters" produced the most laughs, Sam wrote an entire lecture about Ward, which he delivered for the first time on October 23, 1871, in Washington, D.C. Without the time to memorize the new piece, he mistakenly took to the stage with manuscript in hand, but his attempt to present Mark Twain and Artemus Ward simultaneously proved a greater mistake than lecturing from notes. Ward had been dead four years, and his persona and jokes had become hallowed in the public mind. Mark Twain's rendition of his humor forced a comparison between the ideal dead comedian and the real live one. Most reviewers attacked Twain as a fraud. A critic in Wilmington, Delaware, stated flatly that "there are few more unsatisfactory efforts in the lecture field." The rout continued for days. After a week of tinkering, Sam thought the lecture improved, but he recognized that "the same old practicing on audiences still goes on—the same old feeling of pulses & altering manner & matter to suit the symptoms." He fretted especially about Boston's response to Mark Twain, as he had two years before.

His normal preoccupation about Boston's audience had increased because the literary excitement over Bret Harte had begun to fade; Sam hoped he might use that opening to find his way into the ranks of the Hub's elite. Harte, however, was in Boston too, for the same reason as Sam, to lecture for money. The $10,000 *The Atlantic* had given Harte for a year of monthly contributions had dwindled quickly in Newport and New York, and his failure to fulfill the contract made it impossible for the magazine to renew it. Still, Sam deeply envied the respect with which

William Dean Howells, now *The Atlantic*'s editor, had welcomed Harte to Boston, including a dinner with literary gods Longfellow, Holmes, and Emerson. Though Sam owed the dandified Harte for the success of *Innocents Abroad*, he thoroughly resented the fact that he worked hard for crumbs from the silver platter at which Harte carelessly picked. In Boston in early November 1871, Sam often dined with Harte, Howells, Thomas Bailey Aldrich, James Fields, and others of the literary establishment. Ralph Keeler, a writer and *Atlantic* proofreader Sam knew from San Francisco, hosted a dinner to thank Harte for running a piece of his in the *Overland Monthly*, but Harte deflated Sam's pleasure at being included at the gathering by touching Sam on the shoulder and—puncturing a precious image he held of himself—saying to the others, "Why, fellows, this is the dream of Mark's life."

Harte's bite wasn't the only insult that galled Sam during his stay in Boston. Aldrich brought him home for dinner, slurring his name in introducing him to his wife. Sam's sealskin coat, flamboyant diamond ring, violet bow-tie, and shambling manner convinced Lillian Aldrich that this visitor was an outlandish drunk. She refused to serve dinner until he left. At least the Boston lecture attracted full houses and cordial, if not excited, reviews, and Sam cultivated his personal relationships with Aldrich, Howells, and Boston publisher James Osgood. As a comrade, at least, he compared favorably with Bret Harte, though the Boston jury still deliberated his literary fate. His competition with Harte inflamed his ambition for acceptance.

Back in Hartford in November for little Langdon's first birthday, Sam lectured for his new home audience, which gave him the same polite praise he had received in Boston. The pressures of running a household by herself again were troubling Livy. Her kind and generous nature made it difficult for her to fire recalcitrant servants, but Sam's brief stay strengthened her resolve to take charge of the household, including Langdon's dubious health and the family's mixed-up finances. Livy wrote Sam, "Youth in certain things you must teach me a 'don't care' spirit, as regards cooks and the like . . . —I believe there is nothing that sooner ruins the happiness of a family than a worrying woman." Langdon's failure to progress in his efforts to talk, teethe, or walk by his first birthday gave Livy good reason to worry.

Sam worried too, not only about Langdon and money, but about the lecture. He wrote Livy that he was "patching at my lecture all the time—trying to weed Artemus out of it & work myself *in*. What *I* say, *fetches* 'em—but what *he* says—*don't*." By the end of November, after successes at Henry Ward Beecher's Plymouth Church in Brooklyn and failures in making up the lectures canceled earlier, he concluded that improvisation was the key to Mark Twain's stage success. He not only had to appear natural; his performance had to have enough flexibility to hide from the audience the fact that it was a performance. "A great fault with this lecture is that I have no way of turning it into a serious & instructive vein at will," he wrote Livy. "*Any* lecture of mine ought to be a running narrative-plank, with square holes in it, six inches apart, all the length of it, & then in my mental shop I ought to have plugs (half marked 'serious' & the other marked 'humorous') to select from and jam into these holes according to the temper of the audience." Sam meant this comment to allay Livy's concerns about Mark Twain's lack of seriousness, but his Boston experience showed him that she was right to encourage a more substantive presence in Mark Twain. Clowning would not get him published in *The Atlantic Monthly.*

Clowning paid well, however, and he hadn't yet found a way to make seriousness profitable. Livy had her own solution to this problem: "We will either board or live in a small cottage and keep one servant, will live near the horse cars so that I can get along without a horse and carriage—I *can not* and I *will not* think about your being away from me this way every year, it is not half living—if in order to sustain our present mode of living you are obliged to do that, then we will change our mode of living." Still, Livy enjoyed the Nook Farm life. She flourished at the Monday Evening Club's women's auxiliary, which frequently discussed women's rights, the key issue of the day. She and Lilly Gillette Warner became good friends, and in good weather they wandered around Nook Farm discussing architecture and religion. Lilly told Livy that her uneven feelings about God no longer bothered her very much; her feelings toward her husband George varied, too. Livy wrote Sam, "I told her if I felt toward God as I did toward my husband I should never be in the least troubled—I did not tell her how almost perfectly cold I am toward God." After so much tragedy, Livy's religious conviction had dimmed during the past two years; she hoped that Sam's dreams of wealth and fame could dim to a similar extent. Sam received Livy's letter while taking a day from his tour to visit his mother and sister in Fredonia. Proximity to his family always brought out the worst in Sam, and this experience with them only confirmed that he had come too far from where he had started to yet surrender his highest ambitions.

After his lecture in Geneva, New York, Sam received some unexpected visitors, who gave him a glimmer of how to combine humor and seriousness. "Two ladies came forward heartily & shook me by the hand & called me 'Sam Clemens, the very same old Sam'—& when the explanations came out, by & by, they were two little-girl friends of my early boyhood," he wrote Livy. "They seemed like waifs from some vague world I had lived in ages & ages ago—myths—creatures of a dream." Both were married now and had children, but their present lives didn't hold much interest for Sam. He wanted to talk to them about their childhood together, and even backed out of another more pressing engagement in order to explore the past with these one-time waifs. In his early years, Sam had always seemed more interested in escaping his past; but in writing about his life out west, he relished transforming it into something mythic. Here, in the form of two middle-aged women, were living sprites from Hannibal, the Missouri town they had all abandoned years ago. Before his evening with Mary Bacon and Kitty Shoot, his boyhood had seemed ripe only for burlesque, as in "Boy's Manuscript," but these middle-aged women sparked in Sam a new way of reinventing his childhood: to turn it into myth. They inspired the mix of dreamy nostalgia and legendary violence that became *The Adventures of Tom Sawyer*.

Toward the beginning of December, he finally gave up on the Artemus Ward lecture. After Elisha Bliss copyrighted *Roughing It*—Bliss chose the title when Sam couldn't—Sam decided to construct a new lecture from his book material. He skipped a planned visit with Mother Fairbanks in Cleveland and alternated between the *Roughing It* and Artemus Ward lectures until he had memorized the new one. With his new material in place and audiences showing more appreciation, Sam felt much better in Chicago. He stayed up late with his Chicago host and "then turned in & slept like a log—I don't mean a brisk, fresh, *green* log, but an old, dead, soggy, *rotten* one, that never turns over or gives a yelp."

Sam would have stuck with Nevada and California for the remainder of his tour if the *Chicago Tribune* hadn't spoiled his success by publishing a synopsis, which ruined Sam's triumphant mood. "If these devils incarnate only appreciated what suffering they inflict with their infernal synopses, maybe they would try to have humanity enough to refrain." Livy assuaged his anger. "I am *so sorry* that you have been annoyed by those reporters again, but I don't believe people often read those long reports."* Sam's perpetual anxiety over synopses exaggerated their effect. People came to *see* Mark Twain, the iconic author of *The Innocents Abroad*, more than to *hear* what he had to say. His platform success depended on his performance, not his material. His uncertainty about where to situate the character of Mark Twain when talking about Artemus Ward had undermined his previous lecture. In his new lecture about the West, Mark Twain occupied center stage. People wanted to see Twain tell stories about himself; Mark Twain was always Sam's best subject.

Mark Twain met with more success on his homeward swing in late December and January, but his exhaustion with travel soured Sam's pleasure in the circuit. Inconvenient train schedules infuriated him; he once hired a locomotive for seventy-five dollars because taking the only scheduled train meant getting up at two in the morning. He also fretted about how Livy fared; in late December, she sent him two telegrams in rapid succession, the first telling him that Langdon was dying, the second that the boy was in the clear. As he wound up the tour, he thought more about what had driven him to the road. He wrote Livy in early January 1872:

> My lecture business, up to the end of January, yields about $10,000—& yet, when I preach Jan. 30, it is well I am so close to Hartford, for I would not have money enough to get home on. It has all gone & is going, for those necessaries of life—debts. Every night the question is, Well, who does *this* day's earnings belong to?—& away it goes. . . . The rest of my earnings will go to Ma & Redpath, principally—& then what are *we* going to do, I don't reckon?

After the tour concluded, however, he calculated for Mother Fairbanks' benefit that he "paid off all my debts, squandered no end of money, & came out of the campaign with less than $1500 to show for all that work & misery. I ain't going to ever lecture any more—unless I get in debt again. Would you?" Sam mixed his boasts about money with self-deprecation, especially when writing to his family, to Hannibal friends, or to Fairbanks. In one hundred days of "this lecturing penance," as he termed the tour to Livy, he earned more than ten times the average working person's yearly income. Sam prided himself on only having to work a few months to erase debts most people could not even hope to accumulate. His father's lifelong struggle against debt had only dug his family a deeper hole, but in a few months Sam had piled up enough cash to have saved his father several times over. It gave him great satisfaction to confront a great debt, and then stare down what had destroyed his father. Mastering his fear of debt moved him to expand; he planned to buy a good-sized lot in expensive Nook Farm and build a Nook Farm-style house on it.

By the middle of February, Sam ended "the most detestable lecture campain that ever was." He was back on Forest Street in Hartford with his beloved Livy and their "Cubbie," Langdon. Langdon had sprouted his first tooth in January, while Sam was away, and another had begun poking through his sore gums. He had begun to speak, saying "Pa" to indicate, not his famous father, but his nurse. He still could not walk. Livy, in her eighth month of pregnancy, could not walk much, either. Apprehensive about the coming childbirth, both she and Sam worried whether the new baby would be as frail as Langdon. Youth and Angel, as Sam and Livy called each other, stayed in Hartford only a few weeks before retreating to Elmira to await the arrival of their second child.

21 | ## A Birth, a Death, a Book

Every one is a moon, and has a dark side which he never shows to anybody.
—"Pudd'nhead Wilson's New Calendar" (1897)

There isn't a Parallel of Latitude but thinks it would have been the Equator if it had had its rights.
—"Pudd'nhead Wilson's New Calendar" (1897)

SAM'S SHORT STAY in Hartford brought a return to business worries. Two unconnected publishing matters consumed his attention after the publication of *Roughing It*. First, the long-standing disagreement with Bliss about how Orion should discharge his duties as editor of *The American Publisher* proved insoluble. Orion and Elisha Bliss parted company barely a year after Sam had secured his brother the job. Orion, in the throes of invention, obsessed far less about his editorial duties than about his drilling machine requiring some 5,000 chain links and 800 connecting parts. Second and more important, Orion had learned about Bliss' shady business practices and suspected that his brother had become a victim of them. The contract for *Roughing It* gave Sam a 7½ percent royalty, a percentage that Bliss swore equaled half the profits, but Orion knew that Bliss had grossly overestimated production costs in an effort to hide the company's actual profits. In conflict between his duties to his employer and his loyalty to his brother, Orion waited until Sam returned to Hartford to spill the facts; once Bliss had published the book, however, Sam could do little. Sam did not take Orion's good turn with undiluted gratitude. Accusing his brother of disloyalty (whether to him or to Bliss remains uncertain), Sam wrote,

"The fact that I condemn the *act* as being indefensible does not in the least blind me to the virtue of the *motive* underlying it, or leave me unthankful for it." As ever, he could not bear Orion in the role of his bigbrotherly protector.

Still, Orion's testimony bothered Sam enough to make him bring his objections to Bliss on March 12, 1872. With *Roughing It* now on the market, Sam did not want to give Bliss cause to diminish his publicity and sales efforts, so he indirectly brought up the questions Orion had placed in his mind. He patiently sat through Bliss' explanations of publishing costs, which he supported with an account ledger—apparently a false one, though nothing in the books themselves indicated dissembling. Sam wrote Bliss, "I *was* troubled a good deal, when I went there, for I had worried myself pretty well into the impression that I was getting a smaller ratio of this book's profits than the spirit of our contract had authorized me to promise myself." Still, he asked Bliss to alter the contract to reflect Sam's half-profits assumption. When Bliss neglected to do so, Sam consulted a lawyer, his Nook Farm neighbor and Monday Evening Club member Charlie Perkins, who told Sam that Bliss had no obligation to change the contract. Orion thought Sam might squeeze Bliss by calling on testimony from his own bookkeeper, but Sam decided against it.

Instead, Sam determined to buy into the American Publishing Company, to reap as a stock owner the profits he had bargained away as an author. By acquiring enough stock, he became a director of the company, which meant he had an interest in expanding the company's list to include other popular authors. Sam immediately pitched subscription publishing to Anna Dickinson and Bret Harte. He also prepared a volume of his sketches, an expanded version of his first book, to be issued by subscription with Mark Twain's fame to boost sales. Bliss wanted to wait until *Roughing It* had peaked before even considering a volume of short works, an untried form in the subscription market, but Sam was already collecting his sketches for a British publisher and wanted to issue the books simultaneously, to protect against losses through transnational piracies.

Piracies, especially in England, but in North America too, were spreading Mark Twain's fame without providing a cent to Sam Clemens. Weak and inconsistent copyright laws made it nearly impossible to stop the financial hemorrhaging caused by unauthorized editions of Mark Twain's works. Within a few months of Charles Webb's April 1867 publication of *The Jumping Frog of Calaveras County and Other Sketches*, British publisher George Routledge and Sons had reprinted it. The recipient of frenzied reviews, the volume had sold over twenty thousand copies in England, several times what Webb managed in America. Sam had to buy back his copyright from Webb, but he had no copyright at all in England. British law accepted an international copyright only if the originating nation had a reciprocal agreement. The United States publishing industry had pirated Britain's books for so long that no voice rose up to defend the rights of foreign authors. Only recently had any American writer attracted enough British readers for turnabout to seem unfair play.

After another British publisher, John Camden Hotten, brought out another, equally successful version of *Jumping Frog*, George Routledge's American representative bought the rights to a Mark Twain short story, so they could republish their edition claiming a "New Copyright Chapter." Because of this, Sam thought he might be able to secure a British copyright and thus payment, for *Innocents Abroad* as easily as selling the rights overseas, but he could not; a contract with one publisher did not restrict the actions of another. Routledge and Hotten both brought out versions of *Innocents* that did nearly twice the business of the sketches. Routledge and Hotten raced to bring out more volumes of Mark Twain. Sam's efforts to help Routledge did not deter Hotten, who published more Twain volumes, such as the embarrassingly titled *Screamers* and *Eye-Openers*. Routledge printed ten thousand copies of *Roughing It* by the end of February, cementing his position as Mark Twain's British publisher. Hotten conceded indirectly by writing to Sam asking for selections from the book, promising to pay him "whatever is fair & equitable."* Sam did not answer. With Hotten's piracies under control, Sam now wanted to tame the Canadian thieves whose knockoffs had dented sales of *Innocents* and taken a big bite out of *Roughing It*.

Unfortunately, Sam had very little time to defend his rights. After his discussion with Bliss on March 12, Sam took Livy and Langdon to Elmira to await the new baby's arrival. The long trip induced Livy's labor. Olivia Susan Clemens was born on March 19, 1872. Although not much larger at birth than Langdon had been, Susie appeared hearty and healthy, and even the mother came through this delivery feeling stronger than she had after her first child. Up and around within a few weeks of the birth, Livy began the habit of going out for a ride with Langdon every morning. One April day, she didn't feel up to it, so Sam offered to accompany his son. Ruminating, Sam did not notice the blankets slip from the boy until Langdon's lips had turned blue from the cold. With Sam berating himself for imperiling his son through his foolish disregard, they rushed back to the warmth of the house. Despite this incident, both Susie and Langdon seemed well enough for Sam and Livy to leave them in Elmira during their visit to Fredonia and Cleveland—to the latter, to make amends for Sam's having missed a promised stop there on his lecture tour.

Sam's and Livy's relief at the birth of a healthy child eventually gave way to exhaustion; the stress of keeping their apprehensions at bay for months finally caught up with them. Both in profound need of a vacation, they picked up Jane in Fredonia and brought her to Cleveland. This meeting of Sam's real and adopted mothers—Jane Clemens a quirky, flighty, good-hearted gossip; Mary Fairbanks an intellectual woman younger than Pamela—made for a lively, odd visit, and left Sam feeling thankful for having left his old family for his new one. From Cleveland, he wrote to his new baby daughter, "Many's the night I've lain awake till 2 oclock in the morning reading Dumas & drinking beer, listening for the slightest sound you might make, my daughter, & suffering as only a father can suffer, with anxiety for his child. Some day you will thank me for this." Once back in Elmira, Sam wrote Orion that Jane "enjoyed Cleveland & is flourishing," but that Langdon had a nasty cough "& the suffering & irritation consequent upon developing six teeth in nine days. He is as white as alabaster and is weak; but he is pretty jolly about half the time. The new baby is as fat as butter, & wholly free from infelicities of any kind."*

Sam wrote very little during the spring of 1872; preparing the collected sketches took most of his work time. He halfheartedly told his partner James Henry Riley, who was fighting illness at his family home near Philadelphia, that he still had plans for their travel-by-proxy book about the South African diamond fields. *Roughing It* moved briskly, selling fifteen thousand copies a month in March and April; in May, Bliss sent him a royalty check for over $10,000. His niece Annie thought him immensely rich, but Sam denied it, poor-mouthing his finances while at the same time parading the stunning actual numbers. "Livy and I each have about $30,000 in the bank and $10,000 royalties, so you will see we are not as rich as the papers think we are."* His fame brought sacks of adulatory letters and appeals for help, as well as offers. Perhaps most gratifyingly, Boston publisher James Osgood asked to publish a volume of short pieces. Though Sam regarded that as a sign of welcome into Boston's literary club, at least in the matter of sales, he had to refuse because "unfortunately my contracts with my present publisher tie my hands and prevent me." Sam closed his reply to Osgood, "Much love to the boys," referring to Thomas Bailey Aldrich, William Dean Howells, and the others. Howells sent Sam a copy of his first novel, *Their Wedding Journey*, and delighted Sam with another positive review in *The Atlantic*, calling *Roughing It* "singularly entertaining, and its humor is always amiable, manly and generous." Sam wrote his thanks, in language representative of his gritty style: "I am as uplifted and reassured by it as a mother who has given birth to a white baby when she was awfully afraid it was going to be a mulatto."

Sam had small reason to fear for *Roughing It*, however. It was, in some ways, a sequel—and a necessary balance—to *The Innocents Abroad*. Where Twain's first travel book pointed out the shortcomings of myths inherited from Europe, the second work replaced those tarnished ones with myths grown in native soil. In place of the disgraced European virtues of refinement, tradition, and craft, Mark Twain proposed vastness, wealth, and speed. The endless land, the riches under it, and the thrill of crossing it became cardinal virtues. Twain described watching the distant speck of a Pony Express rider as he approached the speedy coach:

> In a second or two it becomes a horse and rider, rising and falling, rising and falling—sweeping toward us nearer and nearer—growing more and more distinct, more and more sharply defined—nearer and still nearer, and the flutter of the hoofs comes faintly to the ear—another instant a whoop and a hurrah from our upper deck, a wave of the rider's hand, but no reply, and man and horse burst past our excited faces, and winging away like a belated fragment of a storm.

This was the American Sphinx, carrying messages but offering not a single word himself.

Roughing It advanced from *Innocents Abroad* in developing a more vital portrait of Mark Twain. In the earlier book, Mark Twain was more of an attitude than a person. He observed what hundreds of others had observed before him, and offered his own appraisal of what he had seen. Very little of what Sam reported of Mark Twain in *The Innocents* comprised unique or even unusual experiences. In *Roughing It*, Mark Twain became more than a set of eyes. Not only passing judgment on what he saw, but also taking real-world consequences for those judgments, Mark Twain was both victim and beneficiary of the new myths proposed in *Roughing It*. He not only crossed the continent, but sailed to Hawaii, too. He struck it rich, *prospectively*, for ten days. His life underwent sudden massive changes, so dizzyingly swift that they left Mark Twain uncertain of who he was or what he was doing. But still, he survived the experience and returned, a contemporary Orpheus, with a smart mouth in place of a lyre.

No one could miss the fact that these recorded events were lived experience, though Sam had dressed them up to be nearly unbelievable. Mark Twain came alive in the pages of *Roughing It*, and lecture audiences happily accepted these fantastical experiences as the actual life of the man who stood before them. The western experience represented the future that Mark Twain had promised his public in *Innocents Abroad*. *Roughing It* offered details of that plan. The wistfulness behind Sam's composition of the book—now encumbered with a wife and growing family, he could not help but think of his wild years with some longing—came through as a dreaminess entirely in keeping with Mark Twain's mythification of the West. The public image of Mark Twain expanded from the witty and wise iconoclast of *The Innocents Abroad* into a hapless, hopeful adventurer, a fool sometimes, but only by the will of fate. The curmudgeonly critic from the cultural sidelines had proved himself to be as rough-and-ready as America itself.

The newly enlarged Clemens family returned to Hartford at the end of May. Langdon's cough, however, did not improve. Livy sat up with him for days until, on June 2, 1872, the sickly and underdeveloped nine-teen-month-old died in his mother's arms.

Diphtheria and not the April chill had killed him, but Sam, prepared long ago by the deaths of sister Margaret and brother Henry, assumed full guilt, as he had whenever death demanded one of his family. Feeling like Midas, with a golden but fatal touch, Sam told Lilly Warner that he was "full of rejoicing for the baby," as she reported to her husband. "He kept thinking it wasn't death for him but the beginning of life." He and Livy returned to Elmira, where they buried Langdon beside the grand-father he never knew. Livy had a death mask made; when she returned to Hartford, she placed it in the same box in which she kept her love letters from Sam.

Most Nook Farm residents went away in the summer, and Hartford's loneliness and oppressive humidity made Sam look for a cooler retreat for his sorrowful family. Leaving Mollie and Orion, now unemployed, in charge of the house, they removed to Saybrook, Connecticut, where a number of other Hartforders summered. "Our Susie is doing famously *here*, but the case was different in Hartford, the moment the warm weather set in. We had to pack our trunks mighty suddenly, the 5th of July & rush down here—& none too soon, for the succeeding week wilted Hartford children away like a simoom," Sam wrote Mrs. Fairbanks. "Mrs. Langdon will reach here in a day or two, & she & Livy will remain till cool weather." Though he pre-ferred to experience his guilt and sorrow at Langdon's death in isolation, Sam gave himself over to helping Livy through her mourning. Livy, though, did not leave the hotel room, wanting to stay close to Susie. She also couldn't bear the sympathetic gazes of the Hartford people she knew. Sam thought swimming would buoy her, and she indulged his desire, but his lev-ity, always increased by emotional strain, did not suit her. Deeply distraught over Langdon's death, Livy would not and could not allow Sam's love and humor to relieve her depression.

Sam also had the mixed blessing of Bret Harte as a houseguest to help him with his recovery for much of the late spring and summer. Harte visited Hartford in June and later spent a week or more with the Clemenses in Saybrook. In a joke based on fact, Sam listed "F. Bret Harte, Poet and Author" as his boarder in the Hartford City Directory. Harte dropped his wife and two small children with his sister in New Jersey while he took to the road on his lecture tour, but despite his profitable tour, his debts mounted quickly. Once, in Boston, he had to string out a performance for nearly an hour until the constable waiting in the wings to arrest Harte could take some hastily found money to one of his impatient creditors. Though Harte's egotism made him an unwelcome guest in a house of mourning, his elegant wit and impressive capacity for alcohol made him a fit companion for Sam in his attempts to escape from guilt and sadness.

After delivering Harte to Hartford on August 5, Sam returned to Saybrook and settled into a bout of invention. He wrote Orion of his design for a "*self-pasting scrap-book*—good enough idea if some juggling tailor does not come along and ante-date me a couple of months, as in the case of the elastic vest-strap." An inveterate keeper of newspaper cuttings, Sam found most scrapbooks worthless or foolishly labor-intensive. His idea was to put gum stickum in columns on bound pages, alternating stripes on facing pages so they wouldn't adhere when closed. By moistening the glue as the paper scrap required, one could permanently and without mess or bother assemble a scrapbook. Sam wanted to turn the scrapbook idea over to Dan Slote, his *Quaker City* cabin mate who kept Sam's personal financial accounts and whose blankbook business could use a new product. He told Orion, "Preserve, also, the envelope of this letter—postmark ought to be good evidence of the date of this great humanizing and civilizing invention."

Always both writer and entrepreneur, Sam also cast about for his next book idea. The success of *Innocents Abroad*, which finally sold its one-hundred-thousandth copy after three years, and of *Roughing It*, which had sold sixty thousand copies in eight months, stimulated Sam to plan several more books. Composing a preface for the official British edition of *Roughing It*, he wrote Routledge's American agent that he was trying to decide whether to "spend my winter either in the rural part of England or in Cuba & Florida—the latter most likely."* The year before Sam had posed the possibility of going to England to research a book, as an invitation for Livy to travel, but now he intended something quite different: He planned to go somewhere alone. The agent leapt to the bait and painted a glorious picture of the welcome Mark Twain would receive in England. Without delay, Sam made up his mind to sail to England on August 21, 1872.

Exactly seven weeks passed between the death of Langdon Clemens and Sam's letter declaring his intention to leave the country. Though Sam had earlier explained that he had not gone to see his dying collaborator Riley because his son's death had so affected Livy's health "that I can hardly be able to absent myself from home for some time yet,"* Livy had not improved; she had suffered three deaths in the first three years of marriage: her father, her dear friend Emma Nye, and her firstborn child. Sam found himself extraneous to his wife's grief, not merely helpless to salve her but perhaps even deleterious to her recovery. Something about Livy's grief made it impossible for Sam to be near her. No sooner had Mrs. Langdon arrived in Saybrook than Sam left. His hasty departure seems heartless, but even six weeks after he left for England, Livy wrote ambivalently to Mother Fairbanks, "I do miss him so much and yet I am contented to have him away." We cannot be certain what Livy knew: She claimed to believe that Sam went to England to gather notes for a book, but she was probably disguising the fact that he had wanted to remove himself from Livy and her sorrow.

| *To England!*

There comes a time in every rightly constructed boy's life when he has a raging desire to go somewhere and dig for hidden treasure.
—*The Adventures of Tom Sawyer* (1876)

There is no such thing as "the Queen's English." The property has gone into the hands of a joint stock company and we own the bulk of the shares!
—*"Pudd'nhead Wilson's New Calendar"* (1897)

Before setting sail for England on August 21, 1872, Sam procured a notebook with detachable pages interleaved with carbon so that he could take notes about his journey and send the copies to Livy as letters. He obtained this curious notebook from Dan Slote in New York, where he went a few days prior to his departure. While waiting for the boat, Sam conducted high times and big business with Dan, the latter concerning his new invention, which Dan's company would soon issue as Mark Twain's Scrap Book.

Sam's ship, the *Scotia*, left New York sparsely occupied, with only a few dozen passengers making its ten-day journey to England, a nation currently gripped by a fever for American humor. The British had first fallen in love with New World wit in the person of Artemus Ward, whose sold-out shows had been the must-see event of 1867. When Ward had died a still-rising star, they hungered for more and eagerly awaited Mark Twain's arrival as Ward's heir apparent. Nearly two dozen volumes of Twain's work had already been published by Routledge and by Hotten, and Sam felt a flash of pleasure when he noticed the man sitting across from him on the train from Liverpool to London reading *The Innocents*

Abroad. This joy dissolved into dread, however, when in the course of an hour the diligent reader did not so much as crack one smile.

Sam Clemens had vexed himself about his reception unnecessarily. After checking into the large Langham Hotel, a favorite among Americans, he marched over to the offices of his publisher. The Routledges, beginning lunch in a private room upstairs, invited Sam to join them. No one left the table until after dinner. Mark Twain proved every bit as funny and charming in person as on paper, and that night the Routledges proudly hosted him as their guest at the Savage Club. From then on, London was a round of luncheons, dinners, and parties feting Mark Twain. Sam was besieged with invitations—to lecture, to dine, to foxhunt, to go to the theater—and could hardly step outside without a squib appearing in the press about how he looked, walked, and spoke. If he said something funny, as he did daily, each newspaper rushed to print it ahead of the others.

Mark Twain's triumph in England received steady press at home. Mary Fairbanks wrote, "They are treating you handsomely in England— we are glad—everybody is watching you here—and I your anxious Mother am stretching my neck over all the great audience." Since colonial times, America had revered English culture and regarded its own output as meager and third-rate, but now Great Britain embraced and exulted over an indisputably American product. Mark Twain received a welcome due only the most celebrated men of letters, which convinced some people back home to reconsider his value.

Sam noticed this difference. Time and again he found himself singularly celebrated. He attended "the great dinner given by the new Sheriffs of London to the several guilds & liverymen of London," an event that attracted an impressive list of dignitaries, whose names were read off and applauded during dinner. Engaged in conversation, Sam clapped ritually with the others during a massive storm of adulation that interrupted the flow of names. He asked his neighbor, "Whose name was that we were just applauding?" Came the inevitable answer: "Mark Twain's." Leaving out the embarrassment, Sam wrote Livy of his reception, "I did not know I was a lion." He compared his reception with that given almost simultaneously to another American, Henry Stanley, recently returned from his legendary trek into the heart of Africa where he found the lost Dr. David Livingstone. The Royal Geographic Society disputed the validity of his claim, but after Livingstone's family testified for him, Stanley received thanks directly from Queen Victoria. Still, he refused to forgive his detractors, even when the Royal Geographic Society gave a dinner in his honor. Sam felt relief that the ungrateful Stanley wasn't born in America, "though indeed he *must* have learned his puppyism with us." Ten days after arriving in London he wrote Livy, "I would rather live in England than America—which is treason."

Sam embraced the English as assiduously as they embraced him. Always susceptible to slang, he picked up Britishisms indiscriminately and his letters to Livy displayed his new argot, including "welly-well-well," "jolly," and "whereby." Sam's interest in British medieval history received a boost when he dined "with a splendid fox-hunting squire named Broom," who was a Plantagenet, descended from kings. "[I]t had all the seeming of hob-nobbing with the Black Prince in the flesh!—for this fellow is of princely presence & manners, & 35 years old." English gentleman-liness charmed Sam, whose rough frontier manners had long since given way to those of the American bourgeois, which in turn worshiped the courtly assurance of the British Empire.

In the social whirl, Sam gave up taking notes, though he had not put much effort into a book on England, other than writing Livy letters of his triumphs and social engagements. His primary work in London was defending the Routledges' right to publish his writing. He composed three vituperative excoriations of John Camden Hotten, but printed only the mildest, in which he called the pirate "John Camden Hottentot," and noted that "publishers are not accountable to the laws of heaven or earth in any country, as I understand it." An unpublished version berated Hotten as malignancy itself, with "only a 'fatty degeneration' where his heart ought to be, and a hole in the place where other people carry a conscience." Despite these exercises in defamation, Sam actually respected Hotten's editorial judgment; he used Hotten's versions of some of his own sketches while preparing Routledge's forthcoming official edition of them. In the newspaper battle, however, Hotten remained an unredeemed pirate of Mark Twain's authorial rights, a position Sam maintained publicly essentially because the Routledge clan had agreed to pay him a royalty, though they were not bound to do so. With no legal protection for Mark Twain in England, Sam could make no sounder deal.

Perhaps Sam reached a parallel conclusion about his more private relationships as well: Since he could not achieve complete union with Livy, it would be better to accept whatever she would give him. Compromising to save his marriage, he came to terms with Livy across the water. In November 1872, he wrote his mother and sister, "Livy is willing to come here with me next April and stay several months—so I am going home next Tuesday" to spend the winter together and prepare for their journey. Sam also issued invitations to join the English adventure to Susan and Theodore Crane and to Mary Fairbanks, in order to buffer his relationship

This is the earliest known photograph of Samuel Langhorne Clemens, taken when he was fifteen and working as a printer's apprentice. The image is inverted so that the typeface he holds in his hand reads correctly. *Reprinted by permission of the Mark Twain Papers, Bancroft Library, University of California, Berkeley.*

Clemens cut a dashing figure in the wheelhouse of a steamboat, even when he was still a lowly steersman, the job he had when this picture was taken. He was always vain about his hair and preferred it wild and luxuriant but carefully groomed. Later in his life, when he could afford it, he had a barber come to his house every morning. *Reprinted by permission of the Mark Twain House, Hartford, CT.*

Sam Clemens' brother, Orion, ten years his senior, became Sam's guardian after the death of John Clemens. Orion, similar in temperament to their hapless father, was the target of Sam's ambivalence and resentment of authority, just as their father had been. *Reprinted by permission of the Mark Twain Papers, Bancroft Library, University of California, Berkeley.*

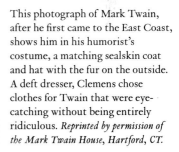

This photograph of Mark Twain, after he first came to the East Coast, shows him in his humorist's costume, a matching sealskin coat and hat with the fur on the outside. A deft dresser, Clemens chose clothes for Twain that were eye-catching without being entirely ridiculous. *Reprinted by permission of the Mark Twain House, Hartford, CT.*

This is possibly how Sam Clemens first saw Livy Langdon's face, in an ivory miniature her brother Charlie carried with him on the *Quaker City* tour. Sam later claimed to have fallen in love with Livy via this picture while sailing off the coast of Turkey in the Mediterranean Sea. *Reprinted by permission of the Mark Twain Papers, Bancroft Library, University of California, Berkeley.*

When Sam met Livy (*center back*) she was a serious student who sometimes read with a group of young women when her health prevented her from attending class. Here she is surrounded by her closest friends (*left to right*) Alice Hooker, Alice Spaulding, Emma Nye, Clara Spaulding, and Mary Nye. *Reprinted by permission of the Mark Twain House, Hartford, CT.*

Sam and Livy built this house on a promontory in Hartford, Connecticut, within five years of their 1870 marriage. Taken from Farmington Avenue, this photograph captures the splendor that made this mansion a landmark in Hartford. In the early 1880s, the Clemenses expanded the servants' wing (*far right*). *Reprinted by permission of the Mark Twain House, Hartford, CT.*

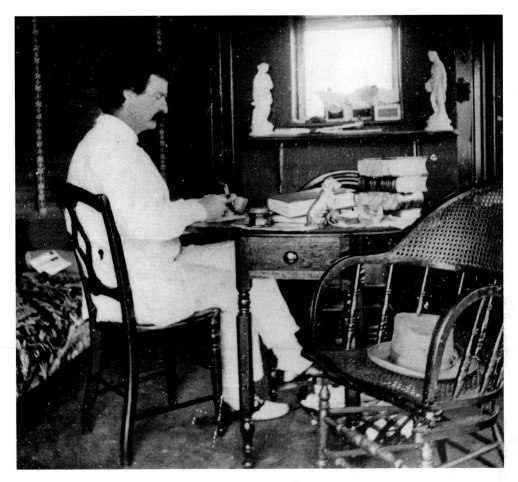

While the Hartford house was under construction, Livy's sister, Susan Crane, commissioned an octagonal study to be built for her brother-in-law on a hill above Quarry Farm, the Cranes' Elmira house and the Clemenses' summer retreat. The window above the fireplace is a motif copied from the plans for the Hartford house. This study was the site of Clemens' most productive writing. *Reprinted by permission of the Mark Twain House, Hartford, CT.*

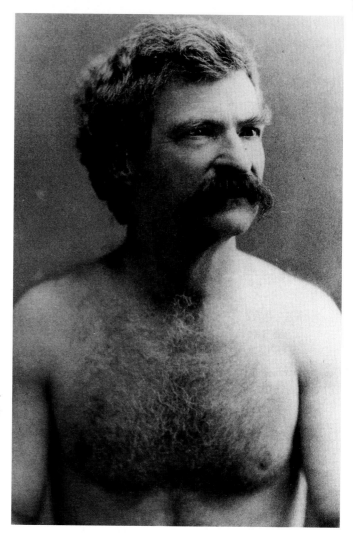

Beneath his bushy mustache Clemens is smiling at some long-lost joke made during the taking of this photograph in the 1880s when he was near fifty. He ate very little and gained barely an ounce between his youth and death. *Reprinted by permission of the Mark Twain Papers, Bancroft Library, University of California, Berkeley.*

Livy with (*left to right*) Susy, age twelve, Clara, age ten, and Jean, age four, in 1884. Clemens was a mostly absent father during this period, beginning with his attention to the publication of *Adventures of Huckleberry Finn* by Charles L. Webster and Co., continuing through his tour in support of the book, and concluding with the massive publication of Ulysses S. Grant's *Memoirs. Reprinted by permission of the Mark Twain House, Hartford, CT.*

Clemens towers over the diminutive George Washington Cable in this photograph promoting the 1884–1885 Twins of Genius tour. While the tour brought popular attention to *Huck Finn*, it also allowed Clemens to proclaim Mark Twain's radical position on race through his association with Cable, acknowledged as one of the most progressive men of the era. *Reprinted by permission of the Mark Twain House, Hartford, CT.*

Charles Luther Webster, shown here at the pinnacle of his career, led a life worthy of a book
by Clemens, his famous uncle by marriage: Having accidentally killed a neighbor child, he went
on to become a con man and publisher. He married Clemens' favorite niece, Annie Moffett,
in 1875, and became his uncle-in-law's mortal enemy before dying at age thirty-nine. *Reprinted
by permission of the Mark Twain Papers, Bancroft Library, University of California, Berkeley.*

with Livy with a circle of adult companions. Sam sailed November 12, 1872, in excited anticipation of his reunion with Livy and the Muggins, as he called his infant daughter Susie. His infectious excitement at discovering England hit the right note for rapprochement with Livy and the restrictions of family life. Livy, too, had grown more bold socially during Sam's absence, spending time with her mother and with Susan Warner, Harmony Twichell, and other members of the Monday Evening Club's auxiliary.

The greatest satisfaction Sam derived from the trip was the respect shown Mark Twain.

> [I]t was flattering, at the Lord Mayor's dinner, tonight, to have the nation's honored favorite, the Lord High Chancellor of England, in his vast wig & gown, with a splendid, sword-bearing lackey, following him & holding up his train, walk me arm-in-arm through the brilliant assemblage, & welcome me with all the enthusiasm of a girl, & tell me that when affairs of state oppress him & he can't sleep, he always has my books at hand & forgets his perplexities in reading them!

While such adulation for Mark Twain did not make the chronically uncertain Sam Clemens any more secure, it did embolden Sam's faith in the power of his persona, who not only outsold Bret Harte, but also enjoyed a firmer reputation. If hallowed Britain adored Mark Twain, why should Sam accept snubs from literary Boston?

By the time Sam reached Hartford, a dramatic scandal had provoked a gale of gossip at Nook Farm. The Reverend Henry Ward Beecher, it was reported, had had an affair with Elizabeth Tilton, the wife of one of his leading parishioners. First to speak about the famous minister's conduct was Victoria Woodhull, the notorious free-love suffragist running an independent campaign for President of the United States, charging Beecher with hypocrisy during a speech at a September convention of spiritualists. Printed reports appeared in *Woodhull and Claflin's Weekly*, Woodhull's politically progressive investment newsletter, in November 1872, although rumors of Beecher's affair had echoed in the ears of women's rights activists for over a year already. Victoria Woodhull's exposé on the scandal resulted in her arrest for obscenity. Copies of the issue containing the allegation soon sold for as much as forty dollars. Beecher, Lib Tilton, and her husband Theodore maintained silence on the matter, but Nook Farm's Isabella Beecher Hooker could not keep her peace. She tried to get her brother to advocate free love, which would at least mitigate the shame of his hypocrisy, but he could not risk alienating his following with so radical an opinion.

Isabella Hooker's belief that her brother had slept with Lib Tilton split the Nook Farm community. Her sisters, Harriet Stowe and Mary Perkins, rose to their brother's defense, while Thomas Beecher, Livy's Elmira pastor, wrote Isabella, "In my judgment, Henry is following his slippery doctrines of expediency." Sam had the inventive interpretation that he, along with the rest of the American public, were victims of the scandal. He wrote his mother-in-law:

> Whoever feels uncertain about the truth or falsehood of those slanders (& I would extremely like to know who feels certain) is suffering shame & defilement, & is continuing to carry a filthy subject in his mind, to his further defilement, when possibly the Beecher party are all the while able to sweep away his doubts & purify his mind with a breath. *I* think the silence of the Beechers is a hundred fold more of an *obscene publication* than that of the Woodhulls.*

But Sam was also a beneficiary of the hubbub. Isabella Hooker's public condemnation of her famous brother effectively ended the Hookers' dominance at Nook Farm. By forcing her neighbors to choose sides—those who would admit her to their homes and those who would not—Hooker turned the national scandal into a Nook Farm family quarrel.

From their place in the Hooker home, the Clemenses used this social disarray to assume some of the prerogatives of leadership that the Hookers had surrendered. While not wholly recovered from the death of Langdon, Livy enjoyed Susie and relished a return to balance with Sam. For himself, Sam began to rethink both the private and public men he had become. The Sam Clemens who had so easily gained the smoky and drunken confidences of men out west seemed inappropriate to the family-centered, intellectually driven, moneyed world of Nook Farm. Sam needed to become a gentleman, akin to the British style he had so admired in the wealthy country homes. He adopted the essential Hartford outlook of a forward-thinking conservative, for example contributing to the Monday Evening Club an argument against a reckless freedom of the press. He even chose a name for this social identity: S. L. Clemens.

Absorbed in the communal life of Nook Farm, hosting parties, and embracing his role as paterfamilias, he took steps to make Hartford his permanent home. Sam and Livy bought a prominent lot at the crest of a hill on Farmington Avenue, the main road leading west from the center of Hartford. This lot, including several acres, bordered on a stream, "traditionally called the Hog or Meandering Swine but variously renamed by the genteel as the Riveret, Little, Woods, or Park River," to the banks of which the land fell steeply from the east. Approaching Hartford along Farmington Avenue, travelers could see nothing of the city until topping this rise, so it gave the Clemenses a view of both Hartford and farmland. Livy sketched a layout for the house, though her enthusiasm for the project dimmed in light of the price of the land itself, more than $30,000. Sam, however, allowed no monetary concerns to obstruct his move into the landed gentry. Livy wrote to Sue Crane, "Mr. Clemens seems to glory in his sense of possession; he goes daily into the lot, has had several falls trying to lay off the land by sliding around on his feet."

Lilly and George Warner recommended their architect, Edward Tuckerman Potter, whose approach matched Livy's and Sam's sensibilities perfectly. Born into a legacy of Episcopal bishops, Potter had specialized early in his career in designing churches, and he had a knack for investing his projects with a conscientious solidity. He took Livy's sketches of her ideal layout and converted them into an unusual but magical floor plan, spacious and intimate at the same time. Knowing that the Clemenses intended to leave for several months in mid-May, Potter worked quickly to produce plans and sketches his clients could approve before their departure. Sam had little interest in the interior, as long as it satisfied Livy's sense of luxury, but he wanted a stone or brick structure that was modern looking, though not so inventive as to invite ridicule. Sam could suit S. L. Clemens to any image of Victorian wealth inside the house, but he wanted the outside to say something about Mark Twain: It had to be grand, durable, fanciful, extraordinary.

To make him worthy of so grand a mansion, Sam embarked on a campaign to gain Mark Twain the same literary reputation at home as he possessed in England. Frustrated that Elisha Bliss had not distributed copies of *Roughing It* to the press, Sam wrote John Hay, an old friend now working for Whitelaw Reid's *New York Tribune*, encouraging him to belatedly review the book. Aware that the literary Brahmins of Boston respected fiction much more than Mark Twain's sort of popular personal narratives, Sam dove into writing a novel of a boy growing up in a Mississippi River village in 1840s Missouri. He rooted his narrative in the reminiscences unearthed by the childhood friends with whom he had become reacquainted while on tour, transforming the manuscript burlesquing romance that he had begun during his courtship into a soothing nostalgia. The novel also converted his early memories into a metaphor of his more recent experience. The main character came from a fractured family; he witnesses a death, a murder in a graveyard; he escapes to an island, where he has nothing but high times; then he returns home triumphant, in the middle of his own funeral, reborn. Sam masked the current elements of his own life—Langdon's death, the break with Livy, his escape to England, and his return home determined to remake himself—into the plot of *The Adventures of Tom Sawyer*.

Sam's work on this book suffered many interruptions due to his myriad projects. Dan Slote's company had made a great success of the Mark Twain Scrap Book. The death of King Kamehameha V revived interest in the Sandwich Islands, then facing annexation as a United States territory, a move Mark Twain now publicly protested on the premise that Americans would simply poison the place. Public acclaim for his articles about Hawaii induced Sam to revive Mark Twain's old lecture on the subject, which he delivered three times in New York City. As a result of these presentations, incredible lecture offers seduced him away from work a few days at a time. He also traveled to Boston regularly to see William Dean Howells and Thomas Bailey Aldrich, ingratiating himself with the nation's literary taste-makers. He extended himself on behalf of the needy, speaking to benefit charities and listening to appeals for various causes. People sometimes called on him with no other agenda than to spend the afternoon with a famous man.

On one of these occasions, Livy, unhappily deprived of Sam's company, wrote her mother, "I should like to put my head in your lap and cry just a little bit. . . . I have four servants to manage, I have a glorious husband to try and be a woman for, but sometimes I would like to lie down and give it all up—I feel so incompetent for anything."* In her darker moods, Livy felt unequal to her role as wife of Mark Twain, though friends always praised her grace and capacity in handling her responsibilities and Sam cherished her as his editor and manager. She coached him constantly on the construction of his public self, vetoing several proposals for him to lecture, not only to get him to focus on writing, but also to keep him home. Sam "knows that he will make more in the long run by writing than by lecturing, but it is a great temptation to him when they offer him such enormous prices," Livy noted to her mother. "It is splendid to see him so heartily love his work, he begrudges every moments interruption."*

One evening that winter, Livy also fulfilled the more traditional nineteenth-century woman's role: that of muse. Over dinner with Charles Dudley and Susan Warner, the men berated the novels their wives read for entertainment. The women responded by challenging the men to do better. Accepting the challenge, the men outlined a plot. Sam dropped his

Mississippi River boy's story and swung into the new project full steam ahead. In a week-long burst of creativity, he produced the first fifth of the novel, eleven chapters concerning a family named Hawkins, which, like his, had moved to Missouri and gone broke. The father dies in debt, except for a mass of property in the hills of Tennessee. An uncle, Colonel Eschol Sellers, convinces the children to adopt his plan for the Tennessee land as a site for a federally funded technical school for liberated slaves.

Warner then took over, composing a more conventional narrative concerning incipient romances, stock characters, and a villainous seduction and abandonment of the beautiful Laura Hawkins, named for his first Hannibal sweetheart. When Sam got her back, he revived her as the heartless essence of ambition. As the two men wrote, the news of the day supplied material for the plot. When Senator Samuel Pomeroy of Kansas attempted to bribe his state legislature to reelect him, Sam, employing his own special knowledge of Washington life, re-created him as Senator Dilworthy. Brokenhearted Laura Hawkins rises as Dilworthy's icy dealmaker, pushing to pass a bill founding the technical college on her family's land. Only slightly recast and renamed, portraits of other leading real-life politicos filled Sam's pages. Laura and her uncle's scheme to use Congress to convert their useless land into a fortune became a savage satire of American political corruption and an indictment of our debased democratic process.

Warner struggled to keep up with Sam, but his stale story line interacted only incidentally with the Washington narrative; his conventionally plotted tale of frustrated love had only a female doctor and an Amish setting to give it spice. Mark Twain's muscular and immediate language easily overmatched Warner's delicate, distant prose. Despite their differences, however, the men quickly piled up the necessary pages. Together they read their drafts to their wives, who settled disputes by voting for one man's narrative over the other's. In three months, *The Gilded Age* was ready for the press.

Sam's uneasiness about writing a novel had two root causes. First, in spite of the beginning he had made on what would become *Tom Sawyer*, he did not believe he had the capacity to compose a compelling fictional narrative, not without demolishing the drama with some wholly inappropriate and destructive humorous passages. Having Warner as his coauthor answered these doubts; Warner could provide plot elements when Sam got stuck and could rein Sam in when he turned antic. Second, Sam worried about how such a book would affect the relationship between Mark Twain and his audience. Would the people who read *Roughing It* also read *The Gilded Age*? Would the publication of this book lose his audience not only for his backlist but also for more traditional Mark Twain narratives? Fans of his shorter work accepted Mark Twain's satirical edge; they would appreciate a roman à clef of Washington that combined the witty critical tone of *Innocents Abroad* with the domestic subject matter of *Roughing It*. The sentimental features of the narrative, however, might well seem ridiculous coming from Mark Twain. When Laura murders the man who ruined her, the trial exposes her political machinations, and her shame kills her. Wouldn't readers take the whole thing as Twainian satire and simply laugh? Sam also fretted that the reading audience would not distinguish chapters written by Charles Dudley Warner from those composed by Mark Twain. Warner's literary persona might muddy the image of Mark Twain that Sam had worked so hard to develop. Sam shelved these concerns for the probable profit, in both money and reputation, the novel would generate.

The two writers took the manuscript to Elisha Bliss, who accepted the project in the hope that the combined reputations of Warner and Twain would at least repay the expense of production. Sam's growing influence as a director of the American Publishing Company encouraged Bliss to make the company the first subscription house to issue a novel, but Bliss took advantage of Sam's business ineptitude by writing a new 10 percent royalty contract for *The Gilded Age*. Sam would have been wiser to convert one of the two contracts Bliss already had in his files, in particular the diamond-mine book, which could never be written: Riley, Sam's deputy in South Africa, had died before Sam found time to debrief him. Ignorantly prolonging his obligation to Bliss, Sam instead focused his attention on getting the great caricaturist Thomas Nast to illustrate *The Gilded Age*. In order to obtain a better deal from Bliss, he threatened to publish the novel with Isaac Sheldon as a trade book, but since his boat was leaving for England on May 17, Sam had no time to negotiate. Warner accepted responsibility for seeing *The Gilded Age* through publication in the States, and Sam would carry the manuscript to England to secure the prior publication necessary for a valid English copyright.

Sam shifted his focus from production to promotion, getting Whitelaw Reid to print an advance notice of the novel in his *Tribune*. Sam then complained that Reid's offhand notice "carries the impression to the minds of other editors that we are people of small consequence in the literary world, & indeed only triflers; that a novel by us is in no sense a literary event."* He asked Reid first to follow up with a more ringing announcement, and then to let their mutual friend Ned House review the book. Reid grudgingly obliged the first request, but he refused the second, on the principle that no good newspaper should publish a book review by a friend of the author. Reid abused Sam to House, who gleefully passed along some of the editor's comments.

Turning over responsibility for the construction of the new house to his lawyer Charles Perkins, Sam spent a few days in Elmira before returning to New York City. In a busy week, he met with his architect and builder, and enjoyed a quick visit with Mother Fairbanks (on the East Coast to visit her children). Then, in a brash defense of his Mark Twain persona, he initiated a $20,000 lawsuit against a publisher who had promoted a miscellany containing some early Twain material by using his pseudonym. Sam sued not for infringement of copyright, because the published material had none, but for trademark infringement. The idea that a nom de plume might be a trademark had never been tested and this case proved a swift success. Sam had demonstrated he had a proprietary interest in his invented persona to the satisfaction of the judge, who granted an injunction. This pioneering interest in the trademark status of an artist's name continues to bear fruit a century later, as prominent pop music stars register their names as trademarks.

He assembled his cohort, including Susie, her nurse Nellie, Livy, Livy's friend Clara Spaulding, and a theology student Sam hired as a shorthand secretary, and they set sail again for England. If anything, the British reception for Mark Twain this time around proved even warmer and more enthusiastic. After a few days in a quiet London hotel that Livy preferred, Sam moved his family to a suite of rooms at the more public Langham. A six-week parade of dignitaries and dinners kept the whole family in a social tumult. Sam dined with novelists Anthony Trollope and Wilkie Collins, social theorist Herbert Spencer, and others. All of literary London turned out to meet Mark Twain and secure his company for a meal or an overnight at one country estate or another.

Sam ran around town with fellow San Francisco Bohemian Joaquin Miller, who gave fifteen-month-old Susie a new nickname, the Modoc, based on his recently published *Unwritten History*, a fictionalized version of his adventures among the Modoc Indians; the toddler's hair and behavior reminded Miller of his Native American friends. Sam attended the races at Ascot, frequented the affairs of the rich and influential, and became a visiting member of the Athenaeum Club. Both he and Livy were overwhelmed by the attention. Sam wrote to Mother Fairbanks, "Tomorrow night I am to meet two or three of England's great men—& I find that the *really* great ones are very easy to get along with, even when hampered with titles. But I will confess that mediocrity with a title is (to me) a formidable thing to encounter—*it* don't talk, & I'm afraid to." Miller concurred, calling Sam "shy as a girl . . . and could hardly be coaxed to meet the learned and great who wanted to take him by the hand." He had not suffered from shyness during his first visit, but this time Livy was watching him perform. In their lives together, Livy had seen him on the platform as Mark Twain and seen him at home as Sam. She had not yet seen his new hybrid—S. L. Clemens, gentleman, a sort of Mark Twain dressed up for the society pages—and he was reticent to parade this new invention in front of her.

Sam's experiment with having a secretary failed; by the middle of July, Sam released him. Only after he had set aside any expectation of writing did Sam begin touring Great Britain with energy. Accompanied by Livy when she felt fit, he went to all the tourist spots in London. Sam especially enjoyed attractions relating to the tortuous history of British royalty and nobility, a history that continued while the Clemenses were in England when a man named Arthur Orton, a cockney butcher, claimed in court to be Roger Tichborne, the long-missing heir to a title and a fortune. Since family legend linked Jane Clemens' family, the Lamptons, to the Lambtons who had held the earldom of Durham, the Tichborne case gave Sam a chance to see a familial claim to nobility, similar to his own, undergo a test by British justice. In mid-July, Sam and Livy left London to tour Ireland and Scotland. Sam loved the palpable sense of history in York, from the half-timbered houses harking back to Queen Elizabeth's reign to "the melancholy old stone coffins and sculptured inscriptions, a venerable arch and a hoary tower of stone" dating from the Roman occupation a millennium and a half before that. In Edinburgh, the Clemenses befriended Dr. John Brown, whose sentimental dog-story, *Rab and His Friend*, enjoyed enormous popularity with both children and adults. Brown, a bachelor physician, romped for hours at a time with Susie, whom he dubbed Megalopis, for her large eyes. They spent a month in Scotland and two weeks in Ireland before returning to London. Their journey was as joyful as it was pleasant; by the time they reached London, Livy was again pregnant.

Once in London, business affairs claimed much of Sam's attention. What would be named the Panic of 1873 had hit the United States, caused primarily by the collapse of Jay Cooke's banking house, which had speculated heavily in western railroads. Money suddenly became scarce and expensive, especially for Americans abroad. Sam spent a few sleepless nights before ascertaining that he was still solvent, but months would pass before he and Livy could learn how the Panic affected the Langdon business interests. Fearful that they would not have enough money in England to pay the prodigious debts they had amassed, Sam consented to a lecture tour. Also, though the death in June of John Camden Hotten cooperated with Sam's resolve to prevent British piracy of *The Gilded Age*, difficulty back in Hartford threatened Sam's plan for prior publication of the novel in England. Typically slow, Bliss neglected to send proof sheets as they became ready, stringing book production through the fall. Since Sam had a copy of the manuscript, he knew Routledge could secure his copyright by issuing a book without illustrations at any time, but at the cost of transatlantic coordination of the novel's release.

By October, when Sam signed his contract with Routledge, Livy was "blue and cross and homesick. I suppose what makes me feel the latter is because we are contemplating to stay in London another *month*." Balancing Livy's homesickness and his need to be in England when Routledge published *The Gilded Age*, Sam decided to split his lecture series into two parts, with a week of shows to excite public appetite and then a longer engagement after taking Livy home. The prospect of a long lecture engagement without Livy became more pleasant when Charles Warren Stoddard, another San Francisco Bohemian, surfaced in London to see to the publication of his *South Sea Idyls*, a collection of travel essays rich with strong, if subtle, homosexual themes. Sam asked Stoddard to share his hotel rooms and play secretary for him when he would return to London in November. Stoddard, perpetually at loose ends and short of cash, agreed.

The first week of London lectures went better than Sam could have hoped. He chose to deliver his reliable workhorse, the Sandwich Island lecture, which he promoted a week before the opening with another humorous Mark Twain letter in a popular paper. His promoter took a risk in booking the high-society Queen's Concert Rooms in Hanover Square instead of a more popular outlet, but Sam felt confident that the elite would pay the higher prices to see him in that environment. Mark Twain's languid English irritated some upper-class Londoners, but the elegant audiences and perceptive critics soon turned Mark Twain into a sellout. The *Spectator* analyzed him, saying that "the unconscious, matter-of-fact way in which he habitually strikes false intellectual notes, the steady simplicity with which he puts the emphasis of feeling in the wrong place, [and] with which he classified in the most unassuming way, as families of the same tribe of things, the most irreconcilable of common nouns" made his humor irresistible. The same techniques that made Mark Twain so effective in the United States assured his success in England. He lectured in Liverpool before boarding the *Batavia*, bound for New York, with Livy, the Modoc, the nurse Nellie, and Clara Spaulding.

Sam stayed in America only six days, during which time he saw his brother, now just scraping by setting type at a New York daily. He "meant to make a proposition to Orion in New York, but was hurried and lost the opportunity." He wrote his mother that "if he will live in Fredonia & will make no effort to leave there, I will pay him a pension of $15 a week." Though Sam regarded his proposition as "kindly meant, as from brother to brother, & is simply a plain unvarnished common-sense view of the situation,"* his brother, mother, and sister did not agree. What Sam saw as generosity to his hapless brother, the rest of his family took as paternalistic gloating over the disparity in the siblings' levels of success; the majority view of the matter was the more accurate.

Sam reboarded the *Batavia* to return to his interrupted lecture series, moving into the Langham with Charley Stoddard ten days before his lectures resumed on December 1, 1873. In London, Sam ignored demands for his company, instead spending his time with Stoddard, the publication of whose *South Sea Idyls* caused a small stir. Critics praised his blend of Romanticism and modernistic invention, rarely referring to the erotic underpinning that made the collection infamous. Although his biographer assumes that he engaged in full sexual relationships with men, Stoddard's endless flirtation with a religious life implies that he sought in his male friendships the sort of spiritual oneness he desired with Christ. His weeks in England with Sam left only scant evidence as to the nature of the bond.

In any case, as Sam's secretary, Stoddard had nothing to do other than penning a few letters from Sam's dictation and keeping a scrapbook of the Tichborne claimant trial. His primary job was to keep Sam company. "We talked and talked and talked," Stoddard wrote a friend. "He saw few people; he was nervous and ill and irritable, and no one suited him but me, and sometimes I didn't exactly suit. But we were together night and day, and we went deep into each other's lives." Sam and Stoddard settled into a pleasant routine, rising about noon to read their mail and eat a hearty breakfast in their rooms, then spending the afternoon out walking and taking care of business. Sometimes when they returned to the Langham, Sam would play the piano and sing spirituals, always his favorite music. At seven-thirty, they repaired to Hanover Square, where Charley counted the gleaming carriages at the window and Sam paced nervously. After the performance, Stoddard joined Sam's crowd of admirers in the greenroom for a social hour until the promoter accompanied the two of them to their rooms. The three would swap stories until midnight and then Sam and Charley would talk a few hours more. The lectures themselves went extremely well. Mark Twain completed his London run on December 20, 1873, and would have taken his show to Glasgow, Edinburgh, and elsewhere, but there were no theaters large enough to make the tour pay. Sam spent two weeks rambling around London and the countryside with Stoddard before giving three more lectures, in Leicester and in Liverpool.

The appearance of *The Gilded Age* in England produced much less excitement than Sam expected, given the enthusiasm for his presence and persona. Despite Mark Twain's introduction to the British edition, intended to bridge the cultural gap, the satire of American life left most British readers mystified. The novel sold fewer than ten thousand copies in an inexpensive edition. In America, however, the book took off on the strength of the authors' names and the barely disguised caricatures of public figures. Early sales averaged almost twelve thousand copies a month. Even the advent of an actual inventor-speculator named Eschol Sellers, who gently requested the name of Laura's uncle in the book be changed in all future printings, could not quell Sam's happiness. American sales eased Sam's displeasure with the limited demand for the novel in England, as did his satisfaction that, despite the difficulties of coordinating publication across an ocean, the Routledge edition had appeared first, securing a British copyright he hoped would handcuff the Canadian pirates. He read the novel again and liked it, or part of it anyway. When Mother Fairbanks responded tepidly to the book, he answered, "That's because you've been reading *Warner's* chapters." Listing his own contributions, he told her, "You read *those!*"

Although his stay in London was both a pleasure and a success, Sam missed Livy more than he had expected. They had rediscovered their love for one another, traveling together for four months in the summer. Whatever pleasure Sam got from his companionship with Charley Stoddard, he found himself craving Livy's company, too. His letters home, almost devoid of news, gushed with affection. He wrote on December 11, "If I'm not homesick to see you, no other lover ever *was* homesick to see his sweetheart." The next day he told her how much more he would enjoy the applause if only he could share it with her. He expressed his sexual desire more frankly than ever, avowing "I do *love* you, Livy darling, & my last word is (when I come) 'Expedition's the word!'" Apologizing for his earlier reticence, he wrote, "You must forgive me for not talking all I feel when I am at home, honey, I *do* feel it, even if I don't talk it. Will you remember that?" Two weeks later he confessed: "I am not demonstrative, except at intervals—but I *always* love you—always admire you—am always your champion."

Sam and Livy had difficulty bringing into harmony their different capacities for displaying physical affection, formed by the ways they were raised. The Clemens household seldom hugged and never kissed, and Sam always flinched at friendly touching. He simply could not bear to be touched by strangers; even close friends kept a physical distance. But Livy showered Sam with kisses, pets, and hugs; the Langdons all hugged and kissed in greeting and parting and relished displays of affection. Though he appreciated his friendship with Charley Stoddard, Sam's time in the company of such an effete and religious man made him pine for Livy's warm-bloodedness. Sam wrote ten days before he left for home, "Stoddard & I have been talking & keeping a lonely vigil for hours—but I won't talk of it any more. It is *so* unsatisfying. I want *you*—& nobody else. I do love you so."

After his final lecture in Liverpool, Sam stayed up all night with Stoddard, who later recalled that "his last words were, that if ever he got down in the world—which Heaven forbid—he would probably have to teach elocution; but this was at five o'clock in the morning." He presented Charley with his notes for his Nevada lecture, a small card with hiero-glyphic drawings which reminded Sam of the order of his anecdotes. Sam signed it "Mark Twain" and scribbled on it, "We're done with *this*, Charles, forever!" a note referring ambiguously to either the lecture or the relationship with Charley Stoddard. Stoddard felt bereft. He wrote Sam from Venice several months later, "The day I left you in Liverpool I took the ferry for New Brighton and saw you go out to sea with a strange mingling of pleasure and regret: You had been longing so for Home that I rejoiced when I saw you actually on your way; but my life had to begin all over again. It seems to me that I am always doing that sort of thing; I get just so far and then somebody or something rubs it all out." After a few hours' sleep, Sam boarded his ship and was gone, his last bohemian interval completed.

| A Man of Parts

> *I have no special regard for Satan; but I can at least
> claim that I have no prejudice against him. . . . A person
> who has for untold centuries maintained the imposing
> position of spiritual head of four-fifths of the human race,
> and political head of the whole of it, must be granted the
> possession of executive abilities of the highest order.*
> —"Concerning the Jews" (1899)

"IF THERE IS one individual creature on all this foot-stool who is more thoroughly and uniformly and unceasingly *happy* than I am I defy the world to produce him and *prove* him," Sam wrote to his Edinburgh friend, Dr. Brown. "I was a mighty rough, coarse, unpromising subject when Livy took charge of me 4 years ago, and I may *still* be, to the rest of the world, but not to her." With *The Gilded Age* promising to outsell both *Innocents* and *Roughing It*, and his castle atop a hill under construction a hundred yards away from the Hooker house, where he and Livy and the Modoc lived in luxury, Sam felt himself climbing. The declines of his brother Orion and of Bret Harte, while sad, gave him confidence in his more abiding glory. Wanting to capitalize on *The Gilded Age*, Sam yielded to James Redpath's urgings that he lecture. He soon regretted his decision and in the end delivered the "Roughing It" lecture only once, in Boston, selecting that city partly because it had suffered patiently through his Artemus Ward piece during the last tour, and partly because he longed for another foray into that literary fortress. Sam and Warner invited William Dean Howells, Thomas Bailey Aldrich, and James Osgood to visit. After Sam's March 5 lecture, he escorted Howells, Aldrich, and Aldrich's wife to Hartford.

Howells described the Clemenses' existence in Nook Farm as "quite an ideal life. They live very near each other, in a sort of suburban grove, and their neighbors are the Stowes and Hookers, and a great many delightful people." He wrote a friend, "They go in and out of each other's houses without ringing, and nobody gets more than the first syllable of his first name—they call their minister *Joe* Twichell." Sam impressed his literary visitors with a stellar display of both his personal charm and his wanton disregard for social convention. He evened the score with Lillian Aldrich for her unwillingness to serve him dinner a few years before by telling her husband that the noise the Aldriches made in the night disturbed Livy, who—six months pregnant and liable to a headache—needed her rest. Sheepishly begging Livy's pardon at breakfast, the Aldriches were dumbfounded when Livy said she had no headache, slept well, and couldn't have heard them from their room if she tried. One evening, Sam regaled the company with spirituals and then left the party to get more beer from a tavern. He came home with neither the beer nor his sealskin hat, so he sent the butler out to retrieve them. Donning a pair of hairy black-and-white moccasins, he mimicked an old Negro dancer until Livy stopped him with a cry of "Oh, Youth!" He behaved like a wild boy playing a civilized, immensely generous grown-up.

What Howells recalled most acutely of his visit, however, was "the satisfying, the surfeiting nature of subscription publication." Sam "lectured Aldrich and me on the folly of that mode of publication in the trade which we had thought it the highest success to achieve a chance in. 'Anything but subscription publication is printing for private circulation,' he maintained." Aldrich and Howells had reached the top of the American literary pyramid through their association with the Boston Brahmins and the houses that published such people, yet they still had to economize by walking instead of taking public transportation. Mark Twain and Charles Dudley Warner, both fine and accomplished craftsmen though they lacked the cachet of acceptance by the Boston literati, earned startling amounts of money. Their collaborative novel had earned each man nearly $10,000 in three months, without any notice by Howells in *The Atlantic*. Sam resolved to gain literary acceptance not by supplicating Howells and Aldrich directly for it, but by converting their values, beguiling them away from an idolatry of the literary tradition to an idolatry of lucre.

If Sam's talk persuaded them halfway to the virtues of subscription publishing, his new house awoke in them a covetous greed that brought them closer to desiring his kind of success. None of the Nook Farm houses competed with the Newport and Hudson River palaces then being constructed by the era's great fortune-makers, the industrial robber-barons, but they were lavish homes. The Clemenses' yet-unfinished house, its nearly twenty rooms and five modern bathrooms occupying Nook Farm's most prominent spot, redefined the Bostonians' notions of a family home. Edward Potter had designed a wild yet solid exterior, an exuberance of turrets, balconies, woodwork, and brick which gave the house a look both overblown and graceful. It was rapidly becoming a Hartford landmark; a drawing of the new house had already appeared in a design magazine. Eager for Howells' good opinion after his visit to Hartford, Sam wrote him that there was a Nook Farm house for sale at reasonable terms: "You or Aldrich or both of you must come to Hartford to live." If Howells and Aldrich regarded the mansion with envy, Sam looked on it with glee, an emotion Livy shared but mitigated with some anxiety over its cost.

Soon after the visitors left, Livy had a miscarriage scare and took to her bed. It had been a stressful winter for her, awaiting Sam's return and then falling in with the feverish activity that always accompanied him. The departure of nurse Nellie relieved Livy of one source of tension; at least she didn't have to fire her for her disrespectful attitude. The new nurse, a German woman named Rosina Hay, not only handled the Modoc better, but could help Livy with her German lessons. A brief visit by Mary Fairbanks—her first look at Susie, her "grandchild"—helped break the tedium of confinement. Sam proved to his second mother what he had written her a few weeks before: "I am the busiest white man in America— & much the happiest." He was simultaneously working on two books and two plays—including a burlesque of *Hamlet* in which a modern character comments on the actions around him, an idea Sam forwarded to the eminent actor Edwin Booth after he'd seen his production a few months before. Fairbanks' only serious concern was that her cub had no private place to write. After Fairbanks' departure, Livy undertook to remedy this situation by setting aside a little nook, but Sam had no use for her arrangement. "Since that day I have gone back to precarious letter-writing, with a pencil, upon encumbered surfaces & under harassment & persecution, as before. But convenience me no more women's conveniences, for I will none of them."

Heady with success and the promise of more, Sam tossed himself into business, which fired back its own barrage of harassments. He contemplated a libel suit after a newspaper squib accused Mark Twain of giving himself a complimentary dinner, forgetting that he *had* proposed just that promotional technique to celebrate selling 100,000 copies of *Innocents Abroad*. A pamphlet of sketches, to be sold as a series through newsstands, first suffered impossible delays and then appeared to no notice and minuscule trade. He mixed himself up in trying to arrange the publication of

Aldrich's and Howells' books by the American Publishing Company. Former Utah Territorial Governor Frank Fuller came to Hartford brimming with moneymaking schemes in which he wanted Sam to invest. The Mark Twain Scrap Book sold well, but the relatively small profits made Sam wonder if his friend Dan Slote knew his business. Demand for *The Gilded Age* suddenly collapsed, leaving a troubling trend of decreasing sales for each of Mark Twain's three subscription books. Sam attributed the novel's relative failure to the ongoing economic distress of the Panic of 1873, but the incoherent narrative had eventually produced an unfavorable word-of-mouth, which Sam did not counter by sending Mark Twain out to lecture.

In the middle of April 1874, Sam escaped these difficulties by taking the family to Elmira in preparation for the birth. The delicacy of Livy's health during this pregnancy brought back unwelcome reminders of little Langdon's long struggle and death. Though the unseasonably cold weather kept them at the house in town, Sam anticipated the removal to the Cranes' hilltop Quarry Farm. Sue Crane had commissioned the building of a special study for her brother-in-law. The enclosed octagonal gazebo had windows on every side, including above the fireplace and in the door, and "sits perched in complete isolation on top of an elevation that commands leagues of valley and city and retreating ranges of distant blue hills. It is a cosy nest, with just room enough for a sofa and a table and three or four chairs." The Cranes accommodated Sam's preferred schedule, with a hearty breakfast at nine, a retreat for work until the late afternoon, and then dinner and socializing. He was hungry to get back to work on the novel about the Mississippi River boy, which he had set aside to meet the challenge of writing a popular novel with Warner. By May 5, the weather cleared and the family gathered under the Cranes' lofty roof.

By then, Sam had also discovered that Gilbert Densmore, a San Francisco acquaintance who had once expanded a Bret Harte story into a book without permission, had dramatized *The Gilded Age*, centering the drama on Colonel Sellers. "It is a one-character play, like Rip Van Winkle," Sam wrote Warner, proposing that they amend their partnership contract to split the rights to any drama generated by the book according to which author's creations most dominated it. Sam went to New York City in mid-May to explore getting *The Gilded Age* on stage. Orion still dallied there, but when an opportunity arose to obtain a chicken farm near Mollie's hometown of Keokuk, Sam gladly bought them the property, hoping that a small place might keep Orion's dreams to a manageable size. He told his mother that he advised "them to furnish their house with the very cheapest stuff they could find, with no pretentious flummery about it—*be* chicken farmers & not hifalutin fine folks."*

He returned to Elmira to wait for Livy to deliver the new baby, and on June 8, 1874, Clara arrived. They named her for Clara Spaulding; had she been a boy, the Clemenses would have named him Henry, for Sam's brother. She "is the great American Giantess—weighing 7¾ pounds. We had to wait a good long time for her," Sam told Joe and Harmony Twichell, "but she was full compensation when she *did* come." The Modoc seemed pleased with the interloper and called her Bay, because she couldn't quite say "baby"— and the whole family accepted the new name. At the end of June, Sam went to Hartford to check on progress at the house and to secure his new agreement with Warner regarding dramatic rights. He wrote to Livy, "You may look at the house or the grounds from any point of view you choose, & they are simply exquisite. It is a quiet, murmurous, enchanting *poem* done in the solid elements of nature."* Sam was less communicative about his arrangement with Warner, by which he squeezed his partner out of a profitable deal. Sam got himself rights to a play that had already enjoyed popular success in San Francisco; Warner got the right to take only his own characters and turn them into a drama, assuming he could find time before traveling to Europe and Egypt.

Returning to Elmira, Sam threw himself into his work, finally confident he could write a novel on his own. But first, he turned his attention to Gilbert Densmore's play. He paid Densmore $200 for the work he had done in dramatizing *The Gilded Age* and felt he got more than his money's worth. While Densmore did not invent much dialogue—the novel provided that for him—he did have to construct a plot and add connective scenes. Sam used most of what Densmore had invented and by mid-July, Sam finished retouching the script and copyrighted the play. He wrote Howells, "I don't think much of it, as a drama, but I suppose it will do to hang Col. Sellers on, & maybe even damn him." (Howells had himself been refining his skills as a dramatist by translating an Italian play. Sam had arranged the job with a producer he knew, to direct some money Howells' way.) Sam then put his effort into getting the Sellers play staged. In the star-driven American stage of the 1870s, a successful actor could command a theater for any play he chose. Sam offered the play to comedian John T. Raymond, who saw a star vehicle in Colonel Sellers.

Remarkably, the novel about Tom Sawyer also progressed. Sam enjoyed combining imagination and reminiscence so much that "I have been writing fifty pages of manuscript a day, on an average," he wrote his sister, "and consequently have been so wrapped up in it and so dead to anything else, that I have fallen mighty short in letter-writing." By early September, he had the book nearly halfway done and found he could not write any more. Tom Sawyer and two of his friends had escaped the demands of their St. Petersburg life and set up camp on an island near the far bank. Sam was uncertain what to do with them next. "It was plain that I had worked myself out, pumped myself dry," he wrote to his Scottish friend, Dr. Brown.

Setting aside the novel in favor of short pieces, in the hope that something would suit Howells' *Atlantic*—Charley Stoddard had raised Sam's competitive fire with his articles about theater, running in the July and August issues—Sam literally discovered a story on the porch of the Quarry Farm house. Mary Ann Cord, the Cranes' cook, had suffered terribly in slavery, having watched her family be sold away from her, person by person. She told the Cranes and the Clemenses the story of her trials, concluding with how during the war she and her youngest son, then attached to a Northern military unit, had found one another again. Sam framed Cord's tale with a question and an answer. The narrator asks, "How is it that you've lived sixty years and never had any trouble?" And after her tale she answers, "Oh, no, Mr. C——, *I* hain't had no trouble. An' no *joy*!" Sam called this transcendentally sympathetic portrait "A True Story, Repeated Word for Word as I Heard It." He offered it to Howells with the note that it "has no humor in it. You can pay as lightly as you choose for that, if you want it, for it is rather out of my line." Howells thought it was "extremely good and touching with the best and reallest kind of black talk in it," and he decided to run it in the November issue. A former slave's painful and glorious account of her life's tragedy and redemption had at last put Sam at the portals of the American literary establishment.

Neither Sam's success nor his new baby could eliminate his periodic displays of rage. In August, Sam and Livy went to Fredonia to visit Jane, Pamela, Sammy, and Annie. While there, he managed to insult a banker friend of his family's. He wrote Jane and Pamela:

> I came away from Fredonia ashamed of myself;—almost too much humiliated to hold up my head and say good-bye. For I began to comprehend how much harm my conduct might do you socially in your village. I would have gone to that detestable oyster-brained bore and apologized for my inexcusable rudeness to him, but that I was satisfied he was of too small a calibre to know how to receive an apology with magnanimity. . . . [A] guilty conscience has harassed me ever since, and I have not had one short quarter of an hour of peace to this moment.

Sam, almost thirty-nine, could not control his childish behavior around his family. More enraged than contrite, his double-edged apology distributes as much blame as it accepts. He offered a tyrannical, child's fantasy solution to his family's embarrassment. If he ruined their lives in Fredonia, why not relocate them to another small town in upstate New York? Despite his money, success, and fame, Sam needed to assure himself of his own power by exerting an arbitrary control over the lives of the people who meant the most to him.

By the end of the second week in September, Livy had recovered from the strenuous, tense journey, and the whole family left Elmira. Sam and Livy stopped for a week in New York City, Livy to buy carpets and furnishings for the house, Sam to attend to business. Sam immersed himself in the tangled finances of the Mark Twain Scrap Book, which surpassed his capacity for figures, and the stage production of *The Gilded Age*, scheduled to open September 16, 1874. He found the rehearsals of the play fascinating. "I staid on the stage 2 to 4 hours several days in succession showing them how I thought the speeches ought to be uttered,"* he wrote his brother, taking credit for the play's opening night success. The play exactly suited the theater of the day, a lighthearted star vehicle which succeeded on the strength of John Raymond's comedic conception of Sellers' character.

By September 20, 1874, the family had moved into their new home, part of it anyway. "We occupy the study, nursery & mother's bedroom— the carpenters have the rest of the house," Sam told Mother Fairbanks. Still, it was a delight to live in their own place, on their own land—even if it would cost them $120,000 to buy the property and build and furnish the place. Much as Sam and Livy enjoyed the house's views and furnishings, especially the massive library mantelpiece, purchased from a Scottish castle, for Sam the finishing touch for it was William Dean Howells' cover note which arrived there with the proofs of "A True Story." "This little story delights me more and more: I wish you had about forty of 'em!"

24

A Man of Letters

I find that principles have no real force except when one is well fed.
—"Extracts from Adam's Diary" (1893)

We have not the reverent feeling for the rainbow that a savage has, because we know how it is made. We have lost as much as we have gained by prying into that matter.
—A Tramp Abroad (1880)

Sam concluded to Mother Fairbanks, after several months in Hartford, "I work *at* work here, but I don't accomplish anything worth speaking of." Even after his large second-floor study was finished, he had trouble settling down to writing in the new house. Family provided the bulk of the distractions, but living on a construction site also contributed its share. Sam added to a letter Livy sent her mother and sister in Elmira:

I have been bullyragged all day by the builder, by his foreman, by the architect, by the tapestry devil who is to upholster the furniture, by the idiot who is putting down the carpets, by the scoundrel who is setting up the billiard table (and has left the balls in New York), by the wildcat who is sodding the ground and finishing the driveway (after the sun went down), by a book *agent*, whose body is in the back yard and the coroner notified. Just think of this thing going on the whole day long, and I a man who loathes details with all his heart!

In fact, Livy attended to the details of construction. Sam merely meddled.

Despite the aggravation, the house was magnificent. It crested the hill perfectly, and Mark Twain's house became a beacon from both the eastern and western approaches. The casually sculpted grounds gave the structure a domestic appearance, notwithstanding its size and prominence, a modesty reinforced by the fact that the front door faced toward the side yard, stretching to the Stowes' house and not busy Farmington Avenue; only the service wing occupied the portion of the house closest to the street. The tinted mortar between the bricks gave the house a solid facade the architect had enlivened with accenting rows of black- and vermilion-enameled bricks. Inside, small features echoed the grandness of the exterior—the window set in the split flue in the dining room, so that from his seat at the table Sam could see snow fall into fire; the elaborate Scottish mantelpiece, so large that the top portion had to be placed as a decorative lintel above a door. Livy did economize on decoration. She had the walls painted white until they could afford the treatments the house deserved. At more than twice the cost of their Buffalo home, their Nook Farm mansion absorbed all the money Sam could earn writing and much of Livy's assets besides.

Mark Twain was enjoying unprecedented literary success, even without a new book on the market. John Raymond's Colonel Sellers became such a hit that President Grant called on Raymond after a performance to offer congratulations. The drama's success not only increased Mark Twain's fame, but also bolstered Sam's income with a royalty for each performance. Like his smash play, Twain's appearance in the November *Atlantic* was a new conquest, and Howells gave Sam an immediate opportunity to augment that victory. Livy pushed him to contribute to *The Atlantic*, but Sam came up empty. He wrote Howells that "it's no use—I find I can't. We are in such a state of weary & endless confusion that my head won't 'go.' So I give it up." Two hours later, after a long walk in the woods with Joe Twichell, Sam posted an addendum proposing a series "about old Mississippi days of steamboating glory & grandeur as I saw them (during 5 years) *from the pilot house*. . . . I hadn't thought of that before."

Sam had had the notion of a Mississippi River book for nearly a decade; only using the idea for magazine pieces was new. Having endured so many rejections from *The Atlantic*, he wanted a subject that would please Howells. Howells had grown up on the Ohio River, and many of his uncles had been pilots. Like Sam, he had witnessed the decline of the riverboats; his boyhood heroes now were all victims of the railroads' greater efficiency. But as a champion of literary realism, a photographic fidelity to human detail, Howells favored firsthand reports; he had little aesthetic sympathy for Mark Twain's romantic mythologizing. Sam's proposal bridged these two literary approaches perfectly, however, using a narrative of experience to evoke the vanished ideals of prewar, prerailroad river life. Howells snapped up the idea, promoting Mark Twain into the top rank of literary men, despite his anchor in second-class publishing and stage humor. Sam wrote Stoddard that the twenty dollars a page he was being paid—far above *The Atlantic*'s going rate—did not satisfy him. "However the awful respectability of the magazine makes up." He forgave the insulting fee in order to gain the crown of Man of Letters.

Sam went right to work—both he and Howells wanted the series to begin with the new year—and he had completed a draft of the first number by the second week in November. Claiming to Howells that if he didn't get mentioned in the magazine's promotion he "shall be as uppish & airish as any third-rate actor whose name is not made loud enough in the bills," Sam also contrived to advertise his contribution himself by carrying the manuscript to Boston on foot.

Walking all day, he and Joe Twichell expected to cover the distance from Hartford to Boston in three days. Sam notified James Redpath of his means of transportation; Howells, he felt, might not publicize the event properly. Sam and Twichell left early on Thursday morning, November 12, 1874, and expected to stay at Young's Hotel in Boston on Saturday night. They made twenty-eight miles Thursday, slept fitfully at a way station, and rose the next morning expecting to go on. Unfortunately, Sam ached from hip to ankle. They hobbled six more miles and then boarded a train. Sam cabled Redpath, "We have made thirty-five miles in less than five days. This demonstrates the thing can be done. Shall now finish by rail. Did you have any bets on us?" The duo headed to Howells' house that evening, where they found a party in progress. Sam held forth about the journey in fully heroic terms.

They stayed in Boston through Monday evening, gathering with Howells and other literati whenever possible. Howells took Sam to meet the era's reigning poet, James Russell Lowell, who wanted to gossip about Henry Ward Beecher's increasing difficulties. The agreement of silence between Beecher and Theodore Tilton had broken down. Tilton had sued Beecher for alienation of affection. The scandal had devolved from its original form as an opportunity for a public exegesis on hypocrisy to a full-blown soap opera captivating the public's imagination. People licked their lips in anticipation of the trial, which might, Sam thought, reprise the illicit pleasures he had found in Richard Blennerhasset's conduct of the Hart-Wise murder trial in Palmyra, Missouri, two and a half decades before.

Sam wrapped up his visit by writing a fantastical projection of life fifty years into the future, when instant communication makes telegraphic transmission quaint and slow, when airships travel between cities, and when Howells, Aldrich, and Twain all have titles of nobility. Though written as a letter addressed to Livy, Sam composed it to impress Howells—and he succeeded. His whimsical purchase of an exciting new writing machine, the typewriter, awed Howells, too. Howells did worry that Sam would find writing for this new magazine audience unnerving, but Sam responded, "It isn't the Atlantic audience that distresses me; for *it* is the only audience that I sit down before in perfect serenity (for the simple reason that it don't require a 'humorist' to paint himself stripèd & stand on his head every fifteen minutes)."

Sam returned to Boston for a December 15 dinner given by *The Atlantic*'s publisher for a select group of contributors. Though Mark Twain's inclusion in the small party more reflected Howells' hopes for his future contributions than the publisher's gratitude for his past ones, the events of these few days left no question of Sam's acceptance into the ranks. He owed his membership in this club to the literary ascension of William Dean Howells and Thomas Bailey Aldrich, whose dominance of Boston's literary scene encouraged them to impose a new aesthetic order. Plain language, humor, and realism were in; lyricism, scholasticism, and transcendentalism were out. Aldrich and Howells made Sam feel welcome by giving him neckties more in keeping with contemporary style, to replace the western string ties for which he affected favor. Sam answered this teasing by promising to send Aldrich a photograph of himself, and then making good by sending photo after photo, one each day. Aldrich laughingly responded to this photographic assault, "The police are in the habit of swooping down upon a publication of that sort." The photos kept coming until New Year's Day, when twenty various pictures of Sam, his family, his house, even his belongings, landed at Aldrich's house in Ponkapog, outside Boston. Sam also returned from Boston with the idea of visiting the Mississippi River with Howells come spring.

As his stock in the conventional publishing world rose, Sam's relationship with Elisha Bliss and the American Publishing Company grew more tangled and unsatisfying. Nearly two years had passed since he had had much to do with Bliss, even though Sam still sat on the company's board of directors. Orion's earlier accusations concerning Bliss' dishonesty during the publication of *Roughing It* remained unresolved, however, so

Sam talked about giving his long-delayed book of sketches to James Osgood, who with Boston luminary James Fields was Howells' and Charley Stoddard's publisher. But if Sam had chosen to forget that he was still under contract to the American Publishing Company, Bliss had not. Sam wrote to Osgood that Bliss, confronted with Sam's intention to publish Mark Twain elsewhere, "went to his safe and brought back a contract *four years old* to give him all my old sketches, with a lot of new ones added!—royalty 7½ per cent!" Sam settled for a compromise: Bliss would pay the contract rate until fifty thousand copies sold; after that the company would pay 10 percent, not only on each subsequent copy but on all the previous copies as well. He thanked Osgood for allowing himself to be used as a crowbar, and asked the publisher to join him and Howells on their trip down the Mississippi.

Sam continued to fish among his friends for good subscription books, which would benefit him as a stockholder. In March 1875, he received a letter from his old Nevada reporting partner Dan De Quille. He announced to Livy that he could tell "the contents of this letter without breaking the seal; and yet I have held no communication with this friend in eleven years. This letter will ask advice and information of me about publishing a book concerning the Comstock lead." Sam had queried Dan just days before about writing a book on the Big Bonanza, and the letters crossed in the mail. With this simultaneous inspiration, the contract was swiftly arranged.

Sam believed that his and Dan De Quille's spontaneously confluent ideas indicated the existence of "mesmeric current." Skeptical concerning conventional religious claims, Sam flirted, along with the mass of his Nook Farm neighbors, with a spirituality that accepted clairvoyance and faith healing as legitimate phenomena. Isabella Beecher Hooker, rehabilitated into society now that her brother's scandal was out of her hands and headed toward the courts, led this mystical parade with a complex theory about the spirit world, which she believed would become manifest on earth through a matriarchal regime, with herself as president. Spiritualism among Sam's set occupied a social and psychological role. The Warners had regularly attended Isabella Hooker's séances, before their departure for Egypt. The Stowes regarded spirit manifestations as matters of everyday life. Twichell accepted spiritualism as evidence of God's complex and unknowable will. Sam, however, remained dubious about life after death, unconvinced about the existence of God, and dismissive of the doctrine of an ethereal balance of good and evil. While it seemed laughable to Sam that a divinity cared a whit about human beings, it appeared possible to him that what people saw as spiritualism was only an as-yet-undiscovered physical law, the way the facts of electricity had been a little more than a century before. His and De Quille's synchronic interest in a Big Bonanza book appeared to confirm the existence of a paranormal world, but Sam regarded it as "mental telegraphy," which he viewed as merely a little understood device.

Sam's hard-edged limitations on belief in the existence of anything beyond the material world had grown in him for many years. He thought of himself as a complete pragmatist, though he understood that even pragmatism required a leap of faith, a belief in the wrongness of belief, and acknowledged that his early religious training limited his ability to practice pragmatism. Still, once his acceptance of Christianity had resulted in his marriage to Livy, he resumed his old ways, from his hard-edged agnosticism to his consumption of liquor. Livy, who had once desired his abstinence, now mixed him an old-fashioned, made of Scotch, lemon, sugar, and angostura bitters, several times a day and even began "to drink a bottle of beer every night." This laxity in matters of alcohol paralleled both Clemenses' abandonment of Christianity. They still attended Joe's services, because Livy found comfort in the ritual, but as Sam told Howells, "Oh yes, I go. It 'most kills me, but I go." Sam's participation in Joe's church represented a contribution to the community, not an assent to its religious principles. Privately, the men argued their religious precepts with the passion they each held for good conversation. Twichell's Christian explanations of the supernatural helped Sam refine his own definitions of a world without it.

Sam's clear-eyed pragmatism harmonized with the most progressive American thinkers and put him at the forefront of a cultural shift away from deism, a change whose effects have continued for more than a century. This philosophy also served his ambition; he seldom suffered much compunction about doing what he must to accomplish his goal. His brother Orion's deeply ethical sensibility and seemingly capricious pursuit of a permanent spiritual truth, on the other hand, challenged Sam's beliefs. Orion, a failure by almost any measure, was undeniably a good man, something Sam could not candidly say about himself. The more severely Sam ridiculed Orion's metamorphoses, the further he grew from the self-exploration so central to his hopeless brother's identity. By rejecting Orion's willingness to change with every new discovery about himself, Sam also rejected his brother's style of self-inquiry as a means to gaining insight. Without this tool for self-understanding, Sam obligated himself to self-discovery through perception of external reality, a method that necessarily valued image over identity.

Sam's preoccupation with the issues of image and identity burdened him with practical as well as spiritual considerations. His reluctance to lecture created an opportunity for Mark Twain impersonators. Honest imitators delivered a Mark Twain lecture and paid their hotel bills, while the others simply absconded with the fee. To some, Mark Twain was a detachable persona, a stock figure invented by one man but playable by many, like Hamlet or Oedipus. Mark Twain had become a public possession and Sam had lost absolute control over him. Though Sam retained enough proprietary interest in Mark Twain to produce substantial income, his persona as well as his manuscripts could be pirated, a dangerous prospect for a man who felt that his pseudonymous self had more authenticity than the personality with which he was born.

At home, Sam began to wear the trappings of his Hartford gentleman, S. L. Clemens, with greater ease. With the house nearly finished, he reveled in company there. In March, Howells came to visit with his wife Elinor. He reported to his father, "The Clemenses are whole-souled hosts, with inextinguishable money, and a palace of a house." Sam even mimicked the British gentleman's pride in his idiosyncrasies, sometimes appearing in company in the long nightgowns he preferred to pajamas. Having hired someone to follow John Raymond when he took *The Gilded Age* on the road, Sam received daily dinnertime reports of the day's take, which he bellowed to the assembled. To Sam, gentlemanliness meant generosity, kindness, charm, and presence, and he executed each of these qualities to the utmost of his considerable ability. The unique presentation of S. L. Clemens, of Farmington Avenue, Hartford, was a public performance akin to his stage presentations as Mark Twain, only less formal and far more regular, a show that promised never to close.

Sam now had two public personas to manage. Mark Twain—author of *Innocents Abroad, Roughing It*, and the successful *Atlantic* series "Old Times on the Mississippi"—specialized in autobiographical fictions. A beneficiary of the new and unfamiliar construct called fame, Sam could mold the image of Mark Twain as he pleased, as long as he did not contradict the public conception of him and was in print as he was on stage, the simulacrum of a real person. Even in dinner speeches, Mark Twain constructed false biographies for himself, making himself an orphan or else giving himself two living parents; creating a cousin Mary in place of his sister Pamela; or assuming the narrator's role in invented or appropriated first-person stories. On the other hand, S. L. Clemens, as he frequently signed his correspondence now, was a gentleman and man of letters. As S. L. Clemens, a humble and rather conservative inhabitant of America's social and cultural elite, Sam could go out in public without having to become Mark Twain.

Sam further disguised his personal experience—that is, the life of his essential identity—by adding another persona: Writing under Mark Twain's byline about his own domestic life, he gave his family the name McWilliams. In the McWilliams stories, Mark Twain reports a disquisition by Mr. McWilliams about the comic foibles of Sam's actual home life. For example, Susie came down with a cough, which sent Livy into a panic, since membranous croup had raged through the community, killing some children. Sam burlesqued Livy as the hysterical Mrs. McWilliams, who issues contradictory orders to her suffering husband. When the child finally coughs up a splinter, acquired from chewing on a stick, the crisis is resolved. Noting the supposed rarity of Mortimer McWilliams' tale, Mark Twain says that he "thought that maybe the novelty of it would give it a passing interest to the reader." Mark Twain offered McWilliams as public cover of Sam Clemens' private life, itself already obscured by the social persona of S. L. Clemens.

His own family reinforced this happy, gentlemanly identity. Susie's third birthday party was a complete success. After the Modoc had distributed pieces of her candy around to the guests and taken the last piece for herself, the liveryman Patrick McAleer, who'd been with the family since Buffalo, arrived with a present. When he asked if there was no candy for him, Susie gave him the piece from her mouth. Sam gave her a wooden Noah's Ark with two hundred animals and Susie shared one of her new dolls with Bay. Livy, reporting the proceedings to her mother, conceded that such concern with a three-year-old was "silly, but you know Susie is so large a part of my life and I am so desperately fond of her." Such a relationship with one's children was a Nook Farm ideal. Sam and Livy were happy again. He felt joy in her girlish fear of storms—though he burlesqued the way she would hide from thunder and lightning in another McWilliams story—and took pride in her capacity to manage him, the house, and the children. Free from her own politically progressive but socially codified childhood, Livy delighted in Sam's unconventionality.

Home life was not perfect, of course. Livy canceled Sam's March trip down the Mississippi. She rarely slept well without Sam in bed with her; Howells had dropped out anyway, minimizing Sam's disappointment. The children and servants presented constant challenges. Despite her prime performance at her birthday, the Modoc was more typically "addicted to sudden & raging tempests of passion,"* which neither her parents nor her caretakers could curb, as her father recorded in his journal of his girls' young lives. Clara turned blue and seemed close to dying when they tried to feed her condensed milk or pabulum, and she ran through a series of wet nurses. The one she liked and who had a sufficient supply of milk also had an appetite for alcohol. Sam described her to Howells as a goddess: six feet tall, stately, and beautiful; but she smoked, ate ghastly food, drank to excess, "whooped like a Pawnee and swore like a demon." The mix "ought to have killed [the baby] at thirty yards, but . . . only made it happy and fat and boozy."

The family also hired a new butler, George Griffin, who came to wash windows one day and never left. He had a hundred faults for every virtue, but those virtues were so valuable that Sam kept him. An unredeemed gambler and womanizer, George was also a leader in Hartford's African-American community and an appreciative audience for Sam's humor. He laughed with abandon at Sam's jokes, even when he ought to have been serving dinner instead, and Sam loved him for it. The two men developed an intense loyalty. As Howells later recounted it, Sam said that he preferred a black butler because "he could not bear to order a white man about, but the terms of his ordering George were those of the softest entreaty which command ever wore." George excelled at refusing entry to the beggars, graspers, and fans who flocked to 351 Farmington Avenue. He would faithfully bring all calling cards to Sam in his third-floor billiard room. Sam would loose a string of profanity at the hopeful guest, which George would translate into a kind refusal.

In April 1875, the independent persona of S. L. Clemens allowed Sam to attend—or attempt to attend—two public events in which he played no role, something he had found difficult as Mark Twain. Early in the month, he went to Brooklyn with Joe Twichell and sat in on the trial of Henry Ward Beecher. Sam left feeling that no matter what Beecher said now, most people were already convinced of his guilt. Later that month, Sam went to Boston to attend the festivities at Lexington and Concord that kicked off the centennial celebration of the War of Independence. He and Howells intended to go together from Boston, but they instead traipsed around through the bitter wind looking for a ride. Back in Hartford, Sam listened to Joe Twichell boast of riding to the centennial atop a crowded train, but wrote to Howells, "He is welcome to the good time he had—I had a deal better one."

This layering of invented selves—Mark Twain, S. L. Clemens, and Mortimer McWilliams—almost completely obscured the original Sam Clemens. In "An Encounter with An Interviewer," a comic piece Sam wrote around this time, a young reporter comes to interview Mark Twain, who replies to his questions with an idiotic barrage of blatant lies and contradictions. He claims to have drowned as an infant, but the family was never sure if it was him or his twin brother. Eventually, the young reporter gives up his goal of uncovering the truth and accepts Twain's absurd and sentimental tale. If the story amuses, Twain argues by implication, of what possible value is truth?

Hiding behind McWilliams, Twain, and S. L. Clemens, Sam could now write knowing that no one could decipher the degree of fact in his romanticized recollections of boyhood. This freedom allowed him to explore his memory, and his reminiscences about his days training on Mississippi River steamboats refreshed his ability to conjure up a boyhood like his own. He wanted to finish his book about Tom Sawyer now, but family pressures threatened that plan. They had "determined to try to sweat it out, here in Hartford, this summer, & not go away at all. That is Livy's idea," Sam wrote Mother Fairbanks, "not mine; for I can write ten chapters in Elmira where I can write one here." Being a gentleman had its costs.

25 | *Taming a Shooting Star*

> *Man is the only animal that blushes. Or needs to.*
> —"Pudd'nhead Wilson's New Calendar" (1897)

SAM'S TIME IN Hartford proved far more productive than he expected it to be. After completing the last of seven *Atlantic* installments of "Old Times on the Mississippi" in mid-May, he settled back to work on his novel. In six weeks, he had nearly finished it, but he remained uncertain as to what the shape of the book ought to be—how the plot would develop, and how old Tom would grow in the course of the narrative—and equally uncertain what to do with it when it was done. Howells came down to Hartford for an overnight stay on June 12, 1875, to discuss these matters. Other writer friends helped too; he had always benefited from close working relationships with friends. When Bret Harte gave his advice, so valuable during the revision of *The Innocents Abroad*, Sam helped arrange a deal with Elisha Bliss for his novel, *Gabriel Conroy*; acquiring Harte was a coup for the American Publishing Company. Responding to Sam's earlier invitation, Dan De Quille came to Hartford to write his history of the Comstock Lode. He did not stay with the Clemenses, but the men spent time writing side by side, as they had in Virginia City.

Like these men, most writers of this period labored under the onus of having avoided service in the Civil War; very few literary men had titles or wounds from the conflict. While Sam had waited out the war in the West, for example, Howells had been consul to Venice, a reward for writing Lincoln's campaign biography. Their wartime absence separated them from their peers. A startling percentage of men retained their military titles into civilian life; even a greater number bore disfiguring wounds from the war. Especially since the Panic of 1873, beggars who had lost limbs at Gettysburg, Bull Run, or some other bloody site crowded most cities' streets. Writers who had escaped the war had to find a way to bridge the divide between those who served, on either side, and those who did not. Sam took his inspiration from Thomas Bailey Aldrich's 1869 book *The Story of a Bad Boy*, which was the first of a flood of novels featuring endearing boys of imperfect virtue. These authors' books created a communion with their audience by representing a prewar solidarity among all boys, transending the period which had splintered them into supporters of the Union, adherents to the Confederacy, and shirkers.

Howells had advised him to make a *bildungsroman* of the story, but Sam wrote that he couldn't, perhaps sensing that Tom Sawyer's charm lay not in his becoming a man but in his being a boy. "If I went on, now, & took him into manhood, he would be just like all the one-horse men in literature & the reader would conceive a hearty contempt for him." Despite the age of his main character, however, Sam wanted to aim the novel at adults, mostly because he felt the book would earn more by targeting that larger audience. Sam told Howells that though he wanted *The Atlantic* to publish the story first, he didn't think the magazine could afford the privilege. Not only were Sam's "household expenses . . . something almost ghastly," as he explained his "vile, mercenary view of things," but he was in direct competition with *Gabriel Conroy*. Bret Harte's novel had sold for serial publication to *Scribner's* for $6,000, and Sam dearly wanted his book to produce more money than Harte's. Nonetheless, Sam begged Howells to read the manuscript for him, in spite of his unwillingness to publish it in *The Atlantic* at any terms the magazine might afford. Howells agreed, adding, "You've no idea what I may ask you to do for *me* some day." To assuage his guilt at loading the role of literary midwife onto Howells' shoulders, Sam turned the favor into a paying proposition: Howells could dramatize the book and take half of the first $6,000 the play produced, in exchange for his editorial advice on the novel. Howells refused the deal, but renewed his promise to read the manuscript.

Productive as he was, Sam did more than write over the summer. He and Joe Twichell frequently attended baseball games; professional baseball had become a popular spectator sport in Hartford. The men also argued about the Beecher trial, in which the court had effectively stone-walled Theodore Tilton's claims of alienation of his wife's affection by refusing to admit Lib Tilton's testimony against the minister. More pleasantly, promoter extraordinaire P. T. Barnum launched a barrage of correspondence at Sam, which Sam happily answered; the men admired one another's capacity for publicity. Discovering that each kept a library of their most pathetic and humorous begging letters, they began exchanging them. Sam also initiated another lawsuit to assert that Mark Twain was his trademark, this time challenging a Boston publisher who had used his name to advertise a collection of humor. He tried to persuade Howells and Osgood to move in the same suit with him, for the good of all publishing men, but they declined.

The summer allowed Sam more time to focus on his children. The Modoc—now called Susie most of the time—was a spunky child, verbal and quick-tempered. She could easily make the many household visitors laugh with her imitation of her father's drawl. Her fits, however, eventually drove Sam and Livy to spank her, although their principles had kept them from corporal punishment until then. Paddlings became a daily feature of the little girl's life, continuing for several months with decreasing frequency as she improved her conduct to avoid them. Her exasperating behavior once made Sam so angry he kicked a chair, without noticing that Clara was on it; the baby went flying, but landed without serious harm. Bay developed characteristics opposite her sister's. Where Susie talked early and walked late, Clara walked early and by her first birthday showed no inclination toward language. Susie was skittish and Bay brave to the point of recklessness. In late June, an accident with the baby carriage "caught the baby's middle finger, nipping the end of it nearly off,"* as Sam wrote his sister. The parents were beside themselves, but Clara remained relatively calm, a marked difference from what Susie's reaction would have been; she panicked even at splinters.

Together, though, the children created family traditions. Even as a very young child, Susie would interrupt her father's work just to ask him to tell her a story, and Bay soon joined in. They insisted that Sam incorporate all the objects in the room in his tales, usually in a certain order. He also encouraged wildness in his daughters by leading them into activities specifically prohibited by their mother. Livy's deliberate and thoughtful consistency with the children impressed Sam, who was liable to alter his parenting style with his mood, from towering rage to wild playfulness. His changeability both delighted and frightened the children, who were as vulnerable to the Mark Twain magnetism as anyone. He was the center of family life, and when the girls tired of striving for his approval, they reposed in Livy's unvarying love. She never liked to leave the children for long when they were well; when they were sick, she sat up all night rocking them. Acknowledging his own inconsistency, Sam declared of Livy, "She is a perfect mother, if ever there was one."*

July found Livy and the children sick. Howells suggested that the family retire to Newport, Rhode Island. "You'll find my friend Col. Waring, a capital fellow, and most usefully learned in everything a stranger wants to ask about Newport." An *Atlantic* contributor, Waring welcomed the Clemens family to Newport a week later, introducing Sam—or, more properly, S. L. Clemens of Nook Farm, Hartford—to his elite friends of the Town and Country Club and the Bellvue Dramatic Group. Sam eased his way into the Town and Country Club by supplying the champagne for their August picnic meeting. He enjoyed Newport society, though in *The Gilded Age*, he had satirized the resort. "Newport is damp, and cold, and windy and excessively disagreeable," an upper-class woman nasalizes, "but it is very select. One cannot be fastidious about minor matters when one has no choice." Now, two years later, he wanted to hobnob with Newport's wealthy summer patrons whose society he had ridiculed. Though he knew he could not gain full membership into this summer high society, an occasional welcome as an honored guest meant that Mark Twain had infiltrated the same level of American society he had in England. Since the family's provisional acceptance into Newport society depended on Mark Twain's fame, at least twice during the month of August Sam appeared as Twain in public, sharing the Town and Country Club podium with ex-Vice President Schuyler Colfax, and reading at a Bellvue Dramatic Club benefit. The sea air refreshed Livy, and the girls frequently stayed on the sand until dark, and on very warm nights they slept on the beach. The Clemenses extended their stay into September.

As Sam absorbed the manners of the upper class, he also assumed some of their political postures. As a Republican, from a family of Whigs, he blamed public corruption on the election of incompetents and criminals by an uneducated, unsophisticated populace. In his view, formed in Hannibal and reinforced by his community of wealthy progressives, the Democrats were slightly more sophisticated Know-Nothings, who typically occupied the lower social and moral rungs of society. Because these people were more numerous, he objected to the democratic principle of apportioning the vote equally, even among the relatively select citizenry—male and property-holding—empowered to vote in the nineteenth century. In "The Curious Republic of Gondour," he portrayed a utopia that extends voting rights to everyone, including women and the poor, but provides more votes to individuals with higher education or greater wealth. In Gondour, "a university education entitled a man to nine votes, even if he

owned no property." Nothing limited the number of votes a citizen of
Gondour might acquire through wealth, but since such votes existed only
as long as one owned the requisite property, they did not garner the same
respect as the "immortal" votes won through education. In Gondour, the
educated checked the power of the wealthy. Sam asked Howells to publish
"Gondour" in *The Atlantic* without a byline. Despite Mark Twain's success
with "Old Times on the Mississippi" and his deepening reputation, Sam
feared that readers would regard anything from his pen as a joke. The
anonymous *Atlantic* publication of this piece protected Mark Twain's pop-
ulist persona, while allowing Sam to forward this aristocratic idea just as
he knocked at the door of aristocracy itself.

Back in Hartford, Sam moved onto a political concern with more
practical implications. He wanted writers of note to sign a petition asking
the government to honor international copyrights. Outlining his plan for
the passage of a law to Howells, he claimed, "And *then* if Europe chose to
go on stealing from us, we would say with noble enthusiasm, 'American
law-makers *do steal*—but not from foreign authors, not from foreign authors!'" Sam did not want to lead the fight for the law because he was
its most obvious beneficiary. The easiest way for him to protect Mark
Twain was to persuade the United States itself to outlaw such international piracy, thus meeting England's requirement for reciprocity. Then
Sam would not have to worry further about copyrighting books there.

Sam also worked to publicize his collection of sketches, which came
out in September, but very few newspapers other than the *New York
Tribune* showed much interest. Only faithful Howells among editors of
major journals published a review, but he pleased Sam and gratified
Livy with his praise for Mark Twain's "growing seriousness of meaning
in the apparently unmoralized drolling, which must result from the
humorist's second thought of political and social absurdities." Sam wrote
in thanks:

> That is a perfectly superb notice. You can easily believe
> that nothing ever gratified me so much before. The news-
> paper praises bestowed upon the Innocents Abroad were large
> & generous, but I hadn't *confidence* in the critical judgment
> of the parties who furnished them. . . . Yours is the recog-
> nized critical Court of Last Resort in this country; from its
> decision there is no appeal; & so, to have gained this decree
> of yours before I am forty years old, I regard as a thing to
> be right down proud of.

Sketches sold well enough at first, but the slender press notice and Mark Twain's long absence from the lecture platform hurt sales, which dropped off very quickly after twenty thousand copies. Despite its flattery, the *Atlantic* review could not revive interest in the volume, much as Sam hoped it would. His faith in *The Atlantic*'s power was somewhat misplaced. His fulsome compliment to Howells about his journal's standing in the literary community specifically contradicts an opinion he expressed in a letter earlier in the year, in which he paid the same compliment elsewhere: "The 'Nation' *always* snarls. It would think it was impairing its reputation as our first critical authority if it failed to do that."* The fact that he needed to laud Howells so hollowly implies that the relationship between the two famous writers was, as late as fall 1875, still more professional than personal.

Partially in an attempt to change the nature of this friendship, Sam and Livy visited the Howellses in Cambridge in late September, choosing to skip the wedding of Sam's niece Annie Moffett to Charles L. Webster, also of Fredonia. That choice was odd, especially since Pamela had permitted Annie's wedding only after Sam overcame her objections to the groom, whom she found arrogant, grasping, and coarse. Annie felt, and Sam concurred, that a man hoping to make a mark in American business needed those qualities to which Pamela objected. Pamela relinquished her objections, but Sam's presence at the nuptials would have welcomed Charley Webster into the family more emphatically. Much as he enjoyed the weekend with the Howellses, he would come to regret skipping the wedding.

Right after the weekend, however, Sam wrote Howells that he and Livy "had a royal good time at your house, & have had a royal good time ever since, talking about it, both privately & with the neighbors." While in Boston, Sam poured his high spirits into "A Literary Nightmare," another creative tour de force intended to impress Howells, about the difficulty of shaking an infectious piece of doggerel out of one's head. Two weeks later, Howells had finished *Tom Sawyer*, "sitting up till one A.M. to get to the end, simply because it was impossible to leave off. It's altogether the best boy's story I ever read." This last remark was pointed: Howells' enthusiasm for the novel went hand in hand with his belief that the book was for children. He warned Sam that "if you should put it forth as a study of boy character from the grown-up point of view, you'd give the wrong key to it." If it were published to appeal to adults, the novel risked becoming a burlesque, like the mocking sketch Sam had composed during his courtship, in which he had satirized the rituals of courtship and which he incorporated in *Tom Sawyer* in describing the budding childhood romance between Becky and Tom.

Sam turned the first section of *The Adventures of Tom Sawyer* over to Bliss, so that he could get True Williams, the principal illustrator for most of Mark Twain's books, to begin work. Assured of Howells' strong review of his first solo venture into fiction, Sam sought mastery of the book's publication. He wrote Bliss regarding De Quille's book and his own, "I think you had better rush Dan's book into print, by New Year's, if possible, and give Tom Sawyer the early spring market. I don't want to publish in the summer—don't want to wait till fall—shall have a bigger book ready then." The few thousand dollars of profit brought in by *Sketches, New and Old* could not support the Clemenses Nook Farm life, and Sam had high hopes for young Tom. He wrote Howells:

> [True] Williams has made about 200 rattling pictures for it—some of them very dainty. Poor devil, what a genius he has, & how he does murder it with rum. He takes a book of mine, & without suggestion from anybody builds no end of pictures just from his reading of it.
>
> There [never] was a man in the world so grateful to another as I was to you day before yesterday, when I sat down (in still rather wretched health) to set myself to the dreary & hateful task of making final revision of Tom Sawyer, & discovered, upon opening the package of MS that your pencil marks were scattered all along. This was splendid, & swept away all labor. Instead of *reading* the MS, I simply hunted out the pencil marks & made the emendations which they suggested.

True Williams was not the only alcoholic in Sam's world. Dan De Quille also suffered from bouts of severe drinking. Anticipating that Dan's book, *The Big Bonanza*, would generate a sudden rise in the value of the Comstock mines, in February Sam sent him $1,500 to invest as he saw fit. Dan, on a bender, never invested the money. Sam feared that he had misplaced his faith in Bliss as he had in Dan. Though he anticipated imminent publication, Dan's book suffered the typical deflating delays, shrinking its effect on the market and forcing back the publication of his own volume. Sam's carefully planned schedule for the publication of *The Adventures of Tom Sawyer* seemed as though it might easily fall to pieces, along with the fortune he dreamed it would bring him.

26 | Compromising the Past

Gratitude and treachery are merely the two extremities of the same procession. You have seen all of it that is worth staying for when the band and the gaudy officials have gone by.
—"Pudd'nhead Wilson's Calendar" (1894)

O NE OF SAM'S first projects after recovering from an early winter cold was to create the Saturday Morning Club. Based on a similar club in Boston, dedicated to promoting intellectual training not typically available to young women, this group of teenage girls met weekly at the Clemens house to discuss a prepared paper. Young women had always appealed to Sam. Livy's girlishness had attracted him as much as her womanliness, but the burden of raising two children, managing a household staff of six, and performing as the wife of a famous man had frayed her friskiness and made her more of a stolid adult. The Saturday Morning Club of young women replenished the household's lost girlishness. Much as Sam complained about his inability to work while in Hartford, he put tremendous effort into supporting the Saturday Morning Club, seldom missing a meeting and often reading papers or insisting that his notable friends and visitors speak to the membership.

Early in 1876, there were visitors aplenty for Sam and his club, such as Moncure Conway, an expatriate American living in London who had amused Sam and Livy there a year and a half before. Sam turned over to Conway the responsibility for arranging his publications in England. Resentful of the relatively small percentage of profit he had received from his books, he wanted to experiment with the publication of *The Adventures of Tom Sawyer*, covering the costs of production himself and paying his publisher a sort of royalty for distribution. Inverting the typical arrangement between publisher and writer, Sam would assume the risks of the enterprise in exchange for greater profits. Conway floated the proposition not only to Routledge but also to Chatto and Windus, the successor to John Camden Hotten's firm. Andrew Chatto accepted Sam's inventive alternative, but then Sam wrote Conway, "I finally submitted the matter to Mrs. Clemens, and she said, 'Take the royalty; it simplifies everything; removes all risk; requires no outlay of capital.' "

William Dean Howells came to visit the vast house in March with his young son John, whose awe overwhelmed his tongue, causing him to speak the era's unspoken attitude on race. "When he found the black serving-man getting ready for breakfast, he came and woke me. 'Better get up, papa. The *slave* is setting the table.' " His host's fame, which so exceeded even his own father's distinguished reputation, excited the boy's expectations. Letters arrived by the dozens, at least one addressed as vaguely and grandly as "Mark Twain, The World." During the visit, Sam appealed to Howells with the intriguing idea of getting each author in *The Atlantic*'s stable to write a story inspired by the same plot. Sam thought that the writers could make money by issuing the collection as a book, but the inclusion of Mark Twain along with Howells, Aldrich, Harte, Henry James, and other literary lights would mean more to him than any financial gain from the project. Livy had money, and if *Tom Sawyer* sold half as well as *Roughing It* and *The Innocents Abroad*, Sam would possess enough of it as well, but success in the fiction market would secure him a reputation beyond that which the earlier books, lectures, and occasional *Atlantic* pieces had established. *The Gilded Age* had exploded on the scene and as quickly disappeared. The success of the play based on the book almost persuaded Sam that the book's relative failure had resulted from Charles Dudley Warner's flaccid contributions, but Sam still doubted his own capacity as a writer of fiction. *Tom Sawyer*'s success would confirm his skills.

The Adventures of Tom Sawyer was an utter departure for him—one that would stir up the contradictions between his past and his present in discomfiting ways. In some respects, the book was more like *Roughing It* than *The Gilded Age*, notwithstanding the differences in genre. What plot the book contained developed slowly, almost as an afterthought to its primary purpose, the representation of a lost American world in nearly mythic terms. When Tom takes an unannounced vacation with Huck Finn on the island across the Mississippi from St. Petersburg—Hannibal, during the time of Sam's own boyhood—the townspeople think he's dead. Tom and Huck sneak back to town to hear their own funerals and appear only after the funeral sermon on the text, "I am the resurrection and the life." Tom's world was like the world of *Roughing It*, a vibrantly heated greenhouse in which was revived an intense and urgent life. Fantasy didn't merely augment Tom's existence; it *was* his existence. He affection for Becky Thatcher didn't merely amuse him; it consumed him. Injun Joe is not merely a murderer; he is a demon. Even Huck says, when they encounter the villain and his pals in the cemetery, "I'd druther they was devils, a dern sight."

Despite the mythic American boyhood embodied in the book, *Tom Sawyer* invoked an underlying realism, just as had *Roughing It*. His western adventures had already given the Mark Twain persona a historical depth. "Old Times on the Mississippi" established the narrative of his early adulthood. The chronicles of a river-town boyhood extended Mark Twain's history even further back. Twain's preface reinforced this autobiographical quality of the book: "Most of the adventures recorded in this book really occurred; one or two were experiences of my own, the rest those of boys who were schoolmates of mine. Huck Finn is drawn from life; Tom Sawyer also, but not from an individual—his is a combination of the characteristics of three boys whom I knew." Despite his misdirection in suggesting the composite nature of the character of Tom Sawyer, Sam clearly intended his readers to identify the boy with Mark Twain. Like *Roughing It*, *The Adventures of Tom Sawyer* combined literal history and conscious mythologizing, with Mark Twain as the somewhat hapless mythic hero of both narratives. Sam was dressing up his public persona with a complete, though hyperbolic, reality.

Sam Clemens used his own history as the inspiration for his characters in *Tom Sawyer*. Huck Finn was based on Tom Blankenship. Becky Thatcher recalled Laura Hawkins, the beautiful blond child who lived across Hill Street from Sam. There was an actual Injun Joe in Hannibal, though he was more of a wild drunk than a violent evildoer. Huck calls Tom late at night just as Tom Blankenship called Sam, and Tom's angelic younger brother Sid chastises Tom Sawyer just as Henry chastised Sam. But Sam transformed the reality in a strikingly consistent way, portraying the docile civilization of St. Petersburg as a mask for the untamed world. The mixed-breed Injun Joe becomes an incursion of the savage into the hothouse of St. Petersburg. The town's grown-ups' civilized ways seem almost entirely incomprehensible and irrelevant to Tom and his friends. The boys appear to be the only inhabitants of the town able to abrogate the walls of civilization, not only in their literal voyages to the island and to the cave, but also in their knowledge of superstitious rituals for eliminating warts and summoning ghosts. No girl's corpse hangs in St. Petersburg's cave, as the body of the doctor's daughter did in the cavern outside of Hannibal. Instead, Sam reconfigured reality by separating sex and death as Tom and Becky get lost together in the cave's sexualized underworld, where it turns out that Injun Joe has hidden himself to escape judgment passed against him on the basis of Tom's eyewitness testimony. In Mark Twain's world, even a real-life cave can become a repository for mythical abstractions of lust, fear, and justice. Tom and Becky barely escape from the underworld; Injun Joe dies trapped there, "his face close to the crack of the door, as if his longing eyes had been fixed, to the latest moment, upon the light and the cheer of the free world outside."

Howells wrote a thunderingly positive review of *Tom Sawyer*. "The story is a wonderful study of the boy-mind," he explained, "which inhabits a world quite distinct from that in which he is bodily present with his elders, and in this lies its great charm and its universality, for boy nature, however human nature varies, is the same everywhere." Sam was immensely grateful. Nervous about the novel, he was trying to coordinate British and American publication while stirring the publicity machine for both. He told Howells that his review "will embolden weak-kneed journalistic admirers to speak out, & will modify or shut up the unfriendly." Moncure Conway told Sam that Chatto and Windus could publish by early summer and Sam believed that Elisha Bliss would have the book bound by the beginning of May. The publication of Howells' review in the May issue would work perfectly.

Except, of course, that Bliss was nowhere near ready to publish. While True Williams had completed most of his drawings, the engraving and electrotyping processes meandered along with more than their usual slowness. By mid-April, Sam realized that the American Publishing Company could not release the book before summer. Summer being a dreadful time to sell a subscription book, Sam believed it would be better to delay until fall and "make a Boy's Holiday Book of it," as he wrote to Moncure Conway. "I am determined that Tom shall outsell any previous book of mine, and so I mean that he shall have every possible advantage." For that, he willingly sacrificed coordinated publication on both sides of the ocean. As long as *Tom Sawyer* came out first in England, the copyright there was secure. Sam could publish in America when he deemed the time best. Having put Howells out considerably by allowing *The Atlantic* to review a book long before anyone could buy a copy, he tried apologizing by letter but gave up, planning instead to explain it all to his friend in person. Meanwhile, he wrote, "I shall print items occasionally still further delaying Tom, till I ease him down to autumn without shock to the waiting world." Howells assured his friend he was unperturbed. "I know I shall do you an injury some day," he wrote, "and I want a grievance to square accounts with."

Sam suggested that he help Howells round out a one-act of his own he had recently run in *The Atlantic*, with Sam adding a comic character and then, of course, sharing in the rights. After a year and a half, John Raymond's traveling production of *The Gilded Age* had stopped bringing in such delicious royalties, and Sam put most of his creative thought into developing another play for the ridiculously profitable theater. Sam wanted a writing partner who could disguise his own weak skills as a dramatist. Though Howells' plays had not been professionally produced, they reached appreciative audiences as people staged readings in their homes, a common form of entertainment at the time. This project was mere preparation, however, for a play based on *Tom Sawyer*, the dramatic venture that promised the greatest return. He wrote to Moncure Conway requesting that he find a dramatist in England with whom Mark Twain could share a copyright. Sam had already accepted, even looked forward to, the indignities forced on novelists selling their stories for adaptation to a different medium. He began to scout for unconventional actors for the anticipated production, telling Conway

> I have a young genius of a girl in my eye, here, to take the part of Tom or Huck (whichever turns out to be the principal character—for I want the play to depart from the book as widely as the dramatist chooses, even though he leave the book's incidents out entirely). I would enlarge that part myself, if it did not already preponderate in the play, & try to make a lucrative "one-character" drama of it— wherein lies the cash. "Sellers" has paid me $23,000 clear, this season.*

Even before the publication of the novel in the United States, Sam saw the possibility of generating a series of stories in a variety of media based on either Tom or Huck.

Writing *Tom Sawyer* had brought the past into the present for Sam, and this uneasy relationship continued throughout the spring. An old Hannibal friend, now in charge of relocating the town's cemetery, had written to ask what to do with the graves of his brother and father. Soon after, those ghosts materialized for him in an extended visit from Jane

Clemens and Pamela Moffett. Family inhibited Sam's creativity, however; they obligated him to remain Sam Clemens, and to his own mind Sam Clemens did not amount to much. For two years, he had self-protectively decided not to go to Fredonia. Now, during Jane's visit to Hartford, he tried to persuade her to relocate to Keokuk, near Orion and far away from him. One of the few things Sam wrote that month was a letter to Mother Fairbanks.

> What a curious thing life is. We delve away, through years of hardship, wasting toil, despondency; then comes a little butterfly season of wealth, ease, & clustering honors.— Presto! the wife dies, a daughter marries a spendthrift villain, the heir & hope of the house commits suicide, the laurels fade & fall away. Grand result of a hard-fought, successful career & a blameless life. Piles of money, tottering age, & a broken heart.

Though feelings of desolation hounded Sam his whole life, he most frequently responded with humor and forbearance. But now, with humor assigned to the role of Mark Twain and forbearance to his role as the gentlemanly S. L. Clemens, Sam had given away his best and most private defenses against sorrow. In the presence of his family, who insisted that he be just Sam, these figures could not protect him. Moreover, it was the family itself, as an embodiment of the past, against which Sam felt he needed the most protection.

On June 15, 1876, the entire family rode up to Elmira. Sam's octagonal study, perched above the old quarry at Quarry Farm, allowed him to concentrate on his writing as he could in no other place. Manuscript pages almost flew out of him: first, attempts to work the "Old Times on the Mississippi" series into a book-length manuscript; then, after a now-unidentified "double-barreled novel" went "torpid" in the middle of July, Sam told Howells he "began another boys' book—more to be at work than anything else. I have written 400 pages on it—therefore it is very nearly half done. It is Huck Finn's Autobiography. I like it only tolerably well, as far as I have got, & may possibly pigeonhole or burn the MS when it is done." Sam invested in Huck Finn's book as a sequel to Tom Sawyer's, counting on good sales of the first book. Even before the publication of an American edition of *Tom Sawyer*, Sam had cards printed up to respond to his mail asking for a sequel. He thought he might be able to turn Tom's adventures into a lucrative series; Ned Buntline's successful children's books had formed the core of his own childhood reading.

Unfortunately, Bliss could not tell Sam when he expected to have *The Adventures of Tom Sawyer* on the market. This book represented the execution of Sam's final contract with Bliss, and Bliss wanted to prolong the relationship with his most popular author. From his position on the board of the American Publishing Company, Sam determined to wield some power. In three years, the business had moved from shabby offices to luxurious ones and had gone from issuing only two or three books a year to putting out three times that many. With so many books to handle, Bliss could not supervise the production of *Tom Sawyer* as closely as Sam preferred, so Sam wrote the other directors suggesting that the company go back to selling primarily books by Mark Twain and perhaps a few others. Sam would willingly sacrifice his investment in the publishing house, an investment that had not recently paid many dividends, to ensure the success of his novel.

Of course, the other books now threatening to squeeze *Tom Sawyer* out of public notice included Bret Harte's *Gabriel Conroy*, Dan De Quille's *Big Bonanza*, and Charles Dudley Warner's Egyptian travel-book *Moslems and Mummies*, all contracted under Sam's influence. Putting the good of the business ahead of his personal feelings, Bliss answered the charges by criticizing Sam for traducing him. "Even the poor drunken [True] Williams comes and boastingly taunts me with what you tell him—while another of my help gets letters from N.Y. stating what he says you told there. For myself I care nothing, but it seems poor policy to injure the stock this way." Sam then tacitly admitted his own responsibility for the problems in marketing *Tom Sawyer* by secretly proposing to Bliss that he head up a new joint publishing company Sam wanted to establish, built on the plan he had suggested to his fellow directors. Despite Sam's growing belief that Bliss robbed him on behalf of the American Publishing Company, he had faith in Bliss' capacity to sell books. Only Bliss' divided interests made him dangerous. Bliss turned him down, but Sam's threats cleared a small space in the fall for company book agents to sell *Tom Sawyer* with only Harte's *Gabriel Conroy* as competition. This may have been Sam's desire, a western-style showdown with his western competitor; Sam may have even conspired with Bliss to push his novel at the expense of Harte's. In any case, there was gossip around Virginia City, Nevada, as Sam acknowledged to his old friend Denis McCarthy, that "I had persuaded Dan to adopt a plan in the writing of his book which I knew would kill it!"* The gossip may have been a disgruntled author's sour grapes, but if Sam interfered in any way with the writing, canvass, or production of Dan De Quille's *The Big Bonanza*, he may have done the same with Bret Harte's *Gabriel Conroy*.

In a mixed blessing, the British edition came out in June, securing an English copyright for Mark Twain. The book had no illustrations, since Chatto had been negotiating with Bliss through Sam for copies of True Williams' work, and they had not arrived on time. As it happened, the coveted British copyright did Sam no good in Canada, where a firm called Belford Brothers printed up inexpensive copies of the novel for sale through newsstands and bookstores on both sides of the border. Watching the market for his delayed American Publishing Company edition disappear in Belford's seventy-five-cent paperbacks, Sam determined to prosecute the thieves. Unfortunately, contradictory Canadian laws made it difficult to determine if Mark Twain held a copyright on *The Adventures of Tom Sawyer* there, while American law prohibited selling a pirated book only if the seller had been personally informed that the edition was a piracy. Sam had no recourse. His plan for launching his precious literary vessel lay in pieces.

His frustration and impatience with publishing *Tom Sawyer* overflowed into his response to the nostalgic visions of the past the novel itself provoked. He wrote biting letters to old friends moved to contact him in his fame. Even Will Bowen, with whom Sam had been friends since childhood, received a savage blast for the maudlin dreaminess of his recent letter. "Man, do you know that this is simply mental & moral masturbation? It belongs eminently to the period usually devoted to *physical* masturbation, & should be left there & outgrown." He explained to Jacob Burrough, his St. Louis roommate during his vagabond typesetting days, that he had told Bowen to shelve his sentimental drivel. "When I get a letter like that from a grown man and he a widower with a family, it gives me the stomach ache," he wrote. "I told him to stop being 16 at 40; told him to stop drooling about the sweet yet melancholy past, and take a pill. I said there is but one solitary thing about the past worth remembering, and that was that it *is* the past." The virulence of Sam's resolution against the past threatened to overwhelm the genial Mark Twain. When Howells wondered why people hated the past so much, Sam replied, "It's so damned humiliating." The promise for the future, embodied in the publication of *Tom Sawyer*, battled with the past that suffused the book itself. Sam risked his psychic balance by attempting to earn his fame through propounding the very past he was desperate to elude.

The past kept calling in the form of Bret Harte. Harte's work had steadily declined in quality. His debts mounted. Friends who had at first admired his wit now resented his sting. Even his personal habits deteriorated: He continued to dress with foppish refinement, but his drinking had become excessive and his hours even more irregular. Harte had two projects in which he placed great hope, *Gabriel Conroy* and a play called *Two Men of Sandy Bar*, based on some of his short-story characters. Harte nervously anticipated the opening of the play and offered tickets to Sam, who stopped in New York on his way home from Elmira to see it. Critics disliked the play thoroughly, but Sam felt "Harte's play can be doctored till it will be entirely acceptable & then it will clear a great sum every year," as he wrote Howells. "The play entertained me hugely, even in its present crude state."

In early October, after the failure of the play, Harte again came to Hartford and "asked me to help him write a play & divide the swag, & I agreed." The two men blocked out a play involving Buck Fanshaw, a slang-slinging western archetype from *Roughing It*, and Ah Sin, a Chinese cameo character from the flop *Two Men of Sandy Bar* who stole the show when the role was performed by Charles Parsloe. Parsloe would re-create the character, who would be the focus of the drama and give it its new title. Howells warned his friend about the collaboration. "I think Harte has acted crazily about the criticism of his play, but he's been shamefully decried and abused. Of course no man knows till he's tried how absurdly he'll act, but I wish Harte had not been tried."

Howells meanwhile had spent his summer vacation exercising his political interests. His early success in writing Lincoln's campaign biography and the fact that his wife Elinor was a cousin of Rutherford B. Hayes made him the perfect man to write the life story of the 1876 Republican candidate for President. Sam read the biography right after publication, in early September. He praised Howells, "It is a marvelous thing that you read for it & wrote it in such a little bit of time, let alone conduct a dysentery at the same time." Howells tried to seduce Sam into campaigning for Hayes against Samuel J. Tilden, but Sam preferred to keep Mark Twain out of politics. "When a humorist ventures upon the grave concerns of life he must do his job better than another man or he works harm to his cause." Eventually, though, he agreed to speak out if Howells promised to get Charley Stoddard a consulship somewhere if Hayes won. "I am mighty sorry that book [the campaign biography] does not sell better; but don't you worry about Hayes," Sam reassured Howells three weeks before the election; he felt certain about Tilden's impending defeat "since my brother went over to the enemy." In fact, the popular vote went to Tilden by a small margin, but delays in the returns allowed vote trading in the electoral college, which tipped the presidency to Hayes—an irony since Hayes had campaigned as a reformer but gained the White House by old-fashioned horse-trading. His election, with the help of southern Democrats, marked the end of Reconstruction and a temporary burial of white America's most acrid animosities resulting from the Civil War, accomplished by disenfranchising freed blacks and returning white rule to the former Confederacy.

Bret Harte visited frequently during the several months of anxious waiting for election results, astonishing Sam with his complete political indifference. The old friends worked on *Ah Sin* around Mark Twain's light schedule of public readings that Sam had arranged for November in a halfhearted attempt to garner some attention for the December release of *The Adventures of Tom Sawyer*. He performed in Brooklyn on November 13 on a joint bill with some musicians, an arrangement Sam disliked completely. The public now clamored for author readings, but that was not a form with which Sam felt at ease. Mark Twain was not an author in the regular sense of the word. He was a name on the spine of a book. He was a performance. Sam transformed what began as an author's reading into a performance, but the conflicting expectations of the audience and the performer made the evening difficult. Sam tried the format twice in Boston and once in Providence, before abandoning it.

Harte had also come to Hartford so that he could bemoan the further collapse of his fortunes with a friend. His earlier play had made him little money and damaged his reputation, and *Gabriel Conroy* had embarrassingly sold fewer than five thousand copies. Even *Tom Sawyer*, sustaining heavy damage by the Canadian piracy, sold three times that number. Sam offered Harte his sympathy, but the modest success of the crippled *Tom Sawyer* in its head-to-head competition with *Gabriel Conroy* culminated years of his passionate and secret struggle against Bret Harte. Sam's victory was a mastery over his past, in which Bret Harte had been his mentor. Despite his triumph, Sam still allowed himself to be amazed by Harte's startling facility with language. During one visit in December, Sam appointed Harte guest artist for the Saturday Morning Club, and yet late Friday night he had nothing to present. When Sam went to bed, Harte retired to his room with a bottle of whiskey and some paper. By morning, the pages were full and the bottle empty. His story, "Thankful Blossom," impressed Sam with its charm and polish.

Harte then ruined the glow by asking to borrow more money. Sam had fronted him nearly $3,000 over the past year, not including the money he had convinced Bliss to extend on Harte's American Publishing Company account. To top off the visit, Harte also offended Livy severely enough to have to later write to Sam, "Tell Mrs. Clemens that she must forgive me for my heterodoxy—that until she does I shall wear sackcloth (fashionably cut,) and that I would put ashes on my head but that Nature has anticipated me." The awkward relationship did not bode well for the

success of their play, but Sam still felt confident that the names Bret
Harte and Mark Twain, their western subject matter, and Charles Parsloe's performance could win *Ah Sin* an audience. Theatrical profits seemed
a certainty compared with the dicey prospects of a book. He wrote to
Moncure Conway after the anticlimactic release of *Tom Sawyer*, "We find
our copyright law here to be nearly worthless, and if I can make a living
out of plays, I shall never write another book. For the present I have
placed the three books in mind, in the waste basket."

27 | *Feeling Poor*

*There are two times in a man's life when he should not
speculate: when he can't afford it, and when he can.*
—"Pudd'nhead Wilson's New Calendar" (1897)

On THE NEW Year's Eve welcoming 1877, the Clemenses attended the most peculiar party of their married
lives. Isabella Beecher Hooker hosted a double-barreled
gathering, for her neighbors and friends, and for her spiritualist comrades.
Hooker and her followers believed that the New Year would usher in her
new order, the transcendental matriarchal government she had envisioned,
with herself as President. An involved séance among devotees, held simultaneously with the party for those more secular neighbors, would reveal this new regime. The spiritualist junta would then emerge from
seclusion with an aura of authority obvious even to their nonbelieving
subjects. Unfortunately for Hooker, the revelation never came.

Sam felt some sympathy with Hooker's disappointment. While not
wrapped up in a full-blown spiritualist delusion like his neighbor, he too
struggled to reach the top of an invisible order and found himself coming
up short. For a couple comprised of an heiress and popular author, money
had grown tight. Strikes among Pennsylvania coal miners, part of a wave
of labor unrest affecting the industrial North, were severely pinching
Langdon coal interests. The relative failure of *Tom Sawyer*, whose sales had
lingered under ten thousand copies in its first month of release and then

fell off rapidly, also forced Sam and Livy to consider reducing the scale of their lives. The Clemenses lived expensively, spending about $30,000 a year to run their household. Salaries for their domestics were close to $2,000 annually, excluding food and board. They entertained frequently and elegantly and went first class whenever they traveled. Sam tried to persuade Livy that the family should spend at least a year in Germany starting the next summer, so that they could temporarily suspend house-keeping—the typical Nook Farm solution to the economic impracticality of their ideal community. Livy did not see the need to relocate overseas, preferring to economize less drastically; the fact that the girls, going on three and five, could now play well together increased her desire to give them a summer in Elmira. "I don't know who will come out ahead," she wrote her mother of the debate about retiring to Europe. "But I think I shall."

A popular play would ease the financial shortfall that had provoked the disagreement. *Ah Sin* promised not only to lift Sam out of his economic doldrums, but to finalize his victory over Bret Harte. Harte's name was the faltering writer's only valuable property, and Sam already secured that for promoting the play; now he would attempt to make the play work without distraction from his cowriter. Sam used Harte's lack of money as a way to keep him on the sidelines as *Ah Sin* moved toward its opening. His advance on *Gabriel Conroy* and loans from Sam made up financially for his inability to produce short stories while working on the book and play, but not enough to compensate for the flat-out failure of the novel. In February, Sam wrote Harte a letter offering him a twenty-five-dollar-a-week salary to come to Hartford and collaborate on another play. "I had not the slightest idea of your speculating out of my poverty," Harte haughtily wrote. Vitriolicly accusing Sam of shrewd practice, he added that "either Bliss must confess that he runs his concerns solely in *your* interest, and that he uses the names of other authors to keep that fact from the public, or else he is a fool."

Though the collaborators had a contract with Charles Parsloe, the actor who would take the role of Ah Sin, they as yet had no theater or opening date for the production. In March, while Sam flirted with sending Parsloe to California to study how to perform the western Chinese character, Harte arranged for a tryout in Washington, claiming that "if we fail—it is a local failure and will not hurt our other work as much as a metropolitan *fiasco*." Dissension between the men had already rendered the collaboration a disaster. Earlier in the year, when Harte ran into Parsloe on the street in New York, Parsloe had fended off questions by informing Harte that there was nothing he needed to know. Parsloe and

Sam, meanwhile, kept in regular contact concerning every detail of the play.

Sam's coldness even infected the character of Mark Twain, who had been notably humorless early in 1877, writing little and publishing less. One of his funniest pieces was a cruel attack on Charles C. Duncan, captain of the *Quaker City* a decade before. While lecturing about the tour, Duncan had recently insulted Mark Twain. When the press asked for a reply, Mark Twain blistered Duncan. "I know him to be a canting hypocrite, filled to the chin with sham godliness, and forever oozing and dripping false piety and pharisaical prayers. I know his word to be worthless." He also echoed gossip that Duncan, in his current position as shipping commissioner for the port of New York, had lined his pockets with gold stolen from poor sailors. Duncan sued. Although accurate, Sam's attack was pointlessly ferocious, the result of the rage Sam always experienced when circumstances spun past his control. He exempted a few relationships from his vitriol, such as those with Livy, Howells, and Joe Twichell, but their father's unpredictable rants and curses terrified Susie and Bay. Other friends knew they might come in for a savage shot at any time. Frank Fuller, for example, persuaded Sam to invest in a steam generator he was representing, and when it failed Sam broke off their friendship. Sam settled Captain Duncan's lawsuit out of court for a few hundred dollars, writing to tell Howells that he "got off admirably well." Sam's explosion at the flawed but harmless Duncan was an expensive amusement for a man worried about money.

Looking for a quick release from his tightened financial condition, Sam invested more speculatively. Before the failure of *Tom Sawyer*, he had preferred to buy stock in existing companies, but now he looked for ventures whose vast prospects might make the success or failure of his literary work financially irrelevant. All of these projects followed the pattern of Fuller's steam generator, a promising invention that nonetheless fails to find a market. Invention was a national craze in the late nineteenth century: Machines were remaking society, breaking the shackles of dangerous and repetitive labor; advances in power generation promised a future in which electricity replaced muscle in every endeavor except the creations of the human mind. But still, inventions providing merely a refined version of an existing technology had short lives, and those which promised to alter the technology entirely were difficult to finance. Sam, completely enchanted with visions of both a new world and personal wealth, invested an average of $25,000 each in a steam pulley, an improved method of marine telegraphy, and a new insurance company, money which in each case disappeared when the project proved unworkable. The money came from Livy, since between 1866 and 1876, Sam earned approximately $150,000, not enough to cover the family's living costs for the same period, even excluding the $120,000 it cost Sam and Livy to build their house. His failure rate in investing in new inventions was due to Sam's surprisingly limited vision of technology. Like many southerners, Sam liked the past too much for a man who thought of himself as an unsentimental visionary. He invested in machines that mechanized human activity, not machines that reconceived it. The future belonged to machines which transcended the past, such as the telephone and the automobile, both rooted in inventions of the 1870s, both using radically new technologies to accomplish traditional tasks such as communication and transportation. Sam's recurring embarrassment about the past handicapped his capacity to see the future.

Sam steeped himself in history books much the way a man in prison studies his cell, to look for an escape from it. Having given himself over to the memories of an earlier America in composing *Tom Sawyer* and "Old Times on the Mississippi," he now turned his attention to the lore of another land he loved: England. He was especially caught up in the monarchical power struggles that followed the death of Henry VIII. So far, his reading had produced only one bit of writing, a scatological "fireside chat" among Queen Elizabeth, William Shakespeare, Ben Jonson, Francis Bacon, Walter Raleigh, and assorted other notables, which Sam shared in manuscript with his male friends. Though he could not publish *1601*, he found in the boyhood of Edward VI a prime subject for a switch-of-identity story concerning the prince and his lowliest subject. Intrigued by Scottish historian W.E.H. Lecky's contention, forwarded in his *History of European Morals*, that ethical progress determined the path of history, Sam wanted his book to uncover any moral lessons learned by both the prince and the pauper after taking up one another's roles.

While Lecky's argument about moral progress countered Sam's long-standing conservatism, it echoed Thomas Paine's ideology, as expressed in his *Age of Reason*, a volume to which Sam traced his own moral and religious sensibility. By giving the traditional romantic plot of highborn and lowborn trading places this moral and political underpinning, Sam could explore his own uncertainty about whether history improved the level of a nation's morality. He had his doubts. When he first read Thomas Carlyle's history of the French Revolution, he found the radicals' central ideals unappealing. "Republican government, with a sharply restricted suffrage, is just as good as a Constitutional monarchy with a virtuous & powerful aristocracy," he wrote Mary Fairbanks' daughter Mollie, "but with an unrestricted suffrage it ought to perish because it is founded in wrong & is weak & bad & tyrannical." He found the underlying principles of most European democratic movements equally unsatisfying. Still, Sam looked forward to using Edward VI's enforced education in social justice as a way to explore the ideas of Lecky and Paine.

Although Sam's reading showed up in his writing, he did not read to write. He simply loved to read. He consumed his monthly *Atlantic* and other magazines and typically had a dozen half-read books scattered around him. In the winter of 1877, he at last moved his Nook Farm study from the second floor room designed for that purpose to the third floor billiard room, using an array of old crates to store his books and papers. Invariably before the ritual meeting of his Friday Night Club—in contrast to Monday's intellectual meeting, Friday was devoted to billiards, cigars, whiskey, and talk—he would have to clear from his pool table the books that wouldn't fit in his cubby. "Of all the literary men I have known," Howells later described him, "he was the most unliterary in his make and manner." Though Sam "was always reading some vital book," he had little patience for most fiction and almost none for poetry, and he knew no Latin or Greek. To Sam, these conventional sources for literary material were bones long since picked over, but history offered an untried cuisine through which he could feed both his hunger for knowledge and his imagination.

In late April, Sam went to Baltimore for the rehearsals of *Ah Sin*. He had intended to travel to Washington, where he told Mother Fairbanks the play would "be hurled at the public" on May 7, 1877, and where he could take the opportunity to introduce himself to Elinor Howells' cousin, President Hayes. Instead, he left on May 1, before the opening. He wrote Howells that he "found I was not absolutely needed in Washington, so I only staid 24 hours," and he later claimed to have succumbed to a sudden attack of bronchitis, but in fact it was Bret Harte's presence in Washington that drove him home. Parsloe, entrusted by Sam to read his curtain speech for him, complained to Sam later that "the excitement of a first night is bad enough, but to have the annoyance with Harte that I have is too much for a beginner." The producer begged Sam to return to Washington and work on the play, which he felt would succeed with revisions. Instead, Sam took Joe Twichell on a five-day trip to Bermuda.

Within two weeks of his return, the Clemenses relocated to Quarry Farm for a summer of work and play. First, Sam wrote up his "Rambling Notes of an Idle Excursion," about his trip to Bermuda, as a four-part article for *The Atlantic*, and then began work on his sixteenth-century royal-switch tale; his joy in his own family had also fueled a desire to write something for children. Then, turning his attention to the stage, he composed a play featuring an "old fool detective [who] pervades the piece from beginning to end—always on hand & busy," he explained to his prospective collaborator Howells. "I *meant* it for a comedy—but it is only a long farce." Detective fiction had become popular and Sam could not resist travestying it. Howells wanted to see the script, to judge Sam's capacity as a playwright before agreeing to compose a play together. He had recently leased a play of his to an actor, and Sam advised Howells to write the contract "from the standpoint that he is the blackest-livered scoundrel on earth. That is the standpoint of our contract with Parsloe, who is a mighty good fellow & as gentle as a lamb."

Ah Sin opened on Broadway on July 31, 1877, and Sam left Elmira a few weeks before to attend rehearsals. Rumors of a prowler in Hartford derailed his plans. Sam raced home to investigate. Other than the police chief's racist opinion that George Griffin, the butler, planned to gut the house, witnesses provided a muddle of small accusations: The cook said the housemaid Lizzie slept with her boyfriend in the house; Lizzie said George played billiards with his friends; George said Patrick McAleer, the coachman, wore Sam's shoes. Sam finally concluded that Lizzie's lover had set off the alarm. She tearfully confessed, heartbroken that her man would not marry her. Consumed by the detective drama in which he saw himself as the central character, Sam plotted the climax. For over an hour, Sam tried to convince Lizzie's man to marry, but he refused—until Sam announced that he had a policeman in one room and a preacher in the other, and the man could choose between them. Joe Twichell married the couple and Sam gave them each a $100 gift and sent them on their way. Newspapers everywhere reported Mark Twain's paternalistic lark just two weeks before *Ah Sin* opened, which contributed to strong ticket sales— which may have been Sam's intention from the beginning of this escapade.

Tacitly agreeing that they should not meet, Bret Harte remained in Washington during the opening, lobbying for a consular post; his partner could make whatever adjustments he felt the play needed. Sam tried to permit "hardly a foot-print of Harte in it anywhere. But it is full of incurable defects: to-wit, Harte's deliberate thefts & plagiarisms, & my own unconscious ones," he told Howells. "I don't believe Harte ever had an idea that he came by honestly. He is the most abandoned thief that defiles the earth." Livy cautioned Sam, "Don't say harsh things about Mr. Harte, don't talk against Mr. Harte to people, it is so much better that you be reticent about him, don't let anybody trap you into talking freely of him—We are so desperately happy, our paths lie in such pleasant places, and he is so miserable, we can easily afford to be magnanimus toward him." In fact, Sam spoke where he thought it would hurt the most, urging President Hayes not to consider Harte for an appointment overseas. Howells could not help but concur with Sam's assessment of Harte's character, though he did so without Sam's vehemence when he discussed it with the President when they met in Boston at the end of June.

The fall brought a series of minor catastrophes leavened with pleasant visits. After a tremendous opening, *Ah Sin* slowly failed. Charley Stoddard came to commiserate, but he also reported to Sam that, despite the fame attendant on the publication of his *South Sea Idyls*, he had made only six dollars on the book. In November, Sam installed a direct telephone line to offices of the *Hartford Courant*, so he could send telegrams from there, but he subsequently had to battle rumors that he was about to become the editor of the paper. Howells came to town twice, once for a reception at the Clemenses for pioneering Chinese-American activist Yung Wing, who ran a Hartford-based educational organization. Orion reported that someone in Keokuk was selling by subscription a book attributed to Mark Twain; strangely, the book turned out to be by Max Adeler, the Philadelphia writer who as John Quill had tussled with Sam over plagiarism seven years before. Even the Mark Twain Scrap Book, which had been the year's most lucrative venture, began to lag. On Dan Slote's request, Sam loaned the company $5,000; only after he had done so did he learn that its debt was so large that the loan would do nothing to assuage it. The new insurance company into which Sam had put $23,000, guaranteed by Nevada Senator John P. Jones, folded; but Jones had not returned Sam's money. Sam's relationship with Elisha Bliss had entirely frayed, and he felt uncertain where he might publish his next book, or even if he might finish one.

As always whenever money grew short, Sam reconsidered his pledge not to lecture. He revived a plan the famous cartoonist Thomas Nast had proposed ten years before, for Nast to "stand on the platform and make pictures, and I stand by you and blackguard the audience." Sam proposed going only to large towns, hiring a tour manager on a salary, and splitting the profits, which he estimated would reach at least $60,000 for four months. When Nast turned him down, Sam's last hope for an infusion of cash disappeared. The Clemenses decided to go abroad in the spring.

A week before Christmas, a single event capped this pile of frustration and uncertainty. Sam spoke at a dinner to honor John Greenleaf Whittier, sponsored by *The Atlantic*. Holmes was there, and Longfellow, and Emerson; Sam sat midway down one leg of the U-shaped table and spoke near the end of the celebration, after midnight, when many of the brilliant minds there had been dulled by champagne. After Howells introduced him as "a humorist who never makes you blush to have enjoyed his joke," Sam spoke of visiting a miner in 1864, when Mark Twain was just beginning to be known as a writer. The miner begrudgingly gave him hospitality and then explained that he'd recently been the victim of three literary types, a Mr. Holmes, a Mr. Emerson, and a Mr. Longfellow, who fought over cards, drank his whiskey, and stole his boots. The miner says:

> "Mr. Twain, you are the fourth in twenty-four hours—and I'm a-going to move—I ain't suited to the littery atmosphere."
>
> I said to the miner, "Why, my dear sir, *these* were not the gracious singers to whom we and the world pay loving reverence and homage; these were imposters."
>
> The miner investigated me with a calm eye for a while, then said he, "Ah—imposters, were they?—are *you*?"

The audience's ambivalent reaction to the story deflated Sam in the telling. Without Mark Twain's legendary insouciance, the joke foundered. He could not communicate both the honor he was paying to the eminent writers at the head table, and the hoax he revealed in himself, that Mark Twain occupied a place between the thieving impostors and the great poets. Instead of wild laughter, his conclusion met with some guffaws and mostly silence.

Back at the hotel, Charles Dudley Warner revealed the rotten core of the episode by solemnly chiding Sam, "Well, Mark, *you're* a funny fellow." His moral reasoning and literary skill notwithstanding, the Mark Twain persona succeeded on its humor; he had received an invitation to speak at the dinner because William Dean Howells championed his humor in Boston's literary Valhalla. Only three years had passed since Mark Twain's first story appeared in *The Atlantic*, and he had yet to persuade the literary establishment that he belonged among them; mocking the giants on their own turf could not gain him favor. Howells had bestowed the blessings of literary glory upon Mark Twain, but in this brief after-dinner speech, Sam had betrayed the trust of his defender by embarrassing his audience. Sam worried that if Howells dropped him, Mark Twain's literary ambitions would be finished. But Howells had staked his claim on his literary judgment and felt responsible for Twain's blunder. Howells refused Sam's offer to withdraw from *The Atlantic*, telling him "not to exaggerate the damage. You are not going to be floored by it; there is more justice than that even in *this* world." He suggested that Sam apologize to Whittier, Emerson, Holmes, and Longfellow by letter, which he did, noting as he did to Howells himself, "Ah, well, I am a great & sublime fool. But then I am God's fool, & all His works must be contemplated with respect."

The Clemenses soon began their preparations to leave America. They would close the house for more than a year, crating and storing all possessions to reduce the house's temptation for thieves, and dismiss all the servants but Patrick McAleer. Sam hammered out a secret contract for his next book with Frank Bliss, Elisha's son. Frank had tired of working for his father and wanted to strike out on his own; he agreed to the partnership with Sam that his father had rejected, for a new firm publishing primarily Mark Twain's book. Trying to salvage his business endeavors, Sam gave Dan Slote a few short pieces for a pamphlet littered liberally with advertising for the Mark Twain Scrap Book. The Aetna Insurance Company paid $300 for the remaining lot of his "Mark Twain's Sketches, No. 1" pamphlet—which he had intended as a series to be sold through newsstands but which never got past the first issue—for use as a promotional tool. He pursued Senator Jones for his vanished $23,000, but had no success. In March, he turned to his late father-in-law's Buffalo associate John D. F. Slee, who not only got the money back but also brought the Clemenses' unstable finances to the attention of Sam's brother-in-law Charlie Langdon, now managing the Langdon holdings. Charlie regarded Sam's expenditures as profligate, especially in the light of the family's diminished fortunes.

None of these negotiations brought Sam much money or satisfaction. He wrote to his mother, now living temporarily with Orion in Keokuk, "Life has come to be a very serious matter with me. I have a badgered, harassed feeling, a good part of my time. It comes mainly of business responsibilities and annoyances, and the persecution of kindly letters from well meaning strangers." Sam asked her to come as far east as Fredonia, so that he could see her before he left for Europe. He tried to write, making some progress on his tale of the prince and the pauper. Doubting his capacity to write for the stage in the wake of his failure with *Ah Sin*, he hired a playwright to repair his unusable farce concerning the bumbling detective. He also wrote one short piece for *The Atlantic*, satirizing those instructive little fables, typical of religious publications, in which a simple act of generosity produces a miracle. In Mark Twain's versions, acts of generosity only bring on greater claims against the benefactor. Claims on Sam's generosity grated not only because they rolled in incessantly but because, with money tight, every dollar he gave away diminished his own solvency.

Before they left Hartford to make their farewells in Elmira and Fredonia, Sam and Livy received a visit from the Howellses. Livy's friend Clara Spaulding, who had helped close up the house, decided to accompany the family to Europe. Sam arranged with Joe Twichell, his favorite walking partner, to join him in August for a hiking tour of Switzerland. Livy had constructed an itinerary calling for a few months in Germany, followed by a fall tour of Italy, a winter in Munich, and spring and summer in Paris. At the end of March, they closed the house and on April 11, 1878, sailed on the *Holsatia* for Hamburg. Sam was looking forward to a vacation from business worry, from financial constriction, and from Mark Twain himself, who had produced very little joy or prosperity over the past several years.

28 | *Hiding Out in Europe*

*Let us be thankful for the fools. But for them the rest of
us could not succeed.*
—"Pudd'nhead Wilson's New Calendar" (1897)

It is your human environment that makes climate.
—"Pudd'nhead Wilson's New Calendar" (1897)

"I SHALL BUDGE no more until I shall have completed
one of the half dozen books that lie begun, up stairs," Sam
told his mother before he left for Europe. In addition to
finishing at least one of his incomplete manuscripts—which included Huck
Finn's autobiography, the prince-and-pauper switch story, and a visit to
heaven via comet by a figure based on West Coast sea captain Ned Wakeman—Sam wanted to learn German and refine his taste in art. The era's
international center for advanced learning, Germany attracted Americans
pursuing scholarship in science and letters. America in 1878 had no uni-
versities, and its colleges primarily harbored children of privilege. Amer-
ican-trained physicians attended small independent schools and American
lawyers learned by apprenticeship; training in Germany was far more rigorous and of much higher quality. Sam, Livy, and Clara Spaulding decided
to learn German and immersed the children in the language with the help
of their Hartford nurse, Rosina Hay, who spoke only her native tongue
with the children.

After a rough sea passage and a slow overland trip from Hamburg,
the family settled into a beautiful hotel in Heidelberg. They had a suite
of rooms, with a common room that occupied a corner of the building and

featured two glassed-in balconies offering different views of the mountain and the River Neckar. Across the river and down a hill lay a clatch of several houses, one of which, with a solitary third-floor window over-looking Heidelberg, caught Sam's eye, and he began to refer jokingly to it as his study. The house had a room to rent; it turned out to be the workspace he had imagined. Still, Sam found writing difficult. He told Howells, "I have waited for a 'call' to go to work—I knew it would come. Well, it began to come a week ago; my note-book comes out more & more frequently every day since; 3 days ago I concluded to move my manu-scripts over to my den." But within a week he abandoned his workroom because "it was no exercise to trot down there, & the exercise of climbing up here again was valueless because I got it at the wrong end of the day."* He found a new room which took him over an hour to climb to. It cost "five dollars a month, the family to teach me German, & presently [I] found that they imagined they were to lodge me & furnish me my meals also!"*

Even as he maintained his habit of working from breakfast until late afternoon, Sam could not easily settle down to writing. Learning a new language interfered with his ability to think smoothly in his own. Still bothered by the course of his professional life back home, he felt uncertain of Frank Bliss' capacity to succeed with a Mark Twain volume sold by subscription. In June, Howells reported that Bret Harte had at last re-ceived a consular appointment—to Germany. "To send this nasty crea-ture to puke upon the American name in a foreign land is too much," Sam responded. "Harte shan't swindle the Germans if I can help it. Tell me what German town he is to filthify with his presence; then I will write the authorities there that he is a persistent borrower who never pays." Sam did not know that Howells, having received reports of Harte's efforts to control his drinking and repay his debts, had recommended the ap-pointment. Although Howells knew that his efforts on Harte's behalf would haunt his relationship with Sam, he could not allow Sam's slanders to poison Harte's chances to redeem himself.

The children provided Sam with a joyful release from his creative frustration. Susie, age six, made progress with her German, though she found Rosa's fidelity to her Teutonic roots wearisome, complaining, "Mama, I wish Rosa was made in English." Bay, now four, blithely ig-nored the rules concerning what language she must speak, but being young enough to absorb a new language naturally she acquired German at nearly the rate of her sister. Livy and Clara Spaulding also worked on their German lessons with more diligence but less success than the girls. One morning at breakfast, a German man adjusted the blinds to let in the sun,

to which his wife said, *"Wunderschön!"* Livy said, gratefully, "There—
Gott sei dank, I understood *that,* anyway—*window-shade!"** Meanwhile, Bay
was becoming as willful as Susie had been. Told she had lost a privilege
simply because her mother said so, Bay replied, "That isn't any *why."**
Livy paid the children to keep quiet during her lessons; she rewarded
them with candy for a day of not fighting. Once, after thinking about it
a moment, Susie returned her reward. Sam inquired: If she fought with
Bay, hadn't Bay fought, too? Susie insisted Clara keep her treasure because
"I don't know if she felt wrong in her heart, I only know I didn't feel
right in mine."

For the most part, Livy expressed content with Europe as a temporary respite from the United States, where the hurly-burly of public
life grew ever more unsettling. The growing American labor union movement erupted frequently into violence, as government and industry
worked in concert to suppress what they regarded as a revolutionary
threat. Though the continuing strikes and riots in the Midwest concerned
her, she was thankful to be a citizen of her native land. "I only hope that
we shall always have money enough so that we can continue to live
there,"* she wrote her mother. When the annual report of the coal firm
arrived in June, both Sam and Livy sighed with relief. *"We've quit feeling
poor!"* Sam confided in Howells. "Yesterday we fell to figuring & discovered that we have more than income enough, from investments, to live
in Hartford on a generous scale." Satisfied with their prosperity, Sam left
money matters in Livy's hands. She found that the family's European
expenses were $250 a month, a fraction of what they spent at home. Her
mother sent her regular disbursements as well, which gave Livy the freedom to buy some fashionable European furnishings for the Hartford house.

Joe Twichell met the Clemens clan in Baden-Baden on August 1, 1878,
prepared to spend six weeks hiking with Sam, but in July Sam had experienced a rheumatism in his legs that forced him to stay horizontal for
a few days. The medicinal baths at Baden-Baden provided him some relief,
and during August and the first week of September, he and Joe took a
variety of short hikes around Germany and Switzerland, returning to the
family whenever comfort required. Sam began to feel the release that
travel had always brought him. "I think I foretaste some of the advantage
of being dead," he had written Howells soon after arriving on foreign soil,
about the happy hibernation of his alternate personas, Mark Twain and
S. L. Clemens. Twichell noticed a child's fresh delight in his friend.

> Mark is a queer fellow. There is nothing that he so
> delights in as a swift, strong stream. . . . [A]s we were on our

way back to the hotel, seeing a lot of driftwood caught by the torrent side below the path, I climbed down and threw it in. When I got back to the path Mark was running downstream after it as hard as he could go, throwing up his hands and shouting in the wildest ecstasy, and when a piece went over a fall and emerged to view in the foam below he would jump up and down and yell.

The trip furnished great literary material. Resorting to wheeled transportation despite their avowed intent to walk supplied Sam a running joke for Mark Twain's book of travel. Joe's personality gave Sam an alternative literary sidekick with whom he could replace the crass Brown whom he had used in his Hawaiian and Mediterranean correspondence. He wrote Joe after his September departure, "I am putting out of my mind all memory of the times when I misbehaved toward you and hurt you; I am resolved to consider it forgiven, and to store up and remember only the charming hours of . . . a companionship which to me stands first after Livy's."

The family traveled from Switzerland to Venice, which reminded Sam of Howells, who had served as consul there during the Civil War. Looking up Howells' connections, Sam realized he hadn't heard from his friend for months. Howells had let enough time pass for Sam's fervent disgust with Harte's consular appointment to die down, so he would not have to choose between responding to the attack on Harte and maintaining a peculiar silence on that one subject. "Have I offended you in some way?" Sam worried. "The Lord knows it is my disposition, my infirmity, to do such things."

For the remainder of the fall, the group went on an Italian tour, with long stays in Rome and Florence. In Italy, Sam found his efforts to appreciate art hampered by his discontent with the realism of the paintings and his ambivalence about nudity. It galled him that the body could be depicted but not written about; at the same time, he was disgusted by the frank sexuality in much of southern European art, even in portraits of saints. He noticed that "the fig leaf & private members of statues are handled so much that they are black and polished while the rest of the figure is white & unpolished," and asked in his journal, "Which sex does this handling?" He appreciated some of the work, especially that of Titian, but wrote to Twichell that "Rome interests me as much as East Hartford could, and no more. Livy and Clara Spaulding are having a royal time worshipping the Old Masters, and I as good a time gritting my ineffectual teeth over them."

They worked their way back to Germany in mid-November, planning to settle in for the winter in Munich. At first Munich seemed a dreadful mistake, and they "decided that we would rest 24 hours, then pay whatever damages were required, & straightway fly to the south of France." Clara's bed had a habit of collapsing, and the house's courtyard proved the workshop for noisy craftsmen. Sam wrote Livy's mother, "There was but one thing we took solid & healing comfort in, & that was our gentle young colored girl who waits on our table.—But alas, day before yesterday she fell in the cistern & the color all came off."* They stayed nonetheless, uncertain they could find anything better. By his forty-third birthday— "I broke the back of life yesterday and started downhill toward old age," he wrote his mother and sister—he had rented a room a mile away to work in. He hit an immediate snag: He misplaced one of the notebooks he had kept while traveling with Joe Twichell. He had completed fifty thousand words, but in discrete anecdotes, some elaborating on his European experiences and some tall tales recalled from California. Without the notebook to create structure, he had only a collection of sketches. Around the New Year, the notebook showed up again and Sam could finally turn the sketches into a book he had already titled *A Tramp Abroad*. He wrote Twichell, "I haven't the slightest desire to loaf, but a consuming desire to work, ever since I got back my swing."

He titled the book to recall *The Innocents Abroad*, challenging himself to make it compare favorably. To that end, he planned to write perhaps twice the material needed to fill a subscription book and then cut and rearrange it. Unlike *Innocents* and *Roughing It*, books for which he struggled to complete the requisite number of pages, Sam wanted *A Tramp Abroad* to represent judicious editing and sensitive pacing as it waltzed from travelogue to sketchbook. With less fidelity to fact than to the demands of entertainment, he invented legends to go with German castles, depicted some experiences exactly, and recast others to fit the text. For example, in Munich, Sam woke in the middle of the night, "and after raging to myself for 2 interminable hours, I gave it up." He got out of bed, but could not locate a sock. Crawling around the dark room getting more and more lost and angry, he finally found one. In his joy, he stood up suddenly, upending the stand with the washbowl and pitcher. Livy woke at last, "screamed, then said, 'Who is that? what *is* the matter?' I said, 'There ain't anything the matter—I'm hunting for my sock.' She said, 'Are you hunting for it with a club?' " In the book version of the anecdote, Harris— actually Twichell—gets Livy's line. Sam seldom published Livy's wit, instead disguising Mrs. Mark Twain as a worried mother or a frightened child.

But *A Tramp Abroad* lacked "sharp satires on European life," because, as Sam noted to Howells, "a man can't write successful satire except he be in a calm judicial good-humor—whereas I *hate* travel, & I *hate* hotels, & I *hate* the opera, & I *hate* the Old Masters—in truth I don't ever seem to be in a good enough humor with ANYthing to *satirize* it." At least the uncertainty of who would publish the book seemed to diminish. As Elisha Bliss stepped up his campaign to get Sam's next book, gossip around Hartford informed him that his son already had the contract. The senior Bliss had an old contract in his safe, for the Riley-diamond field book, and since the American Publishing Company had fronted $2,000 for Riley's expenses, Bliss felt he had already paid for Sam's European manuscript. Usually shrewd, Bliss chose to forget that he had published *Tom Sawyer* without a contract. Sam forced Elisha to retroactively apply the Riley contract to *Tom Sawyer*, agreeing to repay the $2,000 the company had put up for the original project. Mark Twain's defection from Elisha Bliss was at last complete.

By the end of February 1879, the Clemenses relocated to Paris, which attracted people Sam liked and admired, like the Aldriches and painter Frank Millet, who had done a portrait of Sam a year and a half before and had become an adopted member of the family in the process. Sam stood up for Millet at his wedding in his secluded studio, and then rented the studio while the Millets honeymooned in England. The studio provided respite from the parade of visitors to Sam's rooms at the Hotel Normandy. Sam relished most of his visitors, including his German publisher Bernhard Tauchnitz, the Russian writer Ivan Turgenev, and Norwegian emigrant and Cornell professor Hjalmar Boyesen. He also dined regularly with a group of Americans known as the Stomach Club, to which he presented a speech, "Some Thoughts on the Science of Onanism," noting of the practice, "As an amusement it is too fleeting; as an occupation it is too wearing; as a public exhibition there is no money in it." Still, the unbroken social stream reminded both Sam and Livy of the relentlessness of company they entertained in Hartford, and they sometimes retreated to the studio without leaving word of where they had gone.

"France has neither winter nor summer nor morals," Sam wrote in his notebook. He did not much like France or the French. Paris did not warm all spring and they had to light a fire daily, with wood at ruinously high prices. At the Louvre, he found himself appalled at Titian's "Venus," who stares frankly back at the viewer while apparently masturbating. She "is thinking bestialities. She inflames & disgusts at the same moment," he remarked in his journal. "Young girls can be defiled by looking" at her. He plotted out a satire of French morals, a sentimental farce in which a French mother of several children dies surrounded by their fathers, all the while commiserating with her husband that she never had a child by him. Sam, a student of French since his river days, now regarded the language as "a mess of trivial sounds. . . . If one tried to be in earnest in such a language he could only be sophomoric & theatrical." He detested the food. "I can't quite make out," he wrote Joe Twichell, "how Americans live on this flat infernal European food several years at a time without a run home now & then to fill in with something wholesome & satisfying." He regarded the French as savages covered with a veneer of civilization; the excesses of their Revolution proved that fact to his satisfaction.

Then Charlie Langdon wrote to report reverses in the coal business, primarily due to labor disputes. Livy wrote her mother that she regretted her expensive house. "I seem only able to save at the spigot and the waste goes on at the bung just the same." Sam, meanwhile, pondered the more theoretical considerations behind the Langdon troubles. He dismissed arguments that eliminating oppression would result in a more just society; the Jews, he reasoned, "have endured these oppressions about 2,000 years—and yet . . . they are the world's intellectual aristocracy." He viewed the emerging social philosophy of communism as idiocy; no matter how wealth might be redistributed, it would soon end up in few hands. These opinions were consistent with Sam's praise to Howells for an *Atlantic* paragraph that had proposed disenfranchising blacks and immigrants, suppressing most newspapers, and replacing public high schools with elementary ones teaching basic skills. Though careful to express his political conservatism in moral terms when speaking as Mark Twain, privately Sam came to those positions less from his philosophy than from his upbringing. His self-protective reactionism battled with the upper-class liberal progressivism he had learned from the Langdons and from his Nook Farm neighbors, and adversity always made him favor the familiar old ways of his Whiggish father.

He also reacted self-protectively to Orion's plan to go out on a lecture tour as "Mark Twain's Brother," speaking on the subject of the development of character. Precious as the relief from being Mark Twain had felt, Sam would soon go back to his public life and could not have his ne'er-do-well brother muddying the origins of Mark Twain with his insights into the development of Sam Clemens' character. He first wrote an ill-tempered response, which Livy suppressed. Instead, Sam told Orion not only to give up on the idea of lecturing, but also to say nothing at all about him. "Mother Fairbanks, Mollie Fairbanks, you, & other close friends, have printed stuff from my private letters, & I have never had the courage to say 'Respect my privacy,' but have taken refuge in writing ten-line letters with nothing *in* the ten lines."* At the same time that he begged for Orion's respectful silence, he shared his brother's letters with Howells, often encouraging him to write up the feckless Orion as a character in one of his plays or novels.

The bad financial news pressured Sam to assemble a winning book. Poor engravings and print quality had always before made Mark Twain's books look cheap, so Sam exerted extra effort upon that aspect of *A Tramp Abroad*. He commissioned an American artist in Paris to make illustrations for the book and asked a French engraver to make the plates, but European technology didn't satisfy him. Though Dan Slote's stationery business had recently failed, Sam wrote Frank Bliss that "Slote has the best process in the world" for engraving, in which "the pictures are not transferred, but drawn on a hard mud surface." He pressed on with his manuscript and by the end of June felt that he had nearly completed it. After a ten-day pleasure trip through Belgium and the Netherlands, the Clemens crew reached London on July 20 to begin a month-long stay. Livy wrote her mother the day they arrived, "Doesn't that address sound (or look) as if we were nearing home?"* Sam did not find England nearly as entrancing as he had before. The English seemed rude to him, he found the English accent laughable, and the weather remained cold all summer. But the trip did allow Sam to meet a hero of his, Charles Darwin, who returned the compliment of Sam's admiration by confessing that he relaxed with Mark Twain's books. On August 23, 1879, surrounded by their mounds of luggage and crates of articles purchased in Europe for their Hartford home, the Clemens family sailed for America. They'd been absent nearly a year and a half. Sam had given Mark Twain a needed rest, and now he was returning with regained humor, a new manuscript, and refreshed ambitions for his persona.

| *The Return of Mark Twain*

> *Man will do many things to get himself loved, he will do all things to get himself envied.*
> —"Pudd'nhead Wilson's New Calendar" (1897)

THE CLEMENSES STOPPED briefly in New York City, to clear customs and get their land legs back, and then continued on, not to Hartford, but to Elmira. An article in the *New York Sun* described Mark Twain on his return to America as a changed man: "His hat, as he stood on the deck of the Cunarder, *Gallia*, was of the pattern that English officers wear in India, and his suit of clothes was such as a merchant might wear in his store. He looked older than when he went to Germany, and his hair had turned quite gray."

One factor that aged Sam was the continuing uncertainty concerning the publisher of *A Tramp Abroad*. Frank Bliss' effort to establish his own firm hit rocky shoals with its first book, the autobiography of "Wild Bill" Hickok, at the same time that Elisha Bliss' health fell into a sharp decline. Frank felt obligated to return to his father's company with his most valuable asset, the contract for Mark Twain's next book. From Elmira, Sam explained his crucial condition of reconciliation with the American Publishing Company: "They shall not canvass *any* book *but mine* between this present date and a date *9 months after the actual publication and issue* of my forthcoming book." This was the term he had tried to impress on Elisha

Bliss before the publication of *Tom Sawyer*, but it took that novel's weak showing, Sam's three-year hiatus, and his defection to carry his point.

After a week in Elmira, the entire family went to Fredonia for a brief visit. Four generations of Clemens women lived there: Jane, Pamela, Annie, and Annie's baby daughter Jean Webster. Sam at last met the baby's father, Charley Webster, who impressed him with "his energy, capacity & industry." Sam thought so much of his niece's family, in fact, that he bought the Websters a lot for a summer house at Van Buren Point on Lake Erie, after a pleasant group outing there. He was less impressed with his nephew Sammy, also recently returned from Europe and doing very little. Sam thought his nephew "had better look out or he'll be another Orion. This may be a false alarm & I hope it is—but isn't it really time Sam was getting at something?" Back at Quarry Farm, Sam Clemens settled down to rework *A Tramp Abroad*. "I did not expect to like it, but I do," he wrote Joe Twichell. "I believe it will be a readable book of travels. I cannot see that it lacks anything but information."

Staffing the Hartford house occupied part of Sam's attention, because Livy's was focused on how to redecorate it modestly, as fit their finances. Despite George Griffin's "disposition to gallantry" with the Clemens kitchen help, Sam rehired him, but he wanted Joe Twichell to help get a cook who could resist George. "You see, George is going to live with his wife again,—unless we get a cook to his taste. I *want* him to live with his wife; it curtails her immoralities, by diminishing her time for them."* Immediately upon their return to the house in late October, Livy contracted for the work, but repainting turned out to be the smallest labor in reopening the house. Kitchen implements needed repair, the chimneys did not draw properly, and no one could remember where the bedding had been stored. All this labor fell to Livy, who said she would happily give up housekeeping if not for the children. When she told Sam she felt daunted, he turned the problem against Susie, asking, "Why do you let mamma get low?" Despite the domestic distractions, Livy made time to read Sam's work, an activity that always brought her intimacy with her husband. The variety of ideas and cultures she had encountered in Europe made her simple childhood faith in Christianity seem small-minded. Though she missed the solace of her old religion, she felt full recompense in a closer philosophical companionship with Sam. They encouraged one another's ideological progressiveness.

Sam turned over most of the pages to the Blisses before leaving for Chicago the second week of November 1879. Ulysses S. Grant, like Sam, had just returned from overseas; he had been in Asia, and his progress east from California was festooned with testimonials, banquets, and parades—all part of a campaign to return the former President to the White House in 1880. Mark Twain had been asked to speak at a massive gathering in Chicago, to honor Grant. Sam informed the organizers that he would give a toast to babies, a subject close to his heart now that Livy was pregnant again and due the next summer. The Chicago festivities included quantities of drink, food, and talk that amounted to "a solid week of unpareleled dissipation," according to Sam's report to Howells. As a featured guest, Sam enjoyed special privileges, such as small parties with other dignitaries. Grant trumped Sam's memory of the awkward silence between them when they had met a decade before by saying, "I am not embarrassed. Are you?" The banquet organizers gave Mark Twain the final spot, on the roster of speakers, so as to keep the audience in their seats till the end of the ceremony. Grant sat placidly on the dais throughout the entire evening, but broke into a deep rumble of laughter in response to Twain's. "The biggest part of the success of the speech," Sam wrote Livy, "lay in the fact that the audience *saw* that for once in his life he had been knocked out of his iron serenity."

At home, proof sheets for the early parts of *A Tramp Abroad* had mounted up in Sam's absence. With them came increased pressure to resolve the book's conclusion. He begged off a visit to Boston, which would have included two speeches, one to Howells' Saturday Morning Club and another at a small breakfast in honor of poet, physician, and Harvard professor Oliver Wendell Holmes on his seventieth birthday. It was this latter that made Sam uneasy; his folly at the Whittier dinner still clanged in his memory, and he felt no desire to risk an appearance before the same audience. A week later, after discussions with Livy and Charles Dudley Warner, Sam reconsidered. Warner regarded Sam's reluctance to go "a great mistake" and told Howells that "he should act just as if nothing has happened." Sam quickly completed *A Tramp Abroad* and wrote Howells that he preferred to speak early in the proceedings, submitting everything he planned to say to his friend for editing.

Sam redeemed himself gracefully at the Holmes breakfast, an act of strong will in front of an audience that again included Emerson, Longfellow, and Whittier. In his speech, which Howells introduced as "a few words of truth and soberness from Mark Twain," he confessed to having unconsciously plagiarized the dedication of *The Innocents Abroad* from Holmes. He apologized to Holmes, who replied in a letter, "You will be stolen from a great deal oftener than you will borrow from other people." Ending with praise for Holmes' continued brilliance, Sam exonerated Mark Twain with this elegant display of crow eating.

Back home, Sam again received a run of visitors, including Frank Fuller and Dan Slote, both recently rehabilitated from enemies into friends, both looking to further Sam's investments with them. Livy had the house in order at last, so that she could throw herself into her extensive holiday preparations, which always included more gifts for the city's poor than for members of her own circle. She adored the Christmas festivities, much as they tired her; now that Susie and Bay could accompany her on her errands of charity, she viewed them not only as good in themselves but also as valuable lessons in noblesse oblige. They attended a vast party for nearly a thousand at Mrs. Samuel Colt's mansion. Livy's dressing for this affair was an elaborate ritual little Susie watched with longing. When Livy had finished, Susie "drew an envious little sigh and said, 'I wish *I* could have crooked teeth and spectacles!' " In a late autobiographical note, Sam credited "a guest" with these physical flaws, to preserve his wife's reputation for beauty.

Writing to her mother, Livy explained the modern pressures on women of their class.

> I told Mr. Clemens the other day, that in this day women must be everything, they must keep up with all the current literature, they must know all about art, they must help in one or two benevolent societies—they must be perfect mothers—they must be perfect housekeepers and graceful, gracious hostesses, they must know how to give perfect dinners, they must go and visit all the people in the town where they live, they must always be ready to receive their acquaintances—they must dress themselves and their children becomingly and above all they must make their houses "*charming*" & so on without end—then if they are not studying something their case is a hopeless one.

This list neglected to mention her continuing roles as Sam's editor and his adviser in formulating Mark Twain and his public presentation. Though she confided in her mother that she felt very "rebellious about" these expectations, everyone who met Livy praised her for exactly the qualities she satirized, and for the aplomb with which she manifested them.

Her holiday preparations, her editorial duties, Sam's short temper over completing *A Tramp Abroad*, and the early months of her pregnancy all combined to weaken Livy. Sam, working on his book through Christmas and the New Year to get "that Old Man of the Sea off my back, where he has been roosting more than a year & a half," nagged her to rest. One day while he was working, his neighbor, Mary Beecher Perkins, interrupted him in his billiard-room warren. "You will never get any woman to do the thing necessary to save her life by mere *persuasion*," she told Sam. "You see you have wasted your words for 3 weeks; it is time to use *force;* she *must* have a change; take her home & leave the children here." Sam packed Livy up for Elmira and they stayed away nearly three weeks. Relieved at last to have *A Tramp Abroad* out of his hands, Sam took out the historical switch novel he had set aside before going to Europe. His European experience now lent sixteenth-century England a vitality in his imagination. Despite his inexperience with fiction set in the distant past and the picturesque antiquity of the language he used for direct discourse, Sam found himself rejuvenated by the freedom to write as the story required, instead of having to force his thoughts into the prescribed form of a book of travels.

Regarding *The Prince and the Pauper*, Sam wrote to Howells that he enjoyed his work so much he didn't want to hurry it, for fear it would end too soon. "My idea is to afford a realizing sense of the exceeding severity of the laws of that day by inflicting some of their penalties upon the king himself & allowing him a chance to see the rest of them applied to others." This instructive quality gave fiction legitimacy, Sam felt; it was more than just entertainment, like *Tom Sawyer*. Livy enthusiastically approved this new story, and Sam read his daily production to her and the children, who were now old enough to appreciate writing with a serious purpose.

With *A Tramp Abroad*, the Blisses had at last realized what would keep Mark Twain happy. They allowed no delays in typesetting, engraving, or binding, and they canvassed for no other books that winter. The results lagged at first—Sam blamed Canadian pirates for the failure to sell as many initial copies as *Roughing It*—but sales picked up steadily, with more than twenty-five thousand orders before its March release date. Although he wrote Frank Bliss that he liked the book "exceedingly well," he described his feeling more fully to Howells: "My joy in getting the book out of my hands fills me up & leaves no room for trivial griefs." Pleased that he'd be receiving nearly fifty cents for each of the many copies sold, he felt even greater happiness that his obligation to the American Publishing Company and the Blisses neared an end. Only Howells' praise rekindled any joy in the finished product itself. "You are a blessing," he wrote Sam in an informal summary of his *Atlantic* review. "You ought to believe in God's goodness, since he has bestowed upon the world such a delightful genius as yours to lighten its troubles."

As a book, though, *A Tramp Abroad* had little to recommend it. It flaunted its origins as a collection of shorter works, despite Sam's intention of editing a mass of unrelated pieces into a cohesive whole. While many of the set pieces, anecdotes, and legends equaled Mark Twain's best writing to date, the obviously contrived thread of connection among them revealed the lack of relevance of the pieces to one another or to a larger theme. The composition of *A Tramp Abroad* differed from that of *The Innocents* and *Roughing It* in that the earlier volumes were conceived as books only after the experiences they recounted. Writing the new book as he traveled through Europe, Sam could construct neither a larger purpose for the narrative nor a perspective on the events in it. For example, Mark Twain's discussion of the bloody sword duels that formed both the entertainment and initiation rites of Heidelberg college men is inherently interesting, but does not relate to any narrative pieces around it and reveals nothing of what he thought of such a brutal tradition.

The financial success of the book, on the other hand, plainly reflected the public's gratitude for Mark Twain's return to America, as well as his return to the amusing genre in which he had his popular roots. Readers could easily imagine how Mark Twain would deliver any of the book's anecdotes from the stage. The work's major cultural contribution was the yoking together of rich European legends and traditions and piquant American tall tales and unconventionality. Putting the two on equal footing in his disparate narrative, Sam gave Americans a higher regard for their own folk traditions and gave Mark Twain a more international and cosmopolitan flavor.

Beginning in February 1880, Sam tried to settle all his business worries, so that he could get back to writing. "When one is writing literature," he told Orion, "he must purge his mind clean of other interests before he tackles his work, else his mind will be sure to wander." Haggling with Dan Slote over his new engraving process called Kaolatype, Sam at last bought a four-fifths interest in it. His enthusiasm for any patentable invention caused him to neglect his own advice to Mother Fairbanks, whose husband's speculations were causing such a crisis that Sam had wired her $1,000 from Europe the year before. He wrote her at Christmas, "Confound speculation, anyway! It nips us all sooner or later; but it won't nip me any more." Still, Sam plunged $20,000 into Slote's process, which involved engraving a picture into a thin layer of fine mud, which then dried to a very hard clay. Sam believed that the process, much easier than engraving on metal and much cheaper to correct, would "utterly annihilate & sweep out of existence one of the minor industries of civilization, & take its place." The fact that the more advanced technological innovation of photography threatened all engraving did not occur to Sam; he believed in mechanizing the existing process, not in reinventing the technology.

Meanwhile, the annoyances of fame, which he had avoided during the many months he had retreated to Europe, surpassed Sam's patience. Infuriated by the stream of requests for money and autographs, he scribbled angry denials on the envelopes or had someone else—Livy, Howells, or a houseguest, it didn't matter who—sign his autograph card "S. L. Clemens, per" followed by his or her name. The uneasiness Sam felt with fame induced him to make a striking suggestion to his brother Orion: that he write a book under the title, "The Autobiography of a Coward," the text to be an absolutely unremitting admission of his shams, embarrassments, and failures. Sam held up as models Rousseau and Casanova, praising the latter because "he frankly, flowingly, & felicitously tells the dirtiest & vilest & most contemptible things on himself, without ever suspecting that they are other than things which the reader will admire & applaud." In fact, in one of his European notebooks, Sam remarked that he wanted to try this type of autobiography himself, but he found that he could not. He shifted this brash idea onto Orion's shoulders because Sam did not believe that he *could* write with such uncompromising honesty—and because he had too many flaws he *might* confess. Burdened with guilt and insecurity, Sam considered himself a failure and a coward. He had constructed Mark Twain as a brave and successful alter ego. Now the gulf between his private identity and his public image made it impossible for Sam to write as Mark Twain about his inner self, at least not with the frankness he admired in Casanova.

More frequently, since his return from Europe, this disjunction between his public and private selves provoked Sam to insist on appearing incognito, as he did on an April trip to Boston with Livy. He also delivered a benefit speech in Hartford, on the condition that no newspapers report his presence, even at a time when publicity might have sold more copies of *A Tramp Abroad*. This reluctance to appear in public as Mark Twain did little to hurt sales, however. Sam made sure that newspapers reprinted many of the independent stories from *A Tramp Abroad* and, spurred by those free samples the book sold nearly fifty thousand copies before the Clemenses headed off to Elmira for the summer, the best sales he had managed in so short a period since the release of *Innocents Abroad*. Despite his unsettled feeling about the relationship between Sam Clemens and Mark Twain, he could not resist playing the dangerous game of publishing Twain's veiled exposure of the Clemenses' private life in the form of another McWilliams short story, like the one he had published in *The*

Atlantic a few years before. This one concerned Mrs. McWilliams' fear of lightning and her husband's efforts to calm her, a lightly disguised tale of Sam's own domestic irritations.

Looking to the past in hopes of finding a Sam Clemens he could live with, he answered a letter from a Texas schoolboy named "Wattie" Bowser. Sam typically would have tossed this letter, but he responded to it because Wattie's school principal was Laura Wright. As Sam's passionate ideal since they had split up years before, Laura Wright reappeared regularly in his dreams. Though he wrote down some of these dreams, Laura represented Sam's private past, and he bristled at adding it to Mark Twain's public one. This secret access to a time which preceded the existence of the public facades of Mark Twain and S. L. Clemens intrigued him. Communicating with Wattie folded together his own boyhood, recollected and mythologized in *Tom Sawyer* and in its unfinished sequel, and his later romance on the river. These thoughts and dreams, it seemed to Sam, might allow him to transcend the gulf between image and identity.

Sam's dreams of his former love did not produce any major rifts in his relationship with Livy, however, though the couple had one of their periodic showdowns over Sam's impressive swearing. Frustrated while dressing in the bathroom, Sam gushed a stream of invective before noticing that the door was ajar. When he emerged, Livy caught his eye and leveled the stream back at him. "There, now you know how it sounds." Sam could not hold his laughter. "Oh, Livy, if it sounds like that, God forgive me, I will never do it again! You know the words, but you don't know the tune."

Sam pressed on with *The Prince and the Pauper.* As he noted to Cornell professor Hjalmar Boyeson, a Norwegian scholar he'd met in Paris, "There is a fascination about writing even for my waste-basket, which is bread & meat & almost whiskey to me—& I know it is the same with all our craft."* But distractions of his own making crowded him. Orion had actually begun work on his autobiography on the terms that Sam had suggested to him, and Sam forwarded the daily installments to Howells. "It wrung my heart, and I felt haggard after I had finished it," Howells responded. "But the writer's soul is laid *too* bare: it is shocking. I can't risk the paper in the *Atlantic*." Orion had managed what Sam could not, but what he had written could not be printed. Sam kept the manuscript for decades, though eventually Orion's confessions disappeared.

Sam kept up his literary grudges. In May, he proposed a new club for people of sparkling modesty, such as Howells and himself, that would have as its goal, "by superior weight, character & influence, to impair & eventually destroy the influence of Bret Harte—not from any base feeling, but from a belief that this is a thing required in the interest of the public good." The Kaolatype business nosed its way into his life again, and, together with Dan Slote, Sam developed the idea of carving through the clay to the steel sheet below and casting in the hollow. The resulting plate would have a very deep bite, perfect for printing on leather or wallpaper; now they needed to develop a way to cast metal that would work with this process. Sam ponied up the salary for a German metallurgist Slote had found. Exasperated by his own ineptitude meddling in negotiations between Chatto and Windus, his British publishers, and the American Publishing Company, he wrote, "*Dam* business of *all* sorts!—that's my only religious creed."* Despite all these interests pulling him from his own work, Sam cautioned his brother, "The bane of Americans is overwork—and the ruin of *any* work is a divided interest. Concentrate—*concentrate*. One thing at a time. Yrs in haste."

After a brief foray to Washington to lobby for copyright protection, still a self-serving preoccupation, Sam returned for the summer to Elmira to a book he loved writing, to a delightful family growing, and to feeling rich again. Even the political news pleased him: Though his beloved General Grant had not won the Republican nomination for President, James A. Garfield—a political apostle of Howells' father and the husband of Mary Fairbanks' cousin—had. In truth, the whole summer in Elmira was a delight for the entire family. For Bay, a rugged outdoorsy child to whom the hills and animals meant more than any book could, the time at the farm was heaven. Livy valued this family time free of the worry of housekeeping, and Sam found the perfect balance between work in his octagonal hillside study and company with extended family. He and Theodore Crane talked books, and he always tried to get Saint Sue to react to some heretical point, sometimes developing theological arguments to spring on her as she snipped wildflowers along the stone wall that ran beside the steep road toward town.

The birth of the new baby girl brought more joy to the family. Named for Sam's mother but immediately dubbed Jean, the baby "arrived perfectly sound but with no more baggage than I had when I was on the river," he wrote Howells. She "weighs about 7 pounds. That is a pretty big one—for us." The older children were fascinated with their new sibling, which cost Sam caste in the family popularity rankings. "I have dropped from No. 4, and am become No. 5," he told Joe Twichell. "Some time ago it used to be nip and tuck between me and the cats, but after the cats 'developed' I didn't stand any more show." Mother Fairbanks heard about the birth through Charlie Langdon and offered her best wishes to break the long silence caused by her borrowing money from Sam. She unflinchingly resumed her role as literary adviser: "The time has come for your *best book*. I do not mean your most taking book, with the most money in it, I mean your best contribution to American literature." Sam turned his attention back to *The Prince and the Pauper*, a work he knew she would approve. He read the manuscript to the family at night and by the middle of September felt he had finished it. Compared with *A Tramp Abroad*, the composition of this new book brought him genuine pleasure.

Still, *A Tramp Abroad* provided its own rewards, netting Sam approximately $30,000. As his eleven-year affiliation with the American Publishing Company neared its end, he could look back on six books, 400,000 copies sold and royalty payments in excess of $100,000. On the other hand, Elisha Bliss' accounting sleights of hand, and outright lies, had cost Sam nearly $50,000, while his ineffective protection of Sam's copyright had robbed from Sam half again as many copies sold, twice his potential earnings, and quantities of time and aggravation that defied calculation. More important, however, Mark Twain had become the brightest star in the American cultural firmament, an international figure. When Elisha Bliss died on September 28, 1880, he had done more to create that star than anyone but Sam himself.

It takes your enemy and your friend, working together, to hurt you to the heart; the one to slander you and the other to get the news to you.
—"Pudd'nhead Wilson's New Calendar" (1897)

If the desire to kill and the opportunity to kill came always together, who would escape hanging?
—"Pudd'nhead Wilson's New Calendar" (1897)

ELISHA BLISS' DEATH gave Sam his freedom. Sam believed he had made his last contract with the American Publishing Company and that any loyalty owed to Bliss for his help in creating Mark Twain died with him. Now new ventures could and would increase his wealth, fame, and reputation. A falling-out between two Boston partners serendipitously created an opportunity. Henry O. Houghton and James R. Osgood had been in business together since Houghton had bought *The Atlantic* from Osgood in 1874. When they separated, Houghton had kept the magazine, but Osgood wanted the book contracts. Osgood had published—for bookstores only—Sam's 1877 slap at Bliss for his failure with *Tom Sawyer* the year before, a small volume containing two of Mark Twain's best short stories: his *Atlantic* debut, "A True Story," and "The Recent Carnival of Crime in Connecticut," a comic masterpiece about a man literally at war with his conscience, represented as a moldy green dwarf shrunken from long disuse. A trade book publisher with solid status in the Boston literary world, Osgood could confirm Mark Twain's standing in the world of letters.

For *The Prince and the Pauper*, Sam revived the idea he'd had for the British edition of *Tom Sawyer*—he would finance production himself and pay Osgood a 7½ percent commission to sell it by subscription. Gambling on Osgood's ability to manage an army of canvassers, Sam stood to realize a dollar a copy, twice his largest royalty when publishing through the American Publishing Company. He also got to keep his own copyright, which Bliss had always purchased outright. These changes made Samuel L. Clemens Mark Twain's publisher. In the chain of publication, he relinquished direct control over only sale and distribution of the book. Controlling production of the books by his purse strings put him in the position of wanting the book to look better than his past ones, but also of wanting to reduce the costs that now ate into his profits. Decisions concerning price, print run, paper, binding, and commissions to agents resided in Sam's hands, each decision engendering the same contradictions. After a decade of second-guessing his publisher, Sam now could habitually and unhappily second-guess himself.

No matter how successful *The Prince and the Pauper* became, however, it could not match the profits Sam expected from Kaolatype. As it turned out, clay's advantages over metal as an engraving medium were lost by its inability to withstand the pressures of a printing press, but the idea of casting a printing plate in the engraved clay mold—that is, inverting Kaolatype's intended process—seemed a simple stroke of genius. Dan Slote's young German metallurgist, Sneider, produced hard effective plates through some new processes that Sam believed to be patentable in and of themselves. Sam wrote his brother, "I have had him under wages for 3 months, now, night & day, & at last he has worked the miracle." Slote and Sneider were "wild . . . over this invention—& they might well be if the thing were absolutely *proven*—I mean for *fine* work." K-type itself, as Sam called it, might not generate cash, but these new methods of working brass would surely bring Sam a fortune.

Sam also involved himself in a number of smaller projects. A Philadelphia subscription publisher proposed an encyclopedia of humor edited by Mark Twain. Sam liked the idea, as long as he didn't have to do the work. He offered the bulk of the editorial duties to Howells for $5,000; Sam felt certain the project would net him considerably more than that, no matter who published it. General Grant had begun stumping for James Garfield's presidential campaign, and Sam sat on the committee that brought the general to Hartford. He went to Boston in mid-October to escort Grant to town and then joined him for a parade passing right by Sam's house, which had been decorated for the event. Foot-high letters announcing HOME OF MARK TWAIN had been made, but Sam declined to restate the obvious. To Sam, and to most of America, the impassive Grant embodied a laissez faire serenity and power that made him the prime exemplar for America after the Civil War, when the nation's gigantic industrial growth led to its development as an international force. Emerging from a somewhat tattered presidency as an American landmark, Grant caused Sam to regard Mark Twain's huge fame as a comparatively hollow thing.

In late October 1880, Sam at last made amends to his brother concerning the allegations Orion had made when employed at the American Publishing Company. A letter from his mother brought his guilt to the surface again when she reported that Orion's "mind is not right" since Sam had allowed his autobiography to go unpublished. "We have been very particular not to let it be known that there is anything between the brothers but brotherly love," Jane wrote. "It is so mortifying to a mother." Instead of publishing Orion's book, Sam created a scheme to enhance his brother's pride and purse. If he had believed Orion instead of Bliss and followed his own convictions instead of the advice of his lawyer, Sam told his brother, he would have made a far more advantageous contract for half profits as early as *Roughing It*. "I have lost considerably by all this nonsense—sixty thousand dollars, I should say—and if Bliss were alive I would stay with the concern" and exact repayment through each future book. He had been providing Orion with "loans" for years; a check would go to Keokuk and a check for the interest on the loan would come back. Sam reasoned that the contract for *A Tramp Abroad* had specified half profits and thus brought in $20,000 more than he would have earned by a stipulated royalty. From now on, Orion would get the interest on that extra $20,000—$75 a month. Sam added that his brother should forget his past indebtedness, considering it instead "interest charged against the heavy bill which the next publishers will have to stand who gets a book of mine."

The softening of Sam's treatment of his brother mirrored a shift in some of his other opinions. He even relaxed his view of copyright legislation. Although irritated enough at Canadian pirates to hire lawyers to stop them, Sam doubted that international reciprocity on copyright would truly benefit anyone—except himself. He wrote Howells:

> I can buy a lot of the great copyright classics, in paper, at from 3 cents to 30 cents apiece. These things must find their way into the very kitchens & hovels of the country. A generation of this sort of thing ought to make this the most intelligent & the best-read nation in the world. International copyright must becloud this sun & bring on the former darkness & dime-novel reading.

> Morally, this is all wrong—governmentally it is all
> right; for it is the *duty* of governments—& families—to be
> selfish, & look out simply for their own. International copy-
> right would benefit a few English authors, & a lot of Amer-
> ican publishers, & be a profound detriment to 20,000,000
> Americans.

This progressive view of a matter close to Sam's pocket oddly conformed
with his antidemocratic politics. Widespread suffrage was unwise because
voters were unwise; educating the public would solve the problem more
equitably than limiting the vote.

The 1880 presidential election a few days ahead might have started
Sam's thoughts on this path. Garfield's chances did not look good. Garfield, however, managed a surprising victory, which meant continued Republican spoils. Several officials who were friends of Sam's kept their posts,
although this also meant that Bret Harte would retain his consular appointment. Sadly, John Hay—who had recently seen to the private printing of half a dozen copies of *1601*, Mark Twain's obscene Elizabethan
fireside chat—stepped down as assistant secretary of state. Garfield's election also meant a continuing influence for Ulysses S. Grant. Sam took
advantage of this connection and brought Joe Twichell down to New York
so that he could ask Grant to support Yung Wing, whose unique Chinese-
American educational exchange mission Twichell embraced. Twichell had
prepared an involved argument for his cause, but "before Joe had more
than fairly got started, the old man said: *'I'll write the Viceroy* [of China]
a letter— . . . it will be a labor of love.' " Sam also wrote a rare letter
supporting a political appointee—activist, writer, and orator Frederick
Douglass. Sam wanted him retained as marshal of the District of Columbia
"because I so honor this man's high and blemishless character and so
admire his brave, long crusade for the liberties and elevation of his race."

Life at home was a trifle quieter in the fall and winter, perhaps
because of the new baby. Livy had returned from Elmira with two new
servants in tow, a wet nurse for Jean and a young woman from an excellent
Elmira family named Katy Leary, who became Livy's special factotum in
domestic matters; with three children, a dozen pets, and cigar smoke
continually pouring from Sam, the Clemenses could always use more servants. Jean, meanwhile, proved herself a delightful, healthy baby, "as fat
as a watermelon, & just as sweet & good, & often just as wet."* Once
Livy felt well enough, she taught the older girls "Reading, writing, Geography—Arithmetic & a little United States History—I really don't
teach Clara reading," she wrote to Mollie, "for she has picked English

reading up herself and reads very nicely indeed."* Sam instituted a family tradition that required the girls to come to breakfast each morning with one new fact, proof of their continuing learning; for Sam, the most satisfying facts were dates of particular historical occurrences. Other family traditions were also established. They had acquired the German habit of saying *"Unberufen!"* whenever they had any piece of good news, in order to prevent bad luck; loosely addressed to demons, the phrase meant "You are not called!" When their parents entertained, the girls sat on the stairs listening to the conversation taking place around the dining room table. They could imagine their father ignoring his food to jump up and narrate a story, complete with facial expressions and gesticulations. They always knew what course George served by what story Sam was telling. These gatherings were as close as Mark Twain got to public performance of late; Livy showed her love and her patience by appearing amused at stories she had heard a hundred times before.

By the end of the year, Howells had read *The Prince and the Pauper* and made several suggestions for changes and improvements. He had obtained the manuscript from Osgood; Sam had not sent it directly to him, wanting to spare him the labor since his friend's life had turned suddenly bitter. William Dean Howells had become an object for Houghton and Osgood to fight over once they separated *The Atlantic* from their company's book division. After many anxious months, Osgood resolved the problem of who owned the rights to Howells' services by guaranteeing him an annual income if he quit Houghton's employ and gave Osgood the right to publish his books. Howells wistfully left *The Atlantic* editor's chair early in 1881, installing Thomas Bailey Aldrich as his successor. A second, more personal problem offered no solution: Howells' eldest daughter, Winnie, now seventeen, suffered a nervous breakdown. She did not return to school in the fall of 1880, but her "rest cure," considered the era's most progressive treatment for psychological disorders, did little to relieve her.

Sam and Livy barely escaped domestic tragedy themselves. In the space of ten days, fire nearly extinguished the Clemenses' good fortune. Just as the new year of 1881 began, a lamp set fire to the canopy of Clara's bed. Rosa, the nurse, tossed the burning fabric out the window and saved the girl. A few days later, a crackling log sent a spark onto Jean's netting; her nurse found the fire and screamed, and Rosa again came to the rescue. Soon after, while Susie practiced piano in the schoolroom, originally built as Sam's study, the fireplace spread its flames to the wooden molding supporting the mantel. This time, a barber, who came to the house daily to groom Sam, noticed the flames and

doused them with a pitcher of water. One child after the other had
been at risk; all were spared.

These events made Sam and Livy grateful for their good fortune and
sparked a run of Clemens generosity. For example, one morning they
received a visit from a beautiful young woman of perhaps twenty. She
explained that her husband, Karl Gerhardt, worked in a machine shop,
but wanted to become a sculptor. He had no formal training and no money
to get any, but he was too proud to ask advice as to what he should do.
Though he knew nothing about art, Sam accompanied her to the studio
and was charmed, especially when the young Hattie Gerhardt placidly
posed beside the nude statue her husband had made of her. Sam asked
two artist friends to view the work, both were impressed, and one said
that the city of Hartford should send Gerhardt to Paris for two years'
training. Livy told Sam to "go privately & start the Gerhardts off to
Paris, & say nothing about it to anyone else."

This generosity did not spread to business matters. The Philadelphia
publisher who had approached Sam with the idea of assembling *Mark
Twain's Library of Humor* proved unreliable, so Sam and Osgood took up
the project themselves. Howells agreed to work on it, with the assistance
of *Hartford Courant* editor Charley Clark, but only "in the most leisurely
way." A distant cousin of Sam's named Jesse Leathers wanted Sam to
finance a claim in the British courts that he was the rightful earl of Dun-
ham, as Lampton family legend had long held. Leathers sent Sam an autobiographical manuscript telling the story of his lost nobility, and Sam
fobbed the manuscript off on Osgood, to whom Sam wrote that he ought
to use his influence with new *Atlantic* editor Aldrich on behalf of the
manuscript. But, he added, "you are as dainty and effeminate as Howells;
so I know perfectly well that you will simply urinate on the Earl's MS
and send it back to him without other comment. It is what Howells used
to do with poems of sentiment when I sent him any."

In the middle of March, Dan Slote sent an encouraging report about
the Kaolatype brass business. The news emboldened Sam to pay $12,000
for the land across the stream from his house, so as to preserve the Clemenses' western prospect. He wrote to Slote about the purchase, "Old
Kaolatype is a bit expensive; but if it hadn't been for K., we shouldn't
be in the bully brass business, you know." He also told Livy to go ahead
with plans not only to redecorate the house, but also to remodel it by
doubling the size of the servants' wing and tearing out the reception room.
Livy hired Associated Artists, Louis Comfort Tiffany's organization of fine
crafts people.

Soon after Sam received Slote's enthusiastic report, Charley Webster, Annie Moffett's ambitious husband, came to Hartford to sell Sam some stock in a watch company based in Fredonia, New York. Sam bought the stock without question and then hired Webster to handle some Kaolatype business Dan Slote could not get to. Webster ran to Providence, Rhode Island, to discuss brass founding with a company there and then down to New York. There, he met with Slote and Sneider—and discovered that Kaolatype, which had some modest legitimate trade, was mostly a con. Sneider had created no patentable inventions for founding brass. He and Dan Slote had simply hoodwinked Sam.

When Webster relayed the news to his uncle, Sam was devastated. Dan Slote had been a trusted friend for more than a decade. Slote tried to cover himself with the lie that Sneider had conned him, too. Suspecting that Dan would sacrifice Sneider, Sam played along, planning with Charley Webster to turn the tables on Dan once Sneider had been dealt with. In April 1881, as a reward for uncovering the swindle, Sam gave Charley Webster complete control of Kaolatype and its related operations. Less than two weeks after Sam's explosion of confidence drove him to buy his neighbor's property at an exalted figure, he wrote Dan Slote again that "my hopes are not high—they have had a heavy jolt. I feel pretty sore & humiliated when I think over the history of the past few months. The book I was at work on & intended to rush through in two months' time, is standing still."

But hiring Charley Webster to look after his personal business for him soon freed Sam to focus his attention more completely on his most immediate concern, *The Prince and the Pauper*. He pressed ahead with final revisions, even as he worried about his new publishing arrangement. Osgood's experience in trade publishing had taught him nothing he needed to know for his end of the subscription business. With whatever his 7½ percent commission amounted to, Osgood had agreed to sell Mark Twain's *The Prince and the Pauper* through an army of agents, but he had no idea where to begin. General agents—that is, people who hired the actual door-to-door salesmen and took a percentage of their earnings—existed across the country, but finding reliable ones and establishing contracts with them took time. Sam agreed to let Osgood take a shortcut: He hired the American Publishing Company's system of agents wholesale, a weird display of faith in Frank Bliss' integrity, since Sam had crippled Bliss' company by leaving it. By May, with production of the new book under way and agents beginning their canvass, Sam and Charley Webster began a vindictive crusade against the now-broke and broken Dan Slote. Sam demoted him to vice president and Charley demanded to know where the money had gone. Revenge took precedence over Kaolatype's actual business. Sam determined to use Kaolatype for printing a deeply embossed cover for the new book. His friend had betrayed him with an unworkable company, but if the company's process worked, he could salvage what Slote had taken and leave Slote out.

The experience did not entirely sour Sam on either investments or inventions. The year before, he had put a few thousand dollars into the prototype of a mechanical typesetter devised by a Hartford mechanic named James Paige. Now that his dreams for Kaolatype foundered in dissembling and bad feeling, he turned his ambitions for grand wealth to Paige's machine. Unlike the new and patentable brass processes Sneider claimed to have perfected, Sam understood the typesetter. A man struck a keyboard, and a font would slide onto a stick. When it worked, the machine sped up typesetting tremendously, but it had the same flaw as most inventions in which Sam invested: It mechanized the movements of an actual compositor, but did not reconceive the typesetter's work. Still, Sam could not rein in his enthusiasm. He invited his newspaper friends to witness the technology. "I never saw such an inspired bugger of a machine," Sam told the *New York Herald*'s John Russell Young. "A man who owns a newspaper can't look at this creature unmoved."*

In early June, the family left for six weeks at Branford, on Long Island Sound, choosing to summer close to home so that Livy could run up to Hartford to supervise the construction and redecoration of the house and Sam could keep his eye on his various ventures. Totaling up the costs of Kaolatype, house reconstruction, book production, and other investments in the previous year, Sam had extended himself by $100,000, or about twice what *A Tramp Abroad* had paid him. He was risking more and more of his family's assets on his dreams of a new world in which he was his own publisher and a grand capitalist. In escaping the past and living for his imagined future, he had made the present a dangerous place.

31 | *The Distribution of Wealth*

We should be careful to get out of an experience only the wisdom that is in it—and stop there; lest we be like the cat that sits down on a hot stove-lid. She will never sit down on a hot stove-lid again—and that is well; but also she will never sit down on a cold one any more.
—"Pudd'nhead Wilson's New Calendar" (1897)

T HE SHOOTING OF President James Garfield, on July 2, 1881, disheartened the nation. Unlike John Wilkes Booth's attack on President Lincoln sixteen years before, this act did not originate in mad national passion, but in banal party politics. The assassin, Charles Guiteau, resented that his faction of the Republican party had lost to Garfield's; Chester A. Arthur, chosen as Garfield's Vice President as the result of convention negotiations, represented the wing of the party the assassin favored. Guiteau's political, and not ethical or patriotic, motivations cast the public drama as tragic farce.

During the somber summer, as the President slowly died, Sam's mood matched the nation's. Business worries robbed him of writing time, for which he so valued the season. The result of Charley Webster's work with Kaolatype was the discovery that the business did not pay. Charley thought it best just to close it down, but Sam refused, mostly because Dan Slote had not contritely repaid the money he swindled. Sam sold his stock in the American Publishing Company and removed himself from the board, at which point the company insulted him by declaring its first dividend in years. Since only Mark Twain's backlist kept the company alive, Sam wanted his copyrights returned in lieu of further inquiry into the company's shenanigans. Sam timed his dispute foolishly, given that his old publisher's agents would soon be selling *The Prince and the Pauper*.

That Howells and his other early readers liked the novel gave Sam hope that the book might become a bonanza, and he paid close attention to the quality of printing, illustration, and production. He encouraged the illustrators to render the buildings and clothing with historical accuracy, a fact he insisted on noting in the book agents' prospectus. Although he typically found reading page proofs drudgery, Sam awaited them eagerly, but when they arrived he got so irritated that he sent "Chapter VI back unread. I don't want to see any more until this godamded idiotic punctuating & capitalizing has been swept away & my own restored." Near the end of summer 1881, Sam hurried to Boston to plan for the protection of his copyrights with Osgood, who proved responsive to his author's determined prepublication planning. Concerned about Canadian incursions into the American market, Sam dearly wanted to avoid the difficulties Elisha Bliss had run into while trying to coordinate publication with Chatto and Windus. More important, the men plotted the book's prospectus. Much as Sam delighted in a novel so obviously suited to bourgeois tastes, he knew his audience would have trouble reconciling it with what they expected from Mark Twain. He flirted with the idea of issuing *The Prince and the Pauper* anonymously or under a different name, but Howells' encouragement and simple financial self-interest persuaded him to publish it as a Mark Twain book.

When it became clear that house renovations would drag on into the fall, Sam put Charley Webster in charge of the project and took the family up to Elmira. Sam arranged for Howells to get *The Prince and the Pauper* proofs after he had finished with them, so he could both edit them and write a review. Since Howells no longer had *The Atlantic* outlet, Sam asked John Hay, occupying the *New York Tribune* editorial chair while Whitelaw Reid honeymooned in Europe, to give Howells a platform from which to publish his glowing review. Reid believed that a review of Mark Twain by a literary friend and partner shouldn't appear "in a paper which has good reason to think little of his delicacy and highly of his greed." Hay approved the project anyway, informing Reid, "If it does not please you— wait for his next book and get Bret Harte to review it. That will be a masterpiece of the skinner's art." Sam assisted other admirers in landing their reviews in other leading periodicals. Hjalmar Boyesen wrote one for *The Atlantic*, Joel Chandler Harris for the *Atlanta Constitution*, and his Friday Night Club crony Colonel Parker for the *Hartford Courant*. After a wearying trip to see his mother and sister in Fredonia, Sam and Livy read the last of the proofs. They finished before leaving Elmira around the first day of fall, returning to their still-unfinished house.

Though the unsettled conditions at home prevented him from writing, Sam did not let his thoughts veer far from literature. He acted on Howells' numerous suggestions on *The Prince and the Pauper* proofs and some of the book's anachronistic references noticed by his bohemian buddy Ned House, now back from Japan. The technical accomplishment of *The Prince and the Pauper* gave evidence of Sam's mature mastery of his craft. He wrote a letter of literary advice to a young aspirant, defining the two essential ingredients for success as a writer: "*experience of life* (not of books)" and "a good, honest, diligent, pains-taking *apprenticeship* of 15 or 20 years with the pen."* Howells' review in the October 25, 1881, *New York Tribune* emphasized the artistic and moral earnestness of the novel as proof that Mark Twain always provided more than laughs for the careful reader. Despite this praise, which other reviewers echoed, Sam received a well-reasoned dissent from his Nevada friend Joe Goodman, who was disappointed in the book. "It might have been written by anybody else— by a far less masterly hand, in fact. You went entirely out of your sphere."

Goodman seemed right about *The Prince and the Pauper*, which has no obvious literary connection to either Mark Twain or Sam Clemens. The direct voice of Mark Twain, who appears in some ways to be the subject of all of Sam's earlier books, only comes through in a jocular 150-word preface and in the notes, which made explicit the novel's implicit theme about the moral improvement of society over time. Neither does this book reveal much more about Sam Clemens than any of the earlier books. Yet there are two ways in which it is not quite so much of a departure as it may at first appear.

Mark Twain's political sensibilities, so different from the deeply conservative instincts harbored by Sam Clemens, subtly infused all of his work. Though Twain's books and lectures avoided promoting explicit political views—except where, as in parts of *Roughing It*, they formed an essential part of the narrative—the Mark Twain persona was deeply political. Twain represented an instinct for social justice that animated the moral conscience of America. From Mark Twain's origins as a political reporter, few subjects energized Sam's prose like straightforward outrage over injustice. His indictments of politicians who betrayed the public trust and his defenses of oppressed minorities vitally informed his vision. He translated his outrage into comedy in *Innocents Abroad*, lampooning American respect for a European culture that he regarded as less fair, clean, and moral than that grown on our native soil. A moral outrage against respect unjustly allocated was fundamental to his construction of the Mark Twain persona.

The Prince and the Pauper reflected his vision of justice more explicitly than any of the earlier books. The unwashed and marginally educated Tom Canty lives in "a foul little pocket called Offal Court, . . . small decayed and ricketty, but it was packed full of wretchedly poor families." Tom suffers at the hands of his drunk and violent father and grandmother. "He had a hard time of it," Mark Twain pointed out, "but did not know it." As Mark Twain portrays it, Tom's experience appears at first to be mere misfortune—until we see the wider frame of existence, the political structure that determined the apportionment of fortune in his society. Then it becomes clear that Tom's unhappy life results from a Dickensianly abusive social system. In Mark Twain's view—a radical one for the 1880s, and one still divisive a century later—systematic misfortune is injustice. When chance puts Tom Canty before Prince Edward, the boys find they are nearly twins beneath Tom's rags and dirt, Edward's robes and jewels. The boys switch clothing and roles. We laugh at Tom's ignorance of the ways of court, but we learn from the Prince's hardship that who you are in fact matters far less than where you appear to fit into the system of injustice. The brief notes force Mark Twain's political intention into his reader's consciousness. "There has never been a time," his notes conclude, "when above FOURTEEN crimes were punishable by death in Connect-icut. But in England, within the memory of men who are still hale in body and mind, TWO HUNDRED AND TWENTY-THREE crimes were punishable by death! These facts are worth knowing—and worth thinking about, too."

Apart from its social intentions, *The Prince and the Pauper* leads the reader into a greater awareness of the symbolic power of twinship: two divergent personalities sharing identical bodies. Readers following the work of Mark Twain had to notice the parallels in the relationships be-tween the Prince and Tom and Twain and Sam Clemens. Prince Edward lived in a palace; he was a figure of immense power, wealth, and respect-ability, a public leader despite his playful childishness. Much the same could be said of Mark Twain. Tom Canty occupied his role only because of his likeness to the Prince. His personality differs so radically from Edward's that the Prince's advisers all believe the Prince to be ill when they witness Tom's behavior. Even the author's choice of the name Tom, as in Sawyer, implied a personal confession amid the mythmaking. Mark Twain and Sam Clemens may occupy the same body, the book seemed to say, but they are not a single person.

In his own life, this was a difficult move for Sam to make, to distance himself from Mark Twain while trying to deepen the character of Twain with an explicit social consciousness. As the fall wore on, he began to feel as though he were "detained in purgatory," divided against himself. "The house is full of carpenters and decorators; whereas, what we really need, here, is an incendiary," he wrote Charley Stoddard, who had determined to escape to Hawaii. "Maybe you think I am not happy? The very thing that gravels me is, that I am. I don't want to be happy when I can't work; and I am resolved that hereafter I won't be."*

Sam's lighthearted resolution in favor of unhappiness took on a savage edge when he found out from Elinor Howells that her husband had been ill for weeks, and periodically near death. Despite his regular contact with Howells, this news came as a complete surprise. Howells' worry over money and his daughter's health, his overwork from relinquishing steady employment, and his natural nervousness had led to a mental collapse and concomitant physical ailments. Sam could only count and recount his blessings.

Immediately after Thanksgiving, Sam went to Montreal for ten days. *The Prince and the Pauper* was ready to be issued, and this "Canadian raid," as Sam reported it to Howells, was meant to secure the new book some international protection. British copyright law only extended its covenants to books originated in England while the author resided in a British territory. Canada had its own copyright provisions that coexisted with British imperial and provincial ones, but obtaining that protection required more preparations and machinations than a quick journey would allow. Sam could have received protection from the Dominion simply by lying on his application, but he declined. "There are reputations that can stand a strain like that," he wrote in a newspaper column on the matter, "but you know, yourself, that it would not answer for you or me to take any such risk." Sam remained uncertain whether the novel's prior publication in England shielded him, because "possible suits for damages and felony would be no more restraint upon [Canadian pirates], I think, than would the presence of a young lady be upon a stud-horse who had just found a mare unprotected by international copyright." The American edition was issued soon after the Canadian one, with a handful of copies printed on expensive paper as gifts for Clemens' favorite youngsters.

Grander business also absorbed some of his attention. James Paige's typesetter had generated interest from some large-scale investors, whom it needed to make it a real success; building the machine required a plant and someone to manage its sale and distribution. Sam told Charley Webster that he had $5,000 in the project and regarded it "safe, there, & is very much the best investment I have ever had." Webster and Sam helped arrange meetings with New York financiers. Sam wanted to know the moneymen's opinion quickly, so that he could buy more stock in the invention. At Christmas, 1881, Charley and Annie Webster came up from New York for a mix of business and pleasure.

Soon after, Sam tore off into another ill-starred crusade. Charles Dudley Warner told him that the *New York Tribune*, now safely back in Whitelaw Reid's hands, had been running almost daily slurs against Mark Twain. Never one to let an insult pass unavenged, Sam determined to write an explosive biography of Reid, pretending it to be serious and adulatory, but revealing the sordid history of his acquisition of the *Tribune* and his recent marriage to a wealthy Californian. In Sam's mind, Reid had sold his journalistic soul to robber baron Jay Gould in order to obtain financing to buy the newspaper. Gould's subsequent sale of his share of the paper to Reid's new father-in-law had a similarly opportunistic and unpleasant taint. After dedicating a solid month to this project, Sam finally listened to Livy's suggestion that he ascertain if the *Tribune* had in fact attacked him. It had—but only once. "Nobody knows, better than I, that there are times when swearing cannot meet the emergency," Sam wrote Howells. "Can you conceive of a man's getting himself into a sweat over so diminutive a provocation?"

In mid-February, Dan Slote died. Sam vented the spleen he had built up against Reid on a more deserving object. "If Dan had died thirteen months earlier, I should have been at the funeral, and squandered many tears; but as it is, I did not go and saved my tears," he wrote Mary Fairbanks, who met both men on the *Quaker City*. "Dan was . . . not a robber. There is a sort of robust dignity about robbing. He was only a pick-pocke[t], more base than ordinary pick-pockets, who merely filches from strangers." He reported to Mother Fairbanks that at least Dan had returned a portion of what he had stolen. She warned him in response to say nothing publicly against Dan Slote, whatever his flaws; she attended his funeral and observed "hundreds of friends who buried Dan Slote with honor." Either her argument, Livy's restraining hand, or Sam's own common sense moved him to refrain from any public attack on Slote or his estate, either in print or in the courts.

Sam had written this letter to his honorary mother on a typewriter; the new versions had much smoother works than the one he had bought with Howells a few years before. He acquired the new machine in preparation for his long-delayed trip to the Mississippi River Valley. He had decided, at last, to write the book about the region; it was an idea that had intrigued him ever since his California days, becoming a clear intention since the success of his *Atlantic* series about his training as a pilot.

The sales of *The Prince and the Pauper*, while adequate, disappointed him. The favorable reviews hardly moved more than twenty-five thousand copies, and the production had been more costly than he had anticipated. The dollar-a-copy profit made up somewhat for the short sales, but Sam thought that a return to travel literature, his monetary mainstay, would produce even greater rewards. In April and May 1882, he and Osgood would travel the Mississippi River Valley with a companionable secretary, Roswell Phelps, in tow to copy the conversations and observations in shorthand. The secretary would type up the notes from which Sam could construct his new book.

Sam wanted Howells along on the trip, but Howells could not afford the time, the cost, or the emotional drain. His illness had delayed his completion of *A Modern Instance*, running serially in *Century* magazine; the editors had just published a long essay of praise for Howells' literary achievement, and he naturally felt obliged to complete the novel. He found, however, "that every mental effort costs about twice as much as it used, and the result seems to lack texture. I ought to have had a clean rest of three months when I began to get well." He planned instead to go to Europe for several months, to allow himself and Winnie their needed rest. In mid-March, Howells did accompany his friend on a trip to New York to capitalize on Sam's access to General Grant. Howells' father, the American consul at Toronto, feared that since he had been Garfield's mentor, President Arthur would want to replace him. Perhaps because of Grant's influence, Howells' father retained his position. In repayment for Sam's help, Howells took on another editorial chore for Sam, assembling a collection of short Twain pieces for Osgood to publish. When Sam wasn't practicing with his typewriter or dictating to his new secretary, he wrote letters in imitation of Joel Chandler Harris' character Uncle Remus, whose tales recalled Sam's boyhood summers at the Quarles farm, listening to the slaves' stories. For example, Sam wrote Osgood in faux-Negro dialect: "I's gwyne to sen' you de stuff jis' as she stan', now; an' you an' Misto Howls kin weed out enuff o' dem 93,000 words fer to crowd de book."

In the spring, the redecoration of the house was finally completed and Sam's mother and sister came to Hartford to see it. The enlarged entrance hall had intricate silver-leaf stenciling, and Tiffany leaded-glass panels graced various rooms. The original quirky plumbing now operated smoothly, though the new burglar alarm proved every bit as unreliable as the plumbing had been before. Jane and Pamela stayed more than three weeks, during which time it was decided that Jane would go to Iowa to live with Orion, and Pamela would join Sammy, who had moved to California, where he was a student at the University of California in Berkeley and working part-time for an Oakland newspaper. Now that Annie had joined Charley in New York, it seemed silly to keep their big Fredonia house, and both women would be happier with their children. Livy waspishly criticized Charley Webster's conceitedness and Sammy Moffett's wastefulness, the only threat to the rare pleasant peacefulness of the visit. Livy's typically saintly patience had been temporarily fractured under a long siege of company and illness; between January and April 1882, the house had seemed more a hospital and hotel than a home.

After a quick trip to Boston, where Sam presented his hypothesis on mental telegraphy to Howells' Saturday Morning Club, he set off for the Mississippi River with Osgood and his secretary. Sam planned his book as a standard work on the river valley, from its days before settlement to the present battles to contain the river itself. He gleaned some new insights about the geologic formation of the river from recent publications, and more facts about the early days from the writings of observant travelers to the region. He also wanted use his own experiences in learning how to pilot the river to represent the natural history of the Mississippi as an avenue of commerce while this trip would yield up the personal flavor of contemporary life along the river, so changed since Sam's days. He found, among other things, that the federal government had altered the river, redirecting its flow, marking the channels with buoys, and securing the unstable banks. Now, a pilot merely followed traffic signals. River traffic itself had become passé. Where the boys of Sam's day could name all the boats on the Mississippi, now they knew all the railroad lines.

Sam invited Joel Chandler Harris to join him in New Orleans, cautioning him to keep the letter "dreadfully private and confidential because my movements must be kept secret, else I shan't be able to pick up the kind of book-material I want." Using the name C. L. Samuel, of New York, Sam maintained the cover-up only a few days, because once he arrived in St. Louis he constantly ran into people he knew. Fearing pursuit by reporters, he stuck close to the river, but even there he had the same trouble. One pilot "recognized my voice, after 21 years, though I did not remember him or his name either. He waited a while for confirmation of his suspicions; & presently when I raised my hat & passed my fingers up through my hair, he had no further doubts, & just called me by name."

Sam and his companions had a grand time in New Orleans. After chasing down his favorite haunts, he met both George Washington Cable and Joel Chandler Harris for the first time. Cable wrote stories and novels of Creole life, with a sharp moral edge; Harris attracted the local children who, as Sam wrote Livy, "were grievously disappointed to find he was white & young." Sam induced the writers to imagine themselves becoming part of a traveling authors' menagerie, reading to packed houses across the country; only Harris demurred, because he was too shy to read in public. A tugboat carried them around the delta, and Sam himself took a hand at steering. Despite warnings from Livy not to "be too ready & cordial to invite people to visit you," Sam secured agreements from both Harris and Cable to come to Hartford. Sam left New Orleans on board the *City of Baton Rouge*, captained by his old master Horace Bixby.

His three-day stop in Hannibal was a continual celebration. Sam stayed with his old friend John Garth, who had made a fortune in New York and returned to live in the old town. Hannibal had fared well in the period of transition from steamboats to railroads; a handful of lines converged there. Many of Sam's childhood friends had disappeared, but the Hill Street house remained. He wrote Livy of his twin feelings of delight and dismay: "That world which I knew in its blossoming youth is old and bowed and melancholy, now; its soft cheeks are leathery and wrinkled, the fire is gone out in its eyes, and the spring from its step." The visit gave Sam a double vision of Hannibal and the river: their shadowy history, which he needed to capture for his new book, and that vanished youth he remembered so vividly. After six weeks away from home, he was ready to return to his present-day life with his family.

Sam had only one very busy month between his return to Hartford and the family's summer removal to Elmira. His absence had been a test period for Charley Webster, to determine if his nephew could reduce Sam's business burden to simple daily reports and occasional yes-or-no questions. Although it took Webster a while to learn what Sam wanted, he satisfied Sam that he was competent enough to become his business agent; Sam confidently gave him almost all tasks connected with making or investing money. Instead of finances, Sam turned his attention to writing, friendships, and family. In Fredonia, Jane Clemens took ill, and the doctor expected her to die before the end of summer. In Hartford, Sam and Livy threw Clara an eighth birthday party for more than sixty children. Sam and Livy took two days in Boston to bid farewell to Howells and his family before they departed for Europe.

Howells had penned a critique of Mark Twain for the *Century* and gave Sam the essay to read and forward to the magazine. The article, accurate in most details, erred in one startling particular. Howells wrote that Mark Twain allowed himself only one bit of sham, that of a false name; the remainder of his identity was utterly true to his work. Whether due to blindness or collusion with his friend, Howells' critical assessment matched what Sam intended the world to believe of his public persona. If the reader "leaves out of the account an indignant sense of right and wrong, a scorn of all affectation and pretense, an ardent hate of meanness and injustice," Howells wrote, "he will come infinitely short of knowing Mark Twain." Sam returned the favor modestly with an effusive letter of praise for Howells' *A Modern Instance*. Revealingly, Sam saw himself in Bartley Hubbard, the novel's lead scoundrel, a writer whose early self-indulgence develops into a resolute amorality. Howells in fact modeled Hubbard not on Sam but on his nemesis Bret Harte.

Sam began writing his Mississippi book as quickly as he could, reviewing first his *Atlantic* series on piloting, and reading his own notes and those Roswell Phelps had typed from his shorthand. He even dug out the novel he had begun as a sequel to *Tom Sawyer* five years before, finding in it a wild flight of boast and insult between bargemen that he could use to portray river life back before his piloting days. Leaving for Elmira, he packed it in his crate of raw sources, including books, maps, notebooks, and manuscripts, which he would open when he got to his octagonal hilltop study. He composed a handful of chapters during those weeks and felt he could complete the rest over the summer. Illness and malevolence changed his plans, however. First, Jean contracted scarlet fever. The dread disease ran rampant around Hartford that season, as close as Patrick McAleer's rooms above the stable, leaving one of Patrick's children deaf. With no effective defense but hygiene, Livy, Sam, Rosa, and the doctor kept Jean isolated, trying to prevent the spread to Clara and Susie. Then, Susie succumbed to something soon after, though not scarlet fever; and soon after the anxiety felled Sam. He claimed to his Hannibal host John Garth to be "stretched on the bed with three diseases at once, and all of them fatal."

Then, just as the family had recovered enough to make the trip to Elmira in mid-July, another catastrophe struck. Orion, in Fredonia to attend Jane, reported that the Independent Watch Company, stock in which Charley Webster had sold to both his uncle Sam and his mother-in-law Pamela Moffett, was a con. In Orion's opinion, Webster knew this and had swindled his own family by selling them the stock. Pamela's modest means were strained by this development, as was her already uncertain faith in her son-in-law. In New York on their way to Elmira, the Clemenses pretended ignorance when they saw Webster at their hotel.

On the train north, Sam weighed his response to his brother's allegation. Orion had been right about Bliss and could well be right about Webster. But Sam thought highly of Webster's acuity; as he confided to Mother Fairbanks about Dan Slote's thievery, "I did not find him out then, but a sharper man than I am, did." Webster managed Sam's business affairs capably. He was Annie's husband, father to her children, and a member of the family. Sam decided to buy Pamela's bogus shares and to tell Orion to mind his own business, but this nastiness would not disappear so easily. Livy confided in a letter to Sammy Moffett that Sam was so affected by the combined pressures of his work and this family crisis that he "often comes down at night, with his head so sore & tired that he cannot bear to have the simplest question asked him, or be compelled to talk at all."*

At the end of August, Charley Webster promised to require the company to make restitution. Annie wrote Sam a letter defending her husband, and Sam replied, "Let this queer nightmare dissolve & pass away—give it no further thought. You have borne your part in the long trouble well, Annie. . . . We call off the inquisitorial dogs, now, & send love to you & Charley, & best wishes for a better time henceforth." The excitement brought about an unexpected recovery in Jane, who left for Keokuk. "Seldom has such an eloquent & imposing array of slanders come to so grotesque an end, I suppose," Sam wrote Orion in his careful, tight-rope-walking summary of the resolution to the crisis. "I was in a fine fury over these foolishnesses for a spell—cost me heaps of cash, in time, which is money & worth its face—& after all, it was sheer waste, no occasion for it."* As thanks, to cover the inconvenience of Jane's care, and as a kind of bribe against further meddling, Sam raised Orion's monthly stipend to $100. In the end, the Independent Watch Company returned Sam's money—but only under threat of public humiliation by Mark Twain.

Sam now had no choice: Firing Charley Webster meant he believed him to be a crook, which would have led Pamela to insist that Annie separate from him. Instead, in a foolish but necessary display of confidence, Sam turned over greater responsibility to Webster, who sought to repay his uncle-in-law's demonstration of faith by becoming his shining knight in the world of business. He negotiated with Sheldon and Company for stolen profits on the (*Burlesque*) *Autobiography* pamphlet Sam had gotten up to gall Elisha Bliss years before. Working with a friendly conspirator from western New York, Daniel Whitford, now a lawyer with a prestigious Manhattan law firm, Alexander and Green, Webster prosecuted publishers who assembled books of early, uncopyrighted material or who pasted Mark Twain's name on work authored by someone less well-known. Daniel Whitford's review of Sam's contracts with the American Publishing Company provoked Sam to fire Charlie Perkins with the remark "I had the monumental fool of the 19th century for a lawyer." The agreement to let *Tom Sawyer* stand in for the Riley–diamond mine contract also gave up Sam's right to protest the previous contracts, all of which enjoined Mark

Twain from going to market with any book while his old publisher still sold any previous volume. Technically, since his old publisher still sold Mark Twain's early works, Sam could not have sold *The Prince and the Pauper* or any future book. Webster explained, "The less we bother the Amer. Pub. Co. the better off we are."

The time Sam lost chasing a peaceful resolution to Webster's betrayal ought to have gone into his new book, *Life on the Mississippi*. When the family returned home in late September, Sam realized he was thirty thousand words short. Lying that illness had delayed the completion of the book over the summer, he told Howells "I am going to write all day and two thirds of the night, until the thing is done, or break down at it. The spur and burden of the contract are intolerable to me." The book, however, proved recalcitrant. Sam's efforts to finish it, made sluggish by a persistent illness in the fall, dragged on into December. Writing became an ugly chore as Sam searched for a way to complete the manuscript, which had a natural beginning in its geologic history, but no natural conclusion.

Sam's position as his own publisher only made the task more difficult. After Osgood's trade publication of Mark Twain's collection, *The Stolen White Elephant*, met with minimal success, Sam gave Webster the responsibility for managing the subscription and distribution of *Life on the Mississippi* and turned over the general agency for the New York area to him. Osgood knew trade publishing—he had taste and sense and he appreciated a well-made book—but the nuances of directing a squadron of booksellers spread across the country escaped him. When canvassing for the book began in December 1882 and Osgood asked Sam what premiums to offer agents, Sam wrote Webster, "Charley, if there are any instructions to be given, you may give them—I will not interest myself in *any*thing connected with this wretched God-damned book."

His problems finishing the book exacerbated his impatience with his scattered family. Sam rebelled against Pamela's requests for signed copies of books for friends. If a stranger asked for a book, Sam simply sent "his letter to the publisher and have not a trifle of trouble about it; if he wanted an autograph in it, I should put his letter into the waste paper basket,"* rather than find a copy, sign it, wrap it, address it, and send it. Then Orion asked him to support his new project, electrifying Keokuk's streetlights. When Sam did not respond, Orion took his silence as assent. Sam snapped angrily, "I could have written you a week ago that I did not want anything whatever to do with the electric business, and I would have done so if I had supposed your own interest in it would keep alive a whole week."* Sam saw civilization as a metaphor for family, so it pained him to expunge the following line from his Mississippi manuscript: "All 'civilizations' are legitimate matter for (private, not public) jeering & laughter, because they are so conspicuously made up of about three tenths of reality & sincerity, & seven tenths of wind & humbug."

Letters from Howells reporting his high times in Europe with John Hay and Thomas Bailey Aldrich did nothing to make Sam content at home. He wanted to join them, but he had to keep on the harness for the duration of writing the book. He wrote Howells, "I never had such a fight over a book in my life before. And the foolishest part of the whole business is, that I started Osgood to editing it before I had finished writing it. As a consequence, large areas of it are condemned here and there and yonder, and I have the burden of these unfilled gaps harassing me and the thought of the broken continuity of the work, while I am at the same time trying to build the last quarter of the book." The visiting George Washington Cable assisted Sam in writing the chapters concerning New Orleans. Cable, a tiny man and very religious, quickly became a family favorite. He spoke with such elegance that he astounded even Sam, a remarkable conversationalist himself. Cable's fluency of talk lent Sam an ease in bringing his interminable book to an end without really concluding it. Using the latter part of the formless project as a sort of conversational catchall, he reprinted long passages from other sources and tossed in stories left out of *A Tramp Abroad*. He even included the invented tale about how he got his pen name, claiming that he harvested it from the venerable river pilot Isaiah Sellers after his death, a story to which he obligated himself to adhere for the remainder of Mark Twain's life. By the end of the year, the manuscript was complete and Sam committed *Life on the Mississippi* to Osgood's and Webster's hands.

Writing Huck Finn

Even popularity can be overdone. In Rome, along at first,
you are full of regrets that Michelangelo died; but by-and-
by you only regret that you didn't see him do it.
—"Pudd'nhead Wilson's Calendar" (1894)

WHILE SAM FELT relief at finishing *Life on the Mis-*
sissippi, he did not derive much pleasure from the book
itself. Like *A Tramp Abroad*, the book more resembled a
collection of unrelated short pieces than a coherent whole. The mutability
of both the Mississippi and the lives of people around it formed a theme
for the book, but Sam did not exert his authority over the material sufficiently to fashion it into a unified entity. His desire to create a standard
work on the history of the river conflicted with his interest in artistic
cohesion.

More dangerous was that *Life on the Mississippi*—perhaps as an exten-
sion of the confession of twinship buried in *The Prince and the Pauper*—was
a book with two personalities bound in a single volume. "Old Times on
the Mississippi," the section written originally for *The Atlantic* and copied
wholesale in the new volume, was in Mark Twain's voice, as were several
shorter pieces incorporated in the later chapters. The remainder of the
book appears to be spoken not by Mark Twain but by some version of
Sam Clemens, a voice that bobs back and forth between the assured Samuel L. Clemens, middle-aged Hartford gentleman, and the tinny, uncertain
man reflecting on the losses time and change have wrought. Sadly indis-

tinct, this other voice came as close to Sam's own voice as anything he had yet published. *Life on the Mississippi* betrays the uneasiness of its narrative identity and the instability of its divided purpose and origins. Sam had only small confidence in it as a literary production.

He felt more confidence in it as a product to be marketed under Mark Twain's name. Still, he worried about turning his fortunes over to James Osgood and Charley Webster. Since Osgood wanted to make beautiful books and Sam wanted to sell thousands of copies, their goals never converged. Osgood's efforts on *The Prince and the Pauper* had resulted in a lovely book that sold barely a third as many copies as *A Tramp Abroad.* Sam wanted, even expected, *Life on the Mississippi* to sell 100,000 copies, as had Mark Twain's three previous books in that genre. Publishing under the same terms as *Prince*—bearing the cost of production himself while paying Osgood a premium for distribution—Sam issued directives he felt would bring the success he needed to maintain both his style of living and Mark Twain's preeminence in the literary marketplace. "We must give Webster all the thunder-and-lightning circulars and advertising enginery that is needful," Sam ordered Osgood and Company. "We must sell 100,000 copies of the book in 12 months, and shan't want him complaining that we are the parties in fault if the sale falls short of it." No Twain book had reached the 100,000 plateau so quickly, and Webster cautioned his wife's uncle to temper his expectations. "I think you will sell as many of the new book as of *any* you ever wrote *not excepting Innocents*, but it can't be done in a minute," he answered, "but it *will* be done in the same time." Sam's ambivalent faith in Webster's business sense did not extend to his knowledge of subscription publishing, however, and his uncertainty showed in the confusion between Webster and Osgood about which man was in charge. Technically, Webster was just one of eleven general agents, but it was he who had hired the other general agents. While Webster ran his own New York area agency and Osgood produced the books, the other agents dangled undirected. As financier of the new operation, Sam approved printing 50,000 copies even before the canvass began. Then he sat waiting for the canvass to reach 40,000 units, Elisha Bliss' magic signal to publish.

When the artists hired to illustrate *Life on the Mississippi* refused to draw without a guarantee that the publisher would reproduce their work by photographic process and not engraving, it signaled the end of Kaolatype, and with it a loss of $50,000, which Sam hoped the sales of the book could offset. He also transferred his hopes to the other invention he had invested in, the mechanical typesetter. As he wrote Howells, "I must speculate in something, such being my nature." Already, James Paige had charmed Sam out of many more thousands of dollars with his recital of how his Compositor, which handled type at several times the speed of human hands, solved the most glaring technical difficulties of other similar machines. His gift for poetically describing his inventions exceeded even his undeniable engineering genius. As 1883's winter melted into spring, Sam also speculated on the future theatrical success of Hartford neighbor Will Gillette, fronting him $3,000 for a stage production to be performed at the Madison Square Theater, run by Marshall Mallory and his brother. The Mallorys also published a religious magazine, which gave them a respectability unusual in show business; but after the play closed, Gillette found that their supposed religious beliefs did nothing to blunt the sharp trading practices, typical of less religious-minded producers. Only when Sam intervened did the Mallorys give Gillette his share, hoping they might get a playable property from Mark Twain.

Between Livy's bout with diphtheria and the children's with scarlet fever, "the persistent enemy of this book," Sam reveled in his leisure. "I have been an utterly free person for a month or two; and I do not believe I ever so greatly appreciated and enjoyed and realized the absence of the chains of slavery as I do this time." His trip back to the Mississippi and the prospect of his fiftieth birthday, a year and a half distant, made him philosophical. He argued in a paper presented to the Monday Evening Club called "What Is Happiness?" that altruism did not exist. People acted generously as a mechanical response to their guilt or need for pleasure, Sam maintained. This hypothesis undermined the Nook Farm policy of social responsibility, which made luxurious lives morally acceptable by encumbering the wealthy with a duty to the poor; without altruism, there was no social responsibility, only individual guilt. For Sam, though, living with his invented personas complicated the problem. What responsibility did Sam bear for the thoughts and actions of Mark Twain? His denial of altruism eliminated his responsibility for them entirely. The human machine named Sam Clemens responded to the circumstances of his life by producing Mark Twain. Raising self-interest to a moral law erased the immorality of selfishness. If all actions are selfish, one can judge their morality only by how the actions benefit others. Mark Twain's actions—his books and performances—obviously did.

This moral questioning was a Clemens family trait; but while Jane, Orion, and Pamela shifted their religious allegiances in their search for truth, Sam changed his personality. The philosophical quandaries raised by this indeterminacy of self led Sam to the character of Huckleberry Finn, whose story he had pawed at for seven years. Even more since Sam's return to the Hannibal home of his model Tom Blankenship, Huck seemed to be the very emblem of uncertainty. Floating south into slave territory while hoping to free the runaway slave Jim, the boy who made a life out of escaping place, responsibility, and self would soon collide with an inescapable choice: fidelity to society or fidelity to himself. Sam faced this identical problem, feeling that he would soon have to choose between his socially successful invented selves and his fundamental identity, his true self, which had not seen daylight in years. He picked up Huck's manuscript again.

The publication date for *Life on the Mississippi* fell in early May 1883. With Clara Spaulding serving as a companion to Livy at home, Sam went to Montreal to secure his British copyright. In Canada, he was the frequent guest of the marquis of Lorne, governor-general of Canada, whose wife, Princess Louise, was Queen Victoria's daughter, playing tennis, cards, and billiards with the royals and their friends. At the Literary and Scientific Society Dinner, Sam told Livy, the princess didn't mind "that I was the only male creature in the drawing room who hadn't patent leathers on" or notice the shabbiness of Sam's ties or the moth hole in his dress coat, which he disguised with ink. While Sam danced with royalty, Livy had her hands full at home. Eleven-year-old Susie ruminated on the sour relationship her Aunt Ida, Charlie Langdon's wife, had with her own mother. Livy wrote Sam of Susie's fixation, "I have been afraid that she might begin to feel that it would be rather interesting not to get on quite well with me." Patrick McAleer, meanwhile, had convinced Clara that Jumbo, her pet calf, would grow into a horse if only she curried it enough. Jean proved less tractable. "She needed a whipping," Livy wrote Sam, "but I was too cowardly to give it to her." The servants, meanwhile, fell to bickering when Sam was not around. Only summers at Quarry Farm relieved Livy of housekeeping and provided Sam with the time and isolation he needed to write.

In June, just before the family left for Elmira, Sam once again squabbled with the onetime *Quaker City* captain, Duncan, who was still commissioner of the port of New York. Duncan had nepotistically provided his sons with jobs on the federal payroll, and a reporter caught Mark Twain gloating over the reports while eating strawberries and cream on the veranda of his Hartford house. The *New York Times* gave front-page space to Mark Twain's characterization of Duncan as "an old piece of animated flatulence . . . a canting hypocrite, filled to the chin with sham godliness and forever oozing and dripping false piety." Duncan promptly filed a libel suit against the paper. To save himself, Sam denied the accuracy of the report. "There is not a sentence in the interview that ever issued from my mouth," he wrote instructing Webster on how to handle the suit. "As a rule the interviewer has invented both the ideas & the language." Sam escaped the imbroglio, in which Duncan won a judgment against the paper of only twelve cents, but in the process Sam destroyed his relationship with the *Times*.

Though the Quarry Farm quarters were cramped—Susie and Clara slept together, and Jean slept with the nurse—that did not affect the joy Sam, Livy, and the girls felt in being with the Cranes. In the evenings, everyone played charades by creating elaborate tableaux for each syllable in the mystery word. The adults played cards or talked about books late into the night. During the day, while Sam worked, the children ran after cows, showered affection on the cats, and patiently suffered through lessons when Livy felt up to them. Though recovered from her diphtheria, Livy remained dangerously thin. "It's been like sleeping with a bed full of baskets," Sam confided in Howells. Whenever Livy weakened, pain returned to her back, a frightening reminder of her early brush with paralysis, but the fresh air, good food, and loving attentions of her sister and her mother always restored her.

Sam set himself right to work in his glassed-in study. Howells fed Sam's creative fires with a puff of praise from British novelist Thomas Hardy: "Why don't people understand that Mark Twain is not merely a great humorist? He's a very remarkable fellow in a very different way." In mid-July, Sam wrote to Howells, recently returned from Europe:

> Why, it's like old times, to step straight into the study, damp from the breakfast table, & sail right in & sail right on, the whole day long, without thought of running short of stuff or words. I wrote 4000 words to-day & I touch 3000 & upwards pretty often, & don't fall below 2600 on any working day. . . . I have finished one small book, & am away along in a big one that I half-finished two or three years ago. I expect to complete it in a month or six weeks or two months more. And *I* shall *like* it, whether anybody else does or not.

The first book was a long-winded burlesque in which Scheherazade talks King Shahriyar to death on the 1002nd Arabian night. The second was *Adventures of Huckleberry Finn*.

For the first time in fifteen years, Sam wrote with no contract, delivery date, or idea of how the book might make its way to his public. He even flirted with the notion of giving the finished book to Frank Bliss at the American Publishing Company. He only knew for certain he would not publish with Osgood again. *Life on the Mississippi* had sold barely thirty thousand copies. The absence of central control of the canvass had led to chaos. By the middle of the summer, two major general agents, in Cincinnati and in Philadelphia, had dumped copies of *Life on the Mississippi* into bookstores. By October, the agents no longer canvassed for the book at all. There remained well over ten thousand unbound copies, each one representing a dollar of unearned profit for Sam. For Sam to end his business relationship with Osgood while remaining friends with him proved nearly impossible. He broke off the relationship and then asked Osgood to settle for less than the agreed-upon 7½ percent of the receipts, "based upon the fact—and it is unquestionably a fact—that the publisher who sells less than 50,000 copies of a book for me has merely injured me, he has not benefitted me. Legally one pays the same rate for an injury as for a benefit, but not morally." Believing contracts to be flexible documents, Sam asked Osgood to accept the smaller percentage to reach the intended half profits. Osgood agreed. Sam compared working with Osgood to enduring a bout of scarlet fever, and concluded "I believe I would almost rather have Osgood publish a book for me."

Sam's freedom extended to his schedule. In mid-July, he took a day off to set up a whimsical history game for Susie and Clara, driving stakes into the ground, each stake representing the ascension of a British king, each foot between them a year of royal reign. The children started at the bottom of the hill and ran up, calling out the names of the rulers as they passed each stake, racing on to Queen Victoria. That night, after the children went to bed, Sam—ever the entrepreneur—tinkered with a way to bring the educational fun inside, finally settling on a board with pin-holes and a book of dates to go along with it, a game structure he could use for any collection of facts. He turned the fact collecting over to Orion, who needed the occupation, and he sent for Charley Webster, to have him explore the feasibility of patenting and manufacturing games. But Joe Twichell published parts of Sam's letter to him describing the game in the *Hartford Courant*, deflating Sam's passion for it by endangering its market and risking the loss of Sam's friendship. Sam was, in every genre, absolutely proprietary about his creations.

Still, thinking about history helped Sam get his literary locomotive back on track. He had interrupted his composition after Huck discovers that the family that imprisoned Jim, the slave he befriended and helped free, is coincidentally expecting a visit from his St. Petersburg buddy Tom Sawyer. To save his friend Jim, Huck becomes Tom, which forces Tom to become his own brother Sid. In order to secure Tom Sawyer's cooperation in freeing Jim, Huck allows his white friend to torture his black one, in the hallowed name of Tom's beloved romantic fictions. At the novel's end, Tom explains that Jim was already free via a deathbed manumission by his St. Petersburg owner.

This ending robs Huck of his power as the novel's moral center, but it capitulates to the facts of the era. Sam realized that no hero, no matter how magical or pure of heart, can countermand history. Exploring this large underlying theme brought Sam a special pleasure to the composition of the novel. He told Howells, "I used to restrict myself to 4 & 5 hours a day & 5 days in the week; but this time I've wrought from breakfast till 5.15 p.m. six days in the week; & once or twice I smouched a Sunday when the boss wasn't looking. Nothing is half so good as literature hooked on Sunday on the sly."

After completing the first draft of *Huck* in Elmira, Sam was hungry to see Howells. The two had plans to write a play together, certain that with their combined imaginations and drawing power they could expect a shimmering success. Howells wrote, "As soon as I mentioned our plan for a play, Mrs. Howells nobly declared that she would do anything for money, and that I might go to you when I liked." They plotted a dramatic sequel to *The Gilded Age*, featuring Colonel Sellers, who had vast commercial value in the hands of comedian John T. Raymond. Before he could begin work with Howells, however, Sam ruined his relationship with Raymond. Sam felt obliged to offer Raymond an option on the sequel, but he also instructed Webster to get Daniel Whitford to make the contract so restrictive the actor could not wrangle any unintended benefit from it. As he wrote Webster regarding the option, "*I wish to God he would not take it.*" Meanwhile, Charley looked for another actor to take the lead role.

Sam and Howells began work in early November. Now in his seventies but still seeing millions in every crackbrained scheme, Sellers wears a fire extinguisher he invented strapped to his back during the whole play, waiting for a fire to break out, and wears wings so he can fly to a fire at any altitude. He drunkenly leads a parade of temperance women. A spiritualist, Sellers believes in spontaneous materialization of people and objects, which naturally gets him into trouble when a new character suddenly appears on stage. "It was not possible for Clemens to write like anybody else, but I could very easily write like Clemens," Howells later remembered. "No dramatists ever got greater joy out of their creations." They laughed themselves silly generating one wild idea after the other, but the farce was chaos.

While Howells and Sam goaded one another into collective insanity in Hartford, the sophisticated British poet and critic Matthew Arnold appeared in Boston. Arnold, disappointed to have missed Howells, was surprised to hear he had gone to see Mark Twain. "Oh," Arnold replied, "but he doesn't like *that* sort of thing, does he?" Arnold met Howells at a reception in Hartford a few days later. "While his hand laxly held mine in greeting," Howells recalled after a quarter of a century, "I saw his eyes fixed intensely on the other side of the room. 'Who—who in the world is that?' " Howells introduced him to Mark Twain, and the men did not part company for the rest of the evening. Over dinner, Sam persuaded the dubious Englishman of Mark Twain's utter brilliance.

Later in the month, George Washington Cable came to read in Hartford. Sam revived his idea of a traveling menagerie of readers, including Howells, Aldrich, and Cable, whose presentation now impressed Sam; he had "been training under an expert, & he's just a rattling reader now— the best amateur I ever heard; & with 2 seasons of *public* practice, I guess he'll be the best professional reader alive." Cable had made a name for himself as a novelist with his finely wrought explorations of the complex tides of race, culture, and caste among Louisiana Creoles. His resolute belief in the equality of all people, fueled by his passionate adherence to Christianity, formed the ethical foundation of his books. Cable stayed with Sam, but fell ill with mumps while in Hartford and became an almost permanent guest. Soon after, first Jean and then Susie contracted the disease. Setting aside their feelings about Cable's infection of their children, Sam and Livy hired nurses for him, answered his mail, and coddled him.

Confined to his bed in the Clemenses' guest room for several weeks, Cable was, as Sam reported to Howells, a poor patient but "a marvellous talker on a deep subject," race relations in America. The entire country wrestled with the question of what privileges of citizenship ought to be accorded freed slaves. Cable believed fiercely in the fundamental equality of all Americans, but he also believed that allegiance to African ways held blacks back from assimilation into American life, a view of race not only far ahead of typical southern ideas, but well beyond northern liberal thinking. Sam felt that Cable, a southern man like himself, had evolved a refined perspective on race issues. Conversations between the men helped Sam resolve some of the same issues that were embodied in *Huckleberry Finn*.

The conversations also alerted Sam to the market for a novel that touched on matters of race, as did many of Cable's books. Sam decided to publish the novel himself under the imprint of Charles L. Webster and Company, which Sam owned and financed. Webster received a salary and a percentage of the company's profits. He delighted in negotiating the price of paper and drawing up strong contracts. In early April, Sam and Webster settled on a new illustrator, Edward Kemble, whose humor matched Mark Twain's. Though he had more confidence in Charley Webster than he had in Osgood, he still issued him the same edicts. "Get at your canvassing early, and drive it with all your might, with the intent and purpose of issuing on the 10th (or 15th) of next December (the best time in the year to tumble a big pile into the trade)—but if we haven't 40,000 orders then, we simply postpone publication till we've *got* them. It is a plain, simple policy, and would have saved both my last books if it had been followed." Webster began assembling a canvassing force to sell *Huck Finn.*

Howells offered to read proof, a generous offer made in hopes of bringing the relationship between the writers back onto purely literary terms and so relieve some of the tension caused by continuing negotiations over the play. Howells' emotional unpredictability had affected the progress on that project. After first refusing to change the name of the character Sellers, to avoid the identification of Sellers with Raymond in case another actor took the role, Howells reversed himself with little explanation. Sam, annoyed, had Webster reply. Howells coldly told Webster, "If Mr. Clemens is disabled, or in trouble, or has some unknown offence with me, I can understand his preferring to write his friend by the hand of his agent; but not otherwise."

The moment word circulated that they had a script, the famous authors had become attractive playwrights in a business driven almost entirely by names. Despite the dispute, the Colonel Sellers play was only one of a half dozen Sam and Howells intended to write. Marshall Mallory, of the Madison Square Theater, offered to find an actor for the new farce while taking all production risks and splitting the profits in thirds, but that left the writers only a third to share between them. Sam preferred to own the property and hire the actor himself. He rejected Mallory's offer and instead offered to open negotiations with him on a dramatization of *Tom Sawyer.* "I am now writing a new play by myself (while Howells & I are kept asunder by Cable's illness,) & that if I finish it to my liking maybe we can strike up some terms for it which will be mutually satisfactory." Worse than merely neglecting Howells' interests, Sam actively undercut them. While apprising Howells regularly of the progress of negotiations for the sale of their joint project, Sam told Webster, "I never meant that this Sellers business should stand for a moment in the way or take precedence of Tom Sawyer." Howells did not suspect Sam of double-dealing, and his willingness to help with *Huck* returned warmth to their correspondence. Sam finished revising *Huck Finn,* relying heavily on Howells for his final refinements of the book.

The promise of quick money from the theater enchanted Sam. He wrote Charley, "If the book business interferes with the dramatic business, drop the *former*—for it doesn't pay salt; & I want the latter rushed."

When it came to projects involving huge capital, however, Sam excluded Webster: His trust only went so far. One big project came his way in the form of Yung Wing, the former head of the American Chinese Educational Mission, on whose behalf Sam and Joe Twichell had enlisted President Grant's support. Grant's letter had not kept Yung Wing in America, but now, two years later, Yung Wing had returned from his native land with the idea of building a railroad in China. The American railroad boom had pretty much subsided, but the export of the technology had not yet begun. This enterprise appealed to Sam, and he took Yung Wing to New York to consult with Grant about the project. Grant had an investment partnership with experienced stock trader Fred Ward; Sam thought that their company, Grant and Ward, which had made a fortune in American railroads, might be interested in an overseas speculation.

Despite his business interests and Cable's and his family's illnesses, Sam kept up an active social life in the winter and spring. Henry Irving, the renowned British actor, came to dine in Hartford, as did the noted sculptor Augustus Saint-Gaudens. This parade of friends and the complaints Cable and Sam shared about the pestilence of autograph seekers led Cable to construct an elaborate April Fool's Day joke on his benefactor. He asked 150 of Sam's friends to send a letter begging for an autograph. Several, poking Sam where it hurt, affected to confuse Mark Twain and Bret Harte by begging an autograph from the famous author of "The Heathen Chinee." Others put absurd strictures upon their requests, defining the paper and the ink Sam should use. Still others desired autographs by the pound. Livy, in on the plan, brought him the absurdly high stack of mail that day and watched while Sam's boiling anger turned into an appreciation of the joke. The story of the prank made it into almost every newspaper in the country. Mark Twain could not take a deep breath without becoming more famous for doing it.

Sam's life was now full of everything, except money. He constantly scratched after cash. As he wrote to Karl Gerhardt, the art student he had supported in Paris, the Clemenses wanted to go to Europe, "but we can't well afford it. We have made but few investments in the last few years which have not turned out badly."* None of his plays found a producer or an actor. He shared a script he wrote from *The Prince and the Pauper* with Howells, who pronounced it "altogether too thin and slight. . . . It's not more than half long enough; and the parlance is not sufficiently 'early English.' "

Without a play running, Sam risked his capital on *Huckleberry Finn*, fully knowing that his earlier fiction had not sold well. Sam threw himself into every aspect of the book's production, showing a special concern for the illustrations. He went so far as to tell Charley that in the cover picture "the boy's mouth is a trifle more Irishy than necessary." As more pictures came, he became less comfortable with them. "As a rule (though not always) the people in these pictures are forbidding and repulsive. Reduction will modify them, no doubt, but it can hardly make them pleasant folk to look at. An artist shouldn't follow a book too literally, perhaps—if this is the result." He worried every detail.

Sam loved to gamble, but speculating on Mark Twain fretted him. Having accepted arguments from Elisha Bliss and insecurity from his own heart, he believed that Mark Twain's fame was a sham, not the result of any substantial accomplishment but the result of manipulation of his public image. Sam Clemens was merely the undeserving beneficiary of this laughably ephemeral sham. Sam could more easily believe in a railroad in China.

33 | *His Own Publisher*

> *All I care to know is that a man is a human being—*
> *that is enough for me; he can't be much worse.*
> —"Concerning the Jews" (1899)

THE CREATIVE ENERGY Sam had enjoyed during the summer of 1883 in Elmira failed to reappear in 1884. "This is the first summer which I have lost," he told Webster. "I haven't a paragraph to show for my 3-months' working season." Reading the proofs for *Huck Finn* and undergoing painful dental treatments consumed all his time, except when he relaxed by falling off his bicycle, America's latest recreational rage.

Determined to market his novel aggressively, Sam decided to put Mark Twain on the platform again, though the idea of returning to the long railroad trips and the loneliness of lecturing nauseated him. His idea of a circus of writers proved unworkably expensive, but one other performer could reduce his platform time and make travel congenial. With Livy's guidance, Sam made overtures to organize a series of readings with George Washington Cable, contacting Major J. B. Pond, Redpath's successor and Cable's manager. Charley Webster negotiated the contract according to Sam's long list of requirements, including accounting methods, dates, and travel conditions. "Pond must attend to everything which comes under the head of *business*—halls, route, printing, prices, &c, deciding all business questions himself, & asking no advice of me," Sam demanded. "It is Pond's menagerie, not mine; & he must put himself to the front, all the time, as boss & head-ringmaster." In fact, Sam set the terms of the tour, which would generate between $25,000 and $30,000 profit in four months. Sam would pocket two or three times what Cable received. No one doubted that the show belonged to Mark Twain, both as headliner and proprietor.

Without a consuming literary project to distract him, Sam pushed his nose into every corner of his financial affairs. At the beginning of the summer, when Webster found an Alabama firm advertising cheap versions of Mark Twain's American Publishing Company books in the *New York World*, Sam wrote Webster, "Notify Bliss that I expect him to protect and defend my copyrights." Sam hoped and believed that Frank Bliss' failure to act breached the company's contracts with Sam, so that he could reclaim ownership of the books. "When you send me pirate ads which are calculated to enrage me, I wish you would also send me a form for a letter to the Am. Pub. Co to fit the case," Sam wrote Webster, concluding that he would soon have to turn the matter over to his lawyer. "I have foolishly gone so far with the Am Pub Co that I must now go on, if Whitford thinks it a winning case—which he won't." At the same time, Sam commanded Webster to ask Bliss for the right to market *Tom Sawyer* in tandem with *Huck Finn*, continuing his contradictory habit of asking favors from people he wanted to take to court. At the same time that Sam would not relinquish authority to Webster, he refused to occupy himself with small business matters. A frustrated Webster continued to brave this impossible arrangement.

When the reality of Mark Twain's lecture commitment settled on Sam, he wrote Ned House, now back in Japan, "Think of the insanity of it! I wish I hadn't promised; but it is too late, now, to cry about it."* For a month before the tour began, Sam threw himself into politics to relieve his anxiety. His Republican party nominated James G. Blaine for President, but Blaine's shady record in Congress made it impossible for Sam to back him. Usually of a political mind with Sam, Howells disbelieved the allegations of Blaine's graft and besides found the Democratic nominee, Grover Cleveland, not only morally repugnant—he'd had a child with his mistress—but also monstrous, with a "hangman-face" he found "dull and brutal." Cleveland, chief of police in Buffalo while Sam lived there, had since moved to New York's governor's mansion. Sam scoffed at the hypocrisy of "arguing against a bachelor's fitness for President because he has had private intercourse with a consenting widow!" He and Joe Twichell became Hartford's only prominent Cleveland supporters. Known as Mugwumps, defectors from the Republican party became Cleveland's most powerful allies, and Mark Twain spoke frequently and publicly against Blaine's campaign. Even Sam's butler, George Griffin, got involved, taking bets on a Blaine victory against his employer. Days before the election, a Blaine partisan categorized the Democrats as standing for the three Rs—rum, Romanism, and rebellion. George heard the remark and hedged by making book on the other side of the election. When Blaine refused to repudiate the statement, Cleveland won.

"*Isn't* human nature the most consummate shame & lie that was ever invented?" Sam marveled to Howells about the wretchedness of electoral politics. "Isn't man a creature to be ashamed of in pretty much all his aspects? Is he really fit for anything but to be stood up on the street corner as a convenience for dogs?" His characterization of the human race included himself, since he had recently confronted one of his own moral shortcomings, an arrogance born of vanity. When Mark Twain received an invitation to lecture at a church benefit, Sam reported to Howells that

> I began to rage over the exceedingly cool wording of the request, when Mrs. Clemens said "I think I know that church; & if so, this preacher is a colored man—he doesn't know how to write a polished letter—how should he?"
>
> My manner changed so suddenly & so radically that Mrs. C. said: "I will give you a motto, & it will be useful to you if you will adopt it: "Consider every man colored till he is proved white."

Livy had given Sam a valuable tool for putting his theory of human equality into practice. Sam had an instinctive generosity to the downtrodden, but it was born of a race prejudice instilled in him in childhood that all of his reading, thinking, and moral evolution could not entirely erase. He contributed generously to the education of African Americans; he gave money to a Negro college in Pennsylvania and helped a particularly brilliant young black man earn his law degree at Yale. More forward-thinking on race than most of his contemporaries, he nevertheless understood his actions as reparations for an underlying bigotry that he tried to manage and combat. Though Cable did not persuade Sam to accept religion—Cable's social consciousness relied on his belief in each person's equal access to God's grace—he did convert him to a faith in the fundamental equality of all people. To this ideology, Sam added his own variation: that all people were equally inconsequential. He had begun to think of human affairs as infinitely small and he noted in his journal, "I think we are only the microscopic trichina concealed in the blood of some vast creature's veins, & that it is that vast creature whom God concerns Himself about, & not us."

These issues of race and human folly formed the backbone of *Huckleberry Finn*. Sam had begun the novel as a sequel to *Tom Sawyer*, but ran out of steam once he got Huck to the same island where he and Tom had hidden while the townspeople of St. Petersburg thought them dead. He returned to the manuscript with the ironic inspiration of sending the escaped slave Jim and Huck—on the lam from the "sivilizing" beneficence of the widow Douglas—downriver in their quest for freedom. The remainder of the novel flowed from that perverse decision: The trashy white boy and the noble black man would have to find their freedom deep in a region of the country that in the 1840s tendered very little of it. Sam infused their progress southward with the panorama of life he had seen from the texas of his steamboats, memories revived by his recent Mississippi trip. Along the way, Huck finds himself in the middle of a feud, becomes the unwilling accomplice of some ridiculous con men, and learns to accept Jim's humanity. The con men sell Jim back into slavery and Huck determines to free him, until a charade of false identities forces Huck and Jim to act out a burlesque plucked from Tom Sawyer's mental library. When the absurd escape plan fails, Tom saves Jim by explaining that he was already free, manumitted by the will of his owner. Gratified by the result of Tom's efforts but frustrated by the foolishness underlying it, Huck determines "to light out for the Territory ahead of the rest, because aunt Sally she's going to adopt me and sivilize me and I can't stand it. I been there before." The realization of the character of Huck Finn is the work of a master.

But what raises the novel to greatness is the presence of Mark Twain in the text. He does not appear as a character, per se, but he dominates the perspective so thoroughly and so sympathetically that he appears to mediate the relationship between Huck Finn and the reader. For example, when Huck is asked if anyone is hurt in a steamboat explosion and answers, "No'm. Killed a nigger," we recognize a distance between Huck's moral system, which still does not wholly embrace slaves as human, and Mark Twain's, who has revealed this shortcoming in Huck, something he can only do from a higher moral position. This moral difference between Huck and Twain becomes more complex as Huck becomes more heroic. When he discovers that the con men have sold Jim back into slavery, Huck writes Jim's owner to tell her where to find him, but then feels qualms about returning Jim to the world from which he so desperately wanted to escape. The letter represents Huck's capitulation to a social order he otherwise rejects. Holding the paper in his hands, he makes a

dangerous moral choice, telling himself, " 'All right, then, I'll go to hell'—
and tore it up. It was awful thoughts, and awful words, but they was
said. And I let them stay said, and never thought no more about reforming." Huck continues, "I would go to work and steal Jim out of slavery
again; and if I could think up anything worse, I would do that too." At
first, readers cheer Huck along, relieved that he is willing to accept eternal
damnation rather than accede to a power structure he abhors. But savvy
readers then recognize that, despite the virtue of Huck's choice, he still
believes in a moral system that recognizes some people as the property of
others. Believing that Jim belongs to someone, he resolves to steal him;
and not only to steal, but then to perform any other immoralities that
occur to him, since the act of stealing Jim is already morally culpable. It
is a moving passage, but it is also intentionally deceptive. Mark Twain,
morally hovering over the scene, applauds Huck's moral growth, but by
qualifying the reasoning by which Huck makes his choice he also cautions
readers to recognize how paltry a step it really is. To accept Huck's
ideology, Twain seems to say, only replaces one immorality with another
only slightly better.

Mark Twain capitalized on Huck's appealing immorality. Serious
moral ambiguity on the part of a novel's narrator was a technique fresh
to most readers, but Sam had packaged Huck's contradictory character
with his typical humor and skill. He thought he had made Mark Twain's
progressive agenda on race unmistakable in the novel's moral hierarchy.
Pap, Huck's father, occupies the bottom rung with his drunken tirade
against an educated freeman: "When they told me there was a State in
this country where they'd let that nigger vote, I drawed out. I says I'll
never vote again." Mark Twain sits at the top, advocating a uniform racial
blindness. The novel uses the same didactic sophistication that marked
David Ross Locke's performance as Petroleum Vesuvius Nasby, educating
others by revealing the dubious logic at the root of certain ethical choices.
Because *Huck Finn* tries to represent all the positions in between as Huck
himself makes his ascent toward Twain's position, careless reading has led
to blaming Mark Twain for his characters' immoralities.

Sam did not just want to reinforce Mark Twain's position as Moral
Phenomenon, as he'd called himself nearly two decades before as he sailed
to Hawaii; if that had been his purpose, he would have written a treatise.
Instead, he wanted to explore the ambiguity of storytelling, even if the
exploration undermined Mark Twain. Tom Sawyer comes into the novel
at the end and resets its moral compass. Suddenly the plot becomes preeminent, not the moral. Huck proposes a simple plan for liberating Jim,
the right thing to do, but Tom regards his plan as "too blame' simple;

there ain't nothing *to* it. What's the good of a plan that ain't no more trouble than that?" Tom wants the enterprise to be more literary, more elaborate, more grand; it is the process that appeals to Tom, not the result. Just as Huck climbs the moral ladder in the course of the narrative, trying to reach the zenith at which Mark Twain sits, Tom scales the storyteller's ladder of narrative sophistication. Tom drives the conclusion of the novel as an amoral artist, threatening both Huck's narrative progress and the book's moral fabric. He does not care so much what happens, as long as the story is good. Like Tom, Sam Clemens hides behind the scenes of *Huck Finn* pulling the narrative strings, and he does not mind weakening Mark Twain's authority in the process. Tom's incursion at the end of the book, which challenges the moral foundation carefully set by Mark Twain, represents Sam's disguised effort to secure recognition for himself as both the author of *Huck Finn* and the inventor of its titular author. Unable to ask for the recognition more boldly, it is no wonder he thought of himself as mere microscopic trichina.

Minuscule or not, Sam wanted his novel to sell well, and that meant taking Mark Twain on the road. Soon after the election of the first Democratic President since before the Civil War, Sam began his reading tour with Pond and Cable. Major Pond advertised Mark Twain and George Washington Cable as "Twins of Genius," and the men did in fact exert efforts to come to terms with issues of race through fiction. Cable's thoughts on race were at the core of his fame, and the issue of race occupies the heart of *Huck Finn*, the novel Sam wanted to sell through his appearance on the platform. Magazines of all political stripes published articles wrestling with questions concerning the racial integration of American life. The liberal perspective on what *The Atlantic* called "The Negro Problem" argued that "if the negro is thoughtfully cared for, if his training in civilization, begun in slavery, is continued in his state of freedom, we may hope to find abundant room for him in our society." Twain and Cable represented the radical position of free integration. As southerners, their voices carried extra authority. The differences between the men—Cable religious, delicate, and refined; Mark Twain heretical, illkempt, and unpredictable—faded in the light of the fundamental twinship they presented on the thorny issue of race.

Sam was, however, not at ease on this tour, and the largest part of his anxiety floated around Cable. His apprehension stemmed more from the high stakes for *Huck Finn* and the unfamiliar format of this double performance than from his relationship with Cable, but Sam could not express his anxiety about his novel or his performance. On the other hand, he could freely vent his worry on Cable. Livy noticed it within two weeks of Sam's departure. "Don't allow yourself to get awry with Mr. Cable," she cautioned; "he is good and your friend and it is an advantage to have him."* Sam behaved well to Cable, but his dissatisfaction with him became a refrain in letters to Livy.

In New York with the tour, Sam dined with Richard Watson Gilder of *Century*. There he heard that the Century Company planned to publish Ulysses S. Grant's memoirs. Sam felt he had a prior interest in the project: Three years before, he had suggested to Grant that he tell his life story, but Grant waved off the idea. In the interim, however, Grant's business partner had walked off with not only the firm's assets but Grant's personal holdings as well. The ex-President and his family found they possessed less than $1,000 cash. Grant then agreed to write reminiscences of his role in the Civil War for $1,500 and also to compose his life story. Sam went to Grant the next morning, offering to review the rough, unsigned contract with Gilder, which had offered Grant a 10 percent royalty. Sam was insulted on his behalf, and offered twice that, certain that Webster and Company could sell three times as many copies of Grant's memoirs as of the best of Mark Twain's books. Committed to Gilder, Grant demurred, so Sam suggested taking the offer back to Gilder; if Gilder couldn't match it, the general could look for another publisher.

When he and Grant broke out of their private conference, General Lew Wallace, whose novel *Ben-Hur* had reached enormous popularity, was waiting for the former President.

> Mrs. Grant got up & stood between Gen. Wallace & me, & said, "There, there's many a woman in this land that would like to be in my place & be able to tell her children that she had stood once elbow to elbow between two such great authors as Mark Twain & General Wallace." We all laughed & I said to Gen. Grant: "Don't look so cowed, General; you have written a book, too, & when it is published you can hold up your head & let on to be a person of consequence yourself."

Sam continued his tour, leaving negotiations for Grant's memoirs to Webster, who was already struggling with a difficult assortment of labors. In addition to small matters such as Sam's old accounts with Osgood, Slote and Company, and the American Publishing Company, he was working to sell forty thousand copies of *Huck Finn* by the middle of December. Gilder's *Century* published selections from the novel in December and January as the tour gathered steam, but the book sold no better than Mark

Twain's previous fiction. Nonetheless, Webster sat down with General Grant and his sons to work out fair terms for publishing his memoirs.

On tour, Sam maintained a level demeanor for most of December 1884. In New Jersey, he and Cable stayed with Tom Nast. Annoyed by Nast's collection of ticking and cuckooing clocks, Sam went around the house stopping them all, going so far as to drag the most offensive outside. Nast discovered him and sketched Mark Twain carrying a grandfather clock in his nightshirt, a drawing he soon published. In Albany, Sam visited President-elect Cleveland at the governor's mansion; as one of the nation's most prominent Mugwumps, Mark Twain had helped make Cleveland's victory possible. In the course of his sociable conversation with the President-elect, Sam lounged on a corner of the desk, accidentally sitting on several electric buttons, which "summoned four pages whom nobody had any use for." Cable introduced Sam to Malory's *Morte d'Arthur*, which the writers and their promoter read aloud to one another to while away hours on the train or in their hotel rooms. Cable, Pond, and Sam spoke to each other in Malory's quaint English and gave one another courtly names.

Over his week-long Christmas hiatus from the tour, Livy surprised him by arranging a staging of Sam's "thin and slight" adaptation of *The Prince and the Pauper* at George and Lilly Warner's house. Susie Clemens, who now insisted on spelling her name "Susy," and her friend Daisy Warner played the lead roles, and most of the other children in the neighborhood took part. Livy made the costumes with the help of Katy Leary, and Karl Gerhardt, back from Paris, designed the sets. Though Sam, tired from his two months of travel, tried to beg off the mysterious evening out, Livy dragged him to the Warners', ushering Sam to a first-row seat, just in front of Gerhardt's drop curtain. The junior actors' performance delighted him, especially his eldest girl's turn as Prince Edward. Livy had hinted of her surprise in a letter she wrote her husband in November, praising "Susy's lately developed powers" of storytelling. "She informed me tonight that she should like to be an actress. I think she seems on the way to it."

Otherwise, with the *Huck Finn* canvass bringing only modest returns, Sam became combative and gloomy over the holiday. Bookstores, which were not supposed to have the novel until well after the opportunity to subscribe had passed, nonetheless advertised *Huck* at a price below Webster's. He instructed Charley to begin a lawsuit against the usually reliable Boston bookselling firm of Estes and Lauriat, but their courteous reply bothered Livy, who chastised Sam, "How I wish that you were less ready to fight, and more ready to see other people's side of things."* But such piracies bled him of money, and no matter how much of it he had, Sam always felt he needed more.

And he sometimes saw Cable as a pirate. Resuming their tour, Sam wished he had listened to Major Pond the summer before, when he argued that Mark Twain would draw better alone. "I thought Cable would be a novelty, but alas he has been *every*where, & is a novelty nowhere. I wish I could pay him $200 a week to withdraw." He objected to Cable's parsimony—he even saved his laundry from the holiday break, so that it could be cleaned at Sam's expense—and his unerring observation of the Sabbath, on which he refused to ride in a carriage or have his shoes polished or do anything but attend church. Sam argued against Cable's "constant disposition . . . to *lengthen* his pieces—he never shortens one."* Cable crowded Mark Twain off the stage, and since in Sam's view the audience mostly came to see Mark Twain, Sam wanted Cable curtailed. During the moments when he realized the irrationality of his irritation with Cable, Sam delighted in his conversation. Though he tired of Cable's studied effects in performance, he enjoyed the Creole songs Cable interspersed between his readings. For their own pleasure, Sam and Cable performed the Mississippi River boatmen's game of boast and insult, which Sam had originally composed for *Huck Finn*, but lifted for use in *Life on the Mississippi*.

In Kentucky, Sam saw his cousin James Lampton, whom Cable easily identified as the model for Colonel Sellers. He went on to revisit Hannibal: "You can never imagine the infinite great deeps of pathos that have rolled their tides over me. I shall never see another such day. I have carried my heart in my mouth for twenty-four hours." Sam also spent a day in Keokuk. Jane had begun to sink into senility; her manner remained pleasant, but her mental decay became obvious when she began telling outrageous stories, such as a tale about Orion chasing Mollie's lover through the house with a pistol. Mollie wanted Sam and Livy to contribute more than money to Jane's care, but Sam pleaded Livy's ill health in explaining the impossibility of having Jane come to Hartford any time soon. Since Livy's mother came to Hartford for several weeks at a time, Sam's true motive was to keep Jane in Keokuk; the time Orion took to care for Jane kept him from projects that might get him—or this more famous brother—in trouble. Still, seeing his mother's condition grieved Sam. He mused to Livy, "What books she could have written!—& now the world has lost them." Major Pond's brother Ozias, on the road with the show just after they left Keokuk, noted about Sam that "although one unacquainted with him might think him almost totally indifferent to [suffering], the close observer can always see the sadness in his eyes and the aching heart."

These contradictions followed Sam into business, which distressed Charley Webster, who never knew how much detail to provide his employer. Sam crossly wrote in response to a request from Webster, "No, it is *business*—& so I don't want anything to do with it. You are there to take care of my business, not make business for *me* to take care of." Sam wanted simple, dollars-and-cents reports, but Webster increasingly proved himself incapable of managing his own office, much less the business affairs of Samuel Clemens and Mark Twain. For example, one of Webster's assistants sold a piece of *Huck Finn* to the *North American Review* without authority, and both Sam and Charley had to work hard to undo the damage. Charley could not get the American Publishing Company to honor its obligations to defend Sam's copyright; Frank Bliss had also set the price for selling *Tom Sawyer* so high that Webster could not offer the novel as a companion to *Huck Finn*. Webster had neglected to send review copies of the book to magazines—Sam had forgotten to tell him to—and so tried to quickly hustle some good reviews long after the novel first appeared. Sam himself veered from optimism about his publishing company's first project to despair at the fate of Mark Twain's masterpiece. At the end of January, he wrote to Webster, "I ought to have staid at home & written another book. It pays better than the platform." Two weeks later, he contradicted himself, moaning that he couldn't "see that anything can save *Huck Finn* from being another defeat."

As the tour closed and he pocketed $17,000 from four leisurely months on the road, Sam began to accept the divided nature of fate. He assessed the experience for Howells:

> It has been a curious experience. It has taught me that Cable's gifts of mind are greater & higher than I had suspected. But—
>
> That "but" is pointing toward his religion. You will never never know, never divine, guess, imagine, how loathsome a thing the Christian religion can be made until you come to know & study Cable daily & hourly. . . . He has taught me to abhor & detest the Sabbath-day & hunt up new & troublesome ways to dishonor it.

Sam wanted nothing more than to rush home to Livy and the children, but he had to linger in New York because General Grant had signed a contract with Charles L. Webster and Company for the publication of his memoirs. Sam set aside his uncertainty about Charley's capacity to drive as huge an enterprise as the Grant book because *Huck Finn*, against all Sam's expectations, had developed a strong postpublication sale. Only two weeks after Sam arrived home, he received a telling lesson in life's unpredictable duality. As he prophesied to Charley Webster, "The Committee of the Public Library of Concord, Mass., have given us a rattling tip-top puff which will go into every paper in the country. They have expelled Huck from their library as 'trash and suitable only for the slums.' That will sell 25,000 copies for us sure."

Grant

*The very ink with which all history is written is merely
fluid prejudice.*
—"Pudd'nhead Wilson's New Calendar" (1897)

*Courage is resistance to fear, mastery of fear—not
absence of fear. Except a creature be part coward it is
not a compliment to say it is brave.*
—"Pudd'nhead Wilson's Calendar" (1894)

GENERAL GRANT SIGNED on with Charles L.
Webster and Company in part because he felt obligated to
Sam. Once the Century Company admitted they could not
come close to matching Sam's offer, publishers flocked to Grant with new
and varied contracts, some with terms even more favorable than Webster's. But Grant concluded that only Sam's company could carry out the
plans. Charley's publishing savvy impressed Grant, who would have felt
satisfied to sell as many copies of his memoirs as Mark Twain had of *Huck
Finn*, fifty thousand copies by the end of April. But Grant was never much
of a judge of businesspeople. His trouble with his partner Fred Ward had
been presaged during his presidency, when the people he hired to help
him govern appeared to regard the federal bureaucracy as their own private yard sale. Sam had relayed to Charley his considerably higher expectations "as regards the General's book. [*Huck's* sale] *insures* a sudden
sale of 250,000 copies of the first volume. Pity but that first volume were
completed."

The general's progress on his memoirs became a constant worry.
Grant was dying of throat cancer, and a crisis at the beginning of April
1885 brought his work on the book to a halt. Once Grant regained his

strength, the company hired a secretary, Fred Hall, to take dictation from him. Grant finished the first volume and, with the encouragement of his son, Colonel Fred Grant, moved ahead swiftly on the second, despite his failing health. Sam edited the book and read proof on the first volume himself, when only a few months before he had refused even to look at some of the *Huckleberry Finn* galleys.

Now that he was publishing someone whose significance and sales exceeded his own, Sam was forced to reorganize his business. *The Personal Memoirs of Ulysses S. Grant* promised to be an enormous enterprise, an operation on a scale that matched Sam's dreams. Though few people now carped at Mark Twain's artistry, it was Sam Clemens' entrepreneurial ambition that had fueled his ascension in the literary ranks. He did not dream of himself as an immortal bard, only as a capitalist of fame, turning notoriety into towering piles of money. Grant's book gave Sam the opportunity to consolidate his assets under the Webster and Company rubric. So when James Osgood's company failed, he bought the few rights Osgood had held on Twain's books, such as the contract for *Mark Twain's Library of Humor*, which Howells had edited. Webster and Sam drew up a new partnership contract, giving Webster full control of the office, a $2,500 annual salary, and a portion of the profits. Charles L. Webster and Company could accept books for publication only with consent from both principals, and Sam provided $75,000 working capital for the firm. Grant's memoirs, the largest publishing effort the world had ever seen, also required Sam to borrow $200,000 for production and distribution. Webster obtained admirable prices for paper and binding; he reserved every available press in New York City to keep up with the expected demand. In the space of a month, Sam Clemens had transformed Mark Twain from best-selling author and lecture attraction into hardworking publisher. As with his marriage fifteen years before, the public perceived that Mark Twain had become the ex-President's publisher, without concern that it was Samuel Langhorne Clemens' name on the contract.

Gossip surrounded Mark Twain's transition. One rumor claimed that General Grant had not written the memoirs at all, but had only made an outline for his aide to flesh out. With other publishers hurrying versions of Grant's life into press, the autobiography had special value only if actually written by Grant himself. Sam persuaded Grant to answer this charge directly. Then, some newspapers condemned Sam for having stolen the Grant book from the Century Company. According to Sam's distillation of these articles, Mark Twain had an industry reputation "of being a pushing, pitiless, underhanded sharper."* Defending both his persona and himself, Sam used the public's knowledge about the general's financial reverses to claim that he had saved the Grants from an impoverished future. Sam believed he had pursued the memoirs honorably, but he did not confess in his replies to these charges that he expected to make a fortune on the book himself.

Sam felt a deep personal affinity with Grant: Both of them were poor boys, unlikely successes, with hard-drinking pasts, who had succeeded through a combination of genius and hard work. Sam alluded to this parallel in revealing his own military service in "The Private History of a Campaign that Failed," published in *Century* as a combined promotion for the memoirs and a declaration of peace with Gilder. The article tried to erase the distance between the young Sam Clemens, who had spent the Civil War dressed as a West Coast Bohemian, and the towering Grant, commander of the Union Army's western forces. According to Mark Twain, only a few hours separated Sam's desertion of the Confederacy and Grant's arrival at his abandoned camp in Florida, Missouri; in fact, it had been a matter of several weeks, far longer than Sam even belonged to the Marion Rangers. Even in his notebook, Sam imagined the two men had come closer than they had in fact. "How near he came," Sam wrote, "to playing the devil with his future publisher!" Sam felt he was fated to publish Grant's book; the newspaper censure he received meant little to him when compared with what he regarded as meeting his destiny.

Five weeks after signing the contract with Grant, Webster and Company began receiving orders. Sam explained to Livy in a letter from New York in early April:

> General Grant's book is not in type—indeed, the work on it is only fairly begun, & not a scrap of advertising has been done; & yet 20,000 sets are already in effect sold. . . . This affords a clear profit to *us* of $13,000—& over $26,000 to Mrs. Grant. You were a little afraid to have me venture on the book & take all the risks for so small a share as 30 per cent of the profits. I did not think there was any risk. These 40,000 books are ordered for only 2 States—Michigan & Iowa—wait till you hear from the other 37.

If Sam's predictions held true, Webster and Company would reap a $250,000 profit from the project. General Grant's wife Julia, the beneficiary of the contract, would receive twice that. Desire for the book was so strong that Sam wanted to publish a limited, high-priced version, with manuscript pages bound into the book itself, in an edition of a few hundred.

This project absorbed Sam's every waking thought. He regarded publishing Grant's memoirs as the most significant achievement of his life. His own accomplishments and fame became minor matters, except as they led to his becoming Grant's publisher. In Sam's mind, the general, who had risen improbably from early embarrassments in his military career to huge success on the battlefield and eventually to the post of Commander in Chief, still directed the fate of the nation. Grant embodied history; Mark Twain, at his very best, merely commented on it, fluttering like a moth in its bright light. In early spring, Sam's thirteen-year-old daughter Susy began a biography of her father—Livy found the beginning pages and shared them with him, secretly at first, but then with Susy's approval—so Sam brought Susy to meet the general, which provided several pages for her biography. He even began his own autobiography, hiring James Redpath, who had returned to an earlier vocation as a shorthand transcriptionist, to record his story of how he came to publish Grant's memoirs. Once he had finished telling that tale, however, Sam lost interest in telling more of his own story.

His encouraging calculations impelled Sam to further speculations. He brought Karl Gerhardt to the Grants' house one day, supposedly to show the Grant family a bust the young sculptor had made of the general from photographs, but with the actual intention of getting Grant to agree to a sitting. After the family critiqued the bust as a worthy effort that did not entirely capture the general's humanity, someone suggested Gerhardt work from life in the room where Grant wrote. Gerhardt and Sam then planned, together with Fred Grant, to market a small bronze casting of the bust through an organization of Civil War veterans, which had put themselves at Sam's disposal after the 1879 banquet for Grant in Chicago. Sam saw another fortune in this project, but only if it were kept separate from the book, the purchase of which was being presented to Americans as nothing less than a patriotic duty. Sam worked directly on the arrangements for casting the bust and marketing it, but in strict secrecy.

In addition, Sam's abiding aspirations for James Paige's typesetting machine seemed near fruition. Paige had added a type tester to the machine to prevent unsound type from breaking inside it; it now set type at three times the speed of a human compositor, with fewer errors, and then redistributed the type, work normally done by an apprentice. In partnership with Hartford attorney William Hamersley, Sam bought limited rights to the invention. Then, he asked Charley Webster to establish yet another company, capitalized with a minimum of $2 million, which would buy *them* out and produce the machine. This task was beyond Charley Webster's capacities, especially while he was preoccupied with coordinating the manufacture and sale of the Grant book. To spare Charley, Sam turned over the care of his personal finances to his near neighbor—and Friday Night Club pool-and-booze buddy—Franklin Whitmore.

Delaying the summer move to Elmira, Sam often drifted down to New York City to check on the progress of production and sale of the memoirs, but by late June 1885, the Clemenses had set up at Quarry Farm. The children found a little hollow in the hill far below Sam's study and Aunt Sue had a one-room cabin built there; she deeded the land to the Clemens children, who called the retreat Ellerslie. In his own retreat, imagining the fortune and greatness publishing the Grant memoirs would bring, Sam could not concentrate on writing anything substantial; instead, he sent letters, read history, romped with the children, and played cards and tennis endlessly. When his friend Charley Stoddard confessed his uneasiness about publishing *A Troubled Heart*, his memoir of his religious quest, Sam answered with a description of his own pragmatist's spiritual quest.

> Peace of mind is a most valuable thing. The Bible has robbed the majority of the world of it during many centuries; it is but fair that in return it should give some to an individual here & there. But you must not make the mistake of supposing that absolute peace of mind is obtainable only through some form [of] religious belief: no, on the contrary I have found that as perfect a peace is to be found in absolute unbelief.*

Responding to Howells' new novel, *Indian Summer*, Sam told his friend, "You are really my only author; I am restricted to you; I wouldn't give a damn for the rest." To make his point, he savaged George Eliot, Nathaniel Hawthorne, and Henry James. "I see what they are at, a hundred years before they get to it, & they just tire me to death."

Webster's publishing office became even more frenetic as the canvass for Grant's *Memoirs* shifted into high gear, with 100,000 two-volume sets sold before Sam reached Elmira. Charley had forged close relationships with nearly a dozen general agents across the country, and they reported back to him that the book was selling itself, especially as the newspapers regularly reported Grant's simultaneous progress in composition and toward death. No one had a greater interest in this race than Sam. Three days after he brought his family to Elmira, Sam went to Mount McGregor, where the Grant family had moved for the hot season, to edit the manuscript on which Grant worked steadily, despite his decline and his family's apprehensions. Sam wrote Livy that Grant was "as placid, serene, & self-possessed as ever, & his eye has the same old humorous twinkle in it, & his frequent smile is still the smile of pleasantness & peace. Manifestly, dying is nothing to a really great & brave man."

Over the next two weeks, Grant completed his memoirs; his steadfast style would have benefited little from revision, so Sam edited with a light hand. Sam wrote Livy, "The second volume . . . was formally delivered to Charley Webster at Mt. McGregor last Saturday [July 18, 1885]. General Grant having not another interest in this world to live for, died. He would have died three months ago if his book had been completed."

The entire country mourned Grant, even the South, which both resented the man and admired the dignity with which he had prosecuted the war. Even his political enemies, who despised the corruption that had infested the presidency under his watch, grieved the death of a hero. Cities across the country held vigils and draped public buildings in black crepe. Placards with a portrait of Grant framed in black showed up everywhere. Sam kept an unobtrusive profile during the period of mourning, but he never strayed far from the Grant family. He arranged for Karl Gerhardt to take Grant's death mask.

Once actual production began on *The Personal Memoirs of U. S. Grant*, Sam assumed his role of full-time publisher. While Charley Webster secured enough paper, press time, and bindery space, his boss worried that the time between the release of the two volumes would leave the company with thousands of unclaimed second volumes. Sam wanted to break the contract stipulating the delay, but Webster explained that in any case they could not obtain all the paper and machinery to print the second volume before the end of the year. Grant's death sparked the canvass, which quickly reached the 300,000 mark Sam had anticipated when he first approached the general about serving as his publisher. Representing purchase by one American home in thirty, this sale earned a royalty of over $400,000 for Grant's heirs and a profit of about half that for the publishing company.

Success brought dangers. At the end of July, when Charley had to leave the country for two months to arrange publication of the memoirs in Europe, Sam showed a rare solicitousness for Charley's health, warning "overwork killed Mr. Langdon, & it can kill you." Webster at last seemed to be erasing the stain left on his reputation by the earlier incident of fraud, but his efforts had taken their toll. Sam wrote to his niece Annie, set to accompany her husband, "I have a special message for Charley. Leave *all* work behind . . . & devote the sea-voyage to solid rest."

Larger, but more theoretical, dangers threatened Sam. Had the enterprise failed, as the secret plan for marketing the small bronze bust did, he could have lost everything: He had jeopardized his personal fortune, his career as a writer, and the carefully built reputation of Mark Twain by backing this enormous project. Yet Sam's masterful manipulation of Mark Twain's fame paid off handsomely in the success of the Grant memoirs. The success of the book even enhanced Mark Twain's public standing. In a culture that pursued wealth without apology, Mark Twain's successful control of his own publishing firm, following on the heels of his own lucrative reading tour, only reinforced his reputation as a writer. In the public mind, Mark Twain was not so much a gifted artist as a prosperous literary entrepreneur. If he could have, Sam would have frozen his life at just that moment, when fame, success, and money had all come together. But time is inexorable. Fearful of losing what he had gained, he felt he had to drive forward still harder. He wanted more money; he believed that the typesetter would provide that. But he mostly wanted greater fame, and to achieve it, he had to return to writing.

35 | *Going for Broke*

> *When people do not respect us we are sharply offended; yet deep down in his private heart no man much respects himself.*
> —"Pudd'nhead Wilson's New Calendar" (1897)

O N NOVEMBER 30, 1885, Samuel Langhorne Clemens turned fifty. Testimonials to Mark Twain deluged journals around the globe. Oliver Wendell Holmes wrote a poem of tribute, and various writers and critics added their hosannas. Mark Twain had become the nation's leading literary man by acclamation. William Dean Howells was a superb literary photographer, as Sam thought of him, a practiced delineator of the American scene, but Mark Twain embodied the American soul. Imbued with the transcendent dreaminess of legend, his novels of boyhood captured the country's nostalgic optimism. A pragmatist capable of looking contemporary reality in the face—but with laughter in his eye—Mark Twain wrote nonfiction that tapped a concurrent stream of the American psyche, the unwillingness to sentimentalize the present, by combining human experience with statistics, arcane facts, and hard research. Balancing sentimentality and realism, he explicitly equated childhood with history, by representing America's romanticism through Tom Sawyer, for example; then further equated history with fables, by blending them into a portrait of a place, as he had done in *A Tramp Abroad*.

With a businessman's head and a philosopher's heart, Mark Twain had become everything Sam could dream for him. He said, "I am frightened at the proportions of my prosperity. It seems to me that whatever I touch turns to gold." Sam Clemens was earning a fortune from Mark Twain's books. *Adventures of Huckleberry Finn* generated close to $50,000, and its success boosted Mark Twain's backlist. Yet Sam worried about Midas' curse and thought that, perhaps, his very popularity was his payment for his good fortune. Unpersuaded of Twain's enduring worth, he wrote in his notebook, "My books are water; those of the great geniuses are wine. Everybody drinks water."

The popularity of water notwithstanding, even Mark Twain's sales could not make Sam rich enough to live as he aspired to and work only as he pleased. The Clemenses lived like wealthy people—with a half-dozen servants, private tutors, and travel on the grandest scale—but Susy, Clara, and Jean could not continue in that style if Mark Twain stopped generating money. Sam thought that the publishing company might survive him, but abundant money would only come with the success of the Paige typesetter. As he turned fifty, Sam expended his efforts in proportion to their likely return: more to the typesetter than to the publishing firm, and more to Charles L. Webster and Company than to his writing. The higher the return, the greater the risk, but Sam Clemens speculated exactly because of the danger: His hierarchy of concern was also a hierarchy of hazard, both of his family's financial fortunes and of his persona's continued reputation.

Her father's hierarchy bothered young Susy. She wrote in her biography, a document that more and more took on the aspect of a journal of her father's activities:

> Mamma and I have both been very much troubled of late because papa, since he has been publishing Gen. Grant's book, has seemed to forget his own books and work entirely, and the other evening as papa and I were promonading up and down the library he told me that he didn't expect to write but one more book, and then he was ready to give up work altogether, die or do anything, he said he had written more than he had ever expected to.

Of course, Sam couched his confession to his melodramatic thirteen-year-old daughter in such a way as to excite her. He liked toying with his children's anxiety, teasing them into passionate excesses. But he was telling his daughter the truth: He did expect to kill off Mark Twain at some point, if he could find the courage to claim his accomplishments for his own identity. First, though, Sam wanted to glory in his persona's successes.

But those successes came freighted with troubles. Sam had spent most of the fall in New York City reading proofs for and coordinating production of Grant's memoirs; by Sam's fiftieth birthday, Webster had shipped more than 300,000 copies of the first volume. But then Webster claimed to need $100,000 to cover the costs of production, and Sam had to spend weeks borrowing that enormous sum at very high rates. Subscribers paid for their books on receipt, and the publisher had to wait for the general agents to return their share. Sam asked Howells to wait for the money owed for work on the *Library of Humor:* "I am not in financial difficulties, & am not going to be. I am merely a starving beggar standing outside the door of plenty—obstructed by a Yale time-lock which is set for Jan. 1st."

But it was never entirely clear that the company needed the $100,000. Charley Webster had either lost control of his enterprise, and therefore simply did not know how much cash he needed, or he had lied to his uncle about the deficit in order to occupy him elsewhere. Already tending toward arrogance, Charley was not quite thirty-five years old, managing his own publishing firm, and hobnobbing with the socially prominent. Having directed the largest single book sale in history, he forgot that it had all resulted from Sam's generosity. He even allowed himself to upstage his famous uncle by presenting the Grants' first royalty check, for $200,000, himself. Mark Twain could have used the opportunity to memorialize Grant and trumpet himself as having saved the general's family from poverty, but Charley made the presentation without fanfare. He even flirted with disaster in the publication of the book itself. He had awarded one firm an exclusive contract for printing and binding the book, but he had not carefully monitored the manufacturing process. By the time Sam investigated the matter, Webster was nearly 100,000 copies short, when his boss had warned him repeatedly to stay 25,000 copies ahead. In order to catch up, the firm needed to farm out the book to other printers, violating the exclusive contract.

When Sam tried to influence the management of the firm, Daniel Whitford, the firm's lawyer and Webster's friend, explained the contractual limits of his control. According to their agreement, Sam and Charley both had to assent to the publication of any book, but Charley could write the terms of a publishing contract alone. Though the future of the firm was a constant source of uneasiness to Sam, he acquired more properties for Webster to sell. He arranged for the authorized biography of Pope Leo XIII, certain that every Catholic would buy a copy as a sacred duty to the Church. To follow up on the Grant success, Webster and

Company bought the right to publish all Grant's correspondence. In addition, Civil War generals lined up to have their memoirs published by the firm. Sam also contracted with his old Nevada friend Rollin Daggett, former congressman and most recently minister to the Sandwich Islands, to publish a book of Hawaiian myths and legends, told by King Kamehameha V and translated by Daggett.

Webster's health declined, and his frequent absence due to neuralgia, a pain of obscure origin, allowed the firm to grow moribund. Sam could have fired Webster, but the cost in money and in family harmony seemed too high. He kept peace between himself and his sister and niece by holding his tongue, but in his notebook he vented with page after page of angry scribbling about Webster's malfeasance. He could not decide whether to blame the firm's stagnation on Charley's incompetence, his ill health, or his drug use. The last of these seems most likely. Sam later noted that Webster took phenacetin, an aspirinlike medication, for pain, "with increasing frequency and in increasing quantity. It stupefied him and he went about as one in a dream." Phenacetin in quantity would sicken, not stupefy, but in its early years of use it was frequently combined with codeine or cocaine. A startling fact from Webster's childhood supports the notion that Webster succumbed to addiction: When he was nine, he accidentally shot and killed a three-year-old girl, a trauma that might lead an adult to numb the painful memory through medication.

These projects and emotions affected Sam's creative life, which was in fact continuing despite Susy's and Livy's concerns to the contrary. "For the first time in a long while, I am so situated that I can't well leave home. I have begun a book, whose scene is laid far back in the twilight of tradition," he wrote Webster the day after Susy noted her father's literary inactivity. "If I peg away for some weeks without a break, I am safe; if I stop now for a day, I am unsafe, & may never get started right again." The book blended his reading of history and of *Morte d'Arthur*, with a book set in Hawaii that he had begun a few years before. In the original manuscript, a practical, scientific nineteenth-century man finds himself in a primitive world of superstition, faith, and ignorance. Sam shifted the scene of his original conception from the Sandwich Islands to Arthurian England to avoid competing with Daggett's volume.

Home life cooperated with Sam's renewed creative drive. In January, the family staged *The Prince and the Pauper* again, with nearly one hundred guests crowded into the dining room and library. Howells came down from Boston with his daughter Mildred, called Pilla, a friend of Susy's and Clara's. The snowy winter gave ample opportunity to use the toboggan Sam had bought while in Canada the winter before, replete with colorful tobogganing outfits, on the steep hill leading down to the river behind the house. In February, Clara "conducted a misunderstanding" with a tree and mangled her ankle, an accident that halted sledding for the season. Sam cited Clara's injury as an excuse to stay close to home. For a period that winter, Sam left the house only to play chess two hours a day with Susan Warner, the wife of his former collaborator on *The Gilded Age*.

During Howells' visit, James Paige and William Hamersley interrupted Sam with an unscheduled meeting to discuss their new plan for the typesetter. The machine could have gone to market then and had the field to itself, since no other mechanical typesetter could match Paige's invention for accuracy or speed. Paige, however, had ideas for improvements—a small motor and an automatic justifier—and he and Hamersley wanted Sam to underwrite this work in exchange for greater ownership of the machine. Sam had already accepted responsibility for Paige's $7,000 annual salary and for marketing the machine. Now, in January and February 1886, the men negotiated a contract committing Sam to support Paige's improvements, which he maintained would cost no more than $30,000. The contract did not stipulate an upper limit on his investment; Sam's business adviser Franklin Whitmore warned him that the clause could bankrupt him. Sam, more engaged by storytellers than businessmen, believed Paige's estimate of expense. He signed the contract on February 6, 1886.

Soon after, Sam received a letter from A. P. Burbank, a professional public speaker with a yen for the theater, who wanted to perform the Sellers play Sam had written with Howells. Sam declined, fearing that the confused history of the play would generate "a fire of newspaper criticism," but Howells urged Sam to dive back into the project. After a furious rewriting session, Sam left for New York determined to sign a contract for the play to open on May 24 at Daniel Frohman's Lyceum Theatre. Howells took that time to reconsider the wisdom of mounting a play "which every manager has put out-of-doors and which every actor known to us has refused, and now we go and give it to an elocutioner. We are fools." Before he knew that Howells wanted out, however, Sam signed the contract. Then he wrote Howells a letter "purposed to shrivel you up," but his recognition of the truth of Howells' position impaired his effort. "Therein lies the defect of revenge," Sam concluded; "it's all in the anticipation; the thing itself is a pain, not a pleasure." By the time the two of them backed out, the whole fiasco had cost the men about $1,000 and some lying: Howells wanted to keep his share of the loss a secret from his wife.

After a difficult two-week swing west to see Sam's mother and siblings in Keokuk, the clan settled into Elmira for the summer, during which Sam again did not write much except letters. He corresponded unenthusiastically but regularly with Ned House, now returned from Japan where he had served as that land's official spokesman to the English-speaking world. Sam had seen him in New York City a few times during the spring, and House had come to Hartford with his Japanese "daughter" Koto; people suspected that the relationship was not quite filial. House, who had partaken in the wildest excesses of bohemian New York twenty years before, was now unable to walk, "his knee-joints . . . bent so long by gout that they have solidified." Livy and the children were devoted to House and Koto. Once Sam declared that he envied a compliment Livy had paid House; Livy replied she would compliment Sam the same way, "if you ever deserved it."* Perhaps because of his greater knowledge of the man, Sam himself never quite trusted House, but, as he later confided to a mutual friend, "I was the only ostensible friend the man had in the world, & I had to keep up appearances, or be a brute."*

Rather than write, Sam delved more deeply than ever into history. He no longer saw history as a string of kings, battles, and technological innovations for the improvement of the human condition, though his children still had to bring a fresh historical fact to the breakfast table every day. Instead, he began to appreciate the complex movement of European history as an evolution toward the American political perspective that valued individual freedom, dignity, and labor as a continual balancing of power relations. In March, he had presented a paper to the Monday Evening Club identifying labor unions as a locus of power that capitalists could resist only at risk of violence; in May, the Haymarket Riots in Chicago and the increasingly strident and bitter rhetoric that culminated in pitched battles between unions and management gave evidence to Sam's prediction. The reactionary arrest and kangaroo trial of six anarchists in connection with Haymarket radicalized even Howells, to whom government now seemed stupidly and harmfully self-protective. Sam's cynicism about government, born of both his reading of history and his direct experience with democracy, induced Howells to doubt his earlier patriotic precepts.

Sam balanced his devotion to history with his speculations on the future, in particular the mechanical typesetter. His hopes for the investment received a solid blow in July when he found that one competing machine had progressed so rapidly that it was in experimental use in the composing room of Whitelaw Reid's *New York Tribune;* the *Washington Post* and the *Baltimore Sun* were also backing the Mergenthaler Linotype. The Linotype cast its own type in response to keyboard strokes, laying this new type in a matrix that formed a printing plate. Sam conceded that the "machine is a most ingenious & capable marvel of mechanism: & so is a racehorse; but he can't run no competition with a railroad."* Studying the columns of the *Tribune*, Sam spotted those set by the Linotype and identified its problems: The alignment wavered; the expensive matrices wore out quickly. As astute as Sam became at detecting what transpired in secret at the *Tribune*, he remained resolutely blind to the one important fact: The flawed Linotype was setting type for a major daily newspaper while Paige's machine, running up bills of $5,000 a month, lay in pieces most of the time. Despite this disparity, Sam dreamed of a head-to-head demonstration against the Mergenthaler, to be witnessed by financiers who would immediately construct a multimillion-dollar company to build and sell Paige's perfect typesetter.

Sam's Elmira working season lost a few weeks at the beginning to Keokuk, and a few weeks at the end in preparation for the marriage of Livy's friend Clara Spaulding, on September 6, 1886, to John Stanchfield of Elmira. "Out of the accumulated riches of my seventeen-years' married experience I tender to you folks one offering," Sam wrote Clara. "There isn't *time*—so brief is life—for bickerings, apologies, heartburnings, callings to account. There is only time for loving—& but an instant, so to speak, for that."*

John Stanchfield, considerably younger than Clara, had a virile charm affecting even Susy and Clara Clemens, now fourteen and twelve. Though Susy had more of a crush on her schoolmate Mary Foote, as the first man they knew entering matrimony Stanchfield represented a romantic reality the girls had just begun to imagine. Though Sam and Livy were devoted partners, they did not communicate the kind of passion that might inspire an adolescent. In all probability, the sexual component of their relationship had dwindled with Sam's unreliable performance due to age and business worries. As he wrote later, the male "is competent from the age of sixteen or seventeen thenceforward for thirty-five years. After fifty his performance is of poor quality, the intervals between are wide, and its satisfactions of no great value to either party; whereas his great-grandmother is as good as new." Despite this waning, the love between the two strengthened on the basis of their common projects: Mark Twain's career and the raising of their children. The late marriage of Livy's closest friend reminded Livy of the treasure she had in her own husband.

On the way back to Hartford, the family stopped in New York for a week, meeting Charley and Annie Webster on their triumphant return from Rome, where they had enjoyed an audience with Pope Leo XIII and obtained his imprimatur for the biography of him. Sam tried to reestablish warm relations with Charley, but during this visit he did not waste much time with him; the family had other interests to pursue in the city. The prospective fortune the company would make from the biography of the pope encouraged Sam to allow himself considerable freedom with money. Livy wanted some new furniture and other objects for the house, since her mother planned to spend the winter in Hartford. Clara, who had inherited her mother's crooked teeth, began a $400 course of treatment with Dr. J. N. Farrar, the world's leading orthodontic authority. The girls' affection for animals created a special fervor for the work of Henry Bergh, whose Society for the Prevention of Cruelty to Animals successfully had campaigned to protect the city's dray horses. Sam took the girls to the organization's headquarters.

Back home, the members of the family entered their active rounds of visiting, projects, and school. Every Wednesday morning, Sam read Robert Browning's poetry aloud to a gathering of women including Livy, Susy Warner, Lilly Warner, and some others; Sam lost Mark Twain's trademark drawl entirely when reciting verse. The young women of the Saturday Morning Club still made demands on him, which the fraternal pleasures of the Friday Night Club made easier to bear. Susy and Clara went to dancing school, music lessons, and their embroidery club. Everyone in the household began to practice the latest Nook Farm enthusiasm, mind cure. This nondenominational form of faith healing, advocated from the platform by the girls' former governess, taught people to use their minds to control their physical health; by exertions of will, the Clemenses tried to correct everything from stomachaches to nearsightedness.

During the fall of 1886 the celebrated explorer Henry Stanley and his wife, artist Dorothy Tenant, dined at Farmington Avenue, but Sam had an ulterior motive for inviting them to this social evening: He wanted Stanley's next book. Grant's *Memoirs* had surfeited public interest in Civil War literature; the firm's expensive contracts with Generals Logan, McClellan, Crawford, and Sheridan, whose books could only add background detail to Grant's panorama, now seemed like business mistakes. Sam pressured Charley to acquire books that fell outside the military realm, such as Henry Ward Beecher's autobiography. Sam and Charley's meetings and letters consisted mostly of debates about what books to pursue on what terms.

Sam wrote very little. His King Arthur book had hardly progressed, though in November 1886 he read the beginning of it aloud to a gathering of military men. The typesetter kept swallowing thousands of dollars at a time; as winter came, Sam's outlay had already passed the $30,000 mark James Paige had set as the cost for developing his improved machine. The project appeared no closer to completion, while the competition continued to set cleaner type more reliably at better speed. Franklin Whitmore supervised the expenses with a nervous hand; his warning seemed to be destiny now.

As his financial condition grew more strained, so did life in his home circle. "Yesterday a thunder-stroke fell upon me out of the most unsuspected of skies," he reported to Howells in mid-December 1886, probably after locking horns with his temperamental adolescent, Susy. He explained, "I found that all their lives my children have been afraid of me! have stood all their days in uneasy dread of my sharp tongue & uncertain temper. The accusing instances stretch back to their babyhood, & are burnt into their memories: & I never suspected, & the fact was never guessed by *anybody* until yesterday. Well, all the concentrated griefs of fifty years seemed colorless by the side of that pathetic revelation." Sam's heart was broken by this news, though he had suspected that his rage—what Clara later called "the liberation of the caged wild animals of the earth"—terrified his children.

This experience only began a period of consuming weirdness during the first half of 1887. The Clemenses' venerable neighbor Harriet Beecher Stowe declined colorfully after the death of her husband, at times sneaking away from her burly Irish nurse and stepping into various Nook Farm houses to play the piano or cut some flowers. She stopped people on the street demanding to know if they had read *Uncle Tom's Cabin*. As Mark Twain later recounted, "She would slip up behind a person who was deep in dreams and musings and fetch a war whoop that would jump that person out of his clothes." Jesse Leathers, the Clemens relative whose pursuit of the supposed Lambton earlship inspired Sam to include the same theme in the Sellers sequel, died of tuberculosis in a charity hospital in New York, leaving Sam uncomfortably responsible for his remains. A month later, Sam went to Boston for a program of authors' readings to benefit the Longfellow Memorial Fund, dining there with two coordinators of the event, writer Sarah Orne Jewett and her live-in companion Annie Fields, the widow of James T. Fields. Fields and Jewett had what was known as a Boston marriage; however much the younger Sam may have roughed it in the bohemian West, a generation later such same-sex relationships had the power to unnerve the Hartford gentleman S. L. Clemens had become.

Clemens' publishing house became a strange mix of money and hostility. Beecher had signed a contract for his memoirs, and then promptly died without writing them. Sam, refusing another author's book, wrote "I think I could write a pretty good moral fable about an author who

turned publisher in order to get a better show, and got shut up entirely."
Sam seldom pulled money out of the publishing firm, even when entitled
to it: Though he personally profited more than $60,000 from the Grant
book, he left most of the money in the firm's coffers in deference to the
expected expenditures of the pope's biography. When Howells offered to
publish *Mark Twain's Library of Humor* with Harper and Brothers, Sam
floated the idea to Charley Webster, who responded that "it would never
do to publish that out of our house, as you are a partner it would look
as though we had had a row, or as though you doubted the ability of
your own house." Colonel Fred Grant confirmed those sorry appearances
by casting serious doubts on Charley's honesty. An independent account-
ant hired by the Grant family turned up a discrepancy of more than
$100,000.

At the same time, it came out that the publisher's bookkeeper, Frank
M. Scott, had embezzled $25,000. After Scott's arrest, investigators found
only a third of the stolen money, and Webster pointedly ignored Sam's
request that he hire a private detective to find the remaining sum. Nearly
20 percent of the general agents for the Grant book had defaulted on their
payments, with accounts in excess of $80,000; more than a year later
Charley had taken no steps to reclaim the money. When Sam demanded
an accounting, Charley replied he could make none because Scott had
destroyed the books. Why was his nephew-in-law so recalcitrant? It is
probable that Webster, with the help of Daniel Whitford, colluded with
the general agents through the bookkeeper for his own benefit. It is also
possible that the other two thirds of Scott's embezzled funds had already
made their way into his cohorts' accounts. Sam suspected, but did not
know, the range of Webster's betrayal.

These suspicious peculiarities led Sam and Charley to a hostile re-
negotiation of their contract. Sam wanted several new terms: regular reports on the firm's accounts, an agent on the premises, and severe limits
on his financial commitments to the firm. He threatened to abandon the
house and establish the Mark Twain Publishing Company with other people's money, but that meant leaving several of his works in the hands of
a nephew whom he viewed as at least incompetent and possibly criminal
and drug addicted. Sam, caught in a snare with Webster, paid for his
escape. As he described the negotiations to his brother Orion, Webster
was frightened that the typesetter would bankrupt his uncle and so "demanded and *required* that I put up a permanent cash capital of $75,000 for
the publishing-house to save it from destruction in case I ruined myself.
(Formerly I had to furnish *limitless* capital and be responsible for everything.) It was offering me my emancipation-papers." The contract raised

Charley's salary and also made the Grant stenographer Fred Hall a minor partner. Sam reluctantly allowed Webster to undertake a multivolume *Library of American Literature*, for which Charley designed a payment plan that would require the firm to summon up vast capital to see the series into the black. After signing this agreement, Sam seldom wrote directly to Charley, preferring to communicate either via Fred Hall or through Frank Whitmore. Charley Webster's neuralgia returned in force and he medicated himself heavily. He came to the office even less often than he had previously.

Amid the peculiar tides of Sam's fortune, he found enough quiet in Elmira during the summer of 1887 to return to the story of the New England mechanic in Camelot. Sam and Livy left Farmington Avenue in the hands of Ned and Koto House, though many other members of the Nook Farm community had cooled to House after he had repaid hospitality with insult on more than one occasion. House spent part of the summer dramatizing *The Prince and the Pauper*, a project he had undertaken at Sam's suggestion nearly a year before. When they were not studying, Clara and Susy camped out at their little Ellerslie estate. Sam told his sister that Jean thought she was "studying too, but I don't know what it is unless it is the horses; she spends the day under their heels in the stables—and that is but a continuation of her Hartford system of culture." Sam seemed not to think much of Jean's intelligence, nor all that much of Jean herself; he absented himself on her seventh birthday. Livy spent her summer days in town with her failing mother and with Clara Spaulding Stanchfield, who delivered a healthy baby girl on July 3, 1887.

Despite this confusion, Sam took to his novel with passionate energy, fueled by his reading. He reread Carlyle's *French Revolution* and wrote Howells how different the book seemed from his first reading in 1871. "Now I lay the book down once more, & recognize that I am a Sansculotte!—And not a pale, characterless Sansculotte, but a Marat. Carlyle teaches no such gospel: so the change is in *me*." With his confirmed faith in human equality and a growing belief in the effects of training, Sam had entirely abandoned his reactionary conservatism. Society could be remade, he now believed, though it would take a radical reeducation, much like the one he had himself experienced. This change in his political perspective gave his new book a fine edge of rage. What had begun as a comic fancy, with the vision of a modern man desperately uncomfortable in a suit of armor, had developed into a seriocomic contrast between democratic and hierarchic political systems. Sam regarded it as "an uncommonly bully book."

A Connecticut Yankee in King Arthur's Court also balanced its politics with the hero's romanticized attachment to mechanical gimcrackery, which paralleled Sam's increasing obsession with the typesetter. He ciphered competitive schemes to market the machine—selling it outright, leasing it, putting a counter in it, and charging per em of type—but none of his calculations went outside the circle of men building the machine. Mergenthaler's Linotype had improved its speed and reliability. It required a steely, perhaps foolish, independence of mind for Sam to continue to pump thousands of dollars monthly into Paige's machine when it had yet to set a single line for print. He realized that success would make him a millionaire several times over, an industrial hero as well as a cultural one, but he revealed his anxiety to "Brer Whitmo' " with almost daily requests for progress reports, pleading with him to shut off the financial spigot and ready the typesetter for a demonstration. In mid-August, after telling Whitmore to hold back on his reports for a while, he wrote, "I got no sleep last night. I suppose this type-setter is going to break this forty-thousand-dollar book up & ruin it ANYway, so you may as well resume your letters to me."* Sam just could not shut Paige down.

In truth, he did not want to. He regarded Paige's machine as poetry in steel, a harmony of nearly twenty thousand parts that had the capacity to set type faster than human hands could manage its keyboard. Sam filled his notebook pages with rich fantasies about beating the competition, about setting type faster than had ever been conceived, about how much money a single machine could save, and how much it should cost. Whatever the virtues of the machine, a self-destructive stubbornness pushed him to court disaster. Part of him had had enough of success. He had mounted high pinnacles of honor, wealth, and fame, but he could not accept them as his just rewards. Perhaps Mark Twain by now deserved some respect, but Sam Clemens did not, and Sam's uncertainty toward his essential self made him not only risk defeat, but actually crave it, as proof that the world had misplaced its faith in him. As a sign of this hidden desire, he began to sign his names oddly: "S. L. Clemens" straight across the page and "Mark Twain" running over it at an angle, making a dark, almost illegible X, a double signature that looked like a simple cancellation.

Needing cash, Sam fought against Webster's destruction of the publishing firm. In New York during Jean's birthday, he instituted some new company protocols after discovering "that there was no more system in the office than there is in a nursery without a nurse." American Catholics had disappointed Sam with their lack of interest in the biography of the pope, so Sam hurried the *Library of Humor* into print, in the hope that it would generate enough capital to keep the firm afloat. In two years, Charley, racked by incapacitating headaches, produced nothing while spending nearly $200,000 of the firm's assets. He had not capitalized on the success of the Grant book, he had not found another book to replace the lost Beecher autobiography, and he had not pursued other books Sam believed in. If Sam had any hope that illness and failure might moderate Charley's arrogance, he must have given it up when a letter came from Rome proclaiming Webster by "Pontifical consideration . . . a Knight of the Order of Pius." The only lasting benefit Sam derived from his renewed involvement with Webster and Company was a startling and utterly new truth about the book business: that publishers should pay a higher royalty percentage as the number of copies sold increased, now standard in the industry.

The family's September return to Hartford allowed them to develop a friendship with Grace King, a New Orleans short-story writer favored by Charles Dudley Warner. Sam and Grace shared a dislike for George Washington Cable's prudish religiosity, and Livy felt a kinship with this literate and patrician woman. With astonishing accuracy, King evaluated life in the household, quickly perceiving the differences between Mark Twain and S. L. Clemens and sensing Sam's comprehensive genius. She enjoyed his warmth as Sam stretched out on the hearth rug and offered a troubling disquisition on his vision of the coming, dollar-driven American century. "He seems to have made a slave of his soul—," she noted, "& condemned it to trudge along with him as he shakes his cap & bells."

Sam aired his eccentric manner in Washington in the fall of 1887, when he went to renew his copyright fight. At a White House reception, he foisted a note card on President Cleveland's young wife, asking for her signature. The card said only, "He did not." Mrs. Cleveland resisted signing without an explanation, but Sam pleaded with her. She finally agreed, saying, "I will take the risk. But you must tell me all about it, right afterward, so that you can be arrested before you get out of the house." Then Sam pulled another note out of his pocket, put there by Livy before he left home, which read, *"Don't wear your arctics in the White House."* After ascertaining that the great writer wore conventional shoes, Mrs. Cleveland had a messenger send the card with her signature to Hartford immediately.

Livy developed many methods for refining Sam's social demeanor. Naturally charming, most of his life Sam simply ignored social forms, taking advantage of the license to flout society that was granted humorists and eccentric geniuses. Pressure from his teenage daughters at last convinced him to accept some training; he especially dreaded disapproval from Susy, whose intensity nearly overmatched her father's. The family developed a system for signaling Sam at the dinner table, whereby Livy would mention one color when she wanted Sam to change the subject and another to get him to speak to the person on his left. Susy referred to this correction of his social behavior as "dusting off Papa."

While his manners struggled under constant supervision, his financial management went unrestrained. By the end of 1887, Sam had tightened his own fiscal noose. His recurrent urge to risk disaster not only imperiled his own family's security, but also jeopardized that of the large group he assisted, such as Wales McCormick, his typesetting friend from Hannibal days, and his sister-in-law's father, whose medical care he paid for. The Clemenses' pension list totaled close to $3,000 a year, but he wrote in his Christmas letter to Jane, Orion, and Mollie, "Will you take this $15 & buy some inconsequential trifle that will help you to remember that we remember you? We are scrimping like the devil this year, on account of the type-setter, or we would send check enough to buy a horse, or part of one. I almost think the type-setter will be finished some day or other."* Despite Sam's declaration that in a few months the investment would end, no printer or publisher had even been solicited to order any machines, no factory for building them existed, and there wasn't even a company behind the Paige Compositor. There was only Sam, who pretended not to notice that his grand dream of wealth had become a nightmare. While showing the world his patient optimism, he confessed to himself a strange blend of desperation about the future and satisfaction with his past. He had climbed to the top of the mountain, and now he had set his mind to tumbling down.

36 | *The* Connecticut Yankee

*A monarch, when good, is entitled to the consideration
which we accord to a pirate who keeps Sunday School
between crimes; when bad, he is entitled to none at all.*
—Notebook (1888)

As 1887 BECAME 1888, Sam's courtship with financial
disaster led him to increase his consumption of cigars
above his typical thirty a day, and cut his normally light
eating down to almost nothing. In the house on Farmington Avenue, the
cigar odor mixed with the odors of the several dogs and cats that milled
underfoot, the fresh-cut flowers from the Clemens greenhouse across the
stream, and the cleaning products wielded by an army of domestics. Jean
now had a tutor, while Susy and Clara combined private lessons with a
more general education. Clara, going on fourteen, had an enthusiasm for
music; Susy's own sharp interest in performance seemed blunted by the
challenges of being the fifteen-year-old daughter of a famous man. Only
Livy's bouts with quinsy and diphtheria slowed the procession of company
and travel. Sam went to New York frequently. In January, he attended a
luncheon to organize the Players Club, primarily the brainchild of actor
Edwin Booth and producer Augustin Daly, but endorsed by Sam, Thomas
Bailey Aldrich, actor Joe Jefferson, critic Brander Matthews, publisher
Laurence Hutton, and a handful of other men known and admired by Sam.
Booth bought a brownstone on Gramercy Park and paid for its redecora-
tion by architect Stanford White to make it suit the club's purpose. The

bylaws intimated that the membership wanted to help down-and-out performers, but the club truly catered to its elite founding corps. Sam would come to use it as a second home in New York.

Sam had reached his limit with Webster and Company. The resources of the firm had dwindled to nearly nothing. Struggling to maintain control, Charley handpicked W. E. Dibble as his successor for the New York area general agency, because Charley had bought the failing *Library of American Literature* from Dibble and could expect loyalty from him. Webster's apparent neuralgia and his continued mental decay gave Sam and Fred Hall an apparently compassionate excuse to squeeze him out of the president's chair. Their agreement called for Charley to take a one-year leave of absence, beginning April 1, 1888. Charley departed toward the end of February, taking vital papers with him and leaving the office in confusion, well aware that he had been dismissed.

With young Fred Hall piloting the firm back into solvency, Sam served both as captain and stoker: He had to write a book Hall could sell. Hall demoted Charley's lackeys, such as Dibble, and soon established a harmonious working relationship with Sam, something none of Sam's other publishing partners had accomplished. But Hall could not overcome some of Webster's errors. Because Charley had often dumped books out of the canvass and into the bookstores quickly, many of the better agencies for selling books by subscription feared that the firm would undercut them. Marketed by unreliable agents, *Mark Twain's Library of Humor* had foundered. The lawsuits against the general agents who had defaulted on payment for the Grant *Memoirs* produced only small settlements.

The firm's premiere hope was Mark Twain's as yet unfinished *A Connecticut Yankee in King Arthur's Court*, but the book's political theme, its fine outrage against injustice, made it difficult for Sam to complete. He felt inclined to write a revolutionary treatise, but he knew perfectly well he could not sell one. "The very title of the book requires fun," he had written the summer before, "and it must be furnished." The story, however, brought blood, not fun, to Sam's mind. Whenever he started the book off in a new direction, his Yankee ran into some arbitrary, malicious authority. Offended at the carelessness of a young page, Morgan Le Fay, the enticing sister of the King, "slipped a dirk into him in as matter-of-course a way as another person would have harpooned a rat!" The Church imposed gruesome penalties for minor offenses. Freemen were slaves to their own conception of caste. Sam would begin a chapter with a funny digression about the discomfort of armor and end with an outraged diatribe against nobility.

Sam comprehended that Mark Twain was caught in a fine-toothed trap. America's famed sense of humor, Sam believed, derived from "a bright sky, a general freedom from the depressing bread-and-meat cares of life, and every man entitled to hold his head as high as his neighbor's." America especially demanded humor from Mark Twain. At the same time, those very qualities that encouraged humor—freedom, prosperity, and dignity—obligated Americans to engage in a serious crusade to ensure that those qualities existed elsewhere. Sam's attempt to join humor and duty exasperated him. Even when, in the spring of 1888, Matthew Arnold gave him patriotic fuel with a fiercely Anglocentric attack on the level of civilization in America, Sam found it difficult to spring wholeheartedly to his culture's defense. The honorary master of arts degree Yale University awarded him that spring, at the instigation of alumnus Joe Twichell, only increased his sense of obligation to produce funny but serious literature, blending the lightness of American humor and the gravity of American duty.

Sam thought that the joys and duties that came from freedom, prosperity, and dignity had crystallized in the union movement, to which he felt great allegiance. Even there he perceived an irony lost on those most directly affected. He wrote to the politically sympathetic Howells, "Every great invention takes a livelihood away from 50,000 men—& within ten years *creates* a livelihood for *half a million.* But you can't make Labor appreciate that: he is laboring for *himself,* not the breadless half million that are issuing from his loins." Sam himself participated in this contradiction: If it ever succeeded, his Paige typesetter would put fifty thousand compositors out of work. He struggled with this problem in an address to an organization of compositors. He wanted to realistically discuss his primary interest, the machine that would erase their jobs, but his nerve failed, and he instead made a nostalgic claim to membership in the typesetters' club. Sympathetic with the working class that bought Mark Twain's books, Sam as a financier and inventor wanted to become a capitalist, the natural enemy of labor.

In an implicit admission that he could not write the revolutionary *Connecticut Yankee* and raise several million dollars in capital simultaneously, Sam asked a friend to arrange new financing for the machines for a percentage of the profits. The book and the machine were linked in Sam's mind, both in theory and practice: Sam believed that both he and Paige could bring their troublesome progeny into the world at the same time. During the summer of 1888, he wrote as productively as he had during the summer of 1883, when he had completed *Huckleberry Finn,* but now his project was a big, ambitious novel for adults, the political subtext of which made it unsuitable for children. He piled up nearly as much manuscript as he had before, interrupting himself now and again to satisfy alternative creative urges with an attack on British monarchy or a venomous campaign against the city of Hartford's ineptitude regarding public safety. But Sam's high-spirited freedom while composing *Huckleberry Finn* had disappeared under his new obligation to save his publishing company, which could then generate more capital for the Paige Compositor to devour.

Sam planned to knock off from his summer labors early and travel to Chicago for a speech and then on to Keokuk to visit his mother. Orion wrote pathetic weekly reports about Jane's decline. For example, she agitated for days to go to a parade, but on the way back home forgot she had seen it. In her mind, she played all day with her cousins and her sister—all dead, but not to her—and at night was so overwrought by their games that she couldn't sleep. Sam wanted to see his mother before she died, reemphasizing to Orion and Mollie that Jane could not come to Hartford, but early September brought a new crisis: Theodore Crane had a stroke. Sam's longtime summer friend was just fifty-seven, four years older than Sam, but his health had been unsettled for several years. For the first two weeks after the stroke, Crane's survival was in question. Sam canceled his western trip and the family stayed at Quarry Farm until the danger passed. Sue Crane, Livy, and Sam agreed that once the weather turned, the Cranes would come to Hartford for the winter.

Back home in early October, Sam took over a room in Joe Twichell's house, so that he could work on the book without the typical interruptions. At Joe's, he had a singular problem with which to contend: The Twichell house was under construction at the time. "It's like a boiler-factory for racket," he wrote to Theodore Crane, "and in nailing a wooden ceiling onto the room under me the hammering tickles my feet amazingly sometimes, and jars my table a good deal; but I never am conscious of the racket at all, and I move my feet into position of relief without knowing when I do it. I began here Monday morning, and have done eighty pages since." Sam was so pleased with his progress under the circumstances that he gave the construction crew a dinner, complete with a private reading, when they completed their work. He predicted he would finish work on the manuscript before the end of the month and received assurances that the same would be true for the machine. By instructing Franklin Whitmore to borrow against his securities to pay Paige and the Pratt and Whitney machine shop, he was mortgaging his and his family's future against the success of the machine. He tried to keep a light heart about it, reporting to Theodore Crane that the whole family was behind his investment. When one of the maids wanted some blacking for the children's shoes, Jean chastised her, "Why, Marie, you mustnt *ask* for things now. The machine isn't done."

Grace King came to visit Hartford again that fall. She and Livy had written frequently since their last visit; Susy and Clara, who were very much taken with the lively southerner, also corresponded with her. The Clemens girls had relatively little to do with women writers; Sam did not cultivate mutually creative relationships with women. For her part, though Grace King enjoyed his brilliant conversation and admired his fame, she did not think much of Mark Twain as a writer.

The presence of another novelist in the house made Sam reflect on the nature of writing. Answering a question about his method of composition, he replied, "Let us guess that whenever we read a sentence & like it, we unconsciously store it away in our model-chamber; & it goes, with the myriad of its fellows, to the building, brick by brick, of the eventual edifice which we call our style."* Sam's style represented spoken English, with its Americanisms, shorthand, and rhythms intact.

Sam recognized how distant this written style was from simple transcription, however. When Edward Bok, the new editor of *Ladies' Home Journal*, came to Hartford to interview Mark Twain, submitting the resulting transcript for approval, Sam killed it. "The moment 'talk' is put into print you recognize that it is not what it was when you heard it; you perceive that an immense something has disappeared from it. That is its soul. You have nothing but a dead carcass left on your hands." He added, "I wouldn't talk in my sleep if I couldn't talk better than that." Though this episode reflects Clemens' exacting vision of literature, it also demonstrates his deft control of Mark Twain's image through the press. In the Captain Duncan/*New York Times* furor a few years before, Sam had deflected a lawsuit by claiming a reporter got the soul of his comments, but not the words. He played both sides of the journalistic game of quotation better than almost any reporter's prey.

In November, with neither the novel nor the machine finished, more trouble came from the publishing firm. First, the bookkeeper hired by Webster after the defalcation by Scott wrote to Sam claiming that he was "not allowed to keep the books in a proper manner." Then, in what was probably part of a coordinated plan to reinstate himself, Webster himself reappeared by letter claiming that "by April 1st I shall be able to resume business with my old time activity." Hall and Sam moved in concert to prevent Webster's return, while Sam privately looked into pulling out of the firm, his best option if Webster succeeded. His health overtaxed,

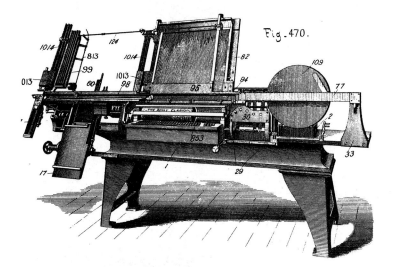

This mechanical drawing of the Paige Compositor was probably part of its patent application and was used to promote investment in the machine. Sam Clemens was the primary backer of this project for a decade; the machine swallowed close to $200,000 of his money before it failed completely in 1894. *Reprinted by permission of the Mark Twain House, Hartford, CT.*

During the summer of 1890, while the Paige Compositor imperiled Clemens' financial position, the family retreated not to Quarry Farm but to an artists' colony in Onteora, New York. Susy (*left*), in the carriage beside her sister Clara, spent the summer preparing to enter Bryn Mawr College. Sam was often absent. *Reprinted by permission of the Mark Twain House, Hartford, CT.*

Clemens was in Onteora for this comical take on *Hero and Leander*, performed with Susy, who seems ill at ease with her father's mockery. Sam did not always enjoy the hokey atmosphere at the retreat, and took many opportunities—some rude and others merely unsuccessful—to deflate what he regarded as aesthetic claptrap. *Reprinted by permission of the Mark Twain House, Hartford, CT.*

Samuel Langhorne Clemens in 1894, in the midst of his bankruptcy proceedings. In later photographs, he typically raised his chin, giving his face an air of courage, joy, and insouciance. Here, with his head straight on, he seems overwhelmed by care. He signed this photograph S L Clemens. He was at this point uncertain of the future of Mark Twain. *Reprinted by permission of the Mark Twain House, Hartford, CT.*

Clemens, dressed for his evening performance in Seattle, Washington, on August 13, 1895, in a photograph aboard the SS *Mohican*, which took the family on to Vancouver, where they stopped before crossing the Pacific. Nephew Sam Moffett (*far left*) is sitting next to Livy, and Clara (*center*) is at her father's elbow. *Reprinted by permission of the Mark Twain House, Hartford, CT.*

Henry Rogers was Sam Clemens' guardian, adviser, and close friend throughout the collapse of Clemens' finances, Mark Twain's rebirth during the world tour of 1895–1896, and Clemens' further hardships and eventual economic revival. Clemens loved and admired Rogers, who had, in Clemens' mind, a power of almost supernatural significance. *Reprinted by permission of the Mark Twain Papers, Bancroft Library, University of California, Berkeley.*

Sam and Livy resting on the porch at Quarry Farm in 1903, their last visit before retiring to Florence, Italy, where Livy's heart disease ran its course. She died in Florence a year after this picture was taken, having never recovered from the death of Susy in 1896. *Reprinted by permission of the Mark Twain House, Hartford, CT.*

Clemens and the Reverend Joseph Twichell took a trip to Bermuda in 1906, a frustrating attempt to re-create the pleasure of their May 1877 Idle Excursion, about which Mark Twain wrote a four-part article for *The Atlantic*. Twichell and Clemens were friends for over forty years, and neighbors for almost twenty of those years. *Reprinted by permission of the Mark Twain Papers, Bancroft Library, University of California, Berkeley.*

Henry and Emilie Rogers gave Sam a billiards table when ill health prevented him from taking a voyage to Egypt during the winter of 1906–1907. Rogers himself stopped by every morning, but Albert Bigelow Paine (*at Clemens' right*), Mark Twain's official biographer, was his most reliable billliards partner. Clemens tended to make up his own rules for the games, often accommodating to his cats, who liked to sleep on the table. *Reprinted by permission of the Mark Twain House, Hartford, CT.*

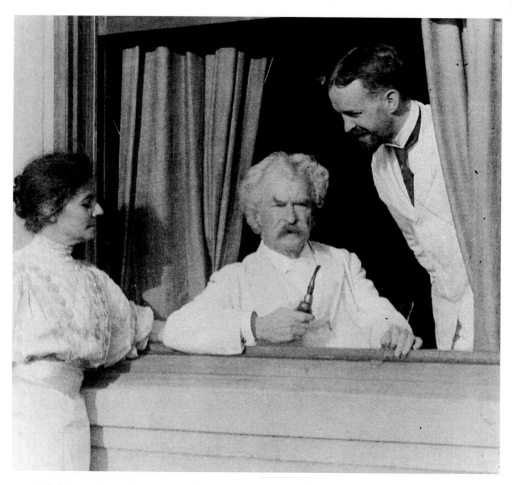

Isabel Lyon, Clemens' secretary, and Ralph Ashcroft, his business manager, with Clemens at Stormfield, his final home, in Redding, Connecticut. When Ashcroft established the Mark Twain Company as a repository for Clemens' copyrights and Mark Twain's endorsement, his daughter Clara worried that the pair had designs on her father's fortune. *Reprinted by permission of the Mark Twain House, Hartford, CT.*

Clad in his white suit, Clemens plays cards on the piazza of Stormfield. With him (*left to right*) are Angelfish Dorothy Harvey and Louise Paine, the daughter of Clemens' neighbor and biographer, Albert Bigelow Paine. Paine's younger daughter, Frances, while too young to be an official Angelfish, completed the foursome that summer day in 1908. *Reprinted by permission of the Mark Twain Papers, Bancroft Library, University of California, Berkeley.*

William Dean Howells came to Redding in 1909 to see both his friend Mark Twain and his friend's house, which had been designed by Howells' son John. Their friendship, arguably the most remarkable in American letters, survived thirty-five years of writerly squabbles. *Reprinted by permission of the Mark Twain Papers, Bancroft Library, University of California, Berkeley.*

This is the photograph described in the prologue. Notice the carved wooden angel above, which the girls played with and were allowed to sleep with when ill. Clemens is perched against the bed's footboard, which is how he and Livy always slept, though he occupied the far side of the bed when his wife was alive. An ashtray to his left is overflowing with his cigar ends. *Courtesy of the United States Library of Congress.*

Webster at last sold Fred Hall his share of the company. "The substitution of brains for guesswork," Sam called Hall's arrival at the helm of Charles L. Webster and Company. "We are not sailing a pirate ship any longer; we have discarded the pirate ways and the inalterable pirate laws, along with the pirate himself." Still, Sam felt uneasy about the *Library of American Literature*, which sold well, but under such long payment terms that the firm required a constant infusion of capital to cover up-front costs.

Then another crisis arose. The writer Abby Sage Richardson approached Sam with the idea of getting child-actress Elsie Leslie for *The Prince and the Pauper*, on the condition that Richardson write the drama; having been enchanted by Leslie's New York performance in *Little Lord Fauntleroy*, Sam accepted. Unfortunately, Ned House was alarmed to hear of this arrangement, since Sam had asked him to dramatize the novel years before. Sam now wrote House, "I remembered that you started once to map out the framework for me to fill in, and I suggested to this lady that possibly you would collaborate with her, but she thought she could do the work alone." Sam offered to find a way out of the bind, even asking Richardson to withdraw, and then had Daniel Whitford attempt, unsuccessfully, to settle with House. In April, when Sam and Richardson drew up a new contract, Daniel Frohman—the producer of their version of *The Prince and the Pauper*, who had suffered through the sudden withdrawal of the Colonel Sellers sequel a few years before—insisted on a clause indemnifying him against House's claims. House looked for a producer to stage his version and for a lawyer to represent him.

New Year's 1889 did bring Sam cause to celebrate. "At 12.20 this afternoon a line of movable types was spaced and justified by machinery, for the first time in the history of the world." Within a month, Sam had the machine ready for exhibition. William Laffan of the *New York Sun*, already on board as a fund-raiser, tried the machine himself and then ordered fifteen of them. Sam pleaded with newspapermen from Boston and New York, "All we want is a couple of hours, & we can make a convert of any man in the world who understands type-setting,"* but the potential customers only sent congratulations. He put shares of the machine on the market for forty-eight hours only, but no one stepped forward to purchase. Sam was undeterred: Paige, he believed, had captured in steel the essential grace of human movement without the imperfection of the human mind or the bloody, muscular limits of human speed. His machine set type faster and more precisely than any five compositors combined. Yet Paige's typesetter could not reach those people who might have been inspired by it: They had already committed themselves to the grimy, hot-lead process of the Mergenthaler Linotype. It may not have captured in steel the workings of a human compositor, but it got the work done just the same.

Sam finished *A Connecticut Yankee in King Arthur's Court* despite the unhappy turns even his victories took, but his life crept into the work. As the novel closes, the Yankee claims victory over the ruling class, but his victory requires the destruction of all the nineteenth-century technology he has brought to Arthurian England. Not only that, but the carcasses of the ruling knights form a wall of death around the Yankee, trapping him and his small, faithful band. His victory is hollow, sad, impossible, and Sam's frustration is palpable in it. Just like the Yankee fenced in by his triumph, Sam had created a wall of his many selves, a wall that could only be torn down by erasing the boundaries separating those selves. He wrote in his instructions to a man set to introduce him for an after-dinner speech to use the name "Mr. Mark Twain (not Clemens, for my private name embarrasses me when used in public)."* Sam dropped famous names in a letter to his mother, when typically he kept the particulars of his social life out of family correspondence. Having tied all three of his identities to a high-stakes gamble on a new invention, he risked not only his financial security, but his very self. It was too late for him to write a new persona, his surest means of escape. Like his most recent invention, the Connecticut Yankee, Sam looked out from his cave, walled in by his own success, and surveyed the dread cost of his victories.

| # A Season of Death

Why is it we rejoice at a birth and grieve at a funeral?
It is because we are not the person involved.
—"Pudd'nhead Wilson's Calendar (1894)

IN MARCH 1889, the Cranes left Hartford after wintering there. Thanksgiving Day had brought so much stimulation that Livy worried it would threaten Theodore's health, but he only wished to have that much fun each of his remaining days. Sadly, his decline persisted unabated, and the infrequent good days would presage a handful of bad ones. This sweet-tempered man, half his body frozen into disuse, cursed and spat not only at his wretched fortune but also at those who loved him. The Clemenses expected his death soon.

They did not expect the death of William Dean Howells' daughter, just twenty-five years old. Winnie had been in a rest home near Philadelphia, under the care of Dr. S. Weir Mitchell; the family hoped she would recover from her "hysteria." Mitchell, both a physician and a writer, conducted an autopsy on Winnie and discovered that her problems were physical, not mental, that her pain had likely been intense, and that nothing could have prevented her early end. The news of this missed diagnosis—after years of treating Winnie as a mental patient—rattled the Howellses. Two months after his daughter died, William Dean Howells lay down beside Winnie's grave "and experienced what anguish a man can live through." Howells was grateful for Sam's company and kindness.

Meanwhile, Will Gillette, the Nook Farm native whose start in the theater Sam had financed in 1883, organized a meeting in New York City between the Clemenses and the family of child-star Elsie Leslie, to persuade them to let her play the dual role of Prince Edward and Tom Canty in Abby Sage Richardson's adaptation of *The Prince and the Pauper*. Jean Clemens and Elsie Leslie were both about nine, but children of vastly different experience. A hit on the New York stage, Elsie traveled widely and partook comfortably of adult society, while Jean was more at home at a doll's tea party. Jean sat silently through dinner until envy loosened her tongue. Someone mentioned *Tom Sawyer* and she spoke up immediately: "I know who wrote that book—Harriet Beecher Stowe!"

Gillette and Sam each designed and needlepointed a slipper for the young actress, but while Sam worked on his, the dispute with Ned House over the right to dramatize *The Prince and the Pauper* became insoluble except in court. House's spite hurt Sam, especially because Richardson seemed unable to produce a playable script. The *New York Times*, still smarting from Sam's refusal to help in their libel defense against Captain Duncan four years earlier, gave House a public podium from which to declare Mark Twain's betrayal.

The publishing firm seemed to run smoothly for once, but to finance production of the *Library of American Literature*, Sam was obligated to reinvest $20,000 due him as author and partner. Hall moved with arrangements for the publication of *A Connecticut Yankee in King Arthur's Court*, looking for reliable agents to sell it and an inventive artist to illustrate it. Sam's revisions of the book ran into a problem, however. Livy developed a painful case of pinkeye, and Sam declared to his sister that "there was nothing left of Livy but semi-blindness & headache."* At this crucial time in Mark Twain's career, Livy could not edit his most daring book. She knew how extreme a risk Sam ran in politicizing Mark Twain's public persona with this adult novel. Her sense of exclusion from this pivotal book comes across in one of her letters to Grace King. "I desperately want a visit with you," she wrote. "It surprises me very much that you care much for me, because I am so deadly common place, and you know yourself that you are not."*

The family retreated to Elmira on June 13, to be present for Theodore Crane's final decline. His pain and paralysis worsened and "a mental depression & hopelessness . . . made him yearn for death every day, & break into impatience every time the sun went down on his unsatisfied desire." Theodore died on July 3, 1889. The children were particularly broken up by it. "Jean's grief was good to see," Sam told Mother Fairbanks, in one of his now infrequent letters to her. "The earned heartbreak of a little child must be high & honorable testimony for a parting spirit to carry before the Throne."

Sam preferred to mourn away from family, so barely a week after Theodore Crane's death, Sam left Livy and the girls in Elmira to return to Hartford for ten days. He tried to entice the grieving Howells to visit with him for a few days' solace of billiards, talk, and work. While waiting for his friend and for an unveiling of the typesetter, Sam wrote love letters to his family. To Livy, who had discarded religion to keep Sam company in his skepticism, but who despaired when confronted with death's metaphysical questions, he wrote that since "what we call God" made people for the most part good, "I am plenty safe enough in *his* hands; I am not in any danger from that kind of a Deity. The one that *I* want to keep out of the reach of, is the caricature of him which one finds in the Bible. We (that one & I) could never respect each other." He described for Clara a Beethoven piece he heard Susan Warner play. He relayed to Susy, with whom he increasingly shared his philosophical and artistic perspectives, some of the hopelessness that filled him after Theodore Crane's demise. "This is a very dark and silent cavern, now—this house. The thick foliage and lowered curtains make deep twilight; the little piano is gone and the big one locked. So, sometimes I have a feeling . . . made up of revery, and dreariness, and lonesomeness, and repentance, and is either the malady called homesickness or is a something which is 'jist contaagious' to it."* Howells could not come and, although the machine seemed to work well, every time James Paige reassembled this instrument of Sam's prospective fortune, it required another adjustment. Now it needed a mechanism to prevent the keys from jamming, which would increase the machine's potential speed to seven times the speed of an average compositor.

In New York, Sam and Fred Hall settled on an illustrator for *Connecticut Yankee*, Dan Beard, a talented young man who felt excited about depicting the novel's astringent political satire. "Tell Beard to obey his *own* inspiration," Sam instructed, "and when he sees a picture in his mind put *that* picture on paper, be it humorous or be it serious. I want his genius to be wholly unhampered." Edmund Stedman, editor of the *Library of American Literature*, read the manuscript for Sam and made suggestions, but that did not give Livy full comfort. Sam wrote Howells, "Mrs. Clemens will not listen to reason, or argument; or supplication: I've *got* to get you to read the book." Because Livy couldn't do her usual share of editing, "she is afraid I have left coarsenesses which ought to be rooted out, & blasts of opinion which are so strongly worded as to repel instead of persuade." Howells replied, "Next time try to ask something of me that I don't want to do." Fred Hall nervously expected to begin canvassing in September and release the book toward the end of November. The failure of any other book merely affected his titular partner's finances, but the failure of *A Connecticut Yankee in King Arthur's Court* would also injure Mark Twain's reputation and Sam's pride.

The pressure on Hall came from Sam, who wrote Howells that he didn't want any copies in the hands of critics, because the novel is "my swan-song, my retirement from literature permanently, & I wish to pass to the cemetery unclodded." Closing in on fifty-four, Sam felt the moist breath of age on his neck. The unlimited energy of his youth had dwindled, and his body, still as thin as it had been when he went west almost thirty years before, was growing more slope-shouldered, gray, and flaccid. When a young British writer came to Elmira to meet Mark Twain, Sam felt how his powers were abrading into silence. After the man left, Sam told Livy's mother, "He is a stranger to me, but he is a most remarkable man—and I am the other one. Between us we cover all knowledge; he knows all that can be known, and I know the rest." Because the man's card named his residence as Allahabad, India, Susy kept it; only a few months later did the family identify the young man as the suddenly famous Rudyard Kipling. In a flash, Kipling had become what Mark Twain had once been, the most promising voice of his generation, a writer who defined his epoch. Just as Mark Twain rose to fame with his incisive portraits of home truths, Kipling rose through a sympathetic universalism, capturing the ethos of a shrinking world by portraying the exotic as familiar. Sam felt time passing him by.

Though he filled his notebook with his typesetting machine's imagined conquests of the printing world, these jottings were only desperate defenses against the years of impending emptiness before him. In a year, Susy would go off to college. Soon after, Clara would leave home, too. He had books he wanted to write, in particular one about his idol Joan of Arc, but he could not envision a way to write them as Mark Twain. The image of his persona had become a cultural icon, a fixture in the public mind, and there was no way Sam could transcend him. Like the other pseudonymous writers born and bred in the newspapers, Mark Twain was a voice of the common people. But Sam felt increasingly uncommon. He had developed ideas it seemed unlikely that common folk would accept. For Sam, *A Connecticut Yankee in King Arthur's Court* was the emblem of those savage and difficult ideas. His mix of radical political ideology and pessimistic determinism drove the book's hero, Hank Morgan, into impossible compromises. Hank's democratic reformation of civilization combated his misanthropic drive to rule it all. Hank, like Sam, wanted to dominate his world through public acclamation of his technological superiority. Both wanted to leave the decision to the people, but neither would accept that there was equal justice inherent in the possibility that his own ideas might suffer defeat.

The novel labored under a theoretical inconsistency: Progressive political ideas depend on a belief in the improvability of individuals. The purpose of making a society more just is to allow its members more readily to accomplish their dreams. Hank's reconstruction of King Arthur's realm accepts this framework, but only up to a point. Hank builds man-factories, where the best of the kingdom's freemen can obtain the knowledge previously forbidden them, such as reading, logic, and science. Hank establishes schools because "the thing that would have best suited the circus-side of my nature would have been to resign the Boss-ship and get up an insurrection . . . : but I knew that the Jack Cade or Wat Tyler who tries such a thing without first educating his materials up to revolution-grade is almost absolutely certain to get left." When the Church and nobles fight back, though, the human products of Hank's man-factories prove themselves incapable of revolution. His faithful assistant Clarence, with him since Hank's arrival from the nineteenth century, points out the flaws of Hank's dream, asking, "Did you think you had educated the superstition out of those people?" In those words lies Sam's theoretical underpinning of the novel: Society can improve—does, in fact—but the people who are a part of it cannot.

Toward the end of the book, Hank notes, "How empty is theory in presence of fact!" This is especially true when two separate personas develop the theory, each for his own purposes. Mark Twain's political progressivism fed his popularity. An unrestrained Mark Twain, like Hank, would push for an even more progressive agenda than the population at large; Twain's visionary quality made him a voice of the people. On the other hand, Sam Clemens' sensibility judged human nature to be somewhere between pitiful and despicable. Such was, after all, the opinion he had of himself, and the low quality of the species as a whole was proved by his very success. Ironically, the tension between Mark Twain's progressivist vision of society and Sam Clemens' cynical view of human nature created a depth of both passion and substance for *A Connecticut Yankee*. A novel that could have turned into an ideological treatise with a time-travel plot instead transformed itself into a serious, dramatic, and engrossing exploration of contemporary faith in technology.

The voice of Mark Twain frames the novel, claiming to be the audience for an odd old man who turns out to be Hank Morgan after his return to his own time. Hank's character during the novel proper—his sardonic wit, his sly self-aggrandizement, his political fervor—differs little from Mark Twain's public persona. In the frame, however, Hank Morgan is a storyteller, an enchanter, perhaps a simple fabricator. Mark Twain reads the man's manuscript, all through the night but when he returns it to him at dawn he finds the man dying. If *A Connecticut Yankee* was Mark Twain's swan song, then the dying Hank Morgan of the frame story is Twain himself, perishing at last so that Sam Clemens might possibly emerge from his shadow to write something more, something else. He told Howells, "Well, my book is written—let it go. But if it were only to write over again there wouldn't be so many things left out. They burn in me; & they keep multiplying & multiplying; but now they can't ever be said. And beside, they would require a library—& a pen warmed-up in hell." Until he could bridge this divide between Mark Twain's image and what Sam Clemens wanted to say, he must remain silent.

In September, the family returned to their Farmington Avenue house and its worries. Livy's eyes did not improve. Susy pushed herself to prepare for college. Clara studied music and Jean had a new teacher to give her the instruction her mother's faltering eyes prevented her from providing. As money grew scarcer than ever, Sam struck a way to raise funds. He arranged to receive a $500 royalty on each Paige Compositor sold in the United States, and then broke the royalty down into $1 shares and sold them at $1,000 apiece. He interested a few people—such as actor Henry Irving and his manager Bram Stoker—and thus paid his immediate bills, but this breathing space only encouraged Sam to allow Paige to disassemble the machine once more in order to make it entirely perfect. He asked his old Nevada editor Joe Goodman to market shares of the machine, whose domination of the field Sam regarded as inevitable. If Goodman sold only two fifths of the royalty shares, Sam would recoup the $150,000 he had so far sunk into Paige's invention. The severity of Sam's debt forced him to ignore the counsel of an experienced financial hand, longtime friend Dean Sage. "To tell the truth I feel anxious about *you*—as I understand it, *you* are the man who will have to furnish the capital, so large in amount that a failure in the business might sweep away all you have, or very seriously embarras you."*

Two other projects progressed falteringly. Abby Sage Richardson's version of *The Prince and the Pauper* failed to impress Sam in any way. By early November 1889, she entered Sam's panoply of nemeses; Howells named her fifth and last on Sam's enemies list, which included Bret Harte, Dan Slote, Charley Webster, and John Raymond. Her unfaithful adaptation of the novel left Sam wondering whose work would go on stage. She invented scenes to recapture the dramatic excitement that having the same actress play the two leads necessarily lost. Her dialogue, which barely resembled Sam's well-wrought early English, often led nowhere and said nothing. More essential, Richardson refused to help Sam keep Ned House at bay. Producer Daniel Frohman, confident in Elsie Leslie's charm if not the play itself, planned to open the show before Christmas in Philadelphia.

A Connecticut Yankee made its way to the public as well. Dan Beard's illustrations proved "extraordinarily sympathetic" to Mark Twain's text, capturing both its human pathos and its political nuance. Beard's illustrations condemned the historical abuses of power described in the book, but also extended Mark Twain's political meanings into a critique of modern society through caricatures of contemporary public figures. "What luck it was to find you!" Sam wrote Beard after the drawings were done. "I went netting for lightning-bugs and caught a meteor. Live forever!" Sam hatched promotional schemes for the book, as well. He relaxed his prohibition against sending out review copies after Hall convinced him that such publicity might sell enough copies of the book to keep the firm out of trouble. He wanted to give critics a cheap paperback volume documenting the novel's historical and political background. The canvass proceeded uninspiringly, however, even as world events appeared to forward the ideas Mark Twain expressed in the book. The emperor of Brazil fell to republican insurgents in November, and Portugal's monarchy appeared to be tottering.

Like many other progressive writers, Sam fell under the spell of Edward Bellamy's utopian novel, *Looking Backward, 2000–1888*, which inspired a movement promoting ethical diplomacy. As the United States rose in international significance, this ideological pressure made the nation an unpredictable player on the world stage. Sam's revolutionary enthusiasm outstripped even Howells' socialist leanings. But Howells saw through their fervent rhetoric, noting that the Howellses and the Clemenses "are all of accord in our way of thinking: that is, we are theoretical socialists, and practical aristocrats." Sam echoed his friend by noting, "I am a democrat only on principle, not by instinct—nobody is *that*. Doubtless some people *say* they are, but this world is grievously given to lying."

Howells crept away from Boston for an overnight with the Clemenses, entertaining Sam and the eye-weary Livy by reading from his newest work, *The Shadow of a Dream*. The novel concerns the tragic effects of a dream in which the narrator's friend, Douglas Faulkner, sees his own funeral followed by the marriage of his widow to his best friend, a minister like Joe Twichell. Faulkner finds his dream disturbing not because of his death or his wife's remarriage, but because of the betrayal of his romantic bond with his friend. Howells probably chose to read the Clemenses this book, alone among his novels, because Sam and Livy were the models for the Faulkners. Sam applauded the work and wanted Howells to join him on a foray to West Point, where Sam went to read from *Connecticut Yankee*. Howells bristlingly refused. "I wish I could go to West Point with you, but I can't, or rather I won't; for I hate to shiver round in the shadow of your big fame."

Susy achieved some small fame herself over Thanksgiving weekend 1889. She wrote, staged, and performed a play for the family's gathered friends. Susy, Clara, Jean, and Daisy Warner took parts in the allegorical drama about art, which they carried off with surprising elegance. All Nook Farm buzzed with excitement over Susy's accomplishment, and most of the praise went to Livy. George Warner called Susy "the most interesting person I have ever known, of either sex," and another admirer praised Susy to Livy, ending the note, "This needs no answer, it is just my tribute to your motherhood." Both Sam and Livy were unspeakably proud of Susy's abilities, concluding that only her French needed work before she could enter college. Sam and Livy planned to spend the summer of 1890 in France, instead of at Quarry Farm.

Sam's mixed dread and anticipation of the future came together in a contract he signed with James Paige in December of 1889, in which he received all rights to the typesetter in exchange for $160,000 and $25,000 a year for the term of the patents. Sam did not have this money, but with exclusive control of the invention he expected to raise it. Believing his beloved machine would soon be "perfecter than a watch," Sam wrote Joe Goodman that the new contract put him "in supreme command; it will not be necessary for the capitalist to arrive at terms with anybody but me." Sam had even picked out his capitalist, Senator John P. Jones, the same man who had in 1877 enticed Sam—with iron-clad guarantees he then did not honor—to invest $23,000 in an insurance company. Jones represented both convenience—Joe Goodman had access to the senator—and self-sabotage. Livy struggled to make a glorious Christmas on a stringent budget. Gifts to members of the family dropped to $5 apiece.

The family went to New York for the premiere of *The Prince and the Pauper*. House had gotten a theater in Brooklyn to produce *his* adaptation, so two versions of the play opened during the winter of 1890, while the combatants battled in depositions, newspaper columns, and the chambers of Judge Joseph Daly, brother of producer Augustin Daly. This painful episode culminated on opening night of Richardson's production, January 20, 1889. At first, Sam "was bewitched by Elsie's acting, & carried out of myself by the pretty stage-pictures & the rich colors of the dresses."*

Later, however, "the infinite repulsivenesses of the piece"* struck him. When Sam tried to improve Richardson's play himself, she objected. Sam questioned producer Daniel Frohman whether Richardson had in fact dramatized the book, rather than merely invented a play based on Mark Twain's material. If he could make this sophism stick, Sam would be able not only to renounce Richardson and her play, but to wend his way out of the legal mess with House. Judge Daly, however, awarded House a temporary injunction against Sam, which Frohman abrogated by agreeing to put all the play's proceeds into the hands of the court. The play, thanks to Elsie Leslie and director David Belasco, succeeded, but no one made a penny from it. Sam wrote to Howells, "In very truth I want to get far, very far away from plays, just now, for any mention of the stage brings House to my mind & turns my stomach."

Both Sam and Livy neglected their twentieth wedding anniversary. Livy did not notice the date until writing it at the top of a letter to her mother; Sam was embroiled in *The Prince and the Pauper* fiasco. Though their strong and loving bond seemed intact, the neglect of their anniversary demonstrated how far Sam's concerns had strayed from the most reliable source of his strength. His attention jumped among various falling objects: the play, the publishing firm, the typesetter. Livy went to New York to consult a physician about her eyes and contracted a devastating case of quinsy, a common infection in the days before most people had their tonsils removed. Clara's torturous orthodontia continued, and Jean, nearly ten, seemed oddly shy and immature. Susy reflected on her passing childhood to her Aunt Sue, "Why, I should be a well-poised woman instead of a rattle-brained girl. I should have been entirely settled and in mechanical running order for two years!" She balanced this dramatic intensity with aggravating humor. Thanking her grandmother Langdon for a gift of silver spoons she wrote, "My lover (if I ever have one, and I *hope* I will!) will be pleased with these lovely spoons to go housekeeping with, I know."

These woes wore Sam down. Everything went into the typesetter, not only money, but his identity and faith in the future. In April 1890, the machine received a renewed attack from an old source. "The Mergenthaler, which was dead, has come to life again," Sam alerted Joe Goodman, in Washington trying to get Senator Jones to back the typesetter. Its backers, including Stilson Hutchins of the *Washington Post*, "make as prodigious claims as they used to when the old machine was a new wonder. Now you see, [Senator John P.] Jones lives in Hutchins's house, & probably keeps his ears full of this talk."* Not only had the Linotype established itself as the leading mechanical typesetter, but Sam realized at last that he had courted, as his only capitalist, a man already beholden to his competition. Sam made some halfhearted overtures to other moneymen, such as Andrew Carnegie, but he knew he had no escape. He made trip after trip to Washington and New York that spring, in vain hope of finding the path out of this maze. Livy tried to calm him. "Youth, don't let the thought of Europe worry you *one bit* because we will give that all up. I want to see you happy *much* more than I want anything else even the children's lessons," she wrote Sam at the beginning of May. "There is no *must* in the case." Livy felt they could sell their assets and live less expensively on the remains of her patrimony and the returns from his books. Sam, though, could not scale back Mark Twain, the life that brought his words and image to the attention of all his countrymen and of readers around the world. Better to obliterate the entire phenomenon than to gradually reduce the towering legend he had built.

Instead of Europe, they chose to summer in the Catskills at Onteora, an artists' retreat presided over by Candace Wheeler, a decorator with Louis Comfort Tiffany's Associated Artists. At Onteora, the Clemenses lived simply and communally. They hired a French tutor for Susy, who had determined to go to Bryn Mawr College outside of Philadelphia, a new and rigorous school, one with a sense of purpose that matched Susy's own intensity. Clara reveled in the artistic atmosphere of Onteora and Jean, whom Livy opined "ought to be a boy," thrilled to the rough terrain, animals, and tree climbing. Despite some trouble acceding to the gentle Onteora aesthetic, Sam made himself popular as a raconteur and performer in the retreat's evening theatricals. Most of the time, business called him away; in July, he even missed a visit with Howells, who had come to the Catskills to see him.

He wrote almost daily to "Brer Whitmo' " in search of ways to reduce his expenses. Whitmore had a table in Sam's billiard room now, and came to work with Sam on nearly a daily basis. He handled most of Sam's mail, after Sam jotted a note of instruction on the envelope. Whitmore, who had spent his life in business and whose sons were the resident experts in setting type on Paige's machine, could see failure as clearly as anyone. By mid-July, Sam and Whitmore had canceled every activity connected with the typesetter except keeping a demonstrator in practice. Sam wanted monthly expenses kept to $600, no matter what. Despite *Connecticut Yankee*'s encouraging reviews in the United States and the outrage the book's antimonarchical rhetoric caused in England, the book sold fewer than twenty-five thousand copies, barely half the performance of *Huck Finn* even before the Concord Library Committee had so salably run *Huck* off its shelves. A trade book selling that many copies brought a nice return to its author, but not a volume sold by subscription.

Webster and Company could only survive by abandoning subscription publication. Urbanization and improved transportation had rendered door-to-door bookselling almost obsolete, except for encyclopedias such as *The Library of American Literature*. Since Mark Twain had made his name in subscription publishing, closing that branch of the business felt to him like a little death. Sam could not endure his financial situation much longer, and so in August he made a suicide pact with Paige. Sam had six months to pay him $250,000 for ownership of the machine; after that time, Sam relinquished control, but not his part ownership, of the invention. Though Whitmore warned Sam that the contract did not provide him any escape, he signed it anyway. He already knew he had no escape. Now at least he knew the torture would end in February.

Heading to Washington in mid-August to meet with Senator Jones, Sam received a call to come to Keokuk: Jane was dying. She had suffered a stroke, just at the time Livy's mother had begun to fail in Elmira. Sam spent a few days at his mother's bedside, and her condition seemed to improve. A telegram on typesetting business summoned Sam from Iowa. On his way east, he met Livy in Elmira to look in on Mrs. Langdon. While he was there, Sam wrote his brother and Mollie, "Livy & I are full of admiration & gratitude to you both for the lovely & patient way with which you have tended & watched over Ma all these trying years. It is beautiful—& beyond me."* The same day, he wrote to Whitmore a letter more metaphorically than literally true: "My own movements are uncertain."* In Washington for the rest of August, Sam merely waited for Jones. In the end, the senator said he would take an option on establishing a company for the Paige typesetter. To Sam, that seemed like a promise. He returned to Onteora for a few weeks to end the summer.

Fall brought three losses. First, Sam and Livy took Susy to Bryn Mawr. She could not move into her residence hall because it was still under construction, so for two weeks, the trio stayed at a hotel with other unfortunate students. A classmate of Susy's later recalled how the young women "were tramping back and forth to lectures and laboratories and missing many of the social and student events on campus. . . . Finally, Mr. Clemens convinced the College authorities that, much as he would like to spend her Freshman year with [Susy] at Bryn Mawr College, he was obliged to get back to work, but added that he would not leave her in a hotel." Susy quickly received a room at the college. Sam wrote his sister, "The last time I saw her was a week ago on the platform at Bryn Mawr.

Our train was moving away, & she was drifting collegeward afoot, her figure blurred & dim in the rain & fog, & she was crying." Sam had difficulty separating from Susy—Livy swore that Sam would take any excuse to go to Bryn Mawr, even just to bring Susy her laundry—and before the month was out he visited her again, this time with Clara.

Then, within days of this visit, on October 27, 1890, Jane Clemens died. Sam went west for the funeral; she was buried in Hannibal, beside her husband, dead already more than forty years. Sam felt frankly envious of his mother's release. Everything in his life tasted bitter, like the success of Elsie Leslie's traveling production of *The Prince and the Pauper*. Frohman now paid a portion of Sam's share directly to House, so that he would keep his version of the play off the boards. House staged his version of *The Prince and the Pauper* again anyway, and never paid his bills for the show besides, which began a wild series of lawsuits, counterclaims, and midnight raids. House published ranting tirades in the *Times*, hired and fired lawyers, and initiated court battles with abandon. His case began to look ridiculous. "Let that dog bark till his teeth drop out," Sam wrote his sister. As he had predicted in May, "a year hence nobody will be able to remember what cur it was that barked, nor who it was he barked at."

Sam could not shrug off other aspects of his professional life so easily. The publishing company's move to trade publication hit a snag when Watson Gill, who handled bookstore sales of the firm's surplus books, objected in court to the firm's move into his business. *The Library of American Literature* sold well, but its success absorbed more capital up front than it brought in, and Hall had to borrow money. Daniel Whitford, the firm's lawyer, arranged a short-term loan from the Mount Morris Bank, on whose board he sat. When the notes Hall had taken fell due, Sam first borrowed $10,000 from Mrs. Langdon, then $10,000 from Livy; Hall got $15,000 from his friends. Meanwhile, Senator Jones stalled on the typesetter. Dependent on a man proven unreliable in business, Sam had designed a predictable finale for his speculative extravaganza.

His personal life, too, spiraled inexorably downward toward its vortex. Sam and Livy kept getting reports of Susy's dreadful homesickness. Clara Stanchfield visited Hartford and volunteered to run down to Bryn Mawr and bring the poor girl home. At last, in mid-November, Sue Crane sent for Livy. Their mother was failing. Sam went with her, but in a few days he was himself called back to Hartford: Jean had had a seizure, and was dangerously and mysteriously ill. After checking in quickly at home and finding Jean "full of life & looking first rate but a trifle pale," he ran down to Bryn Mawr to pull Susy home in anticipation of both Thanksgiving and her grandmother's death. Livy wrote, "We had a bad fright last night, we thought mother was going, but after a time she got quiet and slept about four hours. It is a terrible time."

Sam answered Howells' letter of condolence for Jane's death with news of this latest upheaval. "I ought to be there to [be] a support to Mrs. Clemens in this unspeakable trouble, & so ought Susy & Clara; but Jean pleads to be not wholly forsaken; so, when the death-telegram falls, I think I shall stay with Jean & send Susy & Clara to their mother." Olivia Langdon died on November 28, 1890, a day after Livy's forty-fifth birthday and two days before Sam's fifty-fifth, which dates passed without notice. Their mothers had died barely a month apart, the third and fourth deaths in the Clemenses' circle in just over a year. Tragedy was crowding in on Sam, and he felt devoid of resources to hold it back.

38 | *The End of Mark Twain*

Faith is believing what you know ain't so.
—"Pudd'nhead Wilson's New Calendar" (1897)

Susy WAS NOT nearly so homesick as her letters from Bryn Mawr led her lonely parents to believe. Once settled at Bryn Mawr, she had transformed herself. She assumed her given first name, Olivia, a change both disorienting and disarming to her father, who had made a career out of his own name changes. One college friend viewed her as "very emotional, high-strung, temperamental," but she was also popular, with some attractive eccentricities that growing up in Mark Twain's houschold had fostered. Though just a freshman, Susy so impressed her schoolmates that they decided to mount a production of *Iolanthe* with her as Phyllis, the lead. "Olivia was in her element," her friend remembered, "and all of us were enchanted with our Phyllis."* Blond, thin, and charismatic, Susy also enchanted the unofficial class leader, Louise Brownell, and Louise and Susy became friends and, in time, intimates. Susy's transition to college, troubled at first, turned into a triumph. Only her parents remained anxious about it—an anxiety Susy cultivated, as a means of keeping herself close to her family while enjoying the freedom of her separation from them.

Sam's feelings about Susy were only the most palpable sign of the desolation he felt his life had become. His daughter's independence broke apart the family circle on which he had relied for support. The once-prized Nook Farm neighborhood seemed more like a repository for well-to-do kooks and cranks than a utopian blend of art and commerce. Sam's historic accomplishment as Ulysses S. Grant's publisher had left no tangible benefits; Webster and Company needed more money than Sam had. Two decades had passed without Mark Twain replicating the back-to-back successes of *The Innocents Abroad* and *Roughing It*. Sam worried that Mark Twain was lingering on the public stage, a once-honored performer who did not know that his part of the show had ended. Sam's hopes for future glory resided with the Paige Compositor, but that machine's promise faded as the efficiency of the Mergenthaler Linotype increased. Sam filled his notebooks with calculations of how much money his machine would save, but he could do nothing constructive except wait for Senator Jones to build a company around this mechanical repository of his dreams.

His other projects brought him little hope. His legal appeals concerning *The Prince and the Pauper* play resulted in frustration. He wrote his lawyer, and Webster crony, Daniel Whitford, "I *must* have some rights somewhere, & I wish to know what they are,"* but Whitford kept losing every case he tried for Sam. When the original and exclusive printer for Grant's *Memoirs* sued Webster and Company for using another shop, Charley Webster himself gave testimony in the case that cost the firm a judgment five times the printer's offered settlement. The firm struggled to keep sufficient assets together to see the *Library of American Literature* into the black. In December 1890, Sam wrote Fred Hall, "Merry Xmas to you!—and I wish to God I could have one myself before I die."

As a brave and desperate measure to revive his dwindling hopes, Sam attempted to resuscitate Mark Twain. He gave dinner speeches, published a few lighthearted essays, and began signing letters with that name again. Tinkering in his mind with how to bring foolproof and lingering popularity back to Twain, Sam reconsidered Bret Harte without hostility, reexamining his longtime competitor's route to success. Though Harte was no longer in fashion and had lived in Germany and England for more than a dozen years, he still had regard as a literary man and his books still earned him an income. Limbering up to write short pieces he could sell, Sam made lists of stories he could tell as Mark Twain, including a few he could "smouch" from Bret Harte's original versions.

After Christmas, Sam went to Washington to see Senator Jones, who could not conceal how little he cared about the typesetting machine. He tried to delay Sam by telling him that capitalists he knew were reluctant to speculate on new machines, like the telephone and telegraph. Sam responded that those machines proposed "to occupy an absolutely untried field & supply a want which no man could even say existed," unconsciously parading the very shortsightedness that doomed his investments. "We propose to supply a want which master printers have been imploringly voicing & repeating for more than sixty years."* Jones did come to Hartford in January with some potential investors, but the machine was simply parts and promises; Paige had taken advantage of Sam's absence to tinker with it again. An exasperated Sam sent Jones a note concerning the dwindling term of his option and took to his bed for a week. Jones replied that "within the time named it is impossible to accomplish anything, and that even with time, so far as my investigations had gone, the difficulties seem almost insurmountable." Everyone interested in a typesetter had already invested in the Linotype. Sam tried to write angrily to Jones, but he could only manage a burst of rage to Joe Goodman, calling Jones a "humbug," a "shuffler," and a "fraud."* He wrote to Orion, "I've shook the machine & never wish to see it or hear it mentioned again."*

Sick and disturbed, Sam told Orion that he had resolved "to work to rebuild my wasted fortunes. The task I have set for myself is to earn $75,000 in three months from Feb. 13,"* the final day of his option on the typesetter. Almost at once, he began writing a novel in which *The Gilded Age*'s Colonel Sellers claims ownership to a British earldom. Sam's own body fought against his determination; a painful rheumatism in his writing arm made the labor of composition nearly impossible. He acquired an Edison phonograph, so he could dictate the story for a secretary to transcribe. Forgetting his earlier wisdom concerning the differences between the spoken and the written word, he "filled four dozen cylinders in two sittings, then found I could have said about as much with the pen & said it a deal better," as he told Howells. "Then I resigned." He went back to excruciating longhand.

Immediately after Sam committed himself to earn back his fortune, he oddly began to sign his name S. L. Clemens, not only in his private correspondence, but also in a promotional statement he made for the Merriam-Webster dictionary. He was going to reinvent his public self again, replacing the jovial humorist Mark Twain with the dignified gentleman who occupied his Hartford mansion. That gentleman had never been a writer before. S. L. Clemens was merely a social self, but he was a step closer to Sam's essential identity, and it was on that self Sam hoped the adulation given Mark Twain might land.

While Sam's option on the typesetting machine went through its death spasms, Livy went to Bryn Mawr to help with the production of

Iolanthe. Though impressed by her daughter's success at college, Livy felt uneasy about Susy's relationship with Louise Brownell. Louise and Olivia, as everyone now referred to Susy, possessed between them a heartfelt love and a strong, romantic tie. Although it is not clear how frank they were about the sexual nature of their relationship, Livy returned to Hartford exhausted and unnerved enough to stay in bed for two weeks. At the end of March, Sam went to Bryn Mawr himself, in part to read to the students but primarily to confirm what Livy had told him of what she had seen of Susy and her lover Louise. Before making any decisions concerning their daughter, Sam wanted to witness her in her own milieu. Prior to the performance, Susy made a special request of her father not to tell "The Golden Arm," the slave ghost-story with which he always made an audience jump, but as the program drew to a close, Susy whispered to a friend that she knew he would tell the tale, which she regarded as vulgar and inappropriate. As he began it, Susy fled the room, going across the hall to cry. "She was heartbroken!" a friend recalled. "There was nothing to do or to say, no comfort that I could give her." Sam went to Susy, who tearfully reprimanded him, "You promised! You promised!" Sam made no excuses, noting in his journal that the incident was "an immense mistake." Desiring to please his audience, he had only succeeded in creating so distressing a memory for himself that he would find it difficult to perform as Mark Twain again.

Immediately after his return from Bryn Mawr, Sam agreed with Livy to close the house indefinitely and leave for Europe at the beginning of June. They had several good reasons for their planned hiatus. Both Livy's overall health and Sam's rheumatism would benefit from a prolonged exposure to some health spas. Running the Hartford house cost more money than they had and more attention than Livy could continue to give it, and in any case the charm of the Nook Farm community had faded. Clara had outgrown her New York music teacher and would benefit from a fresh instructor abroad, while Jean would acquire languages more easily in Europe. Sam and Livy decided that Susy would also accompany them, despite the obvious joy she was experiencing at college. Livy wrote a friend that she couldn't bear to have an ocean between Susy and herself; she did not mention that this trip also would put an ocean between Susy and Louise Brownell. The relationship between the women had become more intense and devoted during the winter and spring of 1891 at Bryn Mawr, and Susy wanted to share a home with Louise, a choice unacceptable to Sam and Livy. The Clemenses knew the misery this separation would cause their daughter, but they regarded her homoerotic desires an illness, one that distance and the right spas might cure. At the very least, the move to Europe would make it impossible for the women to set up housekeeping together.

Despite the fact that as early as the beginning of April 1891 Sam had found new employment for most of his servants, he did not tell William Dean Howells about his leaving the country; just two weeks before the family's departure, Howells discovered his friend's plans in the newspaper. Sam had two reasons for keeping the news from Howells. First, like most people in the 1890s, he regarded homosexual attachments such as Susy's to be parallel to the kind of breakdown that Winnie Howells had suffered. This made the subject of his eldest daughter especially difficult for Sam to broach with Howells. Also, and perhaps more significantly, Sam had lifted some fifteen pages from their joint play for his new novel, *The American Claimant*. He excused his rudeness in not telling Howells of their plans directly by pleading Livy's health, saying that the family would perch at some bath. "The water required seems to be provided at a little obscure & little-visited nook up in the hills back of the Rhine somewhere," he wrote. "I don't know how long we shall be in Europe—I have a vote, but I don't cast it. . . . I have seen all the foreign countries I want to see except heaven & hell, & I have only a vague curiosity as concerns one of those."

The European plans soon included Sue Crane, and only Katy Leary from among the servants. Though Sam represented to his friends that the family would be gone no more than a year, he expected they would stay in Europe considerably longer. He did not know where he himself would go, arranging their letter of credit in Livy's name, in part to protect her from his financial problems, but more importantly to give her freedom in Europe if he returned to America. Selling their pew in the left front of Joe Twichell's church and crating their furniture, the Clemenses prepared to leave their beloved but expensive house empty.

At the end of April 1891, before they left for Europe, Charley Webster died at age thirty-nine, of uncertain causes. Occasionally wearing his Knight of Saint Pius robes in the streets of Fredonia, he had become a buffoon people sometimes referred to as Prince Charles. Sam wired Orion asking him to attend the funeral as his proxy, telling Annie, "Your aunt Livy is invalided, & I am debarred from travel by rheumatism." Mollie sent a poignant, chiding letter to Sam and Livy, observing that Webster "was Annie's husband, no matter what he was to anyone else; and she will suffer the sorrows women have to have in losing a husband." But Sam had no intention of offering a posthumous olive branch to Charley, even for the sake of his widow. In her attempt to provoke Sam's guilt for avoiding the funeral, Mollie supplied Sam with new ammunition against Webster, writing, "To me there is a sense of relief in Charlies death—for it has been a fixed thought in my mind that he was not really sound minded. His giving the hired girl a $500.00 check for a Christmas gift—and Annie permitting his taking the same girl on one of his trips to Washington or Philadelphia or both, being away some days and nights." Knowing that Webster had betrayed Annie made Sam regret even more profoundly having smoothed over the Independent Watch Company swindle. To Sam, marriage was an elevated moral state, a fixed universal law. He perceived Susy's determination to establish a same-sex marriage as a sickness, but Webster's infidelity seemed a conscious act of evil. This final piece of evidence against Webster bronzed Sam's view of him as a devil. Only a few weeks before Webster's death, he had suggested that Fred Hall locate some lost papers by requiring "them of Webster, who has without doubt carted them off in obedience to his native disposition to smouch all unwatched property." In the decade between his arrival in Hartford to sell his uncle-in-law bogus stock and his death, Charley Webster had cost Sam over $100,000, much creative peace of mind, and a large measure of pride.

His new novel at last gave Sam some financial relief. The McClure Syndicate offered him $12,000 for serial rights to *The American Claimant*, and $1,000 for any Mark Twain article he might write from overseas. Though the money was less than he had dreamed he would make, he capitulated to the changing realities of American bookselling. The lucrative days of subscription publishing had passed away, and Mark Twain lacked a sales reputation in the trade book market. Becoming more of a literary agent than a publisher, Fred Hall guided Sam's transition—negotiating his contracts, balancing sales and costs for the *Library of American Literature*, and handling the recently rejuvenated history board-game. Sam dredged up some old work to sell, for example, placing his frequently reworked essay on mental telegraphy with *Harper's*. He noted on May 2, 1891, that despite his rheumatism he "finished the book which I began to write Feb. 20. 71 days."

Cleaning out his literary closet, Sam moved toward shutting down Mark Twain. After *The American Claimant* ran in syndication, he could allow his alter ego to disappear. Sam eliminated the chance of some pre-departure publicity for Twain, and the opportunity to boost sales of the novel, by answering "an interviewing proposition from a rich newspaper with the reminder that they had not stated the terms." He filled his notebook with ideas for short pieces he could write while overseas, but writing was his backup plan; he still owned a large, though no longer exclusive, interest in the typesetter, and hoped to sell it for close to the $200,000 he had spent on it over the past decade. If he could not unload the machine, his pen would provide a living. Out of the country, Mark Twain could become nothing more than a byline. Sam could escape the woeful performance his life as Mark Twain and S. L. Clemens had become. The family sailed on June 6, 1891.

39

Farewell, America

*If I'd a knowed what a trouble it was to make a book I
wouldn't a tackled it and ain't agoing to no more. But I
reckon I got to light out for the Territory ahead of the
rest, because aunt Sally she's going to adopt me and
sivilize me and I can't stand it. I been there before.*
—The Adventures of Huckleberry Finn (1884)

WHEN SAM CLEMENS sailed from New York on
the *Gascoigne*, he left the United States much as a high-
stakes gambler leaves a casino after a severe, but not devastating, loss. The Clemenses could not afford the Hartford mansion, now
under Whitmore's care, but they could afford Europe on a luxurious
scale. The itinerary for Sam's troupe called for extended visits to cultural
meccas such as Bayreuth, home of the Wagner Festival, and Berlin, and
to fashionable watering holes such as Marienbad and Aix-les-Bains. Sam
hoped to unload his half interest in the typesetter to Marshall Mallory,
with whom he could never come to terms about a play. When they arrived in Paris, however, he found a cable informing him that Mallory had
declined to bid. Sam wanted that money to finance *The Library of American Literature*, which required an enormous infusion of capital and patience to break its cycle: The more copies the agents sold, the deeper the
company went into debt. Sam wrote Fred Hall after receiving Mallory's
cable, "You will now have to modify your instalment system to meet the
emergency of a constipated purse; for if you should need to borrow any
more money I would not know how or where to raise it." He and Livy
went to Aix with Jean and Sue Crane after having deposited the older

girls in a boarding school in Geneva. They were to study French with a family there while Papa, Mamma, and Aunt Sue took the waters. The waters helped Sam's aching arm, but not quickly or steadily enough for him to write. He told his editor at *Century* magazine, "My! I could write reams & volumes I'm so hungry to get hold of a pen, & the place & the air are so inspiring; but my arm won't let me."* This jovial tone belies the remarkable frustration Sam felt: *Century* would pay him $1,000 per article.

Toward the end of July, the Clemenses gathered in Bayreuth, in Bavaria. Under the direction of Richard Wagner's widow, the festival had become a magnet for the world's greatest musicians and opera aficionados, so much so that the Clemenses needed to buy their tickets for the event a year in advance. The festival thrilled the family, particularly Susy and Clara, but Sam loved spirituals and could only generate a periodic and mild interest in opera. The mechanics of dining in Bayreuth interested Sam much more, and he happily left the opera before the end in order to secure a good table for his party. Despite their divergent tastes in music, his daughters' devotion to high culture had given Sam great pleasure; both Susy and Clara had trained long and hard on the piano. But Sam had been shocked, and Livy disappointed, when Susy declared that she wanted to sing instead—and sing on the stage.

Feeling much better during his course of treatment at Marienbad, though not quite mobile enough to dress himself, Sam wrote three of his promised letters. With the courier Joseph Verey, whose help they had enlisted when in Europe a dozen years before, the family began an almost random tour of Europe. They went to Heidelberg, to relive their delightful stay there, taking the same room at the same hotel they had occupied in 1878. Then Sam had a notion to take a raft trip down the Rhone and write an article about it—a sort of adult *Huck Finn* adventure—so he installed the family at Ouchy, near Lausanne, and bought a boat. Sam, Joseph, and the captain floated down the river for ten days, stopping at night in small village inns. As Sam wrote Joe Twichell, he cherished the "intimate contact with the unvisited native of the back settlements" as he floated from Lake Bourget to Nîmes. He told Livy of the vivid sense of the cruelties of history the tour gave him:

> All the hills on both sides of the Rhone have peaks and precipices, and each has its gray and wasted pile of mouldy walls and broken towers. The Romans displaced the Gauls, the Visigoths displaced the Romans, the Saracens displaced the Visigoths, the Christians displaced the Saracens, and it was these pious animals who built these strange lairs and cut

each other's throats in the name and for the glory of God. . . . These are pathetic shores, and they make one despise the human race.

The sentiments about history this river trip provoked overran the banks of the Mark Twain persona. There was nothing comic about this cycle of bloodshed and, though Sam wrote letters and articles about his journey down the Rhone, he never published them. He saw no market for insightful essays by Samuel Langhorne Clemens on the flow of history.

Determined to winter in Berlin, Livy went with Sue Crane to hunt for suitable quarters. She wanted a modest ground-floor apartment, and ended up with precisely that, but it was in what Clara would later declare "a disagreeable quarter of the city. The street was always full of dirty children playing noisy games. Unkempt, half-clad women were continually leaning out of the windows opposite us." Livy believed she could conserve their thin financial resources more easily by keeping house than by living in a hotel; she even sent Katy home. Sam scrimped too, chastising Fred Hall about the length of his transatlantic cables. Always scouting for profitable ventures, he translated a German children's classic, *Strüwwelpeter*, and urged Hall to get out a cheap edition for Christmas. The apartment at 7 Körnerstrasse proved a false economy, however. Berlin boasted one of the finest social atmospheres in Europe and the Clemenses had access to the highest circles in Berlin through a cousin of Sam's who had married a German officer, Frau General von Versen. Once word spread through the city that Mark Twain had located in Berlin, cultural leaders invited him to every event, but because they were living in a dismal neighborhood, the Clemenses felt they could not reciprocate the hospitality.

By the end of December, they took rooms in a reputable, if modest, hotel, saving on expenses by eating in the public dining room rather than in their own suite. Unfortunately, due to Mark Twain's fame, Sam caused a stir whenever he went out in public. People would often stand just a few yards from the table, watching the great man eat. At nineteen and seventeen, Susy and Clara were at once embarrassed and elated by the attention their father—and they—received. Sam acted entirely unconcerned with his audience; though he wanted to quit being Mark Twain, he willingly accepted the burden of his persona in exchange for the opportunities he could not have without it. An invitation from the kaiser, in the form of a command to Frau von Versen from Emperor Wilhelm II that she invite both Mark Twain and His Royal Highness to dinner, roused Sam. The preparatory commotion caused eleven-year-old Jean to lament in an unintentional insult, "Why, papa, if it keeps on like this, pretty soon there won't be anybody for you to get acquainted with but God." Uncertain of the etiquette at his dinner with the kaiser, Sam said little and left the emperor baffled by the public's interest in Mark Twain.

The Berlin air did not agree with Sam or Livy, and, following a doctor's prescription, they spent most of the month of March in Menton, on the French Riviera. Menton was blessedly quiet in the off season, and Sam had a recuperative month. He reassessed his financial situation, finding it more frightening overall than it seemed when he received information piecemeal from America. Fearful that Paige would sniff out whatever money he had, Sam kept secret from Franklin Whitmore what money he received in royalties from his books and from selling the stage rights for *The American Claimant* to Augustin Daly. The publishing firm, exclusive of *The Library of American Literature*, was in fact a successful small business, but the debt of continuing the ten-volume set became onerous. With help from Daniel Whitford, Hall took out more loans from the Mount Morris Bank, in order to buy the last of *The Library of American Literature* copyrights still in the hands of the original publisher. They could then unload the entire project to someone better capitalized.

Left behind in Berlin, Susy and Clara delighted in their first steps into society without their parents' supervision. Leagues of German officers and international diplomats vied for the attention of the pretty daughters of the world-famous celebrity, and the girls were initiated into customs of genteel European society by attending countless balls, receptions, teas, and dinners. The experience enchanted Clara, but Susy just missed Louise. From Ouchy, while her father floated down the Rhone, she had written her lover, "I think of you these days, the first of college. If I could only look in on you! We would sleep together tonight—and I would allow you opportunities for those refreshing little naps you always indulged in when we passed a night together." Later she wrote, "If you were here I would kiss you *hard* on that little place that tastes so good just on the right side of your nose." In Berlin, she raged against the separation her parents had enforced upon her, and then in a more romantic mood she communicated to Louise the permanent connection she felt with her true love: "I feel infinitely nearer to you over there across the water than I would to any other friend even constantly present and living with me here."*

At the end of March, the family reunited for a two-month swing south to Rome, Venice, and Florence. Wherever they went, Mark Twain attracted notice; Sam could not escape his other self. Everyone wanted to meet the famous writer, who these days was actually writing no more than "an hour a couple of times a week; but anything more than that brings back the rheumatism."* Most of what he composed were letters to Fred Hall or Franklin Whitmore regarding business. Sam wanted money, but Hall could not release his royalty payments until after the middle of the year. The best money news came from Whitmore: The cash generated by selling the flowers grown in the Clemenses' greenhouse paid for the expense of maintaining the Hartford house.

All through Italy, the family held discussions and consultations as to what to do next. If they stuck with their original plan, they would return to America, where Sam would be enveloped in distractions and debt, and where the wear of housekeeping and entertaining on a constrained budget would weaken Livy even more. Since her parents would not let her return to Louise and Bryn Mawr, Susy would find herself a society woman with artistic ambitions but insufficient money to pursue them. The same would hold for Clara, while Jean would attend school. In Europe, Clara could study music, her parents could monitor Susy's mental health, and Sam could take periodic trips home for business. Of all Italy, Florence charmed Sam the most. In addition to the beauty of the city itself, the Americans gathered there promised good company. He saw his *Century* editor Robert Underwood Johnson, as well as Sarah Orne Jewett and her companion Annie Fields. Sam met William James; the well-known philosopher opined of Sam that "one might grow very fond of him" despite his "perversest twang and drawl." Friends, such as Hartford's Trinity College professor Willard Fiske and editor Laurence Hutton—Uncle Larry to the girls— fetched up regularly in Florence. Anticipating a visit from Grace King in the fall, Livy determined to perch in Tuscany for another year of European exile. The Clemenses rented a cavernous old villa, with foundations dating from the fourteenth century, a few miles from Florence in Settignano. Sam kept himself from voicing an opinion on Susy's heartbroken opposition to the plan; as he crudely told his brother-in-law Charlie Langdon, "I am humbler, & have gone up in the gallery with the niggers."* The family returned north to avoid the summer heat, to Bad Nauheim, which promised more magic waters to relieve the family's health.

The two months of togetherness proved too much for this volatile family, however, and they scattered soon after arriving at the baths. Sam sailed to New York in the middle of June, to look after his interests. The typesetter showed signs of life again, at least as Paige spun out more of his golden temptations. Sam wrote Orion from Chicago that while Livy was taking the baths, Susy and Sue Crane toured Switzerland, and Clara returned to Berlin to study piano. Jean, staying with her mother, had begun to act sullen, contrary, and difficult; the severe change from her typical coltish ways alarmed her parents. At least Sam had received good news about his wife's health, which had periodically seemed life threatening: "The bath physicians say positively that Livy has no heart disease, but has only weakness of the heart-muscles & will soon be sound & well again. That was worth going to Europe to find out."*

Sam returned to "Bath No-harm," as he called Bad Nauheim, without any resolution of his financial woes. Lacking an influx of cash from the typesetter, Webster and Company would go bankrupt by producing the successful *Library of American Literature*. Sam did discover that his literary light still shone brightly enough in the American press; that, along with a marked improvement in the condition of his arm, started him writing again. After declining an offer of $5,000 for the serialization of a short novel in Mary Mapes Dodge's children's magazine *St. Nicholas*, he began a fanciful sequel to *Huck Finn* and *Tom Sawyer*, which took the boys and Jim to Africa in a balloon. He completed his syndication arrangement with McClure's and could hunt bids on the open market. Learning that his erstwhile neighbor and cowriter Charles Dudley Warner collected $100 per one thousand words, Sam wrote Fred Hall, "If my market value is below Charley Warner's, it is a case of Since When? I should multiply it by two or three if required to testify."

He overflowed with quirky, offbeat story ideas, such as a farcical romance concerning Siamese-twin Italian counts who visit a Mississippi River town. He started writing a "diary" of Adam's life in the Garden of Eden. Even his comic ideas no longer fit Mark Twain, whose humor had always used the tall tale as its basic platform. No, these were more surreal flights of fancy rendered in earthy American prose. These literary hijinks matched the footloose and unsettled nature of his life. Sam wanted something new.

He seemed of two minds about everything. Sue Crane's departure in early August hampered Livy's progress toward health so severely that Sam cautioned Charlie Langdon, in Europe with his son Jervis, not to visit with his sister. "Lord protect her from any more partings until she has weathered this disease & grown able to bear them! I know you will endorse what I am doing."* On the other hand, the Twichells and others came to visit in "Bath No-harm" with no evil result. Sam and Joe even ran over to Homburg for the day, where they wangled an interview with the prince of Wales. When a vicious outbreak of cholera in Italy delayed the Clemenses' removal to the Villa Viviani, their home for the coming months, Sam waited with atypical patience until the end of September.

The division he felt inside between his self and his persona made these other uncertainties seem unimportant. His fame had brought him notice while the family roamed around the Continent and comfort in many of Europe's most fashionable retreats, but in truth he found Mark Twain superfluous now, and he felt more than ready to retire him.

40

Peace and Panic

> *Adam was but human—this explains it all. He did not*
> *want the apple for the apple's sake; he wanted it only*
> *because it was forbidden. The mistake was in not*
> *forbidding the serpent; then he would have eaten the*
> *serpent.*
> —"Pudd'nhead Wilson's Calendar" (1894)

Sam announced the retirement of his alternate persona to his family in a completely unforgettable way. As the Clemenses traveled through Europe, the figure of Mark Twain had value, but once Sam settled in for a winter of work, with a social life restricted to old friends, he could cast off his public persona. On the day Clara would return to school in Berlin, she and Susy sat talking in their bedroom when suddenly Susy let out "a little stifled cry" and "blushed to the roots of her hair and way down her neck." Clara turned and, in a sight she would recall her entire life, "saw Father standing in the door with his head clipped like a billiard ball. His wonderful hair all gone!" Sam would escort Clara to Germany, but he would make the trip as her father, not as Mark Twain.

The family's hilltop isolation re-created the environment of Quarry Farm, with the additional spice of history; to Sam, the Villa Viviani was built on the very footprints of Boccaccio and Dante. The Clemenses hired a French woman as companion and language tutor for Susy. The "cook, the woman-of-all-work and the coachman" spoke only Italian, Sam reported to Sue Crane, while the serving girl brought from Bad Nauheim spoke only German. The villa itself was so large that Sam insisted the family gather in "the vast central hall" every few hours, to make sure no one was lost. Sam's Quarry Farm creativity came to him at Villa Viviani, with six grandly productive months unhampered by pain in his arm.

He wrote *Tom Sawyer Abroad*, the balloon-travel adventure yarn, in three weeks. He found the enterprise so refreshing that he told Fred Hall he could write a million words, "by adding 'Africa,' 'Europe,' 'Germany,' etc. to the title page of each successive volume of the series." His strange farce about the Siamese twins transmogrified into a tragedy as he wrote it, growing from a small tale to a sprawling novel, as two originally minor characters rose to dominate the action. He penned some short pieces too, most notably "The £1,000,000 Bank-Note," speculating on whether an honest pauper could survive in London with only this perfectly legal, but unbreakable, bill.

This last tale questioned the nature of wealth, an inescapable problem for Sam. Though his books sold well, the move toward trade publication meant a reduced profit margin for his firm. Sam's royalties averaged under $1,000 a month, which he doubled through the sale of new material, while Livy's income from the Langdon holdings had shrunk to nearly nothing. The family's income of $25,000 a year represented unimaginable luxury to most of their countrymen and nearly all their European hosts, but it was their smallest budget in years. They were wealthy, strictly speaking, but they felt poverty as a constant threat.

Money anxiety heightened everyone's emotions. Livy missed Clara terribly. "When I think that for eight or nine months I am not to hear your dear voice say 'of course' or 'that's the point,'" Livy wrote her daughter in Berlin, "it seems as if I could *not live* so long without you." The absent Clara became the focus of family life, even more than Susy had been during her months at Bryn Mawr. They all wrote, addressing her with a bewildering variety of nicknames; her father called her Ben, Benny, and Benkins, while Susy called her Blackie, for Black Spider. In Berlin, Clara took advantage of her distance from home and entertained the idea of making a name as a concert pianist. She led a wild life. Susy was envious. "I *am* blue a good deal, I must confess, and lonely and anxious for a taste of 'the rage of *living*,'" Susy confessed. "Oh that Berlin life is perfection!!!"

Sam and Livy, however, deprived Susy of that experience, feeling that she needed quiet to recover her senses and swallow her romantic affections for Louise. She occupied her time with reading, sewing, and battling with her father. "I have to go down to breakfast now and I don't enjoy this one bit," she wrote her sister, "altho Papa hasn't *stormed* yet. . . . I wouldn't have you back here for anything much as I miss you because I am sure you are better off where you are." Susy did have a more active social life than she confessed to Clara, going into Florence almost daily with her French companion, and to balls and parties with a nearby English girl, Lina Duff Gordon. She refused, however, to take her mother's spot at Sam's side when Livy's health prevented her from going out.

Throughout the fall, Susy wrestled with her powerful feelings for Louise. Turning to religion as winter began, she wrote her sister, in whom she had confided her love for Louise, "I am lonely often but I don't seem to have those strange moods any more. (*unberufen!*) I can feel I am not so queer or so nervous and that mental difficulty has left me." Reunion with Louise seemed so distant that the future she imagined with her was simply impossible. Few parts of her life offered as easy a resolution as her morning confrontation with her father, which she eliminated by having breakfast in her room. Susy was a prisoner, albeit a pampered one. Taking Susy's advice, Clara decided not to come to Florence for her vacation. With her weakened heart, Livy quickly shopped herself into exhaustion. Jean took over as the architect of the family's Christmas.

Sam completed a draft of his novel, now called *Pudd'nhead Wilson*, but it dithered uncertainly between its original farce, about the Italian Siamese-twin counts visiting a small Mississippi River town, and the subsequent unforgiving tragedy, in which a near-white slave woman exchanges her even whiter son for the heir to her master's house. Shutting down for the holidays to mull over how to integrate the two distinct tales, Sam attended to Webster and Company. The firm had become the victim of its own success with *The Library of American Literature;* when Andrew Carnegie proved reluctant to add bookselling to his steel monopoly and a plan to run the set as a separate stock company went nowhere, Sam knew that sometime in the spring he would have to go to America to sell the entire company. Unable to resolve the contradictory narrative intentions of *Pudd'nhead Wilson*, he mapped out an even more courageous and complex book. He had obtained some rare volumes concerning his long-idealized Joan of Arc, including some that reprinted her actual trial testimony. Inspired by the many layers of construction of the Villa Viviani, a modern building on a fourteenth-century foundation, he conceived of a way to elude the problematic voice of Mark Twain by erecting a layered narrative. He would tell the story of Joan of Arc in the form of an imaginary memoir written long after Joan's death by her confidant and second-in-command, a defiant count. Sam interposed on top of this narrator a later translator and annotator, the contemporary man who rediscovered the count's long-lost manuscript. Sam, and Mark Twain, remained out of sight.

In January, Clara's Berlin life caused an explosion in Florence with a report that she had dined at the Von Versens', as the only woman in a room with forty officers. Sam was livid at this scandalous breach of Old World protocol, but tried to write a balanced letter to make Clara see her fault. "An American girl in Europe cannot offend in the least degree against the proprieties of these countries and not get herself talked about. The obscurest girl cannot escape—then what is to be the result with the conspicuous?" he warned her. "We love you, and are proud of your talents, and we want you to be a lady,—a lady above reproach—a lady always, modest and never loud, never hoydenish—a lady recognizable as such at a glance, everywhere." Susy commiserated with Clara over this conservative parental outburst; her sister's actions with the officers didn't shock her. She was more anxious to know what progress Clara had made in her flirtation with her music teacher: *"Hasn't Moskowski turned affectionate YET? Come answer honestly."* Clara did not answer her sister directly, but instead wrote longingly of returning to the family enclave. Still chafing on her gilded collar, Susy warned her to stay away. "You know how you will be fretted by the family discipline, after the freedom of the Willard School. You seem to *forget* the life of the Villa Viviani. What *are* you thinking of?"

Susy soon contradicted her own advice. "I do think it is hard to be young," she wrote Louise. "One is so horribly *Alive* and has so much *temperament* one can't bear things well, and oh dear one never gets any serenity. . . . America looks further & further away, recedes & recedes till I am ready to *scream*."* She saw more of Lina Duff Gordon and even developed some male followers, in whom she evidenced little interest. The one man who did intrigue her, the safely married Count de Calry, behaved like a cad, overflowing with Italian charm one day and ignoring her the next. Susy turned down the opportunity to join a "debating club of which Vernon Lee is president"—Vernon Lee was the pseudonym of popular author Violet Paget, who lived near Florence in an openly lesbian relationship—"from pure abject cowardice."* On the eve of her father's departure for America in March 1893, she wrote Louise, "I have come to a conclusion that will utterly *shock* you, dear, namely that the less we *feel* the better off we are, and the more good we can do. It's a *horrid repulsive* conclusion! but really I believe it. I think that *I* live better when I don't feel." Susy at last achieved the emotional serenity, or suffocation, that her parents seemed to desire for her. In her isolation, she no longer knew what she desired for herself.

Not sharing his daughter's acute loss of self, Sam assembled his plans for transacting business in America. He asked Fred Hall to "Get posted and *keep* posted about the machine," in the hope that the typesetter might at last generate the cash needed to keep the publishing firm afloat. Impatient to get another book to market, he sent Hall the scrambled *Pudd'nhead Wilson*. Though uncertain if Webster and Company could handle another promotion, he knew that publishing anywhere else would destroy his own firm. The contrast between his idyllic Florentine existence and his hopeless business situation at home made him wonder in which Sam Clemens truly resided. He described his life to Sue Crane as a dream that "goes on & on & *on*, & sometimes seems so real that I almost believe it *is* real. . . . But there is no way to tell; for if one applied tests, *they* would be part of the dream, too."*

This odd bifurcation continued after Sam arrived in America in early April 1893. He met up with Howells, now living in New York, and through him the New York literary world opened to welcome Mark Twain. Sam dined with Mary Mapes Dodge, Rudyard Kipling, Andrew Carnegie, and Charles Warren Stoddard. These diversions temporarily distracted him from his financial quandaries. In the middle of April 1893, he traveled to Chicago, where, said Paige, a factory was being built to manufacture ten thousand typesetting machines. There Sam fell ill, and while he lay in his hotel bed for ten days on doctor's orders, Paige sat beside him outlining his vision of the future factory. Yet when Paige left, the vision departed too. Sam remarked in his notebook, "He could persuade a fish to come out and take a walk with him. When he is present I always believe him—I cannot help it."

Meanwhile, back in Settignano, Livy received an anonymous bundle of newspapers from America, folded so as to draw immediate attention to nasty slurs against Mark Twain. Since so many of the notices dealt with allegations of thievery and miserliness in Clemens' publishing of Rollin Daggett's book on Hawaii, Livy wondered if Daggett himself had planted the accusations. "It makes me so desperately unhappy I could lie down and cry my eyes out when there is any word said against you," Livy wrote. "Be generous my darling, even if we are as poor as church mice. Don't let anyone have the chance to say that you look too carefully after your own interest." Sam tried to divert Livy from the bad press with prematurely optimistic news about the typesetter, but he left New York despondent. "I was ill in bed eleven days in Chicago, a week in Elmira & 3 months in New York (seemingly)," he wrote Joe Twichell, "& accomplished nothing that I went home to do." He achieved only a temporary new realism about where his talents lay. "I am by nature and disposition unfitted for [business] and I want to get out of it," he wrote

Fred Hall upon his return to Florence. "Get me out of business! And I will be Yours forever gratefully."

Sam was willing to sacrifice half the firm's value to free himself from its deepening debt, mostly owed to the Mount Morris Bank, which had floated the company on $45,000 of revolving paper. Sam realized that the debt to Mount Morris was a "volcano" that company lawyer Daniel Whitford could blow up at any time by withdrawing his protection; Whitford had engineered the dependency of Webster and Company on the Mount Morris Bank in part as smart business and in part for revenge for Clemens' contemptuous treatment of his friend Charley Webster. Sam's desire for escape from his business life surfaced at a remarkably inopportune moment. What soon became known as the notorious Panic of 1893 struck just as Sam boarded his ship. Capital quickly dried up, and thousands of companies collapsed, forcing hundreds of thousands out of work. In this wretched climate, few investors considered acquiring any business, much less one saddled with so much expensive debt. Desperate as Sam's case appeared when he left America, it had become far worse by the time he reached the Villa Viviani. As investment capital evaporated, so did all dreams of relief from sales of the Paige Compositor.

The Clemenses' shrinking purse impelled them to abandon Tuscany just as its most beautiful season began. They went first to Paris, where a physician could check Livy's heart and Susy could study voice with Madame Marchesi, one of the world's foremost teachers. Marchesi gave Susy a few lessons and concluded that she had beautiful tone but no strength. Thin and nervous, Susy rarely ate full meals and got little exercise. If she spent the summer on a farm at high altitude, eating right, the diva instructor decreed, she might return. Then the family went on to Munich, where "the highest authority in Europe on heart disease has just decided that there is nothing serious the matter with Livy," as Sam wrote Orion and Mollie "—very pleasant news after being told by two American & three European doctors that she had incurable heart disease."* Susy, on the other hand, soon received an alarming threat to her newfound emotional chill. "Did I tell you that Louise Brownell got the European fellowship at B[ryn] M[awr] and is coming abroad next winter very likely?" she confided to Clara. "I am scared to find that the news gives me the blue shivers! I don't want to see her yet at all! I dread the thought of a meeting like poison!" She had hoped to grow immune to Louise's attractions, but she knew she had not yet achieved that necessary level of emotional frost.

More Panic-stricken news from America threatened Sam's equanimity, too. Hall's statement of account for July 1, 1893 indicated that the company's debts exceeded assets by close to $50,000. Hall and Sam agreed to suspend marketing *The Library of American Literature* and unload it at any price. "It is my ingenious scheme to protect the family against the almshouse for one more year—and after that," Sam wrote his partner, "well, goodness knows! I have never felt so desperate in my life—and good reason, for I haven't got a penny to my name, and Mrs. Clemens hasn't enough laid up with Langdon to keep us two months." Though he had lived ten years longer than his father—and had accumulated much more than that hapless pioneer ever dreamed of—the twin demons of speculation and economic uncertainty had snared Sam just as they had John Clemens. Sam decided to return to the States at the end of summer and either revive his fortunes with some Midaslike Mark Twain magic or preside over his own financial funeral.

Writing throughout this crisis, he salvaged *Pudd'nhead Wilson* by separating out the original farce from the tragedy. "I pulled one of the stories out by the roots," he wrote in his very Twainian introduction to the farce, "and left the other one—a kind of literary Caesarean operation." As he related it to Hall, Sam had "knocked out everything that delayed the march of the story—even the description of a Mississippi steamboat. There ain't any weather in it, and there ain't any scenery—the story is stripped for flight." Other than the setting, little in the book signaled the fact that Mark Twain was its author. Attracted by the prevalence of maxims in European literature, Sam had developed a series of them to use as chapter headnotes. In late August, preparing to return to the United States to confront financial problems he could only have acquired in a free-market democracy, he wrote this maxim for the conclusion of the book: "It was wonderful to find America, but it would have been more wonderful to miss it."

41 | *Faustian Bargains*

*Happiness ain't a thing in itself—it's only a contrast
with something that ain't pleasant. . . . As soon as the
novelty is over and the force of the contrast dulled, it
ain't happiness any longer, and you have to get something
fresh.*
—"Captain Stormfield's Visit to Heaven" (1907)

Arriving in New York on September 7, 1893,
Sam stayed with his friend Dr. Clarence Rice. Plagued
with a cold and fretting over the increasingly insistent
calls from the Mount Morris Bank that he repay their loans, Sam ran up
to Hartford and tried to raise money from his friends there. He discovered,
he told Livy, that "money can not be had, at any rate of interest whatever,
or upon any sort of security, or by *anybody*." A few days later, Sam found
he was an exception. Mark Twain's books had been a source of pleasure
and insight to Dr. Rice's friend Henry Huttleston Rogers, who had met
Sam on a yacht two years before. Rogers would help Sam out of his jam
in exchange for contact with his favorite author.

An architect of the Standard Oil monopoly, Henry Rogers had the
power to frame his desire as a demand. Rogers was one of a few men
whose rumored interest in a company could send its stock soaring. He
pursued business with a sharp-eyed gravity, cunning, and ruthlessness
other businessmen envied and feared. He had established his fortune with
a small refinery in Pennsylvania, which was absorbed by the Rockefeller-
Standard Oil juggernaut. A shark in business, he maintained strong ties
to his hometown of Fairhaven, Massachusetts, building roads, schools,

sewers, and libraries. His use of the press in his manipulations of stock prices reminded Sam of similar games, involving much smaller sums, he had himself played with mining stock while out West. After meeting Sam, Rogers insisted Fred Hall come see him, and ten days after Sam's arrival in New York, Webster and Company had the money to keep the Mount Morris wolves at bay.

Dividing his time between offering his company for sale and accepting invitations to dinner, Sam dove into New York literary circles. After moving to a cheap room at the Players Club, on Gramercy Park, he dropped in for dinner frequently at the homes of Rice, William Laffan, and Laurence Hutton, and spent a couple of days on the New Jersey farm of former Governor Frank Fuller, from which Fuller supplied his chic health-food store in Manhattan. Sam even saw his old butler George Griffin, who had taken his loan-sharking business to New York, as a sideline to waiting tables at the Union League Club; these lean days, Sam noted, George was the only sanguine man in New York. Meanwhile, Sam attempted to proofread *Pudd'nhead Wilson* for the *Century*, which had bought the serialization rights, until he realized that their Oxford-educated copy editor had amended his prose. "I said I didn't care if he was an Archangel imported from Heaven," he wrote Livy, "he couldn't puke his ignorant impudence over *my* punctuation."

He worried less over the condition of his punctuation in *Pudd'nhead Wilson* than about the novel as a whole. His retreat to Europe and to Florence did not eliminate Mark Twain; Twain's withdrawal merely allowed Sam Clemens space to breathe. The new distance between his private and public selves gave Sam the room to discover his own creative identity, a way to write without writing as Mark Twain. As he noted himself in one of the aphorisms beginning each chapter of *Pudd'nhead Wilson*, "Habit is habit, and not to be flung out the window by any man, but coaxed downstairs a step at a time."

The easy habit of being Mark Twain had allowed him to toss off *Tom Sawyer Abroad* and made him willing to expand it into an around-the-world series. But the habit hampered his effort to find the correct voice for this more serious and personal novel. *Pudd'nhead Wilson* began its life as a Twainian sort of farce, not terribly distant from the burlesque of romance on which Sam later based *Tom Sawyer*, but it soon became something more astringent and far-reaching. The story of the slave woman Roxy and what happens after she chooses to switch her one-thirty-second Negro infant son with the racially pure son of a wealthy southern gentleman master elbowed the farce aside. In the final revision, when Sam separated the root comedy from the flowering drama, he also squelched the presence of Mark Twain in the narrative. For example, he renamed the town in which the action takes place Dawson's Landing, although the site hardly differs from the St. Petersburg where he had placed Tom Sawyer and his gang. Changing the name allowed him to alter the fictive environment from Tom's land of myth to Sam's land of memory.

Roxy's story harks back to Sam's breakthrough 1874 piece, "A True Story," about the trauma of a slave woman deprived of her family, which William Dean Howells had accepted as Mark Twain's first contribution to the pages of *The Atlantic*. In *Pudd'nhead Wilson*, Roxy—like Aunt Rachel—majestically triumphs over tragedy by willingly estranging herself from her only son in order that he may be raised free. Both women make painful sacrifices for their sons, but Roxy lives to regret her sacrifice. Tom grows up into a nasty, violent young man, whom Roxy can tame only by threatening to expose his racial background. When he needs to raise money to disguise his gambling debts from his wealthy uncle, Roxy agrees to let him sell her into slavery. Her sacrifice turns ironic as her ungrateful offspring sells her into bondage downriver, where large plantations consume black muscle and lives. She escapes and confronts her son, an event that leads to the murder of the uncle, whose property Tom stands to inherit. Tom frames the Italian twins for the crime.

This searing, though melodramatic, portrait of southern slavery formed the moral and potent background for Sam's larger theme, the question of identity. Twenty years pass after Roxy switches the children in her care, and their identities have become a masquerade to everyone but Roxy herself, by now free and working as a chambermaid on a steamboat. What is the essential, inborn difference between Roxy's arrogant, gambling, antisocial natural son, called Thomas à Becket Driscoll, and the young man she raised as her own, the kindly and honest Valet de Chambers? Chambers appears black, but isn't; Tom appears free, but isn't. Sam replicated questions about image and identity several times in the novel, first in the nearly identical Italian twins, whom he divided into two freestanding people when he moved them from the farce to the novel, and then again in the thematic pairing of Roxy and David Wilson, the Pudd'nhead of the title. Roxy herself observes their likeness right after she switches the infants. "Dey ain't but one man dat I's afeard of, en dat's dat Pudd'nhead Wilson. Dey calls him a pudd'nhead, en says he's a fool. My lan', dat man ain't no mo' fool den I is! He's de smartes' man in dis town.' " And she is the smartest woman. As Tom remarks, satisfied that his identity will forever remain a secret, "The man that can track a bird through the air in the dark and find that bird is the man to track me out and find the Judge's assassin—no other need apply."

The novel's structure demands that Roxy and Wilson find one another at the climax. In the course of the twins' trial for the murder of Tom's supposed uncle, Wilson uses his quirky interest in fingerprints— Sam wrote the novel soon after the individuality of these marks was discovered—to reveal Roxy's long-held secret: that in switching the babies she had trifled with identity. But the moral of *Pudd'nhead Wilson* is not nearly as simple as the conclusion of the trial initially makes it seem. The novel demonstrates that Sam did not regard identity as an essential trait: Roxy and her son are Negroes and slaves only "by a fiction of law and custom." In the conclusion of the book, Chambers is restored to his native position as a leader of the town, but, unprepared for this ascendancy, his life is an agony to him. Pudd'nhead becomes a hero, seemingly showing his true genius, but in the end is merely elected mayor of a town of pudd'nheads. Roxy has changed utterly too, "the spirit in her eye was quenched, her martial bearing departed with it, and the voice of her laughter ceased in the land." Sam implies that what we call essential identity is simply a more or less random agreement among other people's perceptions of us.

Unfortunately, once Sam concluded that there is no essential identity, he defeated his own goal of writing as Sam Clemens. The premise led inexorably to the conclusion that Sam was in fact Mark Twain; he could not escape the matrix of images that his life had generated. Surrendering to this conclusion, Sam decided not only to publish *Pudd'nhead Wilson* under the name Mark Twain, but also to include in the same volume the extricated farce, called "Those Extraordinary Twins." The farce follows the adventures of Italian Siamese-twin noblemen in a goofy river town. The twins occupy a single body from the waist down, sort of like the book itself, and the story turns on the impossibility of making one twin serve time for the other's crime. Caught in the web of his own logic, Sam used Mark Twain to undercut the dramatic value of *Pudd'nhead Wilson*. In his introduction to the farce, at the end of the drama, Mark Twain notes, "A man who is not born with the novel-writing gift has a troublesome time of it when he tries to build a novel. I know this from experience." All of Twain's readers recognize this to be a joke, but the question remains: on whom? On readers, who have allowed themselves to be moved by the preceding fiction? On Mark Twain, who admits to being nothing but a "jack-leg" novelist? Or on Sam Clemens, trapped in a false identity he has made for himself?

Although Sam missed his family while trapped by business, he made up for the loss with other pleasures. No social or literary evening in New York seemed complete that fall and winter without the drawl of Mark

Twain's voice or the odor of his cigar. Rogers took him to fights at Madison Square Garden, where the architect Stanford White introduced him to champion boxer "Gentleman Jim" Corbett. When Sam threatened to get in the ring with him, Corbett replied that he wouldn't risk losing to Sam by an accidental blow, because "then my reputation would be gone & you would have a double one. You have got fame enough & you ought not to want to take mine away from me." He drifted from testimonial to dinner party to billiard table to all-night parties at the studios of artist friends. He never seemed to tire, frequently crawling into bed at four in the morning only to awaken at nine. He expanded his range of acquaintances to include Coquelin, the famous French actor, and Nikola Tesla, the visionary inventor. Old friends, like Bram Stoker, Henry Irving, and Nevada silver magnate John Mackay, returned to his life. Dancing at the very edge of disaster, Sam reaped what he feared might be the final harvest of Mark Twain's fortunes.

Most days he ran from meeting to meeting, hoping to buy a little more time to find a permanent solution to his financial quandary. Realizing he could accomplish nothing on his own, he made frequent visits to Henry Rogers' office downtown. Sam assured Livy that by chatting in his inimitable way he managed to get "the best and wisest man in the whole Standard Oil group of multi-millionaires a good deal interested in looking into the type-setter." Rogers' researchers concluded that the machine had promise, but the business around it had become a hopeless jumble. If he could iron out the business relationships, he would capitalize the company. Sam quoted the mogul to Livy: "Then the thing will move right along and your royalties will cease to be waste paper. I will post you the minute my scheme fails or succeeds. In the meantime, *you stop walking the floor.*" Sam kindly objected to Rogers taking time from his own business, but Rogers replied, "It rests me to experiment with the affairs of a friend when I am tired of my own," and added that he needed Sam in New York. Sam wrote Livy, "I absolutely must not budge one step from this place *until we are safe from the poorhouse.*"

Sam and Henry Rogers made remarkably good teammates in their efforts to wrestle the business of the Paige Compositor into shape. They snaked concessions out of the New York-based participants of the enterprise by implying that the writer and the millionaire would deal each other out. They arranged for Sam to take an ample finder's fee for any capital Rogers put into the project, which provided Sam with pocket money, stock in the new company, and influence in its direction. Sam enjoyed playing "games with a partner who knows how to play & what to play & when to play it";* Rogers enjoyed business games, especially when his continued association with Sam was the real payoff. Rogers also appreciated that, for Sam, the stakes were enormous. Success in this venture meant the difference between the freedom to live and write as he wanted and slavery to a world platform tour as Mark Twain. Ridiculously lucrative lecture offers came to Sam constantly, and if the typesetter fell through, he would have to clown around the globe.

At last, around Christmas, 1893, Rogers' scheme came to a head. Proving that the New York-based portion of the organization did not have the capital to finance the construction of the typesetter, he and Sam traveled to Chicago in a private railroad car with a parlor and a bedroom, which Sam claimed for sleeping, and "a darling back porch—railed, roofed & roomy; & there we sat, most of the time & viewed the scenery & talked." On the train, they hammered out what each would say, when they would pretend to be at odds, and which terms were negotiable. Everyone involved—James Paige's lawyer, the Chicago manufacturer, and the New York managers—fell in with Rogers' plan to resurrect Paige's machine under the auspices of a new company. Only Paige himself needed convincing. The duo's entire Chicago campaign took under four days, but in the end they could only wait for Paige to make up his mind. At Christmas Sam told Livy, "I was vaguely hoping, all this past week that my Xmas cablegram would be *definite*, & make you all jump with jubilation; but the thought always intruded itself, 'You are not going out there to negociate with a man, but with a louse. This makes results uncertain.'"

While Sam waited for results, Mark Twain's name cropped up in newspaper reports of events he attended as more of his work appeared in magazines: *Pudd'nhead Wilson* premiered in *Century* while *St. Nicholas* carried *Tom Sawyer Abroad*. Sam traveled to Boston, where Sarah Orne Jewett and Annie Fields hosted a dinner for just him and octogenarian Oliver Wendell Holmes. Holmes "said he wanted to 'have a time' once more with me. Mrs. Fields said [Thomas Bailey] Aldrich begged to come and went away crying because she wouldn't let him." In Boston, Sam also saw his old Mother Fairbanks, now broke, infirm, and living with her daughter.

The nagging cough he developed in Berlin returned, and Sam doublepunched it with some homeopathic powders dispensed by Henry Rogers and with visits to a mind curist in New York. Mind cure, a less religious version of Christian Science, was still the rage among the upper class, and Mary Foote, the Clemenses' governess in the mid-1880s, was its preeminent proselytizer. She held that mind cure did not touch disease, but rather helped patients develop the psychological ease that reduced their predilections toward disease. Sam dubiously told Livy that his mind curist "sits silent in the corner with his face to the wall, & I walk the floor &

smoke." But after his treatment, Sam hardly coughed and went away convinced. Elinor Howells, who went to a mind cure "doctor" behind her husband's back, shared William James' view that mind cure and hypnosis were much the same. Sam wrote Livy that Charcot, the originator of hypnotherapy, had disciples everywhere in Paris. Wouldn't it help Susy?

Susy certainly needed help. Though she was remarkably robust when she returned to Paris, her health declined again in the fall. She ate and slept irregularly and lightly; as a result, her voice weakened and she attended to her lessons only occasionally. Susy's preoccupation filled Livy's letters and worried Sam, who desperately wanted to get back to Europe. "Every night I say to myself 'I *must* see the wife & the children, if only for one day'—but have to follow it with 'Hold your grip & don't be a fool—you've *got* to stay here till this thing is settled.' " Sam was happy to hear that Livy had allowed Susy to visit Louise Brownell at Oxford, a trial by fire for Susy's sought-after serenity. His "distress about Susy" returned when he received Livy's "letter telling me that her English trip had done her no good. Oh, if I were only there!"* He had hoped, with Susy herself, that she had gotten over Louise; and perhaps she would have if she had not found that Louise's interest in her had waned during their separation. At least the rest of the family seemed well. Jean attended a French school, Clara was back in Berlin, and Livy received electrical treatments that seemed to improve her heart condition.

Meanwhile, telegrams shot back and forth between New York and Chicago. Listening to Paige, the Chicago manufacturer wired apprehension that the inventor would tire of the delays. Rogers replied, "At this end we are *already* tired waiting."* Finally, on February 1, 1894, Paige signed the contract. Sam cabled an anniversary message to Paris, "Wedding news. Our ship is safe in port. I sail the moment Rogers can spare me." Sam needed first to straighten out his own complex mess of stock and royalties in the typesetter.

Then, the situation at Webster and Company had become desperate again. Reluctantly, Sam explained its true condition to Rogers. He was slow to be completely honest with Rogers because he saw his involvement with Rogers in a Faustian light. Sam knew that Henry Huttleston Rogers was a devil of a businessman. What exactly had he bargained away by picking the brains behind the Standard Oil trust? Though his soul and his creativity seemed intact, either Rogers or fate would some day require compensation for this assistance. The ambiguity of Rogers' relationship to Sam—was he an angel? a devil? both?—moved him to hatch a story about a visit to Earth by a mysterious and otherworldly stranger. Though long familiar with the Faust legend and accustomed to tales that transcended the human realm, Sam had rarely used supernatural strangers in his fiction until after he met Henry Rogers. A fiery February visit to Fairhaven, where Mark Twain spoke at the dedication of a public library Rogers had built for his hometown, drove home the Faustian dimension of this arrangement. During the ceremony, word came that Rogers' "country house here had just burned down after it had been painstakingly put in beautiful order for us guests."* Part of Sam felt sure he had made a pact with the devil.

Despite the moral uncertainty of their relationship, Sam was grateful to Rogers not only for helping him through his business muddle but also for including him in his family during Sam's long separation from his own. Like Livy, Mrs. Rogers was ill but spritely, and Rogers' children, nearly the same age as the Clemenses', had their share of high-spiritedness and trouble. Devil or not, Rogers was intensely companionable. He and Sam talked of forgoing business and traveling with their families to Japan. Rogers offered to buy Sam a lot beside his own on the ocean in Fairhaven, if Sam would build a house there. Sam told Livy, "Assemble the family now and drink long life and happiness to Henry Rogers," and he wrote a letter of thanks directly to Rogers, leaving it so that his new friend would receive it only after Sam sailed from New York on March 7, 1894.

Sam expected to remain in Paris, but soon after he landed he received word of a crisis in his affairs. Though the typesetter progressed smoothly, with plans to build a prototype for use in the office of the *Chicago Herald*, Webster and Company hit deep water: Mount Morris Bank would accept no more delays in the repayment of their loans. After only three weeks with his family, Sam returned to New York, where he discovered that Daniel Whitford had pressed the bank to close in on the firm, though Fred Hall, whom Sam admired for his levelheadedness, refused to believe that Whitford had used him as a pawn to avenge Sam's supposed mistreatment of Charley Webster. Whitford believed his bank to be the firm's primary creditor and therefore the most powerful claimant of its assets, primarily Mark Twain's copyrights. But Whitford did not count on having to negotiate against Henry Rogers. Swiftly excluding Hall from decisions regarding the future of the company, Sam followed Rogers' advice and filed for bankruptcy.

Livy ruminated to her sister Sue, "I have a perfect *horror* and heartsickness over it. I cannot get away from the feeling that business failure means disgrace. I suppose it always will mean that to me. We have put a great deal of money into the concern." That very money, however, was the key to saving the family. According to Rogers' accounting, by a large margin Livy, not Mount Morris Bank, was the firm's major creditor. Rogers assigned her the copyrights while the rest of the creditors had to content themselves that Webster and Company could pay back only fifty cents per dollar of obligation—more than most creditors had salvaged during the Panic the year before. Privately, apart from the legally enforceable agreement, Sam assured them all that they would eventually be paid in full, "*excluding* the bank," Sam muttered to Livy. "I shall be a very old person before I pay the bank any more than half of their claim unless it can be clearly shown that I *owe* more."

Unlike Livy, Sam had little trouble accepting the collapse of Webster and Company. For him, the greatest challenge was remembering to refer to his assets as "Mrs. Clemens'." He wrote Livy, "I was even able to say with gravity, 'My wife has two unfinished books, but I am not able to say when they will be completed or where she will elect to publish them when they are done.' " He told Mary Fairbanks, who read of Mark Twain's financial collapse in the newspapers, "I enjoy it. It keeps me stirring, & is new." He also felt a Faustian confidence that the publishing debt amounted to pocket change next to the typesetter profits that would flood his accounts now that Henry Rogers was in charge. On May 7, 1894, after three weeks in New York, Sam sailed away from his American home, back to his beloved family, now perched in a safely distant place.

The Clemenses found it difficult to shrink its budget to $20,000 a year. Sam and Livy had gone to Europe to restrict their expenses, but the family's medical treatments and education further drained their resources. They could have decided, as early as 1891, to live as Sam expected Orion to do, as the Howellses did—simply, quietly, and privately—but neither Sam nor Livy could accept retirement from public life. Opting for retrenchment, they chose to live in Paris, but they did not occupy the best hotel or take the largest suite of rooms. They did not pursue the sort of company that required costly entertaining, socializing instead with old friends. The Howells children, Pilla and John, were in Paris and enjoyed establishing their relationships with the Clemenses as adults. John, studying architecture, introduced Susy and Clara to his clique of art school friends and also harbored aspirations that Susy would develop a romantic interest in him, a hope shared by the rest of the Clemenses. Livy felt rejuvenated by her heart treatment, and was so grateful to have Sam back home that she accompanied him out to dine with friends, something she had not done for nearly two years. She had found Sam's absence "a great trial. Then of course his business perplexities have greatly weighed upon us all,"* as she wrote to her childhood friend Alice Hooker Day, also in Europe with her family.

The Days stopped in Paris in June, on their way to the fashionable seaside resort of Étretat on the Atlantic coast; Alice's description of the place convinced the Clemenses to spend August and September there, too. William Dean Howells came to Paris in June as well, but soon after he arrived he heard that his father had suffered a paralytic stroke. As a result, his "head in a mist of care and dread," Howells spent a disconcerting week with Sam, and "Clemens was very kind and brotherly through it all." Henry Rogers also received a devastating blow during this time, when all Sam's friends seemed to be falling victim to bad fortune: His beloved wife went under anesthesia for surgery and never regained consciousness. Sam wrote his guardian angel, "It seems impossible; and yet for all my grief I must believe it. When I think of yours, words fail; they cannot measure your loss."

The doctor caring for Susy recommended a fashionable spa, La Bourboule-les-Bains, so after sending Clara to live on a Swiss farm and study music for two months, Sam escorted the remainder of the family south, planning only to settle them before returning to America. Within a few days of their arrival, however, news arrived of the assassination of the French president by an Italian anarchist. Sam amused Rogers with the story of how a crowd of Marseillaise-singing Frenchmen armed with stones surrounded the Clemenses' hotel and "demanded the Italians, proposing to hammer them; but the landlord refused to give them up." He waited a week, to see if he should remove the family to a safer location. Rioting quickly subsided at La Bourboule and by the middle of July, Sam had returned to his room at the Players Club in New York.

Sam made Henry Rogers' office in the Standard Oil Building at 26 Broadway his base camp. The complex of interconnecting conference rooms, waiting areas, and corridors seemed like an architectural metaphor for business. Sam found explaining Rogers' advice to Livy equally complicated. Livy believed that separating their assets into his and hers had law but not morality on its side and felt that their first obligation was to their creditors. "We want to treat them all not only honestly but we want to help them in every possible way. It is money honestly owed," she wrote Sam. "My darling, I cannot have any thing done in my name that I should not approve."

Where Livy considered her financial role inseparable from Sam's, Sam recognized that division as their lifeline. "My first duty is to you & the children—my second is to those others," he responded. "I must protect you first—protect you against yourself." He even played his emotional trump card: "Suppose father had been here in Mr. Rogers's place? Would he have advised me differently? Indeed, no." Rogers tutored Sam toward a wider perspective on his financial position. Mark Twain's copyrights and future writings could provide the family with a steady livable income if they made the proper long-term arrangement with a prosperous publisher such as Harper and Brothers. The typesetter had at last begun construction in Chicago. The nearly $100,000 of unpaid debt—until the receiver could sell the publishing firm's assets, no one could say just how much Sam owed—amounted to very little of Sam's likely income from these sources.

The lumbering pace of business kept Sam in the States until the middle of August. Lonely, he spent his weekends at the ocean homes of his friends and admirers. When Harry Harper did not offer enough money for the *Joan of Arc* manuscript, the first part of which Sam had revised on the voyage to New York, Sam went to retrieve it and met Harper. "He is a very lovely man & we came to an understanding in five minutes. Then he wanted me to go home with him—down on the seashore on Long Island—& I have been there ever since till a few minutes ago," Sam wrote Livy. "It is a charming family, & I am to let them know when you come, so that they can know you." He also visited a well-known palm reader; Sam had previously demonstrated his faith in palmistry by giving the hero of *Pudd'nhead Wilson* the art. He wrote the palm reader's reassuring news to Susy: that Sam made good decisions quickly, but faltered if he had time to think; that he felt "little troubled" by bad press; and that his "affections are strong and deep, but they don't show, much, on the outside." His palm also reassuringly declared he would "be enormously rich at 68—earlier, indeed—but that is the summit."*

These forecasts calmed him somewhat, but Susy still worried him, and he looked forward to rejoining his family in France. Writing Clara, he told her how pleased he was that she enjoyed her farm life, and also noted, "You are laying-in a stock of health & vigor that you can draw upon for many a year to come. I do wish we had put Susy through a course like that instead of sending her to that deadly college." Sam reached Étretat at the end of August, happy to learn that the seaside resort agreed with Susy. She was happy to have childhood friends—the Days and the Howellses—for company. She had also developed a new faith in work. As she told Clara, "*Anything* to keep one busy and useful and prevent one's being a fearful . . . society gal!!!!!" Her work was writing fiction, which gratified Sam, who believed Susy's talent lay in literature, not public singing. Her determination to work disguised her true goal of gaining her independence, the only chance to regain the interest of, and perhaps reunite with, Louise, who was set to leave Europe without seeing Susy again. Susy wrote desperately to her beloved friend, "Please come in to me and let me lie down in your arms, and forget everything but the joy of being near you.—Write me THAT YOU WILL LET ME SEE YOU once, one *little* once before you go."

Buckling down to his work on *Joan*, Sam steadily produced a hundred manuscript pages a week, ten thousand words. He read the text aloud to the clan, explaining to Rogers how "the madam and Susy are prompt and frank about squelching inferiorities." The confluence of Susy's troubles and his work on the life of Joan resulted in his secretly using his own daughter as his model when describing the martyred saint. Despite this practical approach to depicting the transcendence of a young woman dead for half a millennium, Sam also often fell back on concepts of God, forgiveness, and eternal life, not because he consciously believed in them but because he could not eliminate his belief completely. Joan of Arc fascinated him for the same reason that thought transference did: The saint's very existence disproved pragmatism. Joan represented a denial of Sam's disbelief rather than a confirmation of his belief.

He found Étretat an excellent retreat for his writing, "a kind of paradise; it is beautiful, and still, and infinitely restful." They left at the end of September, intending to reside in Paris for the winter, but Susy developed a serious illness that detained the family for a month in Rouen. Sam wanted to absorb the atmosphere of the town where Joan of Arc had been tried and executed but, as he wrote Rogers, "there is no scrap or stone in Rouen that she ever saw. Even the spot where she was burned is not as definitely located as one would expect it to be."

During the month, good news did come from Chicago: The Paige Compositor was efficiently setting type in the *Herald* office, with only seventeen minutes of "cussedness" in an eight-hour shift. Renting a four-bedroom house, at 169 rue de l'Université on the Left Bank, which an American let to the family at only $250 a month, he reported to his financial watchdog Rogers, "We expect to save $200 a month, housekeeping, *but*—we'll wait and see." Sam got sick just as the family moved to the new house, with gout and a long, virulent cold. He fretted about Rogers' discomforting reports about the test in Chicago, where the machine's delicacy showed itself and errors and downtime for repairs increased. By Sam's fifty-ninth birthday, he and Livy were anticipating the failure of his "fine ten-year-old dream." They decided to live cheaply in Elmira once the lease on the Paris house expired in May, while Sam prepared his "books for a uniform edition. . . . The mother and the three children spent two francs on birthday presents for me, and we have begun life on a new and not altogether unpromising basis."

Regrettably for Sam, this new start meant the full-force return of Mark Twain. Without the typesetter, it would take years to repay Webster and Company's creditors, even with a uniform edition selling well. Only a return to the lecture platform could earn the money he needed. More discouraging words, about the impending collapse of the Paige Compositor, reached Paris. "By George," Sam wrote Rogers, "that wolf does seem to be approaching my door again! I wish he would apply somewhere where he hasn't worn out his welcome." Looking to hedge his speculation, Sam suggested that Rogers secretly buy stock in the Mergenthaler Linotype machine before publicly bowing out of the typesetter competition. He proposed that Rogers could go into partnership with Mergenthaler, if Paige could be persuaded to relinquish his patents. These desperate ideas came too late. Everyone concerned already knew that, whatever its virtues, the Paige Compositor failed to withstand daily use.

Despite Sam's long anticipation of the machine's demise, the news itself "hit me like a thunderclap," as he told Rogers. "It knocked every rag of sense out of my head." For a day, he felt a wild need to preside over the machine's ashes; he made plans to sail to America. The next morning, he regained some equanimity and proposed some ways in which the machine might be simplified and tried again, but Rogers had seen enough. He only worried that scrapping the project would terminate his friendship with Sam. Sam reassured him, "I shall keep your regard while we two live—that I know." Rogers offered to personally negotiate Sam's publishing contracts, keep his accounts, and oversee the placement of his short pieces. Sam embraced the offer and decided to return to America to help arrange publication of *Joan of Arc* and negotiate for the uniform edition.

The death of his dream of gargantuan fortune challenged Sam's conception of himself as had no other crisis since his bout with poverty in San Francisco. His darkest realization was that the family could never return to the Hartford house, a fact that "would break the family's hearts if they could believe it." Livy still felt hopeful, and her hope led to his survival. "Nothing daunts Mrs. Clemens or makes the world look black to her—which is the reason I haven't drowned myself." He wrote to Rogers that random luck and not the supernatural apportionment of fortune had determined his life. "All my life I have stumbled upon lucky chances of large size, and whenever they were wasted it was because of my own stupidity and carelessness." Luck had left him at last, and he needed "to teach myself to endure a way of life which I was familiar with during the first half of my life but whose sordidness and hatefulness and humiliation long ago faded out of my memory and feeling." As the first gesture of the return to this scraping way of life, he gave Livy only a new five-franc piece for their silver wedding anniversary.

Livy at last approved the round-the-world lecture tour by Mark Twain, an option for raising funds that they had held in abeyance since Sam and family had relocated to Europe more than three years before. The hopelessness of ever paying the creditors without lecturing finally persuaded her. For once, too, the family all seemed in good enough health to undertake such an arduous journey. Kismet endorsed the plan, in the form of the mental telegraphy Sam grudgingly accepted: The very night that Sam wrote to Henry Stanley's Australian lecture agent proposing that he manage the Southern Hemisphere portion of his tour, he received a letter from the very same man answering his questions. With fate smiling on this plan, Livy agreed to rent out the Hartford house to Alice Day, an ironic turn since Sam and Livy had rented Alice's family home when they first moved to Hartford more than twenty years before. At the end of February, Sam sailed for America. Through the graying, almost ghostly shadow of Sam Clemens, Mark Twain would speak again.

42 | A Respite for the Bankrupt

If you pick up a starving dog and make him prosperous, he will not bite you. This is the principal difference between a dog and a man.
—"Pudd'nhead Wilson's Calendar" (1894)

D URING HIS SIX-WEEK stay in the United States, Sam attended fewer dinners and saw fewer people than he had before the collapse of his fortunes. Staying with Henry Rogers, eating with Rogers, attending to business with Rogers, and occupying a room in Rogers' office, Sam looked after his publishing interests, which had become miserably tangled. The fate of a uniform edition of his works, and the long-term financial salvation that project promised, rested in the hands of Frank Bliss and the American Publishing Company, which held the copyrights on most of Mark Twain's early works, including *The Innocents Abroad*, *Roughing It*, and *Tom Sawyer*. Watson Gill, with whom the publishing firm had had such trouble as they moved into the trade business, still held the trade distribution rights for *Life on the Mississippi*. Bliss, Harper, and Rogers' son-in-law William Evarts Benjamin all wanted to publish the uniform edition, but Sam's distressed financial condition, widely reported in the press, worked against him in negotiations. "Oh, I *hate* business—& so these days do drag along most wearily," he wrote Livy. "I miss you; & I often wish we lived out of the world where one might never more hear of business or worry about money."*

The only relief came in a trip he took to Hartford in late March. He went to the house, fearing that the old place would torment him, but—with Livy's elegant decor reconstituted by Katy Leary—"the place was bewitchingly bright & splendid & homelike & natural, & it seemed as if I had burst awake out of a hellish dream, & had never been away." Sam stayed with the Twichells, and on every side people offered him sympathy and Livy praise. "Words cannot describe how worshipfully & enthusiastically you are loved in this town," he assured Livy; "& the wash of the wave reaches even to me, because I belong to you; it would wash to your dog, if you had a dog." Despite the difficult emotional currents of returning home a bankrupt, Sam did feel an underlying happiness at being in the United States. He had traveled to Europe in part to escape Mark Twain, but now that he knew how much he needed his alternate persona, he regretted life without him. "I can't describe to you how poor & empty & offensive France is, compared to America—in my eyes," he told Livy. "The minute I strike America I seem to wake out of an odious dream."

Once he returned to Paris, Sam shut himself up at the house on rue de l'Université to read the proofs for *The Personal Recollections of Joan of Arc*. He lifted his head out of the galleys long enough to sign his lecturing contract with R. S. Smythe for a tour of the Southern Hemisphere; Major Pond would handle his American engagements. Outlining to Harry Harper his exhausting global itinerary, Sam concluded that when it was done he would "then die, I reckon."

The sheer size of his undertaking, of his debt, and of his reversal of fortune combined with his completion of *Joan* to cultivate Sam's doubts about the presence of a divinity on earth. His own luck had always proved to him there existed no God with an interest in human affairs, because he felt certain that he was unworthy of such interest and yet was among the most fortunate men on the planet. He expanded his questioning, wondering about the worth of his fellow humans. Writing to his nephew Samuel Moffett, now editing a newspaper in San Francisco, about his anticipated lecture stop there, he observed the hopelessness of human goodness: "Once more we are forced to admit that it was a mistake & a misfortune that Noah & his gang were not drowned."* As the Clemenses prepared to move once again, he received a small but painful reminder of his childhood abandonment that he related to Rogers: He emerged from his study one day in late April to discover that "the baggage has all disappeared, including the family. I reckon that in the hurry and bustle of moving to the hotel they forgot me." When he ought to have had opportunity to glory in his accomplishments, Sam felt more like the young boy his father had neglected to bring to the Quarles farm one summer, pathetically draining meal from a burlap sack.

The Clemenses left Europe on May 11, 1895, after four years' absence from America. In New York, they lodged at the modest Everett House, rejecting Charlie Langdon's offer to host them at the Waldorf because, as he told Rogers, "people would think we were splurging there on our own footing and it wouldn't look modest for bankrupts." They planned to stay at Quarry Farm until the tour began in July. Sam and Livy had originally thought that all three girls would join them on the tour, but the expense dissuaded them. Also, Susy declared that she would rather stay in America because she didn't like ocean travel, but she harbored private hopes of seeing Louise Brownell on a romantic basis once again. And Jean needed to return to conventional schooling, and her parents feared more that the irregularity of travel would worsen the unexplained blackouts she had begun to suffer. Susy and Jean agreed to stay in Elmira with Aunt Sue, and then meet their parents and sister in England after they'd circled the globe. Only Clara would travel with them.

Sam settled down to work. He had to finish reading proofs for *Joan* and he wanted to prepare several different readings for the tour, because he would deliver a number of lectures in each of the larger towns on his itinerary. Unfortunately, first he was delayed by an attack of gout, and then he developed a carbuncle on his leg, so painful he couldn't wear anything but a loose-fitting nightgown. Business—in the form of letters from publishers, partners, and creditors—also bothered him. Newspapers offered $1,000-a-month contracts for correspondence, which Sam declined, as he did a deal for the book he planned to write about the global journey. Unwilling to sign any agreement, he lied to Rogers, now serving as his literary agent, misrepresenting himself as a perpetually unencumbered artist. "I have never written with chains on, in my life, and wouldn't know how to manage it." Sam's nearly daily business letters heaped so many obligations on Rogers that Sam wrote, after a particularly long list of provisions and assignments, "Look here, don't you think you'd better let somebody else run the Standard Oil a week or two till you've finished up these matters of mine?"

The most exasperating business interference came in late June, while Sam still lay in bed with his gaping carbuncle. A printer and bookbinder owed money by the publishing firm served Sam with papers that would have forced his appearance in a New York City courtroom on July 19, by which time he ought to have started his tour. The lawyer handling the bankruptcy said Sam had made himself liable to the state court by residing in New York. Livy shuddered at the thought of her husband's name appearing in the paper as having ignored the court order and fled the country, as Rogers advised doing, so despite his pain Sam went to New York

City the second week in July and settled out of court. Only after reaching this agreement did Sam discover that he was under no obligation to honor the court order. The ineptitude of his attorney made Sam moan to Rogers, "What cheap, cheap material one can make a New York lawyer of." Rogers sarcastically replied that New York lawyers were not all so bad: Even "poor old [Daniel] Whitford melted to tears over your troubles." The debacle at least secured some public sympathy for Mark Twain on the eve of his lecture tour. By that time, Sam and Livy and Clara were on the road west, prepared once again to leave home behind for perhaps another two years.

43 | Around the World

The low level which commercial morality has reached in America is deplorable. We have humble God fearing Christian men among us who will stoop to do things for a million dollars that they ought not to be willing to do for less than 2 millions.
—Source unknown

SAM'S AMBIVALENCE ABOUT Mark Twain's return to the platform appeared not only in his intemperate moods and sieges of illness, but more remarkably in an area he seldom allowed indecision to affect: his fame. In April 1895, *The Personal Recollections of Joan of Arc* began running serially—and anonymously—in *Harper's*, where it caused excited speculation. As women's rights had become more widely debated, Joan's tragic life had become better known, rehabilitated into history after centuries in the shadowland of legend. This version presented itself as a serious and well-researched, though fictional, study of her. Sam's insistence that the book appear anonymously seemed self-destructive—if the tour spurred sales of the book, both endeavors would earn more—but Mark Twain's return brought back Sam's fear that readers would not accept Twain as a serious writer. Before he attached his trade name to a product, he wanted to make sure the product would sell.

He had constructed the novel so that the name Mark Twain would be nothing more than a label. Sam left it purposefully vague where Mark Twain—or Sam himself—resides in the manuscript. The title page cites Sieur Louis de Conte, not Mark Twain, as the author. An introductory note by an invented scholar, Jean François Alden, describes the book as a translation of a recently discovered manuscript: notes the aristocratic de Conte made at the end of long life about his brief and youthful career as Joan's "page and secretary. I was with her from the beginning until the end." Alden's annotations, supposedly the product of Darwin's century, show that he remains incredulous about de Conte's firsthand report of the miraculous life of the Maid of Orleans. Alden's comparison of de Conte's story and the court records—the same records Sam himself used in his composition of the novel—persuades him of the truth behind the legends of Joan. He concludes, "She was perhaps the only entirely unselfish person whose name has a place in profane history."

De Conte's Joan does not differ much from the recent tide of other books about her, which over a decade had turned Joan into a cult figure. In her latest incarnation, Joan of Arc represented a progressivism in Western civilization. She was a precursor to Protestant resistance to papal authority, a force for justice, and Christlike evidence of the Creator's ongoing faith in humanity. The leaders of the vast social changes of the nineteenth century needed a model like Joan, who became a touchstone for suffragists, pacifists, and unionists. As de Conte portrays her, she deserves all these accolades and then some. This Joan of Arc differs from common visions of her only in her American drive and her unmistakable sense of humor. The details of her life are both accurately and strikingly recorded: her calling at a very young age; her successful generalship of French forces comprised of lay soldiers; her amazing performance during her trial; and her execution by burning before the age of twenty. De Conte, remembering back more than sixty years, imbues his recollections with wistful passion.

Though it appeared that Sam wanted to withhold the use of the Mark Twain name on *Joan of Arc* because he feared that people might not take the book seriously, he had other reasons as well. *Pudd'nhead Wilson* had appeared under the name Mark Twain, and it was a serious effort, though undermined by the appending of the separated farce. Apart from the farce, *Pudd'nhead Wilson* actually had less humor than *Personal Recollections of Joan of Arc*, and less of the fantastical detail and idiosyncratic characters that made both *Huck Finn* and *A Connecticut Yankee* so captivating and memorable. It is possible that Sam was not so much hiding Mark Twain's authorship of the book as hoping to claim it as Sam Clemens' own product. The book's narrator shared the same initials with Samuel L. Clemens, and Samuel L. Clemens, like Sieur Louis de Conte, had every right to claim proximity to a figure of myth. The novel attempted to reveal the flesh-and-bone reality of Joan; could it also strip the mask off Mark Twain and reveal Sam Clemens?

One excellent reason for Sam not to try to claim direct responsibility for the book was money. He had no way to estimate how much Mark Twain could earn on this world tour, and whether it would be enough to clear his financial name. By the time he reached the West Coast, however, he sent Henry Rogers $5,000 profit and could imagine earning five times that or more before he finished. Before he left North America, he asked Harper and Brothers to put Mark Twain on the title page of *Joan of Arc*, "for all that I wanted to accomplish by withholding it has been accomplished." What he had accomplished, other than the personal satisfaction that a book unescorted by Mark Twain could garner glorious reviews, remains a mystery. Between the time he requested anonymous publication and the time he wanted Mark Twain restored to the title page, only two important things had changed: The book had been lauded and Mark Twain's world tour had begun. Sam thought that "appearing in print periodically" in *Harper's* would advertise Mark Twain, whose name he wanted "kept alive while I am away on this long journey."

The North American portion of the tour carried him back and forth across the Canadian border, starting in Cleveland and ending a month later in Vancouver, British Columbia. Major Pond brought his wife along, as much to help Livy and Clara in their unaccustomed roles as entourage as to round out the company. Though the hole in his thigh left behind by the carbuncle healed slowly, Sam took to the platform again very quickly. He was a speaker without peer, and he easily remembered his lessons of twenty-five years before: Mix laughter and serious intent; always appear natural; have enough flexibility in the program to suit the audience. This presentation of Mark Twain linked a series of short pieces into a sermon on righteousness, with the short pieces illustrating whichever particular virtue he felt like emphasizing. This loose structure allowed Sam to add new material as he tired of the old and prepare a new performance piecemeal. For the first time, he found the platform endlessly invigorating. He wrote to his nephew Sammy Moffett, as a combined letter to the editor and advertisement, to be published in Moffett's *San Francisco Examiner:* "Lecturing is gymnastics, chest-expander, medicine, mind healer, blues destroyer, all in one. I am twice as well as I was when I started out. I have gained nine pounds in twenty-eight days, and expect to weigh six hundred before January."

The tour also allowed Sam to adjust Mark Twain's public image. The rumors about his reluctance to honor the debts of his publishing firm offered an opportunity to speak frankly about Mark Twain. With the advice of Henry Rogers and the help of Sammy Moffett, Sam published a manifesto of honor, putting a noble face on his bankruptcy. He learned the lesson underlying the document while on the road, when an Anaconda, Montana, theater owner lost money on a thin house. Sam sent him $100, saying, "I'm not going around robbing my friends who are disappointed in my commercial value." Dispelling the notion that he planned to leave his creditors hanging, Mark Twain noted in the manifesto:

> The law recognizes no mortgage on a man's brain, and a merchant who has given up all he has may take advantage of the rules of insolvency and start free again for himself; but I am not a business man, and honor is a harder master than the law. It cannot compromise for less than a hundred cents on the dollar, and its debts never outlaw. . . .
>
> I do not enjoy the hard travel and broken rest inseparable from lecturing, and, if it had not been for the imperious moral necessity of paying these debts, which I never contracted but which were accumulated on the faith of my name by those who had a presumptive right to use it, I should never have taken to the road at my time of life.

He concluded, with Twainian humor, that he had intended to give the creditors all the benefits of his touring, but that the public's reception provided him "dividends [which], if not available for banking purposes, may be even more satisfactory than theirs."

The Clemenses' departure from Vancouver was like a step off the end of the earth. They took their leave of the Ponds and of the mails; they might receive letters in Hawaii, but otherwise, until they reached Australia, communication with their regular lives became impossible. Hawaii, whose society and environment had decayed even from the degraded condition Sam had seen when he had covered the Sandwich Islands for the *Sacramento Union*, frustrated his nearly thirty-year-old dream of returning to that idyllic spot. As the ship neared Honolulu, a message came out from the harbor that cholera had killed a handful of Hawaiians. The captain would not land or take anything on board. All Hawaii felt a disappointment as profound as Sam's; the islands were proud of their connection to the fledgling Mark Twain. As the sea journey stretched on, Sam felt more at home with this forced march. Clara and Livy relieved him of social burdens, such as correspondence and late-night visitors, which always exhausted him while on tour. The cruise itself offered its own pleasures. Sam embraced the ship's shuffleboard championship as a kind of oceanbound billiards, but his intensity in playing the typically lighthearted game reflected what Livy wrote Sue Crane about him: "He is pretty cheerful—in fact he appears entirely cheerful—but underneath he has a steady, unceasing feeling that he is never going to be able to pay his debts."* He wrote Joe Twichell about his coming birthday, "I shall be 60—no thanks for it."

The Clemens trio spent more than three months in New Zealand and Australia, visiting not only principal cities, but also many smaller towns. Sam regarded the whole continent as comically loathsome, a land without refinement in food or lodging, but he found the Australians wildly friendly and enthusiastic. An Australian was also "as vain of his unpretty country as if it were the final masterpiece of God, achieved by Him from designs by that Australian." Sydney set the tone for how the Southern Hemisphere greeted Mark Twain. Town notables in business, politics, and the arts stampeded the Clemenses with invitations, banquets, and interviews. Newspapers reported commonplace movements and opinions of Mark Twain with a fervor Sam had not experienced for many years. One early misstep endangered his entire Australian tour: He let loose on Bret Harte, saying, "He has no heart, except his name, and I consider he has produced nothing that is genuine. He is artificial." Australians, who treasured Harte as they treasured Twain, rose up in anger. Sam apologized for his remarks, and both he and his tour manager had to repair damage to ticket sales. Aside from a few sick days, Sam kept up a frantic pace of interviews and lectures, generating several thousand dollars to send back to Henry Rogers before leaving the island continent at the end of December 1895.

Just before they left Australia, the family went to the theater to see the island continent's early history—especially the hardships of English prisoners exiled a world away from home—presented as melodrama in "For the Term of His Natural Life." Sympathetic to this forced separation, Sam noted that the play "goes far to enable one to realize that old convict life—invented in hell and carried out by Christian devils." Sam and Livy appeared to share sympathies concerning the senselessness of the cruel imposition of British martial law on the transported settlers, but Livy, having no previous experience with indigenous peoples commonly called savages, also felt for the aborigines. In New Zealand, however, she finally had the opportunity to visit a native village and came away repulsed. "I have been very much interested in the Maoris since we came here, and have been anxious to see more of them," she wrote Susy from Wanganui; "now I have had enough, I shall not seek their dwellings any more." Her reaction paralleled Sam's after his first exposure to Indians in Nevada. His earlier belief in a cultural hierarchy based on equality between the sexes, cleanliness, justice, and tolerance had grown more sophisticated since his years in the American West. Sam now doubted the wisdom of imposing the values of one culture on another based on the premise that the dominating culture is superior.

Making a grand circuit of exotic India following a fanciful route organized by Smythe, the Clemenses started at Bombay on India's west coast, traveled across the country to Calcutta on the east coast, and then headed north to begin a return trek including towns along the Tibetan and Afghan borders. Sam lost days here and there from illness, but his progress did not seem determined by any set schedule of appearances, since Smythe altered the plan of the pilgrimage as they went. The Clemenses traveled at a leisurely pace, resting for a few days at a royal palace, rising early to catch a glimpse of the Himalayas, touring the famous Jain Temple with young Mahatma Gandhi as a guide. As tedious as Sam found Australia, he found India stunning, marvelous. If the threat of oppressive heat had not chased them from the subcontinent, Sam would gratefully have extended their stay.

The writer, lecturer, and traveler in distant lands soon grew exhausted. He, Livy, and Clara took refuge on the French island of Mauritius, just east of Madagascar, where for ten days Sam neither lectured nor sought out the press. He wanted only to prepare himself for the final leg. As Sam wrote Rogers, "I have to go to S. Africa, but I suppose that that will end my lecturing in this world. Mrs. Clemens is not willing that I shall continue the risk any further." They needed the rest for an emotional reason, too: They had received word in Colombo, Ceylon, that their Hartford friends, the Whitmores, had lost a child. "Why, Why—we must constantly ask—are we allowed to love and rear these children," Livy wrote in condolence, "and then have to sit by helpless when they are taken away from us."* Sam's mood required lightening: His huge debts and declining health had seemed to conspire against him until, despite the profits and accolades, he finally believed "that we must all our lives live in poverty," as Livy wrote her sister. "He says he never wants to go back to America. I cannot think that things are as black as he paints them."

In South Africa, Livy and Clara accompanied him only on trips to the major coastal cities, and then spent four weeks in May and June camped out in Durban, waiting for Sam to finish his tour of the veldt. Meanwhile, Henry Rogers' news from the States gave Sam and Livy material for contemplation. Negotiations failed between Harper and Brothers, which owned the right to publish Mark Twain's recent books, and Frank

Bliss' American Publishing Company, which owned the early books. Neither company would allow the other to publish the books to which it held the rights. Each forwarded offers the other found impossible to accept. "I have been faithfully at work with Harper Bros. and the Blisses," Rogers wrote Sam, "but I don't know whether we are making progress or not." Rogers easily understood Sam and Mark Twain as separate entities, and he was pleased with his work on " 'Mark Twain's' books. It is fair for me to say now that everybody says that 'Mark Twain' is on the boom." To Rogers, "Mark Twain" was a commodity, not to be confused with his friend Sam Clemens, who promised elephants, giraffes, and anacondas as presents on the occasion of Rogers' second marriage. Mark Twain's manifesto of honor, his world tour, and the final acknowledgment of his authorship of *Personal Recollections of Joan of Arc* had renewed the old master's reputation.

The Republic of South Africa trembled as the British attempted to wrest power from the ruling Boers, with Cecil Rhodes instigating the movement from his stronghold in the north. One of Rhodes' generals, Dr. Leander Starr Jameson, led an unsuccessful raid resulting in an international sensation and the imprisonment of the raiders. Sam made a farcical prison speech to Jameson's mostly well-educated adventurers, many of whom Sam knew through his travels. "I advised them at considerable length to stay where they were—they would get used to it and like it presently; if they got out they would only get in again somewhere else, by the look of their countenances; and I promised to go and see the President and do what I could to double their jail-terms." Because reports of this speech led the annoyed Boer President "Oom Paul" Kruger to treat the prisoners more harshly, Sam did go to see him soon after, and Kruger returned the prisoners to their former state of deprivation. Sam's diplomatic resolution to the uproar led him to flirt with the idea of settling in South Africa as an ambassador. "It is intensely interesting here—," he wrote Rogers, "the political pot is boiling vigorously." Ever the entrepreneur, he saw financial opportunity in Africa, enough so that a well-managed diplomatic post could free him from debt.

Exactly a year after the trio's departure from Elmira, they set sail from South Africa to England, filled with joyful anticipation of the reunion with the family. Reports from Elmira of Jean's progress in school and Susy's state of mind made Sam hopeful that this five-year period of darkness had ended, and that the family might soon reestablish itself on its former terms. At the beginning of August, Sam wrote Howells from England, "We hope to get a house in some quiet English village away from the world & society, where I can sit down for six months or so & give myself up to the luxury & rest of writing a book or two after this long fatigue & turmoil of platform-work & gadding around by sea & land. Susie & Jean sail from New York today, & a week hence we shall all be together again." They found a place in Guildford for a month, and Livy scoured the countryside for a house to take on longer term. Meanwhile, Sam wrote Rogers congratulating him on settling the publication of Mark Twain's future works. The lucrative contract with Harper seemed to promise the end of Sam's debts, even without an agreement on a uniform edition.

Sam's high spirits arrived prematurely, however. The plans in America called for Katy Leary to pack up Susy in Hartford, where she stayed with the Charles Dudley Warners for several weeks, and meet Jean, Sue Crane, and Charlie Langdon in New York. When Katy reached Hartford, however, Susy could not travel. At first, it seemed that the severe August weather had oppressed her, but it soon became clear that she was indeed burning up, from a raging infection. Eventually—too slowly—a doctor was called. A telegram went to England. Sam cabled back anxiously and waited for a reply. Nothing came, and in the morning, Sam, Livy, and Clara went to Southampton, looking for a ship home. A message waiting for them there said that Susy's recovery would be long, but certain. Livy and Clara boarded a boat for America. Sam wrote Livy the next day, "You & Clara are making the only sad voyage of all the round-the-world trip. I am not demonstrative; I am always hiding my feelings; but my heart was wrung yesterday. I could not tell you how deeply I loved you nor how grieved I was for you, nor how I pitied you in this awful trouble that my mistakes have brought upon you. You forgive me, I know, but I shall never forgive myself while the life is in me." Two days later, he had to write Livy again, this time devastated with grief. "I had just sent away a cheerful letter to you about the Joan reviews & such light matters when the cablegram was put into my hands in which Charley and Sue said our poor child had been 'released.' " After several days of delirium and blindness, Susy died, on August 18, 1896, of spinal meningitis. Her mother was still in the mid-Atlantic, sailing toward tragedy.

44 | *City of Heartbreak*

By trying we can easily learn to endure adversity.
Another man's, I mean.
—"Pudd'nhead Wilson's New Calendar" (1897)

Each person is born to one possession which out values all
his others—his last breath.
—"Pudd'nhead Wilson's New Calendar" (1897)

S USY CLEMENS' FINAL year had begun with limited expectations. When her parents and sister left her under the electric lights at the Elmira train station, she had, in her twenty-three years, stepped beyond the protective purview of her family just once, for her seven months at Bryn Mawr. The results had unnerved her mother and father. In September 1895, she wrote to Black Spider, as she called her sister Clara, "I am at Quarry Farm tranquilly living on without you as if I had never been anywhere else," but her letters communicated little tranquillity. In addition to her discontent with her own life, she had found disturbing the relationship between her Aunt Sue and Ernest Köppe, a waiter from the family's Berlin hotel, who had followed Sue Crane from Europe eighteen months before. As a servant, Ernest took great liberties, reading the paper in the living room, eating with the family, and keeping Sue Crane company late in her room. Susy wrote Clara, "My rage almost gave me the apoplexy. But I *never* say or look, or breathe anything and am discretion's very self." She credited Mental Science for her self-control. She wrote Clara, "I have become determined to get hold of a philosophy that will if possible straighten me out morally, mentally, and physically and make me less of a burden to myself and others. I am tired *tired* of all my *sins*, and all myself!" She met with Mary Foote, her old tutor and now proselytizer for Mental Science, as mind cure had come to be called and seriously studied the method.

Both Livy and Sam supported her efforts. Livy wrote, "I am most truly thankful that you are getting interested in Mental Science. I hope it will do you endless good." Two months later, Sam wrote more emphatically, "I have no language to say how glad and grateful I am that you are a convert to that rational and noble philosophy. Stick to it; don't let anybody talk you out of it. Of all earthly fortune it is the best, and most enriches the possessor." Susy saw this less-structured version of Christian Science as her best hope for suppressing the passions she knew her family and her society could not accept. Around the New Year, Susy left Elmira for the New York area, and because of Mental Science she found that her "relations with the people here . . . have been more satisfactory than any I have had at any time or with any people in the past." She and some new friends put on a performance "for the base purpose of 'impressing' Louise" Brownell, in a bald attempt to demonstrate that she had her ardor under control. After New York, she went to Hartford, where many old family friends were also Mental Science enthusiasts. Her new philosophy left Susy little common ground with her peers. The Farmington Avenue house, she told Clara, "is beautiful and Mamma's friends are lovely but the *young people*,—well, there's no use talking,—they don't *exist*, and it's hard to associate with the dead just yet."

Despite this inauspicious start, Susy did find Hartford an attractive place and, after spending the spring in Elmira, moved there with Katy Leary for the summer. She stayed with Charles Dudley Warner, her father's *Gilded Age* collaborator, but spent her days at the Farmington Avenue house, reading, sewing, playing the piano, and singing. Her voice had become strong and clear and so beautiful that neighbors frequently sat outside to hear an impromptu concert. Susy used the jargon of Mental Science to explain the source of her new strength to Clara. The "staff of being (existence)" has "a positive and negative end," she wrote. "The negative end, which is the end swayed and moved and effected ('the soul effected' in other words), we are to extend toward God and the eternal truths, and the *positive* end which is the firm, strong, immoveable end (in other words 'the soul effecting') we must turn toward people and the world." Susy believed she had attained balance, but Jean and Aunt Sue thought she had gone insane. Perhaps they saw in Susy the same disturbance that led her to write Louise what a mutual friend later called "terrible June letters," declaring how much she dreaded the love of her former partner.

Mental Science adherents eschewed conventional medical practice. When Susy fell ill, the Warners favored faith over their responsibility for Susy's health. Even Joe Twichell could not convince her to see a physician. Eventually, Katy Leary solved the problem by sending for the doctor without regard to what Susy said. The delay probably killed her. Susy fell into a raving mania, and her perspicacious sixteen-year-old sister Jean remained convinced that even if she mended physically, she would never have recovered her senses. Jean told her cousin Sam Moffett, now working in New York, "We *said* Susy was sick, but we *knew* she was insane. Mental science, spiritualism, together with her own desire for going away did their work. Poor Susy was too frail to support her brain." In the house her parents had built when she was a toddler, Susy wandered around delirious, furiously scribbling long, illegible notes before succumbing to fever. In those notes, she imagined herself the psychic disciple of Maria Malibran, a Parisian singer of half a century before who had died at Susy's age. Susy was delirious, desperate, and possibly insane when she made this bizarre document; she was also perceptive, bright, and intuitive. This message to her father implies that Livy's "purity and character and peace" were too virtuous to permit her to empathize with Sam in his efforts to understand his own ideological darkness. Instead, Susy believed, Livy should trust Sam, as a "child of great darkness and light[,] to me who can keep the darkness universal and free from sensual taint." She wanted to help her father transcend conventional visions of morality. When the meningitis reached her brain, Susy went blind. Just before she died, she touched Katy's face and said, "Mamma."

Livy and Clara landed in New York to this horrible news. Clara wept. Livy collapsed. Jean, Charlie Langdon, Sue Crane, Joe Twichell, and Sam Moffett supported her on the trip up to Elmira for the funeral and burial in the Langdon family plot. Louise Brownell was not included in the circle of mourners, and her troubled sadness is palpable in a letter of condolence from a fellow student at Bryn Mawr: "Some day Mrs. Clemens will send for you and you will be given a little of that touch with Olivia's Family you were so cruelly robbed of." Susy's forced denial of her homoerotic impulses caused her anguish and provoked the "madness" that her sister Jean saw in her before her death.

The length of a transatlantic journey made it impossible for Sam to reach Elmira in time for the service. Alone in England, he wrote despondent letters to Livy, taking the blame for Susy's death and hoping that his daughter had left behind some crumb to demonstrate that she had loved and forgiven him. He wrote Livy, "I eat—because you wish it; I go on living—because you wish it; I play billiards, and billiards, & billiards, till I am ready to drop—to keep from going mad with grief & with resentful thinkings." When his brother Henry had died almost forty years before, Sam didn't allow himself to think about it, but now, with Susy's death, "I have no disposition or desire to put it out of my mind—I seem to want to think of it all the time. For the present the zest of life is gone from me, which is natural. I have *hated* life before—from the time I was 18—but I was not indifferent to it." Most painful to Sam, after the loss and the separation, was the absence of letters from American friends for more than a week after the tragedy. He wrote Livy, "I sit back & try to believe that there are any human beings in the world, friends or foes, civilized or savage, who would close their lips *there*, & leave me these many, many, many days eating my heart out with longings for the tidings that never come." When letters did flow in, Sam found little comfort in them.

In the middle of September, the family gathered in London to mourn. They took a small house, with Katy Leary to help run it, at 23 Tedworth Square, Chelsea, and closed themselves off from nearly all society, keeping their address secret from almost everyone. Sam wrote few letters of thanks after expressions of sympathy came. He thanked Joe Twichell, saying, "I would have chosen you out of all the world to take my place at Susy's side and Livy's in those black hours." He told Laurence Hutton, "In writing me a kind word you have done the best that any can do—you have paid reverent respect to my dead. That is the value of letters written in such circumstances—I realize it now."* He consoled Sue Crane for the trial Susy had put her through during the year. To Howells he wrote, "Yes, you two know what we feel—but no others among our friends." He added thoughtlessly, "As Mrs. Clemens says, 'they have lost a daughter, but they have not lost a Susy Clemens.' There was not a detail in Susy's make-up that was commonplace."

Within three weeks, Sam could manage his grief enough to work on his book about the world tour, which he now regarded as having rescued his financial soul at the expense of his family. "On my book I work all day—& *every* day in the week, every day in the month," he wrote his sister Pamela at the dawn of 1897. "Save by unavoidable accident I have not lost a day since the 4th day of October."* He corresponded with almost no one, excepting business letters to Henry Rogers. Liquidating the assets of Webster and Company—exclusive of Sam's copyrights—had erased less than a third of the company's debts—exclusive of those owed to Livy. Sam thought he had earned most of the $40,000 he owed during the global campaign, and he had, but the company's debt was $30,000 higher than he expected. He believed that, if he could get the tone of the prose right, he could sell sixty thousand copies of his around-the-world travel book, which he needed to do to earn the extra sum, but the necessary lightness of expression belied the state of his inner self. "I don't mean that I am miserable; no—worse than that, indifferent," he wrote Howells. "We are dead people who go through the motions of life. Indeed I am a mud image, & it puzzles me to know what it is in me that writes, & that has comedy-fancies & finds pleasure in phrasing them." Sam saw only a few friends, such as a long-lost, well-to-do St. Louis relative, James Ross Clemens, descendent of his father's financial savior many years before. He remained dispassionate even when false newspaper reports circulated around the world stating that Mark Twain's family had abandoned him, that he lived in a squalid apartment, that he was broke and broken.

But that indifference hid a rage that flashed when he contemplated Susy's death. Though he privately felt himself responsible for what had happened, he looked elsewhere for the motives that had led him to be so overbearing with Susy and obsessed with money. He blamed Charley Webster. "I am not able to think of him without cursing him," Sam apologized to Pamela in his unapologetic way, "& cursing the day that I opposed your better judgment of the lousy scoundrel & thief, & sided with Annie in her desire to marry him. The thought of that treacherous cur can wake me out of my sleep." He wrote his sister, "He was all dog. And he put me where I am, & Susy where she is."* To Rogers, Sam castigated as fools his former friends in Hartford, believing that if Susy "had had only *one* wise and courageous friend" there, "we should not have lost her." That anger, or his unwillingness to release it, kept the family from acknowledging anniversaries of any sort. The end of November 1896, usually a festive time with Thanksgiving and birthdays, passed without notice. Even Christmas "came and went without mention. No presents were exchanged, and we studiously pretended to be unaware of the day." Paired with this anger came relief, which Sam did not allow himself to feel too pointedly. In the days after Susy's death, he often remarked how fortunate Susy was and how horrible her life would have been "if she had lived & *remained* demented." He had already grown to regard death as a blessing: *A Pudd'nhead Wilson* maxim thanks Adam, "the first great benefactor of our race. He brought death into the world." Having watched Susy suffer throughout the last five years of her life, Sam now fervently hoped that death had released her from herself. Part of him looked forward to his own death as a release from the dreadful responsibility he accepted for his daughter's demise.

Meanwhile, he completed the first draft of his new book, which he spent the spring revising with Livy, whose inactivity worried him. Sam had his writing, he wrote to Joe Twichell, "but Livy! She has nothing in the world to turn to; nothing but housekeeping, and doing things for the children and me. She does not see people, and cannot; books have lost their interest for her." She had even refused a visit from her dear friend Alice Day, in England in the fall. Helping Sam rewrite his book gave her a purpose, as did annulling some of her husband's grand schemes. Fearful that the book might not pay his debts, he flirted with a new lecture format with high-priced tickets, up to $1,000 each. Livy vetoed the lucrative scheme, which would fly in the face of Mark Twain's popular appeal, the true source of his glory and his fortune. She declared to Sam "that if I can go on the platform again I must go in the old way and at the ordinary prices."* Major Pond came forward with an offer of $50,000 for 125 performances, but Sam and Livy turned it down, pleading poor health. Friends started a private fund for his benefit, but when the fund was made known through an editorial in the *New York Herald*, Henry Rogers, Charlie Langdon, and Frank Bliss joined Livy in pleading with Sam to "withdraw graciously." He was reluctant, having already agreed to "stand by it and not repudiate it," as he told Rogers, but the fund had not achieved any startling success.

Sympathy for Mark Twain increased dramatically when newspapers reported him close to death; Sam's newly rediscovered cousin James Clemens had fallen ill, and the similarity of their names and locations confused people. A reporter showed up in May at Tedworth Square with orders for five hundred words if Mark Twain were merely ill, but a thousand if dead. Sam replied that "the report of my death has been grossly exaggerated." Reprinted all over the world, this remark suddenly brought Mark Twain back into the public eye. Sam hurried to finish *Following the Equator*—published as *More Tramps Abroad* in England—in May 1897. In repayment for all Henry Rogers' favors, Sam dedicated the book to his teenage son Harry, "with recognition of what he is, and apprehension of what he may become unless he form himself a little more closely upon the model of the author."

Sam then voyaged back into fiction. Robert Louis Stevenson's *Dr. Jekyll and Mr. Hyde* impressed him, because he believed that it nearly perfectly represented human duality, a fictional replication of a complex human state. He felt he had achieved something close to that replication in his 1876 "Recent Carnival of Crime in Connecticut," in which the narrator's deformed conscience confronts him with his life of conventional lies and minor sins. The narrator, incensed, lulls his conscience into sleep and then kills him, freeing himself to commit greater and grander crimes and immoralities. Now Sam wanted to find exact replications of several other human states: the reality of one's dream world; the problem of scale in human life lived between the teeming microbes and the powerful cosmos; and human reactions to evil. These images were all dark ones, but Sam felt an obligation to Susy's memory to explore the darkness provoked in him by tragedy and advancing age. Honoring his daughter, he recorded his dreams and worked on and off on a philosophical dialogue, "What Is Man?" The purpose of the dialogue, between a wise old man and a clever young one, was to erect an impenetrable wall between human life and the supernatural, proving that people behaved as they did because of training, circumstance, and inborn traits, not because of gods and abstractions. Human beings did not have the transcendent power of self-determination, he argued; the pattern of thoughts that might appear as freedom of mind existed independent of will. For Sam Clemens in 1897, ideas and deities had no place in human existence, since people made no meaningful choices in their lives. Livy loathed this work and forbade its publication, and though Sam accepted Livy's judgment, he considered the dialogue his "Bible." Clarifying these ideas inspired Sam to hunt out the best human dilemmas to represent in fiction.

In the spring, the family decided to move to Vienna. Clara could study music seriously there. Also, Jean's blackouts had become more alarming and more frequent, and Vienna was a great center for medicine. An artistic capital, too, Vienna provided a visible stage on which Mark Twain could reenter public life. Once Livy recovered from minor surgery on her eyes in June, Sue Crane, Ernest Köppe, and Julia Langdon joined them for a summer in Switzerland. The family retired to Weggis, a village in the shadow of Rigi on Lake of Lucerne. Sam wrote most easily in summer, and pages piled up quickly as he worked on several books and stories at once. He relaxed by calculating his accounts, which took on an almost rosy glow. As the Langdon family fortunes improved, he wrote Pond that "the madam & I are well satisfied, now, that we shall have those debts paid off a year earlier than the prophecy" made in his manifesto two years before, and that he could accomplish this "*without any further help from the platform.*"* He had the money in hand to repay his debts now. "Dear me," he wrote Rogers at the end of the summer, "our wealth piles up faster under your handling of it than it did under my labors on the platform."

These financial reflections brought relief, but they did not bring Sam peace. He wrote a British friend, "There will never be an August day, perhaps, in which I shall be sane."* On August 18, 1897, Livy took a boat away from Weggis to a quiet spot and reread every letter Susy had sent her, letters that sounded, she told Alice Day, "much more like a lover's letters than like a daughter."* Sam spent the day writing "In Memoriam," a poem for Susy, in which he tried to accord his departed daughter posthumous fame by casting her as a temple, ignored by the world but cherished by those who recognized "that what seemed brass was gold;/What marble seemed, was ivory." Sam's and Livy's separate experiences brought no real healing.

The closest Sam got to peace came when the Jubilee Singers brought their spirituals on tour to Switzerland. He noted to Joe Twichell, "I think that in the Jubilees and their songs America has produced the perfectest flower of the ages; and I wish it were a foreign product, so that [America] would worship it and lavish money on it and go properly crazy over it." For six years now, Sam had made his principal headquarters overseas, and he had no definite idea how long he would reside in Vienna. Contrasting his financial assets with his emotional losses, he did not feel he would ever be able to call any place his home.

45 | A Jew in Vienna

Grief can take care of itself, but to get the full value of a joy you must have somebody to divide it with.
—"Pudd'nhead Wilson's New Calendar" (1897)

VIENNA PROVED A perfect relief from the cloister of Tedworth Square. In April 1897, the city installed a new mayor, Dr. Carl Lueger, a socialist whose election the emperor had twice previously disallowed, fearing Lueger's rabid followers. In his first few months in office, Lueger undertook a grand modernization of the city, laying conduits to distribute gas, electricity, and water to every home, but only part of his popularity rested on his vision of Vienna in the twentieth century. He appropriated the remainder from the fascists in the form of virulent anti-Semitism. In thirty years, urbanization had swelled the Jewish population of Vienna from a minuscule minority to approximately 10 percent; at least half the city furiously resented this incursion. Lueger's more liberal opponents were equally passionate in their defense of the empire's elaborate cultural fabric. The well-censored press divided themselves according to whether or not Jews wrote for them. There were even two press clubs, one for the anti-Semitic press and one for everyone else. Neither camp supported the fading Austro-Hungarian monarchy now held by the aging Emperor Franz Josef I. All factions jockeyed for position in the democracy likely to follow the collapse of the empire, and the Jewish question always ignited conflict.

Quickly embraced by "the Jewish press," as their opponents called it, in early October 1897 Mark Twain became a target for Jew-haters. Any mention of him would start a contentious blaze. Incited by Clemens' Old Testament first name, the anti-Semitic press attacked "*der Jude Mark Twain*," even while other papers ran welcoming interviews with him. This division grew more venomous as the months passed. The leading paper, *Neue Freie Presse*, owned and staffed by Jews, became almost a public rostrum for Sam, whose comings, goings, and quips they published glowingly. Sam befriended a number of Jewish journalists, such as Eduard Pötzl and Theodor Herzl, a prominent Zionist leader.

Sam reacted to the situation with excitement and did not hesitate to join the fight. A few weeks after arriving in Vienna, he wrote Joe Twichell, "If I had time to run around and talk, I would do it; for there is much politics agoing, and it would be interesting if a body could get the hang of it. It is Christian and Jew by the horns—the advantage with the superior man, as usual—the superior man being the Jew every time and in all countries. Land, Joe, what chance would the Christian have in a country where there were 3 Jews to 10 Christians!" Sam attended legislative sessions considering a minor rule change that would allow civil service workers in Czech-speaking parts of the empire to speak Czech. Though not connected to the Jewish question, a bill granting linguistic, and therefore cultural, respect to one of the empire's tribute regions became a referendum on the acceptance of Jews: Opponents of the Czech-language bill violently attacked Viennese Jews. In late October, Sam witnessed a legislator favoring the bill make a twelve-hour speech; a month later, he watched the Reichsrat's conservative leadership invite police into chambers to suppress a protest by other members of parliament. This action compromised the government's integrity, freeing the emperor to close the legislature. As portions of the city erupted in riots, Mark Twain explained the conflict in a long article for *Harper's*, "Stirring Times in Austria."

Taken under the wing of Countess Wydenbruck-Esterházy, the rich supporter and confidante of Vienna's artists, Sam moved easily in the most select liberal circles. The Viennese art community also thrummed with excitement. Gustav Mahler, recently made director of the capital's dominant opera company, attempted to introduce new music to the populace, fighting the emperor himself, who preferred marches and waltzes. Gustav Klimt led a phalanx of painters and sculptors shunning straightforwardly representational art. The avant-garde of the worlds of science and medicine were also located in Vienna, and drove forward with alarming and bewildering speed. Jan Szczepanik, a Polish inventor living in Vienna, had invented the first television, a primitive closed-circuit affair. Sigmund

Freud challenged the medical establishment, including his mentor Dr. Richard von Krafft-Ebing. Krafft-Ebing's best-selling *Psychopathia Sexualis* had intrigued Sam with its conclusion that homosexuality was an inherited disease of the nervous system. He consulted with Krafft-Ebing, perhaps about Susy's state of mind before her demise.

Sam craved a return to gadding about. "Clara and I had started into society, and were dining and lunching and going to operas, and were getting at times cheerful once more," Sam wrote Henry Rogers. Livy refused to socialize, and so Clara accompanied Sam until sad news came from America in early November: "We are all once more under a cloud, through the death of my brother, and have resumed our former seclusion." Orion's death—at his desk, pencil in hand—registered only a flicker in his sibling's emotional landscape. "It was unjust," Sam wrote Mollie in Keokuk, "that such a man, against whom no offense could be charged, should have been sentenced to live for 72 years." The household reacted more sadly to news that George Griffin, the Farmington Avenue butler, had died at about the same time. These passings made Sam anxious to erase his own recent past. "I throw up the sponge," he wrote Rogers just after his brother died. "I pull down the flag. Let us begin on those debts. I cannot bear the weight any longer."

Sam found a peer in Theodor Leschetizky, who was in many ways the reason the Clemenses had come to Vienna. Leschetizky was the city's foremost piano teacher and the man with whom Clara decided to study. Leschetizky led a piano-study pyramid, with more advanced and impecunious pupils teaching the more numerous beginners, such as Clara. As members of his inner social circle, Leschetizky included Sam and Clara in his weekly salons and in his invitations to the concerts of his most notable students. Leschy, as Sam called him, shared Sam's conversational excellence and habit of monopolizing the attention of a gathering; this similarity, along with his international repute, attracted Clara to him. Leschy also had a reputation for seducing his female students, having married four of them and divorced three. Sam joined Leschy's circle in part to guard Clara's honor. Finding twenty-three-year-old Clara a suitable mate was another goal of the Clemenses' social whirl. Sam dubbed the flurry of interested men who visited Clara at the Hotel Metropole "Delirium Clemens."

Jean, on the other hand, rarely went out. Seventeen when the family arrived in Vienna, she ought to have enjoyed her introduction to adult social life, but she remained childlike and reserved. Her health also contributed to the family's decision to live in Vienna. She had already suffered many serious seizures; her spells of fainting, abstraction, and vomiting increased in frequency. Jean's condition excluded her from Sam's social life. The Countess Wydenbruck-Esterházy rescued the Clemenses by giving responsibility for watching over Jean to her sophisticated thirteen-year-old daughter Clementine. Within weeks of their arrival in Vienna, Sam and Livy consulted several physicians about Jean. They kept the diagnosis of epilepsy a secret from Jean herself.

By January 1898, Henry Rogers had paid out most of the sums due Webster and Company's creditors. *Following the Equator* quickly sold thirty thousand copies and received almost uniformly positive reviews, many more sympathetic to the personal travails of Sam Clemens' life than to the limp narrative of Mark Twain's book. Papers around the globe repeated the news of the repayment, which furthered the sale of *Following the Equator*, but the success of the book made Sam wonder at the inherent falsehood of writing, especially as Mark Twain. "All the heart I had was in Susy's grave and the Webster debts. And so, behold a miracle!" he observed to Rogers, "a book which does not give its writer away." Sam's dismay at his failure to disentangle Mark Twain's persona and his own disappeared in his immense relief at the end of debt. Livy's happiness was greater. "Mrs. Clemens has been reading the creditors' letters over and over again," Sam bubbled to Rogers, "and thanks you deeply for sending them, and says this is the only really happy day she has had since Susy died." The book not only put Sam back in the black, but gave Rogers some working capital to invest on Sam's behalf, which he did with a financial insider's success.

Sam, renewed, returned to work, which he claimed to Howells he did every day for long hours. "I couldn't get along without work now. I bury myself in it up to the ears." Still, he found it more difficult to write satisfying prose, "because of the deadness which invaded me when Susy died. But I have made a change lately—into dramatic work." Sam was befriending theater people in Vienna, collaborating with playwrights successful on the Austrian stage and translating their work. Though sensationally busy with the recent success of *Dracula*, Bram Stoker agreed to serve as his agent in London. Sam told Henry Rogers, "Work is become a pleasure again—it is not labor, any longer." This news brought joy to Rogers, who saw his contributions to Sam's welfare as not only helping a needy friend, but also restoring Mark Twain to the world. By mid-March 1898, Sam had a number of short stories and plays on their way to New York for Rogers to sell. "Be patient, don't get uneasy—" Sam cautioned his friend, "I am hunting up all the work for you that I can think of."

Sam quickly got involved in new projects that would keep Rogers busy. Hearing about an invention by Jan Szczepanik that applied photography to jacquard weaving enabling a loom to weave any image one chose, Sam purchased an option on its American rights. Immediately after, a man representing American carpet interests arrived on a mission to obtain those rights. Meeting with the American several times, Sam noted that he "was afraid he would offer me half a million dollars for [the rights]. I should have been obliged to take it." Sam saved this opportunity for Henry Rogers, who dispatched researchers to look into the market for the invention, which proved disappointing. Sam let his option slip, but soon grew excited by another invention represented by Szczepanik's backer: the manufacture of cloth out of peat.

The Clemenses decided to spend the summer at the fashionable health resort of Kaltenleutgeben, and by the end of May they were comfortably installed in a house there. Both Jean and Livy engaged in the strenuous local cure of early rising, plunging into cold water, followed by calisthenics and another plunge, all before breakfast. Clara decided in June to give up the piano for a career as a singer, imitating her sister's ambitions. Sam and Livy preferred Clara's unpredictability to Jean's contrariness. Sam and Livy disagreed on whether Jean's personality resulted from her disease or from her essential self. Livy was the more forgiving of the couple.

Having engaged the house through the end of October, Sam had a remarkably long season for work. Once he had become fluent enough in German to participate in the aesthetic arguments bandied about the cafés, his work took on an experimental flair in keeping with Viennese currents. He felt uncertain whether he could produce anything for print; as he noted to Henry Rogers, "A literary reputation is a most frail thing—any trifling accident can kill it; and its market along with it." Retiring his well-honed skills as a storyteller and caricaturist, he attempted a new style: impressionistic parable. He reworked his mysterious stranger story, in which a supernatural figure demonstrates some unpleasant eternal truths to a collection of village boys; in one new version, he named a villainous priest Father Lueger, after the anti-Semitic mayor. He also wrote several dream stories in which the dream life takes on unnatural power and reality. In one, a dozing man dreams that his life turns from glory to disaster and wakes moments later a physical and emotional wreck. In another, Sam's varied dreams of love with "My Platonic Sweetheart," Laura Wright, always end abruptly in her violent death. He explained to Howells that writing for him meant finding the way to tell a story so that "the thing slide[s] effortless from the pen—the one right way, the sole form for *you*, the other forms being for men whose *line* those forms are." Sam did not acknowledge that this formal experimentation with his creativity gambled with both his reputation and his market.

Over the summer, Sam allowed the modest Hotel Metropole and the new and lavish Hotel Krantz to bid against one another over his patronage, and so obtained finer accommodations at a trifle higher cost. The Krantz even featured a portrait of Mark Twain in its lobby and "said our being in the house would be the best advertisement they could have." Sam explained the increased expense to Rogers, "I used to be a little ashamed when Ambassadors and dukes and such called on us in that rusty and rather shabby Metropole, but they'll mistake us for millionaires next fall and will probably lend us money."

On his tour around the world, and now in Vienna, Mark Twain had become an at-large American ambassador, representing the American people, their ideas and their culture to a civilization tempted to view occupants of the New World as simple hicks. Sam had regained a measure of pride in his invented self, signing one hotel guest register, "S. L. Clemens, Profession, Mark Twain." Back home, Howells informed him, Mark Twain remained as famous as ever. "You have pervaded your century almost more than any other man of letters, if not quite more; and it is astonishing how you keep spreading." Sam soon found himself in a diplomatic bind when America embarrassed itself in front of Europe by declaring war on Spain, supposedly over Cuban freedom, but in fact to acquire coaling stations, as Howells had acutely observed. Sam deftly managed to support his country without supporting its war, but not everyone saw him as a beneficent force. Stephen Crane, then an ambitious young reporter on his way to cover the end of the Greco-Turkish War, filed a column characterizing Mark Twain as a Viennese "society clown."

Sam took Mark Twain's political efforts more seriously than Crane seemed willing to believe. Sam's failed attempt to translate Theodor Herzl's play *Das Neue Ghetto*, which portrayed the complex social relationships of an assimilated Jew, moved Sam to write "Concerning the Jews," an essay expressing both the solidarity and separateness he felt regarding the tribe to which so many Viennese assumed he belonged. Sam also took a role in the growing international peace movement, headquartered in Vienna. He remarked to an Austrian countess leading the local effort that, although protest would not lead international powers to reduce their armories, this failure would have a positive effect because "even the ignorant & the simple would then discover that the armaments were not created chiefly for the protection of the nations but for their enslavement." In the fall of 1898, Czar Nicholas II of Russia called for a disarmament conference and later offered to disarm, if others would. Although Sam issued a Twainian gibe saying that he too would personally disarm, he privately regarded this as diplomatic foolishness. Never a blind supporter of simple disarmament, he presciently believed that a balance of terror would more successfully promote peace. He put his hope in the eccentric inventor Nikola Tesla, who had already begun work on a massive weapon "against which fleets & armies would be helpless, & thus make war thenceforth impossible."

In addition to meddling with grand matters of state, Sam flirted with the idea of putting himself in debt again by mortgaging the Hartford house, both to buy stock in one of Henry Rogers' lucrative companies and to build a fire under himself to write another book. "I shall never write the Autobiography till I'm in a hole," he wrote Rogers in November, after moving back to Vienna. "It is best for me to *be* in a hole sometimes, I reckon." Sam expressed his ambivalence about money in "The Man That Corrupted Hadleyburg," a story in which a stranger promises a bag of money to the unidentified person who had helped him years before; the rightful owner could claim the prize by identifying the kind words he had spoken to him. Greed corrupts Hadleyburg, prompting honest people to lie, generous people to hoard, and kind people to demean their neighbors.

Avid for money himself, Sam did not object to Henry Rogers' pooling Sam's assets into his own massive stock manipulations, efforts that tripled Sam's money in a few months. "Why, it is just splendid!" Sam wrote in response to the report that Sam's new investments were worth over $50,000. "I have nothing to do but sit around and watch you set the hen and hatch out those big broods and make my living for me. Don't you wish you had somebody to do the same for you?" Comically comparing his guardian's calling with his own, Sam concluded that "literature is well enough, as a time-passer, and for the improvement and general elevation and purification of mankind, but it has no practical value."

After an early-spring visit to Budapest and the surrounding Hungarian countryside, the Clemenses began to turn their eyes toward America. It seemed possible, at last, that they would have enough money to live in a congenial flat in New York City. Although they first thought they would spend another summer in Austria, they decided in the end to go to England before heading home. Blanche Marchesi, the daughter of Susy's Parisian voice teacher, had set up shop in London using her mother's methods and Clara wanted to work with her. Jean's epilepsy had not responded to any Viennese treatment, but in London, Dr. Jonas Henrik Kellgren's Swedish Movements Cure seemed to promise excellent results with that malady. And, flush with cash he wanted to gamble, Sam also coveted the American and British rights to a new German health food called Plasmon, derived from skim milk. At the end of May 1899, Mark Twain gave his parting interviews to a divided, though mostly adoring Austria, where he had been more of a cultural figure than a temporary guest. After delaying their departure so that Sam could have a brief meeting with Emperor Franz Josef I—the only distinguished person in Vienna he had failed to encounter already—the Clemens family left for England.

In Search of Health

There is nothing in the world like a persuasive speech to fuddle the mental apparatus and upset the convictions and debauch the emotions of an audience not practiced in the tricks and delusions of oratory.
—"The Man That Corrupted Hadleyburg" (1899)

E NGLAND SEEMED LIKE a different place to Sam after having spent two years on the Continent. The wound caused by Susy's death, while not fully healed, had begun to close over. Sam's apprehension about money had quieted; Livy could accept invitations without fear that she would not have the means to reciprocate. Most important, as Sam told Howells, his "dread of leaving the children in difficult circumstances has died down & disappeared & I am now having peace from that long, long nightmare, & can sleep as well as any one." Livy calculated that, apart from the more than $100,000 the family had stashed away, Mark Twain's copyrights alone produced an annual income equal to the interest on $200,000. "I have been out & bought a box of 6-cent cigars," Sam concluded to Howells; "I was smoking 4½ before." The money at last freed him from writing for an audience. "At last I can afford it, & have put the pot-boiler pen away. What I have been wanting was a chance to write a book without reserves—a book which should take account of no one's feelings, no one's prejudices, opinions, beliefs, hopes, illusions, delusions; a book which should say my say, right out of my heart, in the plainest language & without a limitation of any sort." He was working on another version of the supernatural stranger's visit to Earth.

The Clemens clan engaged in London life typical for the wholly re-constituted Mark Twain. Clara began voice lessons and Sam went to luncheons, dinners, speeches, and other gatherings. Livy participated more in his public life now than she had at any time since Susy's death. Leaving a luncheon one day in early July, Sam went to pick up his hat and found only one remaining; it belonged to Canon Basil Wilberforce, of Westminster. At his hotel Sam wrote to the divine that, try as he might, he couldn't lie, steal, or behave improperly since wearing this hat. He asked Canon Wilberforce, "Have you developed any novelties of conduct . . . of a character to move the concern of your friends?" But even before receiving Sam's note, Wilberforce had written that he had "been conscious of a vivacity and facility of expression this afternoon beyond the normal and I have just discovered the reason!!" This comic demonstration of mental telepathy delighted Sam.

Only Jean's problem stood in the way of his full participation in society. Dr. Kellgren believed he could help Jean, now almost nineteen, at his clinic in Sanna, Sweden. Because of this, within six weeks of their arrival in London, the family encountered a crisis. Clara had no desire to go to Sweden, but Livy refused to allow the family to be separated. Clara's music teacher resolved the conflict by giving Clara the same advice her mother had given Susy: Gain strength first, and then begin training. Unwilling to capitulate to the family entirely, Clara lingered awhile in London before joining her parents and sister in Sweden.

Located on a lake, miles from any town, the sanitarium did not impress Sam at first. He wrote Clara that he regarded it as hell and the cure as " 'treatment' for the damned." After two weeks under Kellgren's care, however, Jean suffered only infrequent spells and quit the daily doses of bromide that she took to counteract her absentmindedness. Even Sam and Livy undertook Kellgren's regimen, which consisted of a sound diet, fresh air, and a program of daily manipulations of the joints. "Every day," he crowed to a friend, "in 15 minutes it takes all the old age out of you and sends you forth feeling like a bottle of champagne that's just been uncorked." Despite the early success, Kellgren's prognosis for Jean was cautious. By September, Sam had hope enough to remark to Rogers that "an outsider would think Jean is already cured. Her health has blossomed out in the most extraordinary way." By October, the miraculous cures Sam saw at the Swedish sanitarium convinced him that Kellgren had unlocked the secret to health.

The family took a small apartment in a part of London near Kellgren's winter clinic. Sam returned to civilization in time to enjoy the storm over Mark Twain's *Cosmopolitan* article lambasting Christian Science and its founder Mary Baker Eddy. Though Sam believed in the intersection of health and faith, primed by Susy's wholesale surrender to Mental Science, he saw Mary Baker Eddy's manifestation of the practice as a sham and regarded the Church of Christ Scientist as nothing but a shill. His savage attack prompted converts and opponents to write vehement letters to the magazine. *Cosmopolitan*'s editor responded by giving Sam an extra $200 for the article, but he gratified him even more with the comment "It seems to me that you have knocked Christian Science in this country flat." Sam's charge against the religion also impugned some of his contemporaries, like Charles Dudley Warner, who were swept away by their enthusiasm. He took a special pleasure in the controversy now that he had discovered health's true church in Dr. Kellgren's treatments. Sam believed in the Swedish physician's ability to tame epilepsy; he thought he could cure anything not requiring surgery. Kellgren had virtually brought back from the dead Sam's friend, American journalist Poultney Bigelow. Henry Stanley seemed near death when Sam sent Kellgren to his aid.

The long stay in Scandinavia had deprived Sam of a dozen pleasant visitors to England. Though he had seen Rudyard Kipling, he missed Joe Twichell, "Uncle Larry" Hutton, and Henry Rogers' young son Harry, to whom Sam had dedicated *Following the Equator*. Even without them, London still had plenty of enchantment for him, and he met and dined with most of society that appealed to him. He again allowed his social life to interfere with writing, reducing his output to only political essays during the fall and early winter. The war for South Africa occupied the news. England's success now seemed assured, but this knowledge embittered Sam, who regarded the entire sordid enterprise as a commercial incursion on behalf of that British exploiter of Africa, Cecil Rhodes, but using real bullets and expending real lives. He defended the English only because British civilization "is better than *real* savagery, therefore we must stand by it, extend it, & (in public) praise it . . . , for her defeat & fall would be an irremediable disaster for the mangy human race."

Sam could not muster even such deeply qualified support for the United States' war against the Philippines, over which the States sought to extend dominion. He regarded it as even more suspect than America's earlier campaign against Spain. Concluding that American aggression would do nothing for the islanders, Sam wrote Twichell that "the war out there has no interest for me," but it soon interested him enough to protest actively against it. These wars gave Sam further evidence of the worthlessness of humanity. "Why *was* the human race created?" he asked

Howells in one of his first letters in the new century. "Or at least why wasn't something creditable created in place of it. God had His opportunity; He could have made a reputation. But no, He must commit this grotesque folly."

Despite his diminished production, publishing still grabbed Sam's attention. The Harper brothers had ridden their company into a huge financial hole, and its uncertain future provided publisher S. S. McClure an opportunity to rope Mark Twain in as editor of a new magazine at generous terms for very little work. Sam would receive ample pay and partial ownership of the journal for merely approving work selected by others, an offer McClure made because he wanted Mark Twain's books for the Doubleday and McClure Company. During the first several months of 1900, the men wrote long letters back and forth planning the new magazine, but soon McClure called on Mark Twain for more and more work, and Sam had to drop out. The magazine promised a splashy and lucrative way to return to his homeland, which Sam missed severely. "Why, hang it, we haven't seen a home-face for generations," he wrote Laurence Hutton, near whose house in Princeton, New Jersey, he considered living. "I suppose Mr. Rogers is old and fat and wearing a wig, now." He wrote Rogers himself in January 1900 that "I am strongly hoping we may get home the middle of May."

Much as they all desired a return to America, Jean's health came first. Only in Europe had she found any successful treatment. Sometime in the spring, Sam learned that osteopathy, though the poor sister of standard medicine as it was practiced in the United States, shared many characteristics with Kellgren's Swedish Movements Cure. Could they cure Jean at home? It seemed impossible to get reliable answers, since traditionally trained physicians regarded Kellgren and his American osteopathic cohorts as simple quacks.

Pursuing health beyond the norms, Sam believed in Plasmon, the inexpensive dietary substitute, enough to add it to both his own and his family's diet. Sam had tried to buy into the invention when he first found out about it in Vienna, but had failed; now, with his assets spiraling, he risked $25,000 on a syndicate owning the rights outside of Germany. "The pound of powder," Sam wrote Rogers, trying to gain his interest in the project, "contains the nutriment of 16 pounds of the best beef, and will do the same nourishing that the 16 pounds would do, besides being no trouble to digest." Even before capitalizing the company, the backers succeeded in getting the product into hospitals and the British Army in South Africa used it free of charge. Lord Rothschild's Exploration Company promised to capitalize the firm with over $1 million. Knowing the value of having Mark Twain's endorsement, the company guaranteed his investment. Feeling a bit more secure in his speculation this time, Sam promised to help introduce the product to the United States.

In May, Jean turned a corner in her cure. Originally intending to follow Kellgren back to Sweden for the summer, the Clemenses now determined to stay in London. They could have gone home, but they remained undecided about where home would be after so long. Sam's sixty-fifth birthday lay just ahead and he felt the nearness of death. Before, death had seemed a wished-for release, and theoretically he desired it. Practically, however, he abhorred it, and his devotion to the temple of health—built of Plasmon, overseen by Kellgren—proved his determination to live well and long.

He felt less certain about his identity. Nearly ten years had passed since he had lived as Mark Twain at home, except for the brief first leg of the world tour. Planning to reclaim that identity, he protected it from poachers. When an unrelated man named Clemens capitalized on it with a book about Mark Twain, Sam declared to him, "A man's history is his own property until the grave extinguishes his ownership in it. I am strenuously opposed to having books of a biographical character published about me while I am still alive." Mark Twain had already published all he intended to about himself while he lived, in an essay in the last volume of the Uniform Edition, composed by Sam, edited by his nephew Sam Moffett, and published over Moffett's signature.

The Clemenses moved to Dollis Hill for the summer of 1900. This farmhouse, just outside of London proper, had been Prime Minister William Gladstone's favorite retreat. Amid acres of fields, meadows, and sheep, Sam found it easy to work. "I am the only person who is ever in the house in the daytime," he wrote Twichell. "Livy is all so enchanted with the place & so in love with it that she doesn't know how she is going to tear herself away from it." For all the seeming isolation, the center of London lay just twenty minutes away, and Clara and Jean ran into town frequently on their errands of music and health, while Sam and Livy received frequent visitors. As the summer drew to a close, Sam wrote that "Dollis Hill comes nearer to being a paradise than any other home I ever occupied." This sentiment came after the fourth anniversary of Susy's death, and the realization of how impossible that event had made a return to the house on Farmington Avenue in Hartford. He wrote to Twichell on the anniversary—which like birthdays and holidays still went by without family recognition—"Sometimes it is a century; sometimes it was yesterday."

The Clemenses sailed for America on October 6, 1900.

47 | The Sage Returns

Nothing so needs reforming as other people's habits.
—"Pudd'nhead Wilson's Calendar" (1894)

*The radical invents the views. When he has worn them
out the conservative adopts them.*
—Notebook (1906)

MARK TWAIN'S TRIUMPHANT return home in-
itiated a frenzy of newspaper coverage that exceeded even
the press explosion in Vienna. The frequent photos of him
made his wild halo of hair and his full mustache, both gone completely
white, into an icon of literary lionhood. Reporters often complemented
the pictures with comments on how energetic and almost athletic Mark
Twain looked for a man nearly sixty-five years old. Mark Twain, they
wrote, had repaid his debts and returned to his native land healthy and
affluent. Most Americans had suffered under the economic convulsions of
1893 and 1897, but the new century's dawn brought hope for financial
sanity. Mark Twain's return to solvency symbolized a national determination for prosperity. Journals marked the victory with editorials praising
him as "The Hero as Man of Letters." Noting this new infusion of glory,
William Dean Howells wrote Thomas Bailey Aldrich that Sam looked
"younger and jollier than I've seen him for ten years. He says it is all
Plasmon, a new German food-drug he's been taking, but I think it's partly
prosperity. He has distinctly the air of a man who has unloaded."

Sam sensed the national anticipation of his return, and the Mark
Twain who descended the gangplank in New York Harbor bore small

resemblance to the retiring writer he had tried to be in London. This new Mark Twain stepped forward boldly as the embodiment of American virtue. In his first statement after disembarking, Twain criticized American expansion into the Philippines, the direct result of the war with Spain, the islands' prior colonial master. Within weeks of his return, he had become the most recognizable anti-imperialist voice in the country. Avoiding the maelstrom of 1900 presidential politics, except on the comical platform, expressed in newspaper statements, of being in favor of everything, Mark Twain's position against the war in the Pacific coincided with a tenet of William Jennings Bryan's campaign to unseat William McKinley as President. Though McKinley won, he did not do so as handily as most expected. Keeping any taint of party allegiance out of his comments, Mark Twain allowed his presence during the final month of the campaign to enhance public support for Bryan.

The Clemenses settled into a Manhattan hotel and searched for a house to rent. Henry Rogers' investments had put them on firm enough footing to step up from the flat they had envisioned themselves occupying, but they still could not afford to live on the scale they had enjoyed in Hartford. The place's association with Susy's death put Hartford out of contention in any case, as did its distance from the center of American culture. The sudden death of Charles Dudley Warner a few days after Sam's arrival in New York symbolized the end of the Nook Farm life that had originally attracted Sam to Connecticut. While serving as a pallbearer for his old friend in Hartford, Sam looked into 351 Farmington Avenue. Afterward, he remarked to a friend, "I realized that if we ever enter the house again to live our hearts will break. I am not sure that we shall ever be strong enough to endure that strain." Livy stayed in New York; she could not face her Hartford memories.

Despite the appearance of renewed vitality, Sam recognized the hidden fractures in his family. They still did not celebrate birthdays or holidays. Clara, now twenty-six, shared neither her parents' morals nor their belief in their authority over her life. Jean, under the care of a New York osteopath, had improved somewhat, but she still suffered epileptic seizures every six weeks or so. Livy's uneven health remained the primary focus of the family, as it had been when they sailed to Europe nearly a decade before. Recognizing that Sam's objections to Livy's easy Christianity had long ago deprived her of a faith that sustained her health, they pursued a mutually agreeable spirituality by attending occult séances, a practice that had gained greater social acceptance during the previous decade. They especially visited mediums who promised to put them in contact with Susy. The couple also held out hope in the predictions of the renowned palm reader who had told Sam twice over the past five years that he would be rich, at last, at age sixty-eight, three years hence.

The family rented a brownstone just off Fifth Avenue in Manhattan, on West Tenth Street, only a few blocks from where the Howellses lived. The stoop was the gathering spot for neighborhood boys, which Sam appreciated but Livy detested. Since Mark Twain made good newspaper copy, reporters frequently dropped by to ask for a quick quote from Mark Twain, which they typically enlarged into an in-depth interview, a feat Sam regarded as "a miracle equal to the loaves and fishes." Clara would later note, "It always puzzled me how Mark Twain could manage to have an opinion on every incident, accident, invention, or disease in the world." She knew that her father encouraged this manic level of activity: "Every day was like some great festive occasion. One felt that a large party was going on and that by and by the guests would be leaving. But there was no leaving. More and more came." People not only showed up at the house, but Sam also went out to dinners, banquets, and luncheons several days a week. Invitations for Mark Twain to speak flooded Tenth Street every day. Answering the telephone left the butler little time for butler-ing, except when the dependable Katy Leary relieved him.

Sam cultivated Mark Twain's notoriety, right down to the tabloid level. Once, when Katy took a cab home from Grand Central Station, the driver ignored her complaints as he rode her all over town and charged her seven dollars. She took the bill to Sam, who called the man inside. Most cabdrivers ignored city regulations and extorted their customers, so Sam paid only what the fare should rightfully have been, and then gave the cabman a generous tip. As the driver left, however, he muttered, "The damned old fool!" Sam took the man's name and filed a complaint. Grandly pursuing this trivial matter through the courts, Sam pointed out that public good in a democracy depended on the daily practice of citizenship. The publicity surrounding Mark Twain's intervention brought more jus-tice to the business of setting cab fares than any regulations did. The cabman lost his license, but a few weeks later successfully applied to Mark Twain for help in getting it back. The man had served the cause, albeit reluctantly, and Sam was happy for the extra attention he received now for having rehabilitated him.

Challenging extortionate cabdrivers was easy work compared with opposing American imperialism. Anti-imperialism was a radical position, even for Mark Twain, whose politics had always been more progressive than Sam Clemens'. But Sam's experience overseas, especially in South Africa and in Vienna, had radicalized him. In 1898, French writer Émile Zola had taken a courageous stand against the anti-Semitic underpinnings in the espionage trial of Captain Alfred Dreyfus. Sam admired Zola's actions and emulated him in objecting to a political practice that he found entirely unjustifiable. Sam found himself nearly alone in this battle against colonialism; pacifism, not justice, fueled most people's objections to American action in the Pacific. Not only did the government have widespread support for its attempt to dominate the Philippines, but the leadership of the anti-imperialist movement seemed scattered and uncertain. Sam wrote what he titled "A salutation-speech from the Nineteenth Century to the Twentieth, taken down in short-hand by Mark Twain," for use at a series of anti-imperialist Red Cross meetings, but when he could not find out who else was contributing to the meetings, he withdrew the salutation, passing it on instead to the Anti-Imperialist League, which printed it on small cards. It read:

> I bring you the stately maiden called CHRISTENDOM—returning bedraggled, besmirched and dishonored from pirate raids in Kiaochow, Manchuria, South Africa and the Philippines; with her soul full of meanness, her pocket full of boodle and her mouth full of pious hypocrisies. Give her soap and a towel, but hide the looking-glass.

Newspapers across the country republished this indictment, which polarized passions on either side of the issue. Even Joe Twichell, who worried that this unpopular stand would affect Mark Twain's fame, joined the patriotic fervor against his friend's broadside. Sam replied to Twichell, "This nation is like all the others that have been spewed upon the earth—ready to shout for any cause that will tickle its vanity or fill its pocket. What a hell of a heaven it will be, when they get all these hypocrites assembled there!" He pointedly asked his friend, "How do you answer for it to your conscience?"

Sam sought out controversies that would show Mark Twain's moral fiber. Most anti-imperialists, even the pacifistic William Dean Howells, refused to sit on the reception committee for acclaimed, but jingoistic, reporter Winston Churchill, who came to New York to speak about the British efforts to subdue the Boers and dominate South Africa. Sam not only accepted a position on the committee, but also agreed to introduce Churchill, in his own way. "Mr. Churchill and I do not agree on the righteousness of the South African War," he began. "I think that England sinned in getting into a war in South Africa which she could have avoided without loss of credit or dignity—just as I think we have sinned in crowding ourselves into a war in the Philippines on the same terms." It proved nearly impossible to maintain the level of geniality Sam regarded as vital to Mark Twain's popularity while at the same time presenting his unvarnished political ideas.

Not all his speeches required political pronouncements, but the speechmaking and banqueting ran down his health so severely that he suffered three attacks of gout before he at last gave in and withdrew from the social fray. By winter, he accepted fewer engagements, showed up after the food had been served, and left after his speech. Only this conservation of energy got him back to his desk. "I have ended my holiday at last," he wrote, declining an invitation from Columbia professor Brander Matthews, "and put on my overalls and devoted myself to a long and steady siege of work. My work-day stretches from 11:30 a.m. till 7 p.m., and so my lunching days are over." That January, Livy attended Clara's concert debut in Washington, but Sam stayed in New York, socializing with Howells, Rogers, and Rogers' friend "Czar" Tom Reed, the recently retired Speaker of the House of Representatives, with whom Sam particularly enjoyed "billiardizing."

Reducing his public appearances did not induce him to reduce Mark Twain's presence in public debate, however. He completed "To the Person Sitting in Darkness," his first extended piece since arriving home. This critique of both military and cultural imperialism maintained that the responsibilities of nations to the world were identical to responsibilities of individuals to a society, as exemplified by Mark Twain's behavior in the case of the greedy cabman. This indictment of what he called the Blessings-of-Civilization Trust—an unholy alliance of profiteers and Christian missionaries—raised another public storm when it was published in the February 1901 issue of the elite *North American Review*. Publishing this essay then and there hedged Sam's gamble with Mark Twain's public: That issue of the *North American Review* also included an anti-imperialist statement by former President Benjamin Harrison, as well as an essay by William Dean Howells praising Mark Twain for his "comic force" and "ethic sense." Twain's recently published collection of short pieces, *"The Man That Corrupted Hadleyburg" and Other Stories and Essays*, moved other reviewers to concur with Howells in their reconsideration of Mark Twain as a philosopher. Andrew Carnegie thought so highly of "To the Person Sitting in Darkness" that he republished it at his own expense as a pamphlet for free distribution by the Anti-Imperialist League. Sam was a vice president of the organization, always willing to have his name on the board of any group he supported, as long as it expected no work from him.

Sam's retirement from the public field had as much to do with an internal conflict as with his health or his desire for quieter company. He engaged himself in crusade after crusade in part to solidify the image of Mark Twain as a cultural and moral force, but that effort contradicted his belief in the utter absence of free will, which he had developed in his "gospel" "What Is Man?" Why should someone try to change the world, at a high personal cost, when the progress of human events was subject to the more or less mechanical movements of history, and not the efforts of individuals? Though Sam could argue that Mark Twain's role as public moralist was part of this automatic working out of historical forces, the truth was that he had made a conscious effort to enter public debate on American expansionism, and that his contribution had an effect. These facts opened some difficult questions regarding his "gospel." Though this paradox did not immobilize him—he enjoyed skinning missionaries too much to stop—it introduced doubt into public actions, which required unwavering conviction to have their best effect.

By spring 1901, Sam and Livy had decided to take a small cabin in Ampersand, New York, on Upper Saranac Lake in the Adirondacks. Clara planned to stay behind in New York for much of the summer, studying music and enjoying the company of Ossip Gabrilowitsch, a star student of Leschetizky and Clara's favorite Viennese beau. Jean, always a child of nature, remained with her parents. Livy would rest and Sam would write. Without the pressure of having to feed the press gag lines, Sam could concentrate his efforts on more sustained and imaginative work.

48 | *Famous on His Own Terms*

*Good friends, good books and a sleepy conscience: this is
the ideal life.*
—Notebook (1906)

*There are no grades of vanity, there are only grades of
ability in concealing it.*
—Notebook (1906)

T HE CLEMENSES' CABIN on Upper Saranac Lake
had several large porches overhanging the lake itself, and
the foliage crowded in so close that the squirrels regarded
the house as another tree, running back and forth by the rustic table
where the family dined alfresco. Sam named one squirrel Blennerhassett,
for the Missouri lawyer who in 1849 was responsible for explicit love
letters being read into a murder trial transcript, the incursion of the wild
into polite society. Only rare and intrepid visitors interrupted the familial
solitude. Nothing impelled Sam to vary his preferred schedule of a light
breakfast, solid work until evening, a meal with the family, and games or
reading together until bed. He left the lake only once, for the first few
weeks in August, to cruise off the coast of Maine with Henry Rogers and
some cronies on Rogers' fast new two-hundred-foot yacht, the *Kanawha*.
The trip distanced him from Livy on the fifth anniversary of Susy's death,
which remained with them a "sacred subject." He wrote her, "I am with
you in spirit every hour, now, & I know how you are feeling as these sad
anniversaries dawn & drag their course & decay." He told Rogers the
cruise was "the most contenting and comfortable and satisfactory pleasure-
excursion I have ever made."

During the summer, he generated several new essays and reworked stories that had given him trouble for years. Still dwelling on the Faustian implications of his rise in fortune, he recast his "mysterious stranger" story yet again, moving it from the Mississippi River town of Huck and Tom to Austria just after the invention of movable type. In this version, the visitor has no name, only a number, and his only satanic quality is his association with typesetting—the original printer's devil. In another story, "A Double-Barreled Detective Story," a wild send-up of the genre, he let his imagination run amok. He also wrote a rambling tale that put some arguments from his personal gospel into the mouth of a frivolous dilettante, a device that, by mocking his own ideology, distanced him from his own deterministic philosophy whose principles he found impossible to follow.

Sam's difficulty in concluding most of the fiction he began spread into even his most cogent ideas for nonfiction. Reports of a spate of lynchings in the South made him want to publish an encyclopedia of American lynching. He wrote Frank Bliss about getting out a book on the subject for the subscription trade and even penned the introduction, "The United States of Lyncherdom," but, recognizing that the introduction alone would destroy his southern market, the businessman in him soon intervened against the moralist. "I shouldn't have even half a friend left down there, after it issued from the press," he wrote Bliss. Ashamed of this weakness of will, he wrote an essay remembering the woodpile sermons of "a gay and impudent and satirical and delightful young black man—a slave" on his uncle's Missouri farm, who had as his primary text, "You tell me whar a man gits his corn-pone, en I'll tell you what his 'pinions is." He did not publish this piece, either.

Contemplating the September 1901 assassination of President McKinley by an anarchist of questionable sanity, Sam noted to Joe Twichell, "No one is sane, straight along, year in and year out, and we all know it. Our insanities are of varying sorts, and express themselves in varying forms—fortunately harmless forms as a rule." Making an unverifiable allusion to his sudden departure from Hannibal at age seventeen, he claimed that he "bought a revolver once and travelled twelve hundred miles to kill a man. He was away." Just after the President's death, Sam felt like taking up a pistol again, against a publisher. The American Publishing Company had farmed out its rights to market sets of Mark Twain's work to the R. G. Newbegin Company. One Newbegin subagent had bought five hundred sets and then sent out a direct-market appeal with envelopes marked "S. L. Clemens, U.S.A." as the return address, creating the appearance that Sam himself had asked people to buy his books. Further, the Newbegin set represented only part of the complete works, a marketing strategy specifically prohibited by the agreement between Harper and Brothers and the American Publishing Company. Sam found himself where he had been five years before, his books divided between uncooperative publishers. Both publishers soon offered competing sets of selected works, and Sam wanted to do violence to someone.

The family visited Elmira for a week at the end of the summer and then moved, not to New York City, but to Riverdale, half an hour up the Hudson by train, where they rented a furnished mansion a dozen miles north of the city's frantic pace. The city agitated Jean, and Livy's health had declined during the months on Tenth Street. Infrequent trains from Riverdale both made Clara's freedom inconvenient and gave Sam the perfect excuse to decline any invitation he did not strictly want to accept. Without Livy's knowledge, Sam told his old Hartford agent Franklin Whitmore to put the Hartford house on the market. Since Susy's death, and especially for most of the preceding year, Sam and Livy had seldom entertained as a couple or even gone out together. Sam felt younger and more energetic than he had in years; Livy, a decade his junior, felt considerably older. The once-loving couple suffered a growing disaffection, an alienation traceable to their differing means of handling the loss of Susy. This schism led Sam to imagine a story about the "Divorce of the McWilliamses"—Sam's fictional version of his family—which he intended to blame not on grief but on jealousy "on account of his dream-wife." The united family that had occupied the mansion at Nook Farm tore itself apart under Sam's overweening paternalism. When he resurrected Mark Twain as a moralist, he also demoralized his own family by turning his dinner-table performances into something more like sermons and less like stories.

The distance from the city did not keep Sam out of it. In fact, New York's mayoral election in the fall of 1901 consumed him. For the first time in decades, it seemed possible that voters would break Tammany Hall's hold on city politics. Sam campaigned actively and effectively on behalf of the reformers. When Tammany boss Richard Croker lost, Sam forthrightly took credit for the defeat. Nor did Sam limit his efforts to government reform or his speaking engagements to politics. He supported an array of groups helping recent immigrants, particularly Lower East Side organizations that trained primarily newly arrived Jews in language and factory skills. "I am having a noble good time—the best I have ever had. All my days are my own," he wrote Aldrich. "They can't improve on this happiness in heaven." He had made his public life suit him exactly, a true meshing of his own recently developed ideology of determinism and his goals for Mark Twain.

Sam received evidence that his campaign to make Mark Twain America's moral voice was working when Yale University awarded him an honorary doctor of letters in late October. Howells, due to receive the same degree with his friend, wrote teasingly about their habit of missing events together, "What are your plans for getting left, or shall you trust to inspiration?" Theodore Roosevelt, who had succeeded McKinley in the presidency, was present to receive his own honorary degree, but he kept his distance from Sam, in part because of Sam's position on imperialism. "When I hear what Mark Twain and others have said in criticism of the missionaries," Roosevelt said privately, "I feel like skinning them alive."

Sam's success as a public gadfly both impressed and distressed Howells. When he accompanied him to Grand Central Station to catch his train home, Howells couldn't help but notice that Sam

> has no time table, but all the gatemen and train starters are proud to know him, and lay hold of him, and put him aboard *something* that leaves for Riverdale. He always has to go to the W. C., me dancing in the corridor, and holding his train for him. But they would not let it go without him, if it was the Chicago limited! What a fame and a force he is! It's astonishing how he holds out, but I hate to have him eating so many dinners, and writing so few books.

Howells missed having his friend around the corner, and in February 1902 he wrote, "I wish I saw you now and then. I'm getting old even if you're not."

Sam's return to America had brought him so massive a financial improvement that the entrepreneurial spirit rose in him again. He began to speculate, first putting up $25,000 to fund the establishment of the American Plasmon Company and then investing another $16,000 in a new cash register. The cash register, like the Paige typesetter, proved more suitable to fantasy than to manufacture. The Plasmon organization seemed strong, however, with California businessman Henry Butters at the helm and his physician son-in-law lending the outfit medical authority. Ralph Ashcroft, a representative of the British Plasmon group, came to watch over the product's interests as company treasurer. Despite Sam's confidence in the healthful food substitute, Henry Rogers declined to participate.

But Sam could do Rogers other favors. When the oil mogul heard about *McClure's Magazine*'s forthcoming muckraking series, "History of the Standard Oil Company," by Ida Tarbell, he told Sam that "it would be a kindness . . . if you could suggest to [S. S. McClure] that some care should be taken to verify statements which may be made through his magazine." Sam invited the magazine's editor out to Riverdale for dinner—a high honor in New York literary circles—and laid out Rogers' case. As a result, Tarbell interviewed Henry Rogers extensively and in her indictment of the company portrayed him as Standard Oil's sole honest man. Rogers repaid the favor a few weeks later by getting Sam out of jury duty.

Sam continued to write, but not publish, essays that explored the conflict he uncovered between his life and his "gospel." In "The Dervish and the Offensive Stranger," he argued that good deeds and evil deeds do not exist. "There are good *impulses*, there are evil impulses, and that is all. Half the results of a good intention are evil," he wrote. "No man can command the results, nor allot them." Sam's efforts to refine his thinking, as expressed in work his wife loathed, only worsened the alienation at home. From Livy's perspective, the distance between her and Sam reflected a creative dissonance. Just as Susy's deathbed scribblings had revealed, Livy could not perform her usual role of giving shape or form to Sam's work as it became darker and more vitriolic. She felt he had purposely taken leave of her in his efforts to clarify his pessimistic determinism.

> Youth darling, have you forgotten your promise to me? . . . I am absolutely wretched today on account of your state of mind—your state of intellect. Why don't you let the better side of you work? . . . Where is the mind that wrote the Prince & P. Jeanne d'Arc, The Yankee &c &c &c. Bring it back! You can if you will—if you wish to. . . . Why always dwell on the evil until those who live beside you are crushed to the earth & you seem almost like a monomaniac.

This note reads more like a journal entry composed in the midst of emotional upheaval than an attempt to reason with Sam or to appeal to his allegiance to their mutual goal. It proved that their editorial partnership had reached an end. Without her support, his writing lacked the generosity it needed to attract readers. He was struggling to find a way to bring his identity as Sam Clemens, that brooding and uncertain man he had long hidden from the world, to bear on his image as Mark Twain. It was a solitary journey, and an arduous one. It left his family, long his mainstay, feeling bereft.

Livy felt crushed by Sam. For several nights, she sat upright, unable to breathe. Jean, too, suffered from her father's mood change, and her seizures returned. Clara tried to escape into concert tours that never fully materialized; instead, she fled to Europe to join Ossip Gabrilowitsch without telling her parents where she was going, why, or when she would return. Though it was of his own making, Sam too escaped the oppressive family situation, for nearly a month in March and April, sailing with Henry Rogers and a boatload of male friends for a cruise to the Caribbean. Editor Laurence Hutton, physician Clarence Rice, actor Joe Jefferson, and others knocked around from island to island enjoying late-night poker, local rum, and native life. Afterward, Sam wrote in a tribute to Rogers, which the embarrassed recipient suppressed, "He is not only the best friend I have ever had, but is the best man I have ever known." Sam had reason to value Rogers: 1902 promised to bring in over $100,000, half from royalties paid according to contracts Rogers negotiated, and most of the rest from investments in Rogers' hands. It would be the most lucrative year of Sam's life.

Sam's streak of glory continued through the spring with an offer of a doctor of letters degree from the University of Missouri. Leaving New York alone at the end of May, Sam went first to St. Louis, where his cousin James Ross Clemens and his Mississippi River mentor Horace Bixby met him. During five days in Hannibal, Sam spoke to civic groups and at the high school graduation, where he comically awarded diplomas without regard to the names written on them. He spent time with old friends, like Laura Hawkins Frazier, the model for *Tom Sawyer*'s Becky Thatcher, and John Briggs, with whom he had worked so hard more than fifty years earlier to unearth a boulder they sent cascading down Holliday's Hill, over the head of a drayman, and into a cooper's shop. Sam and Briggs walked up the hill and found the hole that still remained where they had pried up the boulder. Regarding it, Sam said, slipping back into the language and worldview of his childhood, "John, if we had killed that man we'd have had a dead nigger on our hands without a cent to pay for him." As Sam bade his old friends good-bye, Tom Nash, who had lost his hearing to scarlet fever after crashing through the ice while skating with Sam more than half a century before, shouted about his neighbors, "Same damned fools, Sam."

At the ceremony in Columbia, Missouri, on June 4, 1902, an ovation by the graduates and their families first choked Sam up and then brought him forward for a speech. Returning to Missouri clothed in glory to meet his past face-to-face, he "experienced emotions that I had never expected, and did not know were in me." On the journey back to New York, degree in hand, Sam conceived a story about Huck and Tom returning to Hannibal in their old age. He looked forward to his summer writing time. The family decided to retreat to York Harbor, Maine, to be near the Howells family, who summered in Kittery Point.

Sam's recent accomplishments and growing wealth emboldened him to think that he had at last overcome his eternal sense of unworthiness. He had come so far from Florida, Missouri, long since disappeared, and from Hannibal, now expanded past recognition. Henry Rogers, for all his wealth, had retained his roots in Fairhaven, Massachusetts, but Sam could not do the same with Hannibal. He felt embarrassed by his past, perhaps especially the parts of it he had mythologized in his writing. But now, he had succeeded for so long that he had at last accepted that his success was no accident. The recent demise of Bret Harte—who by the time of his death had disappeared into the comfortable folds of England's upper classes—renewed Sam's sense of his own skill, luck, and durability. He reevaluated himself and concluded that he deserved to rest on his laurels. Those laurels now had a physical representation in a house in nearby Tarrytown, farther up the Hudson, which Livy had bought while he was in Missouri, and which promised the Clemenses a home after a decade of global rootlessness. After they expanded the place, Sam would again have a perch on which the foot-high letters spelling HOME OF MARK TWAIN would be superfluous, as they had been when he declined to use them during Grant's 1880 parade through Hartford. He wanted a house he could live in with pride; he was willing to perch in Riverdale—or anywhere— until the Tarrytown house could suit his new concept of himself.

Joe Goodman, his old editor on the *Territorial Enterprise*, gave Sam an opportunity to reflect on success when he sent a copy of his recent book, the very first key to decoding prehistoric Mayan inscriptions. Sam congratulated his friend in words he could as easily have applied to himself.

I am lost in reverence and admiration! It is now twenty-four hours that I have been trying to cool down and contemplate with quiet blood this extraordinary spectacle of energy, industry, perseverance, pluck, analytical genius, penetration, this irruption of thunders and fiery splendors from a fair and flowery mountain that nobody had supposed was a sleeping volcano. . . .

You think you get "poor pay" for your twenty years? No, oh no. You have lived in a paradise of the intellect whose lightest joys were beyond the reach of the longest purse in Christendom, you have had daily and nightly emancipation from the world's slaveries and gross interests, you have received a bigger wage than any man in the land, you have dreamed a splendid dream and had it come true.

Sam did not have a chance to adjust to his newfound satisfaction before the summer began. At the end of June, Rogers loaned him the *Kanawha* in order to transport his family to York Harbor. But the summer began harrowingly: Jean had a violent seizure on board the yacht and another one ten days later. "I saw it; I have seen it only three times before in all these five fiendish years," Sam wrote Henry Rogers the next day. "It comes near to killing Mrs. Clemens every time, and there is not much left of her for a day or two afterward." Each terrifying episode weakened Livy's already fragile health. Nor did Clara's continued absence help, although toward the end of July, she abruptly announced that she would soon join the family in Maine. Conveniently, a trolley ran between the Clemenses' and the Howellses' vacation houses, and the men took frequent respite in one another's company. "They used to read to each other the pieces they wrote—their manuscripts—all the time," Katy Leary recalled. "Of course they enjoyed that and laughed and talked by the hour." Howells recalled a decade later that Sam read him his depiction of the return of aged Huck and Tom to Hannibal, an idea he jotted down in his notebook while in Missouri; he intended that the two old men die in each other's arms. The manuscript has disappeared. Howells also told Sam a pathetic story about a family nursing two dying members, and how the healthy ones had to lie to their sick relatives so they would not worry. Sam turned this tale into a sermon on lying and truth-telling called "Was It Heaven? Or Hell?"

A failed offer for the Hartford house forced Sam to break the news to his wife that it was on the market. The fact of the near sale, Clara's imminent return, and the instability of Jean's health proved too much for Livy's heart. In the early morning of August 12, 1902, she suffered an attack. "Mrs. Clemens said she was dying and I was not able to doubt it," Sam wrote Rogers. "But by 7.30 we had the doctor, and he took heroic measures. Before noon the case had ceased to be immediately alarming, though the danger was not past."

From that moment, almost everything but Livy went out of Sam's mind. The prospect of Livy's death restored his full acceptance of his love for his wife of thirty-three years. "My head was all gone & upside down— I could not think of anything," he wrote Howells five weeks later; "of anything but the swift disaster which we believed was hanging over our heads & ready to crush us at any moment." Rogers kept his yacht "ready to fly here and take us to Riverdale on telegraphic notice."

In the end, though, the family could only wait two anxious months in Kittery Point until the doctors felt Livy was well enough to move. Sam and Howells went to Boston together to see about rail transportation to New York; doctors disapproved of the sea voyage. Typically, Sam had had nothing to do with the domestic details of his family's life; he always said that Livy took care of most things and gave him such tasks as might have been done by the cat. When it came to attending to Livy's needs, however, Howells noted how every detail absorbed Sam: "the sort of invalid-car he could get; how she could be carried to the village station; how the car could be detached from the eastern train at Boston and carried round to the southern train on the other side of the city."

The doctors, seeing that Livy suffered from both nervous exhaustion and her heart malady, stunned Sam by prohibiting him from visiting her at all. His presence, the doctor claimed, disturbed her heart. His self-recriminations, which he poured out to the prostrate Livy, hampered her recovery. Sue Crane came to Maine from Elmira and ran the house with Clara, keeping Livy company. Sam and Jean had to stay away. Jean did not have a single seizure during Livy's illness; she spent her time carving wood, her growing avocation. Sam busied himself with a funny gesture that could later be reported to Livy, attaching notes to the trees outside her windows cautioning the birds to keep quiet. He fretted about Livy's doctors and nurses. Toward the end, he became frustrated with both Livy and the treatment she had received, feeling she'd been coddled instead of cured. "I sleep out of the house, and the family keep away from her room and leave her to the trained nurse," Sam wrote Rogers. "The doctors have been babies in her hands—and the rest of us." Nagged by the wretched feeling that his Faustian bargain had not ended with Susy's death in 1896, Sam returned to a dread of his own success. The Clemenses returned to Riverdale by train on October 16, 1902, Sam fussing over the $340 the special car and locomotives had cost.

49 | *The Decline of an Angel*

*When one reads Bibles, one is less surprised at what the
Deity knows than at what he doesn't know.*
—Notebook (1908)

Livy's illness became the organizing force in Sam's life. Despite her declaration, "*I intend to get well,*" no one had confidence that she would. Though the family pulled together once they had returned to Riverdale—Clara ran the house, while Jean handled secretarial tasks—the Clemenses were disrupted at their core. Sam, restricted to seeing Livy for two minutes a day, and then only on a day-by-day basis, "was always waiting by her door long, long before he could get in. He just stood there waitin'!" Katy Leary later said. "And sometimes when he couldn't stand it any longer, he used to write little notes and push them under her door. That seemed to comfort him a little. He couldn't write his stories that winter; he was like a lost soul, really." His separation from Livy and his uneasiness about her health began to close the intellectual distance Sam had felt between them the previous few years. He noted on a letter from an admirer, "Livy never gets her share of these applauses, but it is because the people do not know. Yet she is entitled to the lion's share." Sam determined to give Livy her due.

He got the opportunity in November, when Colonel George Harvey, the head of Harper and Brothers, threw a literary bash in honor of Sam's sixty-seventh birthday. Although Sam grumbled that the publisher held the party only to trumpet Harper's stable of writers, Harvey had a better reason. He knew that the contract to publish Mark Twain came up for renewal the next year and that Sam felt a profound dissatisfaction with all his current arrangements. At the party, Howells, John Hay, "Czar" Tom Reed, and dozens of lesser lights heaped praises on Mark Twain. "A part of me is present; the larger part, the better part, is yonder at her home," Sam declared in response. "We together, out of our single heart, return you our deepest and most grateful thanks." After this event, Sam went to Elmira for the wedding of Julie, Charlie Langdon's daughter, to a rising railroad executive, Edward Loomis. Held in the same house as his own wedding, the nuptials brought "the same joy, the same excitement & hilarity, taken right out of 33 years ago & reproduced unchanged under the same ceilings—lord God, what a sad thing a wedding is!"

Sam otherwise stayed close to home. He hired a secretary, Isabel V. Lyon, recently of Hartford, who relieved Jean and Clara of their most onerous tasks. A pretty, amusing woman of thirty-eight, Lyon had worked for Franklin Whitmore and came recommended by him. Perhaps sensing how much Sam needed her, she quickly made herself a comfortable fixture in the Clemens household and adapted easily to their domestic style. She wrote in her diary that Sam often would not dress until late in the day, working with her wearing only his "nightshirt, blanket gown, bare legs and black felt slippers." Once when Sam wanted to dictate letters, Clara insisted he dress properly first. Instead, he returned to bed and waited until Clara left the house before coming down again, dressed as before.

He worked a bit, revising "Was It Heaven? Or Hell?" for publication. Clara suggested he separate the didactic portions of the narrative, so he tried to "weed enough of the sermon out at one quick sitting to properly and artistically subordinate it." Within a few weeks of the story's appearance in the December *Harper's*, however, Sam and Clara were forced to reenact its theme. Jean developed pneumonia, accompanied with terrifically high fever. Sam feared for her life, but no one dared tell Livy her daughter was ill. "Every day Clara and the nurses have lied about Jean to her mother—describing the fine time she is having out of doors in winter sports!" Sam wrote in his notebook. Both Sam and Livy had looked forward to their first face-to-face meeting in weeks, but Sam did not dare to go alone. Livy "will begin to get impatient, tomorrow or next day; & not long afterward, suspicious," he told Howells. "Then—why then lying would fail! But I *can't* go & see her. We never could explain how it was safe for her to see me & not safe for her to see Jean." Seeing her for five minutes on December 30, 1902, he kept his lie well, but the power he had to endanger Livy intruded itself into his thoughts. "For the first time in months I heard her break into one of her girlish old-time laughs," Sam wrote Joe Twichell, anticipating the next visit. "With a word I could freeze the blood in her veins!" After Jean was out of danger, Sam hid her in a Virginia rest home until she no longer "looked like the victim of a forest fire."*

The attempt to protect Livy succeeded, but spirits remained low all through the house. "I feel so frightfully banished," Livy complained in a note to her husband. "Couldn't you write in my boudoir? Then I could hear you clear your throat and it would be such joy to feel you near. I miss you sadly, sadly." Sam moved there for a while, but his desire to speak through the door overwhelmed their good intentions. Livy's continuing illness also resurrected his feelings of guilt. "I drove you to sorrow and heart-break just to hear myself talk," he wrote Livy. "If I ever do it again when you get well I hope the punishment will fall upon me the guilty, not upon you the innocent." He developed bronchitis; Clara and Jean, returned from Virginia, contracted measles. To make matters worse, the ceiling over Clara's bed collapsed on her in the middle of the night, and she had to wait, immobilized under the debris, until help arrived in the morning. Sam regarded the Riverdale house as a lonely hospital. "I see Howells at wide intervals; the Rogerses every week or two, but I hardly ever have a sight of the other friends," he complained to Laurence Hutton.

Left alone, Sam buried himself in worry about his finances. He was now in his sixty-eighth year, the one the palmist had assured him would see the culmination of his fortune. Instead, he found threats on all sides. Ralph Ashcroft, officially the treasurer of American Plasmon, alerted Sam to the operation's crookedness. Instead of selling Sam $25,000 worth of stock in the new company, Henry Butters had instead transferred to him $25,000 of his own indebtedness to the enterprise. That effectively prevented Sam from getting out of the company when he desired. Ashcroft, maintaining an allegiance to Sam, stayed in his post, in an attempt to prevent any further losses. Sam spent one horrible night calculating and recalculating the family's finances, concluding that they were in debt again. He summoned his daughters, ready to announce the terrible news, and then discovered he had inexplicably multiplied his debits by two. He wrote a friend, "Certainly there is a blistering and awful reality about a well-arranged *un*reality. It is quite within the possibilities that two or three nights like that night of mine could drive a man to suicide."

Meanwhile, Sam's relationship with his publishers had frayed further. He offered Harper and Brothers a book-length imputation of Mary Baker

Eddy's Christian Science business practices. After first accepting and advertising the book, they then withdrew it from their list without explanation. Believing that this action forfeited their contract to publish Mark Twain's works, Sam entertained new offers, but the American Publishing Company would still not relinquish their rights to the early books. Since the company had now dwindled to little more than a repository for Mark Twain's copyrights, Frank Bliss was tempted to misuse those rights, as he had with the Newbegin selected set, and when he did Harper brought suit against him. Earlier that spring, Sam had favored Frank Bliss as his publisher, reasoning that the American Publishing Company was already in essence Mark Twain's personal publisher.

Then Frederick Duneka, editor at Harper and Brothers, met with Sam in Riverdale and pledged to renegotiate their contract from the bottom up, giving Sam whatever he wanted. Only the copyrights held by the American Publishing Company stood in the way. Sam would have called on Henry Rogers to solve this mess, but Rogers had gone on a month-long cruise aboard the *Kanawha*—a trip aborted by an emergency appendectomy. Sam could not get to Rogers, recovering in Massachusetts, because Livy would not let him leave until she felt better herself. Finally, on May 11, 1903, "of her own accord, she proposed to let me go up and spend a night at Fairhaven some time when the yacht is going," Sam wrote Rogers. He rushed up to visit his adviser, who for once affirmed Sam's business sense. In early June, with Rogers' advice and his secretary Isabel Lyon's help, Sam conducted private meetings in Hartford with members of Frank Bliss' board of directors. Sam explained to the directors that Harper would withdraw its lawsuit if the company sold its copyrights for $50,000, but if they refused, Harper would sue them into the ground. The directors agreed to pressure Bliss to go to the negotiating table.

Livy's doctors concurred that she could spend the summer in Elmira, but recommended that the Clemenses winter in a more temperate climate. They decided to move to Italy. Sam accepted $28,000 for the house in Hartford, less than a quarter of its cost, and also rented out the new house in Tarrytown, to which the family had never gotten the chance to move. He then began the bittersweet work of taking apart the Hartford house. On July 1, Sam and Livy went to Elmira, leaving Jean and Clara behind in Riverdale. He made some use of his old study, now overgrown with vines, its view partially obscured by the growing trees.

Jean soon joined her parents, which gave Clara the freedom to arrange a singing tour through New England. Concerned about their daughter's predilection for social irregularity, Sam and Livy had left Richard Watson Gilder, the editor of *Scribner's Monthly*, as Clara's chaperon. Under the guise of taking her to his farm in western Massachusetts for a weekend in August, Gilder and his wife virtually imprisoned her. Mrs. Gilder, "assuming a ferocious air, forbade the young lady to go wandering around into strange New England places when she ought to be taking care of herself quietly at Four Brooks Farm," Gilder wrote Sam. "I told Clara there were moments when young people should allow older people to take their consciences in their hands and act for them." Though Clara had celebrated her twenty-ninth birthday earlier that summer, Sam did not believe that she was free to make her own choices about what to do with her life, especially if such choices showed a disregard for the interests of the family. In Sam's view, single women with artistic pretensions courted scandal; he did not desire scandal for Mark Twain, and he feared its effect on Livy. Sam left Elmira to collect Clara. They returned to New York together, where Sam discovered that plans to rent a villa near Florence had failed. He wrote Jean, "I proposed to send a cable saying 'Take your Papiniano & go to hell with it,' but Clara & I could not agree. She wanted to insert 'dam' in front of Papiniano, but I felt that your mother would not approve." This farcical disagreement only covered a more deep-seated one between father and daughter, who could not come to terms about the limits to her freedom. Sam unsuccessfully tried to impress his fatherly concern upon Clara; by mid-September he was again uncertain of her whereabouts.

Sam met with one of the parties to the publishing agreement every ten days or so throughout the summer, but Bliss resisted all overtures, being unwilling to abandon his family business. Henry Rogers, now fully recovered, himself intervened in the negotiations when Sam could not pull the parties together. On September 15, Rogers telegraphed Sam in Elmira, "Duneka and Bliss are in the other room and are going to agree before they come out." Harper and Sam agreed to split the $50,000 cost of buying back from Bliss the copyrights on Mark Twain's books, and Harper would publish all of Mark Twain's books in the future, guaranteeing him $25,000 a year, though Sam expected his royalties to be double that amount for most years. He wrote in his notebook that he had always kept the palmist's predictions of wealth "in mind and often thought of it. When at last it came true, Oct. 22/03, there was but a month and 9 days to spare. The contract signed that day concentrates all my books in Harper's hands, and now at last they are valuable: in fact they are a fortune."

Sam, Livy, Jean, Clara, Katy Leary, and Livy's nurse left for Italy the day after Sam signed the contracts that sealed his fortune; Isabel Lyon and her mother came two weeks later. Perhaps projecting onto his friend some of his own uncertainties about life in the United States, Howells wrote to his sister, "Clemens, I suppose, will always live at Florence, hereafter. He goes first for his wife's health, and then because he can't stand the nervous storm and stress here. He takes things intensely hard, and America is too much for him."

*Let us endeavor so to live that when we come to die even
the undertaker will be sorry.*
—"Pudd'nhead Wilson's Calendar" (1894)

THE SEA VOYAGE gave Sam time to consider his final
victory over indebtedness. He had at last defeated the
specter of his father, whose approval he had always craved
but could never receive. By bettering the dour, dark image of John Clemens he had carried around his entire life, Sam felt free to remove the mask
called Mark Twain through which he had struggled for fame, wealth, and
approval. He could now receive accolades as Samuel Clemens; he felt worthy at last. Sam could not simply discard Mark Twain, however. The
public would not let him; he had tried before, and failed. Instead, he began
to think about how to make the mask of Twain translucent enough to
reveal Sam Clemens behind it.

The Clemenses moved into the Villa Reale di Quarto near Florence
with trepidation. The massive old pile—over two hundred feet long with
more than sixty rooms—belonged to an American adventuress, married
to an Italian count, who had lavished money on refurbishing the palace.
Unfortunately, "it must have been built for fuss & show & irruptions of
fashion, not for a home," Sam wrote to Howells. "If you were to come I
could not find you a comfortable & satisfactory place." The villa reflected
the personality of the Countess Rebaudi-Massiglia, whom Isabel Lyon

remembered from an earlier marriage in Philadelphia. Instead of leaving the villa grounds when the Clemenses arrived, the countess camped out in the rooms above the stable with "the big Roman steward of the place." No one liked having her around, Lyon noted in her diary, "with her painted hair, her great coarse voice, her slitlike vicious eyes, her dirty clothes, and her terrible manners." Sam found his landlady detestable, especially since a clause in the lease prohibited housing a sick person in the room they had chosen for Livy. Forced to place Livy in the next best room, Sam then discovered that that room put Livy above the stable the family had to use. Within a month, Sam engaged a lawyer to straighten out the problems with the countess, whom he described as in his notebook as "excitable, malicious, malignant, vengeful, unforgiving, selfish, stingy, avaricious, coarse, vulgar, profane, obscene, a furious blusterer on the outside and at heart a coward."

Sam's anxiety over Livy only increased his irritability. The ocean crossing had weakened her, and then in mid-November she received a bad burn from a piece of medical equipment. Though some days she seemed bright and content, on others she could hardly breathe at all. Susceptible to infection, she became dangerously ill in mid-December 1903. Sam saw her infrequently during these bad turns. "I will go down and see her a moment," he sadly wrote Rogers. "Only a moment is allowed. I wish we had stayed at home." Anxious about the family's expenses in order to avoid apprehension about her own health, Livy "was worrying altogether too much about them, and doing a very dangerous amount of lying awake on their account. It was necessary to stop that." Sam allayed her fears by working up thirty thousand words' worth of funny magazine articles. He submerged these conflicts with Livy over money into a story called "The $30,000 Bequest." In the piece, a husband and wife receive false word of an uncle's intention to leave them some money, and each privately imagines what they will buy. In the end, they are broken by their anticipated wealth. Because of their enforced separation and Livy's feebleness, Sam and she could not spend the time together they needed to resolve their discord. Knowingly fooling himself, Sam lived on the anticipation of Livy's return to health; no one but Livy mistook her trajectory. "She comes up again as bright and fresh and enterprising as ever," Sam wrote Joe Twichell, "and goes to planning about Egypt, with a hope and a confidence which are to me amazing." Livy's hopefulness struck Sam as ironic, especially as tidings of deaths came regularly to Florence: Mollie Clemens, Sir Henry Stanley, a son of Thomas Bailey Aldrich. The family kept news of all of them from Livy.

Once he finished his magazine work, Sam began an enterprise that

captured his fancy as nothing had since the typesetter. He wrote to Howells about it:

> You will never know how much enjoyment you have
> lost until you get to dictating your autobiography; then you
> will realize, with a pang, that you might have been doing it
> all your life if you had only had the luck to think if it. And
> you will be astonished (& charmed) to see how like *talk* it
> is, & how real it sounds, & how well & compactly & se-
> quentially it constructs itself, & what a dewy & breezy &
> woodsy freshness it has, & what a darling & worshipful ab-
> sence of the signs of starch, & flatiron, & labor & fuss & the
> other artificialities!

Sam dictated to Lyon all through January and February, for an hour or
more each day. Lyon took down the work in longhand, and when Livy
felt well enough someone read it to her for approval. Sam felt that he had
discovered a new invention, though he had tried this experiment nearly
twenty years before, sustaining it only long enough to record what he
regarded as the historically important facts pertaining to the publication
of Grant's *Memoirs*. He began to record everything, each recollection erod-
ing the wall he had long since erected between Mark Twain and Sam
Clemens. He wrote to Howells that "an Autobiography is the truest of
all books; for while it inevitably consists mainly of extinctions of the
truth, shirkings of the truth, partial revealments of the truth, with hardly
an instance of plain straight truth, the remorseless truth *is* there, between
the lines." He had no real intention of telling the truth, however: After
Mollie Clemens' death, he had instructed the executors of her estate to
destroy his letters to her, Orion, and their mother.

The dictation ceased when Isabel Lyon took to her bed after a violent, foul-tempered donkey belonging to the Countess Massiglia had attacked her. This same animal had recently bit off the thumb of a local
peasant. These attacks and the countess' unconcern regarding them represented the pinnacle of the strife between the landlady and her tenant,
but then the countess shut off telephone service and water to the villa
without explanation. Sam retaliated by backing whatever civil and criminal suits anyone wanted to bring against the countess. The villa became
an armed camp in every arena except Livy's sickroom; the invalid learned
no disturbing news.

Livy declined and rebounded. In February, "her pulse went up to
192, and nothing but a subcutaneous injection of brandy brought her back

to life," Sam told Rogers. In March, "we took the madam out of her bed for the first time in 3 months and she sat in a chair 25 minutes." The strain proved too much, and again her life seemed threatened. Sam reported to Richard Gilder that Livy "all of a sudden ceases to be a pallid shrunken shadow, and looks bright and young and pretty. She remains what she always was, the most wonderful creature of fortitude, patience, endurance and recuperative power that ever was. But ah, dear, it won't last." The next day Sam added that on one of his two visits permitted each day he "found what I have learned to expect—retrogression, and that pathetic something in the eye which betrays the secret of waning hope." This rugged vigil wore Sam down; he began to look older than his sixty-eight years. A visitor noted, "During this hour's interview, Mark smoked three cigars; there was a constant twitching in his right cheek and his right eye seemed inflamed."

Sam tried to keep his spirits up. He read *Daddy Long Legs*, a successful novel recently published by his great-niece Jean Webster, Annie and Charley's daughter. He managed to get away from the Villa di Quarto regularly, making calls in town, searching out doctors for Livy, meeting with lawyers, and, his favorite excursion, looking for a villa to buy. In early June, he reserved two, so Livy could choose between them. Despite this hopeful act, death's impending permanent separation of this loving couple made Sam realize more fully the nature of the gulf between them, a gulf that had widened and narrowed so often over the preceding decades but which had always remained. "Men and women—even man and wife are foreigners," he mused in his notebook. "Each has reserves that the other cannot enter into, nor understand. These have the effect of frontiers."

After a short visit on the evening of June 5, 1904, Livy asked Sam to play the piano and sing some of the spirituals he loved so well. He left her bedroom and went to the piano. She listened attentively, and then not long afterward her heart stopped. Katy Leary ran to get Sam. He touched her. She did not respond. Livy had died.

"Our life is wrecked; we have no plans for the future; she always made the plans, none of us was capable," Sam wrote Rogers. "We shall carry her home and bury her with her dead, at Elmira. Beyond that, we have no plans. The children must decide. I have no head." After spending a night kneeling beside Livy's coffin, Sam told his notebook, "I looked for the last time upon that dear face—and was full of remorse for things done and said in the 34 years of married life that hurt Livy's heart."

Devastated by Livy's death, the children could make no decisions. Clara threw herself into her mother's bed as soon as the corpse was removed from it. Only Katy Leary's insistence impelled her to take to her own room, where she remained immobile for several days. Jean, who had had no seizures for more than a year, now suffered a severe epileptic episode. Once she recovered, she was able to help Sam, who suggested retreating to a cabin near the Gilders' in western Massachusetts. He wanted to be home among his dearest friends. He said, "Why, just the sight of a dog from home that I could lay my hand on and speak to now—would help me."

They booked passage on the second boat leaving Italy—the first happened to be the same ship they had arrived on, and no one wanted to return home with those memories so palpably near. They included with the luggage two horses that had been the most recent gift from Livy to the girls. Sam could not see Clara, who "was strongly threatened with a nervous breakdown, and we are still troubled about her," he confided to Rogers. "We hope to persuade her not to go to Elmira." They boarded ship on June 28, after several long weeks of waiting. "In my life there have been 68 Junes," Sam wrote in his notebook, "—but how vague and colorless 67 of them are contrasted with the deep blackness of this one." Howells wrote his dear friend, "It wrings my heart to think about you. What are you going to do, you poor soul?" Sam did not know. He wrote to Joe Twichell with the nearest metaphor he could find. "I was richer than any other person in the world, and now I am that pauper without peer. Some day I will tell you about it, not now."

51 | Loss

OUT OF RESPECT for Mark Twain's grief, the
Clemens family received a presidential dispensation to pass
unmolested through customs in New York. The family
went directly to Elmira, where Clara justified her father's dark fears by
trying to hurl herself into her mother's grave. After the funeral—conducted by Joe Twichell in the same room of the Langdon house in which
he had presided at Sam and Livy's wedding—Jean, too, was fragile, preoccupied, and liable to mild seizures. Livy had been the family's polestar;
her death left the three remaining members without the gravitational sway
that kept them from explosive collisions with one another. "The family's
relation to her was peculiar & unusual, & could not exist toward another,"
Sam wrote a condoling friend. "Our love for her was the ordinary love,
but added to it was a reverent & quite conscious worship." Sam compared
this worship to that given by subjects to a deserving queen, but in his
case the worship was more that of a believer to his god. To him, she was
a beneficent being whose will one disobeyed only at peril to life and sanity.
Livy had fostered Sam's creation of Mark Twain; to the extent that Mark
Twain was generous, loving, warm, kind, and open, he manifested Livy's
hand. Sam felt uncertain who he could be without Livy beside him.

Joe Twichell wrote Sam after the funeral, asking how he saw the world in his grief. Trying to assess the damage to his psyche long before the full loss could be assayed, Sam replied that at least part of every day he felt that "there is *nothing*. That there is no God and no universe; that there is only empty space, and in it a lost and homeless and wandering and companionless and indestructible *Thought*. And that I am that thought. And God, and the Universe, and Time, and Life, and Death, and Joy and Sorrow and Pain only a grotesque and brutal *dream*, evolved from the frantic imagination of that insane Thought." Sam despaired ever emerging from the disoriented and bodiless state, to a point where he could feel again, not only with the strangely distant intensity of a dream but with his normal emotions. He wanted to be able to write what he felt, but the depth of his grief terrified him so, he feared to pick up a pen.

Clara went to New York and checked herself into a rest home, where her contact with the world could be modulated until she was better able to live in it. Sam and Jean went to Tyringham, Massachusetts, near the Gilders' farm, where Jean calmed herself by going riding. On the night of July 31, 1904, Jean went out with some friends, and while riding through town collided with a trolley. The horse died, Sam told Rogers, but "Jean escaped with a torn tendon, and with 4 wounds on her back and neck, one at the base of her skull, and 5 on her forehead, eyes, nose, and mouth." Her serious but not life-threatening injuries fanned a bonfire of newspaper rumor that she had been killed. Sam, concerned about Clara's reaction to false reports of her sister's death, warned the rest home to keep newspapers from her until he could speak with Clara himself. "He entered my room and, after a brief greeting, handed me a newspaper," Clara later recalled. The headline ballyhooed the unlikeliness of Jean's recovery. Clara "read and reread the sentence, unable to feel anything but a sharp pain in my head. This couldn't be true. Then slowly Father began to tell the story in his most feeling and dramatically impressive way." Sam thought his dramatic tale, leading to a happy ending, would enchant Clara, but she was so distraught by her father's rendition of the accident that she bolted off to Massachusetts to sit by Jean.

Sam stayed in New York to look for a place to live, renting a house at 21 Fifth Avenue, just below Ninth Street, in the same neighborhood where he had lived before. Though it cost nearly as much as his annual rent, he also purchased a player organ equipped with several dozen pieces of music, which he thought might help stave off depression. One needed merely to pump the Aeolian Orchestrelle's pedals to hear music as played by the world's finest musicians. The day Sam returned to the Berkshires,

Clara escaped to her rest home in New York. Believing that he had exacerbated her distress, Clara and her doctors prohibited Sam from contacting her for a year; she accepted no mail from him for many months.

As he always did in grief, Sam isolated himself from those he loved and plunged into the companionship of friends. During August and September, he spent very little time in Tyringham with Jean, who was suffering a long, painful, and solitary recovery. Henry Rogers saw him frequently until Rogers took his wife to Europe, and then Rogers' children adopted Sam. He accepted a small number of other invitations, spending a few days with Harper and Brothers chief George Harvey at his place on the New Jersey shore. Sam's attitude comprised an odd mixture of despair and enlightenment. Henry James wrote to his brother William about listening to Sam talk during afternoons at Harvey's beach house: "Delicious poor dear old M.T. is here and beguiles the sessions on the deep piazza." Richard Watson Gilder, on one of Sam's rare stops at Four Brooks Farm, noted that "Mark, in our cottage next door, is most grim and unhappy, but full of life and abounding in scorn of a mismanaged universe." Sam wrote long letters full of bile and exasperation with life to Joe Twichell, whose gentle patience Sam could count on.

Early September saw the death of Pamela Moffett, but the passing of the last member of Sam's original family left almost no emotional trace; Livy's death had consumed his capacity for grief. Sam went to New York to meet Rogers on his return from France. He moved into the Grosvenor Hotel, from which he watched the slow progress of work on his house at 21 Fifth Avenue, which could not be occupied until December. In enforced social limbo for a year of mourning—and with Howells in Europe, his friends working, and with little inclination to write—Sam had time on his hands. His secretary, Isabel Lyon, joined him at the hotel for endless games of gin. They often played for ten hours a day.

In spite of Sam's obsessive card playing, he did not shirk his other responsibilities. The affairs of the American Plasmon Company reached a crisis. When the company found itself in debt, the only stockholder willing to loan it money had been John Hays Hammond, formerly leader of the failed Jameson raid on South Africa, and a man whom Sam had visited in a Pretoria jail eight years before. When American Plasmon could not repay Hammond's loan, however, he attached the company's assets and found himself opposing Sam's faction for control of their mutual investment. Ralph Ashcroft, Sam's spy, removed all the company's deeds, ledgers, and patents from the office, depositing them at 21 Fifth Avenue. Legal proceedings clarifying ownership took months, during which time Sam funded Ashcroft's nuisance suit against Hammond. Sam invested in another Ashcroft venture, the Spiral Pin Company, which had patented a spiral hatpin that Sam gave out as mementos to his female visitors. Ashcroft assumed responsibility for several of Sam's other business arrangements, reveling in his proximity to Mark Twain.

Isabel Lyon served Sam in more capacities than as secretary and frequent card partner. Though any discussion of Isabel Lyon's role in Sam Clemens' life after Livy's death relies on sketchy and contradictory evidence, it is likely that for more than two years beginning in September 1904, Lyon fulfilled many wifely duties for Sam, a relationship known, though not endorsed, by members of his circle. When Sam had no companionship but Lyon, he found her an exemplary drinking buddy and a feminine boost to his virility. When they did have company, she entertained. She had a talent for making reporters and well-wishers feel welcome, even if they went away without a pithy quote from Mark Twain. Lyon kept up Sam's correspondence with his lawyer in Italy, who continued the various suits against the Countess Massiglia and Livy's physician, who had submitted what Sam felt was an inflated and outrageous bill. Perhaps aspiring to a more permanent place in Sam's heart and home, Lyon coddled him, bringing him lap robes and mufflers and warm drinks to fend off the chill left in the house by the balky heating system. She teased him until he became playful. A bohemian throwback without any art of her own, she adopted Sam's casual attitude toward dress in the house, often appearing in her robe and slippers. She gave members of Sam's circle nicknames, which they happily adopted. She was the Lioness, and Sam was the King. Lyon encouraged him to write, but—not knowing that Sam needed firm criticism and Livy's restraining hand—she praised every word. She told her diary Sam was a genius: "so wonderful—so ennobling."

After New Year's, 1905, Sam wrote some political and social commentary, including censures of Belgian King Leopold's genocidal treatment of native Congolese tribes and Czar Nicholas II's brutal response to uprisings in Russia. He revised "What Is Man?", the gospel of determinism Livy had banished, but Jean, occasionally typing for her father, refused to transcribe his revisions for him. Divided between an obligation to his own ideas and an obligation to Livy's memory, Sam wrote Twichell, "For seven years I have suppressed a book which my conscience tells me I ought to publish. I hold it a duty to publish it. There are other difficult duties which I am equal to, but I am not equal to that one." Perhaps to ease the conflict, he honored Livy by writing "Eve's Diary," a paean to her style of femininity. "It is my prayer, it is my longing, that we may pass from this life together," Eve comments to her diary. "But if one of us must go first, it is my prayer that it shall be I; for he is strong, I am weak, I am not so necessary to him as he is to me—life without him would not be life." Adam responds at her graveside, "Wheresoever she was, *there* was Eden." Having satisfied his obligation to Livy's memory with this tender tribute, he felt he could revise "What Is Man?" without disrespect for his dead wife's objections to the text.

At the suggestion of painter Abbott Thayer, who had married Sam's *Quaker City* flirtation Emeline Beach, Sam considered a summer retreat to Dublin, New Hampshire, where the Thayers had a year-round retreat and where in the summer artists and academics communed in the shadow of Mount Monadnock. In deep winter of 1905, Katy and Jean went to New Hampshire to examine the locale. To tour the rental house, Jean and Katy had to snowshoe several miles and then break into the house through a second-floor window. The Thayers slept out in the snow, making small caverns for themselves each night, and outdoorsy Jean was immediately smitten with the spot. Sam agreed to rent the cabin from May to October.

Sam hoped the whole family would agree to join him in Dublin, but though Clara was again receiving her father's letters, she would not accept a visit from him. She arranged to summer at a rest home in Norfolk, Connecticut, and eagerly planned for visits from Jean, Katy, and even Joe Twichell. Her father would have to wait.

In the absence of Clara's support, Sam accepted Isabel Lyon's pleasant alternative of drink, encouragement, and intimacy, possibly sexual. Late in April, Lyon noted in her journal, "I've known of several men who have married several times—they couldn't live without the companionship and sympathy of a woman, and I like the thought of it." Lyon's faithful support helped Sam out of his alcohol-and-cards haze and back into a productive life. He began a new work of fiction, *The Refuge of the Derelicts*, comprised of short stories told among bums at an asylum from an unlucky and abusive world. In addition to writing more, Sam saw friends more often. Howells, who had been in Europe since before Livy's death, returned to find Sam in a remarkably creative fervor, reaching for pen and paper as enthusiastically as he had during his high-water summers in his study at Quarry Farm in Elmira. With 1905 shaping up as one of Sam's most literarily productive years, he retreated to his New Hampshire mountain cabin for the summer, having constructed a semblance of a family out of the detritus left behind after Livy's death.

52

A Public Man

*We can't reach old age by another man's road. My
habits protect my life but they would assassinate you.*
—"Seventieth Birthday Speech" (1905)

Sᴀᴍ ꜰᴏᴜɴᴅ ᴛʜᴇ cabin and the company in New
Hampshire exactly to his liking. The colony of educated,
artistic, and companionable men and women drew him out
of himself, and he signed on early for the following summer at Dublin.
During the first two months there, he wrote productively on his mysterious stranger manuscript and planned a long narrative about a scientist
who becomes a microbe in an experiment gone awry. Instead of merely
ridiculing the premise of human centrality in the universe, he imagined
that, since microbes feed on humans, humans must be made for them and
not the other way around. In an earlier attempt to communicate this idea
in an essay, he remarked, "If the Eiffel tower were now representing the
world's age, the skin of paint on the pinnacle-knob at its summit would
represent man's share of that age; & anybody would perceive that that
skin was what the tower was built for."

Excited as he was by this premise, Sam's pace of writing slowed down
as summer warmed up. "I lose no day," he wrote Rogers, "but my output
grows smaller daily. It has dwindled from a high-water mark—32 pages a
fortnight ago, one day—to 12 day before yesterday, 10 yesterday, and 8
to-day." When Harper editor Frederick Duneka visited Sam in New

Hampshire, Sam not only described his creative work but also expressed his desire that Clara and Isabel Lyon jointly edit his letters for posthumous publication. This was a valuable gift to Lyon, whose royalty on the project could equal $1,000 per year or more; she was still paid only $50 a month, plus room and board. For that, she read his work, arranged his social life, transferred the Orchestrelle to Dublin, and played it every night for him. She was enchanted with Sam, noting lovingly in her diary, "Hours and hours and hours he sits writing with a wonderful light in his eyes. The flush of a girl in his cheeks, and oh the lustre of his hair. It is too terribly perishably beautiful."

Sam teased Henry Rogers about his "continued popularity" with God when yet another multimillion-dollar deal tumbled through the courts in his favor. "I wish I had your secret. It isn't righteousness, for I've tried that myself, and there's nothing in it." As a gesture of friendship to Sam, Rogers wanted to give the financially strapped Joe Twichell $1,500, but only if Sam would claim he had himself sent the money. This relatively small sum—Sam earned about that much in a week, and Henry Rogers in a day—put the Twichells "where we never were before, and where we are going to be able to stay. The comfort of it—the sweet peace, deep, inward—is past all telling." Despite his uneasiness with the unearned gratitude, Sam assured Rogers "I am keeping the secret and collecting the revenue."

Sam himself benefited by court wranglings. The Count Massiglia, now Italian consul in New York, asked for mercy for his wife, whose health was affected by the lawsuits and the trouble they caused them socially and domestically. Sam had no interest in forgiveness and felt pleased that the countess reaped what she had sown. Sam's faction won control of the nearly valueless American Plasmon Company, and, despite Sam's cautions against it, Ralph Ashcroft sent out an announcement of the fact ornamented with a crowing rooster.

At last, in August, Sam received permission to visit Clara. He rushed off to Norfolk, Connecticut, only to find that a miscommunication made him an unexpected guest. Clara had not wanted to see him until October. His three-day visit, however, stretched into three weeks when Sam had an attack of gout. Livy's lifelong frailty had cemented her position at the center of the family; now, in her absence, Sam and Clara offered competing illnesses in a struggle for family dominance. Sam returned to Dublin feeling broken-down, while Clara went down to New York with Katy Leary to redecorate the house on Fifth Avenue.

In Sam's absence from the mountain cottage, Jean's health took a nasty turn. For most of the summer, she had enjoyed the outdoor life and her new passion, wood carving, but now she had a series of epileptic seizures of savage violence. She was desolate, depressed by the thought that her illness made her, as was commonly assumed at the time, unsuitable for marriage. Sam felt that just as the family had pulled itself back together, it was falling apart again. He took to his bed for much of September and October, rising only to write a tale—to oblige Jean—asking mercy for horses, now rendered expendable by the growth of mechanical transportation. Sam revealed his difficulty in feeling close to his daughter when the girl he depicted in "A Horse's Tale" was not Jean, but Susy.

Sam's ill health and the unsettling family dynamics combined with news of the deaths of several old friends, including Henry Irving and John Hay, to make him short-tempered. Agreeing to speak at a benefit for a cause that interested his Monadnock neighbors, Mark Twain's first public appearance in over a year, he rolled halfway through an anecdote until the clicking of knitting needles arrested Sam mid-thought. He declared, "I have never had the pleasure of playing second fiddle to a sock, so I'll stop speaking! I suggest that you *all* knit more socks and sell them for your charity." Though he was not ready to return to the public, he felt the world crowding in on him, asking him to be Mark Twain once more.

Sam returned to New York in late October determined to resume an active life, but under new terms. The charity episode in New Hampshire had brought him to the painful and difficult realization that he could no longer maintain a clear distance between his public persona and his private self. Without Livy to shape the presentation of his image, he found it difficult to act the role of Mark Twain. On the other hand, he could not erase Twain, whose invention had brought him fame, wealth, and accolades from the wise. All he could do, other than retire from public life and leave the work and image of Mark Twain to ride the tide of public opinion, was to draw his public and private selves together; in short, surrender himself to Mark Twain. By finding a compromise between the image he had created and the man he had become, he could reinvent both into a single persona. Instead of inventing a past for Mark Twain as it suited him, as he had done, he would henceforth stick as close to the facts of Sam Clemens' life as his memory allowed. He would become the self he had begun forming when he dictated his life story to Isabel Lyon in Italy, before the growing closeness between them made it difficult for her to continue as amanuensis.

His seventieth birthday party, held on December 5, 1905, provided him with the perfect coming-out for his new self. George Harvey gathered a gross of guests at Delmonico's: writer friends, powerful men such as Henry Rogers and Andrew Carnegie, and more than sixty women, including Willa Cather and Emily Post. Howells served as toastmaster and concluded his introduction, using the nickname Lyon had bestowed on Sam, "I will not say, 'Oh King, live forever,' but 'Oh King, live as long as you like!' " Sam replied:

> The seventieth birthday! It is the time of life when you arrive at a new and awful dignity; when you may throw aside the decent reserves which have oppressed you for a generation and stand unafraid and unabashed upon your seven-terraced summit and look down and teach—unrebuked. . . .
>
> It is the Scriptural statute of limitation. After that, you owe no active duties; for you the strenuous life is over. . . . You pay the timeworn duty bills if you choose, or decline if you prefer—and without prejudice—for they are not legally collectible.

Laughter and sentiment notwithstanding, it was Sam's emancipation proclamation. No longer imprisoned by either the duality of his selves or a need for cash, Mark Twain had become a free man. Sam, determined to be one with his image, was free, too.

Sam now cared primarily for effect. " 'Wasted time' is no longer a matter of concern to me," he wrote Thomas Bailey Aldrich. "I have worked pretty steadily for 65 years, & I don't care what I do with the 2 or 3 that remain to me so that I get pleasure out of them." He wanted to extend his showmanship to fund-raising. "Give me a battalion of 200 winsome young girls and matrons," he wrote Helen Keller, the amazingly gifted blind and deaf woman whose education at Radcliffe Sam had persuaded Henry Rogers to pay for. "If I could mass them on the stage in front of the audience and instruct them there, I could make a public meeting take hold of itself and do something really valuable for once."

Within a month of his seventieth birthday party, Sam embarked on two projects he expected to carry him through the closing years of his life. Outside Carnegie Hall one December day, he introduced himself to fifteen-year-old Gertrude Natkin, who reminded him of Laura Wright, the girlish young woman he had courted on the Mississippi River nearly fifty years before, and who had returned to him regularly in his dreams. After a brief chat on the street, Sam wrote his new schoolgirl friend, initiating a frequent exchange of letters, phone calls, and visits that delighted the aging writer, an innocent romance that helped him put some distance between himself and the less innocent Isabel Lyon.

Then, during the first week of January 1906, Albert Bigelow Paine, who had attended the birthday banquet at Delmonico's, visited Sam at 21 Fifth Avenue and asked permission to write Mark Twain's biography. Paine, a scholarly man well-regarded in New York literary circles, had recently completed a life of the cartoonist Thomas Nast. "When would you like to begin?" Sam replied. "The longer you postpone a thing of this kind the less likely you are ever to get at it." Giving Paine a key to the house, Sam set up a small study for him and allowed him access to everything.

On January 9, 1906, Paine showed up with a stenographer, and Sam began to tell his stories. Sam paid for the stenographer himself, so that he would own the dictations. Very often, Sam had his own idea of what he wanted to talk about, and he would step right in with a tale from his youth; sometimes Paine would prompt him with an old manuscript or letter. Invariably, one subject would lead to another, and at his drawling rate of speech Sam produced about two thousand words of personal history each day. Spinning his talk into text in this way accomplished three things at once: He answered Paine's biographical questions; he recorded the blending of Sam Clemens and Mark Twain into a single persona; and he provided himself with material he could attach to each of his books as they came due for copyright renewal, so that he could republish them as new texts with new copyrights. Each morning, Paine came and Sam spoke from his bed; in the afternoons, the stenographer typed the dictations while Paine organized the mass of letters, manuscripts, and financial records that made up the physical evidence of Sam's life. Sam amused himself as he saw fit, sometimes with writing. In the evenings, he made his social rounds.

Paine recognized these autobiographical ramblings as a sly sort of fiction. He later wrote that "these marvelous reminiscences bore only an atmospheric relation to history; that they were aspects of biography rather than its veritable narrative, and built largely—sometimes wholly—from an imagination that, with age, had dominated memory." But Paine misunderstood Sam's intention. In truth, he got most of his facts right. What Sam falsified was the atmosphere. He was managing the image of the man these recollections were meant to construct. When the lives of Mark Twain and Sam Clemens veered too far apart—such as those times when Sam had wanted to eliminate his persona, or when he and Livy were at odds—he would alter the dictation to blur the seams between the two.

Paine also made a mistake in not anticipating the trouble he had stirred up with Isabel Lyon. Though impressed with Paine's industry, and reveling in Sam's oral narrative when her time allowed, she worried that Paine's book might endanger her right to publish Sam's letters. Satisfying as Sam found the process of re-creating himself in talk, the pitiful and tense condition of his home life mitigated the pleasure. His only unalloyed domestic joy was Bambino, a kitten Clara had rescued at the rest home the winter before. Sam taught the animal tricks, such as putting out his reading light when he got ready to sleep, a talent he showed off to visitors. Clara, who chafed at 21 Fifth Avenue's restrictive life, turned to Lyon for solace, and to travel for relief. She spent the winter moving from Norfolk to Atlantic City and back to New York for auditions with agents. Her mental disturbance lasted through the winter, and she shared Lyon's affection for bromides to help her sleep.

Jean's situation was even worse. She had seizures as often as three times in a day, followed by weeks of quiet. In a two-week period in November, she had six, culminating in a violent attack on Katy Leary. Lyon noted that "a sadness has settled over her, a gentleness that is pitiful, and you long for the masterful young creature" Jean had been before her relapse. In January, Jean confessed to Lyon that "a terrible thing had happened. In a burst of unreasoning rage she struck Katie [Leary] a terrible blow in the face." Lyon told her diary, "She knew she couldn't stop—she had to strike—and she said that she wanted to kill and was sorry she hadn't." Lyon sent her to a specialist in epilepsy, Dr. Frederick Peterson. When Jean, needing to be with someone at all times, refused to stay at Peterson's sanitarium, much of her care fell to Lyon, who was ill-equipped to handle her.

In the midst of Jean's attacks, Clara's absences, and his own dictations, Sam's mood varied. "When I was 43 and John Hay 41," he wrote in a letter, "he said life was a tragedy after 40, and I disputed it. Three years ago he asked me to testify again: I counted my graves, and there was nothing for me to say." Howells, who normally countered Sam's pessimism, this time agreed with Sam in this comment on his own sixty-ninth birthday: "I was born to be afraid of dying, but not of getting old. Age has many advantages, and if old men were not so ridiculous, I should not mind being one. But they *are* ridiculous, and they are ugly." The death at age sixty of Patrick McAleer, the family's coachman in Hartford, whom Sam described as "an ideal gentleman," only compounded Sam's feeling that his own survival was a tragedy. Like tragedy, though, his survival—Mark Twain's survival—could advance the public weal if put upon the public stage.

So despite his sorrow, Sam imbued Mark Twain with an energetic optimism. He took to the platform for a variety of good causes: Jewish victims of Russian pogroms, the association for the blind, the Tuskegee Institute and its president Booker T. Washington, the Robert Fulton

Monument Association, and Russian revolutionaries, in addition to a number of associations for the print media. His favorite cause was a Jewish children's theater on the Lower East Side; he believed that the arts would elevate young children above the depravity of the slums around them. In his public presentations at gatherings with high purpose, Sam no longer cared about investing his talk with moral substance. His very presence at these myriad functions for good causes was sufficient evidence of his inner seriousness. Now when he stood before his audiences, he did so as an unabashed humorist.

In April, when the Russian writer Maksim Gorky came to New York to build American support for a Russian revolution, Sam and Howells stepped forward as his sponsors. Sam believed, however, that awakening American sentiment would prove nearly as difficult as toppling the Russian monarchy. "We have lost our ancient sympathy when oppressed people struggle for life and liberty," he expressed himself privately in his dictations to Paine. "When we are not coldly indifferent to such things we sneer at them." Out of deference to Henry Rogers, Sam remained publicly silent about the ties between imperialism and capitalism. Instead, he argued that the United States had an obligation to help Russian revolutionaries in their goal of eliminating an oppressive ruler. "Because we were quite willing to accept France's assistance when we were in the throes of our Revolution, and we have always been grateful for that assistance. It is our turn now to pay that debt of gratitude by helping another oppressed people in its struggle for liberty, and we must either do it or confess that our gratitude to France was only eloquent words, with no sincerity back of it." Unfortunately, Gorky trampled his own hopes for American dollars by checking into his hotel with his mistress of many years. Sam and Howells had little choice but to withdraw their sponsorship for the dinner in Gorky's honor after he was hounded from hotel to hotel and forced to leave New York in disgrace.

The episode did nothing to mitigate Mark Twain's popularity, especially since the San Francisco earthquake and fire chased the story out of the newspapers a day later; Sam again mounted the platform, this time to raise funds for the victims' relief. Nothing abridged his fame. Attending a championship billiard match at Madison Square Garden with Henry Rogers, Mark Twain unintentionally stopped play by inspiring a spontaneous ovation. He often paraded on Fifth Avenue, greeting admirers, especially on Sunday when he timed his stroll to coincide with the crowds emerging from the churches along his route. Sometimes he walked from Ninth Street to Ninety-second, to Andrew Carnegie's house, and then rode home prominently in an open bus. Twainian quips and photographs of the grand old man spiced newspaper reports of his speeches. This public life merged Sam's private sensibilities into his thirst for a life lived on an open stage. He brought his public and private selves together emphatically in a long *Harper's* article praising the literary artistry of his friend William Dean Howells. Daring the public to find a gap between his identity and his image, he bylined the article S. L. Clemens, not Mark Twain.

All spring he used his autobiographical dictations to resolve his conflicting inclinations: his humor and his sorrow; his pains and his pleasures; his natural ebullience and his sense of tragedy. "I have led a turmoilsome life this winter," Sam wrote the Aldriches, "and am tired to the bone." The conflicting currents of his joy in society and his need for solitude found expression in his purchase of land in Redding, Connecticut, where Albert Bigelow Paine lived in a rural enclave similar to Sam's summer retreat at Dublin, New Hampshire. Sam wanted a country house there, some day, when he no longer needed the city to distract him from his troubled daughters.

Before leaving for Dublin with Jean, Lyon, Paine, the stenographer, and the Aeolian Orchestrelle, Sam arranged for the private and anonymous publication of 250 copies of "What Is Man?" In the final version of his "gospel," the wise old man proclaims not his innocence, which had been the foundation of Mark Twain's image since his first burst of fame forty years before, but only his guiltlessness. Innocence implies a temporary state, one inevitably replaced by knowledge and guilt; guiltlessness, on the other hand, is permanent, inviolate. Both his determinist gospel and his autobiographical dictations offered the same resolution to Sam's fundamental insecurity: If I can't take credit for the good I have accomplished in this life, at least I can escape blame for the bad.

As he left New York, he felt guilty about his relationship with Gertrude Natkin, the fifteen-year-old girl he had met outside Carnegie Hall around Christmas. During the winter and spring, Sam and Gertrude had written, spoken on the phone, or visited one another virtually every day. Sam had always admired very young women; his relationship with Gertrude was personal and playful, almost romantic, as far as social norms allowed for their fifty-five-year age difference. Gertrude wrote, "Words cannot express the pleasure which you afforded me yesterday," and Sam called her "you dear little rascal." She wrote him a valentine, he wrote her a poem, and their letters always closed with kisses. Gertrude also provided Sam with a safety valve for his ongoing relationship with Isabel Lyon, which threatened to veer into a marriage he did not want. Through Gertrude, he shunted his need for intimate contact in another, unconsummatable direction.

When Gertrude turned sixteen in April, however, he closed his birthday letter to her with a reluctant, written kiss. "Bless your heart it comes within an ace of being improper! Now back you go to 14!—then there's no impropriety." Sam had allowed himself to get carried away with Gertrude. He risked too much when, at a benefit lecture, he had thrown her kisses from the stage, a rather disturbing act for a seventy-year-old Moral Phenomenon. He had to allow his bond with the now perilously adult Gertrude to dissolve in the New Hampshire mountain mists. She wrote him plaintively after his departure, "If you only could realize how I love you. I can not express it but I suppose sending a few blots"—their word for kisses—"will help a little. I hope you will love me just the same."

Dublin did not prove as restful to Sam as it had the year before. Jean's sadness was more palpable than ever. At twenty-six, she was frustrated by her father's alternating unconcern and overprotectiveness, and by her desire to accomplish something on her own and her knowledge that she could not live unaided. Her very body was a metaphor for her situation, trapped between epilepsy and cupidity. "Why must I live on aimlessly, with nothing to do, utterly useless, all my life? I who long so for the love and companionship that only a man can give," she wrote in her diary. "Am I never to know what love means because I am an epileptic and shouldn't marry if I had the chance?" Sam and Lyon treated Jean as a contagion, attempting to isolate her from both themselves and the company she preferred. Gerry Thayer, Abbott Thayer's son, showed an interest in her, an interest she returned, but she noted that "father would at once raise every objection, no matter whether I were better in health, or who the man might be."

Sam also found his publishers distracting. Harper and Brothers issued an updated and altered version of *Mark Twain's Library of Humor* without Sam's knowledge or approval. Sam regarded Harper editor "Duneka, that Jesuit," as his enemy, because his "conduct in the 'Library of Humor' matter convicts him of being not merely a thief," Sam wrote Henry Rogers, "but a particularly low-down sneak-thief. I desire his scalp." He insisted that the company destroy the edition and the plates from which they had printed it. S. S. McClure turned Sam's head by offering him $50,000 for syndication rights to fifty thousand words of his autobiography. Sam spent most of July in New York, often sleeping on Rogers' yacht instead of in the hot Fifth Avenue house to avoid the marriage-minded Isabel Lyon, who meanwhile consulted with Clara and John Howells, their architect, to plan Sam's country house in Redding, Connecticut. Rogers advised patience, maintaining that Sam had to stick to the contract in order to keep Harper honest, but Sam threatened to take his books elsewhere. Even at Fairhaven, where Sam retreated frequently, he picked at this problem over endless games of pool.

While there, he also cemented a close tie with Rogers' daughter-in-law, Mary Benjamin Rogers, young Harry's wife. A vibrant, beautiful, and intelligent twenty-five-year-old mother of two, Mary was a safe replacement for Gertrude Natkin. At last, Sam and Rogers prevailed on George Harvey to intervene in Sam's battle with Duneka. In early August, Harvey held a summit with Sam in New Hampshire. He made Sam a satisfactory offer and outlined his plans to turn his *North American Review* into a more popular magazine, using Sam's autobiography to trumpet the change. Sam was both proud and uneasy. "I'd like to see a lot of this stuff in print before I die," he told Rogers, "—but not the *bulk* of it, oh no! I am not desiring to be crucified yet. Howells *thinks* the Auto will outlive Innocents Abroad a thousand years, and I *know* it will." Sam and Rogers celebrated the happy resolution of the conflict by spending three weeks cruising on the *Kanawha*.

Meanwhile, Clara was apprehensive about her solo debut as a singer, set for September 1906 in Norfolk. Her ambivalent attitude toward her father was perfectly crystallized when she could not decide whether to have him introduce her, have him speak afterward, or have him not attend at all. In the end, she decided to place him unobtrusively in the third row, but after the concert Sam, of his own accord, marched up to the platform to give Clara a kiss. When Clara led her father on stage as she returned for her encore, the audience demanded a speech, which over-shadowed Clara's performance in the newspaper reports. Locked in a strange battle for love, neither Sam nor his daughter realized how far a long talk might take them toward peace. Sam instead filled the day spent in Norfolk writing a letter of devotion to Mary Rogers. "I spoke for twenty minutes," he wrote, "& that is the only speech I have ever made that *entirely* satisfied me." Sam retreated to Mary's company at Fairhaven and then ten days later teased Clara, "perhaps you thought I couldn't leave my niece, Mary Rogers, but I did it. I came away from Fairhaven yesterday." He stopped briefly in New Hampshire to bring Jean and the others back to New York.

Once Sam returned to Fifth Avenue, the enforced proximity of his daughters tried his emotional patience. Clara parlayed her Norfolk success into a series of bookings, which she shook in Sam's face to "prove to me that her time is already worth a thousand dollars a month." At thirty-two, Clara felt the right to govern her aging father, as she had been governed by him. She even objected when he escaped for an afternoon of billiards. Sam wrote Mary Rogers, "The fact is, I have to lead a life of chicane and deception with this end of the family, although it is against my nature and principles." Sam repaid Clara—when she threatened to drop her concert dates and rush off to Vienna, where her teacher Leschetizky seemed to be dying—by "persuading her that she would feel very funny if she attended his [funeral] and missed mine. I guess that that settled it and she won't go; for naturally she wouldn't miss mine for anything." In her diary, Jean noted her sister's difficult relationship with Sam: "I can't help feeling that Clara's love for Father is not what it should be." Yet Jean's own love for Sam received a severe test after their return to New York. Though his presence calmed her, she had had many seizures during Sam's absence from New Hampshire. The rest of the household felt uneasy around her. Isabel Lyon, spurned and drinking, feared her. On the recommendation of Dr. Peterson, Sam decided to put Jean in a sanitarium at Katonah, farther up the Hudson River. She capitulated to her father's request.

Now free of his unhappy daughters, Sam planned a trip to Egypt, but nearly as quickly he fell ill and canceled it. Henry and Emilie Rogers thought a pool table might provide Sam as much amusement as a trip overseas. They intended it as a Christmas present, but Sam begged to have it sooner. Rogers, who stopped in every morning to "furnish advice and abuse," as Sam jokingly told Jean, agreed. The table arrived in November and occupied Sam's study; he moved his own papers to his bedroom, allowing the pool table to both literally and figuratively crowd out his work. Paine was a ready billiard partner, and they played as obsessively now as he and Isabel had played cards in the year after Livy's death.

Without Gertrude Natkin, Sam felt he needed another buffer between himself and the fervent attentions of Isabel Lyon, so he asked Paine to move in with him for the winter. Lyon, believing her relationship with "the King" was under siege, willfully misunderstood Sam's routine agitation about money as legitimate worry, put Clara on short rations, and interrupted the progress on the house at Redding. When Paine worsened the situation by telling Lyon the rumors circulating at the Players Club concerning Sam's relationship with Charlotte Teller, a young writer living nearby, Lyon immediately arranged a meeting with Sam, Teller, Paine, and herself. With little but innuendo to go on, Lyon gained nothing but shot nerves from the experience. She retreated to Hartford for a rest. As Sam had noted a few months earlier, "The course of free love never runs smooth. I suppose we have all tried it." After her return to New York, Lyon wrote that Sam could leave her if he wished, "but I shall not go away from him again unless he sends me."

Hoping to rise above the maelstrom of life at 21 Fifth Avenue, Sam adopted a sartorial change. From now on, he would wear white clothing only, regardless of the season. He chose his December testimony before Congress on a new copyright reform measure as the first venue for displaying his ensemble. Only a row of ever-ready cigars peeking out of his coat pockets and his favorite fountain pen, clipped to his upper vest pocket, interrupted the flow of whiteness. Howells recalled, "Nothing could have been more dramatic than the gesture with which he flung off his long loose overcoat, and stood forth in white from his feet to the crown of his silvery head. It was a magnificent *coup*, and he dearly loved a *coup*." When Paine, who accompanied Sam to Washington, took him to dinner at his hotel by an elevator opening directly into the dining room, Sam asked, "Isn't there another entrance to this place?" Paine led him back upstairs and they rode a different elevator, which deposited them in the main lobby. There Sam sauntered down the showy staircase, through the busy corridors, and into the crowded dining room, contented.

His quest for effect invaded his private life. Sam appointed Paine his literary executor, which irritated Clara. Piqued, she refused to attend Sam's New Year's party. Sam opened his house to more entertaining, especially what he called "buck" and "doe" luncheons, for men and women, respectively. Lyon coordinated all of these gatherings and kept Sam's social calendar, on most occasions sitting in with the guests. In January, Sam took Joe Twichell on a nostalgic trip to Bermuda, but Twichell had gone deaf and showed an old man's focus on his aches and pains. While Sam was in Bermuda, Thomas Bailey Aldrich died. He mourned the loss in a dictation: "Of the gay company of us that used to foregather in Boston, thirty-five years ago and more, not one is left but [Howells] and me." Most of Sam's remaining friends, except Howells and Rogers, merely annoyed him.

When Clara left for a concert tour and Paine went west in February 1907 to interview Sam's old companions, loneliness preyed on the aging man. Though Sam told Rogers that Lyon was "as extraordinarily competent as ever" in her official duties, she could not provide Sam the company he desired. He wanted crowds, adulation, honors, and instead he had only a long solitary winter. "This is too dreadful, this loneliness for the King," Lyon noted. "I telephone in every direction to get hold of people to come in for billiards, but no one is to be reached." William James told his brother Henry that he found Sam "only good for monologue, in his old age." Sam's world grew lonelier, and he again felt like a fraud.

Sam once again escaped for a few days to Bermuda, with Lyon and another young girl he had met, but she did not prove as engaging a companion as Gertrude Natkin. As a reward for her efforts in concocting his future house in Redding, Connecticut—and in compensation for the altered circumstances between them—Sam gave Isabel Lyon a house with twenty acres of land within walking distance of his future home. During the winter and spring, Clara traveled with her accompanist Charles "Will" Wark, rumored to be linked with her romantically; she also made periodic appearances in New York, where Ossip Gabrilowitsch spent the winter. Although she felt the tour had succeeded musically, it failed financially, and Lyon noted that this first leg "has cost at least $2,500.00." Sam only answered, using his nickname for his daughter, "Pay the bills and tell Ben to go ahead." He decided to summer at the luxurious private enclave, Tuxedo Park, near Mary Rogers. Unlike Clara and Jean, who always mixed heartache with their filial affection, his surrogate daughter Mary was sweet and untroubled.

Still, recurrent dreams bothered Sam. Though money was abundant, some of the dreams concerned bankruptcy. In one, financial straits again force him to return to lecturing, but he has nothing to say and ends up addressing an empty hall. In his most bothersome dream, he attends a brilliant gathering wearing only nightclothes; no one hears him explain, "I am Mark Twain!" These metaphors for his uncertainty about his worth recurred when Sam considered that Howells had received an honorary degree from Oxford in 1904, while Sam himself had heard nothing regarding that honor. Then in late May word came that Sam would receive a degree from Oxford the next month. He had mentioned his desire for the honor to a British journalist, and after the announcement Sam wrote to thank him. Sam decided to take Ralph Ashcroft to England as his secretary, and Lyon, feeling left out, cattily wrote that "the King" had cheapened his Oxford crown by asking for it. On June 8, 1907, Sam sailed for England, dressed in white and every inch the public man.

53

Heaven Is Populated with Angelfish

From youth to middle age all men and all women prize copulation above all other pleasures combined, yet it is . . . not in their heaven; prayer takes its place.
—*Letters from the Earth* (1909)

SAM'S FRIENDSHIP WITH Gertrude Natkin whetted his appetite for further association with young girls, who replaced his own children, no longer young, and revived the scintillation of courtship that he had enjoyed with Laura Wright, Emeline Beach, and Livy. He liked trim, well-educated virgins in their teen years, capable of charming conversation and appreciative of his playful humor. Cruise ships offered Sam an excellent supply of the girls he fancied; with parents wealthy enough for travel, the girls were typically articulate, well-mannered, and well-groomed. On the boat to England, Sam met two, Carlotta Welles and Frances Nunnally. Though flattered by Sam's attentions, Welles, whom Sam called Charlie, repulsed his intense attentions. Sam reacted like a spurned lover. "You don't know what you are missing," he wrote to her in her cabin. "There's more than two thousand porpoises in sight, and eleven whales, and sixty icebergs, and both Dippers, and seven rainbows, and all the battleships of all the navies, and me." Francesca, as he called Nunnally, embraced his company and joined Sam on many of his London social calls.

He expected to attend a few necessary events, see some old friends, receive his degree, and then leave, but the reception the English gave

Mark Twain rivaled that accorded him on his return to America in 1900. Most gratifying for Sam, even the stevedores put aside their labor to applaud him when he disembarked. Reporters crowded around him and the hotel lobby became his sitting room, with acquaintances forever pressing for Sam's attention. When the Ascot Cup—the trophy given the winner of Britain's most important horse race—disappeared the day Sam arrived, the British newspapers laughingly accused Mark Twain of the robbery. It became the running joke of his stay.

Ralph Ashcroft found himself much busier than he anticipated keeping Sam in line. The grand old public man went from breakfast meeting, to luncheon, then to tea, a reception and a banquet, and Ashcroft had to find a way to balance visits with the people Sam wanted to meet with those he felt he had to. His old friends usually reserved breakfast with him. He lunched with newer ones, like playwright and critic George Bernard Shaw, who credited Mark Twain with teaching him that "telling the truth's the funniest joke in the world." Whitelaw Reid, the newspaper publisher Sam had long regarded as his nemesis both in print and in the typesetter wars, was now American ambassador to the Court of St. James's and thus responsible for Sam's royal introduction. At a party at the palace, Sam got reacquainted with King Edward VII, whom he had met in Homburg before his ascension, and drew some carping in the press when reporters saw him touch the king and wear his hat before the queen, though Sam explained the king had put his hand on Sam, not the other way around, and that the queen had commanded him to put on his hat. These minor criticisms in any case did little to undermine Mark Twain's universal appeal as a literary man without a trace of elitism, an emblematic American unafraid of pointing out the humor in even the most sacred of European idols. Everyone wanted to be near him: Even the caterer of one dinner dressed as a waiter just to have the honor of serving him.

The presumed faux pas involving gestures of familiarity with royalty were not the only tiny scandals spicing Sam's visit. He also walked across the street from his hotel to the public bath "in his three-piece costume of one bathrobe and two slippers, and had the pleasure of making a lot more people open their eyes very wide," as the *London Times* reported. In New York, Lyon panicked at the news; Clara cabled, "Much worried. Remember proprieties." Sam replied, "They all pattern after me." But even if he actually had stolen the Ascot Cup, Mark Twain would have been forgiven. Though Rudyard Kipling, Auguste Rodin, Whitelaw Reid, and Salvation Army founder General William Booth received Oxford honorary degrees beside Sam, the crowd greeted Mark Twain with the wildest applause. Sam remarked that the commencement parade gave him "ideas for my funeral procession, which I am planning on a large scale." At the Savage Club dinner on July 6, 1907, the club presented Sam with a replica of the Ascot Cup, with a bust of himself in place of the acorn normally at the top.

He sailed out of Liverpool, his thirst for honor temporarily quenched. He even had the good luck to meet another girl on board the return boat, Dorothy Quick, only eleven but bright, attractive, and familiar with his books. When Sam spoke at the ship's benefit of the Sailor's Fund, the program read, "Mark Twain (By courtesy of Miss Dorothy Quick)." On his arrival in New York, photographers couldn't get enough pictures, and the papers ran headlines such as MARK TWAIN HOME—CAPTIVE OF LITTLE GIRL. Though the friendship of a seventy-one-year-old man and an eleven-year-old girl risked opprobrium, the conjunction of Mark Twain's white clothes, his adoration of children as demonstrated by his books, his reputation for honor formed by his repayment of his debts, and public sympathy for his private sorrows made this relationship seem both fitting and enchanting.

Sam went immediately to Tuxedo Park, where Dorothy Quick promised to visit him. Before he could even settle in, though, newspapers reported that Henry Rogers had suffered a stroke. Sam believed the story was simple exaggeration—Rogers' family and Standard Oil denied the reports—and did not discover the severity of the attack until mid-August. Rogers wanted Sam to come to Fairhaven to visit, but Sam stayed at Tuxedo; he was expecting Dorothy. "When Dorothy went away," Sam wrote Clara after her visit, "she took the sun & the moon & the constellations with her, & left silence & solitude & night & desolation behind her." Clearly hurt by such sentiments, Clara had retreated to Norfolk after Sam came back from London. Lyon reported, "He said that he didn't get much good out of Clara." During Clara's visit at Tuxedo Park, when he went "to her rooms he feels like a stranger making an untimely and unwelcome visit. Poor King!"

Only after Dorothy made another ten-day visit in September did Sam go to Fairhaven, where he found that the stroke had rendered the left side of Rogers' body unresponsive and his speech slurred and slow. Sam wrote to Dorothy, to Francesca, and to another girl he had met in England. In this round of correspondence, he found a way to satisfy his desire for youthful innocence without growing too possessive of it, as he had with Gertrude Natkin. By spreading his attentions among many girls, he attached more to their quality of innocence than to the girls as individuals. He wrote them playful gibes, fanciful descriptions of his cats, and foolish romances, but he never mentioned "the damned human race," or microbes, or the carelessness of God; he never even mentioned that his closest friend had suffered a stroke.

Sam could not sustain literary interest in anything except letters to his young friends and his dictations, which had become mainly comments on his present life and expositions on politics or art rather than actual autobiography. He revised "Captain Stormfield's Visit to Heaven," a story Livy had made him shelve thirty years earlier on the pretext of blasphemy; now Colonel Harvey regarded it as too reverent. So instead, Sam worked into a story he called "Wapping Alice" the incident from the mid-1870s, when he had forced a reluctant man to choose between prison and marriage to a maid in Sam's house. Oddly, he transformed the maid into a male transvestite, thereby both subverting his own sexual history and exacerbating his own guilt in this paternalistic meddling. Given a choice between these two tales for its Christmas issue, *Harper's Weekly* not surprisingly selected the godly visit to heaven. The money from the story allowed Sam to expand the Redding house beyond the original plans in order to accommodate Clara's desire for a suite instead of just a room.

Isabel Lyon traveled to Redding regularly to check on the progress of the construction of Sam's house, which he declared he did not "want to see it until the cat is purring on the hearth." She also supervised the improvements on her own place, for which Sam had loaned her $1,500. She arranged the visits of Sam's young friends with their parents and cautioned them against using slang when Sam could hear them; he felt that "slang in a woman's mouth is not obscene, it only sounds so." Lyon also went to Katonah to visit Jean and consult with Dr. Peterson, who gave a dismal report on Jean's condition. Jean was miserable and wanted to come home. She told her diary, "Father can't possibly find any entertainment or interest in me. I am sure he is fond of me but I don't believe that he any more than Clara, really misses me." Lyon still feared Jean's seizures, and Sam did not feel wholly equal to handling her. Lyon's management of his life impressed Sam, but their relationship had changed completely. Rumors, some of them in print, had earlier pointed to an impending marriage between Sam and Lyon, but when Sam denied them publicly, Lyon became merely his underpaid and overzealous employee.

Ralph Ashcroft's competence in leading him around England gave Sam increased confidence in him. Ashcroft, whom Lyon nicknamed Benares, established the Mark Twain Company to handle all his licensing arrangements, endorsements, and investments. The company quickly received patents for Mark Twain Tobacco and Mark Twain Whiskey, creating the equivalent of a trademark for Sam's pen name, a technique he had tried with mixed results three decades earlier. The company seemed a likely place to store his copyrights as well, securing them as surety for his daughters' future. To Sam, it was institutional evidence that Mark Twain would endure beyond the death of Samuel Langhorne Clemens.

Back in New York in the fall of 1907, Sam and Paine tried to resist the lure of the pool table, so that Paine at least could work. Sam sent dozens of letters to his young girl friends. He loved their fawning compliments; he told Francesca, who had visited at Tuxedo Park, that he could live for days on a good compliment. He sent a mock want ad to Mary Rogers:

BUTTER WANTED
Any Kind:
    New; Old;
    Salted; Unsalted;
    Odorless; Fragrant;
Real preferred, but
    Oleomargarine not turned away.

Butter was Sam's code word for compliments, especially the sort he had given up hope of receiving from his daughters. Instead, he found another girl on the street in New York, and others during a trip to Bermuda. Struck by the beauty of the angelfish on the island, he settled on that as the best name for his collection of young friends. To Sam, there was a magical quality to this choice of name, which echoed his nickname for Livy—Angel—and savored of a sensuality that was implied, but also thoroughly subdued, in these ambiguous relationships, unbalanced in terms of their age and his fame. He bought a handful of enamel-and-gold pins in the shape and colors of angelfish to distribute to members of his club, now called the Aquarium.

Hardly a day passed without at least a letter, visit, or phone call from an Angelfish. The Aquarium filled Sam's heart with a joy it had not felt for a decade. When Dorothy Quick came for a weekend in December, she brought Sam a Christmas present, not knowing that he had not acknowledged Christmas since Susy's death. She handed him the present with girlish pleasure and awaited his thanks. Years later, she would describe his reaction:

> A shadow crossed his face as he came back from the far places into which he had been catapulted by my "Merry Christmas"—a shadow that made his countenance seem like that of someone I didn't know at all. I tightened my arm

around his neck and put my face against his. I didn't understand, but I knew something was wrong and instinctively clung to him for comfort.

The shadow lightened; then it disappeared, and his face resumed its natural expression. "Is this for me"? he asked.

As close to his old humanity as his Aquarium brought him, Sam could not sustain it without them being near. In their absence, he frequently drank too much and played cards or billiards until nearly dawn. One January night, he, Lyon, and Ashcroft demolished a quart of Scotch and Sam, drunk, "sailed around the room trying to reach the door and landing up in the corner by the Joan of Arc. He cast a gay little eye over at me in his unsteady gait," Lyon noted, "and said 'I'm just practicing.'" The next night, she found him awake at two-thirty playing pool with Paine "in a drunken haze." Tensions rose between Lyon and Paine, whom Lyon nicknamed Tino, over rights to the letters. With Clara's support, Lyon got Sam to restrict Paine to quoting no more than ten thousand words from his correspondence. He wrote Howells in January, "If Paine should apply to you for letters, please don't comply. I must warn Twichell, too. A man should be dead before his private foolishnesses are risked in print." Howells responded that Sam was too late; Paine had them already. Though Jean at last prevailed on her father to allow her to leave Katonah, Sam would not allow her to come home. Instead, she set up house with a friend in Greenwich, Connecticut, but by spring she had moved to a place near Gloucester, Massachusetts. Her sister as well brought Sam little comfort. Clara gave a recital at 21 Fifth Avenue on January 7, 1908, but "the King didn't come down until the music was over," as Lyon reported; "he listened over the ballusters, and I heard him gently clicking the billiard balls around in between times."

Sam chose to escape to what he liked to call "Bermooda" for two weeks with Ashcroft, and then again for nearly two months, from the end of February until the middle of April, with Lyon and Henry Rogers. Although in January Rogers had seemed almost completely recovered from his stroke, by late February he appeared to Lyon to be once again "a grey feeble man." During his first trip, Sam spent most of his time with new Angelfish Margeret Blackmer, a Bermuda friend of his island buddy Elizabeth Wallace, a dean at the University of Chicago. On the second trip, Henry Rogers and Betsy Wallace formed the Samuel L. Clemens Life-Saving Society, with the comic purpose of saving Sam from himself; whenever they saw him buttonholed by a bore, they would scoop him away. On Bermuda, Sam had no drive to go sightseeing since "he had probably seen the oldest house in the world, the longest street, the biggest city, the most wonderful cathedral, the highest mountain—so why should he bother himself now, in his old age, to see second-rate curiosities?" Instead, Rogers, Wallace, Lyon, and Sam contented themselves with company and cards. Sam and Rogers amused everyone with their patter, in which they would "abuse each other with an earnestness entirely deceptive to the uninitiated." They called one another the King and the Rajah, invoking sanctimonious tones when chastising each other's card playing. The Bermuda freedom from worry or constraint did both Sam and Rogers good. When Emilie Rogers arrived in mid-March, she found her husband quite restored. They all came back to New York together in mid-April.

The Bermuda trip did not give Sam as much relief from his daughters as he had hoped for. Though Clara was on a concert tour in the spring, traveling with her accompanist Will Wark, a violinist, and Katy Leary as her maid, her tour again experienced more artistic than financial success. While Sam was in Bermuda, Lyon received word from Ashcroft that "the good ship Clara Clemens ran ashore yesterday on the No Money shoals, while bound South. Cost of salvage, $300., which please remit." Clara and her entourage sailed for Europe barely a month after Sam returned from Bermuda, and within a few weeks Clara wrote again asking for money. While she was in Europe, rumors about her impending marriage to Wark filtered into the newspapers in America. After Sam's return to New York, lonely, desolate Jean hoped that her father would visit her in Gloucester, Massachusetts, but when he did plan a visit, he was constrained by what Lyon told him Jean's physician had said. "I should like to tarry with you a considerable spell," he wrote Jean, "but Dr. Peterson will not allow that. For your good, he will restrict me to hours, not days." Jean's growing unhappiness in Gloucester led Lyon to develop a new plan for her: Berlin. Much as Jean enjoyed Germany and loved foreign languages, she wrote Lyon that she dreaded going. "I did *so* want to be in Redding." The house there neared completion in the spring of 1908, but construction delays kept Sam in New York until June.

His Angelfish remained the heart of his existence. In a dictation, he noted that after Livy's death, "I was washing about on a forlorn sea of banquets and speechmaking in high and holy causes—industries which furnished me intellectual cheer and entertainment, but got at my heart for an evening only, then left it dry and dusty." He justified his fascination with the girls, "I had reached the grandpa stage of life; and what I lacked and what I needed, was grandchildren." He acted the role of grandfather with his young friends. Once, when Dorothy Quick came for a weekend at Fifth Avenue, Sam showed her a surprise. Her favorite cat, Tammany—

whose regular perch on the pool table meant that players must accommodate their game to her presence—had had kittens, which she kept in the coal bin. Sam and Dorothy, unmindful of their white clothes, climbed over the coals for a look, and then went upstairs to meet Dorothy's mother completely besmudged.

Schoolgirls represented more than grandchildren to Sam. He also said, "I collect pets: young girls—girls from ten to sixteen years old; girls who are pretty and sweet and naive and innocent—dear young creatures to whom life is a perfect joy and to whom it has brought no wounds, no bitterness, and few tears." They replicated both his platonic sweetheart, the dream ideal of romance first embodied in Laura Wright and then realized in Livy until time had abrogated her youth; and the lost girlhoods of his own children, which Sam had missed because of his dedication to writing, publishing, and the typesetter. In his old age, he could recapture a taste of girlishness, a chance to remake opportunities he felt badly about having squandered. Sam designated the billiard room at Redding as Aquarium headquarters and instructed Lyon to frame pictures of the girls alongside illustrations of real angelfish. Each girl as she visited would choose an illustration and sign it as her own. Sam called the Redding house Innocence at Home, representing his Angelfish. The final cost of the house's construction, at $45,000, was nearly double what Sam had anticipated, but with his finances on a sound basis, the cost mattered little. Innocence at Home was his first permanent residence in seventeen years, and his Angelfish promised him serenity there.

Sam moved to Redding on June 18, 1908. The local people, excited by the arrival of their famous new resident Mark Twain, turned out to greet him at the station with wagons, carts, and buggies fully garlanded with flowers and escorted him the three miles to Innocence at Home. Sam toured his new lodgings with boyish excitement, taking the stairs two and three at a time and complimenting Lyon on how superbly she had decorated the house. That night, he held a housewarming party, during which the builder H. A. Lounsbury and Sam's former illustrator Dan Beard set off fireworks; the flashes illuminated the two men, whom Sam called in to join the party, without regard to their dirty clothes. It seemed a "fixed principle," Beard remarked, "that all those to whom the hospitable gates were open stood upon an equal footing." In Sam's first eight weeks of residence in Redding, twenty-one overnight visitors signed the guest book, which had been a gift from the ever-attentive Mary Rogers.

Sam constructed new rules for his Angelfish, institutionalizing their playful conspiracies, all of which had to exclude Ralph Ashcroft, a favorite target of their hoaxes. Ashcroft frequently made the one-and-a-half-hour train trip from New York to consult with Sam and to visit Isabel Lyon, to whom he had grown close. Lyon supported the Aquarium by scheduling visits and arranging Sam's time so that he could have afternoons free. Sam's new home thrilled him, especially the billiard room and the loggia, an open terrace that led to the gardens and paths where Sam and the Angelfish played games. He wrote John Howells, "It is the ideal house, the ideal home." In midsummer, after the senior Howellses had returned from a long sojourn in Europe, Sam asked him to "come, & give us as many days as you can spare, & examine John's triumph."

Then, in August, Sam Moffett, Sam's nephew and lately an editor at *Collier's Weekly,* died while vacationing on the New Jersey shore. Moffett "was drowned in the sight of his little son, and almost in sight of his wife. It is the most heart-broken family I have seen in years," he wrote Emilie Rogers. After he returned from the funeral in New York City, Sam collapsed while playing pool with Paine. Despite his abundant energy in short bursts, his failing health revealed itself in the trouble he had remembering words and in the way he now tired so easily. Doctors instructed him not to leave the house for several weeks.

Sam wrote Howells, "I have retired from New York for good, I have retired from labor for good, I have discharged my stenographer, & have entered upon a holiday whose other end is in the cemetery." Sam disguised the truth for his Angelfish, writing Dorothy Quick of his New York trip, but not disclosing its grievous purpose. After Sam's attack, Lyon and Ashcroft closed in around him. Excluding Paine from Sam's closest circle, Lyon declared her proprietary interest in Mark Twain, telling herself that "Benares and I have a moral obligation, now, in looking after the King. I shall not leave him for an hour unless Benares or another as good is here to look after him." She secured Colonel George Harvey's support in defense of her interest in the correspondence, but she did not secure Clara's. Upon Clara's return from Europe, she and Lyon fell out over Lyon's domination of the new house. Clara refused to occupy the suite built for her and moved to New York. Lyon took the suite herself to be close to Sam, installing her mother at her own small house. Clara came to see her father irregularly.

During one of Clara's rare visits, on September 18, 1908, two burglars broke into the house in the small hours. After the thieves placed Livy's Langdon silver in a bag, one of them made a noise that roused the house. Claude Benchotte, the butler, fired shots to scare off the intruders. When a maid went to rouse Ashcroft, his bed was untouched; he was with Lyon. Sam later claimed to have sleepily regarded the pistol shots as champagne corks popped by Clara's guests at a party to which he was not invited, but in fact, he woke and stayed awake, writing a letter to the New York City commissioner of police identifying the stolen silver. At dawn, the sheriff, with Clara's friend Will Wark and local builder H. A. Lounsbury, tracked the burglars to a New York-bound train, where the sheriff apprehended the felons after a gun battle. An Angelfish arrived for a visit that day and helped Sam post a notice on the door for future burglars: "There is nothing but plated ware in this house, now and henceforth. You will find it in that brass thing in the dining-room over in the corner by the basket of kittens. If you want the basket, put the kittens in the brass thing."

Sam could not take the event as lightly as the notice implied. A week later he wrote to Howells, "Not a woman in this house has had a whole solid hour's sleep since. I mean Clara, Miss Lyon & all the others. They drop into feverish cat-naps, & at the very slightest & almost inaudible noises they spring to a sitting posture, panting & gasping & quaking. It is pitiful." Clara and her friends soon left for New York and most of the servants went too. They disliked the isolation of Redding, resented Lyon's high-handed treatment of the staff, and could not work when authority to direct them was divided between Clara and Lyon. Lyon hired new staff, consolidating her control. Clara took the minor revenge of insisting that her father change the name of the house from Innocence at Home to Stormfield.

54 | Conspiracy Against the King

There are several good protections against temptations, but the surest is cowardice.
—"Pudd'nhead Wilson's New Calendar" (1897)

The principal difference between a cat and a lie it that a cat has only nine lives.
—"Pudd'nhead Wilson's New Calendar" (1897)

ON THE LAST day of September 1908, Sam wrote one of his Angelfish that Isabel Lyon couldn't find anyone for him to play with. He groused, "And so, all day today, & all day tomorrow & all day next day there isn't going to be *anybody* here but *me*, and I don't count, a personal society. *These* aren't the 'bes' g.d. days' for me, for sure." Nearing age seventy-three, Sam knew his physical afflictions would become progressively more severe and his recoveries wretchedly slow. At least his final months would promise some pleasures. His wealth bought him luxury. Clara and Jean gave him what they could, and the Angelfish provided the rest of what he hoped for from his offspring. He had three loving friends in Joe Twichell, William Dean Howells, and Henry Rogers, and the affection of nearly every literate person in the world. He had some special amusements, such as the trial of the men who had robbed his house, and his building of a public library for his Redding neighbors. He felt well enough to travel to New York periodically to visit Howells and the Rogers clan, with whom he stayed. He scheduled trips to Fairhaven, but the plans were broken up by waves of company. Being in school most of the time, the Angelfish could not visit often, but other guests made the foray to Redding for Sam's good company, fine food, and lovely accommodations. Every male guest had to leave a dollar on the mantel for the Mark Twain Library or forfeit his luggage. Sam felt satisfied with his position as a man worth going to see. "I've grown young in these past three months of dissipation here," he wrote Emilie Rogers. "And I have left off drinking—it isn't necessary now. Society and theology are sufficient for me." Sam agreed to perform "the same old string of yarns" to benefit the library. Howells wrote back, disconcerted, "Poor fellow, I thought you went to Redding to get rid of Mark Twain." But Mark Twain was no longer a burden to Sam Clemens; he was not only a source of pride, but Sam's only meaningful promise for the future.

His practical affairs were in the steady and reliable hands of Ralph Ashcroft and Isabel Lyon, who—as if according to a time-worn plot— had found solace and companionship in one another. Sam signed the power of attorney drawn up by Ashcroft authorizing Ashcroft and Lyon to act for him, and placing all of Sam's assets in the Mark Twain Company, under the directorship of Sam, Lyon, and Ashcroft. Establishing a corporation bearing his pen name created a limited immortality for Sam; though he could not prevent his demise, he could enable his public persona to cheat death, transforming Sam into an old Tom Sawyer surviving his own funeral. Such macabre reflections affected Sam's letters to his Angelfish, endangering the very innocence he cherished in them. For example, Sam asked his Angelfish to wear black ribbons on November 30, 1908, supposedly in memory of Sam's cat Tammany, mauled by a dog. The day was actually Sam's seventy-third birthday.

Clara did not trust Ashcroft, and her former affection for Lyon had disappeared. Clara felt hurt that these two interlopers represented a shield between herself and her father; she wanted to control the terms of her contact with him, not submit to Lyon and Ashcroft. She also suspected that the two had designs on Sam's fortune, and thus hers, and the recent reorganization of Sam's assets into the Mark Twain Company only seemed to confirm this. Despite her father's intention that his daughters split the estate, Clara feared that Ashcroft and Lyon might interfere. She already felt an unjust financial pinch from Lyon. Once, when she was shopping for underwear with Katy, Clara fondly handled a beautifully embroidered piece. Katy suggested she buy it, but Clara said she couldn't afford it. Katy observed that Isabel Lyon had many similar articles, and Clara responded, "Yes, but I don't control Father's checkbook."* She tried to communicate her uneasiness to her father, but he would not give her a hearing.

In December, Clara came to Redding for most of the month, and

Ossip Gabrilowitsch was a houseguest for two weeks, through New Year's. Christmas proved a truly happy occasion, for the first time in years. Only Jean, living in Berlin with her friend Marguerite Schmidt, was missing from Stormfield's first Christmas. Jean thrived in Germany, feeling so well that she performed "The Golden Arm" for a benefit there, so the telegram from Redding, dated December 17, 1908, was especially odd. It read, "You sail January ninth steamer Pennsylvania passage prepaid. Send Marguerite home. Dont cable. Father." In fact, Sam never sent this message; cautiously superstitious, he would not have allowed Jean to travel on a steamship bearing the same name as the boat that had killed his brother Henry. Isabel Lyon, however, feared Jean's freedom. She worried that Sam could not resist Clara's pleas to reexamine the disposition of his estate if Jean joined in, and so wanted Jean under closer watch. By February 1909, Jean was hidden away at a farm on Long Island.

Jean was not the only one in transit during that winter. Paine took an extended trip to the Mediterranean, to revisit the places Sam had visited on the *Quaker City* tour more than forty years before. Ashcroft went to England on business, having reorganized the American Plasmon Company as the American Milk Products Company, with Sam as president but with himself in charge. Before he left, Clara suggested to him that an objective person review her father's books. Ashcroft responded, "Are you sure you want to, since it will reveal *your* expenditures?" Clara, uncertain how large her own withdrawals had been, kept her silence. Ossip Gabrilowitsch left for a concert tour and Clara would have gone with him, but she saw an opportunity to press her case because Isabel Lyon had "a sort of nervous break-down, attributable to too much work & care," as Sam wrote Francesca Nunnally. "But she is mending." Lyon was well enough after Ashcroft's return to accept his proposal of marriage, though they kept their plans a secret from Sam. "The psychic moment hasn't come yet for telling the King," she wrote a friend. On February 23, 1909, after a particularly overwhelming run of guests, Lyon left Redding for another ten-day hiatus. She wrote Sam of the wedding plans while she was away.

Lyon's absences gave Clara her opportunity. She returned to Stormfield, prepared to camp out in her father's room until he accepted that Isabel Lyon had embezzled funds and that Ralph Ashcroft intended worse. Day after day, Clara followed Sam as he rambled from his bedroom to his billiard table, arguing that he needed an impartial review of his finances. When Sam scoffed at Clara's accusations, she recalled the duplicity of his past trusted aides: his friend Dan Slote, his nephew Charley Webster, his lawyer Daniel Whitford. Sam had thought he was safe from all of that now, but Clara seemed certain that he was not. She harangued him until

Sam felt desperate. Paine's wife wrote her distant husband that the "poor old man is being driven almost crazy" by the accusations. Sam told her that "until three weeks ago he thought he was happy and well off, but since then it has been h—— and that if things did not get better he would cut his G—— D—— throat."

At the beginning of March, with all the principals on site at Stormfield, Sam sought a balance between the competing agendas. He did not believe that either Ashcroft or Lyon had criminal intentions. "I know Ashcroft & Miss Lyon better & more intimately than I have ever known anyone except your mother," Sam tellingly wrote Clara, in New York for a day, "and I am quite without suspicion of either their honesty or their honorableness." Still, on March 13, 1909, he and Ashcroft held a "General Clean-up Day," codifying the jobs and relationships, such as Ashcroft's role in the Mark Twain Company and Lyon's duties as social secretary. The papers made explicit Sam's knowledge that Lyon had used Sam's money to repair her house and buy the clothes necessary for her job, stripped Lyon of control of Sam's checkbook, and raised Lyon's salary to $100 a month. Ashcroft agreed to a review of the books. With the papers signed, Sam wrote Clara, "Nothing is as it was. Everything is changed. Sentiment has been wholly eliminated. All things in this house are now upon a strictly business basis."

This negotiated settlement brought a brief period of accord. During that peaceful week, Howells visited the house his son had designed, observing both Sam's ill health and how "the Ashcrofts watch over him with tender constancy." On March 18, 1909, Sam attended the wedding of Ralph Ashcroft and Isabel Lyon, and life at Stormfield settled into the new plan. "The Ashcrofts & I were soon very friendly & sociable again, & I hoped & believed these conditions would continue," Sam noted. "Clara hoped the opposite."*

Clara could not support her lack of faith in Lyon and Ashcroft with any evidence, until at last one incident persuaded Sam of his daughter's perspective. Just before accompanying her father on the train to New York on March 31, 1909, Clara, now in charge of domestic management though still living in New York, gave a raise and more time off to Horace, the farmer lad serving as butler only since the burglary in September. A few days later, Ashcroft accompanied Sam and Henry Rogers on the *Kanawha* on a trip to Virginia to dedicate a railroad Rogers had built there, Sam's first opportunity to thank Rogers publicly. After the ceremony, Ashcroft gave Sam a letter from Horace, which claimed that Clara had fired him; Ashcroft admitted he had already drawn a check for the young man's severance pay and that Sam had signed it that morning. Sam was incredulous. Erratic and histrionic as Clara might be, she never flat out lied to her father. Ashcroft's attempt to make Clara seem unreliable backfired on Sam's trusted lieutenant.

On his return to New York, Sam asked Clara what had happened. She had no idea that Horace had been dismissed, but called on Claude Benchotte, the old butler, and secured his agreement to return to Storm-field. At Redding, Sam found the young butler gone back to his family and Lyon managing the house. He dismissed Isabel Lyon from his service on April 15; two days later, Ashcroft came to talk business and then left with his wife. Horace explained that the morning after Sam and Clara left, Ashcroft had come to Stormfield from the city. Making the young butler feel certain that with Clara now in charge he would soon lose his post, Ashcroft told him that if he wrote the letter, he would receive a full month's payment. Ashcroft had himself dictated to Horace the letter he showed Sam in Virginia. Neither Ashcroft nor Lyon appeared at Stormfield again. A week later, Jean moved in, supposedly for an experimental visit, but in fact for as long as she wished.

Overwhelmed with anger and despondency, Sam needed to write out his feelings. Had he been so wrong about Lyon and Ashcroft? Had he allowed himself to be duped again? How much had he lost, if anything? What did they want? What did Clara want? Seeking to cope with his uncertainty of knowledge, he ventured on a new literary program. "My mind's present scheme is a good one; I could not like it better if I had invented it myself. It is this: to write letters to friends *& not send them,*" he wrote Howells. "I will fire the profanities at Rogers, the indecencies at Howells, the theologies at Twichell. Oh, to think—I am a free man at last!"

He began to realign his affinities, rehearsing the betrayal by Ashcroft and Lyon in a long letter to Howells he never intended to send. Over the next several months, this letter grew to more than four hundred pages as Sam attempted to reconstruct the truth, a record of perceptions that became the most concentrated writing project of his final years. This manuscript contains some obvious untruths that have led some scholars to conclude that it is all a fabrication, but it also includes many inter-polated manuscripts from other participants, tells the truth in many places, and makes a convincing, if vengeful, argument against Ashcroft and Lyon. Further, Clara's belief that this document would keep Ashcroft and Lyon quiet implies their guilt: Though they did not know the con-tents of the manuscript, they knew enough of their own behavior to realize that it might accurately record it. When neither Ashcroft nor Lyon ob-jected to being almost completely erased from Clemens' life in Albert

Bigelow Paine's *Mark Twain: A Biography*, they came close to confessing that they had conspired against him.

Sam wrote in the manuscript that though "my paths have never been pleasanter than they were during her reign, [Lyon's] head got turned, you see. She had acquired 'position;' she could freely enter front doors, now, whose back ones she & Ashcroft couldn't enter a few years earlier."* Her proximity to Mark Twain rewarded her sufficiently at first, but then she grew greedy. Once Sam erased the prospect of marriage, Isabel Lyon began supplementing her income. In May, he found out from builder H. A. Lounsbury that Lyon had instructed him to bill $2,000 to the construction of Sam's house for work he actually performed in refurbishing the house Sam had given Lyon. "I used to consider the Countess Massiglia the lowest-down woman on the planet," he wrote. "Well, when I get through examining Miss Lyon I shall realize I have been doing the Countess a wrong."*

Having used the remaining powers of his prose to impose domestic equilibrium, Sam's existence resumed its stability. Claude Benchotte, the old butler, returned to his post at Stormfield. Paine returned from Europe to press ahead with his literary and biographical duties. Jean served as her father's secretary and also undertook the management of the farmland that comprised part of Sam's several hundred acres. Clara gloated only a little. Life hummed along, but Sam missed Isabel Lyon's grasp of the details. For example, he promised to speak at Francesca Nunnally's graduation from her boarding school near Baltimore, and planning the trip himself left him baffled.

In April 1909, Ashcroft finally turned over the ledgers. Still fuming at Clara, whom he sought to blame for his fall from grace, he claimed he resisted this step because "the charges emanated from a brain diseased with envy, malice and jealousy, and it is only when one forgets this fact that one views them seriously." Sam asked Henry Rogers, still fixing the great writer's finances fifteen years after he began, to look into his accounts since his return from England in 1907. Sam hoped that Rogers might find something less damning than Clara's suspicions, a discovery that would relieve Sam of having to hate two people he had loved only six weeks before.

In mid-May, Sam went to New York to meet with Rogers to discuss his ledgers. Clara met him at Grand Central Station in New York with horrible news: Rogers had died that morning. "The expression of grief in Father's face was pitiful to behold," Clara wrote. Reporters were there to record Sam's private sorrow—his tears, his trembling hands, his shuffling walk to the exit under Clara's guidance. "This is terrible, terrible, and I cannot talk about it. I am inexpressibly shocked and grieved," he fumblingly told *The New York Times*. Sam met briefly with the Rogers family and served as a pallbearer at his friend's New York funeral, but he could not bear to go to Fairhaven for the burial because he feared that he could not keep up conversation, even with those he knew and loved so well.

He returned to Stormfield, broken and disconsolate. The discovery of nearly $7,000 in cash disbursements for household expenses, when Sam had insisted all bills be paid by check, rendered Lyon's embezzlement a certainty. Ashcroft responded to these charges by declaring that "during this time $6789. was drawn in cash, an average of $282. per month—a mere bagatelle when you consider the receipts and disbursements passing through her hands, which were: receipts, $342,751.; disbursements, $279,536." Ashcroft's pitiful defense of his wife's innocence—that she couldn't be guilty because she could have stolen more, but didn't—did not move Sam. Even assuming that half the money went to legitimate purposes, since June 1907 Lyon had used Sam's assets to more than quadruple her pay. The audit also found several thousand dollars more charged to Clara, who denied receiving most of it. Sam began proceedings to have the house and land he had deeded Isabel Lyon redeeded back to him. He could not bear having her in the neighborhood.

Victory in Retreat

> *Annihilation has no terrors for me, because I have*
> *already tried it before I was born—a hundred million*
> *years—and I have suffered more in an hour, in this life,*
> *than I remember to have suffered in the whole hundred*
> *million years put together.*
> —Autobiographical Dictation (1907)

IN JUNE 1909, Sam went to Catonsville, Maryland, to speak at Frances Nunnally's graduation from The Misses Tewksbury's School. While at the hotel, after the strenuous day of travel, meeting people, and speaking, Sam had the first twinges of pain in his chest. He returned to Redding white and exhausted. He kept to his bed for most of June and July, though he couldn't resist getting up now and again to play billiards or to add details to his record of the outrages perpetrated by Ashcroft and Lyon. In mid-July, he wrote one of his Angelfish, "I can answer your question definitely, now, Francesca Dear. It is heart-disease. Not the best kind, but good enough for the purpose." Sam had angina pectoris, what the physicians called tobacco heart. He would have preferred something that could kill him instantly, instead of a disease that would slowly wear him and his heart down with unpredictable and excruciating pain. "I was warned to stop smoking, which I did," he wrote Betsy Wallace, his Bermuda friend, "for two or three days, but it was too lonesome, and I have resumed—in a modified way—4 smokes a day instead of 40. This will have a good effect. On the bank balance."

After the death of Henry Rogers, John Stanchfield—the husband of

Livy's childhood friend Clara Spaulding—took over the management of the Ashcroft-Lyon problem. While the pair were in England on a belated honeymoon, Stanchfield attached not only Lyon's Redding house, but also her house in Hartford. Lyon returned to New York to defend herself and her property. Newspapers got hold of the story and telephoned Sam at Stormfield for a response. Jean answered the phone and, unused to the house rule of silence on domestic matters, spoke to a reporter about what happened. In Sam's view, this "gave the Ashcrofts their chance. It lifted them out of obscurity & insignificance, & made them objects of interest & importance."* In July, Lyon and her mother met with Jean and a lawyer. They agreed to relinquish any claim on her house in Redding in exchange for Sam's withdrawal of criminal and civil charges against her. When Ashcroft returned later in the summer, he steadfastly denied any guilt and argued that his wife had been coerced into signing the agreement. The squabbling continued in the courts and in the newspapers.

Sam kept silent publicly about the matter, though in his vituperative manuscript about the betrayal he described Lyon, with a degree of self-conscious prevarication, as "a liar, a forger, a thief, a hypocrite, a drunkard, a sneak, a humbug, a traitor, a conspirator, a filthy-minded and salacious slut pining for seduction and always getting disappointed, poor child." He and Clara spoke frequently about what had happened. She told a story about a long, loving letter Sam had written Jean—"a *real* letter," she called it—which Sam had tried to send without Lyon's knowledge. He gave it to H. A. Lounsbury to mail, but Lyon overheard the conversation between the men and caught up with Lounsbury before he left the grounds. Lounsbury had no choice but to return the letter. Lyon "seemed to have gotten such a hold upon you that she could make you do whatever she pleased," Clara told her father. "She had stopped making requests, she only gave orders. You never denied her anything."* Sam asked if Clara really thought he would marry Lyon in 1907, and Clara responded that she didn't, but she felt certain Lyon would marry him. Sam wrote near the end of his long document on these troubles, "I like the truth sometimes, but I don't care enough for it to hanker after it."* By the anniversary of the burglary, in September 1909, Sam did not want to hear anything about the affair ever again.

Paine took over many of Sam's business affairs, and Jean continued her secretarial and farming duties. To be close to Sam, Paine moved into Stormfield, which made sense since neither man slept especially well. Their rooms connected, and Sam could call for Paine at any hour of the day or night, and the men would read to one another. When a severe chest pain took Sam, only a drink of warm water soothed him, and Paine was always there to fetch it. By August, Sam often felt well enough to walk around the pool table for an hour, talking with Paine. Even without the stenographer, Sam told stories, but he had a harder time sticking to the facts. Paine thought his philosophical turn of mind was making him inattentive to detail, but Sam had simply lost his way. Having invented himself for so long, he could not stick to one story. Now he reinvented himself minute by minute. As Mark Twain's biographer, Paine made Sam's lies his life's work.

At the end of summer, Clara visited New York, where Ossip Gabrilowitsch underwent surgery. Clara prevailed upon her father to allow Gabrilowitsch to recover at Stormfield. In thanks, Gabrilowitsch agreed to give a concert with Clara on September 21, 1909, to benefit the Mark Twain Library building fund, for which Sam opened up the house to over five hundred guests, with scores more scattered on the grounds outside. The paterfamilias was in his element with the horde, which included both his sophisticated New York friends and his Connecticut farmer-neighbors. The celebration went on into the small hours. Clara capped the evening by announcing that, after many years of being asked, she had agreed to wed Gabrilowitsch. Reluctant to leave much time between the announcement and the wedding, the couple was married less than three weeks later; Gabrilowitsch had a European concert tour planned, and he wanted Clara along. On October 6, 1909, Sam opened the house again for the wedding. Howells came to share his friend's joy, and Sam had a good time with the event, preinterviewing himself for the newspapers and personally handing a typed script of the interview to the one reporter who had been invited to cover the event. Clara's marriage delighted her father, but her sporadic but increased presence over the past year had brought a whirlwind of change, and it pleased Sam that she would be gone for a while.

Sam settled down to write again, beginning "Letters from the Earth," in which Satan corresponds with fellow archangels Michael and Gabriel. In most of these letters, the narrator's voice sounds like that of Sam, a reversal of his experimentation with the Faust story in his various and still unpublished tales of a mysterious stranger's visit to earth. With Henry Rogers' death, Sam had come to realize that whatever deal he had made with the devil was a deal he had made with himself. While identifying himself as fundamentally evil was troubling, casting himself as the devil in "Letters from the Earth" compensated him with the freedom to ridicule with unbridled abandon the whole of human history, and especially the Christian conception of the Deity. For example, pointing out the logical inconsistency of restricting women to sexual congress with only one man, though he is physically incapable of fully satisfying her, Sam noted that men make this restriction "without consulting the woman, although she has a thousand times more at stake in the matter than he has. . . . Man is a fool," Satan concludes, and "woman is a damned fool." He wrote Betsy Wallace, "This book will never be published. Paine likes it, but then, Paine is going to be damned anyhow."

Still, there remained some pleasures for Sam in his narrowing world. The foliage at Stormfield "was heaven and hell and sunset and rainbows and the aurora, all fused into one divine harmony, and you couldn't look at it and keep the tears back." He described getting to know Jean as "a surprise and a wonder. She has plenty of wisdom, judgement, penetration, practical good sense—like her mother—and character, courage, definiteness, decision; also goodness, a humane spirit, charity, kindliness, pity." His catalog of her virtues went on and on, as did Jean's energy. Waking early for a cold bath, she handled business for her father and spent the remainder of the day on the farm, she even played billiards.

Sam took a dying man's solace in rereading his favorite books, such as Pepys' *Diary*, Carlyle's *History of the French Revolution*, Malory's *Morte d'Arthur*, and P. T. Barnum's autobiography. He sometimes capitalized on his illness to escape unpleasantness, once manifesting the symptoms of an attack when Jean and Paine criticized an article he had written. Reviewing his life, Sam did not revel in the vastness of his accomplishments, experience, and acquaintance, though most days brought news of the death of a notable figure whom he knew. When he reminisced, he dwelt on his financial errors. "I have always been the victim of somebody, and always an idiot myself, doing things that even a child would not do."

Sam's doctors thought he would benefit from a milder climate for the winter, and so he and Paine left on November 19 for a month in Bermuda. While he was there, the American Plasmon Company collapsed at last, having cost Sam $50,000. At least the Mark Twain Company was now under the sound direction of Paine; Charles Lark, a partner of John Stanchfield's; and Edward Loomis, the railroad-executive husband of Sam's niece Julia Langdon, daughter of *Quaker City* cub Charlie Langdon. Sam's stay in Bermuda featured Betsy Wallace and young Helen Allen, the fifteen-year-old daughter of the American consul, in whose house Sam stayed while on the island. He returned to Redding for Christmas in high spirits.

Jean met Sam and Paine at the docks in New York, but then rushed back home where she planned an old-fashioned Clemens Christmas, as her mother had done every year in Hartford. Sam arrived two days before Christmas and found Stormfield abuzz with preparation. Jean, like her mother, had worn herself out in making Christmas. She went to bed early on the night of the twenty-third and rose at dawn the next day to continue her work. In the tub for her early-morning bath, Jean experienced a seizure. She drowned.

When Paine arrived at Stormfield, Sam remarked to him, "Well, I suppose you have heard of this final disaster." Paine noticed that Sam "was not violent or broken down with grief. He had come to that place where, whatever the shock or the ill-turn of fortune, he could accept it." The Christmas tree stood half trimmed in the loggia and the presents half wrapped. Jean had bought her father a globe; she wanted to give him the world. Sam wired Clara not to come home from Europe; what would be the point? On Christmas Day, Jervis Langdon and Katy Leary took Jean's body to Elmira. Not equal to the trip, Sam asked that Jean's, Susy's, and Livy's favorite music be played on the Orchestrelle and lanterns set so he could see the progress of the body away from Stormfield. He sold a parcel of land Jean had called the Italian farm and used the proceeds to build a Jean Clemens Wing on the Mark Twain Library. Jean had been twenty-nine when she died.

Sam spent the next week writing, writing, writing: an essay called "The Death of Jean," notebook entries, and letters. It was the way he coped with his emotions. He wrote Clara, "I am so glad she is out of it and safe—safe! I am not melancholy; I shall never be melancholy again, I think. You see, I was in such distress when I came to realize that you were gone far away and no one stood between her and danger but me— and I could die at any moment." In this notebook he wrote, "Did I know Jean's value? No, I only thought I did. I knew a ten-thousandth fraction of it, that is all. It is always so, with us, it always has been so." Though devastated, he did not despair. "Shall I ever be cheerful again, happy again? Yes. And soon," he wrote. "My temperament has never allowed my spirits to remain depressed long at a time." He finished his story of Jean's death and told Paine, "It is the end of my autobiography. I shall never write any more." He felt it was the ultimate tragedy of his life, the last inescapable death of a loved one, the final punishment for a lifelong guilt he could never express. But just as he could not sorrow for long, he could not stop his pen, either.

He wanted to return to Bermuda. He left Stormfield with Paine and Claude Benchotte just after the New Year. They stopped in New York for a few days and spent an evening with William Dean Howells. As Howells left, he said to Paine, "There was never anybody like him; there never will be." Paine could not accompany Sam to Bermuda this time, so Benchotte went along instead, keeping a room at the hotel while Sam stayed with the Allens. Pilla Howells was in Bermuda too, and looked in on Sam. Sam's friends received progress reports on his health, which frequently made it into the papers. Well-wishers around the world sent him cures, to which Sam typically responded, "I try every remedy sent to me. I am now on No. 67. Yours is 2,653. I am looking forward to its beneficial results." He tinkered with his essay on Jean and wrote letters, especially when his new Angelfish Helen Allen served as his secretary. His final essay for the public was the first in a *Harper's Bazaar* series called "The Turning-Point of My Life," in which he finally admitted that "the most important feature of my life is its literary feature." Howells praised him, saying "It is a pity to have you dragging along with a wornout material body on top of your soul."

At the Allens', Sam got to see all the distinguished visitors to the island. The president of Princeton University, Woodrow Wilson, came to call on him, and they played golf. After Wilson left, Sam remarked that he believed he would be the next President of the United States. Robert Collier came to look in on Sam. In March, Dorothy Quick visited. It had been nearly a year and a half since they had seen one another, but "the intervening months seemed to have slipped away," Quick later wrote, "and Mark Twain and I met on the same plane of companionship that we had always shared." His friendship with Helen Allen proved unsatisfactory, however. A willful girl, she fought with her parents and often escaped from both them and Sam's unwanted attentions to spend time with her boyfriend. Sam became overwrought by her behavior. The Allens also felt burdened by the presence of this famous dying man, but Sam could not think of a place where he would rather spend what he suspected might be his last weeks. "There are no newspapers, no telegrams, no mobiles, no trolleys, no trains, no tramps, no railways, no theatres, no noise, no lectures, no riots, no murders, no fires, no burglaries, no politics, no offenses of any kind, no follies but church, and I don't go there. I think I could live here always and be contented," he wrote Betsy Wallace. "You go to heaven if you want to—I'd druther stay here."

His pains came more often and more fiercely and Sam's doctors gave him morphine to let him rest. His hosts wrote a panicky letter to Paine, who came immediately and learned how to use a syringe. The Allens hired a tug to help Paine get Sam from their dock to the boat so that Sam could return home; he could not make the trip into Hamilton, Bermuda's capital city. On board the ship, Sam could hardly sleep. He had trouble catching his breath, and when he did drop off, he woke moments later, gasping. He asked Paine to give him enough morphine to kill him. Back in New York on April 14, 1910, he was carried from the boat to a carriage and from the carriage to the train, but when the carriage pulled up to Stormfield, where his household staff waited anxiously outside for him, Sam insisted on walking into his house on his own power. He could not manage the stairs, though, and consented to being carried up to bed.

Paine had cabled Clara to come home. No one was certain she would arrive in time, but when she and her husband arrived on the eighteenth, her father was still conscious. He asked her to sing for him. It was her most difficult performance. Sam, however, glowed with pleasure; Clara was pregnant and he would be a grandfather after all. During his final hours, Sam spoke almost constantly, but in a garbled German that Ossip Gabrilowitsch understood most easily. On Thursday, April 21, 1910, he woke suddenly, took Clara's hand, and murmured, "Goodbye dear, if we meet—." As the sun set that spring day, Samuel Langhorne Clemens died. Halley's Comet was visible in the night sky, its first appearance since the day of Sam's birth nearly seventy-five years before. It had been closest to earth the day before, and it had begun its celestial retreat.

The King Is Dead, Long Live the King

> *Often, the surest way to convey misinformation is to tell the strict truth.*
> —"Pudd'nhead Wilson's New Calendar" (1897)

> *In America—as elsewhere—free speech is confined to the dead.*
> —Notebook (1906)

THE FUNERAL FOR Samuel Langhorne Clemens was held at the Brick Church, at Thirty-seventh Street and Fifth Avenue in New York City, on Saturday, April 23, 1910. It was a brilliant spring afternoon, and mourners began to gather in front of the church long before the three o'clock service; a crowd had even met the casket when it arrived at Grand Central Station. The press of people anxious for a final glimpse of Mark Twain moved the undertaker to open the church doors early, but the large sanctuary could only accommodate three thousand mourners. Hundreds more clogged Fifth Avenue.

The ceremony itself lasted only twenty minutes. The Reverend Dr. Henry Van Dyke addressed the crowd, concluding, "Now he is gone, and our thoughts of him are tender, grateful, proud. We are glad of his friendship; glad that he has expressed so richly one of the great elements in the temperaments of America; glad that he has left such an honorable record as a man of letters, and glad, also, for his sake, that after many and deep sorrows, he is at peace." Joseph Twichell, one of the presiding ministers, could hardly contain his tears long enough to complete his brief prayer. After the service, the casket was opened to reveal Samuel Langhorne Clemens dressed in one of Mark Twain's white cashmere suits. For more than an hour and a half, until the body had to be taken to a train departing for Elmira, New York, where it would be buried in the Langdon family plot beside Livy, Susy, and Jean, people streamed by. Most of them were strangers to Sam, and they seemed to represent every race, faith, and nation. Truly, the world mourned.

Just after delivering his final prayer, Joe Twichell received word that his wife, Harmony, was near death. She died on April 25, 1910. Howells, also present, felt his grief compounded too; Elinor Howells was ill and would die two weeks later, on May 7, 1910. Twichell sent Howells the letter Sam had written him after Livy's death, to share its sad comfort. Howells had described Sam to editor Frederick Duneka as "the most truthful man I *ever* knew." He wrote Twichell, thanking him for their mutual friend's letter, "When Clemens died I felt *desolate*, as I never had before; he had been such a world-full friend."

During the three weeks following his wife's death, Howells compiled his reviews of Mark Twain's books, reflections and anecdotes in appreciation of his talents, and recollections of their conversations and misadventures revealing their shared love and respect into a volume that he called *My Mark Twain*. In his sorrow, Howells wrote the truest portrait of Sam:

> Clemens was then hard upon fifty, and he had kept, as he did to the end, the slender figure of his youth, but the ashes of the burnt-out years were beginning to gray the fires of that splendid shock of red hair which he held to the height of a stature apparently greater than it was, and tilted from side to side in his undulating walk. He glimmered at you from the narrow slits of fine blue-greenish eyes, under branching brows, which with age grew more and more like a sort of plumage, and he was apt to smile into your face with a subtle but amiable perception, and yet with a sort of remote absence; you were all there for him, but he was not all there for you.

Howells' last line defined one of Sam Clemens' two most remarkable talents. He made himself compelling through his inspired ad hoc invention of fame. He transformed almost any situation into a performance, with himself as the star, and he could do this in such a way that most people—even, often, his own family—felt grateful to be included in his audience. His other talent was his power over language. In him, American English realized its greatest strengths: humor, invention, and directness.

Mark Twain was such a masterly work of language and performance that the death of his creator, Samuel Langhorne Clemens, did little to dim his power. By the time Howells' book appeared, a few months after Sam's death, newspapers and magazines had already been crowded with the reminiscences of nearly everyone who had known him. While during his lifetime, the press most frequently referred to him as Mr. Clemens, after his death he became Mark Twain. As the *New York Times* reported the funeral, "The people who passed by the coffin saw not so much the man Samuel L. Clemens, a philosopher through the necessity of bearing misfortune, as Mark Twain, who was everything from Huckleberry Finn to Colonel Mulberry Sellers." This transformation, which Sam had effected so well and so arduously throughout his life, kept his public persona alive. His contemporaries were unwilling to let Mark Twain go, and so Sam Clemens' invented self survived him.

The hunger for Mark Twain has never abated, although the public's interest in him has not always been well served. Albert Bigelow Paine's *Mark Twain: A Biography*, more than half a million words long, came out in 1912. He followed it with an edition of letters, another of speeches, several collections of miscellaneous work, and severely edited versions of the autobiographical dictations and the notebooks. Paine responded to the call for more writing by Mark Twain by patching together, with Frederick Duneka, a bastardized version of "The Mysterious Stranger." With Paine's help, Clara Clemens Gabrilowitsch set herself up as the guardian of Mark Twain's image. She warned Elizabeth Wallace, who was preparing an illustrated reminiscence of Clemens in Bermuda, not to use photographs of Sam and his Angelfish in affectionate poses. Clara also commanded that any reference to Isabel Lyon disappear from the official record; Paine accordingly erased all but minimal vestiges of her in his authorized biography. Clara claimed that her father composed his manuscript about the betrayal by Ashcroft and Lyon to help Clara combat any claims they might make on the Clemens estate. Her preference on this matter had such force that when Dorothy Quick published her memoirs of her friendship with Clemens more than fifty years after his death, she never used Isabel Lyon's name, but called her "the secretary" instead.

Clara gave birth to Nina Gabrilowitsch on August 18, 1910, at Stormfield, but soon after, the family moved to Europe, where they lived until the outbreak of World War I. Ossip Gabrilowitsch became the conductor of the Detroit Symphony Orchestra in 1918, a position he retained until his death in 1936. Clara then moved to Hollywood, and Nina, who had failed to make a career as an actress in New York, joined her mother there. This move also terminated Nina's brief, unhappy marriage to Carl

G. Roters, an artist. In California, Nina struggled with addictions to drugs and alcohol. In 1944, at the age of seventy, Clara married Jacques Samossoud, also a Russian musician, a friend of her deceased husband, and twenty years her junior. Samossoud had a gambling problem and borrowed more than $350,000 from his wife. In 1951, Clara's Hollywood home and many valuable manuscripts were sold at public auction. The Samossouds spent their last years in San Diego, and by the end of the 1950s Clara was borrowing money from friends. Except for her father's papers, Clara willed all her assets to her husband and subsequently to a Dr. William Seiler, a racetrack friend of Samossoud's who reportedly provided Clara with drugs. Nina received nothing but the trust Clara had established before the marriage to Samossoud. After Clara's death in 1962, Nina and Jacques engaged in two years of ugly legal wrangling, and after two years more both Jacques Samossoud and Nina Gabrilowitsch were dead; Nina died childless, of an overdose of barbiturates. Dr. Seiler received a share of the proceeds of Clara's holdings until his death in 1978. Since that time, the Mark Twain Company, later subsumed into the Mark Twain Foundation, has held the remaining family assets, including copyrights on all words written by Samuel Langhorne Clemens. Since most of his published works have now slipped into the public domain, the copyrights still in effect pertain only to words recently published, such as newly discovered manuscripts or letters published for the first time.

By 1978, Mark Twain had become a national industry. Nearly a dozen sites now lay claim to some ownership of Mark Twain. Most significant are the Mark Twain Birthplace, a shack moved inside a museum when a dam on the Salt River threatened to flood the abandoned community of Florida, Missouri; the Mark Twain Boyhood Home in Hannibal, Missouri, where Mark Twain tourism is one of the major industries; Elmira, New York, where the old Langdon home at Quarry Farm is a retreat for scholars and where the octagonal study has been moved to the campus of Elmira College; Hartford, Connecticut, where the Mark Twain House has been carefully restored. There are also the Mark Twain Papers, part of the Bancroft Library at the University of California at Berkeley, which has most of Samuel Clemens' original papers, letters, notebooks, and manuscripts, along with copies of nearly every relevant document held elsewhere. The Bancroft Library is also home to the Mark Twain Project, which aims to publish scholarly editions of all of Mark Twain's letters, works, and notebooks, a goal sadly threatened by budget constraints. The sites in Elmira, Hartford, and Missouri also have some original papers relating to the life of Samuel Clemens, as do archives at Harvard University, the Huntington Library in San Marino, California, the New York

Public Library, Vassar College, the University of Virginia, and Yale University.

New Mark Twain material appears on almost a weekly basis, especially previously unknown letters in the hands of private collectors. With correspondence in Clemens' own hand selling for $1,000 a page, more revelations are likely. In 1990, the first half of the manuscript of *Adventures of Huckleberry Finn* surfaced, having been stored in a trunk in the attic of a California home. Clemens had donated the manuscript to the Public Library of Buffalo, New York, and the man who had solicited the donation died with the first half of it in his possession. It had remained packed away in a trunk until discovered by his now-elderly granddaughters. For over a century, the first half of the manuscript of what has often been called the greatest American novel was thought lost. A complicated legal settlement landed it back in Buffalo, where Victor Doyno, a professor at the State University of New York, past president of the Mark Twain Circle of America, and an accepted expert on the genesis of *Huck Finn*, is attempting to determine its significance. His discoveries, like those of dozens of other able scholars, will help refine and revise the portraits of Samuel Clemens and Mark Twain. A version of the novel, incorporating Doyno's new research and some previously unpublished sections, was published in 1996.

No other American literary figure is as internationally well-known or beloved as Mark Twain. His work continues to win new audiences everywhere. In America, particularly, he is a touchstone of our cultural identity. Born to a large family of indifferent fortune in a run-down shack on the American frontier, poorly educated, but intelligent, ambitious, and adventuresome, he became rich, famous, and respected for his brilliant wit, kindly humor, and staggering insight. He dined with kings and presidents and traveled the world as an emissary of American culture at a point in our history when Americans had only just begun to believe such a culture existed. His fame, his most influential contribution to that culture, became a model for international celebrity and led directly to the world domination of United States' cultural exports. Mark Twain is an American icon, and he will live and breathe in us as long as we can read his books, recall his white clothes, remember his jokes, and imagine ourselves as children.

Samuel Langhorne Clemens, on the other hand, died in 1910. He lives on as the shadow behind Mark Twain and—if I have at all succeeded—in these pages. Sam Clemens was an emotionally unstable, hopelessly insecure narcissist with a remarkable knack for public performance and a dazzling control of the English language. As I have worked on this project, friends and family have asked me, "Do you still like him, after getting to know him so well?" My answer is "Yes!" True, his pettinesses, emotional insufficiencies, and foolish self-destructiveness made him a dangerous partner and a difficult father, but his humor, openhandedness, and compassion made him a valuable friend.

Most precious was his genius. I wish I had known him alive as well as I know him dead. Katy Leary, his servant for over thirty years, noted about one of Sam's late absences from Stormfield, "You always missed Mr. Clemens so. He was one of them people that just filled up the world for you." He has filled my world for many years. I revere Mark Twain, as I have since I first began reading him seriously, but I love Sam Clemens. If he is gazing down on us from a comet somewhere, I hope he can see that love in this book.

Acknowledgments

Iᴛ ɪꜱ ɪᴍᴘᴏꜱꜱɪʙʟᴇ to thank everyone who contributed to this book; even in acknowledging as many people as I have, I will undoubtedly have overlooked some people and institutions without whom this book would be far less than it is. I would like to offer my thanks to the Mark Twain Project, at the Bancroft Library on the campus of the University of California at Berkeley. The scholars there are a crack bunch, assembling the scholarly editions of letters, works, and other papers of Mark Twain, editions that are the model of intelligence, wisdom, and readability. In addition, the entire staff—and Robert H. Hirst and Victor Fischer in particular—embody a kindness and generosity all too rare in academia. Similar kindness and generosity have marked nearly every member of the community of researchers, and I am grateful to every one of them, especially, but not exclusively: John Vincent Boyer and Marianne Curling of the Mark Twain Memorial in Hartford, Connecticut; Gretchen Sharlow of the Center for Mark Twain Studies at Elmira College in Elmira, New York; Henry Sweet at the Mark Twain Boyhood Home in Hannibal, Missouri; P. M. Zall of the Huntington Library in San Marino, California; Nancy MacKechnie at the Vassar College Libraries in Poughkeepsie, New York; John Cunning of the Mark Twain

Birthplace in Stoutsville, Missouri; Gregory J. Higby of the American Institute of the History of Pharmacy in Madison, Wisconsin; and Randy Clark of the Gay and Lesbian Historical Society of Northern California in San Francisco. I thank these people not only for how they helped me in their official capacities, but for the particular warmth they showed me. I offer my special thanks to Brown University for research privileges and a place to roost.

In many ways, this book is a group project. I owe immense thanks to those "Twainiacs"—scholars whose dedication to Twain studies dwarfs even my own—who have given me their guidance and encouragement during this massive project. Most of them kindly acknowledged that I had undertaken the impossible, but at the same time pledged themselves to my aid. I list only the most prominent of them, in alphabetical order: David Barrow, Edgar Branch, Louis J. Budd, Pascal Covici, Jr., Shelley Fisher Fishkin, Alan Gribben, Susan Harris, Michael Kiskis, Steven Mailloux, Suzi Naiberg, David E. E. Sloane, Peter Stoneley, Thomas Tenney, and Harry Wonham. In addition, the entire ethereal Internet community, the Mark Twain Forum, patiently accepted my participation. I thank you all from my heart, above and beyond my scholarly obligations, which are fulfilled in my notes and bibliography. I give a special mention to Cyril Clemens, Justin Kaplan, and Charles Neider, who have welcomed me even as I trespassed upon territory they plowed and planted.

Many people generously read this manuscript. Twain scholars Howard Baetzhold and Earl Briden, writers Judy McClain and Aimée Grunberger, and wise friends Pamela Davis and Michael Ausbrook offered kindly pointers and pointed criticisms, which raised this book from acceptable to something I believe is better than that. To Howard Baetzhold especially I owe more than I could ever hope to repay. Reading the manuscript in its near-final incarnation, philosopher and friend Dave Estlund and physician and cousin Michael Chandler gave me direction and encouragement. Thoughtful editors Sally Arteseros and David Groff helped me transform mere facts into the representation of a life.

I have benefited from a strong network of professional and personal support as well. Professionally, my first obligation is to Ann Dubuisson, my former agent, without whom I would never have considered writing this book; Elizabeth Kaplan, my current agent, has seen the book through production. I would also like to thank Zachary Schisgal, my editor at William Morrow and his multiple predecessors on this project; and Rebecca Wilson, my editor at Weidenfeld and Nicolson. Emilie Sommerhoff has provided constant support as my infallible assistant; this book would be filled with hundreds of embarrassing errors without her sharp eye, excellent company, and occasional baby-sitting. I owe my greatest obligation to my circle of loved ones and readers, very often the same people: my mother, Elaine Hoffman; my wife, Judy Hoffman; and my generous friends. Though I cannot say that they contributed directly to the book itself, my children, Marcus and Alicia, have added immeasurably to my life. They have let me know that, whatever else may happen, I have succeeded.

Notes

I<small>N THESE NOTES</small>, I use several abbreviations that have become standard in Mark Twain scholarship. Letters written by or sent to Clemens are indicated with his initials, SLC; frequent correspondents are noted in the same way: OLC is Olivia Louise Clemens, his wife; CLW is Charles L. Webster, his business partner and husband to his niece; WDH is William Dean Howells, his close literary friend; and HHR is Henry Huttleston Rogers, Standard Oil chieftain and helpful friend to Clemens. I also use coded abbreviations to refer to several collections holding original manuscripts quoted herein. They are:

MTP Mark Twain Papers
University of California
Berkeley, CA 94720

NN Abraham Gilbert Mills Papers
Rare Books and Manuscripts Division
New York Public Library
Astor, Lenox and Tilden Foundations
New York, NY 10018

CtY   Yale Collection of American Literature
Beinecke Rare Book and Manuscript Library
Yale University
New Haven, CT 06520

NN-B   Albert A. and Henry W. Berg Collection
New York Public Library
Astor, Lenox and Tilden Foundations
New York, NY 10018

CtHMTH   Mark Twain Memorial
Hartford, CT 06105

NPV   Special Collections
Vassar College Libraries
Vassar College
Poughkeepsie, NY 12601

CU-MARK   University of California, Berkeley
Mark Twain Collection
Berkeley, CA 94720

DLC   John Russell Young Papers
Whitelaw Reid Papers
Manuscript Division
United States Library of Congress
Washington, DC 20540

NjP   Laurence Hutton Correspondence
Box 3, Folder 22
Manuscripts Division
Department of Rare Books and Special Collections
Princeton University Libraries
Princeton University
Princeton, NJ 08540

UK4   Chatto and Windus Archive
University of Reading
Reading, United Kingdom

ViU   Mark Twain Collection
Clifton Waller Barret Library
Special Collections Department
University of Virginia Library
University of Virginia
Charlottesville, VA 22904

InNd   University Archives
University of Notre Dame
Notre Dame, IN 46556

Lu-Ar   Grace King Selected Papers
Louisiana and Lower Mississippi Valley Collections
LSU Libraries
Louisiana State University
Department of Archives and Manuscripts
Baton Rouge, LA 70803

NNC   Columbia University
      New York, NY 10032

CCamarSJ   St. John's Seminary
           Camarillo, CA 93010
           (Last known holder of quoted MS)

CtHSD   The Stowe-Day Library
        Harriet Beecher Stowe Center
        77 Forest Street
        Hartford, CT 06105

N7   Library of Poultney Bigelow
     Bigelow Homestead
     Malden on Hudson, NY 12453

NCH   Hamilton College Library
      Hamilton College
      Clinton, NY 13323

ODa2   Private Collector

InFw2   Private Collector

CFr2   Tish Scott
       Fremont, CA 94536

Mo2   Private Collector

Abbreviations for these collections are followed in the notes by the Mark Twain Project document numbers as given in Paul Machlis' two volumes, *Catalogue of Clemens Letters* and *Catalogue of Letters to Clemens*. For letters cataloged after the publication of these two volumes, I assign the document number used by the Mark Twain Project. Some notes include the abbreviation *tr* for a letter transcribed by its original recipient; such a notation implies that the quoted words may not be exactly what the writer originally said. Other notes include the abbreviation *ph* for photostat, meaning that no original manuscript has yet come to light, only a photostatic copy of it; unclear copies may have resulted in misquotation. As noted on page 188, Mark Twain's previously unpublished words quoted here are copyright © 1996 by Manufacturers Hanover Trust Company as trustee of the Mark Twain Foundation, which reserves all reproduction or dramatization rights in every medium. Quotation is made with the permission of the University of California Press and Robert H. Hirst, General Editor, Mark Twain Project. Each quotation published here for the first time is identified in the text by an asterisk. Sometimes, to make the text of this biography more readable, I use a capital letter where Clemens' original uses a lower-case one; or I run two paragraphs into a single quotation, obscuring Clemens' original paragraphing. These changes never alter the meaning, of course, but I caution scholars quoting material first published here to go directly to the source to check such capitalization and punctuation.

PROLOGUE

p. ix, l. 11 *Following the Equator*, Vol. 1, Headnote, Chapter 15, p. 137.

p. ix, l. 14 "A Fable," *Collected Tales, Sketches, Speeches, and Essays, 1891–1910*, p. 879.

p. xii, l. 2 "More Maxims of Mark," *Collected Tales, Sketches, Speeches, and Essays, 1891–1910*, p. 945.

1: INVENTING SAM CLEMENS

p. 1, l. 10 *Pudd'nhead Wilson*, Headnote, Chapter 5, p. 84.

p. 1, l. 29 Jane Clemens to OLC, 7 January 1885. Wecter, *Hannibal*, p. 44.

p. 2, l. 15 A document dated 1821 bills the estate of Samuel Clemens for three years of support of Marshall Clemens at $60 per year.

p. 2, l. 30 *Mark Twain's Own Autobiography*, p. 112.

p. 3, l. 6 The Lamptons descended from a much earlier arrival to the New World, Mark Lampton, a distant descendant of the prestigious Lambton clan in Durham. See Lampton, "Twain's Lampton Kin and Colonel Sellers," pp. 24–25.

p. 3, l. 17 Jane Clemens did not tell this story until she reached senility. See SLC to WDH, 19 May 1886. *Mark Twain-Howells Letters*, p. 567.

p. 3, l. 20 Autobiographical dictations, 29 December 1906. Wecter, *Hannibal*, pp. 19–20.

p. 3, l. 36 Wecter, *Hannibal*, pp. 32–33.

p. 4, l. 3 No diagnosis for the disorder can be made from this distance, of course; one can only say that the profile fits the disease.

p. 4, l. 11 Brashear, *Mark Twain: Son of Missouri*, p. 49.

p. 4, l. 30 This cabin, not much more than 300 square feet for a family of eight, including Jennie, the slave and mammy, has been preserved a short distance from where it originally stood.

2: BECOMING TOM SAWYER

p. 9, l. 10 "Remarks at the Opening of the Mark Twain Library," *Mark Twain Speaking*, p. 630.

p. 9, l. 33 Hagood and Hagood, *Hannibal: Mark Twain's Town*, p. 15.

p. 10, l. 6 Now called Cardiff Hill, the name given it by Clemens in *The Adventures of Tom Sawyer*, this landmark is one of many in and around Hannibal which show life imitating art.

p. 10, l. 23 *Life on the Mississippi*, Chapter 4, p. 33.

p. 11, l. 22 "Villagers of 1840–43," *Hannibal, Huck and Tom*, p. 35.

p. 11, l. 24 *Hannibal Journal and Western Union*, 12 June 1851. Wecter, *Hannibal*, p. 60.

p. 12, l. 13 McReynolds, *Missouri: A History of the Crossroads State*, p. 169.

p. 12, l. 28 Wecter, *Hannibal*, p. 77.

p. 12, l. 35 In Wecter, Sanborn, and elsewhere, from "Villagers" and in a random autobiographical note.

p. 12, l. 41 Wecter, *Hannibal*, p. 140.

p. 13, l. 27 Clemens' confusion of his Hannibal boyhood and his summer freedom at the Quarles farm has not been fully addressed in biographical approaches to his fictions.

p. 13, l. 35 See *Mark Twain's Own Autobiography*, p. 112, for his description of the event.

p. 14, l. 8 McCurdy, *Stump, Bar and Pulpit*, p. 153.

p. 14, l. 25 Sweet, *Religion on the American Frontier*, Vol. 2, p. 89.

p. 14, l. 26 *Adventures of Huckleberry Finn*, p. 171. Clemens excised approximately 1,500 words from his description of the camp meeting in the novel. His description, discovered in the first half of the *Huck Finn* manuscript, was recently published in an edition of the novel edited by scholar Victor Doyno.

p. 15, l. 5 McCurdy, *Stump, Bar and Pulpit.*

p. 16, l. 3 *Innocents Abroad*, Chapter 18, p. 231.

p. 16, l. 36 Wecter, *Hannibal*, p. 228.

p. 18, l. 16 *Hannibal Journal*, 19 August 1845. In Wecter, *Hannibal*, p. 148.

p. 18, l. 36 This Dr. McDowell should not be confused with Dr. John McDowell, his son, whose triangular romantic involvement with a member of the Clemens family will be detailed later.

p. 19, l. 7 Evidence for this often repeated resolution to the tale of the corpse remains sketchy.

p. 19, l. 35 *Mark Twain's Own Autobiography*, p. 191.

p. 19, l. 37 Wecter, p. 117, quotes Orion Clemens' comment on the back of a letter sent him by Sam Clemens on 6 February 1861 implying that his father had doctored himself to death. The reference to Cook's pills aroused my curiosity, since John Marshall Clemens' behavior seemed consistent with addiction. Dr. Gregory J. Higby, director of the American Institute of the History of Pharmacy, at the University of Wisconsin School of Pharmacy, advised me on the formula and use of Cook's pills. The use of calomel, or mercurous chloride, was common in the 1840s, as were laxatives of various sorts. Any pharmacist of the period could include other ingredients the patient regularly took in the same pills; given John Clemens' trouble with "sun-pain," we can guess what else the pills included.

p. 20, l. 40 A pair of oblique references in his notebook jottings and letters indicate that Clemens witnessed a postmortem on his father. A manuscript passage by Orion about John Clemens' death prompted William Dean Howells to reply, "Don't let any one else even see those passages about the autopsy. The light on your father's character is most pathetic" (WDH to SLC, 14 June 1880. *Mark Twain-Howells Letters*, p. 315).

p. 21, l. 11 *Mark Twain's Own Autobiography*, p. 94.

3: SEEING WITH HUCK FINN'S EYES

p. 22, l. 10 *Adventures of Huckleberry Finn*, p. 128.

p. 23, l. 21 *Mark Twain's Own Autobiography*, p. 155. He later bowdlerized the incident by describing the women involved as "a poor but quite respectable widow and her young and blameless daughter."

p. 24, l. 2 Hannibal's *Missouri Courier*, 30 August 1849, p. 2. Richard Blennerhassett, a young lawyer famed for his eloquence, is the man Walter Blair could not identify in "Villagers 1840–3," *Hannibal, Huck and Tom*, p. 35.

p. 24, l. 23 *Mark Twain's Own Autobiography*, pp. 53–54.

p. 25, l. 37 The *Liberty* (Mo.) *Weekly Tribune*, 17 December 1847. Lyon, *The Pioneer Editor in Missouri, 1808–1860*, p. 113.

p. 27, l. 15 Wecter, *Hannibal*, pp. 211–12.

p. 27, l. 38 *Mark Twain's Own Autobiography*, pp. 92–93.

p. 28, l. 14 Clemens possibly began a two-year apprenticeship with Ament in January 1849; it may also be that Ament simply released Clemens from his obligations early.

p. 28, l. 23 *Early Tales and Sketches*, Vol. 1, p. 22.

p. 29, l. 26 Lyon, *Pioneer Editor*, p. 89.

p. 30, l. 30 *Early Tales and Sketches*, Vol. 1, p. 75.

p. 31, l. 2 Ibid., p. 86.

p. 31, l. 24 *Life on the Mississippi*, pp. 411–12.

p. 31, l. 32 *The Adventures of Tom Sawyer*, pp. 168–69.

p. 31, l. 37 SLC to William Bowen, 6 February 1870. *Mark Twain's Letters to William Bowen*, p. 7.

p. 32, l. 11   Brashear, *Son of Missouri*, p. 125.

p. 32, l. 15   "My First Literary Venture," *Mark Twain: Complete Short Stories of Mark Twain*, pp. 189–90.

p. 32, l. 26   "Saint Joan of Arc," *Collected Tales, Sketches, Speeches, and Essays 1891–1910*, pp. 584–85.

p. 32, l. 34   Paine, *Biography*, p. 93.

p. 32, l. 40   Wecter, *Hannibal*, p. 264.

4: ON THE ROAD, ON HIS OWN

p. 34, l. 11   "My Boyhood Dreams," *Collected Tales, Sketches, Speeches, and Essays, 1891–1910*, p. 447.

p. 34, l. 39   McReynolds, *Missouri: A History of the Crossroads State*, p. 126.

p. 35, l. 3   *Letters*, Vol. 1, p. 5 n. 4.

p. 35, l. 33   SLC to Jane Clemens, 24 August 1853. *Letters*, Vol. 1, p. 3.

p. 35, l. 39   SLC to Orion Clemens, 28 November 1853. *Letters*, Vol. 1, p. 29.

p. 36, l. 30   SLC to Pamela Moffett, 8 October 1853. *Letters*, Vol. 1, p. 17.

p. 37, l. 3   SLC to Pamela Moffett, 3? September 1853. *Letters*, Vol. 1, p. 13.

p. 37, l. 4   SLC to Pamela Moffett, 8 October 1853. *Letters*, Vol. 1, p. 17. The Ella to whom Sam refers is the wife of his Uncle Jim Lampton, as noted later in this chapter.

p. 37, l. 8   SLC to Pamela Moffett, 5 December 1853. *Letters*, Vol. 1, p. 33.

p. 37, l. 30   SLC to Orion and Henry Clemens, 26–?28 October 1853. *Letters*, Vol. 1, p. 20.

p. 38, l. 17   SLC to *Muscatine Journal*, 17 and 18 February 1854. *Letters*, Vol. 1, p. 40. His reference to Swift gives evidence that he had read him recently.

p. 38, l. 26   Ibid., p. 41.

p. 39, l. 38   Sanborn, *Mark Twain, the Bachelor Tears*, pp. 94–95. This episode is probably based on a reminiscence, possibly invented, of an older Mark Twain; I include it because it seems telling about Orion.

p. 40, l. 12   SLC to Jacob Burrough, 1 November 1876. Paine, *Biography*, p. 103.

p. 41, l. 18   See Gribben, "Mark Twain, Phrenology and the 'Temperaments.' "

p. 41, l. 34   *Notebooks and Journals*, Vol. 1, p. 22.

p. 41, l. 41   Ibid., p. 22.

p. 42, l. 5   Ibid., p. 29.

p. 43, l. 2   Lorch, "Mark Twain in Iowa," p. 420, quoting Orion Clemens' report.

p. 43, l. 35   SLC to Henry Clemens, 5 August 1856. *Letters*, Vol. 1, pp. 65–69.

p. 44, l. 14   Ibid., p. 66.

p. 45, l. 6   Lorch, "Mark Twain in Iowa," p. 439.

p. 45, l. 21   See Baker, "Mark Twain in Cincinnati"; Baender, "Alias Macfarlane: A Revision of Mark Twain Biography"; and Britton, "Macfarlane, 'Boarding House' and 'Bugs' " for a more complete rendition of the differing points of view on Macfarlane. All of these arguments must be tempered by Edgar Branch's discovery that Clemens' stay in Cincinnati occupied considerably less time than has previously been assumed.

p. 45, l. 26   Baker, "Mark Twain in Cincinnati," p. 305.

p. 45, l. 35   Lorch, "Mark Twain in Iowa," p. 447.

p. 46, l. 1   Baker, "Mark Twain in Cincinnati," pp. 304–5.

p. 46, l. 6   See Edgar Branch, "Bixby vs. Carroll: New Light on Sam Clemens's Early River Career." Until recently, scholars accepted as fact that Clemens left Cincinnati on April 15, 1857. The discovery of court documents concerning a disagreement between Captain John W. Carroll and river pilot Horace Bixby confirms the earlier departure date. I am obligated to Edgar Branch for sharing a draft of his paper with me, and much other wisdom besides.

5: LIFE ON THE MISSISSIPPI

p. 47, l. 11 *Adventures of Huckleberry Finn*, p. 183.

p. 47, l. 36 *Life on the Mississippi*, Chapter 14, p. 90.

p. 48, l. 20 Blair, *Hannibal, Huck and Tom*, p. 346.

p. 48, l. 26 Branch, "Bixby vs. Carroll," p. 7.

p. 49, l. 12 *Life on the Mississippi*, Chapter 6, pp. 42–43.

p. 49, l. 12 Ibid., p. 43.

p. 50, l. 2 Reports that Clemens tried to bargain his price for the Snodgrass letters up to $10 per submission imply this happened in Keokuk.

p. 50, l. 12 *Notebooks and Journals*, Vol. 1, p. 43.

p. 50, l. 26 *Life on the Mississippi*, Chapter 13, pp. 87–89.

p. 50, l. 34 Ibid., Chapter 7, pp. 46–47.

p. 51, l. 2 *The Grangerford-Shepherdson Feud*, especially pp. 33–end.

p. 51, l. 20 See McDermott, ed., *Before Mark Twain*, especially pp. 91–111; a collection of writings about Mississippi River travel between 1820 and 1860.

p. 51, l. 26 *Adventures of Huckleberry Finn*, p. 110.

p. 52, l. 15 Marleau, " 'The Crash of the Timbers Continued,' " p. 14.

p. 52, l. 24 SLC to Orion and Mollie Clemens, 9 March 1858. *Letters*, Vol. 1, p. 77. I suspect Clemens wrote more than has yet been credited to him. A great benefit of Edgar Branch's work in settling Clemens' riverboat schedule is that it opens up the opportunity to look for more apprentice writing. By scouring the New Orleans and St. Louis newspapers for the days after we know Clemens to have docked there, we might find a pseudonymous series we can attribute to Sam Clemens.

p. 52, l. 32 Sanborn, *Mark Twain, the Bachelor Years*, p. 122.

p. 52, l. 38 Marleau, " 'The Crash of Timbers Continued,' " pp. 18–19. No one has demonstrated that the owners of the *Pennsylvania* coerced testimony from riverboatmen by promising them jobs, but the continuation of the same staff on the *Pennsylvania* after a ten-week layover indicates that the owners kept the pilots on retainer.

p. 53, l. 19 SLC to Ann Taylor, 1 June 1857. *Letters*, Vol. 1, p. 72.

p. 54, l. 12 SLC to Mollie Clemens, 18 June 1858. *Letters*, Vol. 1, p. 81.

p. 54, l. 26 *Memphis Eagle and Enquirer*, 16 June 1858. *Letters*, Vol. 1, p. 82, n. 1. It seems curious that the *Memphis Eagle and Enquirer* noted Clemens' arrival among the bedlam of meetings; I suspect he was known to the paper prior to the accident. No Clemens contributions to the paper have surfaced yet.

p. 54, l. 32 SLC to Mollie Clemens, 18 June 1858. *Letters*, Vol. 1, p. 82.

p. 55, l. 13 Edgar Branch notes 26 June 1858 as the date of Henry's burial in Hannibal in "Sam Clemens, Steersman on the *John H. Dickey*," though *Letters*, Vol. 1, on p. 86, n. 2, implies 25 June 1858.

p. 55, l. 39 *Early Tales and Sketches*, Vol. 1, p. 59

p. 56, l. 32 SLC to Orion Clemens, 27? June 1860. *Letters*, Vol. 1, pp. 97–98.

p. 58, l. 18 *Early Tales and Sketches*, Vol. 1, p. 133. Despite Horst Kruse's well-researched and informative essay concerning the origin of the pen name Mark Twain ("Mark Twain's *Nom de Plume*"), I continue to doubt that Clemens' one foray as Sergeant Fathom affected his career to the extent Kruse asserts.

p. 58, l. 22 Since none of the aspects of this variable tale that I have included has been shown false yet, I will leave it with the warning that not all of it has been proven true, either.

p. 59, l. 4 It is possible that an impetuous kiss, given by Wright to Clemens, soured the affair. In a late story about Adam and Eve, "Eve, unable to resist the impulse, throws her arms around Adam's neck and kisses him[.]" Her actions "frightened him, and he jumped up, angry and astonished, and flung her off" (Baetzhold,

"Found," p. 427). Clemens probably could not have accepted such a forthright gesture from Laura Wright.

p. 59, l. 6   See *Letters*, Vol. 2, p. 56, n. 7, for details of this relationship.

p. 59, l. 7   Howard Baetzhold gives the fullest rendition of the importance of this relationship in "Found: Mark Twain's 'Lost Sweetheart.' "

p. 59, l. 12   SLC to Susan Stotts, 11 August 1860. *Letters*, Vol. 1, pp. 99–100.

p. 52, l. 26   *Letters*, Vol. 1, p. 121.

p. 60, l. 2   SLC to Orion and Mollie Clemens, 6 February 1861. *Letters*, Vol. 1, p. 110.

p. 60, l. 8   Ibid., pp. 111–12.

p. 60, l. 21   Ibid., pp. 108–11.

p. 60, l. 28   Edward Bates to William Seward, 12 March 1861. *Roughing It*, p. 574.

p. 61, l. 17   Branch, "A Proposed Calendar," p. 21.

p. 61, l. 30   SLC to Worshipful Master, Wardens, and Brethren of Polar Star Lodge No. 79, 26 December 1860. *Letters*, Vol. 1, pp. 106–7.

p. 61, l. 35   Gerber, "Mark Twain's 'Private Campaign,' " p. 39 note. See also Annie Moffett Webster's recollections in Webster, *Mark Twain, Business Man*, pp. 60–63.

p. 62, l. 13   There are several conflicting stories about Clemens' departure from the Confederacy.

p. 62, l. 19   "History of a Campaign That Failed," *Collected Tales, Sketches, Speeches, and Essays, 1852–1890*, p. 880.

6: OUT WEST

p. 63, l. 9   *Pudd'nhead Wilson*, Headnote, Chapter 8, p. 100.

p. 64, l. 9   *Roughing It*, pp. 120–21.

p. 64, l. 11   Stagecoach fare was $300; the brothers owed nearly $200 in cartage and incidental expenses. See *Letters*, Vol. 1, p. 122, for a facsimile of the stagecoach receipt.

p. 64, l. 26   *Roughing It*, pp. 586–87. Although Slade did kill this man, witnesses said it was in self-defense.

p. 65, l. 37   Mack, *Mark Twain in Nevada*, pp. 46–47; Hulse, *Nevada Adventure*, pp. 99–101; Ostrander, *Nevada*, pp. 36, 39.

p. 66, l. 3   SLC to Jane Clemens, 25 October 1861. *Letters*, Vol. 1, pp. 133–34.

p. 66, l. 40   SLC to Jane Clemens, 18–21 September 1861. *Letters*, Vol. 1, p. 124.

p. 67, l. 11   *Roughing It*, p. 172.

p. 67, l. 29   SLC to Jane Clemens, 30 January 1862. *Letters*, Vol. 1, p. 150.

p. 68, l. 32   SLC to Mollie Clemens, 29, 30, and 31 January 1862. *Letters*, Vol. 1, p. 145.

p. 68, l. 37   Orion Clemens to Mollie Clemens, 29, 30, and 31 January 1862. *Letters*, Vol. 1, p. 144.

p. 69, l. 14   SLC to Orion Clemens, 13 April 1862. *Letters*, Vol. 1, p. 187.

p. 69, l. 31   SLC to William Claggett, 18 April 1862. *Letters*, Vol. 1, p. 192.

p. 69, l. 37   SLC to Orion Clemens, 22 June 1862. *Letters*, Vol. 1, p. 221.

p. 70, l. 12   SLC to William Claggett, 9 September 1862. *Letters*, Vol. 1, p. 239.

7: INVENTING THE FIRST MARK TWAIN

p. 71, l. 11   "License of the Press," *Collected Tales, Sketches, Speeches, and Essays, 1852–1890*, p. 553.

p. 72, l. 41   SLC to Jane Clemens, 11 and 12 April 1863. *Letters*, Vol. 1, p. 246.

p. 74, l. 12   *Early Tales and Sketches*, Vol. 1, p. 159.

p. 74, l. 17   SLC to Orion and Mollie Clemens, 21 October 1862. *Letters*, Vol. 1, p. 242.

p. 74, l. 34   See Fatout, *Mark Twain in Virginia City*, pp. 22–27; and Mack, *Mark Twain in Nevada*, pp. 219–29.

p. 75, l. 25   *Early Tales and Sketches*, Vol. 1, p. 173.

p. 75, l. 32   SLC to Jane Clemens and Pamela Moffett, 16 February 1863. *Letters*, Vol. 1, p. 244.

p. 76, l. 10   *Early Tales and Sketches*, Vol. 1, p. 195.

p. 76, l. 20 See especially Kruse, "Mark Twain's *Nom de Plume*," and Fatout, *Mark Twain in Virginia City*, pp. 34–39. Kruse's discussion of Clemens' myth of his pseudonym uncovers a variety of interesting new facts, but does not significantly alter the evidence favoring the gin-mill origin of the name. Kruse's argument that Clemens confused "Mark Twain" and "Sergeant Fathom" depends on Clemens having forgotten key events in his life after a period of less than five years. His argument also depends on his assumption that Clemens misread, misheard, or misremembered the death of Captain Isaiah Russell in October 1862 for the death of Captain Isaiah Sellers a year and a half later. Of course, reports of the subsequent death of Sellers would have made it certain that Clemens knew that his story about the origin of the name Mark Twain was a fabrication.

p. 76, l. 27 *Early Tales and Sketches*, Vol. 1, pp. 192–209.

p. 76, l. 38 *Letters*, Vol. 1, p. 261, n. 3, states that Rice was one of two possible roommates. The regularity with which Clemens mentions Rice implies they lived together.

p. 76, l. 39 For more information concerning Clemens' homoerotic experience and the prevalence of homosexuality in the American West, see my article "Mark Twain and Homosexuality" in the March 1995 issue of *American Literature*. I acknowledge that my hypothesis of Clemens' homosexual behavior, though circumstantially documented, can never be proven.

p. 77, l. 8 *Early Tales and Sketches*, Vol. 1, p. 204.

p. 78, l. 2 A look at the community of writers in early San Francisco proves this point. The leading literary light, George Derby, who wrote under the name John Phoenix and whose work greatly influenced Clemens, conducted a relationship with his assistant Charles Poole before and during his marriage. (See the letters from Derby to Poole in Stewart, *John Phoenix, Esq., the Veritable Squibob*, p. 98.) All the detailed reports of San Francisco's artistic community show at least a social acceptance of homosexuality and quite possibly a cultural norm wherein homosexuality is the dominant, though not exclusive, practice.

p. 78, l. 28 This anecdote, reprinted in the *Eureka* (Calif.) *Humboldt Times* on 18 April 1863, demonstrates just how far Mark Twain's reputation had spread in the mere eight months he had been writing for the *Enterprise*. Its truth, of course, cannot be verified. In Fatout, *Mark Twain in Virginia City*, p. 45.

p. 78, l. 38 *Early Tales and Sketches*, Vol. 1, pp. 246–47. Howard Baetzhold suggested in personal correspondence that this event might be the origin of the cave-climax death of Injun Joe in *The Adventures of Tom Sawyer*.

p. 79, l. 19 Paine, *Biography*, p. 215. Similar anecdotes involving Sam's swearing around a minister can be found elsewhere, but to my knowledge all are secondhand.

p. 80, l. 9 *Early Tales and Sketches*, Vol. 1, p. 248.

p. 80, l. 12 *Letters*, Vol. 1, p. 253 n. 1.

p. 80, l. 26 SLC to Jane Clemens and Pamela Moffett, 1 June 1863. *Letters*, Vol. 1, p. 255.

p. 81, l. 1 Walker, *San Francisco's Literary Frontier*, p. 146.

p. 81, l. 38 *Early Tales and Sketches*, Vol. 1, p. 267.

p. 82, l. 2 Ibid., p. 269.

p. 82, l. 13 SLC to Jane Clemens and Pamela Moffett, 5 August 1863. *Letters*, Vol. 1, p. 262.

p. 82, l. 26 *Letters*, Vol. 1, p. 310, n. 3.

p. 83, l. 8 *Early Tales and Sketches*, Vol. 1, pp. 320–26.

p. 84, l. 15 Born Charles Farrar Brown, he added the final *e* for effect. Browne's homosexuality is generally accepted by scholars and clearly implied by biographer James C. Austin: "Though he was quick to ridicule the mother-love theme in popular songs and stories, his attachment to his own mother is something Freudians could make much of. There is apparently no trace of close affection for any other woman in Browne's life" (*Artemus Ward*, p. 21).

p. 84, l. 29 Paine, *Biography*, p. 240.

p. 84, l. 40 Ibid., p. 241.

p. 85, l. 2 Mack, *Mark Twain in Nevada*, p. 296.

p. 85, l. 15 In Fatout, *Mark Twain in Virginia City*, p. 46.

p. 85, l. 31 Charles Farrar Browne (Artemus Ward) to SLC, 1 January 1864. Sloane, "A Revisionist Perspective on Mark Twain," pp. 135–36. Limited space prohibits reprinting the complete text of the letter here; I have excised some off-color humor about gonorrhea and seduction. Sloane reads this humor as heterosexual.

p. 85, l. 38 SLC to Jane Clemens, 2? January 1864. *Letters*, Vol. 1, p. 267.

p. 86, l. 9 In Fatout, *Mark Twain in Virginia City*, p. 153.

p. 86, l. 12 Mack, *Mark Twain in Nevada*, p. 279.

p. 86, l. 31 SLC to Pamela Moffett, 18 March 1864. *Letters*, Vol. 1, pp. 275–76.

p. 87, l. 3 Ibid., p. 274.

p. 87, l. 10 These "lessons" are my conjecture; Clemens does not make them explicit. On the other hand, he eliminates the sort of behavior he displayed with Artemus Ward: sitting on a barrel at dawn, being fed mustard with a spoon, allowing himself to be thought a comprehensive idiot.

p. 87, l. 17 Dan De Quille, "Neither Head nor Tail," *San Francisco Golden Era*, 6 December 1863.

p. 87, l. 21 In Mack, *Mark Twain in Nevada*, pp. 245, 247.

p. 87, l. 25 *Gold Hill Daily News*, 18 April 1864. Randy Clark, historian with the San Francisco Lesbian and Gay History Project, regarded this newspaper tidbit as dead-sure evidence that a romantic relationship between Mark Twain and Dan De Quille was public knowledge (telephone conversation, 2 May 1993).

p. 87, l. 30 *Letters*, Vol. 1, p. 310, n. 1.

p. 87, l. 41 *Roughing It*, p. 376.

p. 88, l. 60 SLC to Jane Clemens and Pamela Moffett, 17 May 1864. *Letters*, Vol. 1, p. 282.

p. 88, l. 18 In Fatout, *Mark Twain in Virginia City*, p. 188; other sources quote with some minor variations.

p. 88, l. 19 Gridley's flash fame and subsequent obscurity served Clemens as a cautionary tale. Gridley took his sack around the country, netting over $100,000 for the Sanitary Fund and becoming a notable figure for a short time. He died poor and unknown in Paradise, California, in 1870. Clemens ends his description of Gridley's flour trail by saying he "greatly regretted" the death of this man he hardly knew (*Roughing It*, p. 298).

p. 88, l. 29 In Fatout, *Mark Twain in Virginia City*, p. 196.

p. 88, l. 33 In Lauber, *The Making of Mark Twain*, p. 130.

p. 89, l. 9 SLC to Mollie Clemens, 20 May 1864. *Letters*, Vol. 1, pp. 287–88.

p. 89, l. 27 Paine, *Biography*, p. 251.

8: HOSTAGE TO BOHEMIA

p. 91, l. 8 *Following the Equator*, Vol. 2, Headnote, Chapter 2, p. 13.

p. 92, l. 9 See Walker, *San Francisco's Literary Frontier* for a more complete portrait of San Francisco in the 1860s.

p. 92, l. 18 SLC to Jane Clemens, 2? January 1864. *Letters*, Vol. 1, p. 268. Clemens' third-person reference to Mark Twain reveals the relationship he felt with his pseudonymous alter ego.

p. 92, l. 22 *Letters*, Vol. 1, p. 270, n. 8.

p. 92, l. 36 *Roughing It*, p. 396.

p. 92, l. 41 Ibid., p. 397.

p. 93, l. 14 SLC to William Wright (Dan De Quille), 15 July 1864. *Letters*, Vol. 1, p. 304.

p. 93, l. 19 *Roughing It*, p. 397. Given that Clemens accepted a job with the *Call* within days of his arrival in San Francisco, it is safe to assume he had no intention of going to New York for any stock deal, the context for these remarks. I believe that in composing *Roughing It*, Clemens recalled the desperate tone of his unanswered letters and wished to gloss them differently by use of an invented memory. See Lawrence Berkove's article, " 'Nobody Writes to Anybody Except to Ask a Favor': New Correspondence Between Mark Twain and Dan De Quille," for a history of the correspondence between the men.

p. 94, l. 24   SLC to Jane Clemens and Pamela Moffett, 25 September 1864. *Letters*, Vol. 1, p. 313.

p. 94, l. 41   *Early Tales and Sketches*, Vol. 2, pp. 100–7.

p. 95, l. 2   *Letters*, Vol. 1, pp. 252, 254, n. 4.

p. 95, l. 6   SLC to Orion and Mollie Clemens, 28 September 1864. *Letters*, Vol. 1, p. 315.

p. 95, l. 11   SLC to Jane Clemens and Pamela Moffett, 25 September 1864. *Letters*, Vol. 1, p. 313.

p. 95, l. 22   SLC to Orion Clemens, 11 November 1864. *Letters*, Vol. 1, p. 318.

p. 95, l. 29   *Mark Twain's Own Autobiography*, p. 103.

p. 95, l. 41   *Roughing It*, p. 404.

p. 96, l. 10   Ibid., p. 405.

p. 97, l. 4   Walker, *San Francisco's Literary Fontier*, p. 278.

p. 97, l. 9   Ibid., p. 190.

p. 97, l. 16   Steve Gillis said in an interview conducted in 1907, after nearly half a century without contact between the former friends, "Tell Sam I'm going to die pretty soon, but that I love him; that I've always loved him all my life, and I'll love him till I die" (*Biography*, p. 1377).

p. 97, l. 19   Gary Scharnhorst's discoveries of several Mark Twain articles of this period give firm evidence of Clemens' imbroglio with the police and their retaliatory arrest of Clemens for drunkenness. The traditional story tells that Steve Gillis was arrested for fighting and then jumped the bail that Clemens put up for him, necessitating Clemens' escape. More likely, Clemens' set-to with the police combined with debts partially undertaken on behalf of Steve Gillis to motivate his departure.

p. 98, l. 4   Gillis, *Gold Rush Days with Mark Twain*, pp. 65–67. Although Billy Gillis is far from a dependable reporter, his story of the pocket mine comes from direct experience and contradicts Clemens' published stories, with which he normally agrees.

p. 98, l. 13   *Notebooks and Journals*, Vol. 1, p. 82.

p. 98, l. 25   *Early Tales and Sketches*, Vol. 2, p. 268.

p. 99, l. 4   "The Christmas Fireside: For Good Little Boys and Girls," *Collected Tales, Sketches, Speeches, and Essays, 1852–1890*, p. 194.

p. 99, l. 17   *Roughing It*, p. 421.

p. 99, l. 38   "American Humor and Humorists," *Round Table*, 9 September 1865. *Letters*, Vol. 1, p. 325, n. 3.

p. 100, l. 12   SLC to Orion and Mollie Clemens, 19 and 20 October 1865. *Letters*, Vol. 1, pp. 322–24.

p. 100, l. 20   Ibid., p. 322.

p. 100, l. 24   *Letters*, Vol. 1, p. 325, n. 6.

p. 100, l. 37   *Early Tales and Sketches*, Vol. 2, p. 283.

p. 100, l. 40   Ibid., p. 287.

p. 101, l. 21   In *Letters*, Vol. 1, p. 328.

p. 101, l. 26   SLC to Jane Clemens and Pamela Moffett, 20 January 1866. *Letters*, Vol. 1, p. 327.

p. 101, l. 39   Ibid., pp. 329–30.

p. 102, l. 7   Charles Warren Stoddard to Walt Whitman, 2 March 1869. Katz, *Gay American History*, p. 501.

p. 102, l. 19   SLC to Orion and Mollie Clemens, 13 December 1865. *Letters*, Vol. 1, p. 326.

p. 102, l. 30   SLC to Mollie Clemens, 22 May 1866. *Letters*, Vol. 1, p. 341. The details of the offer by Herman Camp and the reasons for Orion's rejection of it depend on Clemens' much later recollection of the events.

p. 102, l. 35 Charles Webb later recalled, "Didn't I get his hat checked to the Islands and back when the *Union* wouldn't advance the money for his fare?" (Charles Webb to Edmund Clarence Stedman, 14? November 1900, *Letters*, Vol. 1, p. 334, n. 1.)

p. 102, l. 41 SLC to Jane Clemens and Pamela Moffett, 5 March 1866. *Letters*, Vol. 1, p. 333.

9: HAWAIIAN CORRESPONDENCE

p. 104, l. 9 "The Facts Concerning the Recent Resignation," *Collected Tales, Sketches, Speeches, and Essays, 1852–1890,* p. 241.

p. 104, l. 40 *Notebooks and Journals,* Vol. 1, p. 189.

p. 105, l. 5 From a population of nearly half a million natives at the time of Cook's arrival in 1778, Kanaka numbered only a few more than 60,000 in 1866.

p. 105, l. 25 *Mark Twain's Letters from Hawaii,* p. 32.

p. 105, l. 39 In Frear, *Mark Twain and Hawaii,* p. 151.

p. 106, l. 9 *Mark Twain's Letters from Hawaii,* p. 46.

p. 106, l. 18 Ibid., pp. 170–71.

p. 106, l. 33 SLC to William Bowen, 25 August 1866. *Letters,* Vol. 1, p. 359.

p. 107, l. 8 See Frear, *Mark Twain and Hawaii,* Chapter 3, pp. 37–54.

p. 107, l. 14 *Notebooks and Journals,* Vol. 1, p. 219.

p. 107, l. 33 SLC to Jane Clemens and Pamela Moffett, 4 May 1866. *Letters,* Vol. 1, p. 337. The missing notebook covering this period would shed light on his associations.

p. 107, l. 37 SLC to Jane Clemens and Pamela Moffett, 21 June 1866. *Letters,* Vol. 1, p. 343.

p. 107, l. 39 SLC to Jane Clemens and Pamela Moffett, 27 June 1866. *Letters,* Vol. 1, p. 347.

p. 108, l. 37 Paine, *Biography,* p. 287.

p. 109, l. 9 A later note about a song sung in Princess Victoria's honor implies that Clemens saw considerably more of the ceremonies than he reported in letters to the *Sacramento Union.*

p. 109, l. 23 *Notebooks and Journals,* Vol. 1, pp. 129, 129, n. 64.

p. 109, l. 29 *Mark Twain's Letters from Hawaii,* pp. 129–32.

p. 109, l. 38 Clemens, copying the journals of the Ferguson brothers and Captain Mitchell, wonders in his own notebook what kept these men alive. Many passages imply that he found inspiration for endurance from their survival.

p. 109, l. 40 Note many references to writing style and stately eloquence in parts of his notebook recorded aboard the *Smyrniote* in *Notebooks and Journals,* Vol. 1, pp. 133–78.

p. 110, l. 3 See note "Be virtuous be happy don't apply to S[andwich] I[slands]" in *Notebooks and Journals,* Vol. 1, p. 156.

p. 110, l. 10 *Notebooks and Journals,* Vol. 1, p. 133.

10: AT HOME, ON STAGE

p. 111, l. 10 *Notebooks and Journals,* Vol. 3, p. 389.

p. 111, l. 27 *Notebooks and Journals,* Vol. 1, p. 163.

p. 112, l. 37 In Lorch, *The Trouble Begins at Eight,* p. 27.

p. 113, l. 6 In ibid., p. 279. Also see Fatout, ed., *Mark Twain Speaking,* pp. 9–10.

p. 113, l. 22 In Lorch, *The Trouble Begins at Eight,* p. 31.

p. 113, l. 32 In ibid., p. 37.

p. 114, l. 8 In ibid., p. 40.

p. 114, l. 26 In *Letters,* Vol. 1, p. 366, n. 3.

p. 115, l. 21 Lorch offers this argument in *The Trouble Begins at Eight,* p. 47. While this was part of Clemens' thinking, the economic necessity of reducing his debt had a greater effect on his decision not to board the boat on 19 November 1866.

p. 115, l. 25 See Lorch, *The Trouble Begins at Eight,* p. 46.

p. 115, l. 32   *Harper's* rare misprint provokes these interesting questions because Clemens wrote with so legible a hand and the name Mark Twain was at the very least familiar in New York publishing circles. I note this unprovable point because Clemens' purposeful alteration of his byline reveals the ambivalent relationship he felt with his Mark Twain persona in the early months of its development.

p. 116, l. 10   SLC to Clemens family, 4 December 1866. *Letters*, Vol. 1, p. 368.

p. 116, l. 24   Lorch, *The Trouble Begins at Eight*, pp. 49–50.

p. 116, l. 29   SLC to Clemens family, 15 December 1866. *Letters*, Vol. 1, p. 373.

11: ON THE MAKE IN THE EAST

p. 117, l. 10   *Pudd'nhead Wilson*, Headnote, Chapter 13, p. 144.

p. 117, l. 28   SLC to Edward Hingston, 25 January 1867. *Letters*, Vol. 2, pp. 8–9.

p. 117, l. 32   *Notebooks and Journals*, Vol. 1, pp. 250–51.

p. 118, l. 5   Ibid., p. 264.

p. 118, l. 9   Ibid., p. 269.

p. 118, l. 15   Clemens' emergence as a public persona on the East Coast in 1867 substantially changes the nature of research about his life. Excepting several periods of intentional public silence, few uncertainties emerge about Clemens' public life or that of his persona Mark Twain.

p. 118, l. 31   *Mark Twain's Own Autobiography*, p. 13.

p. 119, l. 13   In *Letters*, Vol. 2, p. 14.

p. 119, l. 21   The exact terms of the arrangement seem somewhat in doubt.

p. 120, l. 27   In Fatout, *Mark Twain on the Lecture Circuit*, p. 71.

p. 120, l. 33   "Female Suffrage," *Collected Tales, Sketches, Speeches, and Essays, 1852–1890*, pp. 214–15.

p. 121, l. 25   SLC to Clemens family, 1 May 1867. *Letters*, Vol. 2, p. 38.

p. 121, l. 30   In Fatout, *Mark Twain on the Lecture Circuit*, p. 71.

p. 122, l. 2   *New York Tribune*, 7 May 1867, p. 4.

p. 122, l. 10   SLC to John Stanton (Corry O'Lanus), 20 May 1867. *Letters*, Vol. 2, p. 45.

p. 122, l. 22   SLC to Bret Harte, 1 May 1867. *Letters*, Vol. 2, p. 39.

p. 122, l. 24   SLC to Clemens family, 7 June 1867. *Letters*, Vol. 2, p. 57.

p. 123, l. 9   SLC to John McComb, 8 June 1867. *Letters*, Vol. 2, p. 61.

p. 123, l. 17   SLC to Clemens family, 1 June 1867. *Letters*, Vol. 2, pp. 49–50.

12: AN INNOCENT VANDAL

p. 124, l. 13   "The American Vandal Abroad," in Lorch, *The Trouble Begins at Eight*, p. 296.

p. 125, l. 9   *Letters*, Vol. 2, p. 110 n. 4.

p. 125, l. 18   Although Clemens had groups of readers on the *Territorial Enterprise* and among the California Bohemians, no record survives that he shared his work in manuscript with either of these audiences. The only recorded previous instance of such reading comes in the recollections of his niece Annie Moffett, during the period when Clemens was a riverboatman (*Mark Twain, Business Man*, p. 48).

p. 125, l. 27   *Letters*, Vol. 2, p. 123 n. 7.

p. 126, l. 5   *Notebooks and Journals*, Vol. 1, p. 344.

p. 126, l. 21   McKeithan, *Traveling with the Innocents Abroad*, pp. 16–17.

p. 126, l. 36   Ibid., p. 58.

p. 127, l. 20   Ibid., p. 26.

p. 127, l. 33   SLC to Frank Fuller, 7 August 1867. *Letters*, Vol. 2, p. 76. Clemens wrote this as a joke to Frank Fuller, as the immediate context makes clear, but the more complete context of the paragraph concerning Hitchcock implies that Clemens did not jest entirely.

p. 128, l. 9   SLC to Frank Fuller, 7 August 1867. *Letters*, Vol. 2, p. 75.

p. 128, l. 12   SLC to Clemens family, 9 August 1867. *Letters*, Vol. 2, p. 78.

p. *129, l. 10*   McKeithan, *Traveling with the Innocents Abroad*, p. 156.

p. *129, l. 12*   SLC to Clemens family, 26 August 1867. *Letters*, Vol. 2, p. 81.

p. *129, l. 14*   *Notebooks and Journals*, Vol. 1, p. 407.

p. *129, l. 19*   *Innocents Abroad*, p. 322.

p. *129, l. 25*   Roessel, "Mark Twain at Ephesus," p. 27.

p. *129, l. 33*   McKeithan, *Traveling with the Innocents Abroad*, p. 174.

p. *129, l. 40*   Ibid., p. 182.

p. *130, l. 4*   Ibid., p. 184.

p. *130, l. 8*   Ibid., p. 204.

p. *130, l. 12*   Ganzel, *Mark Twain Abroad*, p. 227.

p. *130, l. 30*   McKeithan *Traveling with the Innocents Abroad*, p. 267.

p. *131, l. 4*   See Ganzel, *Mark Twain Abroad*, pp. 261–75.

p. *131, l. 25*   SLC to Joseph Goodman, 24 October 1867. *Letters*, Vol. 2, p. 101.

p. *132, l. 1*   SLC to Clemens family, 20 November 1867. *Letters*, Vol. 2, p. 104.

p. *132, l. 5*   McKeithan, *Traveling with the Innocents Abroad*, pp. 313–14.

p. *132, l. 9*   SLC to John Young, 22 November 1867. *Letters*, Vol. 2, p. 108.

13: A GYPSY AGAIN

p. *133, l. 10*   *Following the Equator*, Vol. 1, Headnote, Chapter 8, p. 80.

p. *133, l. 37*   SLC to Frank Fuller, 24 November 1867. *Letters*, Vol. 2, p. 111.

p. *133, l. 40*   Clemens' correspondence with Emma Beach, a handful of long letters during his winter in Washington, prefigures in form, self-representation, and style his later and more extensive courtship correspondence with Olivia Langdon.

p. *134, l. 14*   Elisha Bliss to SLC, 21 November 1867. *Letters*, vol. 2, p. 120, n. 1.

p. *134, l. 19*   SLC to Clemens family, 10 December 1867. *Letters*, Vol. 2, p. 129.

p. *134, l. 26*   "The Facts Concerning the Recent Resignation," *Collected Tales, Sketches, Speeches, and Essays, 1852–1890*, p. 240.

p. *134, l. 30*   SLC to Frank Fuller, 13 December 1867. *Letters*, Vol. 2, p. 136.

p. *135, l. 13*   SLC to Jane Clemens and Pamela Moffett, 8 January 1868. *Letters*, Vol. 2, p. 144.

p. *135, l. 15*   Ibid.

p. *135, l. 32*   Ibid., pp. 144–45.

p. *135, l. 38*   SLC to Mary Fairbanks, 12 December 1867. *Letters*, Vol. 2, p. 133.

p. *136, l. 2*   Ibid., p. 134.

p. *136, l. 13*   In *Letters*, Vol. 2, p. 153, n. 2.

p. *136, l. 16*   SLC to Clemens family, 14 January 1868. *Letters*, Vol. 2, p. 155.

p. *136, l. 19*   "Woman—an Opinion," *Collected Tales, Sketches, Speeches, and Essays, 1852–1890*, p. 248.

p. *136, l. 40*   SLC to Jane Clemens and Pamela Moffett, 6 February 1868. *Letters*, Vol. 2, p. 178.

p. *137, l. 2*   SLC to Elisha Bliss, Jr., 4 and 6 February 1868. *Letters*, Vol. 2, p. 177.

p. *137, l. 6*   Ibid.

p. *137, l. 14*   *Letters*, Vol. 2, p. 187, n. 2.

p. *137, l. 18*   SLC to Mary Fairbanks, 10 March 1868. *Letters*, Vol. 2, p. 202.

p. *138, l. 6*   SLC to Mary Fairbanks, 17 June 1868. *Letters*, Vol. 2, p. 222.

p. *138, l. 10*   SLC to Charles Henry Webb, 26 November 1870. In Steinbrink, *Getting to Be Mark Twain*, p. 194, n. 5.

p. *138, l. 22*   *Alta California*, 3 July 1868. In Fatout, *Mark Twain on the Lecture Circuit*, pp. 95–96.

14: LOVE AND MONEY

p. *139, l. 12*   "Woman—an Opinion," *Collected Tales, Sketches, Speeches, and Essays, 1852–1890*, p. 248.

p. *139, l. 18*   "Extracts from Adam's Diary," *Collected Tales, Sketches, Speeches, and Essays, 1891–1910*, pp. 107–8.

p. *139, l. 34*   See SLC to Frank Fuller, 12 May 1868. *Letters*, Vol. 2, pp. 216–17. Clemens deserves recognition for the originality of his perception of what has become a marketing mainstay.

p. 140, l. 5   SLC to Mary Fairbanks, 17 August 1868. *Letters*, Vol. 2, p. 241.

p. 140, l. 10   SLC to Charles Langdon, 21 August 1868. *Letters*, Vol. 2, p. 242.

p. 140, l. 15   SLC to Clemens family, 24 and 25 August 1868. *Letters*, Vol. 2, p. 244.

p. 141, l. 17   See Skandera-Trombley, "Mark Twain's Fictionalizing of Dr. Newton's Miraculous Cure."

p. 141, l. 26   In *Letters*, Vol. 2, p. 249, n. 4.

p. 142, l. 7   *Getting to Be Mark Twain*, Jeffrey Steinbrink's authoritative work on this period of Clemens' life, makes a rare misstep in retelling the courtship. Steinbrink misses the fact that, before he began courting Olivia Langdon, Clemens would have discussed the matter with Jervis Langdon. Though it is impossible to know if Jervis Langdon agreed to anything more than permitting Clemens to court his daughter, several factors indicate that Langdon and Clemens worked out their arrangement in detail; for example, immediately following Livy's acceptance, Clemens wrote Jervis Langdon about purchasing shares in a newspaper, implying a written continuation of an earlier discussion. Steinbrink's otherwise excellent book overlooks this transaction and therefore misreads the history of the romance and the progress of the marriage.

p. 142, l. 16   SLC to William Bowen, 25 August 1866. *Letters*, Vol. 1, p. 359.

p. 142, l. 29   SLC to OLC, 7 and 8 September 1868. *Letters*, Vol. 2, p. 247.

p. 142, l. 33   There is some doubt that Olivia Langdon numbered the letters upon receipt, but my research into nineteenth-century courtship rituals indicates that she knew she would accept Clemens, provided he did nothing to shame or alienate her in the interim.

p. 142, l. 38   *Love Letters of Mark Twain*, p. 20.

p. 143, l. 2   SLC to OLC, 21 September 1868. *Letters*, Vol. 2, p. 250.

p. 143, l. 3   SLC to Mary Fairbanks, 24 September 1868. *Letters*, Vol. 2, p. 252.

p. 143, l. 9   Ibid.

p. 143, l. 22   SLC to Mary Fairbanks, 5 October 1868. *Letters*, Vol. 2, p. 257.

p. 143, l. 24   OLC to Alice Hooker, 29 September 1868. *Letters*, Vol. 2, p. 258, n. 3.

p. 143, l. 28   SLC to Mary Fairbanks, 12 October 1868. *Letters*, Vol. 2, p. 263.

p. 143, l. 32   SLC to OLC, 18 October 1868. *Letters*, Vol. 2, p. 266.

p. 143, l. 37   Ibid., p. 268.

p. 144, l. 3   Although this fragment, called "Boy's Manuscript" by Albert Bigelow Paine, has been tentatively dated 1870, further research indicates that Clemens penned it during the early days of his courtship.

p. 144, l. 11   *Letters*, Vol. 2, p. 269, n. 4.

p. 144, l. 31   SLC to Mary Fairbanks, 12 October 1868. *Letters*, Vol. 2, p. 264.

p. 145, l. 14   In *Letters*, Vol. 2, p. 280, n. 1.

p. 146, l. 9   SLC to Joseph Twichell, 28 November 1868. *Letters*, Vol. 2, pp. 293–94.

p. 146, l. 19   SLC to Mary Fairbanks, 26 and 27 November 1868. *Letters*, Vol. 2, pp. 283–84.

p. 146, l. 28   The multiplication factor for translating 1869 dollars into 1996 dollars is approximately 18. Thus, Clemens' 1869 fee of $100 a performance translates to about $10,000 a week gross in contemporary terms, but transportation costs were relatively high, and Clemens spent freely on the road. The tour netted him the contemporary equivalent of $50,000.

p. 146, l. 40   SLC to Mary Fairbanks, 26 and 27 November 1868. *Letters*, Vol. 2, p. 284.

p. 147, l. 14   Olivia Lewis Langdon to Mary Fairbanks, 1 December 1868. *Letters*, Vol. 2, pp. 286–87, n. 3.

p. 147, l. 40   SLC to OLC, 5 and 7 December 1868. *Letters*, Vol. 2, p. 316.

p. 148, l. 10   SLC to OLC, 22 January 1868. *Letters*, Vol. 3, p. 63.

p. 148, l. 23   Ibid.

p. 148, l. 25 SLC to OLC, 2 March 1869. *Letters*, Vol. 3, p. 132.

p. 148, l. 34 SLC to OLC, 21 and 22 January 1869. *Letters*, Vol. 3, p. 58.

p. 148, l. 38 SLC to OLC, 13 and 14 January 1869. *Letters*, Vol. 3, p. 32.

p. 149, l. 7 SLC to OLC, 4 December 1868. *Letters*, Vol. 2, p. 307.

p. 149, l. 13 SLC to OLC, 24 January 1869. *Letters*, Vol. 3, p. 74.

p. 149, l. 39 SLC to OLC, 13 and 14 January 1869. *Letters*, Vol. 3, p. 31.

p. 150, l. 9 In *Letters*, Vol. 3, pp. 47–48, n. 2.

p. 150, l. 18 SLC to Charles Warren Stoddard, 25 August 1869. *Letters*, Vol. 3, pp. 320–21.

p. 150, l. 23 Ibid., p. 320.

p. 150, l. 26 Jervis Langdon forgave Clemens' past much earlier in their relationship than after receiving the horrifying reports of his behavior in California. Little more than a month passed between the time Langdon read the reports and he approved the match, a month during which he saw little of Clemens.

p. 151, l. 2 SLC to OLC, 31 December 1868. *Letters*, Vol. 2, p. 370. For Clemens' biblical reference, see Matthew 7:13–14.

p. 151, l. 22 SLC to Clemens family, 5 February 1869. *Letters*, Vol. 3, p. 85.

15: UNSETTLING DOWN

p. 152, l. 9 *Following the Equator*, Vol. 1, Headnote, Chapter 7, p. 72.

p. 152, l. 14 "Consistency," *Collected Tales, Sketches, Speeches, and Essays, 1852–1890*, p. 916.

p. 152, l. 40 Lorch, *The Trouble Begins at Eight*, pp. 285–86.

p. 153, l. 11 SLC to Mary Fairbanks, 7 January 1869. *Letters*, Vol. 3, p. 8.

p. 153, l. 27 SLC to Olivia Lewis Langdon, 13 February 1869. *Letters*, Vol. 3, p. 92.

p. 153, l. 38 Ibid., p. 91.

p. 154, l. 20 SLC to OLC, 27 February 1869. *Letters*, Vol. 3, p. 115.

p. 154, l. 24 "Open Letter to Com. Vanderbilt," *Collected Tales, Sketches, Speeches, and Essays, 1852–1890*, p. 290.

p. 155, l. 6 SLC to OLC, 12 March 1869. *Letters*, Vol. 3, p. 164.

p. 155, l. 22 SLC to OLC, 8 and 9 March 1869. *Letters*, Vol. 3, p. 153.

p. 155, l. 26 SLC to OLC, 12 March 1869. *Letters*, Vol. 3, p. 162.

p. 155, l. 36 SLC to Mary Fairbanks, 15 April 1869. *Letters*, Vol. 3, p. 196.

p. 156, l. 17 SLC to Mary Fairbanks, 10 May 1869. *Letters*, Vol. 3, p. 211.

p. 156, l. 31 *Collected Tales, Sketches, Speeches, and Essays, 1852–1890*, p. 297.

p. 156, l. 33 Ibid., p. 299.

p. 157, l. 13 SLC to Pamela Moffett, 23 June 1869. *Letters*, Vol. 3, p. 270.

p. 157, l. 35 SLC to Elisha Bliss, Jr., 22 July 1869. *Letters*, Vol. 3, p. 285.

p. 158, l. 6 In *Letters*, Vol. 3, p. 306, n. 2.

p. 158, l. 9 SLC to James Redpath, 14 August 1869. *Letters*, Vol. 3, pp. 297–98.

p. 158, l. 17 Jane Clemens to SLC, 25 July 1869. *Letters*, Vol. 3, p. 277, n. 4. Jane Clemens' spelling is preserved.

p. 158, l. 29 SLC to OLC, 3 September 1869. *Letters*, Vol. 3, p. 333.

p. 159, l. 38 *Innocents Abroad*, Vol. 1, Chapter 25.

p. 160, l. 8 Ibid., Chapter 26. The original is presented as a poster, with centered headlines and varying fonts and typefaces.

p. 160, l. 15 *Innocents Abroad*, Vol. 2, Chapter 19.

p. 160, l. 38 *Overland Monthly*, January 1870, p. 100.

p. 161, l. 2 Howells, *My Mark Twain*, p. 112.

16: ON THE ROAD AGAIN

p. 162, l. 10 *Pudd'nhead Wilson*, Headnote, Chapter 8, p. 100.

p. 163, l. 5 Clemens' route is not absolutely certain, but likely.

p. 163, l. 26 Howells, *My Mark Twain*, p. 4.

p. *163, l. 28*   SLC to ?, 9 November 1869. *Letters*, Vol. 3, p. 392.

p. *164, l. 5*   In *Letters*, Vol. 3, p. 392.

p. *164, l. 18*   Fatout, *Mark Twain on the Lecture Circuit*, p. 127.

p. *164, l. 26*   In *Letters*, Vol. 3, p. 392.

p. *164, l. 39*   SLC to Pamela Moffett, 17 December 1869. *Letters*, Vol. 3, p. 429. Clemens begins a new paragraph with "Purchase."

p. *165, l. 16*   SLC to OLC, 24 and 25 November 1869. *Letters*, Vol. 3, p. 404.

p. *165, l. 27*   SLC to OLC, 27 December 1869. *Love Letters of Mark Twain*, p. 132.

p. *165, l. 35*   Olivia Lewis Langdon to Mary Fairbanks, 25 November 1869. *Mark Twain to Mrs. Fairbanks*, p. 112, n. 1.

p. *166, l. 9*   SLC to OLC, 14 December 1869. *Letters*, Vol. 3, pp. 423–24.

p. *166, l. 15*   SLC to OLC, 15 and 16 December 1869. *Letters*, Vol. 3, p. 427.

p. *166, l. 26*   SLC to OLC, 13 January 1870. *Love Letters of Mark Twain*, pp. 134–36.

p. *167, l. 11*   SLC to OLC, 20 January 1870. *Love Letters of Mark Twain*, p. 141.

p. *167, l. 19*   *Love Letters of Mark Twain*, p. 139.

p. *167, l. 25*   SLC to OLC, 6 January 1870. *Mark Twain to Mrs. Fairbanks*, p. 114.

p. *167, l. 30*   In Fatout, *Mark Twain on the Lecture Circuit*, p. 138.

17: WEDDED BLISS

p. *168, l. 9*   *Notebook*, p. 237.

p. *168, l. 34*   SLC to Elisha Bliss, Jr., 22 January 1870. *Mark Twain's Letters to His Publishers*, p. 30.

p. *168, l. 37*   SLC to Elisha Bliss, Jr., 28 January 1870. *Mark Twain's Letters to His Publishers*, p. 32.

p. *168, l. 40*   SLC to James Gillis, 26 January 1870. *Mark Twain's Letters*, p. 170.

p. *169, l. 7*   Quoted in Ray Morris, Jr., *Ambrose Bierce: Alone in Bad Company*, p. 117.

p. *169, l. 38*   SLC to William Bowen, 6 February 1870. *Mark Twain's Letter to William Bowen*, p. 10.

p. *170, l. 11*   Webster, ed., *Mark Twain, Business Man*, p. 113. Jeffrey Steinbrink notes the unverifiability of this comment (*Getting to Be Mark Twain*, pp. 72, 198, n. 10), pointing out both the unlikelihood of Jervis Langdon making such a confession to a seventeen-year-old and the equal unlikelihood of her subsequently inventing it.

p. *170, l. 25*   SLC to William Bowen, 6 February 1870. *Mark Twain's Letter to William Bowen*, pp. 3–8.

p. *170, l. 32*   SLC and OLC to Langdon family, 20 February 1870. *Love Letters of Mark Twain*, p. 143.

p. *170, l. 35*   SLC and OLC to Mary Fairbanks, 29 May 1870. *Mark Twain to Mrs. Fairbanks*, p. 132.

p. *171, l. 14*   SLC to Charles C. Hine, 10 February 1870. Steinbrink, *Getting to Be Mark Twain*, p. 82.

p. *171, l. 24*   SLC to Mary Fairbanks, 13 February 1870. *Mark Twain to Mrs. Fairbanks*, p. 123.

p. *172, l. 1*   SLC to Mary Fairbanks, 22 March 1870. *Mark Twain to Mrs. Fairbanks*, p. 128.

p. *172, l. 5*   SLC to Clemens family, 26 March 1870. Webster, ed., *Mark Twain, Business Man*, p. 112.

p. *172, l. 15*   *Autobiography*, p. 13.

p. *172, l. 17*   SLC to OLC, 8 July 1870. *Love Letters of Mark Twain*, p. 154.

p. *173, l. 4*   SLC to Pamela Moffett, 12 June 1870. Webster, ed., *Mark Twain, Business Man*, p. 114.

18: THE HORRIBLE YEAR

p. *174, l. 10*   "Which Was the Dream?" *Collected Tales, Sketches, Speeches, and Essays, 1891–1910*, p. 232.

p. 174, l. 24 SLC to Elisha Bliss, Jr., 11 August 1870. *Mark Twain's Letters to His Publishers*, p. 38.

p. 174, l. 32 SLC and OLC to Mary Fairbanks, 2 September 1870. *Mark Twain to Mrs. Fairbanks*, p. 137.

p. 175, l. 8 SLC to Mary Fairbanks, 13 October 1870. *Mark Twain to Mrs. Fairbanks*, pp. 138–39.

p. 175, l. 13 SLC to Mary Fairbanks, 5 November 1870. *Mark Twain to Mrs. Fairbanks*, p. 139.

p. 175, l. 24 Elisha Bliss, Jr., to SLC, 2 November 1870. *Mark Twain's Letters to His Publishers*, pp. 41–42 and n. 1.

p. 176, l. 1 SLC to Elisha Bliss, Jr., 13 October 1870. *Mark Twain's Letters to His Publishers*, p. 40.

p. 176, l. 30 SLC to Elisha Bliss, Jr., 2 December 1870. *Mark Twain's Letters to His Publishers*, p. 45.

p. 176, l. 35 There is good though inconclusive evidence that Clemens used Carl Byng as a secondary cover in the *Express;* little evidence supports his use of Hy Slocum, another candidate. Horst Kruse's impressive article, "Literary Old Offenders," reiterates with precision the complex arguments concerning these pseudonyms.

p. 176, l. 40 It seems probable that Clemens' trip to New York was intended to coincide with Orion's arrival in the East, but I have not found any confirmation that the brothers met.

p. 177, l. 3 SLC to Charles Webb, 26 November 1870. *Mark Twain's Letters to His Publishers*, p. 41, n. 1.

p. 177, l. 29 SLC to Thomas Bailey Aldrich, 27 January 1871. Steinbrink, *Getting to Be Mark Twain*, pp. 5–6.

p. 177, l. 32 SLC to James H. Riley, 3 March 1871. Steinbrink, *Getting to Be Mark Twain*, p. 162.

p. 178, l. 8 SLC to Orion Clemens, 4 March 1871. Webster, ed., *Mark Twain, Business Man*, p. 118.

p. 178, l. 18 Steinbrink's discussion of Clemens' attempts to withdraw his monthly column (*Getting to Be Mark Twain*, pp. 151–54) deserves special attention.

p. 178, l. 21 SLC to Elisha Bliss, Jr., 15 February 1871. *Mark Twain's Letters to His Publishers*, pp. 55–56.

p. 178, l. 33 *The Galaxy*, April 1871, p. 615.

p. 179, l. 2 SLC to Orion Clemens, 11 March 1871. *Mark Twain's Letters to His Publishers*, p. 57.

p. 179, l. 7 SLC to Elisha Bliss, Jr., 17 March 1871. *Mark Twain's Letters to His Publishers*, p. 60.

p. 179, l. 14 SLC to James H. Riley, 3 March 1871. Steinbrink, *Getting to Be Mark Twain*, p. 157.

19: A NEW LIFE

p. 180, l. 11 "What Is Man?" *Collected Tales, Sketches, Speeches, and Essays, 1891–1910*, p. 744.

p. 180, l. 38 SLC to Orion Clemens, 8 April 1871. *Mark Twain's Letters to His Publishers*, p. 63.

p. 181, l. 4 SLC to Isaac Sheldon, 6 April 1871. CU-MARK 00601.

p. 181, l. 16 I credit Jeffrey Steinbrink (*Getting to Be Mark Twain*, pp. 171–80) for this interpretation.

p. 181, l. 21 SLC to Mary Fairbanks, 26 April 1871. *Mark Twain to Mrs. Fairbanks*, p. 153.

p. 181, l. 29 SLC to Elisha Bliss, Jr., 3 May 1871. *Mark Twain's Letters to His Publishers*, p. 66.

p. 181, l. 34 SLC to Elisha Bliss, Jr., 15 May 1871. *Mark Twain's Letters*, p. 188.

p. 183, l. 2 SLC to OLC, 9? August 1871. *Love Letters of Mark Twain*, p. 160.

p. 183, l. 6 In Kaplan, *Mr. Clemens and Mark Twain*, p. 233.

p. 183, l. 12 SLC to OLC, 9? August 1871. *Love Letters of Mark Twain*, p. 158.

p. 183, l. 23 Kenneth Andrews' *Nook Farm: Mark Twain's Hartford Circle* describes the society in which Clemens placed himself—and to belong to which he made great sacrifices—offering incisive perceptions on the man Clemens became while there.

p. 185, l. 23 Hill, *Mark Twain and Elisha Bliss*, p. 39. Hill's admirable account of subscription publishing supports his argument concerning the effects of the business on Mark Twain's writing.

p. 185, l. 28 SLC to Elisha Bliss, Jr., 28 January 1870. *Mark Twain's Letters to His Publishers*, pp. 31–32.

20: HELL ON RAILS

p. 187, l. 9 "More Maxims of Mark," *Collected Tales, Sketches, Speeches, and Essays, 1891–1910*, p. 946.

p. 187, l. 28 SLC to James Redpath, 10 June 1871. Kaplan, *Mr. Clemens and Mark Twain*, p. 142.

p. 187, l. 39 SLC to James Redpath, 8 August 1871. *Mark Twain's Letters*, p. 190.

p. 188, l. 8 SLC to OLC, 17 October 1871. *Love Letters of Mark Twain*, p. 161.

p. 188, l. 12 SLC to OLC, 18 October 1871. CU-MARK 00664.

p. 188, l. 23 In Fatout, *Mark Twain on the Lecture Circuit*, p. 154.

p. 188, l. 27 SLC to OLC, 31 October 1871, *Love Letters of Mark Twain*, p. 162.

p. 189, l. 13 See Howells, *My Mark Twain*, p. 6, and Kaplan, *Mr. Clemens and Mark Twain*, pp. 143–44.

p. 189, l. 34 OLC to SLC, 20 November 1871. *Love Letters of Mark Twain*, p. 165.

p. 189, l. 40 SLC to OLC, 16 November 1871. *Love Letters of Mark Twain*, pp. 163–64.

p. 190, l. 10 SLC to OLC, 27 November 1871. *Love Letters of Mark Twain*, pp. 165–66.

p. 190, l. 22 OLC to SLC, 2 and 3 December 1871. *Love Letters of Mark Twain*, pp. 168–69.

p. 190, l. 30 Ibid., p. 168.

p. 191, l. 3 SLC to OLC, 4 December 1871. *Letters*, Vol. 4, p. 507.

p. 191, l. 26 SLC to OLC, 16 December 1871. *Love Letters of Mark Twain*, p. 170.

p. 191, l. 31 SLC to OLC, 26 December 1871. *Love Letters of Mark Twain*, p. 171.

p. 191, l. 33 OLC to SLC, 30 or 31 December 71. CU-MARK 00700.

p. 192, l. 19 SLC to OLC, 7 January 1872. *Love Letters of Mark Twain*, p. 172.

p. 192, l. 25 SLC to Mary Fairbanks, 13 February 1872. *Mark Twain to Mrs. Fairbanks*, pp. 159–60.

p. 192, l. 27 SLC to OLC, 8 January 1872. CU-MARK 00711.

p. 192, l. 39 SLC to Mary Fairbanks, 13 February 1872. *Mark Twain to Mrs. Fairbanks*, p. 158.

21: A BIRTH, A DEATH, A BOOK

p. 194, l. 9 *Following the Equator*, Vol. 2, Headnote, Chapter 30, p. 327.

p. 194, l. 14 Ibid., Headnote, Chapter 33, p. 366.

p. 194, l. 31 Orion Clemens to Mollie Clemens, 23 October 1871. In Kaplan, *Mr. Clemens and Mark Twain*, p. 151.

p. 195, l. 3 SLC to Orion Clemens, 7 March 1872. David, *Mark Twain and His Illustrators*, p. 149.

p. 195, l. 15 SLC to Elisha Bliss, Jr., 20 March 1872. *Mark Twain's Letters to His Publishers*, p. 70.

p. 195, l. 37 The "Textual Introduction" in *Early Tales and Sketches*, Vol. 1, pp. 501–663, comprehensively outlines Mark Twain's early publishing history in England.

p. 196, l. 22 Hotten to SLC, 3 March 1872. UK4 41296.

p. 197, l. 12 SLC to Susy Clemens, 9 May 1872. *Love Letters of Mark Twain*, pp. 174–75.

p. 197, l. 18 SLC to Orion and Mollie Clemens, 15 May 1872. CU-MARK 00747. The Clemenses spelled their first daughter's name "Susie" most of the girl's life; in her adolescence, she insisted on spelling her name "Susy," and later went by "Olivia." I have tried to spell the name as Clemens himself would have at the time under discussion.

p. 197, l. 29 SLC to Annie Moffett, 17 May 1872. NPV 00750.

p. 197, l. 35   SLC to James Osgood, Sunday Summer (probably 7 April) 1872. *Mark Twain's Letters to His Publishers*, p. 73.

p. 197, l. 40   Howells, *My Mark Twain*, p. 114.

p. 198, l. 2   SLC to WDH, 15? June 1872. *Mark Twain-Howells Letters*, pp. 10–11.

p. 198, l. 20   *Roughing It*, pp. 51–52.

p. 191, l. 21   Lilly Warner to George Warner, 3 June 1872. Kaplan, *Mr. Clemens and Mark Twain*, pp. 149–50.

p. 199, l. 36   SLC to Mary Fairbanks, 11 August 1872. *Mark Twain to Mrs. Fairbanks*, p. 163.

p. 200, l. 31   SLC to Orion Clemens, 11 August 1872. *Mark Twain's Letters*, p. 197.

p. 200, l. 39   SLC to Joseph Blamire, 21 July 1872. ViU 00772.

p. 201, l. 9   SLC to Adolph Sutro, 11 June 1872. ODa2 00755.

p. 201, l. 15   Clemens' letters to Mary Fairbanks and Orion Clemens, both 11 August 1872, indicate that Mrs. Langdon would arrive within two days, and that Clemens would himself arrive in Hartford on 13 August 1872 at two in the afternoon. How plans developed for Mrs. Langdon to come to Saybook remain uncertain.

p. 201, l. 18   OLC to Mary Fairbanks, 25 September 1872. *Mark Twain to Mrs. Fairbanks*, p. 164, n. 2.

22: TO ENGLAND!

p. 202, l. 10   *The Adventures of Tom Sawyer*, p. 175.

p. 202, l. 16   *Following the Equator*, Vol. 1, Headnote, Chapter 24, p. 211.

p. 203, l. 19   Mary Fairbanks to SLC, 26 October 1872. *Mark Twain to Mrs. Fairbanks*, p. 165, n. 1.

p. 203, l. 27   SLC to OLC, 28 September 1872. *Love Letters of Mark Twain*, p. 179.

p. 203, l. 32   Paine, *Biography*, p. 463.

p. 203, l. 34   SLC to OLC, 28 September 1872. *Love Letters of Mark Twain*, p. 179.

p. 204, l. 1   SLC to OLC, 25 October 1872. Kaplan, *Mr. Clemens and Mark Twain*, p. 155.

p. 204, l. 3   SLC to OLC, 11 September 1872. *Love Letters of Mark Twain*, p. 177.

p. 204, l. 11   SLC to Mary Fairbanks, 2 November 1872. *Mark Twain to Mrs. Fairbanks*, p. 167.

p. 204, l. 17   Though it has long been accepted that Clemens' intention of preparing a book on England fell victim to the hospitality of his British hosts, I believe that his journey to England is better seen as an escape than as a purposeful business trip, despite Howard Baetzhold's excellent arguments to the contrary in *Mark Twain and John Bull*.

p. 204, l. 22   *Early Tales and Sketches*, Vol. 1, pp. 596–97.

p. 204, l. 25   In Baetzhold, *Mark Twain and John Bull*, p. 8.

p. 204, l. 39   SLC to Jane Clemens and Pamela Moffett, 6 November 1872. *Mark Twain's Letters*, p. 201.

p. 205, l. 19   SLC to OLC, 9 November 1872. *Love Letters of Mark Twain*, p. 181.

p. 205, l. 32   Victoria Woodhull's card in the 20 May 1871 *New York World* implies that she knew about the relationship eighteen months before publishing anything concerning it.

p. 206, l. 7   Thomas Beecher to Isabella Hooker, 5 November 1872. In Andrews, *Nook Farm*, p. 38.

p. 206, l. 18   SLC to Olivia Lewis Langdon, 3 December 1872. CU-MARK 00991.

p. 206, l. 36   "License of the Press," in *Collected Tales, Sketches, Speeches, and Essays, 1852–1890*, pp. 551–55.

p. 207, l. 3   Andrews, *Nook Farm*, p. 3.

p. 207, l. 12   OLC to Susan Crane, ? January 1873. Paine, *Biography*, p. 480.

p. 207, l. 15   Landau, *Edward T. and William A. Potter*, p. 41.

p. 208, l. 26   OLC to Olivia Lewis Langdon, 19 January 1873. CtHMTH 00859.

p. 208, l. 36   Ibid.

p. 210, l. 38   SLC to Whitelaw Reid, 20 April 1873. DLC 00903.

p. 211, l. 11   Herbert Feinstein's 1968 dissertation, "Mark Twain's Lawsuits," contains the fullest description of this case and its effects.

p. 211, l. 40   SLC to Mary Fairbanks, 6 July 1873. *Mark Twain to Mrs. Fairbanks*, pp. 173–74.

p. 212, l. 1   In *Notebooks and Journals*, Vol. 1, pp. 519–20.

p. 212, l. 16   Paine, *Biography*, pp. 496–98.

p. 212, l. 23   For a complete description, see SLC to Olivia Langdon, 17–25 July 1873. *Mark Twain Letters*, pp. 207–8.

p. 213, l. 10   OLC to Susan Crane, 6 October 1873. In Paine, *Biography*, p. 489.

p. 213, l. 18   Stoddard's biographer, Roger Austen, called his subject "the gayest of the gay" of the American literary scene (*Playing the Game*, p. 11). His poetry and essays bridged a gap between early-nineteenth-century and early-twentieth-century aesthetic.

p. 213, l. 25   Lorch, *The Trouble Begins at Eight*, p. 139.

p. 213, l. 35   In Fatout, *Mark Twain on the Lecture Circuit*, p. 181.

p. 214, l. 6   SLC to Jane Clemens, 6 November 1873. Extract by Mollie Clemens. CU-MARK (tr) 00980.

p. 214, l. 27   Charles Warren Stoddard to "Faithful and Beloved Friend," 30 March 1874. George Wharton James, *California Scrapbook: A Collection of Articles:* "Charles Warren Stoddard."

p. 215, l. 2   Fatout, *Mark Twain on the Lecture Circuit*, p. 188.

p. 215, l. 21   SLC to Mary Fairbanks, 25 February 1874. *Mark Twain to Mrs. Fairbanks*, p. 184.

p. 215, l. 29   SLC to OLC, 11 December 1873. *Love Letters of Mark Twain*, p. 186.

p. 215, l. 32   SLC to OLC, 12 December 1873. *Love Letters of Mark Twain*, p. 186. The last six words were inked out at a later time, probably by Clara Clemens.

p. 215, l. 35   SLC to OLC, 14 December 1873. *Love Letters of Mark Twain*, p. 187.

p. 215, l. 37   SLC to OLC, 29 December 1873. *Love Letters of Mark Twain*, p. 189.

p. 216, l. 9   SLC to OLC, 3 January 1874. *Love Letters of Mark Twain*, p. 189.

p. 216, l. 17   Stoddard, *Exits and Entrances*, p. 72.

p. 216, l. 24   Charles Warren Stoddard to SLC, 12 December 1874. MTP 32076-A.

23: A MAN OF PARTS

p. 217, l. 13   "Concerning the Jews," *Collected Tales, Sketches, Speeches, and Essays, 1891–1910*, p. 355.

p. 217, l. 28   SLC to Dr. John Brown, 28 February 1874. *Mark Twain's Letters*, p. 215.

p. 217, l. 41   Though this visit has entered the Mark Twain lore, contradictions in the sources for it make it difficult to stand by any of the particulars with authority.

p. 218, l. 6   WDH to J.M. Comly, 21 March 1874. *Mark Twain-Howells Letters*, p. 16, n. 1.

p. 218, l. 26   Howells, *My Mark Twain*, pp. 7–8.

p. 219, l. 10   SLC to WDH, 20 March 1874. *Mark Twain-Howells Letters*, p. 15.

p. 219, l. 23   SLC to Mary Fairbanks, 25 February 1874. *Mark Twain to Mrs. Fairbanks*, p. 184.

p. 219, l. 32   SLC to Mary Fairbanks, 24 March 1874. *Mark Twain to Mrs. Fairbanks*, p. 185.

p. 219, l. 40   See "Textual Introduction," *Early Tales and Sketches*, Vol. 1, pp. 608–17, for details of this publication.

p. 220, l. 21   SLC to Joseph and Harmony Twichell, 11 June 1874. *Mark Twain's Letters*, p. 220.

p. 220, l. 40   SLC to Jane Clemens, 10 May 1874. NPV 01087.

p. 221, l. 5   SLC to Joseph and Harmony Twichell, 11 June 1874. *Mark Twain's Letters*, p. 219.

p. 221, l. 12   SLC to OLC, 3 July 1874. Mo4 01105.

p. 221, l. 28   SLC to WDH, 25? July 1874. *Mark Twain-Howells Letters*, pp. 20–21.

p. 221, l. 39   SLC to Pamela Moffett, 23 July 1875. Webster, ed., *Mark Twain, Business Man*, p. 133.

p. 222, l. 3   SLC to Dr. John Brown, 4 September 1874. "Introduction," *The Adventures of Tom Sawyer*, p. 10.

p. 222, l. 17   *Collected Tales, Sketches, Speeches, and Essays, 1852–1890*, pp. 578–82.

p. 222, l. 20   SLC to WDH, 2 September 1874. *Mark Twain-Howells Letters*, p. 22.

p. 222, l. 22   WDH to SLC, 8 September 1874. *Mark Twain-Howells Letters*, p. 24.

p. 222, l. 40   SLC to Jane Clemens and Pamela Moffett, 15 August 1874. *Mark Twain's Letters*, pp. 220–221.

p. 223, l. 17   SLC to Orion, 21 September 1874. CU-MARK 01128.

p. 223, l. 24   SLC to Mary Fairbanks, 21 September 1874. *Mark Twain to Mrs. Fairbanks*, p. 189.

p. 223, l. 27   Calculating the cost of the house in modern dollars is nearly impossible, since many details of the house are now extremely expensive to re-create and the relative cost of labor is so high; also, due to changes in taste and style of living, no one would build a house like the Farmington Avenue structure now. Today, a house of similar size and type in a similar neighborhood of a similar city might cost close to $2 million.

p. 223, l. 31   WDH to SLC, 17 September 1874. *Mark Twain-Howells Letters*, p. 25.

24: A MAN OF LETTERS

p. 224, l. 9   "Extracts from Adam's Diary," *Collected Tales, Sketches, Speeches, and Essays, 1891–1910*, p. 102.

p. 224, l. 16   *A Tramp Abroad*, p. 212.

p. 224, l. 25   SLC to Mary Fairbanks, 23 April 1875. *Mark Twain to Mrs. Fairbanks*, p. 191.

p. 224, l. 41   SLC and OLC to Olivia Langdon and the Cranes, 24 September 1874. Paine, *Biography*, pp. 520–21.

p. 225, l. 30   SLC to WDH, 24 October 1874. *Mark Twain-Howells Letters*, p. 33.

p. 225, l. 34   Ibid., p. 34.

p. 226, l. 10   SLC to Charles Stoddard, 1 February 1875. *Mark Twain's Letters*, p. 248.

p. 226, l. 19   SLC to WDH, 29 October 1874. *Mark Twain-Howells Letters*, p. 35.

p. 226, l. 29   SLC to James Redpath, 13 November 1874. *Mark Twain-Howells Letters*, p. 36, n. 1.

p. 227, l. 15   SLC to WDH, 8 December 1874. *Mark Twain-Howells Letters*, p. 49.

p. 227, l. 34   Paine, *Biography*, p. 537.

p. 228, l. 8   SLC to James Osgood, 12 February 1875. *Mark Twain's Letters to His Publishers*, p. 84. Clemens probably did not tell Osgood the truth when he wrote, "I had totally forgotten the existence of such a contract—*totally*" (SLC to James Osgood, 12 February 1875, *Mark Twain's Letters to His Publishers*, p. 84), since several years later he still remembered the terms of the renegotiated deal with Bliss (SLC to CLW, 8 July 1882, Webster, ed., *Mark Twain, Business Man*, p. 190).

p. 228, l. 20   SLC to William Wright (Dan De Quille), 29 March 1875. Berkove, " 'Nobody Writes to Anybody Except to Ask a Favor,' " p. 7.

p. 228, l. 28   This argument compresses Andrews' discussion in *Nook Farm*, pp. 25–77.

p. 229, l. 16   SLC to Pamela Moffett, 23 July 1875. Webster, ed., *Mark Twain, Business Man*, p. 133.

p. 229, l. 19   Howells, *My Mark Twain*, p. 31.

p. 230, l. 16   WDH to William Cooper Howells, 14 May 1875. *Mark Twain-Howells Letters*, p. 70, n. 1.

p. 231, l. 13   "Experience of the McWilliamses with Membranous Croup," *Collected Tales, Sketches, Speeches, and Essays, 1852–1890*, p. 610.

p. 231, l. 25   OLC to Olivia Langdon, 21 March 1875. Willis, *Mark and Livy*, p. 97.

p. 231, l. 37   "A Record of the Small Foolishnesses of Susie and 'Bay' Clemens." Mark Twain Papers at the Bancroft Library at the University of California at Berkeley.

p. 232, l. 5   In *Mark Twain-Howells Letters*, p. 72, n. 2.

p. 232, l. 16   Howells, *My Mark Twain*, p. 34.

p. 232, l. 33   SLC to WDH, 23 April 1875. *Mark Twain-Howells Letters*, p. 74.

p. 233, l. 12   SLC to Mary Fairbanks, 23 April 1875. *Mark Twain to Mrs. Fairbanks*, p. 191.

25: TAMING A SHOOTING STAR

p. 234, l. 8   *Following the Equator*, Vol. 1, Headnote, Chapter 27, p. 238.

p. 235, l. 1　I am indebted to Alan Gribben for his presentation "Mark Twain and the Making of Boy Books" for this insight.

p. 235, l. 20　SLC to WDH, 5 July 1875. *Mark Twain-Howells Letters*, p. 91.

p. 235, l. 33　WDH to SLC, 6 July 1875. *Mark Twain-Howells Letters*, p. 94.

p. 236, l. 26　SLC to Pamela Moffett, 28 June 1875. CU-MARK 01244.

p. 237, l. 3　"Small Foolishnesses." Manuscript in the Mark Twain Papers.

p. 237, l. 7　WDH to SLC, 19 July 1875. *Mark Twain-Howells Letters*, p. 96.

p. 237, l. 10　John Roche, "Making a Reputation: Mark Twain in Newport." Waring's membership in both groups indicates he introduced Clemens to these organizations. I take the spelling of "Bellvue" from Earl Briden's "Mark Twain's Rhode Island Lectures."

p. 237, l. 16　*The Gilded Age*, Vol. 2, p. 14.

p. 237, l. 25　Briden, "Mark Twain's Rhode Island Lectures," p. 36.

p. 238, l. 1　*Collected Tales, Sketches, Speeches, and Essays, 1852–1890*, pp. 634–38.

p. 238, l. 18　SLC to WDH, 18 September 1875. *Mark Twain-Howells Letters*, p. 100.

p. 238, l. 25　Hill, *Mark Twain and Elisha Bliss*, pp. 95–96.

p. 238, l. 29　Howells, *My Mark Twain*, p. 121.

p. 238, l. 40　SLC to WDH, 19 October 1875. *Mark Twain-Howells Letters*, pp. 106–7.

p. 239, l. 10　SLC to Robert Watt, 26 January 1875. NN-B 02484.

p. 239, l. 28　SLC to WDH, 4 October 1875. *Mark Twain-Howells Letters*, p. 103.

p. 239, l. 31　"A Literary Nightmare" may have been composed in Hartford, but the absence of a cover note implies that Clemens handed the manuscript to Howells directly.

p. 239, l. 38　WDH to SLC, 21 November 1875. *Mark Twain-Howells Letters*, pp. 110–11.

p. 240, l. 11　SLC to Elisha Bliss, Jr., 5 November 1875. *Mark Twain's Letters to His Publishers*, p. 92.

p. 240, l. 28　SLC to WDH, 18 January 1876. *Mark Twain-Howells Letters*, p. 121.

26: COMPROMISING THE PAST

p. 241, l. 11　*Pudd'nhead Wilson*, Headnote, Chapter 18, p. 180.

p. 242, l. 11　SLC to Moncure Conway, 9 April 1876. *Mark Twain's Letters to His Publishers*, p. 96.

p. 242, l. 16　WDH to William Cooper Howells, 19 March 1876. *Mark Twain-Howells Letters*, p. 127, n. 2.

p. 243, l. 4　*The Adventures of Tom Sawyer*, pp. 130–31.

p. 243, l. 11　Ibid., p. 74.

p. 243, l. 22　Ibid., Preface, p. xvii.

p. 244, l. 13　Ibid., p. 238.

p. 244, l. 18　Howells, *My Mark Twain*, p. 127.

p. 244, l. 22　SLC to WDH, 3 April 1876. *Mark Twain-Howells Letters*, p. 128.

p. 244, l. 35　SLC to Moncure Conway, 16 April 1876. *Mark Twain's Letters to His Publishers*, p. 98.

p. 245, l. 3　SLC to WDH, 26 April 1876. *Mark Twain-Howells Letters*, p. 132.

p. 245, l. 5　WDH to SLC, 28 April 1876. *Mark Twain-Howells Letters*, p. 134.

p. 245, l. 32　SLC to Moncure Conway, 24 July 1876. NN 01351.

p. 246, l. 16　SLC to Mary Fairbanks, 3 June 1876. *Mark Twain to Mrs. Fairbanks*, pp. 199–200.

p. 246, l. 36　SLC to WDH, 9 August 1876. *Mark Twain-Howells Letters*, p. 144.

p. 247, l. 24　In Hill, *Mark Twain and Elisha Bliss*, p. 115.

p. 247, l. 27　SLC to Elisha Bliss, Jr., 22 July 1876. *Mark Twain's Letters to His Publishers*, p. 102. Though his letter does not make the nature of the proposition clear, Clemens' interest in self-publishing naturally included the American market.

p. 247, l. 37　SLC to Denis E. McCarthy, 29 March and 7 April 1878. CFr2 11637.

p. 248, l. 23　SLC to Will Bowen, 31 August 1876, in *Mark Twain's Letters to Will Bowen*, p. 24.

p. 248, l. 30　SLC to Jacob Burrough, 1 November 1876. *Mark Twain's Letters*, p. 290.

p. 248, l. 33   Howells, *My Mark Twain*, p. 30.

p. 249, l. 8   SLC to WDH, 14 September 1876. *Mark Twain-Howells Letters*, p. 152.

p. 249, l. 11   SLC to WDH, 11 October 1876. *Mark Twain-Howells Letters*, p. 157.

p. 249, l. 19   WDH to SLC, 18 October 1876. *Mark Twain-Howells Letters*, p. 162.

p. 249, l. 27   SLC to WDH, 14 September 1876. *Mark Twain-Howells Letters*, p. 150.

p. 249, l. 31   SLC to WDH, 23 August 1876. *Mark Twain-Howells Letters*, p. 146.

p. 249, l. 36   SLC to WDH, 11 October 1876. *Mark Twain-Howells Letters*, p. 158. SLC begins a new paragraph after "Hayes."

p. 250, l. 41   Bret Harte to SLC, 16 December 1876. Duckett, *Mark Twain and Bret Harte*, p. 125.

p. 251, l. 8   SLC to Moncure Conway, 13 December 1876. *Mark Twain's Letters to His Publishers*, pp. 106–7.

27: FEELING POOR

p. 252, l. 2   *Following the Equator*, Vol. 2, Headnote, Chapter 20, p. 215.

p. 253, l. 2   Hill, *Mark Twain and Elisha Bliss*, pp. 117–21.

p. 253, l. 3   This figure equals approximately half a million dollars today. Most people familiar with the era regard a multiplier of 15 as modestly correct for 1877; at higher income levels, with today's more expensive taxes and servants, the multiplier should be higher.

p. 253, l. 14   OLC to Olivia Langdon, 2–4 February 1877. Willis, *Mark and Livy*, p. 108.

p. 253, l. 30   Bret Harte to SLC, 1 March 1877. Duckett, *Mark Twain and Bret Harte*, pp. 134–37.

p. 253, l. 38   Bret Harte to SLC, 2 April 1877. *Mark Twain and Bret Harte*, Duckett, pp. 141–42.

p. 254, l. 10   *New York World*, 18 February 1877.

p. 254, l. 22   Paine, *Biography*, pp. 725–26.

p. 256, l. 1   SLC to Mollie Fairbanks, 6 August 1877. *Mark Twain to Mrs. Fairbanks*, p. 209.

p. 256, l. 16   Howells, *My Mark Twain*, p. 17.

p. 256, l. 16   Ibid., p. 15.

p. 256, l. 24   SLC to Mary Fairbanks, 14 April 1877. *Mark Twain to Mrs. Fairbanks*, p. 204.

p. 256, l. 28   SLC to WDH, 1 May 1876. *Mark Twain-Howells Letters*, p. 175.

p. 256, l. 33   Parsloe to SLC, 11 May 1877. *Mark Twain's Letters*, p. 293.

p. 256, l. 34   J.T. Ford to SLC, 8 May 1877. Paine, *Biography*, p. 589.

p. 257, l. 4   SLC to WDH, 4–6 July 1877. *Mark Twain-Howells Letters*, p. 188.

p. 257, l. 10   SLC to WDH, 6 June 1877. *Mark Twain-Howells Letters*, p. 180.

p. 257, l. 25   Paine reported that the couple "lived happily and prosperously ever after" (*Biography*, p. 602), a note immaterial to Clemens' shockingly paternalistic behavior in this incident.

p. 257, l. 36   SLC to WDH, 3 August 1877. *Mark Twain-Howells Letters*, p. 192.

p. 257, l. 41   OLC to SLC, 29 July 1877. *Love Letters of Mark Twain*, p. 203.

p. 258, l. 13   SLC to Mary Fairbanks, 31 October 1877. *Mark Twain to Mrs. Fairbanks*, p. 211.

p. 258, l. 31   SLC to Thomas Nast, 12 November 1877. *Mark Twain's Letters*, p. 311.

p. 259, l. 2   *Mark Twain-Howells Letters*, p. 212, n. 1.

p. 259, l. 15   "Whittier Birthday Speech," *Collected Tales, Sketches, Speeches, and Essays, 1852–1890*, p. 699.

p. 259, l. 25   Paine, *Biography*, p. 605.

p. 259, l. 39   WDH to SLC, 25 December 1877. *Mark Twain-Howells Letters*, p. 213.

p. 260, l. 4   SLC to WDH, 28 December 1877. *Mark Twain-Howells Letters*, p. 215.

p. 260, l. 24   In the absence of convincing evidence of the relationship between Charles Langdon and Clemens after 1874, this argument offers an explanation of the coolness that existed between the men in this period.

p. 260, l. 30   SLC to Jane Clemens, 17 February 1878. *Mark Twain's Letters*, p. 319.

28: HIDING OUT IN EUROPE

p. 262, l. 9 *Following the Equator*, Vol. 1, Headnote, Chapter 28, p. 250.

p. 262, l. 13 Ibid., Headnote, Chapter 9, p. 89.

p. 262, l. 24 SLC to Jane Clemens, 17 February 1878. *Mark Twain's Letters*, p. 320.

p. 263, l. 10 SLC to WDH, 26 May 1878. *Mark Twain-Howells Letters*, p. 231.

p. 263, l. 13 SLC to Charles Dudley Warner, 16 June 1878. CU-MARK 01572.

p. 263, l. 16 SLC to Jane Clemens and Pamela Moffett, 1 July 1878. CU-MARK (tr) 01575.

p. 263, l. 27 SLC to WDH, 27 June 1878. *Mark Twain-Howells Letters*, pp. 235–36.

p. 263, l. 36 Paine, *Biography*, p. 622.

p. 254, l. 2 SLC to Charles Dudley Warner, 16 June 1878. CU-MARK 01572.

p. 264, l. 4 OLC to Olivia Langdon, 9 June 1878. CtHMTH 01569.

p. 264, l. 10 *Papa*, p. 69.

p. 264, l. 19 OLC to Olivia Langdon, 9 June 1878. CtHMTH 01569.

p. 264, l. 23 SLC to WDH, 27 June 1878. *Mark Twain-Howells Letters*, pp. 236–37.

p. 264, l. 36 SLC to WDH, 4 May 1878. *Mark Twain-Howells Letters*, p. 227.

p. 265, l. 7 Joseph Twichell to Harmony Twichell, ? August 1878. Paine, *Biography*, p. 629.

p. 265, l. 18 SLC to Joseph Twichell, 9 September 1878. Paine, *Biography*, p. 632.

p. 265, l. 27 SLC to WDH, 27 September 1878. *Mark Twain-Howells Letters*, p. 239.

p. 265, l. 37 *Notebooks and Journals*, Vol. 2, p. 224.

p. 265, l. 41 SLC to Joseph Twichell, 3 November 1878. *Mark Twain's Letters*, p. 339.

p. 266, l. 4 SLC to WDH, 17 November 1878. *Mark Twain's Letters*, p. 240.

p. 266, l. 9 SLC to Olivia Langdon, 2 December 1878. CtHMTH 01611.

p. 266, l. 11 SLC to Jane Clemens and Pamela Moffett, 31 November 1878. *Mark Twain's Letters*, p. 343.

p. 266, l. 21 SLC to Joseph Twichell, 26 January 1879. *Mark Twain's Letters*, p. 350.

p. 266, l. 38 Ibid., p. 348.

p. 267, l. 5 SLC to WDH, 30 January 1879. *Mark Twain-Howells Letters*, pp. 248–49.

p. 267, l. 30 "Some Thoughts on the Science of Onanism," *Collected Tales, Sketches, Speeches, and Essays, 1852–1890*, p. 723.

p. 267, l. 34 *Notebooks and Journals*, Vol. 2, p. 318.

p. 267, l. 40 Ibid., p. 319.

p. 268, l. 5 Ibid., p. 320.

p. 268, l. 9 SLC to Joseph Twichell, 10 June 1879. CtY 01666.

p. 268, l. 15 OLC to Olivia Langdon, 16 March 1879. CU-MARK (tr) 01640.

p. 268, l. 19 *Notebooks and Journals*, Vol. 2, p. 302.

p. 268, l. 25 SLC to WDH, 18 November 1878. *Mark Twain-Howells Letters*, pp. 241, 244, n. 4.

p. 269, l. 2 SLC to Orion Clemens, 9 February 1879. CU-MARK 01631.

p. 269, l. 14 SLC to Frank Bliss, 10 June 1879. *Mark Twain's Letters to His Publishers*, p. 116.

p. 269, l. 19 OLC to Olivia Langdon, 20 July 1879. CtHMTH 01677.

29: THE RETURN OF MARK TWAIN

p. 270, l. 10 *Following the Equator*, Vol. 1, Headnote, Chapter 21, p. 183.

p. 270, l. 31 In Paine, *Biography*, p. 649.

p. 270, l. 41 SLC to Frank Bliss, 8 September 1879. *Mark Twain's Letters to His Publishers*, p. 119.

p. 271, l. 7 SLC to Pamela Moffett, 15 September 1879. *Mark Twain, Business Man*, p. 139.

p. 271, l. 13 Ibid.

p. 271, l. 16 SLC to Joseph Twichell, 2 October 1879. Paine, *Biography*, p. 650.

p. 271, l. 23 SLC to Joseph Twichell, 2 October 1879. CtY 01696.

p. 271, l. 31 OLC to Olivia Langdon, ? November 1879. Willis, *Mark and Livy*, p. 128.

p. 272, l. 8 SLC to WDH, 17 November 1879. *Mark Twain-Howells Letters*, p. 278.

p. 272, l. 12 *Autobiography*, p. 15. Though Paine treats it as though it happened, this story does not appear in Clemens' letters to Livy from Chicago, and it probably would if it were true.

p. 272, l. 18 SLC to OLC, 14 November 1879. *Mark Twain's Letters*, p. 372.

p. 272, l. 30 Charles Dudley Warner to WDH, 23 November 1879. *Mark Twain-Howells Letters*, p. 282, n. 2.

p. 272, l. 36 Paine, *Biography*, p. 659.

p. 272, l. 39 Oliver Wendell Holmes to SLC, 26 September 1869. In Paine, *Biography*, p. 660, n. 1.

p. 273, l. 13 *Papa*, p. 76. Clemens' letter to William Dean Howells on 28 November 1879 makes it clear that Livy was the object of this childish envy.

p. 273, l. 30 OLC to Olivia Langdon, 30 November 1879. Willis, *Mark and Livy*, p. 131.

p. 274, l. 1 SLC to WDH, 8 January 1880. *Mark Twain-Howells Letters*, p. 287.

p. 274, l. 7 Ibid., p. 286.

p. 274, l. 21 SLC to WDH, 11 March 1880. *Mark Twain-Howells Letters*, p. 291.

p. 274, l. 32 SLC to Frank Bliss, 20 March 1880. *Mark Twain's Letters to His Publishers*, p. 121.

p. 274, l. 34 SLC to WDH, 5 March 1880. *Mark Twain-Howells Letters*, p. 290.

p. 274, l. 41 WDH to SLC, 22 March 1880. *Mark Twain-Howells Letters*, p. 293.

p. 275, l. 29 SLC to Orion Clemens, 26 February 1880. *Mark Twain, Business Man*, p. 143.

p. 275, l. 36 SLC to Mary Fairbanks, 21 December 1879. *Mark Twain to Mrs. Fairbanks*, p. 236.

p. 275, l. 41 SLC to Orion Clemens, 26 February 1880. *Mark Twain, Business Man*, p. 142.

p. 276, l. 17 Ibid., pp. 143–44.

p. 277, l. 6 Pascal Covici, Jr., wrote the key article on this episode, "Dear Master Wattie: The Mark Twain-David Watt Bowser Letters." In "Found: Mark Twain's 'Platonic Sweetheart,' " Howard Baetzhold identifies Wright as the inspiration for Clemens' dream woman in his posthumously published essay "My Platonic Sweetheart."

p. 277, l. 25 Clemens told this story at different times with each of these sentences as his punch line.

p. 277, l. 30 SLC to Hjalmar Boyesen, 23 April 1880. ViU 01792.

p. 277, l. 35 WDH to SLC, 14 June 1880. *Mark Twain-Howells Letters*, p. 315.

p. 278, l. 2 SLC to WDH, 18 May 1880. *Mark Twain-Howells Letters*, p. 308. Howells blotted out Bret Harte's name.

p. 278, l. 11 SLC to Moncure Conway, 1 May 1880. NNC 01797.

p. 278, l. 14 SLC to Orion Clemens, 12 May 1880. Kaplan, *Mr. Clemens and Mark Twain*, p. 237.

p. 278, l. 35 SLC to WDH, 26 July 1880. *Mark Twain-Howells Letters*, p. 318.

p. 278, l. 39 SLC to Joseph Twichell, 29 August 1880. *Mark Twain's Letters*, p. 384.

p. 279, l. 3 Mary Fairbanks to SLC, 26 July 1880. *Mark Twain to Mrs. Fairbanks*, pp. 238–39, n. 2.

p. 279, l. 15 Hamlin Hill calculated Clemens' loss of royalty on books sold based on the difference between his actual contractual royalty percentage and half profits, to which Clemens believed his contracts entitled him.

30: NEW BOOK, NEW BUSINESS

p. 280, l. 10 *Following the Equator*, Vol. 2, Headnote, Chapter 9, p. 84.

p. 280, l. 15 Ibid., Headnote, Chapter 10, p. 98.

p. 281, l. 24 SLC to Orion Clemens, 27 November 1880. *Mark Twain, Business Man*, p. 148.

p. 281, l. 28 Ibid.

p. 282, l. 13 Jane Clemens to SLC and OLC, 2 August 1880. Varble, *Jane Clemens*, p. 321.

p. 282, l. 19 SLC to Orion Clemens, 24 October 1880. *Mark Twain's Letters to His Publishers*, p. 126.

p. 282, l. 28 Ibid.

p. 283, l. 6 SLC to WDH, 30 October 1880. *Mark Twain-Howells Letters*, pp. 334–36.

p. 283, l. 26 SLC to WDH, 24 December 1880. *Mark Twain-Howells Letters*, p. 340.

p. 283, l. 30 SLC to James A. Garfield, 12 January 1881. *Mark Twain's Letters*, p. 394.

p. 283, l. 38 SLC to Pamela Moffett, 11 December 1880. CU-MARK 01870.

p. 284, l. 1 OLC to Mollie Clemens, 7 December 1880. CU-MARK 01867.

p. 285, l. 16 SLC to WDH, 21 February 1881. *Mark Twain-Howells Letters*, pp. 350–55.

p. 285, l. 22 WDH to SLC, 17 April 1881. *Mark Twain-Howells Letters*, p. 361.

p. 285, l. 30 SLC to James Osgood, 30 March 1881. *Mark Twain's Letters to His Publishers*, p. 136.

p. 285, l. 37 SLC to Dan Slote, 16 March 1881. *Mark Twain, Business Man*, p. 151.

p. 286, l. 10 Webster almost certainly discovered the fraud. His sudden promotion to the head of Kaolatype has little basis otherwise.

p. 286, l. 23 SLC to Dan Slote, 31 March 1881. *Mark Twain, Business Man*, p. 152.

p. 286, l. 27 This sequence contradicts the "Textual Introduction" of the Mark Twain Papers' 1979 edition of *The Prince and the Pauper*. Osgood came to Hartford before 3 March 1881 and left with a manuscript copy of the novel that was used only to make illustrations.

p. 287, l. 20 SLC to John Russell Young, 29 April 1881. DLC 01941.

31: THE DISTRIBUTION OF WEALTH

p. 288, l. 13 *Following the Equator*, Vol. 1, Headnote, Chapter 11, p. 107.

p. 289, l. 13 SLC to James Osgood, 23 August 1881. "Textual Introduction," *The Prince and the Pauper*, p. 392.

p. 289, l. 35 Whitelaw Reid to John Hay, 25 September 1881. Kaplan, *Mr. Clemens and Mark Twain*, p. 241.

p. 289, l. 38 John Hay to Whitelaw Reid, 4 September 1881. Kaplan, *Mr. Clemens and Mark Twain*, p. 241.

p. 290, l. 13 SLC to Bruce Weston Munro, 21 October 1881. *Mark Twain: Selections from the Collection of Nick Karanovich*, p. 15.

p. 290, l. 19 Joseph Goodman to SLC, 29 January 1882. "Introduction," *The Prince and the Pauper*, p. 14.

p. 291, l. 6 *The Prince and the Pauper*, p. 49.

p. 291, l. 9 Ibid., p. 51.

p. 291, l. 26 Ibid., p. 342.

p. 292, l. 8 SLC to Charles Warren Stoddard, 26 October 1881. NN-B 02554.

p. 292, l. 29 *New York Times*, 25 December 1881.

p. 292, l. 33 SLC to James Osgood, 28 October 1881. *Mark Twain's Letters to His Publishers*, p. 144.

p. 292, l. 41 SLC to CLW, 26 October 1881. *Mark Twain, Business Man*, p. 173.

p. 293, l. 20 SLC to WDH, 28 January 1882. *Mark Twain-Howells Letters*, pp. 386–88.

p. 293, l. 28 SLC to Mary Fairbanks, 21 February 1881. *Mark Twain to Mrs. Fairbanks*, pp. 247–48.

p. 294, l. 18 WDH to SLC, 31 January 1882. *Mark Twain-Howells Letters*, p. 391.

p. 294, l. 32 SLC to James Osgood, 4 March 1882. *Mark Twain-Howells Letters*, pp. 397–98, n. 1.

p. 295, l. 29 SLC to Joel Chandler Harris, 2 April 1882. *Mark Twain's Letters*, p. 418.

p. 295, l. 36 SLC to OLC, 22 April 1882. *Love Letters of Mark Twain*, p. 208.

p. 296, l. 1 SLC to OLC, 2 May 1882. *Love Letters of Mark Twain*, p. 212.

p. 296, l. 6 OLC to SLC, 3 May 1882. Willis, *Mark and Livy*, p. 148.

p. 296, l. 9 Before they arrived in Hannibal, secretary Roswell Phelps tumbled down the pilothouse stairs, and could not record Sam's observations of his hometown.

p. 296, l. 17 SLC to OLC, 17 May 1882. *Mark Twain's Letters*, p. 419.

p. 297, l. 4 Howells, *My Mark Twain*, p. 141.

p. 297, l. 8 Arguments regarding this are outlined in *Mark Twain-Howells Letters*, pp. 412–3, n. 3.

p. 297, l. 27 SLC to John Garth, 3 July 1882. *Mark Twain's Letters*, p. 459.

p. 297, l. 41 SLC to Mary Fairbanks, 21 February 1881. *Mark Twain to Mrs. Fairbanks*, pp. 247–48.

p. 298, l. 8 OLC to Samuel Moffett, 13 August 1882. CU-MARK 02251.

p. 298, l. 14 SLC to Annie Webster, 29 August 1882. *Mark Twain, Business Man*, pp. 194–95. Samuel Charles Webster's sarcastic defense of his father purposefully eradicates Webster's role in the swindle. Clemens' later castigation of Webster ignores this episode, because by then Webster's mismanagement and Clemens' foolishness had lost them both far more.

p. 298, l. 21 SLC to Orion Clemens and family, 5 September 1882. CU-MARK 02263. Clemens' many emendations indicate the care he took with this letter.

p. 298, l. 39 SLC to CLW, 6 October 1882. *Mark Twain, Business Man*, p. 204.

p. 299, l. 5 CLW to SLC, 23 April 1883. *Mark Twain's Letters to His Publishers*, p. 164, n. 2.

p. 299, l. 12 SLC to WDH, 3 October 1882. *Mark Twain-Howells Letters*, p. 417. Horst Kruse has demonstrated that the editors of this correspondence misdated this letter, misreading the typewritten "3D" for "30."

p. 299, l. 29 SLC to CLW, pencil note on James Osgood to SLC, 3 January 1883. *Mark Twain, Business Man*, p. 207.

p. 299, l. 35 SLC to Pamela Moffett, 21 October 1882. CU-MARK 02293.

p. 299, l. 41 SLC to Orion Clemens, 18 November 1882. CU-MARK 02307.

p. 300, l. 4 In Kruse, *Mark Twain and "Life on the Mississippi,"* p. 55.

p. 300, l. 14 SLC to WDH, 4 November 1882. *Mark Twain-Howells Letters*, p. 418.

p. 300, l. 25 For a dissenting opinion, see Horst H. Kruse's "Mark Twain's *Nom de Plume*: Some Mysteries Resolved."

32: WRITING *HUCK FINN*

p. 301, l. 10 *Pudd'nhead Wilson*, Headnote, Chapter 17, p. 177.

p. 302, l. 20 SLC to James R. Osgood & Co., 6 January 1883. *Mark Twain's Letters to His Publishers*, p. 161.

p. 302, l. 25 CLW to SLC, 9 April 1883. *Mark Twain's Letters to His Publishers*, p. 163, n. 1.

p. 302, l. 41 SLC to WDH, 22 August 1883. *Mark Twain-Howells Letters*, p. 439.

p. 303, l. 29 SLC to WDH, 1 March 1883. *Mark Twain-Howells Letters*, p. 427.

p. 304, l. 17 SLC to OLC, 24 May 1883. *Love Letters of Mark Twain*, p. 215.

p. 304, l. 26 OLC to SLC, 25 May 1883. *Love Letters of Mark Twain*, p. 217.

p. 304, l. 38 *New York Times*, 10 June 1883, p. 1, col. 4.

p. 305, l. 2 SLC to CLW, 18 June 1883. *Mark Twain, Business Man*, p. 215.

p. 305, l. 14 SLC to WDH, 20 July 1883. *Mark Twain-Howells Letters*, p. 435.

p. 305, l. 21 WDH to SLC, 10 July 1883. *Mark Twain-Howells Letters*, p. 434.

p. 305, l. 32 SLC to WDH, 20 July 1883. *Mark Twain-Howells Letters*, p. 435.

p. 306, l. 8 Hamlin Hill maintains that these letters constituted part of Clemens' gradual separation from Osgood as his publisher (*Mark Twain's Letters to His Publishers*, pp. 164–68 notes), but the correspondence between the men argues for a more sudden break.

p. 306, l. 13 SLC to James Osgood, 21 December 1883. *Mark Twain's Letters to His Publishers*, p. 165.

p. 306, l. 17 SLC to WDH, 7 January 1884. *Mark Twain-Howells Letters*, p. 460.

p. 307, l. 11 SLC to WDH, 22 August 1883. *Mark Twain-Howells Letters*, p. 438.

p. 307, l. 17 WDH to SLC, 12 October 1883. *Mark Twain-Howells Letters*, p. 444.

p. 307, l. 24 SLC to CLW, 30 November 1883. *Mark Twain, Business Man*, p. 228.

p. 307, l. 35 Howells, *My Mark Twain*, p. 24.

p. 308, l. 5 Ibid., pp. 28–29.

p. 308, l. 13 SLC to WDH, 21 November 1883. *Mark Twain-Howells Letters*, p. 451.

p. 308, l. 18   This diagnosis remains uncertain, but Clemens believed that Cable had infected his children.

p. 308, l. 24   SLC to WDH, 4 November 1882. *Mark Twain-Howells Letters*, p. 419.

p. 309, l. 6   SLC to CLW, 14 April 1884. *Mark Twain's Letters to His Publishers*, p. 173.

p. 309, l. 18   WDH to CLW, 4 April 1884. *Mark Twain-Howells Letters*, p. 481, n. 2.

p. 309, l. 31   SLC to Marshall Mallory, 10 February 1884. *Mark Twain, Business Man*, pp. 233–34.

p. 309, l. 35   SLC to CLW, 8 February 1884. *Mark Twain, Business Man*, p. 235.

p. 309, l. 41   SLC to CLW, 2 January 1884. *Mark Twain, Business Man*, p. 230.

p. 310, l. 34   SLC to Karl and Josephine Gerhardt, 4 May 1884. CtY (tr) 02969.

p. 310, l. 38   WDH to SLC, 4 May 1884. *Mark Twain-Howells Letters*, p. 485.

p. 311, l. 2   SLC to CLW, 7 May 1884. *Mark Twain, Business Man*, p. 253.

p. 311, l. 7   SLC to CLW, 24 May 1884. *Mark Twain, Business Man*, p. 255.

33: HIS OWN PUBLISHER

p. 312, l. 9   "Concerning the Jews," *Collected Tales, Sketches, Speeches, and Essays, 1891–1910*, p. 355.

p. 312, l. 27   SLC to CLW, 1 September 1884. *Mark Twain, Business Man*, p. 274.

p. 313, l. 2   SLC to CLW, 15 July 1884. *Mark Twain, Business Man*, p. 269.

p. 313, l. 19   SLC to CLW, 1 September 1884. *Mark Twain, Business Man*, pp. 273–74.

p. 313, l. 28   SLC to Edward House, 31 October 1884. ViU 03015.

p. 313, l. 36   WDH to SLC, 4 September 1884. *Mark Twain-Howells Letters*, p. 503.

p. 313, l. 39   SLC to WDH, 31 August 1884. *Mark Twain-Howells Letters*, p. 501.

p. 314, l. 12   Ibid.

p. 314, l. 24   SLC to WDH, 17 September 1884. *Mark Twain-Howells Letters*, pp. 509–10.

p. 315, l. 2   *Notebooks and Journals*, Vol. 3, 12 August 1884, p. 56.

p. 315, l. 25   *Adventures of Huckleberry Finn*, p. 362.

p. 315, l. 32   Ibid., p. 279.

p. 316, l. 5   Ibid., p. 271.

p. 316, l. 27   Ibid., p. 34.

p. 317, l. 2   Ibid., p. 292.

p. 317, l. 30   N.S. Shaler, "The Negro Problem," *The Atlantic*, November 1884, p. 708.

p. 317, l. 35   Critics have yet to consider how the Twain-Cable tour related to the public debate on the role of African Americans in post-Civil War democratic society.

p. 318, l. 3   OLC to SLC, 21 November 1884. CU-MARK 03029.

p. 318, l. 33   SLC to Susy Clemens, 23 November 1884. *Love Letters of Mark Twain*, p. 220.

p. 319, l. 14   SLC to OLC, 3 December 1884. *Love Letters of Mark Twain*, p. 221.

p. 319, l. 33   OLC to SLC, 23 November 1884. *Twainian*, July–August 1880, p. 3.

p. 319, l. 41   OLC to SLC, 3 January 1885. CU-MARK 03100.

p. 320, l. 12   SLC to J.B. Pond, 22 December 1884. NN-B 02601.

p. 320, l. 26   SLC to OLC, 14 January 1885. *Love Letters of Mark Twain*, p. 229.

p. 320, l. 38   Ibid.

p. 320, l. 41   Ozias Pond's diary, 29 January 1885. Cardwell, *Twins of Genius*, p. 54.

p. 321, l. 5   SLC to CLW, 19 January 1885. *Mark Twain, Business Man*, p. 293.

p. 321, l. 20   SLC to CLW, 25 January 1885. *Mark Twain, Business Man*, p. 297.

p. 321, l. 22   SLC to CLW, 10 February 1885. *Mark Twain, Business Man*, p. 300.

p. 321, l. 35   SLC to WDH, 27 February 1885. *Mark Twain-Howells Letters*, p. 520.

p. 322, l. 7   SLC to CLW, 18 March 1885. *Mark Twain's Letters*, pp. 452–53.

34: GRANT

p. 323, l. 9   *Following the Equator*, Vol. 2, Headnote, Chapter 33, p. 366.

p. 323, l. 15   *Pudd'nhead Wilson*, Headnote, Chapter 12, p. 138.

p. 323, l. 38   SLC to CLW, 16 March 1885. *Mark Twain, Business Man*, p. 307.

p. 324, l. 40   SLC to editor of the *Boston Herald*, 6 July 1885. CU-MARK 03254.

p. 325, l. 7   J.B. Pond likely echoed Clemens himself in his detailed comparison of the men (*Eccentricities of Genius*, pp. 197–98).

p. 325, l. 19   *Notebook and Journals*, Vol. 3, p. 153.

p. 325, l. 34   SLC to OLC, 8 April 1885. *Love Letters of Mark Twain*, p. 242.

p. 326, l. 31   The papers relating to this project are in the Mark Twain Papers, in the Bancroft Library, at Berkeley, California; letters to and from Karl Gerhardt in the spring and summer of 1885 give the fullest account of the transaction. I believe this unexplored subject would make an interesting study in the intersection of art and commerce in 1885 America.

p. 327, l. 25   SLC to Charles Warren Stoddard, 1 June 1885. InNd 03234.

p. 327, l. 31   SLC to WDH, 21 July 1885. *Mark Twain-Howells Letters*, pp. 533–34.

p. 328, l. 4   SLC to OLC, 1 July 1885. *Love Letters of Mark Twain*, p. 243.

p. 328, l. 10   SLC to OLC, 24 July 1885. *Love Letters of Mark Twain*, pp. 243–44.

p. 328, l. 36   SLC to CLW, 16 March 1885. *Mark Twain, Business Man*, p. 307.

p. 328, l. 40   SLC to Annie Moffett Webster, 30 July 1885. *Mark Twain, Business Man*, p. 331.

35: GOING FOR BROKE

p. 330, l. 10   *Following the Equator*, Vol. 1, Headnote, Chapter 29, p. 260.

p. 331, l. 3   In Paine, *Biography*, p. 833.

p. 331, l. 9   *Notebooks and Journals*, Vol. 3, p. 238.

p. 331, l. 35   Susy Clemens, *Papa: An Intimate Biography*, p. 187. Quotations from Susy Clemens' biography of her father come from this volume, edited by Charles Neider.

p. 332, l. 13   SLC to WDH, 18 October 1885. *Mark Twain-Howells Letters*, p. 539.

p. 333, l. 17   *Mark Twain in Eruption*, p. 190. The relationship between Clemens and Webster failed as early as October 1885.

p. 333, l. 21   Kirst, "Webster's Childhood Tragedy," p. 17.

p. 333, l. 30   SLC to CLW, 13 February 1886. *Mark Twain, Business Man*, p. 355.

p. 333, l. 35   Winter, "Connecticut Yankee in Kamehameha's Court."

p. 334, l. 2   See *A Connecticut Yankee in King Arthur's Court*, p. 5.

p. 334, l. 22   *Notebooks and Journals*, Vol. 3, p. 195.

p. 334, l. 27   SLC to CLW, 19 March 1886. *Mark Twain's Letters to His Publishers*, p. 196.

p. 334, l. 33   Howells, *My Mark Twain*, p. 26.

p. 334, l. 37   SLC to WDH, 13, 15, 17 May 1886. *Mark Twain-Howells Letters*, p. 562.

p. 335, l. 10   Whitelaw Reid to John Hay, 2 July 1886. *Notebooks and Journals*, Vol. 3, pp. 234–35, n. 26.

p. 335, l. 13   SLC to Edward House, 11 August 1886. ViU 03437.

p. 335, l. 16   SLC to Dean Sage, 5 February 1890. ODa2 04012.

p. 336, l. 3   SLC to Edward House, 11 August 1886. ViU 03437.

p. 336, l. 21   SLC to Clara Spaulding, 20 August 1886. CU-MARK (ph) 03442.

p. 336, l. 24   Details about Susy's relationship with her schoolmate are sketchy, but she expresses her feelings in several letters on file in the Mark Twain Papers. This Mary Foote is not to be confused with the children's governess of the same name. Clara's and Susy's feelings about John Stanchfield are clear from the letters they exchanged in 1892.

p. 336, l. 34   "Letters from the Earth," *Letters from the Earth*, p. 42.

p. 337, l. 8   See *A History of the American Association of Orthodontists* for an overview of Farrar's contributions. Clara accompanied Clemens to New York frequently the following year.

p. 337, l. 12   See Clara Clemens, *My Father, Mark Twain*, pp. 129–30.

p. 338, l. 14   SLC to WDH, 12 December 1886. *Mark Twain-Howells Letters*, p. 575. Many scholars

believe that this revelation was not entirely serious, but Clemens tells Howells
this secret in the same paragraph in which he extends his condolences on the
recent death of Howells' sister. He could not intend the comment as comic without mocking his friend's grief.

p. 338, l. 17   Clara Clemens, *My Father, Mark Twain*, p. 24.

p. 338, l. 26   *Mark Twain's Autobiography*, p. 243.

p. 339, l. 1   SLC to Kate Field, 8 March 1886. Whiting, *Kate Field: A Record*, p. 29.

p. 339, l. 10   CLW to SLC, 17 February 1887. *Mark Twain-Howells Letters*, p. 587, n. 1.

p. 339, l. 17   SLC to CLW, 28 March 1887. *Mark Twain, Business Man*, p. 378.

p. 339, l. 41   SLC to Orion Clemens, 7 September 1887. *Mark Twain's Letters to His Publishers*,
pp. 229–30.

p. 340, l. 21   SLC to Pamela Moffett, 12 July 1887. *Mark Twain's Letters*, p. 489.

p. 340, l. 31   SLC to WDH, 22 August 1887. *Mark Twain-Howells Letters*, p. 595.

p. 340, l. 40   SLC to Fred Hall and CLW, 15 August 1887. *Mark Twain's Letters to His Publishers*,
p. 224.

p. 341, l. 17   SLC to Franklin Whitmore, 13 August 1887. CU-MARK 03626.

p. 341, l. 38   SLC to Orion Clemens, 7 September 1887. *Mark Twain's Letters to His Publishers*,
p. 229.

p. 342, l. 8   M. Cardinal Rompolla to CLW, 7 November 1887. *Mark Twain, Business Man*,
p. 388.

p. 342, l. 12   The policy of stepped royalties appears to have originated with Clemens. This
discovery argues against the long-standing perception that Clemens had no head
for business, however much his failures and wild ambitions disguised his successes.

p. 342, l. 19   Grace King to Sarah Anne Miller King, 8 October 1887. Bush, "Grace King and
Mark Twain," p. 38.

p. 342, l. 23   Grace King, "Mark Twain, First Impression," in Bush, "Grace King and Mark
Twain," p. 39.

p. 342, l. 35   *Mark Twain's Autobiography*, pp. 152–54.

p. 343, l. 16   SLC to Jane, Orion, and Mollie Clemens, 18 December 1887. CU-MARK 03680.

36: THE CONNECTICUT YANKEE

p. 344, l. 10   *Notebooks and Journals*, Vol. 3, p. 399. Spelling altered.

p. 345, l. 31   SLC to CLW, 3 August 1887. *Mark Twain's Letters to His Publishers*, p. 222.

p. 345, l. 36   *A Connecticut Yankee in King Arthur's Court*, p. 144.

p. 346, l. 3   SLC to William Kennedy, ? ? 1886. B.B. Herbert, *The First Decennium of the National
Editorial Association of the United States*, p. 220.

p. 346, l. 23   SLC to WDH, 31 March 1888. *Mark Twain-Howells Letters*, p. 597.

p. 347, l. 32   SLC to Theodore Crane, 5 October 1888. *Mark Twain's Letters*, p. 500.

p. 348, l. 3   Ibid., p. 501.

p. 348, l. 16   SLC to George Bainton, 15 October 1888. M02 03791

p. 348, l. 25   SLC to Edward Bok, ? ? 1888. *Mark Twain's Letters*, pp. 504–5.

p. 348, l. 35   A.H. Wright to SLC, 5 November 1888. *Mark Twain's Letters to His Publishers*, p.
250, n. 1.

p. 348, l. 38   CLW to SLC, 6 November 1888. *Mark Twain's Letters to His Publishers*, p. 251,
n. 3.

p. 349, l. 5   SLC to Fred Hall, 11 January 1889. *Mark Twain's Letters to His Publishers*, p. 252.

p. 349, l. 17   SLC to Edward House, 26 February 1889. Fatout, "Mark Twain, Litigant,"
pp. 36–37.

p. 349, l. 27   SLC to Orion Clemens, 5 January 1889. *Mark Twain's Letters*, p. 506.

p. 349, l. 32   SLC to Sue Crane, 1 March 1889. CU-MARK 03856.

p. 350, l. 16   SLC to Abraham G. Mills, 23 March 1889. NN 10740.

37: A SEASON OF DEATH

p. 351, l. 9   *Pudd'nhead Wilson*, Headnote, Chapter 9, p. III.

p. 352, l. 2   WDH to SLC, 21 May 1889. *Mark Twain-Howells Letters*, p. 603.

p. 352, l. 29   SLC to Pamela Moffett, 1 July 1889. CU-MARK 03905.

p. 352, l. 36   OLC to Grace King, 24 March 1889. Lu-Ar 03877.

p. 352, l. 40   SLC to Mary Fairbanks, 13 September 1889. *Mark Twain to Mrs. Fairbanks*, p. 264.

p. 353, l. 4   Ibid.

p. 353, l. 16   SLC to OLC, 17 July 1889. *Love Letters of Mark Twain*, pp. 253–54.

p. 353, l. 24   SLC to Susy Clemens 16 July 1889. CU-MARK (tr) 03912.

p. 353, l. 35   SLC to Fred Hall, 24 July 1889. *Mark Twain's Letters to His Publishers*, pp. 253–54.

p. 354, l. 1   SLC to WDH, 5 August 1889. *Mark Twain-Howells Letters*, pp. 608–9.

p. 354, l. 2   WDH to SLC, 10 August 1889. *Mark Twain-Howells Letters*, p. 610.

p. 354, l. 10   SLC to WDH, 24 August 1889. *Mark Twain-Howells Letters*, pp. 610–11.

p. 354, l. 18   Paine, *Biography*, p. 881.

p. 355, l. 17   *A Connecticut Yankee in King Arthur's Court*, p. 114.

p. 355, l. 22   Ibid., p. 418.

p. 355, l. 26   Ibid., p. 435.

p. 356, l. 14   SLC to WDH, 22 September 1889. *Mark Twain-Howells Letters*, p. 613.

p. 356, l. 35   Dean Sage to SLC, 19 November 1889. MTP 44772.

p. 357, l. 8   Howells, *My Mark Twain*, p. 166.

p. 357, l. 14   SLC to Dan Beard, 11 November 1889. Paine, *Biography*, p. 888.

p. 357, l. 32   WDH to William Cooper Howells, 2 February 1890. *Mark Twain-Howells Letters*, p. 628, n. 4.

p. 357, l. 34   *Notebook*, p. 357.

p. 358, l. 1   See George Spangler's "*The Shadow of a Dream*: Howells' Homosexual Tragedy."

p. 358, l. 7   WDH to SLC, 29 December 1889. *Mark Twain-Howells Letters*, p. 627.

p. 358, l. 14   *Autobiography*, p. 193. Salsbury, *Susy and Mark Twain*, p. 271.

p. 358, l. 16   Mary Bushnell Cheney to OLC, 8 December 1889. Salsbury, *Susy and Mark Twain*, p. 271.

p. 358, l. 28   SLC to Joseph Goodman, 29 November 1889. *Mark Twain's Letters*, pp. 521–22.

p. 359, l. 1   SLC to Daniel Frohman, 2 February 1890. CCamarSJ 04010.

p. 359, l. 13   SLC to WDH, 1 April 1890. *Mark Twain-Howells Letters*, p. 632.

p. 359, l. 27   Susy Clemens to Susan Crane, 18 March 1890. Salsbury, *Susy and Mark Twain*, pp. 275–76.

p. 359, l. 31   Susy Clemens to Olivia Langdon, 6 April 1890. Salsbury, *Susy and Mark Twain*, p. 276.

p. 359, l. 40   SLC to Joseph Goodman, 18 April 1890. CtY 04041.

p. 360, l. 9   OLC to SLC, 21 May 1890. Harnsberger, *Family Letters of Mark Twain*, p. 79.

p. 360, l. 22   OLC to SLC, 22 May 1890. *Twainian*, September–October 1976, p. 2.

p. 360, l. 24   See *Notebooks and Journals*, Vol. 3, p. 624 n. 189, for an example of how the retreat's gestalt grated on Clemens.

p. 361, l. 24   SLC to Orion and Mollie Clemens, 21 August 1890. CU-MARK 04083.

p. 361, l. 25   SLC to Franklin Whitmore, 21 August 1890. CtHMTH 09831.

p. 361, l. 39   F.W. Andrews, "An Incident," pp. 1–2. Manuscript in the Mark Twain Papers.

p. 362, l. 2   SLC to Pamela Moffett, 12 October 1890. *Love Letters of Mark Twain*, p. 258.

p. 362, l. 19   SLC to Pamela Moffett, 13 May 1890. *Mark Twain, Business Man*, p. 393.

p. 362, l. 39   SLC to OLC, 26 November 1890. *Twainian*, September–October 1976, p. 3.

p. 363, l. 2   OLC to SLC, 27 November 1890. *Twainian*, September–October 1976, p. 3.

p. 363, l. 7   SLC to WDH, 27 November 1890. *Mark Twain-Howells Letters*, p. 633.

38: THE END OF MARK TWAIN

p. 364, l. 8   *Following the Equator*, Headnote, Chapter 12, p. 114.

p. 364, l. 29   E.W. Andrews, "An Incident," p. 2. Manuscript in the Mark Twain Papers. Susy Clemens, *Papa: An Intimate Biography*, p. 12.

p. 364, l. 34   E.W. Andrews, "An Incident," p. 3.

p. 364, l. 39   Correspondence from Susy Clemens to her family during this period has been lost, or was hidden or destroyed, implying that a careful excision of a portion of Susy's life occurred. It seems unlikely that the letters were lost, though it is possible. It is perhaps only a trace more likely that they were hidden, since the value of the letters almost certainly would have flushed them out by now. Most probable is that they were destroyed, though Clemens himself destroyed little. If the letters survived Clemens, then Clara Clemens Gabrilowitsch, inheritor of the family papers, destroyed them. Perhaps Clara viewed Susy's relationship with Louise Brownell as sufficient reason for this severe form of textual editing.

p. 365, l. 18   SLC to Daniel Whitford, 16 October 1890. CU-MARK 04102.

p. 365, l. 25   SLC to Fred Hall, 27 December 1890. *Mark Twain's Letters to His Publishers*, p. 266.

p. 366, l. 4   SLC to John Jones, 20 January 1891. CU-MARK (tr) 04162.

p. 366, l. 11   John Jones to SLC, 11 February 1891. *Notebooks and Journals*, Vol. 3, p. 602, n. 96.

p. 366, l. 15   SLC to Joseph Goodman, 24 February 1891. NN-B 04573.

p. 366, l. 16   SLC to Orion Clemens, 25 February 1891. CU-MARK 04175.

p. 366, l. 19   Ibid.

p. 366, l. 28   SLC to WDH, 4 April 1891. *Mark Twain-Howells Letters*, p. 641.

p. 367, l. 19   E.W. Andrews, "An Incident," p. 5. Manuscript in the Mark Twain Papers.

p. 367, l. 21   *Notebooks and Journals*, Vol. 3, p. 617. This entry is ambiguous. The phrase may refer to his inclusion of "The Golden Arm" or his exclusion of "The Blue Jay Yarn" or both.

p. 367, l. 38   I believe that Susy's stated desire to make a life with Louise Brownell is why her parents insisted she join them in Europe, despite her success at college. In *Papa*, Charles Neider resists concluding that the relationship between Susy Clemens and Louise Brownell was romantic, despite the clear implication in Susy's letters written after their separation.

p. 368, l. 21   SLC to WDH, 20 May 1891. *Mark Twain-Howells Letters*, p. 645.

p. 368, l. 36   SLC to Annie Webster, 26 April 1891. *Notebooks and Journals*, Vol. 3. p. 626, n. 193.

p. 368, l. 39   Mollie Clemens to SLC and OLC, 30 April 1891. *Twainian*, November–December 1976, p. 1.

p. 369, l. 6   Ibid., p. 2.

p. 369, l. 16   SLC to Fred Hall, 9 April 1891. *Mark Twain's Letters to His Publishers*, p. 272.

p. 369, l. 33   *Notebooks and Journals*, Vol. 3, p. 621.

p. 369, l. 39   SLC to WDH, 20 May 1891. *Mark Twain-Howells Letters*, p. 646.

39: FAREWELL, AMERICA

p. 371, l. 12   *Adventures of Huckleberry Finn*, p. 362.

p. 371, l. 40   SLC to Fred Hall, 17 June 1891. *Mark Twain's Letters to His Publishers*, p. 277.

p. 372, l. 6   SLC to R.U. Johnson, 10 July 1891. MO2 04220.

p. 372, l. 13   This fact makes it probable that the failure of the European trip for the summer of 1890 led the Clemenses to buy these tickets in order to commit to making the trip the summer after.

p. 372, l. 33   SLC to Joseph Twichell, 1 October 1891. *Mark Twain's Letters*, p. 558.

p. 373, l. 4   SLC to OLC, 28 September 1891. *Mark Twain's Letters*, p. 553.

p. 373, l. 16   Clara Clemens, *My Father, Mark Twain*, p. 95.

p. *373*, *l. 21* This poem did eventually become a classic in America too; Clemens' version, called *Slovenly Peter*, was not published until 1935.

p. *374*, *l. 4* Paine, *Biography*, p. 936.

p. *374*, *l. 33* Susy Clemens to Louise Brownell, 2 October 1891. *Papa*, p. 15.

p. *374*, *l. 35* Susy Clemens to Louise Brownell, 6? October 1891. *Papa*, p. 15. Neider's dating of this letter is uncertain.

p. *374*, *l. 39* Susy Clemens to Louise Brownell, no date, probably late March or early April 1892. NCH 09136

p. *375*, *l. 4* SLC to Poultney Bigelow, 6 May 1892. N7 (tr) 04288.

p. *375*, *l. 25* William James to Josiah Royce, 18 December 1892. In Kaplan, *Mr. Clemens and Mark Twain*, p. 316.

p. *375*, *l. 33* SLC to Charles Langdon, 7 August 1892. CtHMTH 01660.

p. *376*, *l. 7* SLC to Orion Clemens, 28 June 1892. CU-MARK 04302.

p. *376*, *l. 22* SLC to Fred Hall, 10 August 1892. *Mark Twain's Letters to His Publishers*, p. 315.

p. *376*, *l. 36* SLC to Charles Langdon, 7 August 1892. CtHMTH 01660.

40: PEACE AND PANIC

p. *378*, *l. 12* *Pudd'nhead Wilson*, Headnote, Chapter 2, p. 61.

p. *378*, *l. 33* Clara Clemens, *My Father, Mark Twain*, p. 120.

p. *378*, *l. 39* SLC to Susan Crane, 30 September 1892. *Mark Twain's Letters*, pp. 570–72.

p. *379*, *l. 7* SLC to Fred Hall, 10 August 1892. *Mark Twain's Letters to His Publishers*, p. 315.

p. *379*, *l. 26* OLC to Clara Clemens, 7 October 1892. Salsbury, *Susy and Mark Twain*, p. 309.

p. *379*, *l. 35* Susy Clemens to Clara Clemens, 4 November 1892. *The Family Letters of Mark Twain*, p. 90A. This "book" is merely a heavily edited typescript of some letters between family members that were in Clara Clemens' possession at mid-century.

p. *380*, *l. 1* Susy Clemens to Clara Clemens, 16? October 1892. *The Family Letters of Mark Twain*, p. 94A.

p. *380*, *l. 10* Susy Clemens to Clara Clemens, 6 December 1892. *The Family Letters of Mark Twain*, p. 95.

p. *381*, *l. 11* SLC to Clara Clemens, 24 January 1893. *The Family Letters of Mark Twain*, p. 100B.

p. *381*, *l. 15* Susy Clemens to Clara Clemens, 22 December 1892. *The Family Letters of Mark Twain*, p. 97E.

p. *381*, *l. 20* Susy Clemens to Clara Clemens, 28 February 1893. *The Family Letters of Mark Twain*, p. 103B.

p. *381*, *l. 25* Susy Clemens to Louise Brownell, ? January 1893. NCH 09155.

p. *381*, *l. 32* Susy Clemens to Louise Brownell, 16–20? March 1893. NCH 09158.

p. *381*, *l. 37* Susy Clemens to Louise Brownell, 16–20? March 1893. *Papa*, pp. 31–32.

p. *382*, *l. 1* SLC to Fred Hall, 3 February 1893. *Mark Twain's Letters to His Publishers*, p. 338.

p. *382*, *l. 11* SLC to Susan Crane, 19 March 1893. CtHMTH 04353.

p. *382*, *l. 24* *Mark Twain's Notebook*, p. 232.

p. *382*, *l. 34* OLC to SLC, 21 April 1893. *Twainian*, November–December 1977, p. 3.

p. *382*, *l. 38* SLC to Joseph Twichell, 9 June 1893. *Love Letters of Mark Twain*, p. 266.

p. *383*, *l. 2* SLC to Fred Hall, 2 June 1893. *Mark Twain's Letters to His Publishers*, pp. 343–44.

p. *383*, *l. 31* SLC to Orion and Mollie Clemens, 26 July 1893. CU-MARK (tr) 04425.

p. *383*, *l. 37* Susy Clemens to Clara Clemens, 10 April 1893. *The Family Letters of Mark Twain*, p. 103I–J.

p. *384*, *l. 7* SLC to Fred Hall, 18 July 1893. *Mark Twain's Letters to His Publishers*, p. 351.

p. *384*, *l. 17* *Pudd'nhead Wilson*, p. 230.

p. *384*, *l. 21* SLC to Fred Hall, 30 July 1893. *Mark Twain's Letters to His Publishers*, p. 355.

p. *384*, *l. 28* *Pudd'nhead Wilson*, Headnote, Conclusion, p. 224.

41: FAUSTIAN BARGAINS

p. 385, l. 12 "Extract from Captain Stormfield's Visit to Heaven," *Collected Tales, Sketches, Speeches, and Essays, 1891–1910*, p. 839.

p. 385, l. 29 SLC to OLC, 13 September 1893. *Mark Twain's Correspondence with Henry Huttleston Rogers*, p. 11.

p. 386, l. 15 SLC to Clara Clemens, 15 September 1893. *Love Letters of Mark Twain*, p. 269.

p. 386, l. 21 SLC to OLC, 21 September 1893. *Love Letters of Mark Twain*, p. 273.

p. 386, l. 30 *Pudd'nhead Wilson*, Headnote, Chapter 6, p. 90.

p. 387, l. 38 Ibid., Chapter 3, p. 73.

p. 387, l. 41 Ibid., Chapter 20, p. 206.

p. 388, l. 10 Ibid., Chapter 2, p. 64.

p. 388, l. 16 Ibid., Conclusion, pp. 224–25.

p. 388, l. 33 Ibid., "Those Extraordinary Twins," p. 229.

p. 389, l. 7 Paine, *Biography*, p. 974.

p. 389, l. 22 SLC to OLC, 18 October 1893. *Mark Twain's Letters*, p. 596.

p. 389, l. 27 Ibid.

p. 389, l. 30 Paine, *Biography*, p. 972.

p. 389, l. 32 SLC to OLC, 6 November 1893. *Love Letters of Mark Twain*, p. 276.

p. 389, l. 41 SLC to OLC, 30 December 1893. CU-MARK 04545.

p. 390, l. 13 SLC to OLC, 25 December 1893. *Mark Twain's Letters*, p. 599. Corrected against proofread copy.

p. 390, l. 23 Ibid., p. 598. Corrected against proofread copy.

p. 390, l. 31 Ibid., p. 602. Clemens begins a new paragraph after "with me."

p. 391, l. 1 SLC to OLC, 18 December 1893. *Love Letters of Mark Twain*, p. 285.

p. 391, l. 4 See *Mark Twain's Letters*, pp. 606–7 and *Mark Twain-Howells Letters*, pp. 658–59, for a more complete rendition of his conclusion to direct Susy into mind cure.

p. 391, l. 13 SLC to OLC, 12 January 1894. *Love Letters of Mark Twain*, pp. 289–90.

p. 391, l. 17 SLC to OLC, 11 February 1894. CU-MARK 04692.

p. 391, l. 26 SLC to OLC, 30 December 1893. CU-MARK 04545.

p. 391, l. 28 Paine, *Biography*, p. 979.

p. 392, l. 7 SLC to OLC, 23 February 1894. CU-MARK 04697.

p. 392, l. 18 Quoted in OLC to HHR, 14 February 1894. *Mark Twain's Correspondence with Henry Huttleston Rogers*, p. 39.

p. 392, l. 39 OLC to Susan Crane, ? April 1894. Paine, *Biography*, p. 987.

p. 393, l. 8 SLC to OLC, 4 May 1894. *Love Letters of Mark Twain*, p. 301.

p. 393, l. 14 Ibid., pp. 301–2.

p. 393, l. 16 SLC to Mary Fairbanks, 22 April 1894. *Mark Twain's Letters to Mrs. Fairbanks*, p. 274.

p. 393, l. 39 OLC to Alice Day, 23 May 1894. CtHSD 10518.

p. 394, l. 7 Howells, *My Mark Twain*, p. 85.

p. 394, l. 12 SLC to HHR, 31 May 1894. *Mark Twain's Correspondence with Henry Huttleston Rogers*, p. 58.

p. 394, l. 21 SLC to HHR, 29–30 June 1894. *Mark Twain's Correspondence with Henry Huttleston Rogers*, p. 68.

p. 394, l. 34 OLC to SLC, 31 July 1894. *Love Letters of Mark Twain*, pp. 308–9.

p. 394, l. 40 SLC to OLC, 23 July 1894. *Love Letters of Mark Twain*, p. 306.

p. 395, l. 17 SLC to OLC, 5 August 1894. *Love Letters of Mark Twain*, pp. 310–11.

p. 395, l. 24 SLC to Susy Clemens, 8 August 1894. CU-MARK (tr) 04776.

p. 395, l. 30 SLC to Clara Clemens, 3 August 1894. Salsbury, *Susy and Mark Twain*, p. 353.

p. 395, l. 35 Susy Clemens to Clara Clemens, 10 August 1894. *The Family Letters of Mark Twain*, pp. 124–25.

p. 396, l. 2 Susy Clemens to Louise Brownell, 29 July 1894. *Papa*, p. 28.

p. 396, l. 6 SLC to HHR, 16 September 1894. *Mark Twain's Correspondence with Henry Huttleston Rogers*, p. 77.

p. 396, l. 17 SLC to HHR, 24 September 1894. *Mark Twain's Correspondence with Henry Huttleston Rogers*, p. 78.

p. 396, l. 23 SLC to HHR, 5 October 1894. *Mark Twain's Correspondence with Henry Huttleston Rogers*, p. 80.

p. 396, l. 30 SLC to HHR, 6 November 1894. *Mark Twain's Correspondence with Henry Huttleston Rogers*, p. 91.

p. 396, l. 35 SLC to HHR, 29–30 November 1894. *Mark Twain's Correspondence with Henry Huttleston Rogers*, p. 100.

p. 396, l. 39 SLC to HHR, 16–17 December 1894. *Mark Twain's Correspondence with Henry Huttleston Rogers*, p. 106.

p. 397, l. 6 SLC to HHR, 22 December 1894. *Mark Twain's Correspondence with Henry Huttleston Rogers*, p. 108.

p. 397, l. 15 SLC to HHR, 27–28 December 1894. *Mark Twain's Correspondence with Henry Huttleston Rogers*, p. 112.

p. 397, l. 21 Ibid., p. 114.

p. 397, l. 32 SLC to HHR, 2 January 1895. *Mark Twain's Correspondence with Henry Huttleston Rogers*, p. 115.

p. 397, l. 39 SLC to HHR, 21 January 1895. *Mark Twain's Correspondence with Henry Huttleston Rogers*, pp. 118–19.

42: A RESPITE FOR THE BANKRUPT

p. 399, l. 10 *Pudd'nhead Wilson*, Headnote, Chapter 16, p. 173.

p. 399, l. 40 SLC to OLC, 11 March 1895. CU-MARK 04850.

p. 400, l. 4 SLC to OLC, 20–21 March 1895. *Love Letters of Mark Twain*, p. 312.

p. 400, l. 9 Ibid., p. 313.

p. 400, l. 15 Ibid.

p. 400, l. 22 SLC to J.H. Harper, 23 April 1895. *Mark Twain's Correspondence with Henry Huttleston Rogers*, p. 143, n. 1.

p. 400, l. 33 SLC to Samuel Moffett, 9 April 1895. CU-MARK 04864.

p. 400, l. 38 SLC to HHR, 29 April 1895. *Mark Twain's Correspondence with Henry Huttleston Rogers*, p. 143.

p. 401, l. 5 SLC to HHR, 14 April 1895. *Mark Twain's Correspondence with Henry Huttleston Rogers*, p. 141.

p. 401, l. 28 SLC to HHR, 19 June 1895. *Mark Twain's Correspondence with Henry Huttleston Rogers*, p. 153.

p. 401, l. 32 SLC to HHR, 30 June 1895. *Mark Twain's Correspondence with Henry Huttleston Rogers*, p. 161.

p. 402, l. 4 SLC to HHR, 24 July 1895. *Mark Twain's Correspondence with Henry Huttleston Rogers*, p. 173.

p. 402, l. 6 HHR to SLC, 16 July 1895. *Mark Twain's Correspondence with Henry Huttleston Rogers*, p. 169.

43: AROUND THE WORLD

p. 403, l. 12 "More Maxims of Mark," *Collected Tales, Sketches, Speeches, and Essays, 1891–1910*, p. 944.

p. 404, l. 6 *Personal Recollections of Joan of Arc*, p. 1.

p. 404, l. 12 Ibid., p. viii.

p. 405, l. 19 SLC to J.H. Harper, 17 August 1895. *The House of Harper*, pp. 575–76.

p. 405, l. 39 SLC to Samuel Moffett, 15 August 1895. Kaplan, *Mr. Clemens and Mark Twain*, p. 334.

p. 406, l. 7 Paine, *Biography*, p. 1005.

p. 406, l. 21 Reported in the *New York Times*, 17 August 1895.

p. 406, l. 38 See Zmijewski, "Hawaii Awaits a Legend."

p. 407, l. 6 OLC to Susan Crane, 5 September 1895. CU-MARK (tr) 04958.

p. 407, l. 7 SLC to Joe Twichell, 29 November 1895. *Mark Twain's Letters*, p. 630.

p. 407, l. 14 *Notebook*, p. 265.

p. 407, l. 21 *Sydney Argus*, 17 September 1895, p. 5. Miriam Jones Shillingsburg, *At Home Abroad: Mark Twain in Australasia*, p. 32.

p. 407, l. 33 *Notebook*, pp. 262–63.

p. 408, l. 1 OLC to Susy Clemens, 2 and 5 December 1895. *Family Letters of Mark Twain*, p. 137.

p. 408, l. 24 SLC to HHR, 6 March 1896. *Mark Twain's Correspondence with Henry Huttleston Rogers*, p. 196.

p. 408, l. 31 OLC to Mrs. Franklin Whitmore, 9 April 1896. CtHMTH 05038.

p. 408, l. 35 OLC to Sue Crane, 21 May 1896. Paine, *Biography*, p. 1017.

p. 409, l. 6 HHR to SLC, 29 April 1896. *Mark Twain's Correspondence with Henry Huttleston Rogers*, p. 211.

p. 409, l. 9 HHR to SLC, 22 May 1896. *Mark Twain's Correspondence with Henry Huttleston Rogers*, p. 214.

p. 409, l. 11 SLC to HHR, 18 June 1896. *Mark Twain's Correspondence with Henry Huttleston Rogers*, p. 217.

p. 409, l. 25 SLC to Joseph Twichell, 24 May 1896. *Mark Twain's Letters*, p. 632.

p. 409, l. 31 SLC to HHR, 26 May 1896. *Mark Twain's Correspondence with Henry Huttleston Rogers*, p. 215.

p. 410, l. 4 SLC to WDH, 5 August 1896. *Mark Twain-Howells Letters*, p. 661.

p. 410, l. 27 SLC to OLC, 16 August 1896. *Love Letters of Mark Twain*, p. 317.

p. 410, l. 31 SLC to OLC, 19 August 1896. *Love Letters of Mark Twain*, p. 321.

44: CITY OF HEARTBREAK

p. 411, l. 9 *Following the Equator*, Vol. 2, Headnote, Chapter 3, p. 24.

p. 411, l. 14 Ibid., Headnote, Chapter 6, p. 57.

p. 411, l. 30 Susy Clemens to Clara Clemens, 13 September 1895. *Family Letters of Mark Twain*, p. 132A.

p. 411, l. 38 Susy Clemens to Clara Clemens, 30 July 1895. *Family Letters of Mark Twain*, p. 127. The exact nature of the early relationship between Susan Crane and Ernest Köppe, who either accompanied or immediately followed Crane to Elmira, invites speculation.

p. 412, l. 1 Susy Clemens to Clara Clemens, 13 September 1895. *Family Letters of Mark Twain*, p. 132A.

p. 412, l. 6 OLC to Susy Clemens, 2 December 1895. *Family Letters of Mark Twain*, p. 136.

p. 412, l. 10 SLC to Susy Clemens, 7 February 1896. *Love Letters of Mark Twain*, p. 316.

p. 412, l. 17 Susy Clemens to Clara Clemens, ? ? 1896. *Family Letters of Mark Twain*, p. 122.

p. 412, l. 23 Ibid., p. 125C.

p. 412, l. 37 Ibid., p. 123A.

p. 412, l. 40 Elizabeth Ware Winsor to Louise Brownell, 16 September 1896. NHC 37478.

p. 413, l. 11 Quoted in Samuel Moffett to Mary Moffett, 20 August 1896. MTP 31106.

p. 413, l. 22 Susy Clemens, *Papa*, pp. 44–47. Editor Neider acknowledges that his transcription of the delirious writings of Susy Clemens must be considered uncertain.

p. 413, l. 33 Elizabeth Ware Winsor to Louise Brownell, 16 September 1896. NCH 37478.

p. 414, l. 2 SLC to OLC, 21 August 1896. *Love Letters of Mark Twain*, p. 323.

p. 414, l. 7 SLC to OLC, 26 August 1896. *Love Letters of Mark Twain*, p. 324.

p. 414, l. 13 Ibid., p. 326.

p. 414, l. 21 SLC to Joseph Twichell, 27 September 1896. *Mark Twain's Letters*, p. 635.

p. 414, l. 24 SLC to Laurence Hutton, 6 September 1896. NjP 05104.

p. 414, l. 29   SLC to WDH, 24 September 1896. *Mark Twain-Howells Letters*, pp. 662–63.

p. 414, l. 35   SLC to Pamela Moffett, 7 January 1897. CU-MARK 05166.

p. 415, l. 7   SLC to WDH, 23 February 1897. *Mark Twain-Howells Letters*, p. 664.

p. 415, l. 22   SLC to Pamela Moffett, 7 January 1897. CU-MARK 05166.

p. 415, l. 24   SLC to HHR and Emilie Rogers, 18 December 1896. *Mark Twain's Correspondence with Henry Huttleston Rogers*, p. 255.

p. 415, l. 29   SLC to HHR, 4 January 1897. *Mark Twain's Correspondence with Henry Huttleston Rogers*, p. 259.

p. 415, l. 33   SLC to OLC, 19 August 1896. *Love Letters of Mark Twain*, p. 320.

p. 415, l. 35   *Pudd'nhead Wilson*, Headnote, Chapter 3, p. 69.

p. 416, l. 4   SLC to Joseph Twichell, 19 January 1897. *Mark Twain's Letters*, p. 642.

p. 416, l. 12   SLC to Frank Fuller, 2 July 1897. Kaplan, *Mr. Clemens and Mark Twain*, p. 349.

p. 416, l. 17   HHR to SLC, 16 June 1897. *Mark Twain's Correspondence with Henry Huttleston Rogers*, p. 282.

p. 416, l. 18   SLC to HHR, 16 June 1897. *Mark Twain's Correspondence with Henry Huttleston Rogers*, p. 283.

p. 416, l. 25   Paine, *Biography*, p. 1039.

p. 416, l. 32   *Following the Equator*, Vol. 1, Dedication.

p. 416, l. 36   For Clemens' comments on *Dr. Jekyll and Mr. Hyde*, see *Notebook*, pp. 348–50.

p. 417, l. 33   SLC to J.B. Pond, 17 September 1897. NN-B 05289.

p. 417, l. 36   SLC to HHR, 13 September 1897. *Mark Twain's Correspondence with Henry Huttleston Rogers*, p. 300.

p. 417, l. 39   SLC to Francis H. Skrine, 10 September 1897. ViU 05284.

p. 418, l. 1   OLC to Alice Day, 22 October 1896. CtHSD 10606.

p. 418, l. 5   "In Memoriam," *Collected Tales, Sketches, Speeches, and Essays, 1891–1910*, p. 217.

p. 418, l. 11   SLC to Joseph Twichell, 22 August 1897. *Mark Twain's Letters*, p. 646.

45: A JEW IN VIENNA

p. 419, l. 9   *Following the Equator*, Vol. 2, Headnote, Chapter 12, p. 125.

p. 419, l. 41   Dolmetsch, *"Our Famous Guest,"* p. 166. I have paraphrased Carl Dolmetsch, to whom I am obliged for *"Our Famous Guest": Mark Twain in Vienna*, a model of careful scholarship, clear writing, and comprehension.

p. 420, l. 18   SLC to Joseph Twichell, 23 October 1897. *Mark Twain's Letters*, p. 647.

p. 421, l. 11   SLC to HHR, 16 December 1897. *Mark Twain's Correspondence with Henry Huttleston Rogers*, pp. 307–8.

p. 421, l. 15   SLC to Mollie Clemens, 5 November 1897. Kaplan, *Mr. Clemens and Mark Twain*, p. 350.

p. 421, l. 20   SLC to HHR, 10–11 November 1897. *Mark Twain's Correspondence with Henry Huttleston Rogers*, p. 303.

p. 421, l. 36   Dolmetsch, *"Our Famous Guest,"* p. 144.

p. 422, l. 16   SLC to HHR, 21 December 1897. *Mark Twain's Correspondence with Henry Huttleston Rogers*, p. 309.

p. 422, l. 22   SLC to HHR, 7 March 1898. *Mark Twain's Correspondence with Henry Huttleston Rogers*, p. 325.

p. 422, l. 29   SLC to WDH, 22 January 1898. *Mark Twain-Howells Letters*, p. 670.

p. 422, l. 34   SLC to HHR, 20 January 1898. *Mark Twain's Correspondence with Henry Huttleston Rogers*, p. 316.

p. 422, l. 40   SLC to HHR, 15 March 1898. *Mark Twain's Correspondence with Henry Huttleston Rogers*, p. 326.

p. 423, l. 7   *Notebook*, p. 358.

p. 423, l. 28   SLC to HHR, 31 May 1898. *Mark Twain's Correspondence with Henry Huttleston Rogers*, p. 349.

p. 423, l. 41   SLC to WDH, 16 August 1898. *Mark Twain-Howells Letters*, p. 675.

p. 424, l. 11 SLC to HHR, 28 August 1898. *Mark Twain's Correspondence with Henry Huttleston Rogers*, pp. 360–61.

p. 424, l. 17 *Mark Twain's Aquarium*, p. 115.

p. 424, l. 20 WDH to SLC, 2 August 1898. *Mark Twain-Howells Letters*, p. 672.

p. 424, l. 27 Budd, *Our Mark Twain*, p. 136.

p. 424, l. 39 SLC to Baroness von Suttner, 17 February 1898. Dolmetsch, *"Our Famous Guest,"* p. 185.

p. 425, l. 7 SLC to Nikola Tesla, 17 November 1898. Dolmetsch, *"Our Famous Guest,"* p. 191.

p. 425, l. 14 SLC to HHR, 6–7 November 1898. *Mark Twain's Correspondence with Henry Huttleston Rogers*, p. 374.

p. 425, l. 27 SLC to HHR, 19 February 1899. *Mark Twain's Correspondence with Henry Huttleston Rogers*, p. 389.

p. 425, l. 30 SLC to HHR, 24 January 1899. *Mark Twain's Correspondence with Henry Huttleston Rogers*, p. 386.

46: IN SEARCH OF HEALTH

p. 427, l. 11 "The Man That Corrupted Hadleyburg," *Collected Tales, Sketches, Speeches, and Essays, 1891–1910*, p. 419.

p. 427, l. 31 SLC to WDH, 30 December 1898, 3 January 1899. *Mark Twain-Howells Letters*, pp. 683–84.

p. 428, l. 1 SLC to WDH, 12 May 1899. *Mark Twain-Howells Letters*, p. 698.

p. 428, l. 12 SLC to Canon Basil Wilberforce, 3 July 1899. Paine, *Biography*, p. 1085.

p. 428, l. 15 Canon Basil Wilberforce to SLC, 3 July 1899. Paine, *Biography*, p. 1086.

p. 428, l. 28 SLC to Clara Clemens, 12 July 1899. *Mark Twain's Correspondence with Henry Huttleston Rogers*, p. 406, n. 3.

p. 428, l. 35 SLC to Richard Watson Gilder, 23 July 1899. *Mark Twain's Correspondence with Henry Huttleston Rogers*, p. 406, n. 3.

p. 428, l. 38 SLC to HHR, 3 September 1899. *Mark Twain's Correspondence with Henry Huttleston Rogers*, p. 409.

p. 429, l. 10 John Brisben Walker to SLC, 9 October 1899. *Mark Twain-Howells Letters*, p. 711, n. 7.

p. 429, l. 33 SLC to Joseph Twichell, 27 January 1900. Paine, *Biography*, p. 1096.

p. 429, l. 39 Ibid., p. 1095.

p. 430, l. 4 SLC to WDH, 25–26 January 1900. *Mark Twain-Howells Letters*, p. 716.

p. 430, l. 19 SLC to Laurence Hutton, 18 September 1899. *Mark Twain's Correspondence with Henry Huttleston Rogers*, p. 397.

p. 430, l. 21 SLC to HHR, 8 January 1900. *Mark Twain's Correspondence with Henry Huttleston Rogers*, p. 424.

p. 430, l. 38 SLC to HHR, 8–9 April 1900. *Mark Twain's Correspondence with Henry Huttleston Rogers*, p. 439.

p. 431, l. 20 SLC to Will M. Clemens, 6 June 1900. *Mark Twain's Correspondence with Henry Huttleston Rogers*, p. 447, n. 2.

p. 431, l. 30 SLC to Joseph Twichell, 12 August 1900. Paine, *Biography*, p. 1109.

p. 431, l. 35 In Paine, *Biography*, p. 1109.

p. 431, l. 40 SLC to Joseph Twichell, 18 August 1900. *Mark Twain's Letters*, p. 700.

47: THE SAGE RETURNS

p. 432, l. 8 *Pudd'nhead Wilson*, Headnote, Chapter 15, p. 163.

p. 432, l. 13 *Notebook*, p. 344.

p. 432, l. 35 *New York Times*, 16 October 1900. Kaplan, *Mr. Clemens and Mark Twain*, p. 358.

p. 432, l. 39 WDH to Thomas Bailey Aldrich, 4 November 1900. *Mark Twain-Howells Letters*, p. 723.

p. 433, l. 27 SLC to Sylvester Baxter, 26 October 1900. Paine, *Biography*, p. 1112.

p. 434, l. 9 Paine, *Biography*, p. 1114.

p. 434, l. 11 Clara Clemens, *My Father, Mark Twain*, p. 217.

p. 434, l. 15 Ibid.

p. 434, l. 35 Mary Lawton, *A Lifetime with Mark Twain*, pp. 196–200. Lawton was a friend of Clara Clemens Gabrilowitsch, who arranged for Lawton to turn Katy Leary's reminiscences into a book.

p. 435, l. 20 Zwick, "Who Wrote the Couplet?" p. 35.

p. 435, l. 30 SLC to Joseph Twichell, 29 January 1901. *Mark Twain's Letters*, p. 705.

p. 435, l. 41 "Introducing Winston S. Churchill," *Collected Tales, Sketches, Speeches, and Essays, 1891–1910*, pp. 454–55.

p. 436, l. 13 SLC to Brander Matthews, ? January 1901. Hill, *God's Fool*, p. 23.

48: FAMOUS ON HIS OWN TERMS

p. 438, l. 9 *Notebook*, p. 347.

p. 438, l. 14 Ibid., p. 345.

p. 438, l. 39 SLC to OLC, 14 August 1901. *Love Letters of Mark Twain*, p. 329.

p. 438, l. 41 SLC to HHR, 23 August 1901. *Mark Twain's Correspondence with Henry Huttleston Rogers*, p. 467.

p. 439, l. 22 SLC to Frank Bliss, 29 August 1901. Kaplan, *Mr. Clemens and Mark Twain*, p. 365.

p. 439, l. 27 "Corn-Pone Opinions," *Collected Tales, Sketches, Speeches, and Essays, 1891–1910*, p. 507.

p. 439, l. 32 SLC to Joseph Twichell, 10 September 1901. *Mark Twain's Letters*, p. 713.

p. 439, l. 35 Ibid., p. 714.

p. 440, l. 23 See Hill, *God's Fool*, p. 36, for this notebook entry's relevance to the Clemenses' marriage in the latter part of 1901.

p. 440, l. 40 SLC to Thomas Bailey Aldrich, 30 December 1901. Macnaughton, *Mark Twain's Last Years as a Writer*, p. 176.

p. 441, l. 8 WDH to SLC, 15 October 1901. *Mark Twain-Howells Letters*, p. 730.

p. 441, l. 13 Kaplan, *Mr. Clemens and Mark Twain*, p. 364.

p. 441, l. 25 WDH to Thomas Bailey Aldrich, 8 December 1901. *Mark Twain-Howells Letters*, p. 735, n. 2.

p. 441, l. 28 WDH to SLC, 3 February 1902. *Mark Twain-Howells Letters*, p. 741.

p. 442, l. 6 HHR to SLC, 26 December 1901. *Mark Twain's Correspondence with Henry Huttleston Rogers*, p. 478.

p. 442, l. 11 See *Mark Twain's Correspondence with Henry Huttleston Rogers*, p. 481, n. 1. It is not entirely certain when Rogers did Clemens this service.

p. 442, l. 17 "The Dervish and the Offensive Stranger," *Collected Tales, Sketches, Speeches, and Essays, 1891–1910*, p. 547.

p. 442, l. 33 OLC to SLC, undated, probably January 1902. *Love Letters of Mark Twain*, p. 333.

p. 443, l. 6 While Clemens' essay "Why Not Abolish It?" does seem to be implicitly about Clara's sexual freedom, Hamlin Hill misdates the publication of this essay to make it coincide with Clara's escape to Europe (*God's Fool*, p. 45).

p. 443, l. 15 "A Tribute to Henry H. Rogers," Paine, *Biography*, Appendix T, p. 1569.

p. 443, l. 35 Paine, *Biography*, p. 1170.

p. 443, l. 38 Kaplan, *Mr. Clemens and Mark Twain*, p. 366.

p. 444, l. 2 *Mark Twain Speaking*, p. 435.

p. 445, l. 5 SLC to Joseph Goodman, 13 June 1902. *Mark Twain's Letters*, pp. 721–22.

p. 445, l. 14 SLC to HHR, 7 July 1902. *Mark Twain's Correspondence with Henry Huttleston Rogers*, p. 490.

p. 445, l. 22 Lawton, *A Lifetime with Mark Twain*, p. 220.

p. 445, l. 37 SLC to HHR, 13 August 1902. *Mark Twain's Correspondence with Henry Huttleston Rogers*, pp. 497–98.

p. 446, l. 2 SLC to WDH, 23 September 1902. *Mark Twain-Howells Letters*, pp. 744–45.

p. 446, l. 3 *Notebook*, p. 376.

p. 446, l. 14 Howells, *My Mark Twain*, p. 91.

p. 446, l. 29 SLC to HHR, 26 September 1902. *Mark Twain's Correspondence with Henry Huttleston Rogers*, p. 510.

49: THE DECLINE OF AN ANGEL

p. 447, l. 9 *Notebook*, p. 385.

p. 447, l. 24 SLC to HHR, 24 September 1902. *Mark Twain's Correspondence with Henry Huttleston Rogers*, p. 508.

p. 447, l. 34 Lawton, *A Lifetime with Mark Twain*, p. 221.

p. 447, l. 38 Paine, *Biography*, p. 1180.

p. 448, l. 9 *Mark Twain Speaking*, pp. 458–59.

p. 448, l. 14 SLC to OLC, 30 November 1902. *Love Letters of Mark Twain*, pp. 339–40.

p. 448, l. 23 Isabel Lyon's Diary, 3 January 1903. Hill, *God's Fool*, pp. 57–58.

p. 448, l. 29 SLC to Frederick Duneka, 15 September 1902. *Mark Twain's Correspondence with Henry Huttleston Rogers*, p. 492, n. 1.

p. 448, l. 35 *Mark Twain's Correspondence with Henry Huttleston Rogers*, p. 513, n. 1.

p. 448, l. 40 SLC to WDH, 26 December 1902. *Mark Twain-Howells Letters*, p. 758.

p. 449, l. 4 SLC to Joseph Twichell, 31 December 1902. Neider, *The Autobiography of Mark Twain*, p. 339.

p. 449, l. 6 SLC to Joseph Twichell, 28 January 1903. CTY 06573.

p. 449, l. 11 OLC to SLC, undated, probably January 1903. Clemens, *My Father, Mark Twain*, p. 230.

p. 449, l. 16 SLC to OLC, undated, probably February 1903. Clemens, *My Father, Mark Twain*, p. 251.

p. 449, l. 22 SLC to Laurence Hutton, 18 March 1903. *Mark Twain's Correspondence with Henry Huttleston Rogers*, p. 452.

p. 449, l. 39 SLC to J.Y.M. MacAlister, 7 April 1903. *Mark Twain's Letters*, p. 735.

p. 450, l. 21 SLC to HHR, 11 May 1903. *Mark Twain's Correspondence with Henry Huttleston Rogers*, p. 527.

p. 451, l. 7 Richard Watson Gilder to SLC, 4 August 1903. Hill, *God's Fool*, p. 68.

p. 451, l. 18 SLC to Jean Clemens, 12 August 1903. *Love Letters of Mark Twain*, p. 344, n. 20.

p. 451, l. 29 HHR to SLC, 15 September 1903. *Mark Twain's Correspondence with Henry Huttleston Rogers*, p. 537.

p. 451, l. 38 *Mark Twain's Correspondence with Henry Huttleston Rogers*, p. 540, n. 1.

p. 452, l. 5 WDH to Aurelia Howells, 18 October 1903. *Mark Twain-Howells Letters*, p. 774, n. 4.

50: LIVY

p. 453, l. 9 *Pudd'nhead Wilson*, Headnote, Chapter 6, p. 90.

p. 453, l. 40 SLC to WDH, 4 December 1903. *Mark Twain-Howells Letters*, p. 775.

p. 454, l. 6 Isabel Lyon Diary, 1903. Hill, *God's Fool*, p. 72.

p. 454, l. 14 Hill, *God's Fool*, p. 72.

p. 454, l. 22 SLC to HHR, 16–18 December 1903. *Mark Twain's Correspondence with Henry Huttleston Rogers*, p. 546.

p. 454, l. 25 SLC to Joseph Twichell, 7–10 January 1904. *Mark Twain's Letters*, p. 750.

p. 454, l. 37 Ibid.

p. 455, l. 13 SLC to WDH, 16 January 1904. *Mark Twain-Howells Letters*, p. 778.

p. 455, l. 27 Ibid., p. 782.

p. 456, l. 1 SLC to HHR, 25–26 February 1904. *Mark Twain's Correspondence with Henry Huttleston Rogers*, p. 558.

p. 456, l. 2 SLC to HHR, 21–22 March 1904. *Mark Twain's Correspondence with Henry Huttleston Rogers*, p. 560.

p. 456, l. 8 SLC to Richard Watson Gilder, 12–13 May 1904. *Mark Twain's Letters*, pp. 755–56.

p. 456, l. 14   William Lyon Phelps to unknown, 13 May 1904. Hill, *God's Fool*, p. 83.

p. 456, l. 26   *Notebook*, p. 386.

p. 456, l. 35   SLC to HHR, 6 June 1904. *Mark Twain's Correspondence with Henry Huttleston Rogers*, p. 569.

p. 456, l. 38   *Notebook*, p. 387.

p. 457, l. 7   Lawton, *A Lifetime with Mark Twain*, p. 230.

p. 457, l. 14   SLC to HHR, 13 June 1904. *Mark Twain's Correspondence with Henry Huttleston Rogers*, p. 572.

p. 457, l. 17   *Notebook*, p. 388.

p. 457, l. 19   WDH to SLC, 9 June 1904. *Mark Twain-Howells Letters*, p. 786.

p. 457, l. 22   SLC to Joseph Twichell, 18 June 1904. *Mark Twain's Letters*, p. 760.

51: LOSS

p. 458, l. 9   *Following the Equator*, Vol. 2, Headnote, Chapter 23, p. 246.

p. 458, l. 35   SLC to Thomas Lounsbury, 21 July 1904. *Love Letters of Mark Twain*, p. 349.

p. 459, l. 9   SLC to Joseph Twichell, 28 July 1904. *Mysterious Stranger Manuscripts*, p. 30.

p. 459, l. 22   SLC to HHR, 18 August 1904. *Mark Twain's Correspondence with Henry Huttleston Rogers*, pp. 579–80.

p. 459, l. 31   Clemens, *My Father, Mark Twain*, p. 256.

p. 460, l. 14   Henry James to William James, 31 August 1904. *Mark Twain-Howells Letters*, p. 789, n. 2.

p. 460, l. 17   *Mark Twain's Correspondence with Henry Huttleston Rogers*, p. 573.

p. 461, l. 4   See Hill, *God's Fool*, pp. 101–5, for a more complete rendition of Ashcroft's increasing involvement in Clemens' affairs.

p. 461, l. 10   First-person witnesses to their relationship were either hushed by Clara's later determination that Lyon's name not be mentioned, or so motivated by self-protection as to render them unreliable.

p. 461, l. 27   Isabel Lyon's Diary. Hill, *God's Fool*, p. 100.

p. 461, l. 37   SLC to Joseph Twichell, 14 March 1905. *Mark Twain's Letters*, p. 768.

p. 462, l. 3   "Eve's Diary," *Collected Tales, Sketches, Speeches, and Essays, 1891–1910*, pp. 708–9.

p. 462, l. 25   Isabel Lyon's Diary. Hill, *God's Fool*, p. 94.

52: A PUBLIC MAN

p. 463, l. 9   "Seventieth Birthday Speech," *Mark Twain Speaking*, p. 465.

p. 463, l. 36   "Was the World Made for Man?" *Mark Twain-Howells Letters*, p. 777, n. 2.

p. 463, l. 41   SLC to HHR, 9 July 1905. *Mark Twain's Correspondence with Henry Huttleston Rogers*, p. 589.

p. 464, l. 10   Isabel Lyon's Diary. Hill, *God's Fool*, p. 109.

p. 464, l. 14   SLC to HHR, 9 July 1905. *Mark Twain's Correspondence with Henry Huttleston Rogers*, p. 589.

p. 464, l. 20   Joseph Twichell to SLC, 15 July 1905. *Mark Twain's Correspondence with Henry Huttleston Rogers*, p. 593, n. 1.

p. 464, l. 22   SLC to HHR, 7 August 1905. *Mark Twain's Correspondence with Henry Huttleston Rogers*, p. 595.

p. 465, l. 18   Hill, *God's Fool*, pp. 117–18.

p. 466, l. 4   *Mark Twain Speaking*, p. 462.

p. 466, l. 15   Ibid., pp. 462–67.

p. 466, l. 24   SLC to Thomas Bailey Aldrich, 2 October 1906. Macnaughton, *Mark Twain's Last Years as a Writer*, p. 228.

p. 466, l. 30   SLC to Helen Keller, 23 December 1906. *Mark Twain's Letters*, p. 803.

p. 467, l. 6   Paine, *Biography*, p. 1264.

p. 467, l. 31   Ibid., p. 1268.

p. 468, l. 15   Isabel Lyon's Diary. Hill, *God's Fool*, p. 120.

p. 468, l. 20   Ibid., pp. 120–21.

p. 468, l. 28   SLC to Mr. and Mrs. Gordon, 24 January 1906. *Mark Twain's Letters*, p. 787.

p. 468, l. 32   WDH to SLC, 28 February 1906. *Mark Twain-Howells Letters*, p. 801.

p. 468, l. 34   *Mark Twain Speaking*, p. 494.

p. 469, l. 17   Autobiographical Dictation, 30 March 1906, p. 758.

p. 469, l. 26   Leary, *Mark Twain's Letters to Mary*, p. 32.

p. 470, l. 10   SLC to Thomas Bailey and Lillian Aldrich, 26 April 1906. Hill, *God's Fool*, p. 123.

p. 470, l. 35   Gertrude Natkin to SLC, 10 March 1906. *Mark Twain's Aquarium*, p. 19.

p. 470, l. 36   SLC to Gertrude Natkin, 18 March 1906. *Mark Twain's Aquarium*, p. 21.

p. 471, l. 4   SLC to Gertrude Natkin, 8 April 1906. *Mark Twain's Aquarium*, p. 25.

p. 471, l. 11   Gertrude Natkin to SLC, 5 May 1906. *Mark Twain's Aquarium*, p. 27.

p. 471, l. 21   Jean Clemens' Diary. Hill, *God's Fool*, p. 148.

p. 471, l. 26   Ibid., p. 152.

p. 471, l. 32   SLC to HHR, 17? June 1906. *Mark Twain's Correspondence with Henry Huttleston Rogers*, p. 611.

p. 472, l. 14   Ibid.

p. 472, l. 29   SLC to Mary Rogers, 21–23 September 1906. *Mark Twain's Letters to Mary*, p. 67.

p. 472, l. 32   SLC to Clara Clemens, 2 October 1906. *Mark Twain's Correspondence with Henry Huttleston Rogers*, p. 618, n. 2.

p. 472, l. 37   SLC to Emilie Rogers, 24 October 1906. *Mark Twain's Correspondence with Henry Huttleston Rogers*, p. 618.

p. 473, l. 2   SLC to Mary Rogers, 22 October 1906. *Mark Twain's Letters to Mary*, p. 78.

p. 473, l. 7   SLC to HHR, 24 October 1906. *Mark Twain's Correspondence with Henry Huttleston Rogers*, p. 618.

p. 473, l. 9   Jean Clemens' Diary. Hill, *God's Fool*, p. 160.

p. 473, l. 21   SLC to Jean Clemens, 13 November 1906. *Mark Twain's Correspondence with Henry Huttleston Rogers*, p. 620, n. 3.

p. 473, l. 38   *Notebook*, p. 392.

p. 473, l. 40   Hill, *God's Fool*, p. 158.

p. 474, l. 10   Howells, *My Mark Twain*, p. 96.

p. 474, l. 15   Paine, *Biography*, p. 1348.

p. 474, l. 27   Autobiographical Dictation, 26 March 1907. *Mark Twain-Howells Letters*, p. 824.

p. 474, l. 32   SLC to HHR, 29 May 1907. *Mark Twain's Correspondence with Henry Huttleston Rogers*, p. 625.

p. 474, l. 36   Isabel Lyon's Diary. Hill, *God's Fool*, p. 165.

p. 474, l. 38   William James to Henry James, 14 February 1907. Kaplan, *Mr. Clemens and Mark Twain*, p. 379.

p. 475, l. 11   Isabel Lyon's Diary. Hill, *God's Fool*, p. 170.

53: HEAVEN IS POPULATED WITH ANGELFISH

p. 476, l. 11   "Letters from the Earth," *Letters from the Earth*, p. 17.

p. 476, l. 38   SLC to Carlotta Welles, ? June 1907. *Mark Twain's Aquarium*, p. 40.

p. 477, l. 16   Paine, *Biography*, p. 1398.

p. 477, l. 34   *London Times*, ? June 1907. Hill, *God's Fool*, p. 175.

p. 477, l. 36   Paine, *Biography*, p. 1385.

p. 478, l. 1   Ibid., p. 1396.

p. 478, l. 9   Quick, *Enchantment*, p. 30.

p. 478, l. 27   SLC to Clara Clemens, 11 August 1907. Reported in SLC to Dorothy Quick, 11 August 1907. *Mark Twain's Aquarium*, p. 51.

p. 478, l. 31   Isabel Lyon's Diary. Hill, *God's Fool*, pp. 184–85.

p. 479, l. 20   Paine, *Biography*, p. 1446.

p. 479, l. 24   "More Maxims of Mark," *Collected Tales, Sketches, Speeches, and Essays, 1891–1910*, p. 946.

p. 479, l. 29   Jean Clemens' Diary. Hill, *God's Fool*, pp. 168–69.

p. 480, l. 17   SLC to Mary Rogers, ? October 1907. *Mark Twain's Letters to Mary*, pp. 106–7.

p. 480, l. 27   It seems unlikely, but not impossible, that Clemens ever inappropriately touched any of the young women he called Angelfish.

p. 481, l. 5   Quick, *Enchantment*, p. 143.

p. 481, l. 13   Isabel Lyon's Diary. Hill, *God's Fool*, p. 194.

p. 481, l. 21   SLC to WDH, 22 January 1908. *Mark Twain-Howells Letters*, p. 828.

p. 481, l. 29   Isabel Lyon's Diary. Hill, *God's Fool*, p. 200.

p. 481, l. 35   Isabel Lyon's Diary. *Mark Twain's Correspondence with Henry Huttleston Rogers*, p. 645, n. 1.

p. 482, l. 3   Wallace, *Mark Twain and the Happy Island*, p. 70.

p. 482, l. 7   *Mark Twain's Correspondence with Henry Huttleston Rogers*, p. 645, n. 1.

p. 482, l. 18   Ralph Ashcroft to Isabel Lyon, 5 March 1908. Hill, *God's Fool*, p. 200.

p. 482, l. 27   SLC to Jean Clemens, 14 June 1908. Hill, *God's Fool*, p. 198.

p. 482, l. 30   Jean Clemens to Isabel Lyon, 1 August 1908. Hill, *God's Fool*, p. 199.

p. 482, l. 39   Autobiographical Dictation, 17 April 1908. *Mark Twain's Aquarium*, p. 138.

p. 483, l. 10   Autobiographical Dictation, 12 February 1908. *Mark Twain's Aquarium*, p. xvii.

p. 483, l. 36   Beard, "Mark Twain as a Neighbor." *Mark Twain Journal*, Spring 1987, p. 15.

p. 484, l. 7   SLC to John Howells, 3 July 1908. *Mark Twain-Howells Letters*, p. 831, n. 1.

p. 484, l. 9   SLC to WDH, 12 August 1908. *Mark Twain-Howells Letters*, p. 832.

p. 484, l. 13   SLC to Emilie Rogers, 6 August 1908. *Mark Twain's Correspondence with Henry Huttleston Rogers*, p. 651.

p. 484, l. 21   SLC to WDH, 12 August 1908. *Mark Twain-Howells Letters*, p. 833.

p. 484, l. 28   Isabel Lyon's Diary. Hill, *God's Fool*, pp. 207–8.

p. 485, l. 10   *Mark Twain's Aquarium*, p. 206.

p. 485, l. 16   SLC to WDH, 24 September 1908. *Mark Twain-Howells Letters*, p. 835.

54: CONSPIRACY AGAINST THE KING

p. 486, l. 9   *Following the Equator*, Vol. 1, Headnote, Chapter 36, p. 310.

p. 486, l. 14   Ibid., Headnote, Chapter 27, p. 297.

p. 486, l. 28   SLC to Dorothy Sturgis, 30 September 1908. *Mark Twain's Aquarium*, p. 211.

p. 487, l. 6   SLC to Emilie Rogers, 12 October 1908. *Mark Twain's Correspondence with Henry Huttleston Rogers*, p. 653.

p. 487, l. 7   SLC to WDH, 23 November 1908. *Mark Twain-Howells Letters*, p. 838.

p. 487, l. 9   WDH to SLC, 25 November 1908. *Mark Twain-Howells Letters*, p. 838.

p. 487, l. 38   *Ashcroft-Lyon Manuscript*. Microfilm on deposit in the Mark Twain Papers, Bancroft Library, University of California, Berkeley.

p. 488, l. 8   SLC? to Jean Clemens, 17 December 1908. Hill, *God's Fool*, p. 214.

p. 488, l. 22   *Ashcroft-Lyon Manuscript*, p. 90.

p. 488, l. 27   SLC to Frances Nunnally, 9 February 1909. *Mark Twain's Aquarium*, p. 249.

p. 488, l. 30   Isabel Lyon to Hattie Whitmore Enders, 16 February 1909. Hill, *God's Fool*, p. 218.

p. 489, l. 5   Mrs. Paine to Albert Bigelow Paine, 8 March 1909. Hill, *God's Fool*, pp. 218–19.

p. 489, l. 12   SLC to Clara Clemens, 11 March 1909. *Ashcroft-Lyon Manuscript*. Hill, *God's Fool*, p. 221.

p. 489, l. 21   SLC to Clara Clemens, 14 March 1909. *Ashcroft-Lyon Manuscript*. Hill, *God's Fool*, pp. 221–22.

p. 489, l. 25   WDH to Elinor Howells, 24 March 1909. *Mark Twain-Howells Letters*, pp. 842–43, n. 1.

p. 489, l. 29   *Ashcroft-Lyon Manuscript*, p. 98.

p. 490, l. 3   The original materials relating to this incident are included in the *Ashcroft-Lyon Manuscript*.

p. 490, l. 27   SLC to WDH, 17 April 1909. *Mark Twain-Howells Letters*, pp. 844–45.

p. 491, l. 6   *Ashcroft-Lyon Manuscript*, pp. 42, 73.

p. 491, l. 15 Ibid., p. 37.

p. 491, l. 30 Ralph Ashcroft to SLC, 29 April 1909. Hill, *God's Fool*, p. 225.

p. 491, l. 39 Clemens, *My Father, Mark Twain*, p. 278.

p. 492, l. 1 *New York Times*, 20 May 1909. *Mark Twain's Correspondence with Henry Huttleston Rogers*, p. 648.

p. 492, l. 13 Ralph Ashcroft to John Stanchfield, 30 July 1909. Hill, *God's Fool*, p. 236.

p. 492, l. 17 Hamlin Hill's interpretations of the financial transactions that led to Lyon's dismissal in *Mark Twain: God's Fool* seem very obviously wrong.

55: VICTORY IN RETREAT

p. 493, l. 12 *Autobiography*, p. 428.

p. 493, l. 23 SLC to Frances Nunnally, 15 July 1909. *Mark Twain's Aquarium*, p. 261.

p. 493, l. 40 SLC to Elizabeth Wallace, undated, summer 1909. Wallace, *Happy Island*, p. 130.

p. 494, l. 10 *Ashcroft-Lyon Manuscript*, p. 268.

p. 494, l. 22 SLC to Clara Clemens, 6 March 1910. *Mr. Clemens and Mark Twain*, p. 386.

p. 494, l. 22 *Ashcroft-Lyon Manuscript*, pp. 403–5.

p. 494, l. 29 Ibid., p. 399.

p. 494, l. 33 Ibid., p. 405.

p. 496, l. 3 "Letters from the Earth," *Letters from the Earth*, p. 43.

p. 496, l. 5 SLC to Betsy Wallace, 13 November 1909. Wallace, *Happy Island*, p. 134.

p. 496, l. 9 Ibid., pp. 134–35.

p. 496, l. 12 SLC to Clara Clemens, 18 July 1909. Hill, *God's Fool*, p. 244.

p. 496, l. 25 Paine, *Biography*, p. 1534.

p. 497, l. 6 Ibid., p. 1548.

p. 497, l. 23 SLC to Clara Gabrilowitsch, 29 December 1909. *Mark Twain's Letters*, p. 835.

p. 497, l. 28 Paine, *Biography*, p. 1552.

p. 497, l. 30 Ibid.

p. 497, l. 38 Ibid., p. 1557.

p. 498, l. 4 Clemens, *My Father, Mark Twain*, p. 287.

p. 498, l. 8 "The Turning Point of My Life," *Collected Tales, Sketches, Speeches, and Essays, 1891–1910*, p. 931.

p. 498, l. 10 WDH to SLC, 18 January 1910. *Mark Twain-Howells Letters*, p. 851.

p. 498, l. 14 Colonel George Harvey, Clemens' publisher at Harper and Brothers, directed Wilson's campaign.

p. 498, l. 19 Quick, *Enchantment*, p. 212.

p. 498, l. 30 SLC to Elizabeth Wallace, 12 March 1910. Wallace, *Happy Island*, p. 139.

p. 499, l. 11 Clemens, *My Father, Mark Twain*, p. 291. See Paine, *Biography*, pp. 1577–78.

EPILOGUE

p. 500, l. 10 *Following the Equator*, Vol. 2, Headnote, Chapter 23, p. 246.

p. 500, l. 15 *Notebook*, p. 393.

p. 500, l. 38 *New York Times*, 24 April 1910.

p. 501, l. 12 WDH to Frederick Duneka, 20 April 1910. *Mark Twain-Howells Letters*, p. 854.

p. 501, l. 14 WDH to Joseph Twichell, ? December 1910. *Mark Twain-Howells Letters*, p. 854.

p. 501, l. 33 Howells, *My Mark Twain*, p. 29.

p. 502, l. 11 *New York Times*, 24 April 1910.

p. 502, l. 31 Clara Clemens to Mrs. Franklin Whitmore, 5 August 1910. *God's Fool*, pp. 228–29.

p. 505, l. 10 Lawton, *A Lifetime with Mark Twain*, p. 319.

Bibliography

WORKS BY MARK TWAIN—ORIGINALLY PUBLISHED
DURING LIFETIME OF SAMUEL LANGHORNE CLEMENS

The *Adventures of Huckleberry Finn*. Berkeley: The Mark Twain Library, University of California Press, 1986.

The *Adventures of Tom Sawyer*, ed. John C. Gerber, Paul Baender, and Terry Firkins. Berkeley: University of California Press, 1980.

The *American Claimant*. New York: C.L. Webster & Co., 1892.

A *Connecticut Yankee in King Arthur's Court*. Berkeley: The Mark Twain Library, University of California Press, 1984.

Following the Equator. Author's National Edition. New York: Harper and Brothers, 1911.

The *Gilded Age*. Two volumes. Author's National Edition. New York: Harpers and Brothers, 1915.

The *Innocents Abroad, or The New Pilgrim's Progress*. Author's National Edition. New York: Harper and Brothers, 1911.

Life on the Mississippi. New York: The Heritage Press, 1944.

"*The Man That Corrupted Hadleyburg*" *and Other Stories and Essays*. New York: Harper and Brothers, 1900.

Mark Twain's (Burlesque) Autobiography. New York: Sheldon & Co., 1871.

The *Personal Recollections of Joan of Arc*. New York: Harper and Brothers, 1899.

The *Prince and the Pauper*, ed. Victor Fischer and Lin Salamo. Berkeley: University of California Press, 1979.

Pudd'nhead Wilson and Those Extraordinary Twins, ed. Sidney E. Berger. Norton Critical Edition. New York: W.W. Norton, 1980.

Roughing It, ed. Harriet Elinor Smith and Edgar Marquess Branch. Berkeley: University of California Press, 1993.

Sketches, New and Old. Hartford, Conn.: American Publishing Company, 1875.

"The Stolen White Elephant" and Other Tales. Boston: James R. Osgood & Co., 1883.

A Tramp Abroad. Grosse Point, Mich.: Scholarly Press, 1968.

WORKS BY MARK TWAIN—COLLECTED AND PUBLISHED POSTHUMOUSLY

Collected Tales, Sketches, Speeches, and Essays, 1852–1890. New York: Library of America, 1992.

Collected Tales, Sketches, Speeches, and Essays, 1891–1910. New York: Library of America, 1992.

The Complete Short Stories of Mark Twain, ed. Charles Neider. Garden City, N.Y.: Doubleday, 1957.

Contributions to The Galaxy, *1868–1871*, ed. Bruce R. McElderry, Jr. Gainesville, Fla.: Scholars' Facsimiles and Reprints, 1961.

The Devil's Race-Track: Mark Twain's Great Dark *Writings*, ed. John S. Tuckey. Berkeley: University of California Press, 1980.

Early Tales and Sketches, Volume 1, 1851–1864, ed. Edgar Marquess Branch and Robert H. Hirst. Berkeley: University of California Press, 1979.

Early Tales and Sketches, Volume 2, 1864–1865, ed. Edgar Marquess Branch and Robert H. Hirst. Berkeley: University of California Press, 1981.

Europe and Elsewhere. New York: Harper and Brothers, 1923.

The Grangerford-Shepherdson Feud, with additional commentary by Edgar Marquess Branch and Robert H. Hirst. Berkeley: Friends of the Bancroft Library, University of California, 1985.

Hannibal, Huck and Tom, ed. Walter Blair. Berkeley: University of California Press, 1969.

Huck Finn and Tom Sawyer Among the Indians and Other Unfinished Stories, foreword and notes by Dahlia Armon and Walter Blair. Berkeley: University of California Press, 1989.

Letters from the Earth, ed. Bernard DeVoto. New York: Perennial, Harper and Row, 1974.

Mark Twain of The Enterprise: *Newspaper Articles and Other Documents 1862–1864*, ed. Henry Nash Smith. Berkeley: University of California Press, 1957.

Mark Twain Speaking, ed. Paul Fatout. Iowa City: University of Iowa Press, 1976.

Mark Twain's Fables of Man, ed. John S. Tuckey. Berkeley: University of California Press, 1972.

Mark Twain's San Francisco, ed. Bernard Taper. New York: McGraw-Hill, 1963.

Mark Twain's Satires and Burlesques, ed. Franklin R. Rogers. Berkeley: University of California Press, 1967.

The Mysterious Stranger Manuscripts, ed. William M. Gibson. Berkeley: University of California Press, 1969.

A Pen Warmed-Up in Hell: Mark Twain in Protest, ed. Frederick Anderson. New York: Perennial, Harper and Row, 1972.

Traveling with the Innocents Abroad: Mark Twain's Original Reports from Europe and the Holy Land, ed. Daniel Morley McKeithan. Norman: University of Oklahoma Press, 1958.

"What Is Man?" and Other Philosophical Writings, ed. Paul Baender. Berkeley: University of California Press, 1973.

Which Was the Dream? and Other Symbolic Writings of the Later Years, ed. John S. Tuckey. Berkeley: University of California Press, 1967.

CORRESPONDENCE, NOTEBOOKS, COMMENTARY, AND OTHER PRIMARY SOURCE MATERIAL

The Ashcroft-Lyon Manuscript. Microfilm copy on file in the Mark Twain Papers, Bancroft Library, Berkeley, California.

The Autobiography of Mark Twain, ed. Charles Neider. New York: Harper and Brothers, 1959.

The Love Letters of Mark Twain, ed. Dixon Wecter. New York: Harper and Brothers, 1949.

Mark Twain, Business Man, ed. Samuel Charles Webster. Boston: Little, Brown, 1946.

The Mark Twain-Howells Letters, ed. Henry Nash Smith and William M. Gibson. Cambridge, Mass.: Belknap, 1960.

Mark Twain in Eruption, ed. Bernard DeVoto. New York: Harper and Brothers, 1940.

Mark Twain to Mrs. Fairbanks, ed. Dixon Wecter. San Marino, Calif.: Huntington Library, 1949.

Mark Twain: Selections from the Collection of Nick Karanovich. From an exhibition prepared and described by Nick Karanovich, William Cagle, and Joel Silver. Bloomington, Ind.: The Lilly Library, Indiana University, 1991.

Mark Twain's Aquarium: the Samuel Clemens Angelfish Correspondence, 1905–1910, ed. John Cooley. Athens: University of Georgia Press, 1991.

Mark Twain's Autobiography, ed. Albert Bigelow Paine. New York: Harper and Brothers, 1924.

Mark Twain's Correspondence with Henry Huttleston Rogers, ed. Lewis Leary. Berkeley: University of California Press, 1969.

Mark Twain's Letters, ed. Albert Bigelow Paine. Two volumes. New York: Harper and Brothers, 1917. (Referred to in the notes as *Mark Twain's Letters;* I do not indicate the volume, since the second volume simply continues the first.)

Mark Twain's Letters, Volume 1, 1853–1866, ed. Edgar Marquess Branch, Michael B. Frank, and Kenneth M. Sanderson. Berkeley: University of California Press, 1988. (Referred to in the notes as *Letters*, Vol. 1.)

Mark Twain's Letters, Volume 2, 1867–1868, ed. Harriet Elinor Smith and Richard Bucci. Berkeley: University of California Press, 1990. (Referred to in the notes as *Letters*, Vol. 2.)

Mark Twain's Letters, Volume 3, 1869, ed. Victor Fischer and Michael B. Frank. Berkeley: University of California Press, 1992. (Referred to in the notes as *Letters*, Vol. 3.)

Mark Twain's Letters, Volume 4, 1870–1871, ed. Victor Fischer and Michael B. Frank. Berkeley: University of California Press, 1995. (Referred to in the notes as *Letters*, Vol. 4.)

Mark Twain's Letters from Hawaii, ed. A. Grove Day. New York: Appleton Century, 1966.

Mark Twain's Letters to Mary, ed. Lewis Leary. New York: Columbia University Press, 1961.

Mark Twain's Letters to His Publishers, ed. Hamlin Hill. Berkeley: University of California Press, 1967.

Mark Twain's Letters to William Bowen. New York: Haskell House, 1975.

Mark Twain's Notebook, ed. Albert Bigelow Paine. New York: Harper and Brothers, 1935.

Mark Twain's Own Autobiography: The Chapters from The North American Review, ed. Michael J. Kiskis. Madison: University of Wisconsin Press, 1990.

Notebooks and Journals, Volume 1 (1855–1873), ed. Frederick Anderson, Michael B. Frank, and Kenneth Sanderson. Berkeley: University of California Press, 1975.

Notebooks and Journals, Volume 2 (1877–1883), ed. Frederick Anderson, Lin Salamo, and Bernard L. Stein. Berkeley: University of California Press, 1975.

Notebooks and Journals, Volume 3 (1883–1891), ed. Robert Pack Browning, Michael B. Frank, and Lin Salamo. Berkeley: University of California Press, 1979.

The Twainian. Perry, Mo.: Mark Twain Research Foundation, bimonthly, 1941–90.

SECONDARY SOURCES

Andrews, Kenneth R. *Nook Farm: Mark Twain's Hartford Circle*. Cambridge, Mass.: Harvard University Press, 1950.

Aspiz, Harold. "Lecky's Influence on Mark Twain." *Science and Society*, Winter 1962 (26:1), pp. 15–25.

Austen, Roger. *Genteel Pagan: The Double Life of Charles Warren Stoddard*. Amherst: University of Massachusetts Press, 1991.

———. *Playing the Game*. Indianapolis: Bobbs-Merrill, 1977.

Austin, James C. *Artemus Ward*. New York: Twayne Publishers, 1964.

Baender, Paul. "Alias Macfarlane: A revision of Mark Twain Biography." *American Literature*, May 1966 (38:2), pp. 187–97.

———. "Mark Twain and the Byron Scandal." *American Literature*, January 1959 (30:4), pp. 467–85.

Baetzhold, Howard G. *Mark Twain and John Bull: The British Connection*. Bloomington: Indiana University Press, 1970.

———. "Found: Mark Twain's 'Lost Sweetheart.' " *American Literature*, November 1972 (44:3), pp. 414–29.

Baker, William. "Mark Twain in Cincinnati: A Mystery Most Compelling." *American Literary Realism*, Fall 1979 (12:2), pp. 299–315.

Barrow, David. "The Bound Apprentice." *Mark Twain Journal*, Spring 1991 (29:1), pp. 13–21.

Bates, Allan. "Sam Clemens, Pilot-Humorist of a Tramp Steamboat." *American Literature*, March 1967 (39:1), pp. 102–9.

Beard, Dan. "Mark Twain as a Neighbor." *Mark Twain Journal*, Spring 1987 (25:1), pp. 12–16.

Benson, Ivan. *Mark Twain's Western Years*. Palo Alto, Calif.: Stanford University Press, 1938.

Berkove, Lawrence I. " 'Nobody Writes to Anybody Except to Ask a Favor': New Correspondence Between Mark Twain and Dan De Quille." *Mark Twain Journal*, Spring 1988 (26:1), pp. 2–21.

———. "Life After Twain: The Later Careers of the *Enterprise* Staff." *Mark Twain Journal*, Spring 1991 (29:1), pp. 22–28.

———. " 'Assaying in Nevada': Twain's Wrong Turn in the Right Direction." *American Literary Realism*, Summer 1995 (27:3), pp. 64–80.

Blair, Walter. *Mark Twain and Huck Finn*. Berkeley: University of California Press, 1960.

Bode, Carl, ed. *American Life in the 1840s*. Garden City, N.Y.: Anchor, 1967.

Branch, Edgar M. *The Literary Apprenticeship of Mark Twain*. Urbana: University of Illinois Press, 1950.

———. "A New Clemens Footprint: Soleleather Steps Forward." *American Literature*, December 1982 (54:4), pp. 497–510.

———. "Sam Clemens, Steersman on the *John H. Dickey*." *American Literary Realism*, Fall 1982 (15:2), pp. 195–208.

———. "A Proposed Calendar of Samuel Clemens's Steamboats, 15 April 1857 to 8 May 1861, with Commentary." *Mark Twain Journal*, Fall 1986 (24:2), pp. 2–27.

———. "Three New Letters by Sam Clemens in the Muscatine *Journal*." *Mark Twain Journal*, Spring 1984 (22:1), pp. 2–7.

———. "Bixby vs. Carroll: New Light on Sam Clemens's Early River Career." *Mark Twain Journal*, Fall 1992 (30:2), pp. 3–21.

Brashear, Minnie M. *Mark Twain: Son of Missouri*. New York: Russell and Russell, 1964.

Briden, Earl F. "Mark Twain's Rhode Island Lectures." *Mark Twain Journal*, Spring 1986 (24:1), pp. 35–40.

Britton, Wesley A. "Macfarlane, 'Boarding House,' and 'Bugs': Mark Twain's Cincinnati Apprenticeship." *Mark Twain Journal*, Spring 1989 (27:1), pp. 14–17.

Brooks, Van Wyck. *The Ordeal of Mark Twain*. New York: Dutton, 1920.

Budd, Isabella. "Clara Samossoud's Will." *Mark Twain Journal*, Spring 1987 (25:1), pp. 17–19.

———. "Twain's Will Be Done." *Mark Twain Journal*, Spring 1984 (22:1), pp. 34–39.

Budd, Louis J. *Mark Twain: Social Philosopher*. Bloomington: Indiana University Press, 1962.

———. *Our Mark Twain: The Making of His Public Personality*. Philadelphia: University of Pennsylvania Press, 1983.

Bush, Harold K., Jr. "The Mythic Struggle Between East and West: Mark Twain's Speech at Whittier's 70th Birthday Celebration and W.D. Howells' *A Chance Acquaintance*." *American Literary Realism*, Spring 1995 (27:2), pp. 53–72.

Bush, Robert. "Grace King and Mark Twain." *American Literature*, March 1972 (44:1), pp. 31–51.

Camfield, Gregg. *Sentimental Twain: Samuel Clemens in the Maze of Moral Philosophy*. Philadelphia: University of Pennsylvania Press, 1994.

Cardwell, Guy. *Twins of Genius*. East Lansing: Michigan State College Press, 1953.

———. *The Man Who Was Mark Twain*. New Haven: Yale University Press, 1991.

Clemens, Clara. *My Father, Mark Twain*. New York: Harper and Brothers, 1931.

Clemens, Susy. *Papa: An Intimate Biography of Mark Twain*, ed. Charles Neider. Garden City, N.Y.: Doubleday & Co., 1985.

Cooley, John R. "Mark Twain's Aquarium: Editing the Samuel Clemens-Angelfish Correspondence." *Mark Twain Journal*, Spring 1981 (27:1), pp. 18–24.

Covici, Pascal, Jr. "Dear Master Wattie: The Mark Twain-David Watt Bowser Letters." *Southwest Review*, Spring 1960 (45:2), pp. 105–21.

Cummings, Sherwood. *Mark Twain and Science: The Adventures of a Mind*. Baton Rouge: Louisiana State University Press, 1988.

David, Beverly R. *Mark Twain and His Illustrators*. Troy, N.Y.: Whitson Publishing Co., 1986.

DeVoto, Bernard. *Mark Twain's America*. Boston: Little, Brown, 1932.

——. *Mark Twain at Work*. Cambridge, Mass.: Harvard University Press, 1942.

Dobson, John M. *Politics in the Gilded Age*. New York: Praeger Publishers, 1972.

Dolmetsch, Carl. *"Our Famous Guest": Mark Twain in Vienna*. Athens, University of Georgia Press, 1992.

Doten, Alfred. *The Journals of Alfred Doten*, ed. Walter Van Tilburg Clark. Three volumes. Reno: University of Nevada Press, 1973.

Doyno, Victor A. *Writing* Huck Finn: *Mark Twain's Creative Process*. Philadelphia: University of Pennsylvania Press, 1991.

Duberman, Martin Bauml, Martha Vicinus, and George Chauncey, Jr., eds. *Hidden from History: Reclaiming the Gay and Lesbian Past*. New York: New American Library, 1989.

Duckett, Margaret. *Mark Twain and Bret Harte*. Norman: University of Oklahoma Press, 1964.

Emerson, Everett H. *The Authentic Mark Twain: A Literary Biography of Samuel Clemens*. Philadelphia: University of Pennsylvania Press, 1984.

Ensor, Allison. "The Favorite Hymns of Sam and Livy Clemens." *Mark Twain Journal*, Fall 1987 (25:2), pp. 21–22.

Faderman, Lillian. *Surpassing the Love of Men: Romantic Friendship and Love Between Women from the Renaissance to the Present*. New York: William Morrow, 1981.

Fatout, Paul. *Mark Twain in Virginia City*. Bloomington: Indiana University Press, 1964.

——. *Mark Twain on the Lecture Circuit*. Carbondale: Southern Illinois University Press, 1960.

——. "Mark Twain, Litigant." *American Literature*, March 1959 (31:1), pp. 31–43.

Feinstein, Herbert. "Mark Twain Lawsuits." A dissertation, available at the Mark Twain Papers, Bancroft Library, Berkeley, California.

Ferguson, Delancey. *Mark Twain, Man and Legend*. New York: Russell and Russell, 1965.

Fiedler, Leslie. " 'As Free as Any Cretur . . . ' " *The New Republic*, 15 August 1955 (133:7), pp. 17–18; 22 August 1955 (133:8), pp. 16–18.

Fischer, Victor. "Huck Finn Reviewed: The Reception of *Huckleberry Finn* in the United States, 1885–1897." *American Literary Realism*, Spring 1983 (16:1), pp. 1–57.

Fishkin, Shelley Fisher. *Was Huck Black? Mark Twain and African-American Voices*. New York: Oxford University Press, 1993.

Foner, Philip S. *Mark Twain: Social Critic*. New York: International Publishers, 1958.

Frear, Walter Francis. *Mark Twain and Hawaii*. Chicago: The Lakeside Press, 1947.

Ganzel, Dewey. *Mark Twain Abroad: The Cruise of the "Quaker City."* Chicago: University of Chicago Press, 1968.

Gerber, John C. "Mark Twain's 'Private Campaign.' " *Civil War History*, March 1955 (1:1), pp. 37–60.

Gillis, William R. *Gold/Rush Days with Mark Twain*. New York: Albert and Charles Boni, 1930.

Gribben, Alan. *Mark Twain's Library: A Reconstruction*. Boston: G.K. Hall, 1980.

——. "Mark Twain, Phrenology and the 'Temperaments': A Study of Pseudoscientific Influence." *American Quarterly*, March 1972 (24:1), pp. 45–68.

——. "Mark Twain and the Making of Boy Books." Paper presented at a session on "Mark Twain's Cultural Environment," Modern Language Association annual convention, San Francisco, 30 December 1991.

Hagood, J. Hurley, and Roberta Hagood. *Hannibal: Mark Twain's Town*. Marceline, Mo.: Jostens Publishing, 1987.

Harnsberger, Caroline. *Mark Twain, Family Man*. New York: Citadel Press, 1960.

————. *The Family Letters of Mark Twain*. Unpublished, typescript copy in the Mark Twain Papers, Bancroft Library, University of California at Berkeley.

Harris, Susan K. *Mark Twain's Escape from Time: A Study of Patterns and Images*. Columbia: University of Missouri Press, 1982.

Herbert, B.B. *The First Decenium of the National Editorial Association of the United States*. New York: n.p., 1886.

Hill, Hamlin. *Mark Twain: God's Fool*. New York: Harper and Row, 1973.

————. *Mark Twain and Elisha Bliss*. Columbia: University of Missouri Press, 1964.

Hirst, Robert H., and Brandt Rowles. "William E. James Stereoscopic Photographs of the *Quaker City* Excursion." *Mark Twain Journal*, Spring 1984 (22:1), pp. 15–33.

Howells, William Dean. *My Mark Twain, Reminiscences and Criticisms*. New York and London: Harper and Brothers, 1910.

Hulse, James W. *The Nevada Adventure*, sixth ed. Reno: University of Nevada Press, 1990.

James, George Wharton. *California Scrapbook: A Collection of Articles*. Los Angeles: N.A. Kovach, 1945.

Jerome, Robert D., and Herbert A. Wisbey, Jr. *Mark Twain in Elmira*. Elmira, N.Y.: Mark Twain Society, 1977.

Kahn, Sholom J. "Mark Twain's Philosemitism: 'Concerning the Jews.'" *Mark Twain Journal*, Fall 1985 (23:2), pp. 18–25.

Kaplan, Justin. *Mr. Clemens and Mark Twain, a Biography*. New York: Simon and Schuster, 1966.

Katz, Jonathan Ned. *Gay American History: Lesbians and Gay Men in the U.S.A.: A Documentary History*, rev. ed. New York: Meridian, 1992.

Ketterer, David. "'The Fortunate Island' by Max Adeler: Its Publication History and *A Connecticut Yankee*." *Mark Twain Journal*, Fall 1991 (29:2), pp. 28–32.

————. "'Professor Baffin's Adventures' by Max Adeler: The Inspiration for *A Connecticut Yankee in King Arthur's Court?*" *Mark Twain Journal*, Spring 1986 (24:1), pp. 24–34.

Kirst, Sean Peter. "Webster's Childhood Tragedy," *Mark Twain Journal*, Fall 1983 (21:4), p. 17.

Knoper, Randall. *Acting Naturally: Mark Twain in the Culture of Performance*. Berkeley: University of California Press, 1995.

Krause, Sydney J. *Mark Twain as Critic*. Baltimore: Johns Hopkins University Press, 1967.

Kruse, Horst H. "Literary Old Offenders: Mark Twain, John Quill, Max Adeler and Their Plagiarism Duels." *Mark Twain Journal*, Fall 1991 (29:2), pp. 10–27.

————. *Mark Twain and "Life on the Mississippi."* Amherst: University of Massachusetts Press, 1981.

————. "Mark Twain's *Nom de Plume:* Some Mysteries Resolved." *Mark Twain Journal*, Spring 1992 (30:1), pp. 1–32.

Lampton, Lucius M. "Twain's Lampton Kin and Colonel Sellers." *Mark Twain Journal*, Fall 1989 (27:2), inclusive.

Landau, Sarah Bradford. *Edward T. and William A. Potter: American Victorian Architects*. New York: Garland, 1979.

Lanier, Doris. "Mark Twain's Georgia Angelfish." *Mark Twain Journal*, Spring 1986 (24:1), pp. 4–16.

Lawton, Mary. *A Lifetime with Mark Twain: The Memories of Katy Leary, for Thirty Years His Faithful and Devoted Servant*. New York: Harcourt Brace and Company, 1925.

Leacock, Stephen Butler. *Mark Twain*. New York: Haskell House, 1974.

Leary, Lewis. *A Casebook on Mark Twain's Wound*. New York: Crowell, 1962.

————. *Mark Twain*. Minneapolis: University of Minnesota Press, 1960.

LeMaster, J.R., and James D. Wilson, eds. *The Mark Twain Encyclopedia*. New York: Garland Publishing, 1993.

Long, E. Hudson. *Mark Twain Handbook*. New York: Hendricks House, 1957.

Lorch, Fred W. *The Trouble Begins at Eight: Mark Twain's Lecture Tours*. Ames: University of Iowa Press, 1960.

———. "Mark Twain in Iowa." *Iowa Journal of History and Politics*, July 1929 (27:3), pp. 408–56.

———. "Mark Twain's Philadelphia Letters in the Muscatine *Journal*." *American Literature*, January 1946 (17:4), pp. 348–52.

Lynn, Kenneth S. *Mark Twain and Southwestern Humor*. Westport, Conn.: Greenwood Press, 1972.

———. "Welcome Back from the Raft, Huck Honey!" *American Scholar*, Summer 1977 (46), pp. 338–47.

Lyon, William H. *The Pioneer Editor in Missouri 1808–1860*. Columbia: University of Missouri Press, 1965.

Mack, Effie Mona. *Mark Twain in Nevada*. New York: Scribner, 1947.

Macnaughton, William R. *Mark Twain's Last Years as a Writer*. Columbia: University of Missouri Press, 1979.

Marleau, Michael H. " 'The Crash of Timbers Continued—the Deck Swayed under Me': Samuel L. Clemens, Eyewitness to the Race and Collision between the *Pennsylvania* and *Vicksburg*." *Mark Twain Journal*, Spring 1990 (28:1) pp. 1–36.

McCullough, Joseph B. "Mark Twain and the Hy Slocum-Carl Byng Controversy." *American Literature*, March 1971 (43:1), pp. 42–59.

McCurdy, Frances Lea. *Stump, Bar and Pulpit: Speechmaking on the Missouri Frontier*. Columbia: University of Missouri Press, 1969.

McDermott, John Francis, ed. *Before Mark Twain: A Sampler of Old, Old Times on the Mississippi*. Carbondale: Southern Illinois University Press, 1968.

McKeithan, Daniel Morley. *Traveling with the Innocents Abroad*. Norman: University of Oklahoma Press, 1958.

McReynolds, Edwin C. *Missouri: A History of the Crossroads State*. Norman: University of Oklahoma Press, 1962.

Morgan, Howard W. *Unity and Culture in the United States, 1877–1900*. London: Penguin, 1971.

Morris, Ray, Jr., *Ambrose Bierce: Alone in Bad Company*. New York: Crown: 1995.

Neider, Charles. *Mark Twain*. New York: Horizon, 1967.

Ostrander, Gilman M. *Nevada: The Great Rotten Borough, 1859–1964*. New York: Knopf, 1964.

Paine, Albert Bigelow. *Mark Twain: a Biography*. New York: Harper and Brothers, 1912.

Parsons, Coleman O. "Down the Mighty River with Mark Twain." *Mississippi Quarterly*, Winter 1968–1969 (22:1), pp. 1–18.

———. "Mark Twain in Melbourne." *Mark Twain Journal*, Spring 1984 (22:1), pp. 40–42.

Pettit, Arthur G. *Mark Twain and the South*. Lexington: University of Kentucky Press, 1974.

Pond, James Burton. *Eccentricities of Genius; Memories of Famous Men and Women of the Platform and Stage*. New York: G.W. Dillingham, 1900.

Quick, Dorothy. *Enchantment: A Little Girl's Friendship with Mark Twain*. Norman: University of Oklahoma Press, 1961.

Regan, Robert. "Mark Twain, 'The Doctor' and a Guidebook by Dickens." *American Studies*, Spring 1981 (22:1), pp. 35–55.

Robinson, Forrest G. "Why I Killed My Brother: An Essay on Mark Twain." *Literature and Psychology*, 1980 (30:3–4), pp. 168–81.

Roche, John. "Making a Reputation: Mark Twain in Newport." *Mark Twain Journal*, Fall 1987 (25:2), pp. 23–27.

Rodney, Robert M. *Mark Twain International*. Westport, Conn.: Greenwood Press, 1982.

———. *Mark Twain Overseas: A Biographical Account of His Voyages, Travels, and Reception in Foreign Lands, 1866–1910*. Washington, D.C.: Three Continents Press, 1993.

Roessel, David. "Mark Twain at Ephesus." *Mark Twain Journal*, Spring 1989 (27:1), pp. 27–31.

Salomon, Roger Blaine. *Mark Twain and the Image of History*. New Haven: Yale University Press, 1961.

Salsbury, Edith Colgate. *Susy and Mark Twain: Family Dialogues*. New York: Harper and Row, 1965.

Sanborn, Margaret. *Mark Twain, the Bachelor Years: A Biography*. New York: Doubleday, 1990.

Scharnhorst, Gary. " 'Also, Some Gin': More Excerpts from Mark Twain's 'San Francisco Letters' of 1865–1866." *Mark Twain Journal*, Spring 1988 (26:1), pp. 22–24.

———. "Mark Twain's Imbroglio with the San Francisco Police: Three Lost Texts." *American Literature*, December 1990 (62:4), pp. 686–91.

Sewell, David R. *Mark Twain's Languages: Discourse, Dialogue, and Linguistic Variety*. Berkeley: University of California Press, 1987.

Shaler, N.S. "The Negro Problem." *Atlantic Monthly*, November 1884 (54), pp. 696–709.

Shillingsburg, Miriam Jones. *At Home Abroad: Mark Twain in Australasia*. Jackson: University of Mississippi Press, 1988.

Shugg, Wallace. "The Humorist and the Burglar: The Untold Story of the Mark Twain Burglary." *Mark Twain Journal*, Spring 1987 (25:1), pp. 2–11.

Skandera-Trombley, Laura. "Mark Twain's Fictionalizing of Dr. Newton's Miraculous Cure." *American Literary Realism*, Winter 1994 (26:2), pp. 82–92.

———. *The Company of Women: Mark Twain's Feminine Circle*. Philadelphia: University of Pennsylvania Press, 1994.

Sloane, David E.E. "A Revisionist Perspective on Mark Twain." *Studies in American Humor*, October 1975 (2:2), pp. 135–39.

Smith, Henry Nash. *Mark Twain: The Development of a Writer*. Cambridge, Mass.: Harvard University Press, 1962.

Spangemann, William. *Mark Twain and the Backwoods Angel*. Kent, Ohio: Kent State University Press, 1966.

Spangler, George M. "*The Shadow of a Dream:* Howells' Homosexual Tragedy." *American Quarterly*, Spring 1971 (23:1), pp. 110–19.

Stahl, J.D. *Mark Twain, Culture and Gender: Envisioning America Through Europe*. Athens: University of Georgia Press, 1994.

Stark, John O. "Mark Twain and the Chinese." *Mark Twain Journal*, Fall 1986 (24:2), p. 36.

Steinbrink, Jeffrey. *Getting to Be Mark Twain*. Berkeley: University of California Press, 1991.

Stern, Madeleine B. "Mark Twain Had His Head Examined." *American Literature*, May 1969 (41:2), pp. 207–18.

Stewart, George R. *John Phoenix, Esq., the Veritable Squibob: A Life of Captain George H. Derby, U.S.A.* New York: Henry Holt, 1937.

Stoddard, Charles Warren. *South Sea Idyls*. Boston: J.R. Osgood, 1873.

———. *Exits and Entrances*. Boston: Lothrop Publishing Co., 1903.

Stoneley, Peter. *Mark Twain and the Feminine Aesthetic*. Cambridge, U.K.: Cambridge University Press, 1992.

———. "Signifying Frontiers: Mark Twain, Partnership and Authority." Paper presented at State of Mark Twain Studies Conference, Elmira, New York, 13 August 1993.

Sweet, William Warren. *Religion on the American Frontier*. New York: Harper and Brothers, 1936.

Tenney, Thomas Asa. *Mark Twain: A Reference Guide*. Boston: G.K. Hall, 1977. (Annual Updates in *American Literary Realism*, 1979–90; subsequently in every issue of the *Mark Twain Circular*.)

Varble, Rachel M. *Jane Clemens: The Story of Mark Twain's Mother*. New York: Doubleday, 1964.

Wagner, Jeanie M. "*Huckleberry Finn* and the History Game." *Mark Twain Journal*, Winter 1979–80 (20:1), pp. 5–9.

Walker, Franklin. *San Francisco's Literary Frontier*. New York: Knopf, 1939.

Wallace, Elizabeth. *Mark Twain and the Happy Island*. Chicago: A.C. McClurg & Co., 1913.

Waterhouse, Roger Rilus. *Bret Harte, Joaquin Miller, and the Western Local Color Story: A Study in the Origins of Popular Fiction*. Chicago: University of Chicago Libraries, 1939.

Webster, Samuel Charles. *Mark Twain, Business Man*. Boston: Little, Brown, 1946.

Wecter, Dixon. *Sam Clemens of Hannibal*. Boston: Houghton Mifflin, 1952.

Whiting, Lillian. *Kate Field: A Record*. London: Sampson Low, Marston, & Co., 1899.

Willis, Resa. *Mark and Livy: The Love Story of Mark Twain and the Woman Who Almost Tamed Him*. New York: Atheneum, 1992.

Winter, Kate. "Connecticut Yankee in Kamehameha's Court." Paper presented at the annual Modern Language Association Convention, Chicago, December 1992.

Winters, Donald E. "The Utopianism of Survival: Bellamy's *Looking Backward* and Twain's *A Connecticut Yankee*." *American Studies*, Spring 1980 (21:1), pp. 23–38.

Young, James Harvey. "Anna Dickinson, Mark Twain, and Bret Harte." *Pennsylvania Magazine of History and Biography*, January 1952 (76:1), pp. 39–46.

Zmijewski, David. "Hawaii Awaits a Legend." *Mark Twain Journal*, Fall 1988 (26:2), pp. 21–27.

Zwick, Jim. "Who Wrote the Couplet?" *Mark Twain Journal*, Spring 1989 (27:1), pp. 34–39.

Index